M000304381

TECHTV LEO LAPORTE'S 2003 TECHNOLOGY ALMANAC

Leo Laporte
Laura Burstein

10/5/2003

CONTENTS AT A GLANCE

To

A Division of Pearson Technology Group, USA
201 W. 103rd Street
Indianapolis, Indiana 46290

TECHTV LEO LAPORTE'S 2003 TECHNOLOGY ALMANAC

Copyright 2003 by Que

International Standard Book Number: 0-7897-2829-X

Library of Congress Catalog Card Number: 2002107981

Printed in the United States of America

First Printing: October, 2002

05   04   03   02   4   3   2   1

Trademarks

Warning and Disclaimer

ASSOCIATE PUBLISHER
Greg Wiegand

TECHTV MANAGING EDITOR
Andrew Guest

TECHTV VICE PRESIDENT, STRATEGIC DEVELOPMENT
Glenn Farrell

TECHTV MARKETING COORDINATOR
Anne Leuthold

EXECUTIVE EDITOR
Rick Kughen

MANAGING EDITOR
Thomas F. Hayes

PROJECT EDITOR
Tonya Simpson

COPY EDITOR
Tonya Simpson

INDEXER
Chris Barrick

PROOFREADER
Maribeth Echard

TEAM COORDINATOR
Sharry Lee Gregory

MULTIMEDIA DEVELOPER
Michael Hunter

INTERIOR DESIGNERS
Anne Jones
Sandra Schroeder

COVER DESIGNERS
Anne Jones
Sandra Schroeder

PAGE LAYOUT
Stacey Richwine-DeRome

COVER AND INTERIOR PHOTOGRAPHY
Mark Compton

TABLE OF CONTENTS

DAILY POLLS

Daily Polls, *Continued...*

ABOUT THE AUTHORS

Leo Laporte is the host of *"The Screen Savers"* on TechTV. He has been a television and radio personality for more than two decades, focusing exclusively on high tech since 1991. He won an Emmy award in 1997 for his work as the virtual character, Dev Null, on MSNBC's *"The Site."* Leo lives on a small farm in Northern California with his wife, Jennifer, two children, two goats, two sheep, and two cats. The farm is equipped with high-speed wireless networking, but so far none of the animals has shown an interest.

Laura Burstein is a writer and performing artist who grew up in Silicon Valley. A former Web producer at TechTV, Laura attended college in Ireland and France and holds a B.S. in journalism from San Jose State University. She enjoys music, travel, and gourmet cooking, and is an avid car enthusiast.

DEDICATION

To Henry and Abby.

ACKNOWLEDGMENTS

So many people deserve to have their names on the cover of this book. My co-authors include many of the brilliant and talented people I work with on the show: Patrick Norton, Martin Sargent, Megan Morrone, Morgan Webb, Kevin Rose, Yoshi DeHerrera, Darci Wood, David Prager, Roger Chang, and Alison Strahan, along with articles by some of our best guests over the past year, including Photoshop experts Bert Monroy and Mikkel Aaland, hacker Kevin Poulsen, broadband whiz John Navas, and many more. There's a complete list following the Introduction. I thank each of them for their contributions: The book wouldn't be possible without them. I wrote everything that's not bylined but often it's based on research by these same people.

My able assistant in all this was my co-author, Laura Burstein, who was especially helpful in compiling the historic dates material. Credit also goes to Mike Miller, who put together the "Facts and Figures," "Leo's Black Book," and Glossary in the back; and Andy Guest, who worked on the monthly calendars. Thanks, especially to my editor, Rick Kughen, who filled in all the gaps with wit and style.

Thanks also to the management of TechTV, who are crazy enough to let me do a TV show for them, especially the executive producer of *The Screen Savers*, Paul Block; VP and executive producer, Peter Hammersly; and TechTV's Senior VP for Programming and Production, Greg Drebin. And to the countless producers, directors, assistants, interns, and technical people it takes to put a TV show on the air, I thank you from the bottom of my heart. You guys are the real pros.

Finally, thanks to my wife and life partner, Jennifer. Without her constant love and support this book would not exist.

WE WANT TO HEAR FROM YOU!

As the reader of this book, *you* are our most important critic and commentator. We value your opinion and want to know what we're doing right, what we could do better, what areas you'd like to see us publish in, and any other words of wisdom you're willing to pass our way.

As an associate publisher for Que, I welcome your comments. You can email or write me directly to let me know what you did or didn't like about this book—as well as what we can do to make our books better.

Please note that I cannot help you with technical problems related to the *topic* of this book. We do have a User Services group, however, where I will forward specific technical questions related to the book.

When you write, please be sure to include this book's title and author as well as your name, email address, and phone number. I will carefully review your comments and share them with the author and editors who worked on the book.

Email: feedback@quepublishing.com

Mail: Greg Wiegand
          Que Publishing
          201 West 103rd Street
          Indianapolis, IN 46290 USA

For more information about this book or another Que title, visit our Web site at www.quepublishing.com. Type the ISBN (excluding hyphens) or the title of a book in the Search field to find the page you're looking for.

INTRODUCTION

This is a book for people who love computers but hate computer books. I'm not all that fond of them, myself, although I have to read a lot of them for my job.

Allow me to introduce myself. My name is Leo and I cohost a daily, live, 90-minute television show called *The Screen Savers* on TechTV. I read all those computer books and magazines so you don't have to. Every night on the show, my cohorts and I distill gallons of information into a fun, fast-paced, and informative brew. It's our goal to keep you up to date on what's happening with technology while showing you a darn good time.

This book is that show put on paper. Inside these pages is a year's worth of information—stuff you can really use, surrounded by stuff that's not so useful but fascinating and fun to know nevertheless. Mary Poppins had it right: Just a spoonful of sugar helps the medicine go down. There's lots of sugar mixed in with the medicine in this book.

This is the second edition of the Almanac, and we've really beefed it up for 2003. This time, there's a page for every day of the year. No need to read them in order, by the way, or to wait for the calendar to read that day's entry. We designed this book so you could jump around in it, read a little bit whenever you have the time or inclination, or devour it all at once, if you have a mind to. Each page stands alone, with a feature article, plus a look at this date in technology history, downloads, tips, and more. Each week focuses on a single area in technology: online auctions, hardware, Windows, MP3s, digital photography, and so on. But it's an almanac, not an encyclopedia. You won't find an exhaustive (or exhausting) discussion of any topic inside. You will come away from each week knowing a lot more about the subject than you did before. I've included plenty of links to Web pages where you can learn more if you want to.

A note about those links: To save space (and to save you typing) I've eliminated the redundant `http://` from the Web addresses in the Almanac. I've also shortened the address as much as possible, eliminating www where it's unnecessary. Type the address as printed into your browser, and unless the page has moved or disappeared, it will work. Don't type any punctuation after the address. Many URLs in the book are followed by commas or periods—they're not part of the address, they're to keep Mrs. Kandel, my sixth-grade English teacher, happy. I checked every single Web address just before publication, and they were all working, but the Web being what it is, it's possible that some of them will not be working by the time you get around to trying them. I apologize if that happens, but don't forget that you can always find a similar page by going to a search engine such as google.com. Just leave the period off the end.

Before I wrap this up, I want to thank you—not just for buying this book, but for wanting to learn more about how this stuff works. Computers are remarkable tools. They're probably the most complex machines humankind has ever invented, and yet a six-year-old can use one with seeming ease. For those of us over six, it takes a little more effort, but that effort pays off handsomely. The computer is an amplifier for the mind, giving any individual the power to change the world. It's my mission in life to show people just what buttons to push and dials to twist so they can begin to use technology to make a difference in their own lives. Thanks for your willingness to try. Now, let's get going—I can't wait to see what you're going to do with the stuff you learn in here!

IS THIS BOOK FOR YOU?

If you're just picking this book up in the store, you might wonder whether it's for you. I'll save you the trouble of reading the next paragraph. Yes, this book is for you. In fact, it's for everyone you know. I suggest you buy copies for all your friends. Buy a copy for that guy standing next to you looking at that *Microsoft Excel for Nudniks* book. Buy a copy for the nice bookstore clerk. In fact, buy every copy on the shelf and hand them out to people on the street as you walk by. Spread the Almanac goodness! Hallelujah!

Well, okay, no book is for everyone, not even this fine volume. The *Leo Laporte 2003 Technology Almanac* is for people who spent a lot of money on a computer and are now wondering what to do with that expensive piece of plastic on their desks. Every page contains something fun or useful you can do right now.

It's not just for super geeks, but even computer experts will learn something in here. It's not just for novices, but even a beginner will be able to understand and use the tips inside. It's really for anyone who wants to bring the fun back into tech. We live in an age when the best toys are being designed for grown-ups. This book will help you rediscover how to play with them.

This book is designed for users of all mainstream computer platforms: Windows, Mac OS, and Linux. See "Special Icons Used in This Book," later in this introduction, to see how you can easily identify material that relates specifically to your operating system.

HOW THIS BOOK IS ORGANIZED

Inside, you'll find a page for every day of the year. Each week has a primary focus: MP3s, digital photography, Microsoft Office, and so on. On each page, you'll find a short article related to the week's subject. And because everyone needs a break once in a while, on the weekends I've often included something just for fun. Most pages also have a tip of the day and a daily download. These are tricks and programs I've found particularly useful. It's my evil plan to have you shouting "A-ha!" and "Wow, I never knew that!" on every page.

On each page, you'll also find an historic event in technology—everything from the birthday of the creator of Tupperware to the release date of the first IBM PC. Be sure to visit the related links, which point to a Web site with lots more interesting material about the event. There are many fun surprises, too.

Many pages also feature poll results. These are questions we've posed to our viewers on *The Screen Savers*. The results are unscientific, but revealing, nevertheless.

At the end of the book we've provided one of the best technology glossaries ever. It's new to this year's edition of the Almanac, and I think you'll find it very useful. There's also a statistics chapter that's fascinating to comb through, and I've included a little black book of important addresses and phone numbers you should know.

Leo Laporte's 2003 Technology Almanac is the computer book I've always wanted to read. I know you'll enjoy reading it as much as we've enjoyed writing it.

SPECIAL ICONS USED IN THIS BOOK

Throughout this book, you'll find a variety of icons that help you easily identify information that relates to you and your computer. When more than one icon appears next to a download or tip, this means that the information applies to more than one operating system.

  Windows icon—Tips and downloads specifically for Microsoft Windows users.

 Macintosh icon—Tips and downloads geared toward Mac OS users.

 Linux icon—Tips and downloads for Linux rebels.

 Web icon—Denotes interesting, useful, and sometime peculiar Web sites you won't want to miss.

 Geek icon—For the propeller-heads out there—or at the very least, those aspiring to earn a few extra pens for their pocket protectors.

 Network icon—Tips and downloads designed for networking professionals and wannabes.

Poll icon—Designates viewer polls taken live on *The Screen Savers*. Polls are generally indicated with this icon. However, there are times when I've used a special piece of art that relates to the subject matter of the poll.

ABOUT THE CONTRIBUTORS

Mikkel Aaland is a professional photographer and author of several digital photography books, including *Photoshop Elements 2 Solutions* (Sybex 2002) and *Shooting Digital* (Sybex 2002). Visit him on the Web at www.cyberbohemia.com.

Philip Allingham is a TechTV veteran from the early days. Phil loves surfing the Web and the ocean. He is managing editor at TechTV.

Introduction

Charlie Amter is a former TechTV producer.

Stacee Barcelata is a former TechTV reporter.

Kate Botello is a former TechTV personality. After four years on TechTV's airwaves, Kate Botello opted for a more analog existence in New York City's theater scene, where she currently resides. Keep up to date at `http://www.katebotello.net`.

Chris Breen writes *Macworld*'s "Mac 911," the magazine's monthly tips and troubleshooting column. When not engaged in journalistic pursuits, Chris works as a professional musician in the San Francisco Bay area.

Joshua M. Brentano is a feature-film screenwriter, and currently a segment producer for *The Screen Savers* at TechTV.

Tiffany Bass Bukow is an entrepreneur and founder of MsMoney.com.

Kylen Campbell is a freelance writer for numerous publications, including *New Media* and *Axcess*.

Chris Carle is the editor-in-chief of *IGN Codes, IGN Guides*, `dvd.ign.com`.

Roger Chang has been with TechTV since its launch in May, 1998. He is currently segment producer for *Call for Help*. He hopes to build and fly his own ultralight and raise llamas by the time he is 60.

Hahn Choi is a technical analyst with TechTV Labs, where he covers mobile computing, wireless, and other technologies.

Marina Chotzinoff is production manager for the Web at TechTV. In her spare time, Marina combines her Web skills with her love of all things edible to run savorthis.com.

John Christopher is a data recovery engineer for DriveSavers in Novato, California. Visit Drivesavers.com.

Dale Coffing is the Webmaster of Pocket PC Passion, `www.pocketpcpassion.com`.

Shawn Connally is a freelance writer.

Matt Conover works in R&D for Entercept Security Technologies, makers of a host-based intrusion prevention system, and a founding member of w00w00, the world's largest nonprofit security research group.

Jeff Davis is a former Web editor with *Tech Republic*.

Yoshi DeHerrera is a product specialist for *The Screen Savers*. He spends much of his time building wild and wonderful contraptions for the show.

Chris DiBona works for OSDN. His personal home page can be found at `DiBona.com`.

Bill Dyszel is the author of *Outlook for Dummies*, *Palm for Dummies*, and many other excellent books. He is a regular contributor on *The Screen Savers*.

Bill Elias is a former Web producer for the TechTV Products Lab.

Shannon Entin is co-author *of The Complete Idiot's Guide to Online Health and Fitness*, Penguin, 1999.

Philip Ferrato is the executive chef at *Wired* magazine in San Francisco.

Rich Fisco is technical director at *PC Magazine*, www.pcmag.com.

Bruce Fraser was a columnist for *MacWeek* magazine and is co-author of *Real World Photoshop 5*.

Tom Geller is the founder of SpamCon Foundation.

Charles F. Goldfarb is the inventor of SGML and the author of *The XML Handbook*, www.xmlbooks.com.

Nicole Guilfoyle is Web producer for TechTV's *Call for Help*.

Jon "maddog" Hall is the executive director of Linux International, `li.org`.

Annette M. Hanna is a valued contributor to the Leoville Town Square.

Dan Hantulla is author of the *Pocket PC Handbook*.

Scott Herriott is a comic, former host of *Internet Tonight*, and a regular contributor to *The Screen Savers*.

Woody Hughes is Senior Info Security Analyst at Wells Fargo Bank and a former editor at the late lamented *Maximum Linux Magazine*.

Jane Houston Jones and her husband **Morris "Mojo" Jones** are sidewalk astronomers in San Francisco, `sfsidewalkastronomers.org`.

Jack Karp is a former Web producer for TechTV's *Cybercrime* show.

Donovan Keith is a student and teacher of 3D animation. Learn more about Donovan and his work at `bentplug.com`.

Scott Kelby is editor of *Photoshop User* magazine.

Bobby Kinstle's customized cases can be viewed online at Applefritter.com.

Brett Larson is our resident Mac evangelist at TechTV, trying his best to inform the world on the wonders of the Mac. He runs a small, self-named Web site, www.BrettLarson.com, on which he shares his knowledge of the Mac with other TechTV viewers.

Bob "Dr. Mac" LeVitus is a columnist and resident tipster at OSXFAQ.com.

Mick Lockey is a former product analyst at TechTV.

Rick Lockridge is TechTV's New York City bureau chief.

Roman Loyola is a Web producer for *The Screen Savers*. His Web site is at romansempire.com.

John Lund is a professional photographer and Photoshop artist. His Web site is johnlund.com—visit it for a variety of animal antics.

Bill Manning is an engineer at American Power Conversion, apcc.com.

American McGee is the creative director at Carbon6 (www.carbon6.com) and led the development of *American McGee's Alice*. Parties interested in business development with Carbon6 can contact the company by sending an email to aej@carbon6.com.

Greg Melton spends every working hour at TechTV writing out all of *Call for Help*'s demos and PC tips for the Web site. When not at work, he spends most of his time surfing, playing in a band, or filming live music and posting clips to his Web site, http://www.showpost.com.

Tom Merritt advises TechTV's shows how to integrate the Web into what they do on TV. He is supervising producer at TechTV.

Michael Miller is the author of more than four dozen nonfiction books and numerous magazine articles. He writes about topics as diverse as Internet security, business management, and music theory.

Burt Monroy is a digital artist and author of *Bert Monroy: Photorealistic Techniques with Photoshop and Illustrator*. Visit www.bertmonroy.com.

Don Morelli is a certified professional ergonomist.

Megan Morrone is a contributor on *The Screen Savers*. She doesn't mind being called a *girl* as long as you follow it with the word *geek*. She lives online at jumpingmonkeys.com.

Rachel V. Murray is a licensed mechanical engineer and owner of Safe & Sound Children in the Bay Area, www.safeandsoundchildren.com.

Mike Nadelman has owned his own computer repair business since 1982, Advanced Computer Solutions, www.computer-repair.com.

John Navas is president of The Navas Group, navasgrp.home.att.net, and the author of the *Navas Cable Modem/DSL Tuning Guide*, cable-dsl.home.att.net.

Marty Nemko, Ph.D., is the author of *Cool Careers for Dummies*.

Patrick Norton is a sailor, skateboarder, and all-around good guy. He is the co-host and Alpha Geek on *The Screen Savers*.

Geoff Nunberg is a professor of linguistics at Stanford University.

Rick Oldano is editor-in-chief of *Digital Tourist Magazine*.

Jeanette Pavini is a consumer reporter for KPIX Channel 5 in San Francisco.

Matt Peterson is the founder of the Bay Area Wireless Users Group, www.bawug.org.

Lisa Picarille is a former Web producer for TechTV news.

Chris Pirillo is the host of TechTV's *Call for Help* show and creator of the world-famous Lockergnome, www.lockergnome.com.

Russ Pitts is a former producer of TechTV's *The Screen Savers*.

Lon Poole has written many books about personal computers, including *The Little Network Book, Macworld Mac OS 9 Bible, Using Your IBM PC*, and *Apple II User's Guide*.

David Prager is a producer for TechTV's *The Screen Savers* and claims to be the true genius behind Leo Laporte.

Regina Lynn Preciado is a freelance writer and former Web producer for TechTV. Her Web site is www.wwwritingonline.com.

Joan Price is co-author of *The Complete Idiot's Guide to Online Health and Fitness*, Penguin, 1999.

Introduction

Sue Rabeaux is a Tupperware distributor, Webmistress, eBay seller, and regular contributor to the Leoville Town Square.

Marcus J. Ranum is a security expert and principal of Ranum.com.

Diana Rathbone writes a monthly column for the *San Franciso Chronicle* called "View from the Garden."

Debbie Rich is a designer, illustrator, and teacher. Learn more about Debbie at her Web site, wildbranches.com.

Beth Rimbey is a former reporter for TechTV.

Caryn Roberts is a computer programmer and systems analyst. Before her retirement in 1995, due to Friedreich's Ataxia, a type of Muscular Dystrophy, she designed, operated, and repaired flight simulators.

Corey Roberts is a project manager at STATS, Inc.

Dave Roos is an associate producer for the Web side on *The Screen Savers*.

Alex "Sharky" Ross is the founder of Sharky Extreme (www.sharkyextreme.com) and a columnist for *Computer Power User* magazine.

Avi Rubin is a principal researcher at AT&T Labs and author of *White Hat Security Arsenal* (Addison-Wesley, 2001). Visit him online at avirubin.com.

David Rumsey is a cartographer and map collector. You can see many maps from his collection at www.davidrumsey.com.

Margaret Ryan has worked with America Online since 1993, long before "cyberspace," "online," and "the Internet" had become part of the consumer vernacular.

Adam Samuels is a former writer for TechTV.com.

Roy Santos is a former product analyst for TechTV.com.

Martin Sargent is a regular contributor to, and frequent co-host of, *The Screen Savers*, and is widely regarded as a TV funnyman and internationally recognized Proust scholar.

Blanche Shaheen is a former reporter for TechTV.

Michael Shapiro is a travel columnist for the *San Francisco Chronicle* and author of *Internet Travel Planner*. You can read more of his articles at NetTravel.com.

Richard A. Sherman is better known as Mr. Modem. Visit his Web site at www.mrmodem.net.

Rick Sherman is the director of research for the California Genealogical Society.

John Smiley is author of many books on VB, including *Learn to Program with Visual Basic 6* from Active Path. Visit his Web site at johnsmiley.com.

Scott Smith is an author, filmmaker, and founder of the digital effects company, Silver Planet Studio. He has written and directed 16 short films, including *Carny Tales*, which recently won the Audience Choice Award at the Sundance Film Festival.

David Spark is a comic and writer. His Web site is www.davidspark.com. Please don't call him Sparkles.

Ryan Staake is a high-school student and the president of Melonsoft, melonsoft.com.

Joe Stefan is president of DVDCre8, www.dvdcre8.com.

Matt Stephens is one of the founders of Deviant Art online art community at www.deviantart.com. He's currently a junior at the University of Texas at Austin studying Interactive Advertising.

Bruce Stewart is a freelance writer.

Cynthia Stone was a freelance Web producer for TechTV.

Alison Strahan has filled myriad roles at TechTV, from reporter to line producer, and is a contributing writer to Techtv.com. She is an actor and writer.

Mike Street is a freelance writer who often works for TechTV. He is the creator of "The Supergeek Challenge" on *The Screen Savers*.

Danny Sullivan is a search engine expert and editor of SearchEngineWatch.com.

Mark Swain has been doing special effects and computer animation for more than 12 years, and for the past 7 years has worked at Walt Disney Feature Animation in Los Angeles.

Jim Taylor is the author of *DVD Demystified*, published by McGraw-Hill. Jim created the Internet DVD FAQ, www.dvddemystified.com, and serves as technical director for the DVD Association. Jim now lectures and consults on DVD technology and serves as the DVD Evangelist for Microsoft.

Ryan Vance is a segment producer for TechTV's *Extended Play* show.

Michelle Von Wald is the segment producer for *Call for Help*. Michelle has worked on *Call for Help* for three years helping new computer users get their feet wet with technology.

Morgan Webb is the Windows expert on TechTV's *The Screen Savers.*

Ray Weigel works as a technical analyst to TechTV when not tinkering away at his own site, samuraimind.com.

Mark Willey is director of technical staff at Penguin Computing, www.penguincomputing.com.

Evan Williams is the co-creator of Blogger and CEO of Pyra Labs. He publishes his personal blog at evhead.com.

JANUARY 2003

JANUARY 2003

SUNDAY	MONDAY	TUESDAY	WEDNESDAY	THURSDAY	FRIDAY	SATURDAY
			1 New Year's Day; J.R.R. Tolkien born (1892)	**2** Isaac Asimov born (1920)	**3**	**4**
5 X-rays discovered (1896)	**6**	**7** Transatlantic phone service began (1927)	**8** Stephen Hawking born (1942)	**9**	**10**	**11**
12 First X-ray photo taken (1896)	**13**	**14**	**15**	**16**	**17** Benjamin Franklin's birthday; National Engineer's Week	**18**
19 Oracle AppsWorld 2003: San Diego	**20** Buzz Aldrin born (1930); Martin Luther King Day	**21** First nuclear-powered sub launched (1954)	**22** Apple Macintosh computer commercial airs (1984)	**23**	**24**	**25**
26 Super Bowl Sunday	**27** Apollo I astronauts killed (1967)	**28** Challenger Space Shuttle explosion (1986)	**29**	**30**	**31** First U.S. satellite launched (1958)	

TODAY'S FOCUS: Online Security

BILL GATES TIES THE KNOT

The world's richest man married Melinda French on January 1, 1994, in a high-security ceremony at the Manele Bay Hotel on the island of Lanai, Hawaii. Microsoft CEO Steve Ballmer was the best man. To protect the newlyweds' privacy, security guards arrested members of the media close to the hotel and surrounding area. One television reporter taken into custody near the resort sued Gates and the landowner, Dole Food Co., for being arrested on public property. More than a year later, the two parties reached a settlement for an undisclosed sum.

Related Web sites www.microsoft.com, www.manelebayhotel.com

Disable Unneeded Services

The first rule of computer security is to turn off any unnecessary programs that are running in the background. This is particularly true when those programs are designed to serve up information to the outside world, such as Web, FTP, and Telnet servers.

It's not unusual for a computer to be running services such as these, sometimes even without your knowledge. We rely on the authors of these programs to keep the invading hordes in check, but as the Nimda and Code Red worms have shown, servers often have unexpected bugs that can leave you wide open to hackers. Unless you really know what you're doing, don't run a server.

Unfortunately, many of us leave our systems vulnerable to hacking with the most insecure service of all: Network File Sharing. This service allows networked computers to share files, but a savvy hacker can use it to access your data. If you don't have a compelling need to share files, turn off file sharing.

In Windows 95/98/Me, open the Network Control Panel and uncheck the **File and Print Sharing** box.

In Windows NT/2000/XP, open the Network Connections Control Panel, get the properties for your online connection, and uncheck **File and Print Sharing for Microsoft Networks**.

On Mac OS X, open the Sharing panel in the **System Preferences**, click the **File & Web** tab, and be sure **File and Web Sharing** is off and **Allow FTP Access** is unchecked. Then, click the **Application** tab and be sure **Allow Remote Login** and **Allow Remote Apple Events** are unchecked.

All background services should be disabled unless you have a specific need to run them. If you do keep them running, you'll need extra help securing your system. Check your local experts or visit sites such as www.securityfocus.com to learn more.

For a list of all the services in Windows XP, what they do, and whether you can safely disable them, visit www.blackviper.com/WinXP/service411.htm.

 TIP OF THE DAY   In most versions of Windows, you can see which programs start up when you turn on your system by clicking the **Start** button, clicking **Run**, typing **msconfig**, and pressing **Enter**. This runs the Microsoft System Configuration Utility. You can use it to disable those programs you don't need.

 DOWNLOAD OF THE DAY   Other features of Windows that can open your system to hackers and viruses include the Windows Scripting Host and Universal Plug and Play.

Symantec offers a free program to disable Windows Scripting Host at www.symantec.com/avcenter/noscript.exe.

Security sage Steve Gibson has created a free program that automatically disables Microsoft's Universal Plug and Play. Download UnPlug n' Pray from grc.com/UnPnP/UnPnP.htm.

POLL: Would you sell your town to Microsoft?

16% Yes

39% No

45% How much ya got?

THURSDAY, JANUARY 2, 2003

TODAY'S FOCUS: Online Security

LUNA 1 MOON PROBE LAUNCHED

On January 2, 1959, the USSR launched the first spacecraft to orbit the sun and reach the moon. The silver sphere was about 17 feet long and nearly 8 feet in diameter. Luna 1 carried a tracking transmitter, a Geiger counter, radio equipment, and other devices. One day after launch, the spacecraft released a cloud of sodium gas that created a bright orange trail visible from Earth, which allowed astronomers to track the probe and served as an experiment on the nature of gas in space.

Related Web sites `nssdc.gsfc.nasa.gov, www.nauts.com`

Keep Your Operating System Up to Date

Everyone knows that humans are imperfect, but for some reason we figure that the computer programs humans write are somehow more reliable than we are. I'm here to tell ya, no program is perfect.

Modern operating systems have millions of lines of programming code. There's always a bug or two in there, and some of the bugs make it possible for hackers to break into your system. These "exploits," as they're called, are discovered all the time. In most cases, the security firm that finds the holes notifies the software vendor, then keeps quiet about the problem until the vendor can publish a fix. When the fix is published, however, every hacker from Philadelphia to the Philippines knows about the exploit and begins writing tools to take advantage of it. I'm talking about tools even a 12-year-old can use. We call novice hackers that use these tools *script kiddies*, and their number is legion.

That's why you need to apply operating system fixes as soon as they're made public. It's a race between you and the script kiddies to see whether you can close the holes before they can find a way to exploit them.

Fortunately, both Microsoft and Apple have built automatic updating into their latest OS offerings. In Windows, run Windows Update regularly by selecting it from the Start menu. I'd recommend checking every day and installing all critical updates. Microsoft Windows XP will do this for you automatically, and will even download the updates and tell you when they're ready to install. This is more than a convenience—it's a requirement.

Apple has a similar capability in Mac OS 9 and X. Tell Software Update to check for updates daily, and install them the minute they're available.

There might be other critical software updates you need to perform, too. For example, if you use a router for Internet Connection Sharing you should check the company's Web site regularly for firmware updates that fix security holes.

TIP OF THE DAY Turn on automatic updates in Windows XP by opening the System Control Panel, clicking the **Automatic Updates** tab, and then clicking the **Download Updates Automatically** button.

In Mac OS X, click the **Apple** menu, select the **System Preferences** item, and then open the Software Updates pane. Click the **Automatically** button and select **Daily** from the drop-down menu.

DOWNLOAD OF THE DAY It's a good idea to update all your software regularly, too. Keep track of the latest updates for Windows software with the free CNET Catchup client from `www.catchup.com`.

Mac users can do the same thing with Version Tracker Plus, $20 a year from `www.versiontracker.com`.

TODAY'S FOCUS: Online Security

DRINKING STRAW PATENTED

Marvin Stone was granted a U.S. patent for a wax-covered drinking straw on this day in 1888. The cigarette holder manufacturer wound paper into a manila tube covered with paraffin for strength and to prevent leaks. Stone's design pioneered the way for the spiral-bound wire used in some of the first consumer radios, and can be found today in electric motors, batteries, and many other electronic components.

Related Web sites   `inventors.about.com`, `www.nist.gov`

Don't Open Email Attachments!

If you ever watched my TV shows, you've probably seen me grab a megaphone and shout, "Don't open attachments!" I've been saying this for so long that I can't believe I still need to say it. The primary way viruses and Trojan horses get into your system is through files attached to email messages. Trust no one. These messages often come from friends who are unwittingly infected. If you receive an unexpected attachment, call the sender and ask if they meant to send you something.

Email viruses spread so fast that they can arrive before your antivirus can be updated to protect against them. Don't open attachments. **Don't open attachments**. DON'T OPEN ATTACHMENTS!

And don't send them, either. If you must use email attachments, stick with files that can't spread viruses: that's image file formats such as JPEG, GIF, BMP, and TIF, or plain text files `.TXT`. Do not send Microsoft Word documents (`.DOC` files). They can, and often do, contain macro viruses. Use Rich Text Format (`.RTF`) instead. Most of the fancy formatting will survive, but harmful macros won't. And nearly every word processor on the planet can read and write RTF files.

Beware of files that only seem to be image files. Virus authors often rename their viruses to appear to be pictures; that's how the Anna Kournikova virus spread. Distinguishing between safe and unsafe files is so difficult, even for experts, that it's best to stay away from attachments entirely.

Dangerous File Extensions

.ade	Microsoft Access project extension
.adp	Microsoft Access project
.bas	Microsoft Visual Basic class module
.bat	Batch file
.chm	Compiled HTML Help file
.cmd	Microsoft Windows NT command script
.com	Microsoft MS-DOS program
.cpl	Control Panel extension
.crt	Security certificate
.exe	Program
.hlp	Help file
.hta	HTML program
.inf	Setup information
.ins	Internet Naming Service
.isp	Internet Communication settings
.js	JScript file
.jse	JScript encoded script file
.lnk	Shortcut
.mdb	Microsoft Access program
.mde	Microsoft Access MDE database
.msc	Microsoft Common Console document
.msi	Microsoft Windows Installer package
.msp	Microsoft Windows Installer patch
.mst	Microsoft Visual Test source files
.pcd	Photo CD image, Microsoft Visual compiled script
.pif	Shortcut to MS-DOS program
.reg	Registration entries
.scr	Screensaver
.sct	Windows Script Component
.shs	Shell Scrap object
.shb	Shell Scrap object
.url	Internet shortcut
.vb	VBScript file
.vbe	VBScript encoded script file
.vbs	VBScript file
.wsc	Windows Script Component
.wsf	Windows Script file
.wsh	Windows Script Host Settings file

TIP OF THE DAY   Make file extensions visible so you can tell what kind of file you're about to execute.

In Windows XP, open My Computer, select **Folder Options** from the **Tools** menu, click the **View** tab, and be sure **Hide Extensions for Known File Types** is unchecked.

On Mac OS X, select **Preferences** from the **Finder** menu and check the **Always Show File Extensions** box.

DOWNLOAD OF THE DAY   Email that uses HTML code to add pictures, colors, and fonts can also pose a threat to your system. There's no way to turn off HTML in the most popular email package, Microsoft Outlook, but there is a free download that does the trick. Get your copy of NoHTML for Outlook 2000 and 2002 from `ntbugtraq.ntadvice.com/default.asp?pid=55&did=38`.

You also should disable the Preview pane in Outlook and Outlook Express. Uncheck **Preview Pane** in the **View** menu.

SATURDAY, JANUARY 4, 2003

TODAY'S FOCUS: Keeping Your New Year's Resolutions

INVENTOR OF BRAILLE ALPHABET BORN

Louis Braille was born on January 4, 1809, in Coupvray, France. Braille was blinded at the age of three from an infection caused by an eye injury. When he was 15, Braille created an alphabet using raised dots based on a system developed by French soldiers to communicate in the dark. Today, Braille is used by approximately 1.3 million legally blind people in the U.S. and is the primary reading medium for thousands of blind children.

Related Web sites   www.acb.org, www.afb.org, www.louisbraillecenter.org

New Year's Resolutions

By Alison Strahan

Here we are, four days into the new year, and for many of us, our New Year's resolutions are already as forgotten as yesterday's breakfast. Did you pledge to give up the smokes? Tone up your muscles at the gym? Lose those love handles? It's not too late. Here are some online resources to help you stand by your convictions long term.

Stop Smoking—The American Lung Association (www.lungusa.org) provides articles and recommendations on how to create a personalized plan for quitting smoking. Additionally, the organization's popular Freedom from Smoking program (www.lungusa.org/ffs) is now available online.

Registration in the program is a drag (did I say that?), but registering is a measure of your commitment to giving quitting a serious try.

Shape Up—Keeping that resolution to develop a body to awe Hulk Hogan means you'll need to join a gym. Find the right kind of gym for your exercise and economic needs using the gym locator at FitnessZone, www.fitnesszone.com.

Gym enrollment tends to rise in January, but how do you ensure that you're still working out in September? The American Heart Association (www.justmove.org/home.cfm) will help you develop an exercise program that suits your level of fitness. Chart your progress with the online exercise diary.

Lose Weight—The American Dietetic Association has a comprehensive, alphabetical list of links to nutritional tips at www.eatright.org/ermprev.html. The advice covers everything from preparing a quick nutritious breakfast for your kids to a brief guide on reducing your cholesterol.

If you want more personalized diet help, use the nutritionist locator (www.eatright.org/find.html) to find a dietician in your area.

Many former chubbies swear by eDiets.com (www.ediets.com), a site that helps you lose weight and pick up healthy eating habits. You can access helpful articles for free or subscribe to the service to receive customized meal plans and more.

Finally, here's some offline advice from a seasoned resolution maker: Announce and report your goals to those you care about. Friends and family can be helpful nags when your resolve is flagging.

 TIP OF THE DAY   Resolutions Reminders, at hiaspire.com, will send you a free monthly email reminder to encourage you to follow through with your goals. The email includes a bunch of links geared toward your particular resolution, whether it's finding your perfect mate or clearing up your finances. Although some of the links are advertiser-driven, many include excellent online references. Skip the email reminders and go straight to the advice by using the drop-down menu to find helpful resources related to your resolution.

 DOWNLOAD OF THE DAY   NutriGenie offers a wide variety of health monitoring software for windows, www.nutrigenie.biz.

Keep track of your diet and exercise plan on your Palm with BalanceLog from healthetech.com.

TODAY'S FOCUS: Online Security

FIRST FEMALE BALLOON PILOT BORN

Jeannette Ridlon Piccard was born January 5, 1895, in Chicago, Illinois. In 1934, she became the first woman to ascend into the stratosphere, flying a balloon with her husband, Dr. Jean Piccard, to an altitude of 57,579 feet.

Related Web site   `www.spacefame.org`

Twisted List: Most Notorious Hackers

By Martin Sargent

John Draper, a.k.a. Cap'n Crunch—Draper figured out that the cheap plastic whistles that came inside boxes of Cap'n Crunch cereal produced a 2,600MHz tone—the same tone used to gain access to Ma Bell's long-distance switching equipment—allowing Draper to make free long-distance phone calls.

While serving time for his crimes, Draper created EasyWriter, the first word processor for the Apple II computer.

Mark Abene, a.k.a. Phiber Optik—Abene was a member of the elite hacker group Legion of Doom (LOD) until a tiff with the group's leader, Eric Bloodaxe, inspired him to form a rival group called the Masters of Deception (MOD).

As LOD and MOD battled for supremacy by messing with each other's computers and performing publicity stunts, MOD went a step too far by crashing all the computers at New York public television station WNET, leaving the message "Happy Thanksgiving you turkeys, from all of us at MOD." Abene was sentenced to a year in prison.

Vladimir Levin—Levin, a 28-year-old biochemistry graduate from St. Petersburg University, led a Moscow hacker gang in stealing millions of dollars from Citibank. Levin operated from a laptop computer in London, logging into the network some 18 times over a span of several months. He transferred around $10 million into bank accounts around the world.

He was eventually captured at Heathrow airport and extradited to the United States, where he was sentenced to three years in prison and given a $240,015 fine. Citibank claims to have recovered all but about $400,000 of the stolen money.

Kevin Poulsen, a.k.a. Dark Dante—In 1990, Poulsen took over Pacific Bell's telephone-switching network to ensure that he'd be the 102nd caller to Los Angeles radio station KIIS FM, thereby winning a Porsche 944 S2.

In separate incidents, he used the same method to win trips to Hawaii and thousands of dollars in cash. It's rumored that Poulsen also blocked the tip lines when he was featured on *Unsolved Mysteries*. He was eventually captured and sentenced to five years in prison.

Kevin Mitnick, a.k.a. Condor—Mitnick broke into dozens of computer systems, stole tens of thousands of credit card numbers, and copied millions of dollars' worth of computer software. There's no evidence, however, that he used any of the data for profit.

Mitnick, the first hacker to appear on an FBI "Most Wanted" poster, was eventually captured after two years on the lam. He spent 49 months in jail awaiting a bail hearing—according to Mitnick's lawyers, the longest span of time without a bail hearing in U.S. history. He eventually served five years in prison.

 TIP OF THE DAY   When you buy online, pay with a credit card whenever possible. Under federal law you're only responsible for $50 in losses.

 DOWNLOAD OF THE DAY   Stop email scams with SpamBuster for Windows, free from `www.contactplus.com/products/spam`. An ad-free version is $19.95.

POLL: Do you have the right to know if your bank has been hacked?

97% Yes

3% No

TODAY'S FOCUS: Online Security

FIRST ROUND-THE-WORLD FLIGHT BY COMMERCIAL AIRCRAFT

Pan American Airline's "Pacific Clipper" became the first commercial passenger jet to circle the globe on January 6, 1942. The Boeing B-314 made the trip in four days, leaving from and arriving in New York. The plane was purchased by the U.S. Navy in 1946 and subsequently sold to Universal Airlines. The aircraft was eventually damaged in a storm and salvaged for parts. A round-trip ticket from San Francisco to Honolulu on Pan Am's first Clippers cost about $800 (almost $2,000 in today's dollars).

Related Web sites `www.panam.com, www.flyingclippers.com`

Install a Firewall

If you lived in a dangerous neighborhood, you'd probably install a burglar alarm in your house. If your computer is connected to the Internet, you're in a dangerous neighborhood. Time to install the computer equivalent of a burglar alarm: a firewall.

A firewall restricts traffic into and out of your system, blocking many kinds of hacker attacks. These days, running a firewall is a requirement for any machine that connects to the Internet.

You can use a hardware firewall, like those built into most broadband routers, or rely on a software firewall. You don't need both. Mac OS X and Windows XP come with firewalls built in, but they're not turned on by default.

 To enable and configure the Mac OS X firewall, I recommend a program from Brian Hill called BrickHouse, `personalpages.tds.net/~brian_hill/brickhouse.html`. It's $25 shareware.

 To enable the firewall on Windows XP, open the Network Connections control panel, right-click on your connection, and select **Properties** from the pop-up menu. Click the **Advanced** tab and check the option to **Protect My Computer and Network**. Do this for all the connections in your Network Connections folder.

Unfortunately, the Windows XP firewall is only half a firewall. It controls incoming traffic, but it won't stop outgoing traffic, which means that a malicious program already on your computer can operate unchecked. One of the most important tasks of a firewall is to notify you when a program is trying to access the Net from your system. That's how Trojan horse programs work. A hacker might sneak such a program onto your computer via an email attachment or physically access your system when you're not paying attention. The Trojan horse sits there silently, undetected, for a long time. When it activates, it will try to access the Internet, and that's when your firewall should raise a warning.

No firewall provides perfect protection. To continue to use the Net, you must punch holes in the firewall. Smart bad guys can use these holes to crack your system, but a good firewall makes it much harder.

 TIP OF THE DAY Test your firewall by visiting ShieldsUp, Steve Gibson's invaluable security checker, at `grc.com/x/ne.dll?bh0bkyd2`. You'll find a wealth of security information there, too. Sygate runs an excellent testing service at `scan.sygate.com`, as does Finjan Software at `www.finjan.com/mcrc/sec_test.cfm`.

Test the vulnerability of your email system at the GFI Email Security Testing Zone, `www.gfi.com/emailsecuritytest/`.

 DOWNLOAD OF THE DAY The Windows XP firewall might be less than perfect, but fortunately you can get an excellent Windows firewall free. I recommend ZoneAlarm from `www.zonealarm.com`. I also like the Tiny Personal Firewall from `www.tinysoftware.com`.

TODAY'S FOCUS: Online Security

COMMERCIAL TRANSATLANTIC TELEPHONE SERVICE BEGINS

AT&T president Walter Gifford placed the first call from his office in New York to the Secretary of the British Post Office in London on January 7, 1927. American telephone monopoly AT&T, then known as the Bell System, partnered with the British government to link telephone transmission by converting telephone signals into radio waves to cross the Atlantic, and then reconverting them to telephone signals. Sound quality was extremely poor, and calls cost $25 per minute.

Related Web sites `www.att.com/technology/history`, `www.telecomresearch.com`

Install an Antivirus Program, and Keep It Up to Date

A computer virus is a malicious program that sneaks onto your system, often causing damage. Viruses are sometimes called worms or Trojan horses, but all share the characteristic of operating behind your back. That's why you need an antivirus program patrolling your system for little beasties. When the antivirus finds one, it alerts you and disables the virus. In many cases, it can eradicate all traces of a virus from your system. Antivirus programs can run continuously in the background watching for virus-like activity, or they can be run on a schedule.

New viruses are released every day, so for an antivirus to be effective it must be updated regularly. Most programs offer an automatic update feature—be sure you use it. An out-of-date antivirus is nearly worthless.

When purchasing an antivirus, look for a program that provides automatic email scanning, because that's the most common way systems are exposed to viruses. Updates should be free for at least the first year.

I like Norton AntiVirus from Symantec, but there are many good products to choose from. Windows computers can use a free Web-based antivirus called Housecall from Trend Micro, at `housecall.antivirus.com`.

TIP OF THE DAY Virus names are intended to communicate information about how the virus works and what operating system it affects.

Each virus is assigned a unique name, but the name varies among antivirus vendors. Unfortunately, that makes it hard to track down information about a virus.

For example, the media called one virus AnnaKournikova because it pretended to be an email with an attached picture of the famous tennis star. The antivirus companies have agreed not to use real people's names in virus descriptions, so most of them used another name. If you had searched one of the virus vendors' sites for AnnaKournikova, you might have come up empty.

Fortunately, the Virus Bulletin offers a Web site, VGrep, that helps users find virus information no matter what the name. Visit it at `www.virusbtn.com/resources/vgrep`.

If you think you have a virus, it's worth a visit to one of the antivirus research sites. They're very helpful and often offer free disinfection tools.

Symantec: `www.sarc.com`

McAfee: `vil.mcafee.com`

TrendMicro: `www.antivirus.com/vinfo`

Finjan: `www.finjan.com/mcrc`

DOWNLOAD OF THE DAY Grisoft offers a free Windows antivirus, AVG 6.0, at `www.grisoft.com`.

VCatch is a free antivirus tool for Windows from `www.vcatch.com` that scans incoming files from email, Web mail, file-sharing, and instant-messaging applications, including ICQ. When VCatch finds an infected attachment, it automatically deletes the file and notifies you.

Mac viruses are less common, but it's still a good idea to own an antivirus. Agax is a free Mac Classic application from `www.defyne.org/agax`. Keep it up to date by downloading additives from the same site.

TODAY'S FOCUS: Online Security

AT&T BREAKUP

The American Telephone and Telegraph Company was ordered by the FCC to give birth to 22 "Baby Bell" companies on this day in 1982. The decision split the telecom monopoly into seven regional Bell operating companies, and introduced consumer choice in long-distance telephone service. The AT&T divestiture is considered one of the most important antitrust cases in modern history.

Related Web sites `www.att.com/history`, `www.navyrelics.com/tribute/bellsys/att_divestiture.html`

Encrypt Private Files

It's one thing to keep your most private data on your personal computer; it's quite another thing to connect that computer to the Internet. It's like leaving all your credit cards on the front seat of an unlocked car. And the more you have to lose, the more important it is for you to protect that data.

Even if you've faithfully followed the security guidelines we've discussed so far this month, you're still at risk. No networked computer is unhackable. You could disconnect from the network entirely, but that's not very practical. So, let's take a look at a way to keep your data safe without abandoning the Internet—safe even if the bad guys have physical access to your system. The ultimate key to data security is encryption. Files that are scrambled with strong encryption are safe from prying eyes. Even if a hacker penetrates your defenses, he can't use the stuff he finds on your drive.

There are plenty of free and commercial encryption programs, but Pretty Good Privacy (PGP), by Phil Zimmermann, has stood the test of time… and the CIA. Download a free copy from `www.pgpi.com`. PGP is available for nearly every operating system in existence.

PGP can be used both to lock files and to scramble email. In Windows, for example, once you've installed PGP you can right-click on a document and select **PGP** from the pop-up menu. Picking the encrypt option will scramble a file so well that even the government can't read it.

The free software community has begun work on a version of PGP that doesn't incorporate any patented technologies. This version, GnuPG from `www.gnupg.org`, is in the early stages of development but eventually will eclipse PGP as the encryption tool of choice.

For secure encryption that can't be cracked without a supercomputer and lots of time, look for a product that offers 128-bit or better encryption using Triple-DES, Idea, Blowfish, Skipjack, or RSA-based routines. PGP, for example, combines Idea and RSA technologies and allows keys of up to 4,096 bits.

TIP OF THE DAY   Windows XP Professional comes with encryption built in. To encrypt a file or folder, right-click it and select **Properties** from the pop-up menu. Under the **General** tab, click the **Advanced** button, and then check the **Encrypt Contents to Secure Data** option. The encryption feature is available only on NTFS-formatted volumes. The file or folder is automatically unlocked when you log in—no other user will be able to read it.

If you use this technique, be sure to back up your key; otherwise, you'll lose your data if you reinstall Windows.

DOWNLOAD OF THE DAY   Keep track of your passwords (and automatically create new ones) with *PC Magazine*'s free Password Prompter for Windows, `downloads-zdnet.com.com/3000-2092-5943131.html`.

Mac OS X users can do the same with Markus Mehlau's free Pastor, from `www.mehlau.net/pastor`.

TODAY'S FOCUS: Online Security

FIRST MANNED FREE-BALLOON FLIGHT

Jean-Pierre Francois Blanchard took the first aerial voyage in the U.S. on this day in 1793. George Washington was reportedly among the witnesses of the flight over Philadelphia, Pennsylvania. Blanchard's "flying ship" was equipped with oars suspended below a hydrogen balloon. The French balloonist also became the first person to cross the Channel between England and France. Blanchard died in Paris in 1809 after falling out of his balloon at The Hague.

Related Web site   `www.launch.net`

Back Up Regularly

If the worst happens and you do succumb to a virus or a hacker, your last line of defense is a good data backup. If you have an up-to-date backup, you can format your hard drive, restore your data, and move on. If you don't back up, you'll be out of luck.

Use some form of removable media for your backup. If you can't take it with you, it's not a backup. The best way to back up your data is to record it onto a CD. It's cheap, reliable, portable, and you can read the data on nearly any computer.

The essential rule of backing up is, "Make a copy of anything you can't otherwise replace." In other words, make copies of your personal data. Don't make copies of your operating system or applications; you can restore them from the master discs.

Both Windows and Macintosh store most user-created data files in a special Documents folder (My Documents in Windows). If you save nothing else, copy this entire folder. But not all your precious data is in there. Here are some other places to look.

Email   Locations vary. In Outlook Express, select **Options** from the **Tools** menu, click the **Maintenance** tab, and then click **Store Folder** to reveal the location of your mail files. To find your data in Outlook, select **Options** from the **Tools** menu, click the **Mail Setup** tab, and then click the **Data Files** button.

Internet Bookmarks   Netscape puts bookmarks in a file named `bookmark.htm`, which usually is stored in your user profile folder in the Netscape program directory. Internet Explorer stores favorites as individual files in the `C:\Windows\Favorites` directory.

And don't forget to jot down your network and email server settings, too.

You'll want to back up some files every time you change them. I make a copy of my financial data whenever I balance the checkbook. Other things can be backed up weekly or monthly. I'd strongly recommend backing up all your data at least weekly and saving a copy of that backup offsite. When disaster strikes, you'll be glad you did.

 TIP OF THE DAY   Many programs will automatically save backup copies of your files as you work with them. In Microsoft Word, for example, turn on automatic file backup by choosing **Options** from the **Tool** menu. Click the **Save** tab, and put a check in the box next to **Save AutoRecover Info Every:**. The default save time will be every 10 minutes, but you can make it more often if you like.

 DOWNLOAD OF THE DAY   Second Copy for Windows from Centered Systems (`www.secondcopy.com`) backs up files in the background while you work. It's free to try, $29.95 to buy.

 For Mac OS X, I recommend Synchronize! X Plus, free for 10MB of data or less, $29.95 to buy, from `www.qdea.com`.

FRIDAY, JANUARY 10, 2003

TODAY'S FOCUS: Online Security

INVENTOR OF COTTRELL'S EQUATION BORN

Physical chemistry professor Frederick Gardner Cottrell was born in Oakland, California, on this day in 1877. In 1902, Cottrell created a scientific equation on the principles of static electricity that bears his namesake. He also developed the electrostatic precipitator, which removes suspended particles from gases. His invention is still used today by factories and power plants to reduce pollution. Among the electrostatic laws Cottrell studied most is the phenomenon that causes dust to stick to your computer screen.

Related Web sites www.rescorp.org/cottrell.htm, www.sciencemadesimple.com/static.html

Are You at Risk?

By Marcus J. Ranum

If you're like most people, you've dismissed the threat of getting hacked because you don't think you're a target. You're probably not a target—but your system might be.

The "new school" hackers use broadbased searching tools that scan thousands of machines per hour looking for security holes. When they find a hole, they can take over the machine and use it either as a staging area for further attacks or as a "zombie" system to launch attacks against other sites.

So, although a hacker might not be out to get you, he might be out to take over your machine. It's nothing personal. Next-generation worms break into every machine they can find that is vulnerable. They don't care who you are or whether you're an interesting target. Every target is interesting to them.

Your level of risk depends on how you're connecting to the Internet. If you're on a broadband connection, your machine is more attractive to hackers for three reasons:

- Broadband users tend to leave their machines turned on and connected 24 hours a day.
- Hacker scanning tools can locate your machine more quickly.
- Uploading and downloading files is faster.

Many broadband users' systems are constantly being scanned and probed by hackers. During the Code Red worm outbreak, my machine was getting several dozen scans per hour. Any one of those scans could have gotten through, forcing me to spend hours cleaning up my computer.

The best way to avoid being hacked is to follow the security tips provided this month. If you're curious about what hackers are up to, pay regular visits to the following security sites:

SecurityFocus: www.securityfocus.com

CERT, the Computer Emergency Response Team: www.cert.org

CIAC, the Computer Incident Advisory Capability: www.ciac.org

(Marcus Ranum is CTO of NFR Security, www.nfr.com.)

 TIP OF THE DAY Both Windows XP and Mac OS X automatically create Administrator accounts when you first install them. In Unix operating systems, this Administrator account is often known as the *superuser* or *root*.

The operating system allows the administrator complete access to the system. Admins can delete any file, install software, change system settings, and otherwise wreak havoc. That's why it's best not to use the Admin account for day-to-day computing, even if you're the only user on the system.

Protect yourself from yourself by creating an ordinary user account, and use it most of the time. Log in as Admin only when you need the extra power.

 DOWNLOAD OF THE DAY Hacker is a Windows game that simulates the experience of hacking. Free from www.unrealvisions.com.

Want to play the other side? Try Verado: The IT Security Game for Windows, free from www.intrapromote.com/case_study_verado.html

TODAY'S FOCUS: Online Security

INSULIN FIRST USED ON HUMANS

The first insulin injection was given to a human diabetes patient in Toronto, Canada, on this day in 1922. Canadian scientists Frederick Banting and Charles Best extracted insulin from the pancreas of laboratory dogs and transferred it to 14-year-old diabetic Leonard Thompson. The procedure saved Thompson's life.

Related Web site `www.diabetes.org`

Top Five Most Famous Viruses

By Martin Sargent

1986: The Brain Virus   The first MS-DOS virus was Brain. The story goes that Basit and Amjaad Farooq Alvi, owners of a store called Brain Computer Services, wrote the boot sector virus to stealthily leave their contact information on computers. Basit and Amjaad claimed they wrote the code to ascertain the extent of software piracy in Pakistan, but Brain soon leaked through the Pakistani borders and harmlessly infected computers worldwide.

1988: The Internet Worm   Written by Cornell University Ph.D. student Robert Morris, the Internet Worm quickly writhed its way onto VAX and Sun systems throughout the country. Although Morris had intended for his creation to spread from computer to computer without causing any damage or leaving a trace, a bug in his code caused it to replicate wildly, bringing the fledgling Internet to its knees.

Morris panicked and tried to send out warnings, but the Internet was so clogged no one saw them. He was eventually sentenced to three years of probation and 400 hours of community service, and fined $10,050.

1992: The Michelangelo Media Fiasco   Hysteria swept over the planet as the media proclaimed that on March 6, the birth date of Renaissance artist Michelangelo, up to one-quarter of the world's hard drives would be completely erased by a virus. Even the respectable *Wall Street Journal* carried the headline "Deadly Virus Set to Wreak Havoc Tomorrow." Michelangelo was a dud. When March 6 came, the virus struck only about 10,000 computers.

1999: Melissa   Melissa, a Word macro virus, was the first to propagate itself via email. When people opened the host Word document, the virus sent a copy of itself to the first 50 people in the victim's address book.

The Computer Emergency Response Team estimated that the virus hit 100,000 computers in its first weekend.

Melissa's author, David L. Smith, initially entered a plea of innocent, but after being confronted with a maximum sentence of 40 years in prison, he pleaded guilty and received a much-reduced sentence.

2000: Love Bug   According to Reuters, the Love Bug cost the world $15 billion in lost productivity. It spread far faster than Melissa because it sent itself to everyone in the victim's Outlook address book. It also damaged media files stored on the hard drive. One German newspaper lost 2,000 pictures from its archive.

The perpetrator turned out to be a 23-year-old Filipino computer science student who more or less plagiarized all his code. Because of a lack of computer crime laws in the Philippines, he was never charged.

TIP OF THE DAY   The computer virus FAQ for new users tells newbies everything they need to know about viruses: `www.faqs.org/faqs/computer-virus/new-users/`.

The full-length virus FAQ in four parts:

`www.faqs.org/faqs/computer-virus/alt-faq/part1/`

`www.faqs.org/faqs/computer-virus/alt-faq/part2/`

`www.faqs.org/faqs/computer-virus/alt-faq/part3/`

`www.faqs.org/faqs/computer-virus/alt-faq/part4/`

 DOWNLOAD OF THE DAY   My pal John C. Dvorak's favorite antivirus software comes from Russia. Download a trial version of Kaspersky AntiVirus for Windows, free from `www.kaspersky.com`.

POLL: How long before a virus takes down the Net?

10% Next week

22% Next month

68% Next year

TODAY'S FOCUS: Online Security

AMAZON.COM FOUNDER BORN

Jeff Bezos, founder and CEO of Amazon.com, was born in Albuquerque, New Mexico, on this day in 1964. Bezos launched the shopping supersite out of his garage in July, 1995. A few years later, the Seattle-based company was the most frequently visited shopping site on the Internet, with more than 12 million customers in 160 countries.

Related Web site   www.amazon.com

The Hacker's Dictionary

Like any other specialists, hackers have their own, unique language. Here are the most common hacker terms you might hear the next time you go to Defcon:

- **Exploit**—An attack that takes advantage of a bug or hole in a piece of hardware or operating system. "Code Red was based on a buffer overflow exploit in Microsoft's Web server software."
- **Root**—The most powerful user on a computer; sometimes called the Administrator or superuser. The root account has permission to do anything on the system. Intruders often attempt to "hack root" on a computer to take it over. "Condor hacked root on SWAN, Sun's internal network."
- **Rootkit**—A collection of programs that a hacker plants on a system after he or she has obtained access to it. Rootkits contain programs to monitor traffic and cover the hacker's tracks, and replacements for commonly used programs that are designed to give the hacker easy access to the system in the future. "Silver Surfer planted a rootkit on the mail server, and now he can get in whenever he wants."
- **Packet sniffer**—A program that monitors network traffic. A hacker can use a packet sniffer to find passwords, credit-card numbers, and other interesting bits of information that travel over the network. That's why it's important to send private data over a secure connection. "I put a packet sniffer on the company network, and you won't believe the sites the CEO is visiting."
- **Keylogger**—A program or piece of hardware that captures keystrokes. Like the packet sniffer, a keylogger is used primarily for capturing passwords. Unlike packet sniffers, keyloggers are not thwarted by encryption or secure connections. "The FBI used a keylogger to crack Scarfo's PGP passphrase."

- **Script kiddie**—Unskilled hackers who use scripts and programs written by others. Many hackers write programs for their own use and to show their prowess, and then distribute these programs on the Internet. Less adept hackers can use these programs to cause some damage, but they're usually able to get only so far. "Those script kiddies brought down Yahoo! with Mixter's TFN."
- **Social engineering**—Many hacks don't involve computing at all. Hackers often discover passwords and other vital information by tricking people. Hackers will pose as tech support personnel or other official workers to get the information they need. Never reveal private information without verification.

TIP OF THE DAY   Keep on top of security issues with a visit to these sites:

Security Focus: www.securityfocus.com

The Sans Institute: www.sans.org

Stay Safe Online: www.staysafeonline.info

DOWNLOAD OF THE DAY   Nmap is a free program that can test your security. For Unix systems, including Mac OS X and Linux: www.insecure.org/nmap. A Windows version is in development.

POLL: Why did hackers launch the denial-of-service attacks?

4% Political protest

11% Destroying e-business

40% Because they can

45% All the above

TODAY'S FOCUS: Digital Music

FIRST MUSICAL RADIO BROADCAST

Inventor and radio pioneer Lee de Forest transmitted the first live opera performance on this day in 1910. Italian tenor Enrico Caruso sang Cavalleria Rusticana from the Metropolitan Opera House in New York City, marking the beginning of the use of radio for entertainment. de Forest, while a major player in the history of communications, was often overlooked while other innovators, such as Guglielmo Marconi, received more public attention.

Related Web site `www.leedeforest.org`

Internet Radio

By Phil Allingham

Internet radio comes in two major flavors: online versions of broadcast radio stations, such as National Public Radio (www.npr.org) and Internet-only programming. The Internet-only stations offer the most diverse programming, ranging from Bloomberg European financial news (www.bloomberg.co.uk/ukradio) to all prank phone calls all the time (www.live365.com/stations/funmaster).

To listen, you'll need a fast Internet connection. If you're a home user, cable or DSL is best. Corporate users on a high-speed connection will also be fine. But check with your IT department first, because many have policies against all forms of streaming media. You can listen to Webcasts on a dial-up modem, but the quality will suffer.

You'll also need software. Internet radio comes in a variety of formats. Most services use one of the big three media players: RealNetworks' RealOne (www.real.com), Microsoft's Windows Media Player (www.windowsmedia.com), or Apple's QuickTime (www.apple.com/quicktime). All three players come with built-in radio directories to help you find programming, and there also are many online radio directories.

If you have your heart set on listening to the same radio station you listen to in the car, start at MIT's radio locator, www.radio-locator.com. Enter your ZIP Code or city name, the radio station's call letters (if you know them), or nation of origin. You'll get a list of local radio stations, where each falls on the FM or AM dial, whether it broadcasts online, and a link.

RadioDirectory (www.radio-directory.com) also keeps a list of traditional radio available online and online-only stations.

Yahoo! Radio (radio.yahoo.com) is a great place to start finding hundreds of radio stations that broadcast online. Browse by genre, including sports, news, talk, and even police scanners.

Spinner (www.spinner.com) is my favorite place to go for Internet-only music programming. Dozens of channels are all programmed by paid DJs, and the interface, variety, and quality just can't be beat. The Spinner software is based on RealPlayer, but it has a customized interface that allows you to rate songs, influence song play, and save favorite channels and information about your favorite tunes.

Other great music sites include

Launch: www.launch.com

Live365: www.live365.com

Shoutcast: www.shoutcast.com

(Phil Allingham is managing editor of Call for Help.*)*

 TIP OF THE DAY Apple's free iTunes MP3 player also supports Internet radio. Click **Radio Tuner** in the left column for a list of stations. If you have a dial-up connection, stick with streams at 40Kbps or less. For CD-quality sound, pick 128Kbps streams.

 DOWNLOAD OF THE DAY My favorite music player is also great for Internet radio. Download MusicMatch for Windows or Macintosh, free from www.musicmatch.com. After you've installed it, click the radio button to see your choices. For CD-quality music over a broadband connection, try MusicMatch's Radio MX. It's $4.95 per month or $10.95 for a three-month subscription.

POLL: Would you pay for Internet radio?

3% Yes   97% No

TUESDAY, JANUARY 14, 2003

TODAY'S FOCUS: Digital Music

FIRST SUCCESSFUL C-SECTION

The first-known Caesarian operation in North America was performed by Dr. Jesse Bennett on on this day in 1794. The patient was his wife. The medical procedure dates back to Roman times, and usually was performed to save the fetus when the mother was no longer alive. Dr. Bennett's surgery was successful—both mother and child survived. Reports say during the operation, Dr. Bennett also removed both of his wife's ovaries "so that he would not be subjected to such an ordeal again."

Related Web site `www.childbirth.org`

MP3 101

A musical revolution has begun, thanks to MP3. MP3 stands for MPEG audio layer III, a formula for compressing audio to less than 1/10 the size without audible degradation. An MP3 file occupies about 1MB per minute of music. An entire album can be stored in less than 70MB. The technique, patented in 1989 by Germany's Fraunhofer Institute, was first popularized in 1997 by college students who used it to copy music from their favorite CDs to the campus network for other students to listen to.

Music sharing exploded into the mainstream in 1999 with the creation of Napster, a program that allowed people all over the world to share music files with each other anonymously. While some musicians embraced Napster and MP3 sharing as a way to gain a broader audience, many others complained that users were stealing their music and undermining record sales. Eventually, the recording industry sued Napster out of existence, but once consumers had a taste of the convenience of MP3s they were reluctant to return to CDs and cassettes, and many Napster clones surfaced.

Today, nearly every computer comes equipped with software that can transform tracks from a CD into MP3 files on the hard drive. Users listen to MP3s on their computers and on the road using portable MP3 players or aftermarket car stereos equipped with MP3 playback capability. Many users still trade MP3s over the Internet, and record companies have begun selling MP3s online.

The convenience and quality of the MP3 format has fomented a revolution in the recording industry. It has helped millions of consumers rediscover their love for music, and given many bands a chance to be heard. At the same time, MP3s have caused a dramatic reduction in the sales of CDs and cassettes, costing artists and record labels millions of dollars. But MP3 is only a file format; it's neither good nor bad. It's what we do with it that makes the difference.

Artists deserve to be paid for their work. Music lovers want access to music online and the right to manipulate it as they see fit. Revolutions are never pretty, but in time I believe we'll come up with a system that works better for everybody, and we'll owe it all to MP3.

TIP OF THE DAY MP3 files don't just store music. There's also room in there for information about the song: artist, title, album, and so on. Most MP3 players and recorders will let you modify this information, or you can use a program like one of these:

 PZTagEditor (`www.pztageditor.com`), for Windows.

 ID3X (`www.three-2-one.com/ID3X`), for Mac OS X.

 DOWNLOAD OF THE DAY mp3Trim is a free utility that can trim silence from the beginning and end of MP3s, normalize the volume, and edit your ID3 tags. Download it from `www.logiccell.com/~mp3trim`.

POLL: How much should an MP3 song cost online?
43% Free
20% $.10
34% $1.00
3% $3.99

TODAY'S FOCUS: Digital Music

ELEVATOR PATENTED

The first patent for an elevator was granted on this day in 1861. Elisha Graves Otis created a hoisting machine with a revolutionary brake that greatly reduced the risk of accidents. The mechanism consisted of a steel wagon spring meshing with a ratchet. If the rope or cable broke, the spring would catch and hold the suspended platform. The rigging was originally created to transport equipment, but later was used to carry people.

History does not record when elevator music was invented.

Related Web site   www.eesf.org

Martin's Favorite Winamp Skins

By Martin Sargent

I'm a music nut. From Stravinsky to The Captain & Tennille to The Notorious B.I.G., I love it all. I especially love to listen to music on my computer, and Winamp is my player of choice, partly because it's so easy to change how it looks using *skins*. Today I'd like to share with you my favorite skins for the Winamp audio player. All these skins can be found at www.winamp.com/skins.

Growing up on a soybean farm, one of my morning chores was to ride around the fields on a tractor and do all that farmer stuff we did when we rode tractors. That's why, when I'm pining for the bucolic days of my youth, I use my John Deere Winamp skin. It reminds me of the smell of fresh-cut soybeans, chasing hippies off our land, and coming in after a long day of working the fields to Mom's homegrown tofu dinners.

Whenever I get a hankering to go south of the border, I don't go to beautiful Tijuana as any normal person would; I play salsa music on my Doritos nacho amp. To me, a really good Friday night consists of a big jar of extra mild salsa with corn bits, a ridiculously large sombrero, and my Doritos nacho amp. And if anyone out there knows where I can score a Gardetto's Snack-ems Winamp skin, let me know, because I need it bad.

Sometimes I wish I grew up in the 1950s—before drugs, the casual dress code, and Peter, Paul, and Mary destroyed America. But I can get a little taste of the '50s today, thanks to my Denny's Winamp skin. You know those guys who spend the summer going to every baseball stadium in the country? Well, one year my crazy friends and I tried to hit every Denny's restaurant between Buffalo and Albany. It was a summer none of us will ever forget. One of my friends even works at one of the Denny's we hit outside Utica. It's crazy, because after all the talking we did on that road trip, he's the only one who had the courage to live up to our dream.

And don't forget *The Screen Savers'* very own Winamp skin from www.tsslab.com/downloads/TSSskin.zip.

 TIP OF THE DAY   You might prefer to listen to MP3 files with Winamp, but when you install Microsoft's Windows Media Player or Real Network's RealOne Player, those programs will take over. To reclaim the right to play MP3s in Winamp, open the configuration editor, click **Filetypes**, and place a check next to the type of files you'd like Winamp to play.

 DOWNLOAD OF THE DAY   Get your free copy of Winamp from www.winamp.com.

POLL: Have you ever changed operating systems?

18% PC to Mac

9% Mac to PC

22% Anything to Linux

51% No, never changed

23

TODAY'S FOCUS: Digital Music

AUTOMOBILE TIRE PIONEER BORN

André Michelin, cofounder of the Michelin tire company, was born on this day in 1853. The French-born engineer and former architecture student was the first to use demountable pneumatic tires on automobiles. He and his brother Edouard Michelin created "les pneumatiques," inflatable tires originally used on French racing cars that could be easily installed and removed for quick changes in case of a flat. The technology allowed for smoother, faster car travel.

Related Web site `www.michelin.com`

How to Choose an MP3 Player

By Roman Loyola

There are three major categories of portable MP3 players: solid state, hard drive, and CD-ROM. Each has its merits and drawbacks. Here's how to choose one that's right for your needs.

Solid State These MP3 players use memory chips to hold your music. Some players have the memory built in, which means you are stuck with a fixed storage capacity. Others use removable memory, which allows you to increase their capacity.

Solid-state MP3 players tend to be the most affordable, around $100, but they also have a smaller storage capacity, as little as 32MB or 64MB—that's 30 to 60 minutes of music. Solid-state players have no moving parts, so they're lighter, more reliable, and never skip, which makes them best for active users.

Hard Drive If you want to carry your whole music collection with you, get an MP3 player with a hard drive. Some players come with a 5GB drive, while others go as big as 20GB—that's about 4,000 songs.

When it comes to price, MP3 players with hard drives are the most expensive. Prices can range from about $250 for smaller capacities to $400 and up for 20GB or more. They also tend to offer the shortest battery life; keeping the hard drive spinning takes lots of energy.

Because hard drive players hold so much music, pay attention to how they connect to your computer. It will take all night to fill a 20GB player using USB (unless you're using USB 2.0). You can do it using FireWire in less than an hour.

You also should pay more attention to the user interface on these devices. When you're managing thousands of songs, ease of use becomes very important.

Compact Disc These portable CD players can handle both standard audio CDs and home-recorded CD-Rs jammed with MP3 files. The standard audio CD holds about an hour of music. An MP3 data disk holds 10 times that, more than 100 songs. Bring 10 MP3 CDs with you and you've got enough music for several days without repeating. These babies sport good battery life and infinite capacity at a reasonable price—typically around $150. And if you have a CD burner, it's the easiest way to make your MP3 collection permanently portable.

(Roman Loyola is a Web producer with The Screen Savers.*)*

TIP OF THE DAY Want to understand how MP3 players work? Visit Marshall Brain's How Stuff Works site at `www.howstuffworks.com/mp3-player.htm`.

 DOWNLOAD OF THE DAY PCDJ Silver for Windows is a software mixer that lets you play your MP3 files like a DJ. Free from `www.visiosonic.com`.

 Mac users can play with MP3s too, with That MP3 Game, `www.blackmagik.com/mp3game.html`. It's a Name That Tune-style game that up to eight people can play. Free to try, $14.95 to buy.

POLL: Can anything stop music piracy?

4% Yes

96% No

Today's Focus: Digital Music

FIRST NUCLEAR-POWERED SUBMARINE VOYAGE

The *USS Nautilus* began its maiden journey on this day in 1955. The ship was built by the Electric Boat Company in Groton, Connecticut. First commanding officer Eugene P. Wilkinson was at the helm. The *Nautilus* is now on display at The Submarine Force Museum in Groton.

Related Web sites   `www.ussnautilus.org`, `www.ans.org`

Turning CDs into MP3s

Copying the tracks from an audio CD to your hard drive is called *CD ripping*. It's the first step to joining the MP3 revolution. Here's all you need to know about how to do it.

1. **Get the Software** Windows users should start by downloading and installing the best all-around MP3 tool out there. It's called MusicMatch Jukebox, and it's free, although you might want to pay the $19.95 shareware fee to unlock all the features (lifetime updates are available for a reasonable, one-time fee). `musicmatch.com`.

   Mac users can use Apple's free iTunes for all their CD ripping needs.

2. **Decide on a Bit Rate** *Bit rate* is the number of bits of data saved for each second of audio. The higher the bit rate, the better the sound quality and the larger the file. 128Kbps will give you near-CD-quality sound. I prefer to record my music at 160Kbps. Some golden-eared audiophiles I know use even higher bit rates, but I can't hear the difference. If you plan to use a portable MP3 player, be sure to choose a compatible bit rate.

3. **Enter Track Info** Most programs will notice when you insert an audio CD. If you have Internet access, they'll look up the CD on the Internet and automatically fill in the names of the songs. They do this by querying the CD Database at `cddb.com` or the user-supported FreeDB at `freedb.org`. These databases contain information about nearly every CD ever pressed, but if you have a homemade disc or enjoy exotic recordings from obscure bands, you might have to enter the track info by hand.

4. **Record to Hard Drive** Now begin the ripping process by clicking the record button. You can configure the ripper to play the song while it's recording, or to rip in silence. Silence is much faster. Depending on your processor, CD-ROM, and hard drive you might be able to record a CD in about one-tenth the time it would take to play it.

When you've finished ripping the CD, put it aside. You can listen to the entire disk directly from your hard drive using MP3 players such as Winamp (`winamp.com`), MusicMatch (`musicmatch.com`), and iTunes. These players will let you create playlists of your favorite songs in any order you like, and even copy your new mixes to CD or MP3 players.

TIP OF THE DAY If your CD-ripping software supports it, add the track number to the beginning of the filename for each song you record. That way, your tracks will play in the order they appear on the album, instead of in alphabetical order (provided that you store your MP3s in separate folders for each album).

 DOWNLOAD OF THE DAY FreeRip 1.13 for Windows is an easy-to-use, no-nonsense ripping program that'll let you extract audio tracks from a CD directly to your hard drive in WAV, MP3, or OGG Vorbis formats. Free from `www.mgshareware.com`.

POLL: Are MP3s hurting record sales?

80% No

12% Yes

8% 8-tracks still rule!

TODAY'S FOCUS: Digital Music

INVENTOR OF DOLBY SOUND SYSTEM BORN

Ray Dolby was born in Portland, Oregon, on this day in 1933. Dolby developed the electronics for the first professional videotape recorder for the Ampex Corporation while he was still in high school. He later turned his attention to audio and founded his own company in 1965. His laboratory's first invention was Dolby A-type noise reduction. This filtered out background noise on professional tape recordings by using audio compression and expansion. Today, Dolby Laboratories owns 616 patents in 28 countries and has sold more than 960 million licensed products.

Related Web site www.dolby.com

Where to Download MP3s

Frankly, most of the MP3 files floating around the Net these days are pirated. It takes a little more work to find and download legitimate MP3s, but it doesn't have to cost you. There are plenty of places to get free music without stealing it.

Start at The Internet Music Underground, iuma.com. IUMA is the first, and probably still the best, site for independent artists in every musical genre. You've probably never heard of most of the bands, but that doesn't mean they're not good. IUMA is the place to hear great bands before they're signed to megabucks contracts.

MP3.com is the first place many people go to sample MP3 music. This site was a pioneer in the MP3 movement, but record giant Vivendi Universal bought it in 2001 for $272 million. Like Vivendi's other sites, Emusic.com and GetMusic.com, MP3.com has become more about selling mainstream music than about free downloads. But there are still free MP3s out there if you're willing to dig.

Sister site emusic.com was the first to offer unlimited MP3 downloads for $10–$15 per month. It offers standard, unprotected MP3s ripped at 128Kbps from more than 900 record labels, including Concord Jazz, Fantasy, and KOCH. You might be frustrated if you're looking for multi-platinum albums, but it's a good source for alternative, punk, and indie (slang for musicians who have signed with independent record labels) music. Artists split the revenues from emusic subscriptions 50/50 with the service.

The other big player right now is the BMG-AOL-Time Warner-Real Networks-EMI collaboration, MusicNet, at musicnet.com. MusicNet is home to some of the biggest acts in the business, but you have to listen to their music on the RealOne player and are limited to 100 downloads and 100 streams per month for $9.95. Digital rights management limits what you can do with the songs you download.

The biggest challenge you'll face is finding a particular song. No one site carries everything. Music lovers will first have to figure out which label the recording is on, and then visit the site for that label and hope they're offering it for download. In most cases, they aren't. Or they're offering it in a form that will keep you from burning it onto a CD or putting it on your MP3 player. That's one reason people who really want to buy music end up pirating it instead.

 TIP OF THE DAY Find record labels' Web sites at rlabels.com.

 DOWNLOAD OF THE DAY Looking for music for your MP3 player? Napster is dead but there are many other music-sharing programs to fill the void. Try WinMX for Windows, www.winmx.com.

 On the Mac, your best choice is Limewire, www.limewire.com. But remember, if you like the music, buy the album.

POLL: How much downloaded music do you have?

30% 0GB–1GB

45% 1GB–10GB

19% 10GB–100GB

6% Googolplex and counting

TODAY'S FOCUS: Digital Music

TIN CAN PATENTED

The tin can was patented by Ezra Daggert and Thomas Kensett in New York on this day in 1825. The tin-plated iron can they introduced in the U.S. was invented by Peter Durand in England two years earlier. Throughout history, a method was sought to preserve food for long periods of time. In 1795, Napoleon reportedly offered 12,000 francs (about $1,600) for such an invention. Today, many a computer geek considers packaged food to be a staple of modern-day life.

Related Web site `cancentral.com`

Twisted List: Online Musical Instruments

By Martin Sargent

So, you want to be a rock star to get all the chicks or dudes, do you, little geek? Well, you can incorporate your nerditude into your act by forsaking the usual musical instruments, such as guitars and saxophones, for computerized versions.

Imagine taking your laptop to the campfire and leading a round of "Kumbaya," or toting that Dell Inspiron you're so proud of to the coffee shop for open mic night. Awwww, yeah.

 Virtual Trumpet You want to be the next Chuck Mangione? Who doesn't? Get started by downloading the Virtual Trumpet, `birdwellmusic.com/trumpet/vTrumpet/vTrumpet.asp`, from BirdwellMusic.com.

 Virtual Theremin Lev Sergeyvich Termen demonstrated his crazy instrument at the Eighth All-Russia Electrical Engineering Conference in 1921. Vladimir Lenin was so impressed with it that he sent Termen to show it off in the United States, saying that it was a model of the Communist ideal.

In the U.S., Termen changed his name to the more Anglo-sounding Theremin and the instrument inspired everyone from musicians to Albert Einstein, who reportedly started thinking about the relationship between music and geometry after seeing a demonstration of the instrument.

The theremin is played by moving one's hands across a field of air, and the motion changes the pitch of the sounds that are produced. To understand what I'm talking about, download the Desktop Theremin from the BBC Online, `www.bbc.co.uk/science/playground/theremin1.shtml`.

 Virtual Banjo Desktop Music's Desktop Banjo (`desktopmusic.com`) is a fun way to learn the basics of playing the banjo, primarily chords. Compose banjo music and play it back. Set it up on two computers and play dueling banjos.

 Be an Emcee, Yo Want to write rap lyrics, kid? The Rhymerator (`www.rhymerator.com`) is a dope little program in which you write some hip-hop lines and the app suggests rhymes and metaphors, if you want them. It's worth playing with just to admire the interface.

 88-Keys on a QWERTY Aldo's Pianito (`aldostools.com/piano.html`) might not teach you how to play the piano very effectively, but it's really fun nonetheless. You use your keyboard as the piano keys. This allows you to annoy co-workers in adjacent cubicles for hours on end. The Web site has lots of other great software, too.

 TIP OF THE DAY For the best-quality MIDI music playback in Windows XP, open the Sounds and Audio Devices control panel, click the **Audio** tab, and select **Microsoft GS Wavetable SW Synthesis** in the MIDI music playback section.

 DOWNLOAD OF THE DAY If you're going to play these instruments, you'd better be able to turn down the volume quickly. ZVolume enhances control of your system volume by keyboard or mouse. Free to try, $19.95 to buy from `shelltoys.com/zvolume`.

POLL: Is your PC a musical instrument?

70% Yes

30% No

TODAY'S FOCUS: Macintosh

CAMCORDER INVENTED

The home video camera debuted on this day in 1982. The camcorder was a joint venture by consumer electronics companies Hitachi, JVC, Philips, Matsushita, and Sony. The first camcorders weighed three pounds, came equipped with a 17-pound portable VCR, and sold for $1,500.

What Is Mac OS X?

All computer companies eventually face the same problem. To advance, they must leave older technologies behind. Apple Computer is no stranger to this dilemma. In fact, the company has faced it several times, first in moving from the wildly successful Apple II to the untested Macintosh, and then in advancing the Mac itself from the older 680x0 chip family to the modern PowerPC line. In each case, users of the older tech got left behind, but in the long run the company benefited from the modernization.

Apple did it again in 2001, abandoning the creaky Mac OS 7/8/9 family for the modern Mac OS X. To successfully make the change, Apple will have to convince both users and software developers that X is better. Fortunately for all of us, it is.

The guts of Mac OS X are based on the most robust operating system ever developed, Unix. Apple adapted the FreeBSD flavor of Unix and dubbed it Darwin. Darwin's protected memory architecture and preemptive multitasking finally bring the Macintosh into the 21st century.

The user experience has been completely redesigned, too. Apple calls the new user interface Aqua. Aqua is beautiful and more functional. The Finder has better organizational capabilities. The Dock eliminates desktop clutter.

Mac OS X supports three kinds of applications:

- Classic lets you run all your Mac OS 9 applications in Mac OS X. It does not support Mac OS X's plumbing or the Aqua interface components.
- Carbon makes it easier to update older applications to take advantage of Mac OS X features. Carbon apps have all the features of native OS X programs.
- Cocoa provides developers with an advanced object-oriented programming environment for building next-generation applications that take advantage of all the features of OS X.

The Mac OS X display system combines three state-of-the-art technologies:

- Quartz for 2D graphics is based on the PDF standard and delivers on-the-fly rendering, antialiasing, and compositing of PostScript graphics.
- OpenGL is the industry's most widely supported 2D and 3D graphics API, making Mac OS X a first-class platform for 3D games and graphics.
- The QuickTime architecture is embedded into the operating system, providing QuickTime audio, video, and image services to any application.

Moving to Mac OS X is a gutsy move for Apple. It won't run on many older Macs, and it requires users and developers to learn new ways of doing things. But Apple needed to make the move, and in the long run, everyone will benefit from the transition to this state-of-the-art operating system.

 TIP OF THE DAY   To learn more about Mac OS X, visit these Web sites:

Mac OS X FAQ: osxfaq.com

Mac OS X Hints: macosxhints.com

Mac OS X Apps: macosxapps.com

Stepwise: www.stepwise.com

 DOWNLOAD OF THE DAY   LaunchBar (www.obdev.at/products/launchbar) is a must-have application. Launch any application, document, or Web address, or send an email with just a few keystrokes. Free to try, $19.95 to buy. Don't ask, just get it.

POLL: Would you buy an OS-less PC?

83% Yes

17% No

TODAY'S FOCUS: Macintosh

FIRST CONCORDE FLIGHT

The first supersonic passenger flight took place on this day in 1976. Air France and British Airways began service on the same day—one flight went from London to Bahrain, and the other from Paris to Rio de Janeiro. The jets are nearly 204 feet long, have a wingspan of more than 83 feet, and a cruising speed faster than Mach2 (about 1,350 MPH). Only one fatal accident has occurred within the Concorde fleet to date: A piece of metal on the runway caused a tire blowout on a plane outbound from Paris to New York, causing a fuel tank to rupture in July, 2000. Passenger service was discontinued for more than a year.

Related Web site `concordesst.com`

Darwin: The Evolution of an Operating System

Apple's latest operating system, Macintosh OS X, is built on top of a Unix foundation. You can access the Unix command line by opening the Terminal program. It's hiding in the Application/Utilities folder.

After you open Terminal, you'll see the words "Welcome to Darwin!" That's what Apple calls the Unix layer in OS X. Below that is the command prompt. If you've never used a command-line operating system such as DOS or Unix, you might wonder what to do next. Here are some handy commands to try:

- man—This is probably the most useful of all the Unix commands. Typing **man** followed by a Unix command displays the manual pages for that command. Try typing **man man**. Press the spacebar to read the next page. Press q to return to the command prompt.
- ls—Displays a list of files in the current directory. You always start in your home directory, but you can move to other directories using the cd command (see below). Type **l** to see the directory in long form. The long display is in columns like so:
  ```
  -rw-r--r--  1  leo  staff  123  Jun 5 11:31
  almanac.outline
  ```
  From left to right these are the file's read/write/execute permissions, the number of links to the file, the owner and group name, the size in bytes, the last time the file was modified, and the filename.

- cd—This changes the working directory. Type **cd** / to get to the root directory, or **cd ..** to go up one level.
- top—Get a real-time list of all processes running on your machine. top also shows CPU use, memory use, and a whole lot of other interesting information about what's happening on your machine.

For a list of many useful Unix commands, visit `www.oreillynet.com/linux/cmd`, but note that these commands are Linux specific. Darwin is based on a different Unix variant called BSD, so some commands might operate differently.

 TIP OF THE DAY Speed up application launches in OS X by opening the terminal and typing the following: **sudo update_prebinding -root** /. Press Return. When the terminal asks you for a password, enter the password for the Administrator account for your machine and press Return again.

You can run the command as often as you like—it won't hurt anything—but you need to do it only when you install a new application.

 DOWNLOAD OF THE DAY To easily install Unix applications on Mac OS X, install Fink. It's free from `fink.sourceforge.com`. Read the documentation before installing.

POLL: Should record companies be forced to disclose copy protection on CDs?

84% Yes

16% No

WEDNESDAY, JANUARY 22, 2003

TODAY'S FOCUS: Macintosh

FIRST HUMAN HIT BY SPACE DEBRIS

The first recorded incident of a person to be hit by falling space junk occurred on this day in 1997. Lottie Williams of Tulsa, Oklahoma, was hit on the shoulder by a metal fragment from a U.S. Air Force rocket's fuel tank. The scrap was about the size of a human hand. Williams wasn't hurt.

Related Web site `www.space.com`

Apple's iDisk

Apple's iTools (`itools.mac.com`) is a suite of useful applications available to all Mac owners. At its heart is iDisk. Apple created iDisk when the first floppy diskless iMac shipped. The lack of a disk drive posed a problem for Mac owners who wanted to transfer their files from their old Macs to their shiny new iMacs. Apple's solution: 20MB of online storage offered free to anyone running Mac OS 9 or X.

iDisk lives on, and Mac owners have found many new ways to use it. When you install Mac OS X, you are given an opportunity to sign up for an iTools account. You'll use the name and password you choose to log in to your iDisk (or you can sign up manually at the iTools Web site). In OS X, you can configure your iTools for automatic login by using the Internet System Preference. Or click the **Sign Up** button to create a new account.

To access your iDisk, go to the iTools Web site or, in Mac OS X, select **iDisk** from the **Go** menu. The iTools volume will mount on your desktop ready for you to drag files to and fro. You'll notice premade folders for documents, movies, music, and so on. You can copy your files into the appropriate folders or make folders of your own.

Three of the folders are for special use: Public, Sites, and Software.

The Public folder is the place to store files for other people to download. Many Mac shareware authors use this as a free way to make their programs available to the public. Copy files you want to share into the Public folder, and then give your iTools username to anyone who wants to access the file.

Web pages you create with the iTools Homepage tool are stored in the iDisk Sites folder. iPhoto also uses the Sites folder for sharing pictures on the Web. You can even use other Web design tools, such as Dreamweaver and BBEdit, to create Web sites and store them in the Sites folder. The URL for your Sites folder is `homepage.mac.com/membername` (where *membername* is your iTools logon).

The third and final special folder is the Software folder. It contains popular Mac shareware and freeware programs. To use them, just drag them from your iDisk to your hard drive. The files stored here do not count against your 20MB disk limit.

 TIP OF THE DAY You can't create an iTools account without a Mac, but you can access an iTools disk from Windows XP. Open My Computer, then choose **Map Network Drive** from the **Tools** menu. Enter `http://idisk.mac.com/membername` (replacing *membername* with your iTools login) as the server address.

 DOWNLOAD OF THE DAY Goliath is a WebDAV client for Mac OS 9 and X. Use it to access your iDisk faster. It's free from `www.webdav.org/goliath`.

POLL: Does Microsoft and/or AOL have control over your life?

34% Yes

66% No

TODAY'S FOCUS: Macintosh

WOZNIAK PATENTS APPLE II

Apple Computer co-founder Steve Wozniak was awarded a patent for his "Microcomputer for use with video display" on this day in 1979. Patent number 4,136,359 was the foundation of the Apple II, which Wozniak helped create with Steve Jobs and Atari engineer Rod Holt two years earlier. The Apple II had a CPU speed of 1MHz, 64k of total memory (4k on the motherboard), and a price tag of nearly $1,300.

Related Web site `www.apple-history.com`

Macs Are Better Than PCs

By Brett Larsen, Mac Bigot

Macintosh computers are elegant and easy to use, but scratch the surface of the Mac, and you'll find the best stuff is inside.

Everything you need is in your Mac. There's no need to find a video card, Ethernet card, modem card, USB card, or even a FireWire card. The Mac comes with it, and the operating system can handle it all. On a PC, you could spend days getting your video card to work after installing a new version of Windows.

Macs ship with great software, free. Programs such as iMovie and iDVD bring the creation and distribution of home movies on DVD to the consumer. iTunes, another Apple application, makes music playback, management, and CD burning simple. iPhoto does the same for digital photography.

But it doesn't stop there. OS X is Apple's revolutionary new operating system. It combines a simple yet elegant interface with the power, stability, and performance of Unix. OS X has power and features that are appropriate for every level of experience. Power users can jump in and take control, while first-time users enjoy simplicity. There's no need to change anything to go from user to user.

Mac OS X is a true multithreaded, multitasking OS, using Internet standards that make it a global player. OS X will fit into an existing network (be it Mac, Windows, or Unix) without needing additional software or additional employee training.

There's no shortage of software for the Mac. Although it might seem as though you can't find any software titles, the truth is, you just won't find thousands of titles that do the same thing. Does this limit you to only a few key apps? No, it keeps you away from thousands of applications that might not work correctly, are poorly written, or are just flat-out bad.

Macs hold their value far longer than PCs. It's not because Apple is slow to upgrade its machines, but because Macs are right when they ship, which reduces the need to upgrade or change existing hardware. Furthermore, Macs last longer. They're higher quality. You're less likely to need to replace something.

Now the bad news. Yes, Macs cost more than PCs. However, your Mac will be worth more for a longer period of time. Mac software is not available in as many places as PC software, but this doesn't mean it's not available. Try `www.macmall.com` or buy directly from Apple at `store.apple.com`.

Think differently. Buy a Mac.

 TIP OF THE DAY Looking for a great deal on Mac hardware and software? Dealmac tracks the prices of popular hardware and sends you an email when the price is lowest. `www.dealmac.com` (`www.dealnews.com` for Windows users).

 DOWNLOAD OF THE DAY Put a talking ungulate on your Mac desktop with Uli's Talking Moose, free from `homepage.mac.com/witness/moose.htm`.

POLL: Is Apple's comeback a flash in the pan?

40% Yes

60% No

FRIDAY, JANUARY 24, 2003

TODAY'S FOCUS: Macintosh

MACINTOSH DEBUTS

The first Apple Macintosh personal computer was announced on this day in 1984. The new model replaced the Apple II and had a manufacturer's suggested retail price of $2,495. It was the first consumer-oriented computer to feature a Graphical User Interface (GUI). The Macintosh was much faster than its predecessor, running a CPU speed of 8MHz. The Mac also featured the first 3.5-inch floppy drives and came standard with 128k RAM. Apple launched a famous and controversial ad campaign for its Macs, comparing IBM PC users to mindless drones from George Orwell's novel, *1984*.

Related Web site apple-history.com

Windows PCs Are Better

By Hahn Choi, Windows Bigot

Macintosh users always claim that Macs are easier to use. That's too subjective an argument. People find easiest that which they use most. Neither Windows nor Mac is inherently easier to use.

The key advantage of the PC over the Mac is its 90%-plus market dominance. The bigger the market, the larger the number of products. As a result, PCs can address the needs of a wider audience.

Whether you choose Dell, Sony, HP, or decide to build your own, the PC gives you more choices. Competition helps bring prices down. Apple controls all Mac hardware, offers limited choices, and dictates the price.

Windows supports more applications. Mac users will argue that you can find all the same core applications. Maybe, but there's more variety on a PC, so you're more likely to find a product to meet your needs and budget. And you'll never find a great game selection on a Mac. PC bestsellers come late to the Mac, if at all. If you never want to have fun, go with a Mac.

Don't expect cutting-edge peripherals on the Mac platform, either. The best hardware is manufactured first for PCs. Macs are an after-thought; in many cases, a never-thought.

For PC users, more companies are competing for your dollars, so component prices fall much faster. PC prices are cheaper all around. On the high end, a fully loaded PC will cost almost $1,000 less than a high-end Mac. Cool styling is no excuse for high prices.

Okay, there are some good things about the Mac. OS X is based on Unix and is more stable than Windows. When it comes to high-end multimedia applications such as video editing, the Mac wins hands down. With applications such as Final Cut Pro 2.0, the Mac becomes a powerful editing suite that can rival expensive professional editing suites. If you want to pursue multimedia content creation, Mac wins.

Apple is pushing FireWire (known as IEEE 1394 on the Windows side). FireWire rocks with its true plug-and-play capability. PC manufacturers are beginning to include it as standard. We thank Apple for the cool name and promoting something that is truly cross-platform.

PCs are everywhere. It's the box of choice for most corporations. It can't hurt to learn the ins and outs of both, but focus on the PC. You'll be glad you did.

 TIP OF THE DAY To find the best prices on PCs and parts visit www.pricewatch.com. Before you buy, check www.resellerratings.com for vendor reviews.

 DOWNLOAD OF THE DAY Maybe PCs don't have the talking moose, but Macs don't have talking Elvis. Download Tiny Elvis for Windows free from www.forchetti.org/tinye.

TODAY'S FOCUS: Macintosh

MOUSE INVENTOR BORN

Doug Engelbart was born near Portland, Oregon, on this day in 1925. He worked with NASA in the late 1960s to find a tool that would allow computer users to quickly and efficiently move the cursor on a computer screen. Engineers found Engelbart's mouse to be the most practical among a group of other prototypes such as pens and joysticks. The first mouse had a cord in front, but it was later attached to the back to "get it out of the way."

Related Web site `bootstrap.org/engelbart`

Martin's Twisted List: Nonviolent Sports Games

By Martin Sargent

I hate Super Sunday. Maybe that's because my mother wouldn't allow me to participate in rough sports such as football because she feared I'd bruise my marble-like, snowy skin and jeopardize my career as a boy model for Johnson & Johnson. She also made me wear a dress because she always wanted a girl. I was a disappointment from the first second.

Anyway, because of that experience I was always very skilled at nonviolent sports, or as the neighborhood kids called them, "wussy games." And now, thanks to the advice of my therapist, here are three nonviolent sports games for your computer.

 Ping-Pong Sometimes, when my mother had had too many white wine spritzers in the afternoon while watching *Days of Our Lives*, I'd sneak away like a baby bird escaping the nest. I'd always head toward the neighborhood rec center to play Ping-Pong.

I loved Ping-Pong. It made me feel so manly. I still get those jock-like sensations when I play *Table Tennis Pro* from grassgames.com. This game is one of the finest Ping-Pong simulations you'll find in the western hemisphere, and it's more addictive than *General Hospital*.

 Golf My father often escaped to the golf course to avoid my mother and his dainty son, but on occasion he'd take me along, which allowed his golfing buddies to see whether all the stories were true and laugh at me and burn my fancy pom-ponned hat with cigars.

But I picked up on the game and that's why I'm so good at EA Sports' online links masterpiece, *Pebble Beach Golf*, at pogo.com. The game is an accurate representation of its historic namesake. As with most computer golf games, the gameplay is simple. Just hit the mouse button once, twice, three times to swing, and if you play well you accumulate tokens and tickets for actual prizes from EA Sports.

 Snooker I've always loved felt. It's my favorite fabric. As a child I was often dressed in felt tunics, elf-like. I guess that's why I'm a natural at pool, especially computer pool. *Real Pool 3D* from shockwave.com/sw/content/realpool is a fabulous pool simulation. You pick an opponent, slather on some powder, and ride the rail toward some serious 8-ball action. Just heed the advice of my mom: Stay out of those pool halls. The better sorts don't hang out there, the women are dirty, and you'll pick up a filthy smoking habit, just like your grandmother.

 TIP OF THE DAY Some say the best part of the Super Bowl is the super advertisements. Watch last year's ads at www.ifilm.com/superbowl.

 DOWNLOAD OF THE DAY Super Bowl XXXVI is here tomorrow. Tune up for the big game with *Madden NFL 2002* demo, madden2002.ea.com/downloads.html. But start early, it's bigger than the Packers' front line.

SUNDAY, JANUARY 26, 2003

TODAY'S FOCUS: Macintosh

LOTUS 1-2-3 RELEASED

Lotus Development Company launched its first product, spreadsheet package Lotus 1-2-3, on this day in 1983. Not long after its introduction, 1-2-3 became the most popular spreadsheet program for IBM PC users, surpassing Dan Bricklin's VisiCalc in popularity.

Related Web site `www.lotus.com`

Martin's Twisted List: Weird Sports

By Martin Sargent

The Internet is full of crazies, but do jocks build Web pages? Do they know HTML? Doesn't that defy all the stereotypes? Here are three of the oddest sports-related pages on the Internet.

Appliance Shooting (`singsingsing.com/has.html`)
Shooting is a very popular sport in America. What's not as popular is the sport of appliance shooting, in which participants fire guns at household appliances and computer equipment. Take a look.

Extreme Ironing (`extremeironing.com`) Ironing your clothes is always dangerous. You can burn yourself or develop varicose veins. But ironing in your house is nothing compared to extreme ironing, in which participants iron while mountain biking, rock climbing, scuba diving, and more.

Ohio Valley Wrestling (`ovwrestling.com`) Where do the stars of the WWF come from? You don't just show up at Madison Square Garden and start pile driving or suplexing The Rock or "Stone Cold" Steve Austin. Just as professional baseball has farm leagues and professional basketball has colleges to locate and train talent, professional wrestling has Ohio Valley Wrestling. That's right, semiprofessional wrestling in the heart of the Ohio Valley.

Check out the stars you'll one day be seeing in Wrestlemania XXVI—superstars such as Trailer Park Trash, Kousin Krazy, Redd Dogg, and the ridiculously attired Chris Alexander. Locate upcoming tour dates and more.

Squirrel Fishing (`eecs.harvard.edu/~yaz/en/squirrel_fishing.html`) Harvard University is far better known for academics than for athletics. Unless, of course, we're talking about the burgeoning sport of squirrel fishing, at which students in Harvard's division of engineering and applied sciences excel.

In squirrel fishing, a really bored Ivy League student ties a piece of string around a peanut and tries to make the squirrel rise off the ground, as if it were a bass being lifted out of a Texas pond.

TIP OF THE DAY The Super Bowl can be particularly hard on your computer. If you happen to spill some of your favorite brewed beverage into your keyboard during halftime, here's how to clean it:

1. Turn off your computer and disconnect the keyboard. Write down the locations of the keys (or take a photo) so you can put them back in the right places.
2. Use a thin screwdriver or butter knife to gently pry up the rectangular keycaps. Don't try to remove the spacebar, Shift, Enter, or any other oversize keys—putting them back into place can be difficult.
3. Sop up liquid with a paper towel. Use compressed air to remove hair, dust, and other loose materials. If you find built-up gunk, use a mild household cleaner on a cotton swab to clean it up.
4. Gently but firmly press each keycap back in place, following the layout in your diagram or photo.

DOWNLOAD OF THE DAY Play digital football online with Miller Lite Digital Football, `superbowl.com/xxxvi/miller`. You must be 21 to play.

TODAY'S FOCUS: Video Editing

FIRST TELEVISION UNVEILED

The first public demonstration of a television was given by John Logie Baird on this day in 1926. The "Televisor" used mechanical rotating disks to scan moving images into electronic impulses. Baird used two ventriloquist dummies for his first broadcast, which he operated in front of the camera apparatus, out of the audience's view.

Related Web site `tvhistory.tv`

Shoot Video Like the Pros

Anyone can shoot great video by avoiding just a few common pitfalls. In fact, if you've ever been forced to watch Uncle Joe's travel movies or the outtakes from Little Sally's birthday party, you probably already know exactly what to avoid. Here are some things to keep in mind the next time you shoot a home movie that will make it easier to edit and much more enjoyable to watch.

Hold Still Movement should come from the objects you're shooting. It's tempting to add some movement yourself, but it's almost always a bad idea. Compose your shot, and then hold still for five to ten seconds. You might not use the entire shot in editing, but you'll be glad you have the extra material.

Plan Your Sequence Professional cinematographers always shoot the same scene many times. First, they get a master shot of the entire scene, including all the elements. Then they'll reshoot for close-ups of the participants. And they'll shoot again for "cutaways": close-ups of objects referred to in the script.

You might not have the luxury of shooting everything three times, but keep in mind that it's more interesting to mix long shots and close-ups in editing. Try to get each scene from a distance, then midrange, and then close-up, to give you more editing choices. Keep edit points in mind, too. Close-ups of hands, for example, make it easier to edit dialogue.

Ban the Pan Quick panning or zooming is a sure way to make your audience nauseous. Use it in moderation, and if you must pan or zoom, do it slowly. The zoom is useful as a way of focusing your audience's attention on a detail in the scene, but plan it carefully, practice it, and then shoot several takes. Most consumer camcorders make it hard to zoom slowly, but it's possible with practice.

Avoid the Dark Side Digital camcorders have a particularly hard time in low-light conditions, and no camera handles backlighting or bright contrast situations well. When you're outside, keep the sun at your back. If you're inside, be sure any windows and bright lights are behind you. Use fill lights in contrasting conditions, unless you're aiming for a *film noir* effect. Your audience wants to see what you're shooting: No one wants those graduation movies to look like *The Blair Witch Project*.

 TIP OF THE DAY Performance is everything when editing video on your computer. In XP, go to the system control panel, click on the **Advanced** tab, and then go to **Performance**, **Settings**. Uncheck any of the visual effects you don't need.

 DOWNLOAD OF THE DAY You don't always need a camera to make a movie. CamStudio records screen activity as AVI files. Great for tutorials or capturing streaming video. Free from `atomixbuttons.com/vsc`.

POLL: What is your favorite kind of game?

40% FPS (First-Person Shooter)

22% RTS (Real-Time Strategy)

31% RPG (Role-Playing Game)

7% SME (Solitaire, Minesweeper, etc.)

POLL: How much is your vote worth?

9% $50

7% $500

28% $5,000

56% Priceless (wouldn't sell)

TUESDAY, JANUARY 28, 2003

TODAY'S FOCUS: Video Editing

CHALLENGER SHUTTLE DISASTER

The space shuttle Challenger exploded shortly after launch from Kennedy Space Center in Cape Canaveral, Florida, on this day in 1986. Among the seven astronauts onboard was Christa McAuliffe, a high school teacher from New Hampshire.

Related Web site   www.ksc.nasa.gov

Stand Still, Shut Up, and Focus

By Scott Smith

The fate of a movie is sealed during the shooting stage. By following these three rules, you can dramatically improve the quality of your video.

Stand Still   Patience is a worthwhile trait to cultivate if you plan to make movies—steady, smooth camera movement delivers the best results. Fortunately, most digital camcorders have some kind of image stabilization built in. And most of them are lightweight, so holding the camera in a stationary position shouldn't be too big of a strain.

Although it's not essential, a sturdy tripod helps. If you don't own a tripod and don't want to spend money on one, there are other ways to stabilize the camera. When standing up, for example, place the elbow of your support arm firmly against your body and use the other hand on the camera body for guidance. At the park, try using a seesaw for a tilt shot that gives the look of a professional crane in motion.

Shut Up   DV camcorders are so sensitive that they can pick up the slightest sounds on the set. Computer hard drives, refrigerators, car engines, and windy weather can create low-frequency noises that the human ear often misses but can be distinctly heard on the DV tape. You can use remote microphones or professional sound equipment if you feel compelled to, but silence remains the most effective weapon against unwanted noise.

Focus   Focus is the key to consistently matching your shots in editing. Imagine watching an intense dialogue exchange between two actors in close-up shots, and

suddenly a piece of footage goes blurry and soft. This distraction is too great to ignore, and most viewers resent the disruption. Thankfully, this scenario is becoming rare in the digital age.

DV cameras have automatic focus features that make adjustments too subtle for the human eye to perceive. Most attempts to manually override this sophisticated technology only prevent the camera from achieving maximum clarity. In matters of focus, let the camera do its job.

However, in bustling environments, or even when actors are simply moving from the foreground to the background of the frame, your camera's auto-focus feature might take a few seconds to select the correct lens position. The result is a muddled mess of images that can ruin a great take. In this case, deactivate the auto-focus features and choose a manual setting with a longer focal depth to capture the full range of movement.

(Scott Smith has written and directed 16 short films including Carny Tales, which recently won the Audience Choice Award at the Sundance Film Festival.)

TIP OF THE DAY   For advice on buying a camcorder visit www.camcorderinfo.com. Epinions (www.epinions.com) has consumer reviews of all kinds of consumer electronics. And don't forget the old standby *Consumer Reports*, now on the Web at www.consumerreports.org.

DOWNLOAD OF THE DAY   Your Palm can have a silver screen experience, too, with SilverScreen, a beautiful shareware application launcher for the Palm. Try it free for three weeks, and then pay $19.95 to keep it. From www.pocketsensei.com.

TODAY'S FOCUS: Video Editing

CRT PIONEER BORN

Allen Balcom DuMont was born in Brooklyn, New York, on this day in 1901. DuMont produced the first cathode-ray tubes in the United States. Previously, CRTs had to be imported from Germany and had a life span of 25–30 hours. In the 1930s, the American inventor devised a way to manufacture less expensive tubes that lasted up to 1,000 hours. DuMont later started his own company and was the first to market home television receivers. Today, the majority of computer users still use CRT monitors.

Related Web site `howstuffworks.com/tv2.htm`

Thirteen Steps to a Great Video

By Stacee Barcelata

Today, anyone can edit video like a pro with the right hardware and software. If you have a computer, you probably have everything you need, including software. Windows Me and XP come with Microsoft's Windows Movie Maker. Macintosh owners can use the excellent iMovie. We also recommend VideoWave for Windows from Roxio, `videowave.com`. It's inexpensive and very easy to use.

In most video editors, you'll do the bulk of your work in the timeline. The timeline shows you what clips you're using, where they occur in the movie, what transitions separate the clips, and the length of the movie. You can use the timeline to add, delete, and rearrange clips.

Here's the recipe for creating a great movie:

1. Launch the software.
2. Import your clips. If you're doing this from a digital camera, the software will divide each shot into a separate clip.
3. Drag the clips to a player. Watch each clip and decide how you want to edit it.
4. Pick the beginning and end of each clip. Trim the excess. Keep clips short.
5. Drag the clips to the timeline. This adds each clip to the work in progress.
6. Add stills. You're not limited to video; you also can use still images.
7. Select transitions. Transitions, such as dissolves and wipes, can make your video more professional looking, but use them judiciously. Too many transitions can make your audience queasy.
8. Create titles. Just like a Hollywood film, your movie can have opening titles, credits, and more. Be sure each title is onscreen long enough to read it.

9. Preview. Preview. Preview. It's the only way to judge your progress.
10. Choose the compression. All video is compressed. The higher the compression, the lower the quality. Choose a codec (compressor-decompressor) that balances file size and quality. If you plan to export back to your camera, CD, or DVD, choose a compatible format.
11. Build your video. This is sometimes called *rendering*. Some programs do this in the background so you won't need an extra step.
12. Save your file.
13. Watch your movie! Play it back using the program your viewers will be using to be sure it works right.

With a personal computer and the right software, anyone can be the next Steven Spielberg.

(Stacee Barcelata was a consumer reporter at TechTV.)

 TIP OF THE DAY   For information on video codecs for Windows, visit The Codec Zone at `codeczone.virtualave.net/codec.htm`. Find codec info galore at `moviecodec.com`.

 DOWNLOAD OF THE DAY   Convert those video clips into a form that can be burned onto a CD in the VCD format with the free VCDEasy for Windows from `www.vcdeasy.org`.

POLL: What's the best video-editing platform?

8% Windows

44% Mac

48% Amiga

THURSDAY, JANUARY 30, 2003

TODAY'S FOCUS: Video Editing

SUPERCONDUCTING SUPER COLLIDER PROPOSED

Plans to build the world's largest scientific instrument, the Superconducting Super Collider (SSC), were unveiled on this day in 1987. Congress halted construction in 1993 after spending $2 billion and digging 14 miles of tunnels in Waxahachie, Texas.

Related Web site www.hep.net/ssc/

Adding Music to Your Video

By Chris Breen

A less-than-vivacious video can be made more dazzling with the addition of sound. But sound, when used improperly, can be just as distracting as garish effects and poor lighting. Before adding sound and music to your video, follow these simple rules.

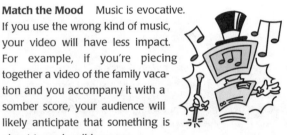

Match the Mood   Music is evocative. If you use the wrong kind of music, your video will have less impact. For example, if you're piecing together a video of the family vacation and you accompany it with a somber score, your audience will likely anticipate that something is about to go horribly wrong.

Watch the Volume   Background music should be just that: background. Keep music audible enough that it conveys the mood, but quiet enough that it doesn't drown out dialogue.

To make a more professional-sounding video, slightly increase the volume of the music during scenes that have no dialogue, and "duck" the music back down when dialogue begins.

Watch the Balance   If you've layered sound—narration, background music, and sound effects, for example—keep the three in balance. Dialogue should be at the forefront, sound effects underneath dialogue, and music the quietest of all.

Watch Those Effects   Just as you can destroy a perfectly good video with cheesy video effects and transitions, so too can you destroy your soundtrack by slathering on the signal-processing effects. Avoid reverb, delay, and extreme equalization unless it adds something to the mood.

Fade   If your video begins by fading up from black or ends by fading out to black, feel free to fade your soundtrack as well. After you try it, you'll find it a completely natural effect. Fading audio in and out makes transitions less abrupt.

Don't Fade   On the other hand, you can create a very dramatic effect by using a soundtrack that suddenly thumps away. For example, if you begin your video with a white title against a black background, it can be very effective to have a dramatic score begin the second that title appears.

Garbage In, Garbage Out   Keep your source sound as clean as possible. This means using an appropriate microphone to record dialogue rather than using the microphone built into your camcorder. Even an inexpensive lapel microphone will work better than your camera.

Also, test sound levels before recording. If the level is too high, your sound will be distorted. If it's too low, boosting it in an audio-editing application might introduce noise.

TIP OF THE DAY   Make it easy to adjust the volume on your computer.

 On Windows XP, open the Sound and Audio Devices control panel, and then check the **Place Volume Icon in the Taskbar** box.

 In Mac OS X, click the **Sound** icon in System Preferences, click the **Alerts** tab, and then check the **Show Volume in Menu Bar** box.

  DOWNLOAD OF THE DAY   The industry's leading audio editor is now free. Download ProTools for Mac or Windows from www.digidesign.com/ptfree. Hurry before DigiDesign changes its mind!

Today's Focus: Video Editing

HEWLETT-PACKARD FOUNDED

Founders William Hewlett and David Packard began the company on this date in 1939 in their garage in Palo Alto, California. The two Stanford University classmates tossed a coin to decide whose name would get top billing.

Related Web site   hp.com/hpinfo/abouthp/histnfacts

A Codec Moment

A video signal contains a huge amount of data, nearly 1GB per minute. So, how does Hollywood get a two-hour movie on a single 4.7GB DVD? The secret is compression. It's the same for computer video. The software used to **co**mpress and **dec**ompress video is called a codec. Let's see how compression can take one minute of video from 1GB of data to a size small enough to send via email.

Step 1: From 1GB to 180MB   Digital video cameras store movies in a compressed format called DV. One minute of video on DV takes up about 180MB on tape. When you transfer video from a DV camera to your computer via FireWire, no conversion is performed. Most computer video-editing programs work directly with DV format files. If you're exporting your edited video back to the camera, there's no need to change the encoding. However, if you want to share that minute of video with others, you must compress it further, ideally to less than 1MB per minute.

Step 2: From 180MB to 18MB   You can cut some of the file size by reducing the picture size. Cut the full-screen video to 160×120 and you've reduced the file to one-quarter its original size. Another common trick is to downsample the video from the normal 30 frames per second. Cutting it to 15fps will reduce the file size by half while only slightly degrading the quality.

For further compression, you must turn to software. One popular software codec is Divx. Divx offers high 10:1 compression ratios at better than VHS quality. If you compress your full-screen DV video with Divx, you'll get down to 18MB per minute, or roughly 1GB per hour of video. That's small enough to trade films over the Net, and,

indeed, that's the most common way Divx is used, much to the annoyance of George Lucas.

Step 3: From 180MB to 180KB   For real file crunching, we turn to the big boys: the codecs most often used in PC video, Intel's Indeo, Sorenson Video, and Microsoft's MPEG4v3. These codecs can achieve compression ratios as high as 100:1. You can use any of them in conjunction with a smaller screen size and slower frame rate to get your one minute of video down well below the magic 1MB mark. The picture will be small, the quality poor, but you will be able to email that video.

And now you know why PC video looks so terrible.

TIP OF THE DAY   Want to know what codec was used to compress that video clip?

 Open the clip in Windows Media Player, and then select **Properties** from the **File** menu. Click the **General** tab.

 Open the clip in QuickTime and select **Show Movie Info** from the **Window** menu.

  DOWNLOAD OF THE DAY   Divx encoders and players are free for almost any platform from divx.com.

POLL: Who's the victim in the dot.com fallout?

39% Workers

5% Employers

13% Venture Capitalists

13% No one

29% San Jose BMW Dealers

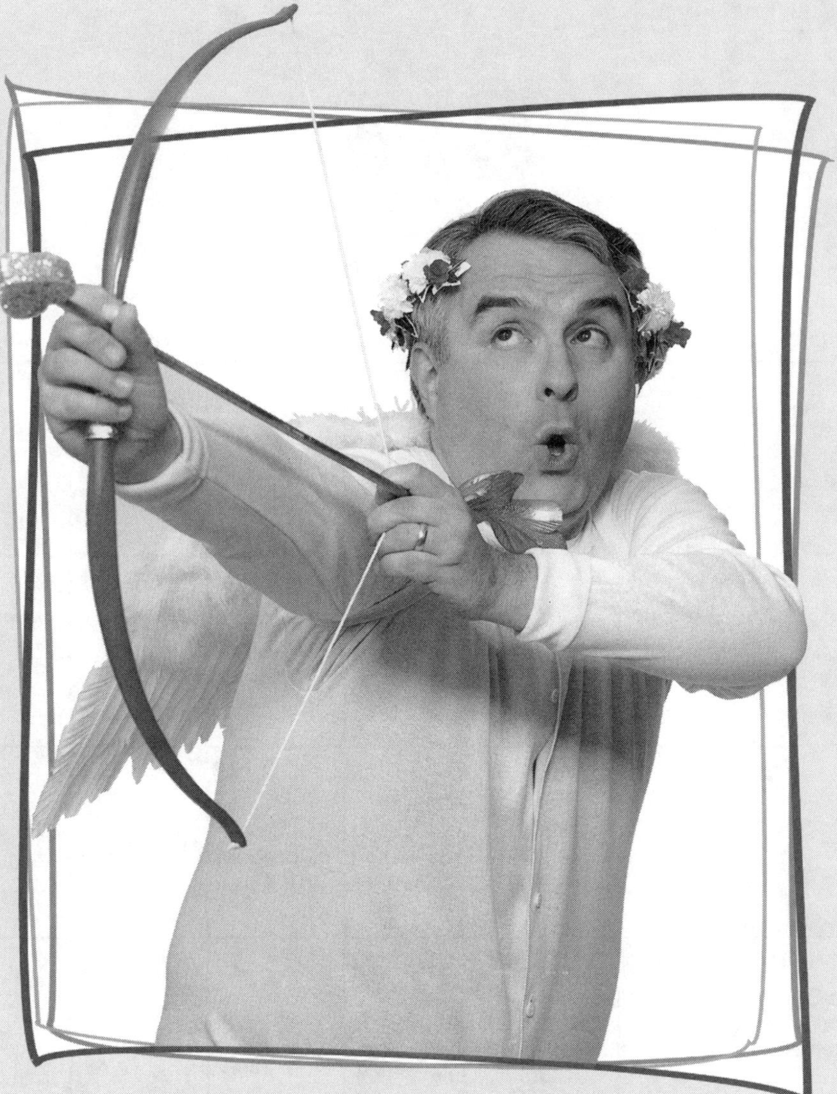

FEBRUARY 2003

February 2003

SUNDAY	MONDAY	TUESDAY	WEDNESDAY	THURSDAY	FRIDAY	SATURDAY
						1
2 Groundhog Day	**3**	**4** Charles Lindbergh born (1902)	**5**	**6**	**7**	**8**
9	**10**	**11** Thomas Edison born (1847)	**12** Charles Darwin born (1809)	**13** Chuck Yeager born (1923)	**14** Valentine's Day	**15**
16 Nylon patented (1937)	**17** Presidents' Day	**18** Pluto discovered (1930)	**19** Nicholas Copernicus born (1473)	**20** First U.S. astronaut orbits Earth (1962)	**21** DNA structure discovered (1953)	**22** George Washington born (1732)
23 Michael Dell born (1965)	**24** Steve Jobs born (1955)	**25**	**26**	**27**	**28**	

TODAY'S FOCUS: Video Editing

FIRST MOVIE STUDIO OPENS

Construction was completed on the world's first film studio on this day in 1893. Thomas Edison's "Black Maria" in New Jersey was the production site for many of Edison's early motion pictures, including such titles as *The Boxing of Cats* and *Edison Kinetoscopic Record of a Sneeze*. Edison's laboratory was responsible for inventing some of the first movie-making equipment: the Kinetograph, a motion-picture camera; and the Kinetoscope, a peephole motion-picture viewer.

Related Web site `tomedison.org`

Star Wars Spoofs

So, now that you're an expert videographer, what are you going to do with this newfound knowledge? Create *Star Wars* spoofs, what else? Here are some of our favorites.

The Tale of Sockpuppetta, Sock Jedi (`thisisgood.com/starwars/sp`) This stop-motion film is brought to you in full color by the folks at *Star Wars* TCG Rebel Base. And a sock.

The 'Star Wars' Gangsta Rap at AtomFilms (`atomfilms.shockwave.com/af/content/atom_1403`) As far as gangsta rap goes, this one's pretty tame. I think they use the word "hell" and that's about it for the cursing. An Audience Award Winner at the 2002 *Star Wars* Fan Film Awards!

Plan 9 from George Lucas (`campchaos.com/cartoons/george_lucas`) If you liked Ed Wood, you'll love this spoof. If you've never seen a film by Ed Wood, this short film probably won't make much sense to you. Great artwork.

Thumb Wars: The Phantom Cuticle (`thumb.com/thumbwars`) Now I finally know why humans have opposable thumbs. Watch the preview and browse through the behind-the-scenes pictures. You'll have to buy the DVD or VHS if you want to see the whole thing. From the very funny Steve Oedekerk, director of *Jimmy Neutron, Boy Genius*.

'Star Wars' ASCIImation (`asciimation.co.nz`) I'm not sure whether to applaud the folks who created the entire *Star Wars* film in ASCII or feel sorry for them. Either way, this is a hoot. If you're not a Jar-Jar fan, you might want to browse this ASCIImation. The film is still a work in progress. Hey, it's not easy typing an entire movie.

(Illustration courtesy of Simon Jansen at www. asciimation.co.nz.)

I'd like to include the most notorious *Star Wars* spoof of all: *Star Wars 1.1: The Phantom Edit* but I can't find a copy on the Net anymore. In 1.1, Mike Nichols, a freelance film editor from Santa Clarita, California, shortened the original by eliminating Jar-Jar Binks and other plot-dragging scenes. Many who saw the re-edit said it improved on the original, but Lucasfilm pushed aggressively to keep Nichols's version off the Net.

 TIP OF THE DAY When you're watching these spoofs, it might become necessary to quickly turn the sound down (aren't bosses a pain?). If you're using Microsoft's Windows Media Player, use your function keys to kill the sound. Punch F8 to mute your player. Hit the F8 key again to bring back the music. F9 turns the volume down a notch; F10 pumps up your desktop sound.

 The QuickTime player also has keyboard controls. Press the up arrow to turn up the sound; press the down arrow to turn it down. To play a movie without sound, hold the Control or Alt key when you click the play button.

DOWNLOAD OF THE DAY Turn your movie into a screensaver with Benjamin Carter's AVI Screen Saver (`downloads-zdnet.com.com/3000-2409-10035640.html`).

POLL: Would you download Star Wars Episode II: Attack of the Clones?

50% Yes

50% No

TODAY'S FOCUS: Video Editing

FIRST MODERN PUBLIC RESTROOMS

The first contemporary public facility with flushing toilets opened on this day in London in 1852. The "Public Waiting Rooms" on Fleet Street were built by Sir Henry Cole and Sir Samuel Peto, and initially were for men only. The fee for using the facilities was two pence (less than two cents in U.S. currency). The enterprise was considered a failure—only 82 people used the public toilets during the first year.

Related Web site `www.restrooms.org`

We can't mock *Star Wars* as we did yesterday and not give equal time to *Star Trek* fans.

Twisted List: Questionable *Star Trek* Sites

By Martin Sargent

Star Trek fans, as a societal type, tend to spend a lot of time on the computer, and often build fan pages devoted to the TV show that they worship so openly, so freely. Some of these sites are wholesome, whereas others are boils on the face of the Internet. Here are the top-five most questionable *Star Trek* sites on the Web.

Leonard Nimoy Should Eat More Salsa (`lnsemsf.com`) At the Leonard Nimoy Should Eat More Salsa Foundation they believe that Leonard Nimoy should eat more salsa. Why? Based on the following equation: Because Leonard Nimoy is excellent, and salsa is excellent, if Leonard Nimoy ate more salsa he'd be an unstoppable force of excellence.

Highlights of the site include a Flash game in which you make Leonard Nimoy eat more salsa—in seven different languages, no less.

The Homepage of Tjark Freese (`pzvd.de/schmidtlef/e-tjark.htm`) For some reason, the home page of Tjark Freese provides me with deep amusement. Maybe it's the endless MIDI music. Maybe it's the photographs (concerning the one of himself, Tjark says: "I had to undergo the nerve-straining procedure of a photocopy of my passing exterior. Unfortunately, my aura remains invisible.") Maybe it's the sense you get that this poor guy has no idea how weird he is. Tjark also says his home page is dipped in blood.

Be sure to check out the family portrait in which Tjark wears his *Star Trek* uniform. And perhaps the weirdest thing is that Tjark's home page is somehow affiliated with a dental group.

Klingon Programming Language (`geocities.com/connorbd/varaq`) One of the geekiest things you can do is learn the Klingon language. But when you stop and think about it, that's nothing compared to writing an entire Klingon computer programming language. That's exactly what Brian Connors has done. It's based on C. So, like, the command `if yes` in the Klingon programming language is `HIja'chugh`. Wow.

TIP OF THE DAY Before you digitize video, or any large file, it's a good idea to optimize your hard drive. A fragmented hard disk is slower, and that can cause you to drop frames.

In Windows, open My Computer and right-click on the hard drive. Select **Properties** from the pop-up menu, and then click the **Tools** tab. Click the **Defragment Now** button.

Macs don't come with disk-optimizing software. I recommend picking up a copy of TechTool Pro, $97.98 from MicroMat, `www.micromat.com`. It can optimize disks and a whole lot more.

DOWNLOAD OF THE DAY Windows comes with Minesweeper, but the Mac does not. Roasted Software has righted the imbalance with Aqua-Mines for Mac OS X, `www.roastedsoftware.com/sw/Aqua-Mines`. Also visit the ultimate minesweeper site, `metanoodle.com/minesweeper`.

TODAY'S FOCUS: America Online

FIRST SOFT LANDING ON MOON

Luna 9 touched down in the Ocean of Storms on the moon's surface on this day in 1966. The unmanned Soviet spaceship was a hermetically sealed container with radio equipment, a program timing device, heat-control systems, scientific apparatus, power sources, and a television system. It was also the first to transmit photographic data and radio signals back to Earth. Researchers were able to assemble the data from Luna 9 into a panoramic view of the surrounding lunar surface.

Related Web site   `antwrp.gsfc.nasa.gov/apod/ap970907.html`

AOL Email Tips

You've Got Mail! AOL is famous for that announcement, but there are other ways to tell whether your mailbox has anything new in it for you. Check the Mail icons in the upper-left corner of the AOL window. If you have new mail, the flag will pop up on the mailbox icon and you'll see a letter sticking out. Click the mailbox to read your mail.

Writing Mail   To create a new message, click the **Write** icon. The composition window opens up with your cursor placed conveniently in the Send To box. Type in the email address. If it's an AOL address, just the screen name will do. For an address outside AOL, be sure to include the full location, including the person's email name and domain. For example, email me at `leo@techtv.com`. To address a message to more than one person, use a comma after each address.

After you've typed in your recipients' addresses, press Tab on your keyboard to move the cursor into the Subject field. There, type a title for your message. Choose a subject that is fairly descriptive; your recipient will use it to decide whether to read your mail. If you make it sound like spam, with lots of exclamation marks and such, don't be surprised if no one answers.

Now press Tab again to jump into the message body, and type your magnum opus. When you're finished, experiment with the row of menus and boxes that run along the top of the message body field. These allow you to change your font, set the font size and color, adjust alignment, bold or italicize certain words, and so on. These formatting commands work only on messages to people on AOL. It's best to stick to plain text for everyone else.

You can also insert pictures, background pictures and colors, and Web links into your messages. Right-click on the message body and select the item you want to insert.

If you like to end your emails with a standard signoff, such as your name, address, Web page, pithy quote, or the like, you can create a signature by clicking the pencil icon just above your message body.

After you've touched up your message to your heart's content, click the **Send** button to wing it on its way.

 TIP OF THE DAY   Want to automatically save mail even after you've read it?

1. Click **Preferences**, and choose **Filing Cabinet**.
2. Put a check in the box next to **Retain All Mail I Read in My Personal Filing Cabinet**.
3. Do the same for your sent mail.

 DOWNLOAD OF THE DAY   eNetBot lets you get your AOL mail from any email program. Free for 30 days; $20 to buy, from `enetbot.com`.

POLL: Why do people stick with AOL?

4% AOL is terrific

39% They don't know where to go

24% They're lazy

33% Because all their friends use AOL

TODAY'S FOCUS: America Online

FEBRUARY 4

CHARLES LINDBERGH BORN

Aviation trailblazer Charles Augustus Lindbergh was born in Detroit, Michigan, on this day in 1902. "Lucky Lindy" is best known for making the first nonstop solo flight across the Atlantic ocean from New York to Paris in 1927. His plane, a 220-horsepower Wright Whirlwind monoplane called the "Spirit of St. Louis," can be found today in the Smithsonian National Air and Space Museum in Washington, D.C.

Related Web site   `lindberghfoundation.org`

Browse the Web with AOL

By Regina Lynn Preciado

Use a URL to Get to a Site   To go directly to a Web site, enter its address (or URL) into the field at the top of the AOL window, the one that reads **Type Keywords or Web Addresses Here**, and then click the **Go** button. Try it: Type `leoville.com` and click **Go** (you never need to type the `http://` you see  in many Web addresses—that's why I leave it out in this book).

The Web site appears in your browser window. It's based on Microsoft's Internet Explorer browser and can do everything that IE can do. Click the underlined links in the window to surf to other pages.

To go back to a previous page click the left arrow to the left of the address box. The right arrow returns to your original page. Click **Reload** to update a page's contents, and click the stop button to stop a page from loading.

Use AOL Search to Find a Site   In many cases, you don't know the address of the site you're looking for. That's when the search box comes in handy. Type **Leoville** in the search field at the top of the AOL window, and then click the **Search** button. A window will open with a list of sites that include the word Leoville. Click the first entry to go to the Web site, just as if you'd entered the address directly. You also can use a more specific search term, such as "The New York Times."

Many people prefer Google to the AOL search engine. You can use it for your searches, too. Just surf to `google.com`, and then enter your search term.

Use Keywords to Find a Site   AOL also uses keywords to get you to AOL-branded content. Instead of typing a URL, you can type a keyword in the **Go** window. Or, click the **Keyword** button to the right to bring up a keyword entry dialog box. Click the keyword link in the box to see a list of AOL keywords. I usually just guess at keywords, and that almost always works.

If you prefer, you can use any standalone browser with AOL. Just dial into AOL as usual, and then minimize the AOL window, open your browser, and surf away.

 TIP OF THE DAY   America Online automatically compresses graphics so that Web pages can load faster. As a result, images often look distorted. To improve their appearance change AOL's compression settings.

Choose **Preferences** from the **AOL Settings** menu and click **Internet Properties**. Click the **Web Graphics** tab. Select **Never Compress Graphics** and click **OK**.

DOWNLOAD OF THE DAY   Momo's AOL Anti-Idle keeps your AOL session active even when you're not. Free from `www.cosmicat.com/software/antiidle`.

POLL: Would you prefer to rent software?

81% No

13% Yes

6% Where's my Blockbuster card?

TODAY'S FOCUS: America Online

FEBRUARY 5

FIRST CALCULATOR PATENTED

Du Bois D. Parmelee of New Paltz, New York, patented the first mechanical adding device on this day in 1850. The little-known inventor's "Machine for Making Calculations in Figures" was a box with keys numbered 1 through 9. Each key would move a lever inside the box when pressed, and would be totaled up on a long stick on the side of the lever. Unlike the abacus, however (which dates back to 500 B.C.), Parmelee's machine could only add, not subtract.

Related Web site   `calcmuseum.com`

Use AOL to Build a Web Page

Are you ready to establish your own little corner of the Web? AOL makes it easy. Click the **People** menu, select **Create a Homepage**, and you're on your way.

Start with AOL's dead-simple 1-2-3 Publish tool. Click the **Beginner's Click Here** link on the right and the tool will launch. Choose a template, fill out the form, add some text, and you're done. Preview your page, tweak it as needed, and then click **Save**. Within minutes you've joined the Internet revolution. Your new Web address is displayed at the end of the process.

Creating a page this way is easy, sure, but your site will look just like thousands of others created in the same way. Now it's time to start customizing. Click the **Edit** link at the top of any hometown page and you'll be able to work on your page directly from within AOL.

When you're ready for more flexibility, click the link for **Easy Designer** (or enter the keyword **Easy Designer**). Easy Designer is a much more full-featured WYSIWYG Web design tool. It's fairly freeform, so it might be a bit bewildering compared to 1-2-3 Publish, but you'll soon appreciate the scope for your creativity.

Try adding some personal images. Click the **Add Images** button. You can choose from AOL clip art or upload your own pictures. If you do upload your own pictures, keep them small—remember, people will be actually visiting your site and you don't want to bog them down with massive images.

Position the images by dragging them around. Resize them by clicking the square handles at the corners and dragging. If you accidentally distort the picture, right-click on it and select **Maintain Aspect Ratio** to fix it.

You also might want to add a counter to tell you how many people have visited your new site. Click the **Insert** menu and select **Counter**.

You also can use your own tools to create Web pages on your computer, and then upload them to AOL. Go to **Keyword Hometown**, click the **Create** button at the top of the page, and click the **Upload** link on the Create and Manage Pages page. AOL limits you to 2MB for all your sites combined, but you can increase that amount to 12MB by registering.

For more ideas and help, enter the AOL keyword "Web Page."

 Tip of the Day   If the Web address `hometown.aol.com/yourscreenname/myhomepage/index.html` doesn't suit you, use a URL redirection service to turn it into something like `i.am.veryweird.com`. Popular providers include `webalias.com` and `v3.com`.

 DOWNLOAD OF THE DAY   One of the best HTML and Web design tools for Windows is completely free. Download 1st Page 2000 from `www.evrsoft.com`.

POLL: Is the Web still fun?

77% Yes

23% No

TODAY'S FOCUS: America Online

FIRST ISP FOR HANDHELDS LAUNCHED

CompuServe unveiled Internet service provider SpryNet on this day in 1996. SpryNet was the first ISP to offer Internet access, email, and supporting software for Windows CE (the first of its kind for any handheld device). Unlimited access was $19.99. The original incarnation didn't last long—SpryNet was acquired by MindSpring about a year and a half later, and 140,000 subscribers were transitioned to the new owner. MindSpring was then bought out by EarthLink in 1999.

Related Web site `www.earthlink.com`

Turn On Parental Controls on America Online

By Nicole Guilfoyle

The Master Screen Name on an AOL account has the power to set limits on Internet use for other users on the account. Use Parental Controls to keep your kids (and other users) from wandering into bad neighborhoods online.

Here's how you find Parental Controls:

1. Click **Settings**, choose **Parental Controls**, and choose **Set Parental Controls**.
2. Choose the screen name you'd like to adjust from the **Edit Controls For** drop-down menu.
3. Go through each of your options and apply the restrictions that make you feel most comfortable.

Here's what each control does:

- **Online Timer**—Sets a limit on the amount of time a user can spend online.
- **Web Control**—Sets parameters for the types of Web sites a user can visit, according to age.
- **IM Control**—If you don't want your child to get instant messages, block them.
- **Email Control**—Decides whether each user can send and receive email, and with whom.
- **Chat Control**—Restricts access if you'd rather not have your child chatting without your supervision. You should at least block member-created rooms and hyperlinks—that's where the really nasty stuff happens.
- **Additional Master**—Gives another user the ability to set controls and change billing information.
- **Download Control**—Says whether the user is allowed to download files from the Internet.
- **Newsgroups**—Keep a user from signing up for newsgroups featuring adult content.

- **Premium Services**—Premium services are charged to your phone bill in addition to your monthly membership fee. It's wise to let only Master account holders have access to these services.

TIP OF THE DAY   Turn off AOL pop-up ads:

1. Sign on to AOL.
2. Go to **Settings**. Choose **Preferences** and click **Marketing**.
3. Click the button next to **Pop Up** and click **Continue**.
4. Choose **No, I Do Not Want to Receive Special AOL Members-Only Pop-Up Offers**.
5. Click **OK**.

You might want to do the same for the other marketing categories, as well.

DOWNLOAD OF THE DAY   You've got mail. It's the signature sound on America Online. But you don't have to stick with Elwood Edwards's dulcet tones (`members.aol.com/voicepro`). AOL offers a variety of other celebrity voices to choose from. Just enter the keyword `You've Got Mail` and choose from dozens of famous voices, from Mr. Moviefone to Britney Spears. Go to keyword "Celeb Voices" for more choices. When you've found a voice you like, click the **Update Sounds** buttons to install it. My favorite is David Letterman.

If you want to add your own AOL sounds manually, you'll find them in the Windows directory in the `AOLSHARE\ sounds\US\Default` folder. Place any WAV you like in the folder using the names `welcome.wav`, `gotmail.wav`, and `goodbye.wav`.

POLL: Which is more important?

26% Safety   74% Privacy

TODAY'S FOCUS: America Online

DOS ATTACKS

A series of denial-of-service attacks on major Web sites began on this day in 2000. Sites such as Yahoo!, eBay, and Amazon.com were flooded with vast amounts of simulated Web traffic from hackers that prevented real users from getting in. The attacks apparently had been planned for months, with hackers secretly co-opting hundreds of computers to create the traffic. This was the first large-scale attack of its kind. Most of the affected Web sites were back up after a few hours, but some estimate the companies hit lost more than $1 billion in revenue.

Related Web site   staff.washington.edu/dittrich/misc/ddos

AOL Anywhere

AOL Anywhere is a service that lets you access your AOL mail, calendar, and popular channels over the Internet. You don't even need to be signed on to AOL to use the service. In fact, you can even customize a My AOL page to use away from home.

Sign in at my.aol.com. AOL starts you off with a default home page featuring news headlines. However, it takes only a couple of minutes to personalize your home page with the information and features you like best. I like to start with a blank Web page and then add content.

1. Click the **Personalize My AOL** button.
2. When the list of content channels appears, uncheck them all.
3. Scroll down to **Settings** to choose how often you want to refresh the page and indicate whether you have a high or low connection speed.
4. When you're finished, click **Save**. With the exception of a tip, you should have a blank page.

Scroll to the bottom of your screen. Use the **Add to Left Side** and **Add to Right Side** drop-down menus to find and add content areas ranging from news and weather to movies and sports. Even add your personal calendar. If you make a mistake, just go into the Personalize AOL area and uncheck the content box.

When you're finished, set My AOL as your browser's start page by dragging the icon in the Address bar to the Home icon in the Internet Explorer toolbar. In other browsers, you'll have to modify your home page in Preferences.

If you want to access your new page from your AOL account, sign on to AOL. Click the **Settings** menu and choose **AOL Anywhere**. Click **My AOL** or choose **My AOL** from the **AOL Services** drop-down menu. You also can enter **my.aol.com** in the address field.

Even if you're not an AOL member, you can still have a customized home page. Many portals offer similar services. Try my.yahoo.com, my.excite.com, my.netscape.com, my.lycos.com, or even mybudweiser.com.

TIP OF THE DAY   To send a copy of an email message to someone without other recipients seeing the address, use the Blind CC, or BCC, field. AOL mail doesn't have a BCC field, but you can do the same thing by surrounding the address with parentheses; that is, (leo@leoville.com).

DOWNLOAD OF THE DAY   AOL PowerTools adds an IM answering machine, customizable email, chat special effects, and a host of other useful features to AOL. Free to try for 20 days, the Lite version is $19.95. PowerTools Pro is $23.95, from www.bpssoft.com.

POLL: Does Web surfing at work increase your productivity?

54% Yes

46% No

TODAY'S FOCUS: America Online

FIRST 747 FLIGHT

The Boeing 747 made its maiden flight on this day in 1969. The first plane had a gross weight of 735,000 pounds, a tail as tall as a six-story building, and a cruising speed of 640 mph. The cabin carried a ton of air when pressurized. The Jumbo Jet is still the largest commercial aircraft in the world, and most of the original planes are still in service.

Related Web site   `www.boeing.com`

Weird Science

By Megan Morrone

I've always been fascinated by the science of food. During my freshman year of college, I put a Big Mac in a blender to see what would happen. Trust me, you do not want to drink a Big Mac. It turns out that the Web is a haven for weird science experiments involving food. Here are my favorites.

The Power of Lemon (`members.aol.com/dswart`) Everyone who's made it through sixth-grade science knows about the food battery, but how many of us have used one since? Dr. Dan has. He has an entire Web site devoted to powering objects with lemons. My favorite is the lemon-powered Texas Instruments TI-30 calculator.

Potato-Powered Web Server (`d116.com/spud`) Fredric White takes the food battery one step further: He decided to run his Web server with a bunch of potatoes. He claims it worked until his potatoes rotted; now he runs the server on a AAA battery.

Meals on the Manifold (`weber.ucsd.edu/~mruben/ cooking.html`) Inspired by the cookbook, *Manifold Destiny*, Matt Ruben tried cooking nachos, hot dogs, and something he calls a Tuna Wiggle on the engine of his car.

Stinkymeat 2 (`thespark.com/science/stinkymeat`) The Stinkymeat Project started out as a form of revenge and turned into a science project detailing the slow deterioration of meat left outside. It's hard to believe that sort of thing could spawn a sequel, but it has. Please do not view this Web site during dinner.

 TIP OF THE DAY   How many times have you heard, "Visit us on the Web at AOL keyword (insert company name here)?" Magazines and newspapers are even starting to include AOL keywords on their covers. But what the heck is a keyword?

A keyword is a simple word or phrase that leads to an AOL content area or directly to a specific Web site. For example, typing **shopping** into the keyword search box will bring you to the AOL Shopping channel. Typing **NYT** will lead you to the *New York Times* home page.

Click the **Keyword** button at the top of your screen to access the AOL keyword search box. If you type a word that's not a keyword, AOL will redirect you to the general search page.

Take the mystery out of keywords by clicking the **Keyword List** link under the keyword search box. Now view the top 10 choices or sort keywords by popularity, channel, or alphabetical order.

Specific AOL content areas also post a keyword in the bottom of the window. Remember the keyword so that you can return to the area quickly at a later time.

 DOWNLOAD OF THE DAY   Window Washer protects your privacy and speeds up performance by clearing your browser cache, cookies, history, mail trash, address bar, auto-complete forms, and downloaded files. It works with all browsers and AOL and CompuServe. Free to try, $29.95 to buy, from `webroot.com`.

TODAY'S FOCUS: America Online

FEBRUARY 9

DAYLIGHT SAVING INSTITUTED

President Franklin D. Roosevelt ordered the beginning of "War Time" on this day in 1942. Clocks in the U.S. were turned ahead one hour to conserve electricity. The concept of daylight saving was conceived by Benjamin Franklin, who believed turning the clocks ahead in the summer would lead to lower energy costs. He was right—the U.S. Department of Transportation estimates that energy use in the country decreases by about 1% each day during Daylight Saving Time.

Related Web site `webexhibits.org/daylightsaving`

African-American Geeks

By Martin Sargent

As part of our salute to Black History Month, I bring you six sites for hard-core afro-geeks.

Black Geeks Online (blackgeeks.com) Black Geeks Online is a 30,000-member "virtual community linking technical professionals, educators, entrepreneurs, students, parents, and community leaders with technology news, information, and resources."

AfroNerds (`www.people.virginia.edu/~rds2u/afronerds.html`) AfroNerds is a mailing list for blacks interested in science and technology. It's geared toward youth.

Sci Fi Noir (`scifinoir.com`) The purpose of Sci Fi Noir is to provide a forum to promote awareness of Afrocentric perspectives within the genres of science fiction and fantasy. If you're a writer, poet, artist, or critic, this is a great place to submit your work and review the work of others.

Black Futurists (`geocities.com/WallStreet/Floor/8647/aboutblack.html`) Black Futurists strives to be a central location on the Internet for deep intellectual discussion, planning, collaboration, and visionary thinking among black people concerned about scientific, technological, and economic development in the 21st century and beyond.

Black Engineer (`blackengineer.com`) If you're an engineer or hoping to become one, be sure to spend time at the Web site of *Black Engineer* magazine.

Computer Scientists of the African Diaspora (`soulsearch.net`) To learn more about the black luminaries of the computer and tech world, search this great Web site set up by the University of Buffalo.

 TIP OF THE DAY Want to chat about African-American geeks? If you're an AOL member, you can create your own chat room on any subject. Here's how:

1. Click the **People** icon in the toolbar.
2. Choose **Start Your Own Chat**. There are two types: Member or Private.
3. If you choose Member, your chat will be listed in the Chat Directory, and other members will be able to find your room.
4. Type a name for your chat.
5. Click **Go Chat**.

This will set up a chat for you.

Another good reason to set up your own chat is to catch up with family and friends. Set up a private chat and tell them the name and time of your room. You can all meet there and have an online reunion. Happy chatting!

A word of warning: We recommend that you don't give personal information over the Internet. It's a good idea not to give your phone number, address, or last name to people you are chatting with—unless you know them, of course.

 DOWNLOAD OF THE DAY Buddy Plus enhances the AOL Buddy List with pop-up notification, logging, custom sounds for each buddy, and more. Free to try, $20 to buy. From `www.tpasoft.com`.

POLL: What do you do with your old computers?

8% Donate	25% Linux server
31% Pass on	6% Resell
15% Doorstop/art	15% Other

FEBRUARY 10

ANTISEPTIC ADVOCATE DIES

Dr. Joseph Lister died on this day in 1912. The English surgeon invented an antibacterial spray to kill germs in the operating room, and was one of the first to sterilize his instruments before performing a medical procedure. Lister's practices drastically reduced the number of deaths resulting from infection and allowed surgeons to attempt new operations, such as open-heart surgery, that were previously too risky. Listerine was named after Dr. Lister in the late 1870s.

Related Web site `www.fordham.edu/halsall/mod/1867lister.html`

Instant Messenger Clients

Instant messengers are the telephones of the Internet age. With one, any user can be in instantaneous touch with any other user, typing instead of talking. Modern IM clients add many other features, including file transfers, application sharing, and person-to-person gaming. But unlike the telephone network, there's no common dial tone. Each client can communicate only with its own kind—it's as if you'd have to have multiple telephones in your home, each serving a different network. What's worse, you'd have to know which system a friend used before you could call her. So, you see why the choice of IM client is so important.

Here's a rundown of the big players; all of them are free. All work on most platforms, including Windows, Macintosh, and PDAs.

ICQ (`icq.com`)   AOL created the idea of instant messaging with its Buddy List feature, but ICQ took the idea and ran with it. It was the first client to work with the entire Internet. Ironically, AOL now owns the company. ICQ has always been the choice for hardcore geeks. But if you're not interested in all those extra features, the interface might be a bit confusing.

AIM (`aim.com`)   America Online's Instant Messenger is, by far, the most popular, especially with teens. You don't need to have an AOL account to use AIM. This client is loaded with advertising, just like the online service.

Yahoo! Messenger (`messenger.yahoo.com`)   This IM client has a large user base among older and corporate users. It also has the most features, including free PC-to-phone calls and elaborate backgrounds and emoticons.

Windows Messenger (Formerly MSN Messenger) (`messenger.msn.com`)   Microsoft is number four, so it tries harder. Every Windows-based computer comes with Messenger. It launches automatically if you just blow on the keyboard. It's loaded with features, including free PC-to-PC calling, video conferencing, application sharing, and more, but for some reason, Windows Messenger just can't get any respect. Kids, the biggest users of IM, see it as way too corporate. Corporations are afraid of the security breaches instant messaging can open. Messenger seems doomed to remain an also-ran.

 TIP OF THE DAY   If you're running an IM client or two, those invitations to chat can quickly fill the screen. Here's how to limit alerts to those from people you know.

AIM   Go to the **My AIM** menu and point to **Edit Options**. Select **Edit Preferences**. In the Category list, select **Privacy**. Select **Allow Only Users on My Buddy List**.

MSN   Under **Tools**, select **Options**. Click the **Privacy** tab. Select **Allow Individuals on My List**.

Yahoo!   Under the **Privacy Settings**, select **Ignore Anyone Not on My Friends List**.

DOWNLOAD OF THE DAY   There are multiplatform IM clients that work with all the above. They're blessedly advertising-free, too.

 For Windows, I like Trillian, free from `trillian.cc`.

 On Mac OS X, go with Proteus, free from `indigofield.com`.

POLL: Which couldn't you live without?
23% Your coffee   77% Your PC

52

TODAY'S FOCUS: Instant Messaging

JOSS SERVICE ENDS

The JOHNNIAC Open-Shop System was terminated at RAND Corporation on this day in 1966. JOSS was the first simple online system to allow multiple users to have access to a single system at the same time. Initially, the system consisted of five terminals, each equipped with an IBM typewriter.

Related Web site `www.rand.com`

IM Made Easy

By Martin Sargent

Let's get started IMing. I'm going to show you how with Yahoo! Messenger because it's simple to use and rich in features, but you can apply these instructions to any IM client with just a few changes.

Create a Friends List A friends list (AOL calls it a buddy list) is the group of people you want to keep track of in your IM client. These are the people you'll be interacting with most, although you're not limited to chatting with them. To add a friend, click the **Add** icon, and fill in the appropriate contact information.

Chat with Your Friends When you go online, a red Y will appear next to those friends who are online and a gray Y will appear next to those who are not. That's the original purpose of a buddy list: to let you know which of your friends are online so you can chat with them.

To send a message to an online buddy, double-click a name from the list. If you don't have any friends yet (awwww), double-click the YahooHelper. An IM window will pop up. Type your message in the bottom field, dress it up with the icons above, and then click the **Send** button. Your message will appear in the top field, along with any responses from your friend. Congratulations—you're instant messaging!

To assemble a whole group of friends in the same IM chat room, choose **Tools**, then **Yahoo! Chat**, and select **Create a Room**. You can invite all your friends to join you.

Voice Chat with Friends With Yahoo! Messenger, if you and a friend have computer microphones, you can voice chat with each other across the Internet. It's like making a long-distance phone call for free. The major drawback is a slight delay time and the fact that only one person can talk at once, much like on a walkie-talkie set.

To start a voice chat, just double-click the friend you'd like to chat with. On the chat window for that friend, click the **Voice** button. If everything is configured correctly, you should be able to voice chat. If you need help, go to the **Help** menu and choose **Audio Setup Wizard**.

For more information, visit `messenger.yahoo.com/messenger/help/voicechat.html`.

Send a File to a Friend You can also use Messenger to transfer files. Right-click a friend's name, and then select **Send a File** from the pop-up menu. Your friend will be asked if he or she wants to accept, and the transfer will begin. As always, be careful accepting files from strangers—or friends with a puckish sense of humor.

TIP OF THE DAY Snazz up Yahoo! Messenger with new skins from `skinstop.com`. They're free and there are hundreds to choose from.

DOWNLOAD OF THE DAY Want to practice chatting with a couple of nice nonjudgmental characters? Meet Billy and Daisy, free from `leedberg.com/glsoft`. They get smarter as you chat, but they'll never tell your secrets.

TODAY'S FOCUS: Instant Messaging

FEBRUARY
12

ARTIFICIAL DIAMOND CREATED

Scientists announced the creation of Borazon, a man-made material nearly as strong as a diamond, on this day in 1955. General Electric chemist Robert Henry Wentorf, Jr. was the first to synthesize diamonds from graphite using a form of boron nitride he invented. Borazon's molecular structure was similar to a diamond, but was much less expensive to acquire and could withstand higher temperatures than its naturally occurring counterpart. Today, it's mainly used for industrial purposes, such as grinding, scraping, cutting, and polishing.

Related Web site   www.ge.com

IM Lingo

By Michelle Von Wald

If you spend much time in chat rooms talking to long-distance friends, or if you are an instant message fan, you might already know these abbreviations. If you don't yet use abbreviations to get your message out quickly, we know you will after you read this list.

AFK: Away from keyboard
ATM: At the moment
B: Back
BBFN: Bye bye for now
BBL: Be back later
B/C: Because
BFN: Bye for now
BFO: Blinding flash of obvious
BG: Big grin
BO: Brain overload
BRB: Be right back
BTW: By the way
BYKT: But you know/knew that
CMIIW: Correct me if I'm wrong
CU: See you
CUL8R: See you later
CYA: See ya
EG: Evil grin
FC: Fingers crossed
FIIOOH: Forget it, I'm out of here
FITB: Fill in the blank
G: Grin
G2G: Got to go
IBK: Idiot behind keyboard
IMHO: In my humble opinion
IRL: In real life
JK: Just kidding
L8R: Later
LMAO: Laughing my ass off
LOL: Laughing out loud
LYLAB: Love ya like a brother
LYLAS: Love ya like a sister
NE1: Anyone
OMG: Oh my gosh
ROFL: Rolling on the floor laughing
TIC: Tongue in cheek
TTYL: Talk to ya later
THX: Thanks
TTFN: Ta ta for now
WB: Welcome back
Y: Yawning

 TIP OF THE DAY   You never know when a friend or co-worker is going to open an email attachment—my messages are often sucked into an abyss created by mail filters. Send files over AOL Instant Messenger to ensure people view them instantly.

When you see your buddy online, choose **Send a File** from the **People** menu option on your buddy list. Type your buddy's screen name. Browse to the file or directory you'd like to send and click **OK**. Write a description of the file and click **Send**.

Your buddy will receive a message asking him or her to accept or deny the file transfer. By default, the file will save to the Download folder in My Documents. Your buddy also has the choice of choosing a different path.

As always, never accept a file from a person you don't know, and always scan for viruses before you open them.

 DOWNLOAD OF THE DAY   Why read your instant messages when your computer will read them to you with SmartButler, from www.smart-butler.com? Works with ICQ, MSN, Yahoo! Messenger, and AIM in many languages. Free to try, $15 to buy.

POLL: Why aren't there more women in tech?

49% Lack of interest

20% Lack of opportunity

31% Fear of geek stigma

TODAY'S FOCUS: Instant Messaging

PILOT WHO BROKE SOUND BARRIER BORN

U.S. Air Force pilot Chuck Yeager was born in Myra, West Virginia, on this day in 1923. Yeager served in the U.S. Air Force during WWII and was later chosen to fly the first X-1 aircraft. Yeager broke the sound barrier over Victorville, California, October 14, 1947. He was lionized in Tom Wolfe's 1979 novel *The Right Stuff*. According to Wolfe, the deadpan Western accent many airline pilots affect is a dead-ringer for Yeager's own voice.

Related Web site www.chuckyeager.com

FEBRUARY 13

Put on a Happy (or Sad) AIM Face

By Joanna Lux

You can personalize your AIM chat by selecting a custom buddy icon. Click the **My Aim** menu, select **Edit Options**, and then click **Edit Preferences**. Select the **Buddy Icons** category. Select **My Buddy Icon** at the top of the Buddy Icons list. In the window to the right, you'll see a huge selection of icons to choose from, but you can also use any icon or image on your system by clicking the **Browse PC** button.

Here are some sites that offer cool ready-made icons:

- For more than 30 categories of cool animated icons, from drinking buddies to celebrities, visit ballericons.com.
- Tons of favorites characters, such as the Flintstones, Fat Albert, Looney Tunes, and Smurfs, are available from draac.com/aimicons.
- Sega heroes such as Dark Savior abound at emulationzone.org/sections/segaforever/downloads/aim.
- Become Chris, JC, Joey, Justin, or Lance at nsyncstudio.com/images/aolims.
- Choose from wrestling's finest muscular visages at 316wrestling.co.uk/multimedia/aol_icons.shtml.
- American Greetings has a wealth of well-produced icons, ranging from stick figures to a cool alphabet, at Icon-O-Rama, aol.americangreetings.com/tribe/iam.

- AIM Icons Net is a pop-culture bonanza at gigahosts.com/~c1003/aimicons.
- Avid gamers and anime fans should head over to dragid.com.

On some sites, you can click on the icon to install it automatically. If not, save it by right-clicking the image in your browser and selecting **Save Picture As**. Save it to the Picture folder inside your AIM folder, or any other location you can remember. Then, go back to the **Browse PC** button to load the image.

You can also use your own photo or a drawing as an icon. AIM will resize it automatically, but it will look best if you size the image to 50×50 pixels yourself. The image file can be in GIF, JPG, BMP, ICO, or XBM format and must be smaller than 7KB.

 TIP OF THE DAY Here's how to transfer your AOL Instant Messenger (AIM) buddy list to a different screen name on your home AOL account.

Sign on to AIM under the screen name with the buddy list you'd like to export. Click **My AIM** and choose **Save Buddy List**. Choose the preferences and sublists you'd like to save and click **Save**. Remember where you put the file on your hard drive. Click **My AIM** again and choose **Switch Screen Name**. Sign on to your alternative screen name so you can import the buddy list. Click **My AIM** and choose **Load Buddy List**. Find the buddy list file on your hard drive and click **Load**.

 DOWNLOAD OF THE DAY AIM+ is a tiny AIM add-on that lets you record all your AIM chats. Free from www.big-o-software.com/software/aimplus-download.php.

TODAY'S FOCUS: Valentine's Day

MOST PROLIFIC FEMALE INVENTOR BORN

Margaret E. Knight was born in York, Maine, on this day in 1838. The "woman Edison" was responsible for several inventions and was awarded 27 patents in her lifetime. Knight supposedly created a safety device for textile looms when she was only 12 years old. She also invented a numbering machine, an attachment that allowed the production of flat-bottomed paper bags, and several devices relating to rotary engines. Later, she patented machines used for shoemaking.

Related Web site `www.invent.org`

Eleventh-Hour Hearts and Flowers

By Alison Strahan

Happy Valentine's Day! Uh-oh. Did you forget? Here are some suggestions that will make you seem more romantic.

The fictional Cyrano de Bergerac was an eloquent scribe of passionate proportions. Although it would be difficult to emulate his heartfelt pronouncements on short notice, you can cheat a little by visiting the Cyrano Server, `cgi-bin.nando.net/toys/cyrano/version2`. This cyber-Cyrano will automatically write a love letter (or a Dear John letter) for you.

Share your ardor with the world by giving a free shout-out to your sweetie at theholidayspot.com, `theholidayspot.com/valentine`. Post to the message board and tell your love where to find the thread or send a 21-page list of remanufactured reasons you love your partner. The site is a cornucopia of Valentine-themed screen savers and wallpaper, and a hub of gifts you can make yourself. It's pretty simple to wrap a batch of cookies in a heart-shaped cardboard bag. Why not get the kids to help you bake? `gamekids.com/gkvalc1.html`.

Whip up something for your love with the help of MakeStuff.com (`make-stuff.com/hollidays/valentine.html`), a site chock-full of fun and romantic crafts. But if hearts made out of Borax don't float your boat, try a gag gift such as Cupid Poop, `make-stuff.com/hollidays/funnygifts.html#valentine`. Honey, I made it myself!

Finally, visit Lovingyou.com for an abundance of romantic inspiration including quotes, poems, and e-cards from the love library. If your last-minute romance ideas aren't well-received, visit the Lovingyou.com message boards. Reading about what others are going through might help situate your romantic dilemmas.

AOL users are just as romantic as anyone. Try these keywords to kickstart your heart:

- **Valentine's Day**—Find out how to find love by searching personals or placing an ad; keep love by planning a romantic getaway or a night out on the town.
- **Family valentine**—Keep your romance alive after having kids: Learn how to make homemade valentines or cook sweet treats the whole family will love.
- **Love**—Learn how to flirt, use the date planner or movie guide, and learn how to create a Web page for your love.
- **Food for love**—Whip up a gourmet meal for the one you love. No time? Order take-out or send a gift basket.
- **Romance**—For women only. Chat about relationships and dating, get advice from love experts, get tips for planning your wedding.

 TIP OF THE DAY   Get off the computer and go out on a date. It's Valentine's Day, fer cryin' out loud!

 DOWNLOAD OF THE DAY   Add Valentine's Day light to your desktop. Choose between cupids, psycho hearts, pink flashing bulbs, and more. They also have bulbs for Christmas, Chanukah, Thanksgiving, and Halloween. For Mac and Windows from `tigertech.com`.

TODAY'S FOCUS: Valentine's Day

FIRST ELECTRONIC COMPUTER DEBUTS

The Electronic Numerical Integrator and Computer was dedicated on this day in 1946. The ENIAC was created at the Moore School of Electrical Engineering at the University of Pennsylvania by John W. Mauchly and J. Presper Eckert. The machine was built using nearly 18,000 electronic vacuum tubes and weighed more than 30 tons. At the time, it was the biggest electronic device in the world. The computer performed 5,000 additions and 300 multiplications per second—as much as 1,000 times faster than existing mechanical computers or calculators, but 1,000 times slower than today's desktop PCs.

Related Web site `www.inventorsmuseum.com`

Love Sites

By Alison Strahan

In the first century, the Catholic church transmogrified the ancient Pagan festival honoring Lupercus, God of fertility and sensual pleasure, into a day to honor the martyrdom of Saint Valentine. Valentine was executed for helping young lovers marry against the wishes of the Emperor, who felt married men made bad soldiers.

The current incarnation of Valentine's Day celebrates romance, love, and commerce—and there's a lot of pressure to do and say the right thing. Here's some advice to ensure your evening out is a success.

Find out whether you and your prospective mate are a match with the Internet Love Test, `lovetest.com/loveteststart.html`. Watch out: You'll need to brave an onslaught of pop-ups and rather probing questions. Even if you're unhappy with the results, I guarantee you'll learn something about your feelings for this person. Use the drop-down menu to select other quizzes to test your numerological compatibility and more.

Should you go out to dinner, meet at a coffee shop, or go for a walk in the park? Whether it's your first date or a surprise for your long-term partner, download the free Great Dating Ideas e-book from `greatdatingideas.com`.

About.com's dating hub, `dating.about.com/cs/ideasfordates`, is filled with romantic advice ranging from inexpensive date ideas to dating do's and don'ts.

Romantic Films Why go out when you can stay in and watch these romantic movies at AtomFilms?

- **Hearts and Hammers** (`atomfilms.shockwave.com/af/content/hearts_hammers_1`)—This short showcases the suspense and anxiety—and utter foolishness—of giving your heart away.
- **If You Loved Me** (`atomfilms.shockwave.com/af/content/if_you_loved`)—In this live-action comedy, two British sweethearts dare each other to new extremes in order to prove their feelings.
- **Pillowfight** (`atomfilms.shockwave.com/af/content/atom_1217`)—One sleepy husband discovers that love really is a battlefield.
- **Radiskull & Devil Doll: Love n' Stuff** (`atomfilms.shockwave.com/af/content/radiskull04`)—Devil Doll, the foil to Radiskull in Joe Sparks' cult hit series, is Candy Angel's object of affection.
- **Girl Go Boom** (`atomfilms.shockwave.com/af/content/atom_356`)—In this former Sundance Film Festival entry, a coffee date goes from pretentious to explosive in a matter of seconds.

 TIP OF THE DAY Send your loved one an instant message kiss.

In AIM 8 or later, open the AIM Today window and click **Kisses and Hellos** on the left for a whole selection of love messages.

In Yahoo! Messenger, open IMVironments, select **Falling Hearts**, and then type Ctrl+G to plant a big wet kiss on the screen.

In MSN Messenger, type **(k)**.

 DOWNLOAD OF THE DAY Get the latest Shockwave player so you can watch all those romantic films at Atom Films. It's free from `sdc.shockwave.com/shockwave/download`.

POLL: Can robot love replace the real thing?

18% Yes   82% No

TODAY'S FOCUS: Valentine's Day

NYLON PATENTED

A patent for nylon was granted to the DuPont Corporation on this day in 1937. The revolutionary synthetic material was developed by organic chemist Wallace Carothers after seven years of experimentation. Carothers called his invention Fiber 66, but DuPont later changed the name to nylon. Urban legend states the name was a combination of the abbreviations for New York and London (NY + Lon). The new polymer was originally marketed in the form of women's stockings but is, of course, used in thousands of other products today.

Related Web site `fibersource.com/f-tutor/history.htm`

Twisted List: Valentine's Gifts You Could Exchange for an iPod

By Megan Morrone

By now everyone knows that Megan wants an iPod, Apple Computer's hot little MP3 player. She spends hours each day dreaming up ways to come up with the $400 she needs to buy one. This list just shows the lengths she's willing to go to. I pity her poor husband.—Leo

Leather Flowers (`leathersuedeskins.com/Flowers1.html`)   Here's a tip for all the men out there. Just because women like flowers and women like leather items, doesn't necessarily mean they'll like leather in the shape of a flower. Chocolate flowers are lame, and leather flowers are tacky. Return them and get yourself an iPod.

Giant Teddy Bear Made of Balloons (`sanbrook.com.au/balloonlink/Images/BalloonCircusTeddyBear.jpg`)   This thing isn't cute—it's just plain scary. Although you'll have little luck returning this inflatable gift, I'm sure you can sell it for $400 on eBay.

My Love Chinese Candies (`www.bad-candy.com/mylove/mylove2.shtml`)   You should never judge a candy by its name. According to the Ultimate Bad Candy Web site, `www.bad-candy.com`, My Love candy is a fruit snack that's "shaved into thin, green, mucous-covered strips, which we believe were, at one point, identifiable as papayas." The site doesn't name a price for these candies, but I'm guessing that if your loved one gave you 400 of these packages, you'd be able to return them and buy that iPod. You should also begin to wonder whether your loved one is trying to kill you.

A Live Monkey   You might be tempted to keep the monkey you received from your Valentine. You might even be tempted to name it Bubbles. But it's just not realistic to keep a monkey. Many zoos would be happy to take your monkey off your hands for $400 or even more.

 TIP OF THE DAY   Microsoft includes ads and links to sponsors in its Money software. If you're tired of being asked to open a brokerage account or buy products, make these links disappear. You'll also clear up a lot of room on your interface.

Choose **Options** from the **Tools** menu. On the **General** tab, put a check next to **Turn Off Sponsorship and Shopping Links**. Click **OK**.

 DOWNLOAD OF THE DAY   Look at email before you download it with the free Email Remover from `eremover.bizhosting.com`. It's also a good way to delete big email attachments without downloading them.

POLL: Will we all have personal force fields one day?

54% Yes

21% No

25% Use the Force, um, 3M?

POLL: Whom do you trust to protect free speech?

5% Corporations

4% The government

58% Yourself

33% An armed Leo-Bot 2000

TODAY'S FOCUS: Broadband Internet

STETHOSCOPE INVENTOR BORN

René Laennec was born in France on this day in 1781. The physician developed the first stethoscope in 1816 to protect the modesty of one of his female patients. The device was made from several sheets of paper rolled into a cylinder. Before this, doctors listened to heart and lung sounds simply by pressing their ears to their patients' chests. Laennec's stethoscope, and many models that followed, were monaural, meaning they were used with only one ear.

Related Web site `antiquemed.com`

A DSL Primer

Digital subscriber line (DSL) service is one form of broadband offered by local phone companies. DSL speeds and prices vary considerably. Typically, you'll pay $40–$50 a month for a minimum of 384Kbps downloads and 128Kbps uploads. The phone company can act as your ISP, although you also can use third-party ISPs such as EarthLink, DirecTV, or AOL.

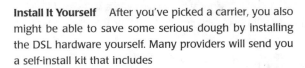

To find a provider, go to dslreports.com and click **Find Service** in the left navigation bar. DSL Reports will give you the names of carriers and prices in your area. I highly recommend you check the user reviews and ratings before you buy. They can steer you away from some real turkeys.

Install It Yourself   After you've picked a carrier, you also might be able to save some serious dough by installing the DSL hardware yourself. Many providers will send you a self-install kit that includes

- A DSL modem. DSL modems connect to your computer in one of two ways: Ethernet or USB. If you get an Ethernet modem, you'll also get an Ethernet networking card to install into your computer. USB is easier to install, but if you're comfortable opening your case, Ethernet will be more flexible. For example, many users purchase Ethernet broadband routers to share Internet access. Plug the DSL modem into the wall, plug the router into the modem, and then connect the computers to the router. If you think you might be doing that, ask for an Ethernet DSL modem.

- A phone splitter, so your modem can share a jack with a phone set.
- Filters for your phones, to reduce line noise. These are very important. Your DSL might not work without them. Be sure you use a filter on every jack that has a phone, but *don't* filter your DSL connection. If you use a splitter, plug the splitter into the jack and connect your DSL modem directly to the splitter. Put the filter between the phone and the splitter only.

PPPoE Versus Static IP   Most big DSL providers require you to use PPP over Ethernet, or PPPoE, to connect to their systems. This allows them to share bandwidth among users more efficiently, making room to crunch more people in. PPPoE requires a dialer and is somewhat slower due to the overhead. If you use a broadband router it can handle the PPPoE negotiation, but avoid PPPoE if possible.

 TIP OF THE DAY   How fast is your broadband connection? Check each of these sites, and then use the highest number as your peak speed:

DSL Reports: `dslreports.com/stest`

Bandwidth Place: `bandwidthplace.com/speedtest`

Cable-Modem.net: `cable-modem.net/features/oct99/speed.html`

MSN Speed Test: `computingcentral.msn.com/internet/speedtest.asp`

DOWNLOAD OF THE DAY   You can also download a free program that will monitor your broadband speed. Mark Thompson's NetStat Live is free from `www.analogx.com/contents/download/network/nsl.htm`.

FEBRUARY 18

PLUTO DISCOVERED

The most distant planet in our solar system was discovered on this day in 1930. The ninth planet from the sun was spotted by Clyde Tombaugh at the Lowell Observatory in Flagstaff, Arizona. Pluto's surface temperature is below −200 degrees Celsius. The planet is nearly 4 million miles from the sun and takes about 249 years to complete one orbit.

Related Web site `kidsastronomy.com/pluto.htm`

What Is DSL?

By John Navas

DSL refers to a group of technologies that deliver higher speeds over standard telephone lines. The most common forms of DSL available to consumers today are

- **ADSL (Asymmetric DSL)**—Designed to deliver much higher downstream speeds at the expense of upstream speeds. Although downstream can be as high as 8Mbps, consumer-class service is commonly limited to 1.5Mbps; upstream speed is commonly limited to 128Kbps.
  One advantage of ADSL is that it can share an existing phone line with voice (and even a conventional dial-up modem), minimizing cost. It's the most common consumer choice.
- **SDSL (Single-Pair HDSL)**—Usually marketed as a business-class service, SDSL normally has the same speeds for upstream and downstream transmission, up to a maximum of about 1.5Mbps in each direction. SDSL cannot share a phone line with voice, so a dedicated phone line is needed, which increases cost.
- **IDSL (DSL Over ISDN)**—IDSL effectively turns ISDN into an always-on data service. Speed is 140Kbps (sometimes 128Kbps) for both upstream and downstream. Although speed is much lower than other forms of DSL, a major advantage of IDSL is its range: roughly double that of ADSL or SDSL, on the order of about 27,000 feet as compared with about 14,000–17,000 feet. Repeaters can further extend the range of IDSL, but not ADSL or SDSL.

How Does DSL Work?   DSL is based on high-frequency transmission between a subscriber DSL modem (which looks much like a conventional dial-up modem) and a DSLAM (digital subscriber line access multiplexer), a relatively large "head-end" box that usually is located at the phone company's central office.

DSL gets around the speed limitations of the standard telephone network by splitting off the high-frequency DSL signal at the DSLAM rather than passing it through the telephone company switch in the central office and over the low-speed voice network. In the case of ADSL, the telephone line can be shared between voice and DSL, because ADSL is confined to different frequencies that are higher than the first 4,000Hz used for voice.

(John Navas is the author of Navas Cable Modem/DSL Tuning Guide, `cable-dsl.home.att.net`.*)*

 TIP OF THE DAY   Here are John's tips for getting the best performance out of any broadband connection:

- Apply all operating system updates, particularly any available updates to Windows sockets (WinSock) and dial-up networking (DUN).
- Set the TCP Receive Window to between 32,000 (enough for typical broadband) and 64,000 (one-way cable modem or satellite).
- The default MTU (maximum transmission unit) of 1,500 is normally best. However, a value of 1,400 might help with certain PPPoE or VPN connections.

 DOWNLOAD OF THE DAY   You can apply these changes easily by downloading small Registry patch files from `speedguide.net`. Click the **Patches** link on the left.

POLL: Where do you use broadband?

50% Home

8% Work

31% Home and work

11% None of the above

TODAY'S FOCUS: Broadband Internet

PHONOGRAPH PATENTED

Thomas Edison was granted a patent for the phonograph on this day in 1878. Less than a month before the patent was awarded, the Edison Speaking Phonograph Company was created to exhibit and market the new invention. Edison reportedly received $10,000 for the manufacturing and sales rights and 20% of the profits.

Related Web site `tinfoil.com`

Myths of DSL

By John Navas

DSL is a fantastic way to get online, but it can also be very frustrating. Here are some common misconceptions, along with some suggestions on how to deal with them.

DSL Is Easy to Get   If only that were true. For the most common form of DSL (ADSL), you can't be more than about 17,500 feet from the central office—that's distance along copper wires, not as the crow flies. In addition, your phone line must be free from a whole laundry list of phone company accessories.

As a result, perhaps a third of people can't get DSL at all, and those who can might have to wait for weeks or months to get service. The only way to find out for sure is to order DSL service—prequalification on a Web site is not terribly accurate.

DSL Is Easy to Install and Won't Interfere with Your Phone Service   As a cost-saving measure, DSL subscribers are increasingly self-installing their own service. Unfortunately, self-install doesn't always work. A whole host of problems—from poor house wiring to lighting dimmers—can make DSL perform poorly, or not at all. The special software that DSL demands might not run properly on your computer. Be prepared to insist on a visit by a service technician if you run into problems.

The Upstream Cap Doesn't Affect Downloading   Although downstream speeds usually are high, consumer-grade DSL service often has an upstream cap of only 128Kbps. This is about three times faster than a 56Kbps dial-up modem. What's not generally well-known is that the upstream cap can also affect your downstream speed.

If you saturate the upstream by uploading (for example, sending a large PowerPoint file to your boss), your downstream will drop to about the same speed. This is due to a weakness in the basic TCP Internet protocol, not DSL.

DSL Is Better Than Cable Internet Because It Isn't Shared   It's true that DSL has a dedicated connection to the head end (DSLAM), whereas cable Internet has a shared connection to the head end (CMTS), and that cable sharing can sometimes be a problem. However, past the head end out to the Internet and beyond, both DSL and cable Internet use the same kind of shared links and other resources, and both can be adversely affected if those links and resources are overloaded.

In general, there are more similarities than differences between DSL and cable. The quality of service depends much more on the service provider than on the basic technology.

TIP OF THE DAY   If Windows XP's offer to send information to the home office after every little crash is driving you crazy, disable error reporting. Open the System control panel. Click the **Advanced** tab, and click the **Error Reporting** button. Change your settings and click **OK**.

DOWNLOAD OF THE DAY   Replace your ISP's lousy PPPoE dialer with RASPPPOE. Free for personal use from `bakwaters.com/raspppoe.htm`.

POLL: Which is better?
59% Cable
41% DSL

TODAY'S FOCUS: Broadband Internet

FIRST AMERICAN TO ORBIT EARTH

John H. Glenn became the first U.S. astronaut to orbit the Earth on this day in 1962. Glenn's Mercury spacecraft, Friendship 7, circled the Earth three times in a 4-hour, 55-minute space flight. The capsule is now on display at the Smithsonian Institution's National Air and Space museum.

Related Web site `history.nasa.gov/friendship7`

How Do Cable Modems Work?

By John Navas

Cable Internet works by using TV channel space for data transmission, with some channels used for downstream transmission and other channels for upstream transmission. Typically, considerably more capacity is deployed for downstream transmission than for upstream transmission, which is why many cable Internet providers prohibit types of use that make heavy use of upstream capacity. The shared nature of cable Internet makes everyone in a neighborhood suffer if the capacity of that segment is overwhelmed.

Cable Internet is based on transmission between a subscriber cable modem (which looks like a conventional dial-up modem) and a CMTS (cable modem termination system), a relatively large head-end box. The range of cable Internet effectively is unlimited, available at any location passed by an appropriate cable network.

Speed The typical downstream cable Internet speed is 1,500Kbps, roughly 25 to 50 times faster than standard 56Kbps dial-up modems. Because it's always connected, cable Internet is more convenient than having to dial up with a conventional modem. In addition, cable Internet doesn't need a phone line. Cable Internet signals have much less transmission delay than do dial-up signals. Although that difference in delay doesn't make much difference when surfing the Web, it can make a big difference in real-time gaming over the Internet.

Modems Cable Internet providers have embraced a standard known as DOCSIS (data over cable service interface specification). If your cable company supports DOCSIS, you aren't necessarily stuck getting your cable modem from it—you should be able to purchase your own cable modem yourself. Ask for a list of approved cable modems before making a purchase.

Of the two basic types of cable modems, external and internal, I strongly recommend external. They're easier to install and generally don't require drivers. External modems are further divided into two types of connections to your computer: Ethernet and USB. Although USB is convenient and works fairly well, Ethernet tends to be more stable and efficient.

TIP OF THE DAY Watching online video is one of the joys of broadband, but if you install RealNetworks's RealOne Player to do so, watch out. Unfortunately, when you install RealOne its default behavior is to take over all the media-playing duties. So, if you want WinAmp to play your MP3s and Windows Media Player to handle AVIs, you'll have to reclaim the file associations by hand.

Click the menu bar on the top of RealOne. Open **Preferences**. Under the CD category on the left, select **Media Types**. On the right, you can check or uncheck media types you want associated with RealOne.

DOWNLOAD OF THE DAY RealOne costs $10.95 a month, but Real Networks still offers free older versions of its player. They're pretty hard to find and who knows how long they will be there. So, run—don't walk—to `proforma.real.com/real/player/blackjack.html` and get your copy now.

TODAY'S FOCUS: Broadband Internet

FIRST ELECTRICAL BURGLAR ALARM

The first automated security system was installed in Boston, Massachusetts, on this day in 1858. Edwin Holmes, a hoop-skirt manufacturer by trade, created a system for wiring doors and windows to a bell that would ring in case of a break-in.

Related Web site www.howstuffworks.com/burglar-alarm.htm

Myths and Truths of Cable Modems

By John Navas

Cable Internet is a fantastic way to join the Internet community, but it can also be frustrating. Here are some common misconceptions, along with suggestions on how to deal with them.

Your Cable Internet Traffic Isn't Safe A common misconception is that cable connection systems are like local area networks (LANs), where it's possible for one subscriber to monitor the traffic of another. In reality, upstream and downstream traffic are carried on different channels. Cable modems are not capable of monitoring upstream channels. Most cable connection systems provide even more security by encrypting traffic with unique subscriber keys.

Running a Server Won't Hurt Other Subscribers Cable connections are vulnerable to an Internet problem known as upstream saturation. If the upstream gets saturated, downstream speeds can drop by 90% or more. It's possible for servers run by only a few subscribers to adversely affect hundreds of other subscribers. This is due to a weakness in the basic TCP Internet protocol, and is why many cable Internet providers prohibit servers.

You Can Get Cable Internet Only If You Subscribe to Cable TV Service It's possible for cable service providers to block TV channels in such a way that a cable connection can be used only for cable Internet service. Hence, some cable service providers offer cable Internet service without cable TV service, although there might be an additional charge. Check with your cable service provider.

Three Truths About Cable Internet Connections

Cable Internet Is Not Limited by Distance Unlike DSL, which is limited to about 17,500 feet from the head-end equipment (along the wire, not as the crow flies), cable connection is provided anywhere on a capable cable system.

It's Easy to Buy a Cable Modem Cable Internet has evolved considerably from the early days of proprietary systems. The DOCSIS standard now makes it possible for subscribers to buy their own modems, potentially saving money in the long run.

Open Access Is Coming to Cable Internet Although it's still true that you don't get a choice of Internet service providers on most cable systems, the industry is moving (albeit slowly) to open access, where you'll have a choice of ISPs. That's good news for consumers, because choice generally leads to lower prices and better service.

TIP OF THE DAY It's not enough to speed up your connection; you must speed up your surfing, too. Add an Address bar to your Windows toolbar by right-clicking the toolbar, pointing to **Toolbars**, and selecting **Address**.

You can enter any Web address into the Address bar, but you can also use it to navigate your hard drive. Try entering `C:` or `My Documents`.

DOWNLOAD OF THE DAY Want to make all your neighbors mad at you? Run your own Internet radio station from your house. It's free and easy. Just download the Shoutcast plug-in for Winamp from www.shoutcast.com and start spinning the hits.

POLL: How does using the Internet at work affect your productivity?

15% It decreases it	40% It increases it
20% No effect at all	25% Too busy surfing to answer

TODAY'S FOCUS: Broadband Internet

HERTZ PIONEER BORN

Radio innovator Heinrich Hertz was born in Hamburg, Germany, on this day in 1857. The hertz, a unit of frequency measurement, was named for him. The physics professor was the first to send and receive radio waves, which led directly to the development of radio, television, and radar. According to legend, a teenage boy vacationing in the Alps read one of Hertz's articles on electromagnetic waves and rushed home to Italy to experiment with Hertz's ideas. The young man's name was Guglielmo Marconi, the future "Father of Radio."

Related Web site `ideafinder.com/history/inventors/hertz.htm`

Myths and Truths of Satellite Broadband Access

By John Navas

Myth: It's Cable, DSL, or Nothing Coverage of cable Internet and DSL is increasing rapidly, but there are still many areas where neither is available, particularly rural areas. In these cases, satellite Internet might be an option. Satellites can broadcast the Internet directly to homes where the signals can be received using the same kind of small-dish antennas used for TVs. You can get satellite Internet wherever you have an unobstructed view of the satellite (located in the southern sky from the United States).

Myth: My Landlord Won't Let Me Put Up a Dish Federal law prohibits undue restrictions on direct broadcast satellite antennas. For more information, see `www.fcc.gov/mb/facts/otard.html`.

Myth: Satellite Internet Still Requires a Modem Connection First-generation satellite systems did require a modem connection for the upstream data. Second-generation satellite Internet systems eliminate the need for the modem by using the satellite for both up- and downstream transmission.

Those are the myths, now for the true stuff.

Truth: Double-Up with Satellite TV StarBand and DirecPC provide a single antenna that can be used for both satellite TV and satellite Internet. In the case of StarBand, the television service is provided by EchoStar's Dish Network. In the case of DirecPC, the combo configuration is called DirecDuo and the TV service is provided by DirecTV.

Truth: Watch Out for Latency It takes a long time, in Internet time, for a signal to travel up to a satellite and back down to the ground. This increases *latency*, lags of up to one second between the time a request is sent and the time the response is returned. Techniques used to minimize the negative effects of increased latency are effective for typical Web browsing, but not for interactive applications such as real-time gaming or remote access.

Truth: Watch Out for the "Fair Access" Policies Satellite Internet is designed for relatively light use. Heavy use can cause the system to slow down for all subscribers. DirecPC imposes a "fair access" policy that throttles back your speed when your use is heavier. StarBand doesn't appear to have an equivalent policy, but it's reasonable to expect that StarBand will limit use as well.

 TIP OF THE DAY Satellite access isn't great for fast-paced games such as Quake and Counter-Strike, but it's fine for many other games. For a great selection of games that work great on slow or high-latency connections, visit `games.yahoo.com` or `www.pogo.com`.

 DOWNLOAD OF THE DAY DALiWorld is an artificial-life screensaver for Windows and Linux. It looks like an aquarium, but you can share the fish you breed with other users across the Net. DALiWorld is free from `www.daliworld.net`.

POLL: Does the Web make you stoopid?
13% Yes
44% No
43% Huh?

TODAY'S FOCUS: Black History Month

DELL FOUNDER BORN

Founder and CEO of Dell Computer Corporation, Michael Dell, was born in Houston, Texas, on this day in 1965. When he was 15, Dell bought his first computer, an Apple II, and took it apart to see how it worked. At 18, he started selling PCs out of his dorm room at the University of Texas. He quit school after his freshman year and started making custom-built computers full time. Dell Corporation was established in 1984. Today, Dell Computers has offices in 34 countries with nearly 36,000 employees.

Related Web site `dell.com/us/en/gen/corporate/michael.htm`

Twisted List: African-American Inventors

By Martin Sargent

We continue with our special lists for Black History Month. Today's topic: great African-American inventors.

Benjamin Banneker (1731–1806) (`web.mit.edu/invent/www/inventorsA-H/Banneker.html`) The son of two freed slaves, Banneker is considered the first black American inventor. While growing up on a tobacco farm, he developed a novel irrigation system that allowed the plants to survive even during terrible dry spells.

Banneker is also remembered for building the first clock manufactured exclusively in America. When Banneker was 21, his friend Josef Levi lent him his watch and Banneker took the thing apart to study how it worked. He carved an enlarged replica of each piece of the clock's mechanism out of wood. Banneker's wooden clock kept accurate time for more than 50 years.

While architect Pierre L'Enfant was designing the layout of the nation's new capital in Washington, Thomas Jefferson appointed Banneker to the planning committee. According to sources, when L'Enfant was fired from the job for his bad temper—and took all his plans with him—Banneker was able to completely reproduce L'Enfant's designs from memory, re-creating complete layouts of the streets. Our nation's capital might look totally different if not for the genius of Banneker.

Sylvester James Gates (1950–) Gates, an MIT Ph.D. in the field of elementary particle physics and quantum field theory, is an expert in the mathematical and theoretical physics of supersymmetric particles, fields, and strings. His work covers topics such as the physics of quarks, leptons, gravity, super and heterotic strings, and Einstein's unified field theory. Gates is particularly skilled at explaining string theory to general audiences. For his wonderful lecture on super string theory, visit the Library of Congress at `www.loc.gov/locvideo/gates/intrgate.html`.

Philip Emeagwali (1954–) (`emeagwali.com`) Philip Emeagwali spent his youth living in Biafran refugee camps and fighting as a boy soldier in Biafran armies. Decades later, after coming to the U.S. with $140 in his pocket, Emeagwali figured out a way to harness the power of 64,000 computers into one intelligent superorganism—a supercomputer. Emeagwali shocked the world by using this network to perform 3.1 billion calculations per second in 1989—that's three times faster than the fastest supercomputer at the time. His Web page is considered by many to be the first personal page on the Net.

 TIP OF THE DAY To see TV shows and Hollywood movies online, visit `intertainer.com`. Pay monthly or by the program. Broadband connections only.

  DOWNLOAD OF THE DAY Travel through the universe to more than 100,000 stars with Celestia. Free for Windows and Linux from `www.shatters.net/celestia/`. Or get the Mac OS X version at `redivi.com/~bob/celestia.html`.

APPLE CO-FOUNDER BORN

Apple Computer CEO and co-founder Steve Jobs was born in Los Altos, California, on this day in 1955. Adopted from birth, Jobs used to attend lectures after school at Hewlett-Packard, and later got a job with Atari in 1974. Two years later, he started Apple Computers with Steve Wozniak, selling personal computers built in Jobs' garage. Jobs left Apple in 1985 to start the NeXT Corporation, but came back to Apple in 1996. He is also CEO of animation company Pixar.

Related Web site `americanhistory.si.edu/csr/comphist/sj1.html`

Great Palm Downloads

By Megan Morrone

Palm Reader (`peanutpress.com`) There are many e-book readers for the Palm OS. This free application from Palm is my favorite. It offers many screen preferences that make reading on a tiny screen a little easier. It also allows you to convert Word documents to the Palm Reader format.

Noah Lite English Dictionary (`arslexis.com`) Never be at a loss for words again. This free dictionary contains more than 122,000 words. For $19.95, you can get more specialized dictionaries and the ability to create your own.

QuizApp (`quizapp.com`) Throw away your flash cards. QuizApp is a handy tool that lets you test yourself on everything from anatomy to world capitals. The coolest thing about this application is that it lets you create your own quizzes.

Bubble Blasters 1.0 (`handheld.hice-dev.org/bubbleblastersAppPage.htm`) Bubble Blasters is another quiz program with an interesting visual interface that adds to the fun of learning. It works great with color Palms or Visors.

GradePoint (`pdaceonline.tripod.com/prod01.htm`) GradePoint helps you keep track of homework, tests, and projects. It reminds you to study, and even lets you beam assignments to friends.

Filez (`nosleep.net/filez.asp`) Just like your PC, your Palm can quickly get overloaded with programs. Use this free download to organize your files with ease. Think of it as Windows Explorer for your PDA.

Vindigo (`vindigo.com`) Before I became a Palm enthusiast, I thought a PDA had to have wireless access to get maps, restaurant reviews, or movie times. How could I be so stupid? Download Vindigo, and every time you sync your Palm you get updated information.

Geeky Alarm Sounds (`palmrat.com/software/palmos`) This is by far the most fun download I have. I can't stand the standard alarm sound for Palm, so I downloaded Justin R. Cutler's GeekSounds. Now I can be reminded of meetings and appointments with the digital sounds of Nena's "99 Luftballoons" or the *Mission: Impossible* theme song.

Note: Geeksounds is not an application; it's a replacement alarm database. The new alarms will show up in any application, such as Datebook, that picks its alarm from System MIDI Sounds.

 TIP OF THE DAY PDA screens scratch easily. All it takes is a piece of grit on your stylus and a Graffiti 'S' will be forever etched on your screen. You can buy commercial screen protectors from companies such as Fellowes (`www.fellowes.com`), or you can make your own.

PocketPC users can get instructions at Dale Coffing's PocketPC Passion, `www.pocketpcpassion.com/General/ScreenProtector/ScreenProtector.htm`.

Palm users should visit Do-It-Yourself Tips for PalmPilot Screen Protectors at `www.geocities.com/SiliconValley/Campus/9054/screenpr.html`.

DOWNLOAD OF THE DAY JR's BigClock is a big clock for your Palm. It includes a small monthly calendar, four alarms, stopwatch, and world clock. Free from `www.rupp.paessler.com/palmpilot.htm`.

POLL: Do you download pirated software?

58% Yes

42% No

FEBRUARY 25

FIRST U.S. TELEVISION STATION

The Federal Radio Commission issued the first television license to Charles Francis Jenkins Laboratories in Washington, D.C., on this day in 1928. The station was assigned the call letters W3XK. The following July, W3XK began broadcasting scheduled programs five nights a week. At first, Jenkins Labs was limited to primitive silhouette images because of its 10kHz bandwidth. Soon after, however, it was allowed to move its carrier frequency to 4.95MHz, with a bandwidth of 100kHz and 5,000 watts of power. W3XK operated until October 31, 1932.

Related Web site `antiquewireless.org`

PDA Viruses

Any computer platform can be attacked by a computer virus, even PDAs. So far, only three viruses have been discovered for the Palm platform: Vapor, Phage, and Liberty Crack, but more are sure to come. You can contract a virus on a PDA in three ways.

- **Synching**—If you open an email attachment containing a PDA virus on your PC, the next time you sync, the virus will be transmitted to your PDA.
- **Beaming**—Most PDAs have the capability to transmit information to and from other PDAs via infrared beaming. Your PDA has an alert to tell you data is being beamed to you, but some viruses can override that alert and infiltrate your system in a covert manner.
- **Network**—If your PDA has wireless access to a network or to the Internet, virus files can reach your handheld via email or other modes of network data transmission.

All the major antivirus companies offer PDA versions of their software, including McAfee, Symantec, Trend Micro, and Finjan. Trend offers a free download for Palm, PocketPC, and Epoc users at `www.antivirus.com/free_tools/wireless`.

I'm tempted to say that PDA viruses are nothing to worry about. So far, they haven't been a huge problem, but they can be destructive. Liberty Crack, for example, will delete files on your Palm. As more of us use wireless PDAs, I expect to see more virus activity.

As always, the best defense is to make regular backups of your data and follow the security advice I offered in January. And for PDA users, I'll add the warning: Don't beam with strangers.

TIP OF THE DAY The screen is the first thing to go on a Palm. If yours gets crunched, here's what to do. First, back up your data if you can. Often, when the screen is cracked everything else still works. You have two options for repair.

Have Palm fix it. It's generally around $100. Call customer service at 1-888-956-7256 for information. They'll send you a shipping container and an RMA. If your Palm is under warranty and you can prove the screen didn't break through your negligence, they might even replace it free.

If you're handy (and cheap), you can do the repair yourself. Buy the parts from Gethightech, `www.gethightech.com`. They have instructions on their Web site. Naturally, fixing the screen yourself voids your warranty.

DOWNLOAD OF THE DAY While your Palm is being repaired, you can run the Palm Emulator on your desktop for that full-bodied Palm flavor. It's free from `www.palmos.com/dev/tech/tools/emulator`. You'll also need Palm ROMs. You can get them from Palm itself by joining Palm's alliance program, `www.palmos.com/alliance/join`, or get them from `www.se-ed.net/palmos`—at least until Palm reads this.

TODAY'S FOCUS: Palm OS

FEBRUARY
26

FCC CREATED

The Federal Communications Commission was formed by President Franklin D. Roosevelt on this day in 1934. The Communications Act of 1934 made the FCC responsible for overseeing radio, wire, and cable communications. Over the years, the agency's role has expanded to also include television and satellite communications. The FCC consists of five commissioners appointed by the President and confirmed by the Senate for five-year terms. Today, there are six operating bureaus: Consumer and Governmental Affairs, Enforcement, International, Media, Wireless Telecommunications, and Wireline Competition. The FCC also has 10 staff offices.

Related Web site   `www.fcc.gov`

Palm Email Tools

If you're on the move and don't have time to sit down at a desktop for extended periods of time to read and compose email, you might want to consider bringing your mail with you on your PalmOS PDA.

You need three things to get email on your Palm: the Palm Desktop, a Palm-based email client, and a desktop email client such as Outlook Express or Eudora. You likely already have all three. Most Palm devices come with Palm Mail, a built-in client, but if you have an older device you can download one from `pda.tucows.com/palm/int_email.html`.

Next, you must configure HotSync to copy the mail from your desktop email client. Palm Mail works with Lotus cc:Mail, Microsoft Outlook and Outlook Express, and Eudora. It does not work with AOL mail or CompuServe. To work with Netscape mail, you will have to configure Netscape to use MAPI and configure HotSync to use Outlook Express.

To tell the Palm which email program you want to sync with, open the Palm Desktop and select **HotSync** from the menus at the top. In the **HotSync** drop-down menu, select **Custom**. When you are in the Custom dialog box, click **Mail** in the **Conduit** list and click the **Change** button. In the next dialog box, select the **Mail Setup** button at the bottom and select the desktop email program with which you want to sync.

To read email on your Palm, you must download all your current email from your desktop email client. This should happen automatically when you HotSync. You might want to set up some conditions in your Palm-based email program first, however.

If you get a lot of mail every day, use Palm Mail's filtering to keep your mailbox to a reasonable size. Open Mail on your Palm, click the silk-screened **Menu** button, open the **Options** menu, and click **HotSync** options. You can choose just to receive mail addressed directly to you, unread mail, or to limit the size of emails. Unless you like to wait a long time for HotSyncs, don't elect to copy your entire email inbox to your handheld.

To send mail, compose messages from within your email program. They'll be copied to your desktop mailer's outbox the next time you sync, and sent out with the rest of your mail when you next run your desktop client.

TIP OF THE DAY   There's more than one way to skin a Palm. Dress up your Palm interface with PalmTheme from `www.shin.nu/~FocV/PPro/index.html#download`.

Choose from many themes at PalmTheme Theme Park `www.shin.nu/~FocV/TP/themepark.html`.

DOWNLOAD OF THE DAY   Your Palm can read e-books with the free Palm Reader from Peanut Press, peanutpress.com. Peanut Press offers hundreds of free books, too, such as Bruce Stirling's classic, *Hacker Crackdown*, `peanutpress.com/free.cgi/0101649104-46717-85248`.

POLL: Do you read the manual?

40% Yes

60% No

TODAY'S FOCUS: Palm OS

APPLE KILLS NEWTON

Apple Computer nnounced it would discontinue the Newton operating system on this day in 1998. The handheld was introduced in 1993, but never succeeded due to its high price tag and poor handwriting recognition. Several Newton employees left the company at the end of 1997 to join 3Com's Palm Computing team.

Related Web site   webring.com/hub?ring=newtonring

FEBRUARY 27

Palm Office Apps

By Roger Chang

You use your PC in the office and your Palm on the road. Wouldn't it be great to take your MS Office Word and Excel documents with you? You can.

One way is to convert a Word document into a format that can be read by a Palm document reader. One such converter is Word-Doc (deepwave.net/ref/palm-wdc2), which converts Microsoft Word files to the Palm document, RichReader, and iSilo formats. This is a read-only solution, however.

If you want to be able to edit Microsoft Office documents on your Palm, consider Quickoffice from Cutting Edge Software, quickoffice.com. Quickoffice comes with a Microsoft Office–compatible word processor, spreadsheet, and chart maker. The program has two parts: one that resides on your Palm and a second that lives on your PC.

Launch the Quickoffice PC software on your PC. Select which Excel and Word documents you want to sync with your Palm. After you've selected the files, they're converted and stored in the Palm HotSync install tool and will be transferred over on the next HotSync you perform. When a document changes on either the Palm or the desktop, it will be automatically updated on the other side.

Quickoffice is $39.95, and you can buy individual components for less.

TIP OF THE DAY   There are four ways to reset your PalmOS device:

1. **Soft Reset**—Reboots the Palm. All your data and settings will be saved. Press the reset button inside the hole on the back panel of your handheld.
2. **System or Warm Reset**—Reboots the Palm. No system extensions are loaded. All your data and settings will be saved. Perform this reset if you've installed system enhancements that might be crashing your Palm. Hold down the top scroll button while you press the reset button inside the hole on the back panel of your handheld.
3. **Hard Reset**—A hard reset erases everything from your Palm. All data will be lost. Your Palm will be as it was when it came from the factory. Back up first! Hold down the power button and press the reset button inside the hole on the back panel of your handheld. When the Palm Computing Platform screen appears, release the power button. You'll get a message warning you that you are about to erase all your data. To continue, press the top scroll button. To cancel, press any other button, which will start a soft reset and your data will remain intact.
4. **Power Down Reset**—This reset is a hard reset for Palms that use removable alkaline batteries. It's equivalent to a hard reset. Remove the batteries from the Palm for at least 30 minutes. If the system doesn't boot, try again for a longer period.

DOWNLOAD OF THE DAY   Take screen shots of your Palm screen with LinkeSoft's ScreenShot, free to try, $12 to buy, from linkesoft.com/english/screenshothack.

TODAY'S FOCUS: Palm OS

NETWORK NOTES CANCELED

A joint venture between IBM and AT&T was called off on this day in 1996. AT&T scrapped Network Notes, a project that linked users of IBM's Lotus Notes over AT&T's phone network, enabling several users to work on a single document from different locations at the same time. The move came at a time when the growing popularity of the Internet was threatening proprietary networks. Not surprisingly, AT&T announced the debut of its new dial-up Internet access service in the same week it discontinued Network Notes.

Related Web site www.lotus.com

Speed Up HotSync

By Megan Morrone

I'm tired of waiting a million hours for everything on my Visor to sync with my PC. And I'm not going to take it anymore. Here are two tips I use to speed up my synching.

Customize Your HotSync Hogs There are a few common programs that, although useful, can waste a lot of time in the sync process. The most popular of these sync hogs are AvantGo and Vindigo. The default configuration for both of these programs is to synchronize files every time you HotSync. With Vindigo, you can change this in five easy steps.

Open the Palm Desktop. Click **HotSync** and highlight **Custom**. Select **VindigoLink**. Click the **Change** button. Click the **VindigoLink** button and change to Daily or Weekly.

Here's another tip about customizing your HotSync hogs. When I first told him about Vindigo, my dad made the mistake of choosing all the cities he was ever interested in visiting. The first time he did a HotSync, it took him more than half an hour. When you set up Vindigo, just choose the city where you live. You can always add more cities as you plan to visit them.

The same goes for AvantGo. The more sources you choose to download, the longer it will take each time you HotSync.

Don't Be Afraid to Purge If you've been adding new items to your date book, address, to-do, and memo databases for a while, you're likely to see some slowness. It's easy to purge old items from your handheld and archive them on your desktop.

Open the Palm Desktop. Choose **Datebook**. Go to **Tools** and select **Purge Events**. Set the time limit for purging and be sure the archive box is checked. Click **OK**. Do the same with your memo pad, address book, and to-do list. Your items will be purged at the next HotSync, and you should notice increased speed.

TIP OF THE DAY Those four buttons on the bottom of your Palm PDA offer easy access to your calendar, memo pad, address book, and to-do list. You can, however, reassign them to different applications that you use more often. To reassign a button:

1. Tap **Applications**.
2. Tap **Prefs**.
3. In the drop-down menu in the upper-right corner, select **Buttons**.
4. Tap the drop-down menu for the button you want to reassign. You'll see a list of installed applications.
5. Choose the program you want to assign to that button.

DOWNLOAD OF THE DAY If you like The Sims, try Dejobaan BeBop, a Sims clone for the Palm OS. The demo is free, but pay the $14.95 for more ways to play, from www.dejobaan.com.

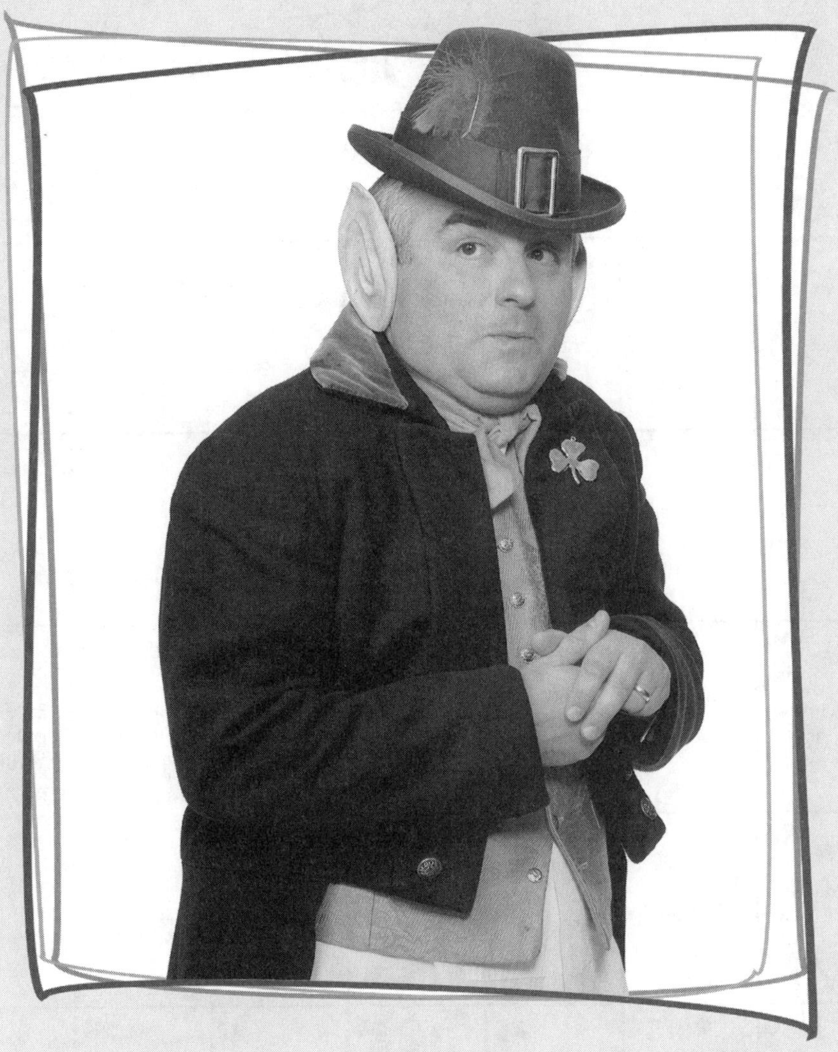

MARCH 2003

MARCH 2003

SUNDAY	MONDAY	TUESDAY	WEDNESDAY	THURSDAY	FRIDAY	SATURDAY
						1
2	**3** Alexander Graham Bell born (1847)	**4**	**5**	**6**	**7** Telephone patented (1876)	**8**
9 Rick Kughen born (1968)	**10**	**11**	**12**	**13** Uranus discovered (1781)	**14** Albert Einstein born (1879)	**15** Escalator patented (1892)
16 First liquid-fueled rocket launched (1926)	**17** St. Patrick's Day	**18**	**19**	**20** Sir Isaac Newton died (1727)	**21** First day of spring	**22**
23/30	**24/31** March 31 – Daylight Saving Time in effect (1918)	**25**	**26**	**27**	**28** Three Mile Island nuclear accident (1979)	**29**

TODAY'S FOCUS: Palm OS

TYPEWRITER INVENTOR BORN

The man who developed the typewriter was born in Pennsylvania on this day in 1819. Christopher Latham Sholes was a printer turned politician who pursued inventing in his free time. The Milwaukee customs collector developed a machine that printed numbers on the pages of books, and eventually applied the same technique for putting letters on paper. Sholes also improved the keyboard, including the QWERTY layout. He and his partners patented the typewriter in 1868 and sold the rights to the Remington Arms Company in 1873 for $12,000.

Related Web site `yesterdaysoffice.com`

Using Your Palm to Buy a House

By Megan Morrone

Who knew that buying your first house could be so confusing? I always imagined fresh paint and picket fences. Instead, I'm mired in percentage points, credit scores, and the idea that I'll be in debt for a very, very long time.

As always, I turn to my PDA for solace. I resist the temptation to play another game of Tetris, and download a few programs to help me keep track of my adventures in real estate. (Note: I searched high and low for a database program to keep track of my thoughts about the houses I looked at, but I couldn't find anything that worked better than the built-in memo pad.)

Top three downloads to help you with your home purchase:

LoanPro (`www.infinitysw.com/products/loanpro.html`) One of the first decisions you have to make when looking for a home is deciding how much you can afford. Unless you're some kind of dot-com millionaire (do they still exist?), you're going to have to take out a loan.

LoanPro lets you enter different prices, down-payment percentages, and interest rates, and then quickly calculate a summary of your loan payments or an amortization table. This tool also can be used for auto loans. LoanPro is free to try, $19.99 to buy.

HomeLoan (`www.palmutil.com`) This download does everything LoanPro does and a bit more. It lets you create and compare different price and payment plan scenarios, and also contains an inflation calculator and a monthly budget tool. If you're worried about qualifying for a loan, use the Qualify Ratios form. HomeLoan is free to try, $10 to buy.

AvantGo (`avantgo.com`) You might already use AvantGo to read the latest news or your stock quotes, but it also supplies Web content that will help you with your home search. Make Homes.com one of your channels, and you can search for available properties, check daily interest rates, and get all the latest real-estate news. I also created a unique channel to view updates on my real-estate agent's page.

AvantGo is an ad-supported free service.

TIP OF THE DAY Want to print from your Palm or PocketPC device? There's no printer port, but you can use the infrared port if you have an infrared-compatible printer and PrintBoy, $19.95 from `bachmannsoftware.com`.

DOWNLOAD OF THE DAY Get down to Spring Training and keep score on your Palm with Scorepad, `www.scorepad.com`. Free to try, $69.95 to buy. For an additional $39.95 per season, you can download the latest stats and sync them with your Palm, so you'll never have to wonder how many home runs Barry and Sammy have.

TODAY'S FOCUS: Palm OS

FIRST OUTERPLANETARY PROBE LAUNCHED

Pioneer 10 was launched from Cape Canaveral, Florida on this day in 1972. The unmanned spacecraft was the first to leave the solar system and to send back close-up images of Jupiter. Scientists estimate Pioneer 10 is currently about 7.5 billion miles from Earth. A drawing of a man and woman, a star map marked with the location of the sun, and a map showing the flight path of Pioneer are bolted to its exterior.

Related Web site   `spacelink.nasa.gov`

MARCH
2

Twisted List: Most Addictive Palm Games

By Megan Morrone

I have an addictive personality. I bite my fingernails, I drink too much Diet Coke, even though it makes me jittery, and when I download a new game for my PDA, I play it nonstop. If you're at all like me (and I hope, for your sake, that you're not), you'll love these Palm games.

SFCave (`meighan.com/sfcave`) Sometimes, the simplest games are the most addicting. SFCave is about as simple as they get. You are some kind of snakelike object trying to make your way through a cave, avoiding rectangular obstructions. Hold down any button on your PDA to go up, let go to go down. The farther you go without hitting anything, the higher your score. My highest score is 1169. What's yours?

Blocks (`electronhut.com`) Why is Tetris so addicting? I asked this very question of Alexey Pajitnov, the inventor of this evil, evil game when he appeared on our show. Because he couldn't give me an answer, I feel perfectly fine using this free Tetris clone instead of the real thing.

TetAttack (`tetattack.com`) TetAttack is like Tetris, with more oomph. If you like Bejeweled (`www.astraware.com/palm/bejeweled`), you'll probably like TetAttack. It costs $8 to register, but your addiction to this one should be soothed by the fact that all royalties go to the Red Cross.

Kyle's Quest (`crmsonfire.com`) Kyle's Quest is one of the coolest portable role-playing games around. You play the role of Kyle, exploring a new land with a click of your stylus. You also can create your own adventures for other people to play. This little piece of shareware costs $15, but you can download bushels of new add-ons absolutely free. Works on PocketPC, too.

TIP OF THE DAY   Here's how to conserve battery life on your Palm:

Change Power Usage Preferences:

1. Choose **Prefs** from the Application launcher.
2. Tap the drop-down menu in the upper-right corner and choose **General**.
3. Set **Auto Off** to one or two minutes.

Adjust Brightness: Hold down the power button to turn down brightness and extend battery life.

Beam Conservatively: Beam only when it's necessary; it takes a lot of power.

Don't Overclock: Utilities to speed up your Palm make it faster, but they also burn up the juice.

DOWNLOAD OF THE DAY   On the other hand, if you don't mind shortened battery life, it's fun to double the speed of your PDA without breaking a sweat. FastCPU, from `megasoft2000.com/palm_division/fastcpu.htm`, is my favorite utility. Free to try, $12.95 to buy. Warning: Overclocking might void your warranty.

POLL: Is the search for extraterrestrial intelligence a waste of time?

23% Yes

72% No

5% I'll be playing the Atari 2600 E.T. cartridge

TODAY'S FOCUS: Photo Editing

ALEXANDER GRAHAM BELL BORN

The inventor of the telephone and many other innovations was born in Edinburgh, Scotland, on this day in 1847. Bell was always fascinated by human communication and began teaching deaf people to speak when he was in his 20s. Bell's mother and his eventual wife—one of his pupils—were also deaf.

Related Web site `lcweb.loc.gov/exhibits/treasures/trr002.html`

Review: Adobe Photoshop 7

By Brett Larsen

Photoshop 7 brings to the table all the power and tools found in previous generations of the application and goes forward from there. Several new tools are designed to take the pain out of daily tasks; many others promise to give you a creative edge.

A new healing tool will assist you in removing dust, scratches, and even wrinkles from faces in photographs. Unlike the stamp tool, which sampled part of your image and then applied it to another portion to cover up flaws, the healing tool uses information from elsewhere in your image but keeps the light and shading attributes of the area being touched up to make the change less noticeable.

Photoshop 7 also saves images for the Web without sacrificing quality. By allowing you to assign higher priority to specific areas of your image, the software lets you boost the quality of key graphic elements—such as text or corporate graphics—relative to background information.

Mac users can now manage files and folders in Photoshop instead of in the Finder. Using Photoshop 7's new file browser, you can quickly navigate your hard drive or network disks that contain needed information.

Not only are you able to see the images, you also can check image data, such as modification date, file format, color mode, file size, and rank. The rank can be modified any way you choose, so you could tag pictures "best take," "good alternative," or whatever your creative needs require.

You also can view EXIF (exchangeable image file) data, such as flash and exposure settings, recorded by digital cameras. Furthermore, you can move, rename, and copy files without leaving the comfort of Photoshop. You can even rotate images.

The best news about the latest edition of Photoshop is that it takes full advantage of both Mac OS X and Windows XP. For Mac users, this means Photoshop finally runs natively in OS X instead of in Classic. Photoshop 7 also takes advantage of digital-imaging features in Windows XP to provide a better user experience.

Photoshop 7 for Windows or Mac is $609 complete, $149 for an upgrade, from `www.adobe.com`.

 TIP OF THE DAY If you're a student or teacher, you can get Photoshop and many other programs at a substantial academic discount. Check with your campus store. Sites such as `academicsuperstore.com` also sell software at academic pricing if you have the proper documentation.

 DOWNLOAD OF THE DAY Still too expensive? How about downloading a Photoshop clone for free? The GIMP (GNU Image Manipulation Program) has many of the features Photoshop users want. And it's free. Download a copy for nearly any operating system, including Windows, from `www.gimp.org`.

To get the GIMP running on Mac OS X you'll have to install X Windows first. Automate the process with Fink, free from `fink.sourceforge.net`.

TODAY'S FOCUS: Photo Editing

CLONING FUNDING BANNED IN U.S.

On this day in 1997, President Clinton said federal funds should not be used for human cloning research. The proposal came less than a few weeks after Scottish scientists announced the first cloning of an adult animal on February 23. Researchers made Dolly the sheep by removing an unfertilized egg cell from an adult ewe and replacing its nucleus with the nucleus of an adult sheep mammary gland cell. The egg then was implanted in another ewe. The success of the experiment has created much controversy over the ethics of cloning.

Related Web site `www.roslin.ac.uk`

Review: Photoshop Elements for Macintosh and Windows

By Roy Santos

 For many casual users, Adobe's high-end Photoshop software has always been too expensive and too complicated. Its baby brother, Adobe's Photoshop Elements, hits the sweet spot for those users.

Photoshop Elements is missing professional tools, such as CMYK separation and channel editing, but it keeps the capabilities consumers want and adds an easy-to-navigate interface. Photoshop Elements is simple for beginners to use but has enough horsepower to satisfy advanced users.

Most noticeable on the interface is the Help Palette. When you place your mouse over an object in the Tool Palette or over one of the tabs, the Help Palette's contents change to show what that object or tab does.

Another convenient user interface improvement is the Filters Browser. Whenever you press this tab, a window opens to reveal thumbnails of filters that you can apply to your picture. The Effects Browser works the same way, condensing to one click effects that normally would take several steps to achieve, such as Blizzard or Drop Shadow.

With the addition of a Recipes Palette, Adobe attempts to reduce the number of clicks it takes to perform common image-editing tasks. For example, to remove scratches from a picture, click the **Recipes** tab. A palette drops down from the tab and lets you select from a palette of common image-editing tasks. Click **Image Cleanup**, select **Remove Dust & Scratches**, and the recipe will walk you through the task.

One feature Adobe has never offered before is Photomerge. It automatically stitches multiple consecutive images into a single panoramic shot.

Adobe Photoshop Elements does lack the advanced Web features that some of its competitors have, such as the rollover and image-slicing support found in Ulead's PhotoImpact. Adobe reserves these features for the higher-end Photoshop. If these are not important to you, you should give Elements a try.

Photoshop Essentials is $99 from `adobe.com`.

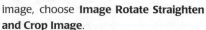

 TIP OF THE DAY   Do your scans often end up crooked, like this one?

 It's easy to fix in Photoshop Elements. Open the crooked image, choose **Image Rotate Straighten and Crop Image**.

If you want to straighten the image but leave the canvas size the same, choose **Image Rotate Straighten Image**. Using this command results in an image with a transparent border at its edges.

 DOWNLOAD OF THE DAY   Paint Shop Pro is nearly as powerful as Photoshop and easier to use. Try it free for 30 days. Buy it for $99 from `www.jasc.com`.

TODAY'S FOCUS: Photo Editing

FIRST GOVERNMENT-MANDATED NET CENSORSHIP

Singapore announced it would filter "morally offensive" Web sites on this day in 1996. The government also outlined a plan to license ISPs and content providers, and admitted it was already preventing about 100,000 users from accessing sites such as Playboy and Penthouse. Singapore officials instituted technology to block normal HTTP requests sent by Web browsers, but users soon discovered a loophole that allowed them to access blocked sites by using a proxy server. The battle between Internet users and the government continues—in 2001, Singapore announced it also would ban certain political Web sites.

Related Web site `www.gov.sg`

Three Simple Photoshop Fixes

By Bruce Fraser

It's rare to find a digital image that you can't improve in Adobe Photoshop or Adobe Photoshop Elements. Both programs are available for download as a 30-day free trial at the Adobe Web site, `adobe.com`. Here are three adjustments nearly any photo can benefit from using Photoshop Elements:

Tip 1: Balance Light and Dark Set the dynamic range to be sure the image contains a full range of tones from light to dark.

1. Open the levels command by pressing Ctrl+L. You will see a histogram, a simple bar chart that shows how many pixels in the image are at each brightness level.
2. If, for example, the histogram indicates that the image has a lot of pixels in the middle ranges, but no light or dark pixels, you can fix the dynamic range of the image by pulling the black and white input sliders inward.
3. Stop when a significant number of pixels start to appear.

Tip 2: Correct Color Does the color of your image still look a little off? You need to balance the red, green, and blue in the image to remove color casts.

A secret the pros know is that if you fix the neutrals in an image, the rest of the color falls into place. The trick is to find a few elements in the image that you know should be close to neutral gray (equal amounts of red, green, and blue) and make them so.

Simply click **Enhance**, **Color**, and then **Color Casts**. Click on gray points in the picture until the image looks right.

Tip 3: Adjust Contrast Optimize the final contrast to make the subject pop. In Photoshop Elements

1. Click **Enhance**.
2. Select **Brightness/Contrast** from the **Brightness/Contrast** menu item.
3. Move the sliders until you're satisfied with your image.

This final tweak adds depth and drama to the final image.

TIP OF THE DAY Like many other programs that handle huge files, Photoshop often uses a scratch disk for temporary storage. Choose a scratch disk with plenty of room (at least twice the size of the largest file you'll ever edit) on the fastest drive you've got. Change the location of the scratch disks in Photoshop's preferences.

DOWNLOAD OF THE DAY My favorite photo editor is not very well known, but Ulead's PhotoImpact does everything Photoshop does, works with Photoshop plug-ins, and costs just $89. It's particularly good for working with images destined for the Web. Download a free trial at `www.ulead.com`.

POLL: Do you verb your nouns?

74% Yes

26% No

THURSDAY, MARCH 6, 2003

TODAY'S FOCUS: Photo Editing

MICHELANGELO VIRUS STRIKES

One of the first widespread computer viruses was programmed to activate on this date beginning in 1992. Michelangelo stayed dormant on infected PCs until March 6 of any year. On that date, the virus would activate upon boot-up and destroy all data stored on hard drives and floppy disks. The boot sector virus was first detected in Sweden and named after the Renaissance artist, who was born on March 6, 1475. Despite much publicity and panic, only a few thousand computers were infected worldwide. Michelangelo's author was never found.

Related Web site   `www.cert.org`

Fix Overexposed (and Underexposed) Images

By Bert Monroy

There are many ways to fix bad shots in Adobe Photoshop, but not all of them are the best solution. With overexposed or underexposed images, the solution most people use is the Levels command. Using the Levels command is a great way to correct the problem, but the downside is that you lose image quality.

In an overexposed or underexposed image, you want to affect all the pixels in the image equally. Follow these steps to fix an overexposed image:

1. Duplicate the background layer into a new layer.
2. Put the new layer in Multiply mode. This will intensify the saturation of the image.
3. Not enough? Duplicate the multiplied layer again, until you get the results you want.

Underexposed images are handled the same way, except you put the new layer in Screen mode instead of in Multiply.

(Bert Monroy is a digital artist. Visit his Web site, www. bertmonroy.com, for more information about his work.)

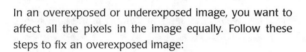

TIP OF THE DAY   Eliminate Red Eye

By Mikkel Aaland

Red eye occurs when light from an on-camera flash reflects off the back of the eye, giving someone a demonic look. Red eye is such a common problem in color images that Photoshop Elements includes an easy-to-use tool

devoted to fixing the problem (this tool really is a color replacement tool and has other uses, as well).

1. Select the **Red Eye Brush** tool from the toolbar.
2. Choose a **Soft Round 65 pixels** brush from the pop-up palette in the Options bar (the brush you choose will depend on the specifics of your particular image). I clicked **Default Colors** in the Options bar to specify black as the replacement color. I selected **First Click** from the **Sampling** pop-up menu and specified a **Tolerance** of **30** percent.

3. By clicking first on the red area of the eye, I automatically specified that color for removal. I then dragged over the eye until the red was replaced with black. Sometimes, the replacement to black is too light. You can fix this by using the Burn tool to darken the pupil. Also, if a person's face is pink, sometimes the Red Eye Brush doesn't work as well. To reduce this problem, use the Lasso tool to select the red eye area, and then apply the Red Eye Brush tool.

(Mikkel Aaland is the author of Photoshop Elements Solutions *(Sybex, 2001).)*

DOWNLOAD OF THE DAY   If that's too much trouble, you can download a free program that can do several photo-retouching tasks, including eliminating red eye, free from `www.ofoto.com`. Ofoto is Kodak's online photo printing service, but their ofotonow software also is an excellent standalone photo management tool for Mac and Windows.

TODAY'S FOCUS: Photo Editing

DISNEY CEO BORN

Michael D. Eisner was born in Mount Kisco, New York, on this day in 1942. Eisner got his start in the television business while in college as a page for NBC, and then worked for the network as an FCC logging clerk. He later worked in programming at CBS, and then ABC. In 1976, Eisner became President and COO at Paramount Pictures. He made the switch to Disney in 1984 and is now one of the richest CEOs in the world. His wife, Jane (a.k.a. "Tasty"), is a former computer programmer.

Related Web site `www.disney.com`

MARCH 7

Restore Old Pictures

By Mikkel Aaland

Most photographs suffer from the passage of time: They fade, crack, wrinkle, or tear. Using a combination of Photoshop Elements' Dust & Scratches filter, the Selection tool, and the Clone Stamp tool we can make those pictures as good as new.

First, apply auto levels to the cropped image to optimize the colors. Then, set the magnification level to 300% and look for dust and scratches and other age spots. You might also notice moiré patterns and other artifacts caused by the scanning process. Select the damaged areas with the Lasso Selection tool and apply the Elements Dust & Scratches filter to this selected area. Set the radius at **4** and the threshold at **0**.

In general, higher radius values effectively remove more dust and scratches but blur other pixels in the image. Depending on the image, you can still remove dust and scratches but diminish the blur caused by higher radius values by selecting higher threshold values.

If larger blemishes remain, use the Clone Stamp tool from the toolbox. In the options bar, select the following options for the clone stamp tool:

> **Brush:** Soft round, 100 pixels
> **Mode:** Normal
> **Opacity:** 100%
> **Aligned:** Checked on
> **Use All Layers:** Checked on

Position the cursor slightly to the side of a scratch or smudge, in an intact area of the same color. While holding the Alt/Option key, click and sample the clean color. Then click and stamp over the flawed area. Be careful not to drag and smear the pixels and cause an unnatural-looking blur. Repeat this process in all the flawed areas.

(Mikkel Aaland is a professional photographer and author. Visit him on the Web at www.cyberbohemia.com.)

 TIP OF THE DAY   Whether in a presentation or on a Web page, adding a shadow to text makes it more dramatic and polished. It's easy to add shadows in Photoshop 7. Here's how:

1. Create a new image and type some 60-point text into it.
2. Click the **Layer** menu.
3. Move to the **Layer Style** menu item and select **Drop Shadow**.
4. You can change the settings in the Layer Style window. If Preview is checked, you can see how changing parameters will change your image.
5. When you have the shadow where you want it, click **OK**.

If you really want to get fancy, add a bevel by clicking **Bevel and Emboss**.

DOWNLOAD OF THE DAY   IrfanView is free, fast, and will open just about any image file you're likely to come across. It also enables you to manipulate images, changing size or color depth, for example, and you can set it up to play slide shows of your favorite pictures. From `irfanview.com`.

POLL: Are you your family's tech support?
90% Yes
4% No
6% Too busy to answer

TODAY'S FOCUS: Photo Editing

MARCH 8

PC-DOS 2.0 RELEASED

IBM released PC-DOS 2.0 on this day in 1983. The computer maker originally intended to use a different operating system in its PCs: Gary Kildall's CP/M. However, Kildall was reportedly out flying his plane when IBM executives came to call. When Big Blue told Bill Gates of its search for an OS for its new PC, the Microsoft founder quickly bought the rights to a program under development for $50,000 and turned around and sold it to IBM. DOS became the foundation of Microsoft's fortune.

Related Web site   `computerhope.com/history/dos.htm`

Surfin' Saturday: Colorful Sites

Clairol's Try It On Studio
If you want to change your hair, but fear the catastrophic social ramifications of a bad cut, experiment with various styles and colors at Clairol's Try It On Studio, `clairol.com/tios_2.jsp`.

Follow these steps to create your color profile:

1. Click **New Users**. Select the color of hair you have now. Choose how long you want your new hair color to last. Register at the site with a username and email address. Uncheck the box for special offers if you don't want to be bombarded with email. Enter the studio, and get ready to have some fun.
2. Now select a picture of a model whose facial features look similar to yours, or upload a digital picture of yourself. If you choose the latter option, be sure your hair is pulled back in the photo.
3. Finally, experiment with short, medium, and long locks, as well as various colors. Use the arrows below your photo to get the new hairstyles centered just right.

Colorgenics   Color's not just for hair. Colorgenics, at `colorgenics.com`, is a whole new way of learning about yourself based on your color preferences.

In taking the Colorgenics test, you select eight colored cubes one at a time, starting with the one you most closely relate to and finishing with the one that you feel least represents your being. You'll be amazed at the results. It's almost as much fun as trying a new hair color.

 TIP OF THE DAY   If you're emailing a picture to friends and family, it's just plain courteous to keep it to a manageable size. No image should be larger than 640×480 or occupy more than 100KB.

Here's how to use Microsoft's Paint program—yes, the one that comes free with Windows—to get your pictures down to size:

First, open the image in Paint. It can read most common file formats, including BMP, JPEG, and GIF. Type Ctrl+E to check the image size. If it's too big, close the window and type Ctrl+W to open the Stretch/Skew window. Here, you can shrink or enlarge an image by a percent. Be sure both horizontal and vertical percentages are the same so you don't distort the picture.

Now it's time to save the picture. The most compact file format is JPEG. If it's not already a JPG, select **Save As** from the **File** menu and choose **JPEG** in the **Save As Type** drop-down menu. In most cases, the file will be small enough to email, but still look great.

 DOWNLOAD OF THE DAY   PicViewer Lite for Windows is another great image manipulation tool. Download it free from `www.anixsoft.com`.

TODAY'S FOCUS: Photo Editing

COMPUSERVE OFFERS INTERNET ACCESS

Online service provider CompuServe announced it would offer access to the Internet on this day in 1994. Previously, the company's 1.7 million members could only view CompuServe's proprietary content online. CompuServe was launched in 1969 as a computer time-sharing service and was the first commercial provider to offer email and technical support. The company was acquired by America Online in 1998.

Related Web site www.compuserve.com

Twisted List: Secret Windows Software You Already Own

By Chris Pirillo

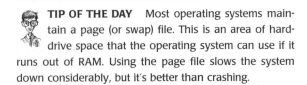

IExpress Have you ever wanted to make a customized self-extracting executable? You already have the tool. IExpress' wizard will step you through the process, and in a matter of minutes, you'll have something ready for download. To use IExpress, open the **Run** box and type `iexpress.exe`.

Vintage Windows Media Player If you're like me, you hate the new Windows Media Player. Sure, it's skinnable, but it also sucks up a lot of resources. Did you know the old one is still there? Yep, it's now called mplayer2.exe. Just type the name in the **Run** box.

Onscreen Keyboard Keyboard stuck? Don't want to reboot? Use the onscreen keyboard. It's an accessibility tool, but it'll work just as well for anybody. Click **Start**, **Programs**, **Accessories**, Accessibility, then select **On-Screen Keyboard**. Or, type `osk.exe` in the **Run** box.

Winchat Instant messaging is fun, but what if you don't want to install any of that kind of software on your machine? Launch Winchat, and then connect with another buddy on your network (your buddy also has to run Winchat). Open the **Run** box and type `winchat.exe`.

(Chris Pirillo is the host of Call for Help *on TechTV.)*

TIP OF THE DAY Most operating systems maintain a page (or swap) file. This is an area of hard-drive space that the operating system can use if it runs out of RAM. Using the page file slows the system down considerably, but it's better than crashing.

Even with scads of RAM, your system still requires a page file. So, it's worth optimizing it for better performance. Start by creating a dedicated hard drive partition for the page file. This keeps it from getting fragmented and mixed in with other data. Doing this on Mac OS X can improve performance by 10%–20%.

If you have multiple drives, put the page partition on a different drive from the operating system to minimize back-and-forth movement of the drive heads. If you can put the page drive on a different IDE chain, all the better. Best yet, put the page partition on the fastest part of the drive, which usually is the first partition.

To move the page file to another partition in Windows XP, open the System control panel. Click the **Advanced** tab and click the **Settings** button in the Performance section. Click the **Advanced** tab again, and click the **Change** button. Here, you can choose which drive or drives hold the page file. You also might want to set a value for the Initial size and Maximum size. Pick a single value for both to keep the system from spending time resizing the page file. 400MB should do.

DOWNLOAD OF THE DAY TealPaint is the best color painting program for the Palm. Free to try and $17.95 to buy, from www.tealpoint.com.

TODAY'S FOCUS: Web Searching

TELEPHONE INVENTED

Alexander Graham Bell made the first successful telephone transmission on this day in 1876. The prolific inventor's first message over the wires was, "Mr. Watson, come here," directed at his assistant Thomas Watson, who was in the next room.

Related Web site   `telecomwriting.com`

Search Strategies

By Martin Sargent

There are some 800 million Web sites out there, but let's say that only one of them holds the information you need. Here's how to sift through the Internet haystack for that one shining needle.com:

Internet Directories Versus Search Engines   To get the most out of Web searching, understand the distinctions between the various search tools, and use the one that's best suited to what you're doing.

Internet Directories   About half of all Internet users rely on Yahoo! to find information on the Web. Yahoo! isn't a true search engine; it's an Internet directory. Internet directories hire people to group all submitted sites into categories, such as San Francisco restaurants.

Underneath this broad category are more precise groupings, such as Chinese, Italian, and Swiss restaurants. Internet directories, therefore, are the best way to go if your search isn't too obscure and if you want a broad range of results.

Search Engines   If you're looking for more precise information, such as Web sites that contain your name, Internet directories aren't as effective as true search engines (unless you're a big star like me).

When you perform a search, engines such as AltaVista send out programs called *bots* or *spiders* that scour the Web looking for pages that contain your keyword. The found pages are then sorted according to relevance.

Search Jargon   No matter what search tool you use, you need to know how to refine your search using tricks such

as Boolean operators. Boolean operators add a little logic to your Web searches. They consist of AND, OR, NOT, and other operators. The best way to explain the Boolean brew is by example. So, let's say I'm having Leo over for dinner tonight and plan to cook a quiche. (No jokes, please.) Thing is, I need a new quiche recipe because Leo hated my last one because of all the red onions in it. I also want only one type of meat, because I'm getting fat.

So, in the search box, I'd type

`recipe AND quiche AND (bacon OR ham) NOT "red onions"`

What I'm looking for is a site that includes the words *recipe* and *quiche* (signified by the AND) as well as either the words *bacon* or *ham* (signified by the parenthetical OR statement), but definitely not the words *red onions* (signified by the NOT in front of the quotation marks–enclosed red onions–the quotation marks tell the engine to not search for the words *red* and *onions* apart from each other).

Get it? With many search engines, you can do the same thing with + and - signs.

So, the search request would read `+recipe +quiche +(bacon OR ham) - "red onions"`.

TIP OF THE DAY   To search for items on a single site, say techtv.com, go to Google.com and type `site:techtv` plus the terms you are looking for.

DOWNLOAD OF THE DAY   SearchRocket searches many search engines to find what you're looking for. Free from `searchrocket.com`.

POLL: What's your favorite search engine?

60% Google	2% Hotbot
15% Yahoo!	2% About
4% Northern Light	17% Other

TODAY'S FOCUS: Web Searching

MEDIA MOGUL MURDOCH BORN

Keith Rupert Murdoch, Chairman and CEO of News Corporation, was born in Melbourne, Australia, on this day in 1931. Murdoch became a U.S. citizen in 1985. News Corp.'s media empire is worth nearly $50 billion, one of the largest in the world. Its holdings in the U.S. include Fox Broadcasting, the *New York Post*, *TV Guide*, and the L.A. Dodgers. Assets world-wide include *The Times of London*, British Sky Broadcasting, and STAR, the first international satellite television service ever allowed in China.

Related Web site   `newscorp.com`

MARCH
11

Google: Everyone's Favorite Search Engine

Google began as a research project at Stanford University in spring 1995. There, two computer science Ph.D. candidates, Sergey Brin and Larry Page, worked together to develop the search technology that would become the foundation of Google, Inc.

"Larry was looking at the link structure of the Web, a sort of mathematical problem about which pages pointed to which other pages," Brin recalls. "I was looking at the concept of data mining—how useful information could be extracted from large quantities of information."

The Founding of Google   After discussions with other portals, Page and Brin decided to start their own search engine. They called it Google, based on "googol," the mathematical name for a huge number represented by a 1 followed by 100 zeros.

"We wanted Google to reflect our mission to search through the immense amount of information available on the Web," shares Larry, "and we wanted it to be fun."

Google officially launched in September, 1999.

How Google's Search Engine Works   Most search engines return results based on how often keywords appear in a Web site. Google is different. It uses what it calls PageRank technology to quickly scan its index and produce highly relevant results to a search query.

PageRank relies on the democratic nature of the Web by using its vast link structure as an indicator of an individual page's value. Google interprets a link from Page A to Page B as a vote.

Google looks at more than the sheer volume of votes, or links a page receives, it also analyzes the page that casts the vote. Votes cast by pages that are themselves important weigh more heavily and help make other pages important.

Important, high-quality sites receive a higher PageRank, which Google remembers each time it conducts a search. Google further combines PageRank with sophisticated text-matching techniques to find pages that are both important and relevant to a search.

Google examines all aspects of the page's content (and the content of the pages linking to it) to determine whether it's a good match for a query.

"Google uses a fully automated, objective mathematical equation that says a Web page is important if a number of pages point to it and if pages that are important point to it," says Larry. "Google does not use any human intervention to judge the value of a page's importance."

Give Google a try at `google.com`.

TIP OF THE DAY   If you don't see Google as one of the choices in your browser's search bar, don't fret. To add Google to your browser surf to `www.google.com/options/defaults.html`.

DOWNLOAD OF THE DAY   Download the Google toolbar and never be far from your favorite search engine. Free from `toolbar.google.com`.

TODAY'S FOCUS: Web Searching

FIRST U.S. PRESIDENTIAL RADIO ADDRESS

President Franklin D. Roosevelt addressed the nation in the first "Fireside Chat" on this day in 1933. Only eight days after his inauguration, the President discussed the "bank holiday" imposed on March 6 (designed to prevent panicked investors from pulling out money during the Depression), and urged Americans to keep money in their accounts. This is one of the first examples of policymakers using mass media to communicate with the public—a practice that might have changed the face of politics forever.

Related Web site `www.fdrlibrary.marist.edu/arch.html`

Dictionaries and Quotations

By Alison Strahan

It's your first day on the TechTV set and someone asks you to watch out for the gobo. You tense. Is there some kind of prehistoric monster on the loose? Or perhaps you're about to trip over a musical instrument? What on Earth do you do? Visit Merriam-Webster OnLine, `m-w.com`.

The site has a lot more information than the print version of the dictionary. Learn how words make it into the dictionary, find out more about the history and etymology of English words, or improve your vocabulary by learning the word of the day (you can also have it emailed to you daily).

Stuck searching for a synonym? Use the thesaurus feature to quickly find the answer you need. For example, gregarious: convivial, sociable. Hmm...sounds like my pal Chris Pirillo could take a leaf out of that book.

Not sure how to pronounce a word? Click the speaker icon next to the definition to hear it.

Add the Merriam-Webster Dictionary Lookup Button (`m-w.com/promos/button/button.htm`) to your links toolbar. It enables you to quickly define words when you're visiting other sites. Just highlight a word and click the Webster's link any time you need a definition.

Quotations "If only I had a little humility, I'd be perfect."— Ted Turner, 1988.

When you're stuck for a good line, or you just can't remember a famous quote, go to Bartleby.com. This amazing literary portal enables you to search dozens of reference works from one page. Everything from *Bartlett's Quotations* to the *Oxford Shakespeare* to the *Columbia Encyclopedia* is online here. Bartleby also has a large collection of verse, fiction, and nonfiction. And it's all searchable.

For extra credit, search Bartleby to find out how it got its name.

TIP OF THE DAY You can use Google to search for more than Web pages. Google can find online documents stored as PDF, Word, Excel, PowerPoint, PostScript, and Rich Text Format files, too. And you don't even need to have those programs to read the information.

To search for a particular file type, add the phrase `filetype:` and the file type to your search string. For example, to find a PDF version of Shakespeare's *Hamlet* type **`filetype:pdf Shakespeare Hamlet`**.

When you have the list of results, you can click on **View File As HTML** and Google will translate the file into a Web page for you. Or, click the main link to view it in its native format.

DOWNLOAD OF THE DAY Add a dictionary search to your Macintosh. The free OmniDictionary (`www.omnigroup.com/applications/omnidictionary/`) is both a standalone application and a Mac OS X service. Highlight a word, and then press Command+= to get the definition.

TODAY'S FOCUS: Web Searching

URANUS DISCOVERED

The seventh planet from the sun was spotted on this day in 1781. English astronomer Sir William Herschel found Uranus using a seven-inch reflecting telescope he built himself. At first the German-born scientist thought he had discovered a comet, and had to continue his observations and calculations for months before he confirmed it was a planet. Herschel also found two of Uranus' moons, and discovered infrared radiation.

Related Web site   `pds.jpl.nasa.gov`

MARCH 13

Increase Traffic to Your Web Site

By Danny Sullivan, Search Engine Watch.com

Here are some great ways to identify your site, market it, and network with sites like yours using search engines:

1. Know how you want to be indexed. You should know the top two or three terms that best relate to your Web site. Incorporate them into a 25-word description that doesn't use marketing hype, and submit it to human-powered directories. You should also know the top 10 to 100 terms that identify content on your site. Be sure you have good, solid content to please the crawlers.

2. Get listed with the human-powered directories of Yahoo!, LookSmart, and the Open Directory. These sites get lots of visitors or power other sites that get plenty of visitors. In addition, getting listed with them helps crawler-based search engines locate your site and help it rank better.

3. Write a 7- to 15-word HTML title description for every page. Think newspaper headlines—be punchy! You want to grab the readers' attention when they see this title in search engine results and convince them to click through, although you don't want to be misleading. Look at the page, think of the top one or two terms you'd like it to be sought out for, and then incorporate those words into a title.
   Don't worry if you go longer than 15 words or shorter than 7. Those aren't hard limits—just guidelines from my experience on making your titles attractive to readers.

4. Be crawler friendly. Avoid using frames or dynamic-delivery systems, and ensure that you have good internal linkage between your pages.

5. Build links. Search the top terms that suggest or identify your site. Review the sites that come up. Visit them, and ask the noncompetitive ones if they'll swap links with you. You might get their visitors to follow their links to you.
   If they are ranked high in a search, you can assume they're important and get good traffic. Studying their links can help you configure links on your site.

6. BONUS TIP: Open your wallet. If you have the money, paid placement and paid inclusion programs can be a fast, easy way to get good listings or better representation. Even if you do this, don't forget to do all the basic things that can help you get traffic for free.

 TIP OF THE DAY   If you're itching to be a game developer, steer your browser to the Game Development Search Engine at `gdse.com`. Search for all kinds of information in any area of game development.

 DOWNLOAD OF THE DAY   CleverKeys is a free download that enables you to highlight a word, press the hotkey of your choice, and look it up directly on Dictionary.com or Thesaurus.com. For Mac or Windows, from `cleverkeys.com`.

TODAY'S FOCUS: Web Searching

EINSTEIN BORN

Albert Einstein was in born in Ulm, Germany, on this day in 1879. Einstein formulated the theory of relativity and won the Nobel Prize for his explanation of the photoelectric effect. Despite his achievements, the mathematician struggled with anti-Semitism—his lectures at the Institute of Physics in Berlin were often disrupted by demonstrations around 1920. Aside from his many awards, Einstein also had a chance at politics: The Israeli government offered him the post of second president in 1952, but he refused. Einstein died in New Jersey in 1955.

Related Web site `www.einstein.caltech.edu`

Specialty Search Engines

By Martin Sargent

Yahoo! and Google aren't always the best tools for finding information on a particular topic. Here's a partial list of some excellent specialty search engines that will help you find exactly what you're looking for:

Art Artcyclopedia (`www.artcyclopedia.com`), is an amazing site. Artcyclopedia offers a database of works by 7,500 artists from the world's art museums and image archives.

Aviation FlightSearch.com (`flightsearch.com`) has everything from aviation pictures and products to information on flight disasters.

Computer Games There are several decent computer gaming directories on the Web, but Gamez.com and GamePages.com are the most helpful.

Computer Security Go to SecureRoot (`secureroot.com`) and search more than 15,000 URLs for information about hacking, cracking, encryption, and anarchy.

Computer Programming Are you a software developer? Want to learn more about programming? SourceBank.com has the goods.

Employment Find postings from the Web's many job-listing sites on FlipDog.com.

Fishing Find everything from learning techniques to buying tackle on FishSearch.com.

Law Trouble with the fuzz? Find legal information using these legal-oriented search engines:
- LawCrawler: `www.lawcrawler.com`
- FindLaw: `www.findlaw.com`

Or, get a definition for a legal term at `dictionary.law.com`.

Medicine Feeling some symptoms? You might know about WebMD, but to really broaden your search try a medical search engine. These specialty search engines find documents about particular conditions and medical issues:
- CiteLine.com: `www.citeline.com`
- NetHealth: `www.nethealth.com`

Money FinancialFind.com provides a comprehensive directory of financial information on the Internet.

Museums MuseumStuff.com has all you need to know about thousands of museums worldwide, nicely parceled into categories.

News Moreover, at `moreover.com`, is perhaps the best specialty search engine in any category. Moreover has headlines from more than 1,800 sources. Most important, the headlines retrieved are up to date.

Politics
- OneWorld.Net (`www.oneworld.net`) offers information on human rights and environmental issues worldwide.
- Google Uncle Sam (`google.com/unclesam`) is your source for everything `.gov`.
- FirstGov.gov is the official front door to all U.S. federal, state, and local government sites.

Software If you want downloadable software, try these sites:
- ZDNet's Software Library: `hotfiles.com`
- Tucows: `tucows.com`
- CNET Downloads: `Downloads.com`

TIP OF THE DAY You can use Google in a variety of languages, from Finnish to Elmer Fudd. From the front page at `google.com`, click **Preferences**, and select a language in the **Display Google Tips and Messages In:** drop-down menu. For fun, try Elmer Fudd; Bork, bork, bork!; or Pig Latin. To return to English at any time, click the **Google in English** link on the front page.

DOWNLOAD OF THE DAY Don't have Microsoft Word or Appleworks, but need to read a document created in them? Try icWord for Mac free for 30 days at `icword.com`. Buy it for $19.95.

TODAY'S FOCUS: Web Searching

ENIAC PATENT CONFISCATED

On this day in 1946, the Moore School at the University of Pennsylvania said engineers must relinquish their patents for equipment developed on school premises. The creators of the ENIAC, J. Presper Eckert and John Mauchly, refused to sign the agreement. The researchers resigned from Moore shortly thereafter and filed an independent patent application later that year. In 1973, a district court judge voided the patent and made the controversial ruling that John Atanasoff—not Eckert and Mauchly—developed the first electronic computer.

Related Web site `www.cs.iastate.edu/jva/jva-archive.shtml`

High-Tech Homework Help

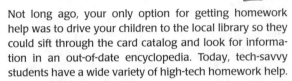

By Teri Rousseau

Not long ago, your only option for getting homework help was to drive your children to the local library so they could sift through the card catalog and look for information in an out-of-date encyclopedia. Today, tech-savvy students have a wide variety of high-tech homework help.

Kid-Friendly Portals

- DiscoverySchool.com: `school.discovery.com`
- BJ Pinchbeck's .Homework Helper: `school.discovery.com/homeworkhelp/bjpinchbeck`
- Fact Monster.: `factmonster.com` from Information Please
- About.com's Homework. Tips: `homeworktips.about.com`
- Lycos Homework. Zone: `lycoszone.com/homework.asp`

Kid-Friendly Search Engines

- Ask Jeeves .for Kids: `ajkids.com`
- Yahooligans.: `yahooligans.com/`
- KidsClick! .: `sunsite.berkeley.edu/KidsClick!`

Reference Sites

- Encarta by. MSN (free): `encarta.msn.com`
- Electric Library's Encyclopedia.com (free): `encyclopedia.com`
- Encyclopedia Britannica Online (subscription): `eb.com`
- Encyclopedia Smithsonian (free): `www.si.edu/resource/faq/start.htm`

Online Q&A Sites

- Ask an Expert: `askanexpert.com`
- Ask A+ Locator: `vrd.org/locator/subject.shtml`
- Star Tribune's Homework Help: `startribune.com/homework_help`

Online Tutoring

- Tutor. com: `www.tutor.com`
- eSylvan: `esylvan.com`
- Tutornet: `www.tutornet.com`

Homework Helpers on CD-ROM

- CD-ROM reference titles
  Homework Survival Kit, by Fogware Publishing: `www.fog-ware.com/product_edu.htm`
  Encarta Encyclopedia or Encarta Reference Library, by Microsoft: `encarta.msn.com/shop`
- Skill-building titles
  Math & Science Excelerator, by Topics Entertainment: `www.topics-ent.com`
  The Children's Skills Test series, by Sylvan Learning Systems: `www.smartkidssoftware.com/test.htm`

High-Tech Gadgets This is an emerging genre for helping students, and LeapFrog (`leapfrog.com`) is leading the way. LeapFrog has developed several products to address the educational needs of preschoolers through preteens. Some of the newest LeapFrog products have an online component, allowing the gadgets' content to be updated and customized.

The best LeapFrog products for helping your child excel in school are the iQuest and the Turbo Twist.

(Teri Rousseau is principal of Multimedia Consulting, specializing in technology for children and families.)

TIP OF THE DAY Webmasters, add search to your site with Google, `www.google.com/services/free.html`. Choose Free WebSearch plus SiteSearch to search your domain and the entire Internet.

Other Webmaster search services you should consider include

- SiteLevel,: `sitelevel.whatuseek.com`
- Everyone. ,net: `www.everyone.net/main/html/search_tour.html`
- Freefind. ,com: `freefind.com`

DOWNLOAD OF THE DAY Atomica is a research tool for Windows that provides definitions, synonyms, and other handy information right from your system tray. Free from `atomica.com/solutions_products_pc.html`.

TODAY'S FOCUS: Web Searching

SECRET SERVICE VIOLATES INTERNET PRIVACY

The ruling in a historic case against the U.S. Secret Service was announced on this day in 1993. A Texas judge said the organization violated privacy laws outlined in the Electronic Communications Privacy Act by seizing email and erasing bulletin-board messages during a computer hacker investigation. The plaintiff in the controversial case, Steve Jackson Games, was awarded nearly $55,000 in damages. The incident also spurred the creation of Internet watchdog group Electronic Frontier Foundation.

Related Web sites eff.org, sjgames.com

MARCH

16

Search Engines That Rival Google

By Martin Sargent

Here are four new search tools that confidently assert they've got the stuff to become the new darling of the Web junkie.

WiseNut (wisenut.com) WiseNut claims to have indexed more than 1.5 billion Web pages—right up there with Google. Plus, it says it can index 50 million pages per day and refresh its entire index once per month. WiseNut places search results into a master list as well as in topical folders—a feature I like. (Google says it thought about using such folders but focus groups shot down the idea.)

Vivisimo (vivisimo.com) Vivisimo means "very lively" and "clever" in Spanish, and in general the search tool lives up to its name. Developed at Carnegie Mellon University, Vivisimo uses many search engines to build one search results list. Unlike standard metasearch engines, however, Vivisimo "clusters" results into logical subcategories based on a text analysis algorithm.

Lasoo (www.lasoo.com) Lasoo is a geography-based search engine that can be of most help when you're looking for businesses in a specific region. When you first start your search on Lasoo, you click the area of a world where you want to find specific stuff. Keep clicking to zoom in on a particular locale, such as San Francisco. When your virtual lasoo is homed in, you perform a keyword search. For example, I looked for Burmese restaurants in the San Francisco area and found two listings (although I know there are more than that). When I clicked on them, a nice map appeared showing me exactly where the restaurants are. This is helpful, but there's no more information than

the address, telephone number, and map location of the businesses. Links to, in my example, restaurant reviews and other resources on Burmese cuisine, such as recipes, would make Lasoo a richer resource.

SpeechBot (speechbot.com) SpeechBot, from HP, stores nearly 11,000 hours of radio interviews, updated daily. In all, about 20 different radio shows are indexed, including some from NPR such as *Car Talk* and *Fresh Air*. When you find the interview you want to hear, you can read a transcript that's constructed using speech-recognition software. Needless to say, it's not too exact. Instead of reading the transcript, listen to a stream of the actual interview using RealPlayer.

TIP OF THE DAY Change Internet Explorer's search settings so you can automatically search using the engine of your choice.

1. Open IE and click the **Search** icon.
2. Click **Change Preferences**.
3. Click **Change Internet Search Behavior**.
4. Select the search engine of your choice from the list of engines and click **OK**.

DOWNLOAD OF THE DAY TrackSeek is a free way to search for MP3s online. Download a copy from analogx.com/contents/download/network/trkseek.htm.

POLL: Should hackers be considered terrorists under Federal law?

32% Yes

68% No

TODAY'S FOCUS: Web Design

ANTI-SPAM EFFORT LAUNCHED

One of the most popular anti-spam tools was introduced on this day in 1998. Eric Allman released a version of his program, Sendmail, which had the capability to reject messages from groups of known spammers. The program also made it more difficult for spammers to conceal their email addresses. Although anti-spam software was already on the market, Sendmail became one of the most widely used.

Related Web site   `www.mail-abuse.org`

Finding a Web Host

by Alison Strahan and Tom Merritt

Before you can have a Web site, you have to have a Web host: a provider that will serve up your pages to the clamoring crowds. You have a few options for picking a host:

- Free hosting, from sites such as Geocities (`geocities.com`) or Tripod (`tripod.com`). Most ISPs also offer free Web space.
- Renting space from a Web host.
- Running your own server.

The first option is a great way to get your feet wet—we'll cover it tomorrow. The last is for hardcore geeks only. Most folks will choose the middle road: paying someone to host their site.

There are several search engines designed to help you find a host that fits your needs. I recommend `hostsearch.com`, `webhostdir.com`, `webhosters.com`, and `hostfinders.com`. Here are some of the terms you'll encounter on your quest:

Disk Space   Almost always listed in megabytes. 50 is plenty unless you're going to host a lot of images or multimedia files. HTML is fairly small; it's the graphics that really take up space.

Bandwidth   Also called *data transfer*. Remember that anytime someone accesses your site, they use up some of your bandwidth. Most companies put a cap on consumption so that if your site gets too popular, they can start charging. Unlimited bandwidth is hard to find, but get a deal that gives you as much per month as possible.

Number of Mailboxes   Each host will give you an email address, but try to get one that will allow you to have unlimited forwarding. This means any email sent to your domain name will come to you. In addition, the more separate pop mail accounts, the better, especially if it'll be more than just you working on the site.

Web Use Statistics Report   A must-have. If you don't know where users go on your site, how can you best serve them?

Telnet Access   This gives you command-line access to your site from any Internet connection. If you are comfortable with Unix, Telnet access is very handy.

CGI Programming   Most scripting for Web sites is done in Perl. Even if you don't program, you can get free Perl scripts that let you run message boards, shopping carts, and other cool features on your site. If that sounds good, look for a host that supports Perl and CGI access.

Server-Side Includes   SSI simplifies page programming. An advanced feature but very handy if you know how to use it.

Now get out there and start hunting!

TIP OF THE DAY   Site Meter offers a free counter and statistics tracker that integrates easily into your Web site. `Sitemeter.com`.

DOWNLOAD OF THE DAY   Platypus Web Builder is an easy way to design your site. Free to try, from `www.c-point.com/webbuild.htm`.

TODAY'S FOCUS: Web Design

FIRST COMMERCIAL ELECTRIC RAZOR

Colonel Jacob Schick marketed the first electric shaver on this day in 1931. It cost $25 (almost $300 in today's dollars). Schick was reportedly obsessed with shaving, and believed the practice could extend one's life to as long as 120 years. By 1937, Schick had sold 1.5 million razors and had made more than $20 million. He died at age 59.

Related Web site   `shaving.com`

Finding a Free Host

By Alison Strahan

Try one of these three easy ways to build a Web site for free.

Lycos Tripod   Tripod (`tripod.com`) will give you 20MB of space for your Web site. It provides its own Web-building tool that runs within your browser—no download required. Try a few different templates, select one, and then add your content. It's that easy. Be sure to test the pages before you upload them.

If you know HTML and want to create your own design, use Tripod's FreeForm HTML editor. For the geek-inclined, Tripod provides a script editor. Webmasters can add their own CGI and Perl scripts. This is handy if you want to add forms or other interactive features to your site.

The quid pro quo is, as one might expect, that Tripod requires you to put advertisements on your Web pages. The cool part is that you can camouflage the ads by choosing colors and shapes that jibe with your Web site's design.

When you're happy with how your pages look, click **Publish to the Web**, and you're set. Unlike the old days of multiple slashes in free Web site addresses, Tripod provides a simple `www.yourname.tripod.com`.

Yahoo! GeoCities   Offering site-building services similar to Tripod's, Yahoo! GeoCities (`geocities.com`) provides Yahoo! PageWizards to assist you in designing simple pages, while Yahoo! PageBuilder provides more sophisticated options.

GeoCities supplies only 15MB of space, but for many users that will be more than enough. Like Tripod,

GeoCities provides an HTML tool for those who want to code their own pages. If you like frills, GeoCities has many free add-ons, including counters, guest books, and stock quotes.

GeoCities also offers complex tracking capabilities and site statistics to help you learn more about your visitors' browsing habits. Bear in mind that you can easily add a free tracker yourself here.

As with Tripod, GeoCities makes you display ads on your pages.

Your ISP   Internet service providers usually provide some free Web space to put up your site and will often offer tools to help you upload your files.

For more free Web site services visit `thefreesite.com/Free_Web_Space`.

TIP OF THE DAY   There's lots of free stuff on the Net for Webmasters. Visit `freebielist.com` or `www.thefreesite.com/Webmaster_Freebies`.

DOWNLOAD OF THE DAY   A good Web design tool should be as easy to use as a word processor but give you the flexibility to insert advanced features such as JavaScript, rollovers, and Flash. It should have built-in graphics manipulation tools. Most importantly, the HTML it generates should be clean. It shouldn't add a lot of extra tags or proprietary features. You should be able to look at it and edit it with any HTML editor.

Macromedia's Dreamweaver fulfills all these requirements. It's not cheap, but if you plan on doing quality Web design, it's the best tool you can buy for Windows or Macintosh. Download a 30-day free trial from `macromedia.com/software/dreamweaver`.

TODAY'S FOCUS: Web Design

IBM 360 GETS GO-AHEAD

International Business Machines executives said yes to the System/360 on this day in 1964. The new line of "compatible" computers replaced all of IBM's previous models (a drastic move at the time). Previously, each computer was built for a specific purpose, and software installed on one machine could not run on another. The System/360 was one of the first general-purpose mainframe computers to remedy that problem. The new line reportedly cost about $5 billion to develop and was very successful—IBM's staff grew by 50% to nearly 250,000 employees within three years.

Related Web site   `www.ibm.com`

Planning Your Web Site

By Marina Chotzinoff

Carefully planning your Web site will save you time and help you make a much better site. To start, think about the following points:

- Consider your motivation and your audience: Why are you creating your site and who will be visiting it?
- Navigation: What's the strategy for navigating through your site?
- Structure: What's the shape of your site? Is it meant to be linear or do you want to encourage roaming?
- Design plan: What will the overall look be? Will the whole site share a look, or will parts have their own designs?

Let's take a look at two sample site ideas and how they would answer these questions.

	The Jones's Vacation	Pooch Palace
Motivation/ Audience	To show family pictures of vacation	To sell fashion clothing for dogs
Navigation	Links to represent compass points for each vacation spot	Doggie accessory icons link to each section of the site
Structure	Welcome page with direction links pointing to second-level pages	Main page links to second-level sections that link to topic-specific pages
Design	Simple design with different background colors for each vacation spot	Overall site will have similar look and feel sharing header styles, icons, colors

Motivation   These two sites were created for different reasons and must be planned differently. The Jones's Picture site aims to show some pictures in an order they can control. The Pooch Palace's creators want people to come into their store, browse, and decide to come back.

Navigation   It might sound trite to think about cute little images or themes for your navigation, but good design and memorable images can really add to the success of your site. Use your images wisely, and be sure they really serve a purpose, even if it's only a decorative one.

Structure   Next to navigation, the structure of your site is the most important decision. Draw a picture of how you think the site should look. Organizing your site will not only help your viewers keep track of where they are, it will help you keep your site tidy.

Design   Now that you have a basic shape to your Web site, think about the look you hope to achieve. A unified look ties the site together, but variations can help users navigate.

TIP OF THE DAY   JavaScript Kit is a great place to learn about JavaScript and DHTML. You'll also find hundreds of free scripts you can use on your site. Visit it at `wsabstract.com`.

DOWNLOAD OF THE DAY   Easy Thumbnails can resize any image with the click of the mouse. Free from `fookes.com/ezthumbs`.

TODAY'S FOCUS: Web Design

FIRST MOBILE RADIO TELEPHONE

The first mobile radio telephone was demonstrated on this day in 1902. Kentucky farmer Nathan Stubblefield used his "groundless antenna" to make the first ship-to-shore transmission aboard a vessel on the Potomac River. Nearly 10 years earlier, he demonstrated a similar invention, a wireless device connected to an electrolytic coil earth battery that allowed two-way conversation. However, it's widely agreed that these demonstrations were a form of wireless telephone communication, not a true radio broadcast.

Related Web site `angelfire.com/nc/whitetho/1902stb.htm`

HTML for Beginners

Web pages are designed in something called Hypertext Markup Language, HTML for short. Browsers interpret the HTML and render it into a Web page. Here's what you need to know to write some HTML of your own.

Essential Tags HTML pages consist of two different kinds of information: the page's text, and the HTML markup commands that tell the browser what to do with it. These commands are called *tags*.

All tags begin with < and end with >. Usually, you need an opening tag and a closing tag, although a few tags can stand alone. Anything you place between the opening and closing tags will take on the attributes described by the tag. For example, using the HTML command for bold text, <B>, a line like this:

```
<B>your text here</B>
```

will show up as

your text here

in the browser.

All pages begin with <HTML> and end with </HTML>. That tells the browser that the enclosed text should be interpreted as HTML. The <HEAD> </HEAD> tags define the page's header information. Within the <HEAD> tags, for example, you can add

```
<HEAD>
  <TITLE>My first web page</TITLE>
</HEAD>
```

to define the page's title. The text will be displayed in the title bar of the browser window and is used for the page's bookmark.

After the <HEAD> tag come the <BODY> </BODY> tags. Within these two tags are the contents of the Web page. Like many HTML tags, <BODY> can contain some additional attributes, including the page's background color, text color, link colors, and so on. A typical <BODY> tag might read

```
<BODY BGCOLOR="white" TEXT="black">
  This is my first Web page!
</BODY>
```

This defines a page with black text on a white background. The page itself displays the text, "This is my first Web page!"

Now that you know what a Web page absolutely needs to have, you can practice inserting some content. Separate lines with <BR> and paragraphs with <P>. Neither of these tags requires a closing tag. When you have finished, save your page with the extension .HTML, and then drag it to the browser window to see your creation.

TIP OF THE DAY You can see the raw HTML for any Web page by choosing **View Source** from the browser's **View** menu. Looking at other programmer's code is the best way to learn for yourself. Find a page you like, and steal the HTML.

DOWNLOAD OF THE DAY HTML must be written using a plain text editor.

The best text editor for the Mac is BBEdit. The Lite version is free from `www.bbedit.com/free/bbedit_lite.html`. I paid for the full version and use it all the time to work on Leoville. I especially appreciate the built-in FTP client.

The best Notepad replacement for Windows is NoteTab Lite, free from `www.notetab.com`. Pay for the full version for even more useful features.

TODAY'S FOCUS: Web Design

TALIGENT OS LAUNCHES

Apple and IBM demonstrated their joint venture on this day in 1994. Taligent was first conceived in 1991 in hopes of establishing an alternative OS to Microsoft Windows that could run on any hardware. Later, it was transformed into Common Point, a layer that could sit on top of any existing operating system, such as AIX, HP-UX, OS/2, Windows NT, and a new Apple OS kernel. The company struggled over the years, and in 1999, Taligent was wholly absorbed into IBM.

Related Web site `www.mackido.com/History/history_of_aim_sw.html`

MARCH 21

Flash Tips

By Debbie Rich

Flash sometimes needs a little help when morphing, or *tweening*, from one shape into another. Shape Hints guides the visual change by identifying points that should correspond in the starting and ending shapes of the animation.

Circle to Square Our example will create a simple tween of a circle into a square using Shape Hints.

Create the Tween Create 36 frames by going to **Insert**, **Frame**. At frame 1, create a green circle. At frame 36, set a keyframe through **Insert**, **Keyframe**. Draw a blue square. Delete the green circle. Click anywhere within the layer, and open the Frame panel. In its pop-up box, choose **Shape**. Flash calculates the in-between steps to morph the circle into a square. Play it back. Looks pretty bad, doesn't it? Let's fix it up with Shape Hints.

Add Shape Hints Select the circle in frame 1 and go to **Modify**, **Transform**, **Add Shape Hints**. A red dot with the letter "A" should appear in the center of the circle. Move the Shape Hint to the top left of the circle along its stroke. At frame 36, a red "A" dot should mark the center of the square. Move that Shape Hint along the top-left corner stroke. It should now become green. Scrub back to frame 1. The red dot will now be yellow. Add a second hint, which appears as "B," and move it to the bottom-left corner of the circle. Go to frame 36 to move the corresponding "B" hint to the corresponding location on the square. Continue clockwise until all corners of both shapes are filled. Click on the image to the right to see what this should look like. The curves of the two shapes now map to each other, which causes the circle to slide rather than roll when morphing into a square.

TIP OF THE DAY Shape Hints:

- Hints are yellow in the start keyframe, green in the end keyframe, and red when not set along a curve.
- Hints play nicely when they are set down one at a time and tweaked from start point to end point.
- Hints work best when they are placed counterclockwise, beginning from top left.
- To remove hints, drag one off the stage or go to **Modify**, **Transform**, **Remove All Hints**.
- Check **View**, **Show Shape Hints** if the Shape Hints aren't visible.
- Right-click on a hint to bring up a contextual menu of choices.
- Keeping **View**, **Snap to Guides** turned on often helps when aligning shape corners.

DOWNLOAD OF THE DAY Flash ain't cheap, but you can still add Flash animations to your site using a Flash generator, such as Swish, $49 from `www.swishzone.com`.

POLL: Is technology getting easier to use for the average person?

71% Yes

29% No

TODAY'S FOCUS: Web Design

LASER PATENTED

"Light amplification by stimulated emission" was patented by Arthur Schawlow and Charles Townes on this day in 1960. The Nobel Prize for Physics was awarded to Townes in 1964, and to Schawlow in 1981, for their work.

Related Web site `www.bell-labs.com/history/laser`

Top 10 Mistakes of Web Design

By Jakob Nielsen

Using Frames Splitting a page into frames confuses users because frames break the fundamental user model of the Web page. Suddenly, the user cannot bookmark the current page and return to it, URLs stop working, and printouts become difficult.

Gratuitous Use of Bleeding-Edge Technology Don't try to attract users by bragging about the latest Web technology. Users care more about useful content.

Scrolling Text, Marquees, and Constantly Running Animations Moving images have an overpowering effect on people's peripheral vision. Give your user some peace and quiet to read the text.

Complex URLs Even though machine-level addressing, such as the URL, should never have been exposed in the user interface, it is there and we have found that users actually try to decode the URLs of pages to infer the structure of Web sites. Users do this because there is often no support for navigation and no sense of location in current Web browsers. Thus, a URL should contain human-readable directory and filenames that reflect the nature of the information space.

Orphan Pages Be sure all pages include a clear indication of what Web site they belong to, because users might access pages directly without coming in through your home page.

Long Scrolling Pages Only 10% of users scroll beyond the information that's visible on the screen when a page comes up. All critical content and navigation options should be on the top part of the page.

Lack of Navigation Support Don't assume that users know as much about your site as you do. They always have difficulty finding information, so they need support in the form of a strong sense of structure and place.

Nonstandard Link Colors Links to pages that have not been seen by the user are blue. Links to previously seen pages are purple or red. Don't mess with these colors, because the ability to understand what links have been followed is one of the few navigational aides that is standard in most Web browsers.

Outdated Information Budget to hire a Web gardener as part of your team. You need somebody to root out the weeds and replant the flowers as the Web site changes.

Lengthy Download Time A user will wait no more than 10 seconds before losing interest. On the Web, users have been trained to endure so much suffering that it might be acceptable to increase this limit to 15 seconds.

(Jakob Nielsen is the king of Web usability. Visit his site at `useit.com`.*)*

TIP OF THE DAY Slicing is used to break images into smaller components for quicker display on Web sites. For a free program that will do image slicing and image maps, and a whole lot more, download PhotoPlus 5 from `www.serif.com/photoplus5/`.

DOWNLOAD OF THE DAY Jakob might not like them, but the easiest way to bring life to a Web site is with an animated GIF. Create them using CoffeeCup's GIFAnimator, free to try, $30 to buy, from `www.coffeecup.com/animator/`.

TODAY'S FOCUS: Web Design

FIRST ARTIFICIAL HEART PATIENT DIES

The first human to receive an artificial heart transplant died on this day in 1983. Dr. Barney Clark lived 112 days with the Jarvik-7 plastic and aluminum heart, implanted at the University of Utah in Salt Lake City. The device, invented by Dr. Robert K. Jarvik, had two pumps, each with a disk-shaped mechanism that pushed the blood from the inlet valve to the outlet valve. The heart was operated by external compressed air hoses that entered the heart through a hole in the chest.

Related Web site   `www.heartpioneers.com`

MARCH 23

Twisted List: Flash Sites That Should Be Illegal

By Martin Sargent

Flash has mostly made the Internet a better place to live, but here are five reasons why the International Internet Governing Body might want to consider making it illegal.

PB&J (`etrata.home.attbi.com/flash/banana.swf`) A banana dances to a song about peanut butter and jelly. And then everyone in your office plays it 4 million times a day to make you mad. I got your baseball bat right here.

Panasonic Ad (`newtown.hi-ho.ne.jp/raibo/raidersei/image/agency/cm/mail.swf`) How Panasonic intends to sell anything with this ad is beyond human comprehension—even if you understand the language. Hi-Ho!

Mr. Nice (`www.csh.rit.edu/~wxs/images/humor/mr_nice.swf`) The armless Mr. Nice is fun for the entire incredibly annoying family! Megan refuses to stop singing this song. She must pay dearly for this.

Chuck E. Cheese (`www.chuckecheese.com/cec2002/games/jukebox`) Have you ever been to a Chuck E. Cheese Pizza Time Theater? Why go when it's just as fun to be there on the Internet? These songs will amaze you.

 TIP OF THE DAY   One of the worst things you can do to your users is keep them waiting for massive graphics or animations on your Web site to download. One way to avoid this is to put big content "below the fold." Give users something to read or look at right away at the top of your page, keeping them busy until the bottom of the page can download. If you do this, be sure to use the height and width parameters in your `<img>` tag so the browser can render the page before those big graphics arrive.

Another solution is to compress your graphics more. Optimize GIFs and JPEGs for your Web page with free online crunchers from `www.spinwave.com/crunchers.html`.

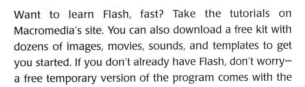 **DOWNLOAD OF THE DAY**   An experienced Webmaster who tries to use Flash without taking a tutorial is like a skier who tries to snowboard without taking a lesson. You've probably got the basics down, but if you're not careful, you're liable to end up flat on your back. Bad Flash animations aren't pretty.

Want to learn Flash, fast? Take the tutorials on Macromedia's site. You can also download a free kit with dozens of images, movies, sounds, and templates to get you started. If you don't already have Flash, don't worry—a free temporary version of the program comes with the download.

Macromedia's Flash Jump Start Kit is free for Windows and Macintosh at `macromedia.com/software/flash/special/startfast/jsk`.

TODAY'S FOCUS: Microsoft Windows

HARRY HOUDINI BORN

Magician and escape artist Harry Houdini was born in Budapest, Hungary, on this day in 1874. Named Ehrich Weiss at birth, Houdini changed his name as a tribute to French illusionist Jean Eugene Robert-Houdin. He reportedly turned to magic at age 17 as an alternative to factory work. Although he is best known for his tricks and escapes, Houdini was also interested in aviation, and completed the first manned flight in Australia. He was also a writer, producer, and actor in many early motion pictures. He died on Halloween, 1926, of appendicitis.

Related Web site   houdinihistory.org

Windows XP: Professional or Home?

Windows XP comes in two flavors, Home Edition and Professional. The first difference you'll notice is the price tag. XP Professional costs $100 more. Here's what you get for your hundred bucks.

Remote Desktop   Windows XP Professional comes with Remote Desktop client software that gives you access to your system over the Internet. The software can be installed on any machine with Windows 95 or later and allows you to see and interact with your remote desktop within a window on the local machine. You can edit local files with remote applications, and then allow the remote applications to access local scanners and printers.

Microsoft claims Remote Desktop works well even over a dial-up connection because only mouse clicks, keyboard strokes, and display information are transmitted over the Internet. However, TechTV Labs found Remote Desktop to be sluggish on slower connections, and recommends a fast connection to avoid Internet rage.

There are other ways to get this kind of functionality on Windows. Symantec's pcAnywhere, $179 from symantec.com/pcanywhere, and Laplink Gold, $139 from laplink.com, are two popular choices. And VNC is free from www.uk.research.att.com/vnc.

Dual-Processor Support   If you have two processors, you need to shell out the extra hundred dollars for Windows XP Professional. Windows XP Home Edition does not support a dual-processor system.

View Network Shares Offline   You can set XP Professional to automatically cache specified network shares at logon for availability offline. Not the most useful feature for the home user, but it's great for business travelers with laptops.

Encrypting File Support (EFS)   XP Professional boasts EFS, a feature first included with Windows 2000. XP Professional can encrypt files and folders with a random and unique encryption key. This is a great feature for theft-prone laptops with personal or sensitive information, but home users can do the same thing just as effectively, if not as easily, with the free PGP encryption program from www.pgpi.com.

Improved Access Control   Because Professional is designed for a corporate environment, it has additional access control features to prevent unauthorized users from accessing files and folders. The privacy features in Home Edition are sufficient for most home users, even if brother and sister share the same PC.

For a chart of the differences, visit microsoft.com/windowsxp/pro/howtobuy/choosing2.asp.

TIP OF THE DAY   In Windows XP and Professional, you can protect your My Documents folder from prying eyes. On the **Start** menu, right-click **My Documents**, and then click **Properties**. Click the **Sharing** tab, and then click to select the **Make This Folder Private So That Only I Have Access to It** check box.

DOWNLOAD OF THE DAY   What's inside your system? The Belarc Advisor will tell you. Free from belarc.com/Download.html.

POLL: Are you considering upgrading to XP?

56% Yes

44% No

TODAY'S FOCUS: Microsoft Windows

HACKER SENT TO THE SLAMMER

Leonard Rose of Middletown, Maryland, pleaded guilty to felony computer-crime charges on this day in 1991. Rose admitted to modifying a copy of an AT&T Unix program by inserting a Trojan horse that allowed him to steal passwords used on the system and distribute them to other hackers. The 32-year-old denied, however, that he was a member of the notorious Legion of Doom, an elite hacker group formed in 1984. Rose was sentenced to two concurrent one-year prison terms.

Related Web site phrack.com

Windows XP: Should You Upgrade?

Microsoft would like you to believe that its XP operating system is a must-have upgrade for anyone with a computer. But everyone might not want or need to upgrade, even though there are many compelling reasons to do so. If you're currently running a system that you're happy with and don't plan on taking advantage of XP's photo, music, networking, or wireless capabilities, or any other of its visual tricks, then stick with what you have until you're ready to buy a new system. If you don't use these features now, you're not likely to use them when you upgrade, although the OS does make working with applications easier.

If you're running Windows 98, 98SE, or Me, you're a good candidate for an upgrade, if nothing more than for XP's stability. XP Home Edition is the OS that Windows Me should have been. Expect to pay $99 to upgrade, and judging from the improvements you'll get, it's worth considering.

Do check your applications first to be sure they're compatible with XP. If not, you might want to wait to upgrade. We recommend doing a "clean" install as opposed to opting for the upgrade directly on top of your existing OS.

And make sure your hardware meets the minimum requirements that Microsoft outlines before you spend your hard-earned money: 300MHz CPU, 128MB RAM, and 1.5GB free hard disk space. Keep in mind that these are minimum hardware requirements, so a faster processor, more RAM, and extra disk space certainly won't hurt. Expect to spend at least an hour upgrading to Windows XP.

Does all this add up to a good value? For Windows 95 users who are happy with what they have or don't think they'll take advantage of XP's features, $199 is too high. In this case, the best overall value would be to buy a new system with XP installed. You can find a well-equipped system, including Windows XP, for less than $1,000. For Windows 98 and Me users, $99 isn't an unreasonable price considering the features and stability.

Despite its limitations, it's an upgrade you'll want either now or later. But if you're skittish, hold off for the eventual updates that will surely come.

 TIP OF THE DAY If you're having trouble getting an older program to run on Windows XP, try the Program Compatibility Wizard. Click **Start**, **All Programs**, **Accessories**, and then select **Program Compatibility Wizard**. It doesn't work with every program, but it can help some make the switch.

 DOWNLOAD OF THE DAY Bring your Windows desktop to life with Drempels. It's more than wallpaper—it's alive. Free from geisswerks.com.

TODAY'S FOCUS: Microsoft Windows

HP CO-FOUNDER DIES

Engineer David Packard died on this day in 1996. He was 83 years old. The Pueblo, Colorado, native and his partner, William Hewlett, started their electronics company in Packard's garage in 1939. In 1968, Packard was appointed U.S. Deputy Secretary of Defense by President Richard Nixon. Three years later, Packard resigned and returned to HP as chairman of the board. The former General Electric engineer was also active in charitable and environmental organizations, such as the California Nature Conservancy and the Monterey Bay Aquarium Foundation. His charitable foundation, The David and Lucile Packard Foundation, has assets of more than $6 billion and awarded grants of $250 million last year.

Related Web site   www.packard.org

One Computer, Two Processors, No Waiting

Most computers have a single processor, just as humans have a single brain. To do more than one thing at a time, the computer must switch its attention rapidly from one to the other. This is called *preemptive multitasking*, and modern computers are so fast that they can do a pretty good job of it.

But what if your computer had two brains? It could assign one processor to, let's say, downloading the mail, while continuing to work doing something else, let's say, burning a CD. Your computer would seem more responsive and less likely to bog down.

Better yet, if a program knows you have two processors, it could use both to divvy up really difficult tasks. That's how Photoshop, for example, can use two processors to speed up a hairy image transformation. It tells one processor to handle all the even lines of the image and the other processor to take the odd lines. Of course, there is some multitasking still going on because both processors have other things to attend to, such as updating the system clock, monitoring the keyboard for typing, and so on. But complicated tasks would get done much faster.

This kind of multiple processor ballet is called SMP, symmetric multiprocessing. The *symmetric* comes from the fact that the processors are dividing the work evenly. Many high-end applications support SMP. So do many operating systems, including most Unix implementations such as Linux and Mac OS X, and, yes, Windows NT, 2000, and XP Professional.

A dual-processor PC is not quite twice as fast, because of the overhead involved in traffic control, but if your software and operating system are designed to support it, a multiprocessor PC can be a relatively inexpensive way to get your work done a whole lot faster.

 TIP OF THE DAY   Windows XP is much more secure than previous versions of Windows. If you forget your password, you're toast. That's why you should create a password recovery disk right now. Grab a floppy disk and launch the Forgotten Password Wizard:

1. Click the **Start** menu, **Control Panel**, and **User Accounts**.
2. Click your user account name.
3. Under Related Tasks on the left, click **Prevent Forgotten Password**.

SECURITY CODE INVALID!

Follow its instructions to create a password recovery disk. Put the disk somewhere safe. Next time you forget your password, log in as usual and insert the disk when prompted.

 DOWNLOAD OF THE DAY   Have you ever forgotten a password? Who hasn't? Password Agent stores all your passwords, secret notes, and data snippets in a secure database. It's free to try, $19.95 to buy from www.moonsoftware.com.

TODAY'S FOCUS: Microsoft Windows

1961: FIRST MOBILE COMPUTER

The first mobile computer center was used on this day in 1961. The setup was essentially a UNIVAC Solid-State 90 computer loaded into a van. This model was one of the first computers to use solid-state components in its CPU, which consisted of 20 vacuum tubes, 700 transistors, and 3,000 FERRACTOR amplifiers. The system also included drum memory, a card reader, a card punch, and a printer. The mobile center was set up by Remington Rand UNIVAC, a division of Sperry Rand, on assignment for the Douglas Aircraft Corporation.

Related Web site `fourmilab.ch/documents/univac`

MARCH 27

Windows XP Product Activation

By David Prager

Microsoft's Product Activation feature, included in the new Windows XP operating system, is the company's latest attempt to fight software piracy. Microsoft says it wants to eliminate what it calls the "casual copying" of Windows.

To ensure that no more than one computer uses a single XP license, Microsoft has taken some extra steps. When you install XP, you will be asked to activate the operating system. If you do not, you still will be able to use Windows XP, but only for 30 days. After that, you will no longer be able to use the OS until it has been activated.

The activation procedure can be performed online or verbally over the phone.

When you install Windows XP and enter the product ID code, it analyzes key hardware components on your computer and creates a 50-digit internal value called the *installation ID*. When you activate the OS, your installation ID code is transmitted to Microsoft (or given verbally over the phone) in exchange for a 42-digit activation ID that activates Windows XP.

No personal information is needed to activate Windows XP. Registration is not required and has nothing to do with activation.

After activation, you can install and reinstall XP using your activation ID as many times as you like, as long as your hardware configuration remains mostly the same. If the hardware configuration changes, you will have to reactivate the OS. Microsoft allows this kind of hardware reconfiguration as many as four times per year without questioning.

 TIP OF THE DAY One of the best new features of Windows XP is ClearType. ClearType dramatically improves the appearance of type on the screen, especially on LCD monitors, although you'll notice some improvements on CRTs, as well. To turn on ClearType and fine tune it, visit Microsoft's online tuner at `microsoft.com/windowsxp/pro/using/howto/customize/cleartype/tuner`.

You can turn ClearType on and off directly from the Display control panel. Click the **Appearance** tab and click the **Effects** button. Choose the method you prefer to smooth screen fonts.

 DOWNLOAD OF THE DAY Why pay for Windows XP when you can look like you're using XP without upgrading to XP?

Start by downloading DesktopArchitect, a Windows 98/Me theme manager, free from `download.com.com/3000-2326-5630015.html?legacy=cnet`.

Then, get the Windows XP theme from `download.cnet.com/downloads/0-1461945-100-6729926.html?tag=st.dl.10001-103-1.lst-7-5.6729926`.

Your friends will never know the difference!

POLL: Would you live in a Windows-free world?

35% Yes

65% No

TODAY'S FOCUS: Microsoft Windows

THREE MILE ISLAND ACCIDENT

The U.S. came 30 minutes away from a nuclear meltdown on this day in 1979. Residents near the plant on the Susquehanna River in Harrisburg, Pennsylvania, were threatened by radioactive contamination after a cooling pump failed. The equipment malfunction was made worse by human error, and within minutes government engineers feared the reactor's nuclear fuel would melt out of its thick steel and cement encasement, or that a hydrogen gas bubble in the core would explode. Although total meltdown was avoided, Three Mile Island is still deemed the worst nuclear accident in U.S. history.

Related Web site `www.libraries.psu.edu/crsweb/tmi/tmi.htm`

Windows XP Power Toys

The Windows XP Power Toys are a collection of free programs that Microsoft distributes but does not support. Two of the programs are must-haves, the rest are kinda-should-haves, maybe. Here's what you get.

Tweak UI   This control panel encompasses a variety of user interface tweaks not found in the default system settings. You can adjust mouse sensitivity and the speed at which cascading menus open, customize the Start menu, and change how applications are grouped. There are so many tweaks in this program that I can't possibly list them all. Suffice to say, every Windows user should have a copy of this program.

Power Toy Calculator   The Windows calculator hasn't changed much since Windows 3.0. The Power Toy Calculator makes up for this oversight and then some. This toy provides a variety of mathematical conversions (length, mass, time, velocity, temperature) and functions (addition, subtraction, and trigonometry, among others) for those who need to use them. There's also a graphing calculator that algebra and trig students will find useful. The History window acts as a paper tape making it easy to recall past calculations.

Image Resizer   Right-click on an image to resize it.

HTML Slide Show Wizard   Automatically create HTML slideshows for the Web.

CD Slide Show Generator   View images burned to a CD as a slideshow.

Taskbar Magnifier   Magnify the area under the pointer. Not as effective as the magnifier that comes with the accessibility tools, but more compact.

Super-Fast Switcher   Quickly switch from one logged-in user to another by pressing Windows+Q.

Alt+Tab Replacement   Adds thumbnails to the Alt+Tab application switcher.

Virtual Desktop Manager   Work on four desktops at once.

Open Command Window Here   Right-click on any folder or disk drive, and then choose **Open Command Window Here** to open a command line in that directory.

Webcam Timershot   Capture pictures from any attached camera and upload them to the Web.

Download Power Toys from `www.microsoft.com/windowsxp/pro/downloads/powertoys.asp`. Be sure to uninstall the old Power Toys before installing the new ones. PowerToys will work only with US-English regional settings.

 TIP OF THE DAY   Here's the fastest way to run Windows XP utilities. Click **Start**, **Run**, and then type the command on the left to run the program on the right.

`compmgmt.msc`	Computer management
`devmgmt.msc`	Device manager
`diskmgmt.msc`	Disk management
`dfrg.msc`	Disk defrag
`eventvwr.msc`	Event viewer
`fsmgmt.msc`	Shared folders
`gpedit.msc`	Group policies
`lusrmgr.msc`	Local users and groups
`perfmon.msc`	Performance monitor
`rsop.msc`	Resultant set of policies
`secpol.msc`	Local security settings
`services.msc`	Services

 DOWNLOAD OF THE DAY   *PC Magazine's* TrayManager consolidates your system tray icons. Free from `download.cnet.com/downloads/0-10106-100-5943070.html?tag=st.dl.10001-103-1.lst-7-1.5943070`.

TODAY'S FOCUS: Microsoft Windows

IBM SUES FOR PATENT INFRINGEMENT

IBM filed a lawsuit against Conner Peripherals on this day in 1995. The PC giant claimed the San Jose, California–based disk-drive maker infringed on its power-management technology patent, which could extend PC battery life. This wasn't the first scuffle between the two companies. In 1993, Conner sued IBM for allegedly infringing on five of its data storage patents, and the computer maker countersued. IBM and Conner ended their disputes in July 1995 with a five-year agreement that gave both companies access to each other's patent portfolios. Conner merged with Seagate Technology in 1996.

Related Web site `ibm.com/history`

MARCH
29

Windows Help Sites

Everybody needs computer help from time to time. Here are some personal sites we think you'll want to bookmark for when your time comes.

Redneck Puters (`redneck-puters.com`)   This site has more style and voice than you can shake a stick at. Bubba Joe and Lester's down-home take on the digital lifestyle gives us a hankerin' for more. They provide daily tech news, help, and excellent tech-support forums.

ComputerProblems.com (`computerproblems.com`) Ken Colburn, brain behind this site, tells us he has an army of geeks-in-training waiting to answer your tech support questions. The geeks are community college students getting college credit for their work.

Newbie.org (`newbie.org`)   Everybody was a newbie once. And no matter how far you've come in the geek world, you probably don't know everything yet. This site offers tips and tricks at all levels of tech expertise.

Practically Networked (`practicallynetworked.com`) If you're setting up your own network, you need this site. Designed for newbies and geeks alike, Practically Networked serves all your niggling networking needs.

PC Mechanic (`pcmech.com`)   Does your PC need a tune-up? You can get free step-by-step guides and helpful tech support at this site. And if you're in the giving mood, you can even volunteer your services to help others.

Geek.com (`geek.com`)   Geek.com proves that it is now officially cool to be a geek. This slick site reviews PC parts, PDAs, and even wireless products.

Chronology of Personal Computers (`www.islandnet.com/~kpolsson/comphist`)   Go back in time and research the origins of the PC (from 1966 to the present) with this carefully researched home page.

Drivers HQ (`drivershq.com`)   Find lost drivers and learn how to install them properly with this easy-to-navigate site.

Navas Cable Modem/DSL Tuning Guide (`cable-dsl.home.att.net`)   New to broadband? You'll find a wealth of free information about DSL and cable modems at this well-organized site. Don't miss the tips and tricks to speed up your connection.

Trish's Escape from Hardware Hell (`hardwarehell.com`) We've all been to hardware hell. Trish shows us the way out with a gaggle of links on every hardware subject imaginable.

TIP OF THE DAY   Tired of typing your name every time Windows starts? Teach it to log in automatically.

1. Click **Start**, **Run**, and type `control userpasswords2`.
2. Uncheck the **Users Must Enter a Username and Password to Use This Computer** check box.
3. Click **Apply**.
4. Enter the username and password you want to automatically log on with, and then click **OK**.
5. Click **OK** again and you're all done.

Remember that by doing this you're giving everyone access to your system.

DOWNLOAD OF THE DAY   *PC Magazine*'s EndItAll shuts down all your programs with one click. Free from `pcmag.com/article/0.2997.s%253D1478%2526a%253D10165.00.asp`.

TODAY'S FOCUS: Microsoft Windows

FIRST ANESTHETIC SURGERY

Anesthesia was first used in surgery on this day in 1842. Dr. Crawford W. Long of Jefferson, Georgia, used sulfuric ether while removing a cyst from his patient's neck. The operation cost $2. Long was known to have "experimented" with ether throughout his career and discovered its capability to dull pain. The implementation of this technology was revolutionary—virtually every invasive medical procedure would not have been possible without anesthesia.

Related Web site `gasnet.org`

25 Things I Love About Windows XP

By Chris Pirillo

1. You can rename several files at one time within Explorer.
2. Use the Tiles view to get quick picture dimensions. When you select an image, its dimensions will also be displayed in the status bar.
3. Check out the Details view if you have many similar files in a folder. In one glance, you can view the number of pages, bit rate, details, and so on.
4. ClearType is a great reason to upgrade to Windows XP.
5. Your removable drives are automatically added to the SendTo menu.
6. EXIF support is built into the Explorer shell. This allows you to see embedded information from untouched digital photos.
7. The Details view in MP3 folders is very revealing.
8. The new Align to Grid feature for the Windows desktop appeals to the neat freak in me.
9. Play with the "Show in Groups" Arrange option.
10. When you see the shutdown dialog box pop up, hold onto the Shift key if you want to flip energy-saving modes.
11. Windows Media Player will now grab cover shots and detailed information for your DVDs.
12. When you put in a CD with MP3s, or a digital camera, or a picture CD, XP asks you what you want to do with it.
13. Icons in the System Tray are now displayed in high color.
14. Zip file support is finally built into the OS.
15. Power Toys!
16. ID3v2 is supported throughout the OS. To edit an MP3's information, pull up its properties and flip to the Summary tab.
17. You can save your current Theme to the My Documents folder.
18. XP's boot (and restart) process is faster than it's ever been.
19. MSConfig is back, baby.
20. In picture folders, the Tasks pane will give you an option to print them.
21. Alpha blending makes those icons look smooooooth.
22. Time synchronization is now built into the Date and Time applet.
23. When Explorer crashes, the icons are restored in the System Tray.
24. XP comes with a slideshow screensaver. Finally.
25. The Task Manager now has Networking performance indicators.

TIP OF THE DAY   After installing XP, you might notice the revamped interface looks nothing like the old one. Miss it? Return to those thrilling days of yesteryear as follows:

1. Right-click your Desktop and select **Properties**.
2. On the Desktop Display properties, click the **Appearance** tab.
3. Under the **Windows and Buttons** pull-down menu, select **Windows Classic**.
4. Click **Apply** to see your new look.
5. Click **OK** to close the Desktop Display properties.

DOWNLOAD OF THE DAY   XP does not provide support for creating MP3s from your CDs, but you can download your own MP3 rippers. MusicMatch Jukebox for Windows is free from `musicmatch.com`. Or try CDex, free from `cdex.n3.net`.

TODAY'S FOCUS: Pranks and Hijinks

MS BOB SHIPS

Microsoft's first "social interface" shipped on this day in 1995. MS Bob was developed under the direction of Microsoft's marketing manager, Melinda French (who also happened to be Bill Gates' new wife). The $99 program converted the user's desktop into a cartoon office complete with animated assistants, including the infamous Clippy, the paper clip. The product flopped, but the cartoon assistants live on in Microsoft Office.

Related Web site `microsoft.com/office/clippy`

MARCH
31

Amuse Yourself at the Office

By David Spark

April Fools' Day is tomorrow. Arm yourself with these wicked tricks.

1. Use Microsoft Word's AutoCorrect feature to replace your subject's name with "I'm a dork."

2. Change Word's NORMAL.DOT file. (Make a backup first!) Open up the NORMAL.DOT template file and type in 72-point text "April Fools!" You might want to throw in a clip-art image of a jester, too. Save the file. When your co-worker starts a new document, he'll see that message.

3. In Windows, set the file properties for an application's file format to open another application. For example, when the user double-clicks on the Word icon, it could start up Tetris.

4. Turn on Marquee screensaver and embed a special message, such as "Nice hairpiece, Leo."

5. Hook up various monitors to the wrong computers, and do the same with the keyboards. Be sure you're in the room to watch the ensuing confusion.

6. Secretly replace your prankee's email .signature file with a blurb advertising the user's extensive Beanie Babies collection.

7. Place clear tape over a user's mouse ball and watch the fury. Better yet, remove the ball entirely.

8. Record the prankee saying something stupid, and then set that as their Windows startup sound.

Of course, you should try these only on people who you know will find the pranks funny, and keep any prank content within the guidelines for appropriate behavior in your workplace. And remember, if you alter anyone's files, remember to always save a backup (.bak) file onto their system—and help your victim fix what you did, after the joke's over. Other than that, have fun!

 TIP OF THE DAY Want more pranks? Visit the newsgroup `alt.shenanigans`: `groups.google.com/groups? group=alt.shenanigans`.

Newsgroups, also known as Usenet discussion forums, are one of the oldest forms of computer message board. There are over 30,000 different newsgroups, covering a wide range of topics from computer help to Hollywood fandom. Beware, the newsgroups are uncensored. Some of the topics are inappropriate for children (and many adults, for that matter).

Search the newsgroups on Google by visiting `groups.google.com`. Google archives 20 years of newsgroup posts—that's more than 700 million messages.

If you decide you want to participate in the newsgroups, you'll need a newsgroup reader. Outlook Express works just fine. Select **Accounts** from the **Tools** menu, click the **News** tab, and add a news server. Most ISPs host free news servers. Check with your provider for the server name. If yours does not, you can subscribe to a newsgroup service such as Supernews, `www.supernews.com`.

 DOWNLOAD OF THE DAY My favorite free Windows newsgroup reader is FreeAgent from `www.forteinc.com`.

 For Mac OS X, I recommend Brian Clark's Thoth from `www.thothsw.com`. Free to try, $25 to buy.

APRIL 2003

APRIL 2003

SUNDAY	MONDAY	TUESDAY	WEDNESDAY	THURSDAY	FRIDAY	SATURDAY
		1 April Fools' Day; Apple Computer formed	**2** First motion picture theater opens (1918)	**3**	**4**	**5**
6 Daylight Saving Time begins	**7**	**8**	**9**	**10** *Titanic* sets sail (1912)	**11**	**12**
13 Apollo 13 disaster (1970)	**14**	**15** Leonardo da Vinci born (1452); *Titanic* sinks (1912)	**16**	**17**	**18**	**19** Oklahoma City, Oklahoma Federal building bombed (1995)
20	**21** Mark Twain died (1910)	**22** Earth Day; TechTrends 2003 (Baltimore, MD)	**23** Administrative Professionals' Day (Secretaries' Day)	**24**	**25**	**26** Chernobyl nuclear accident (1986)
27	**28**	**29**	**30** Commercial TV debuts (1939)			

TODAY'S FOCUS: Pranks and Hijinks

APPLE COMPUTER FOUNDED

Steve Jobs and Steve Wozniak chose April Fools' Day to found the Apple Computer Company in 1976. How the company got its name is up for debate, but the most popular story is that Steve Jobs, who had previously worked in an apple orchard, considered the fruit the perfect combination of nutrition, packaging, and durability—much like he thought his computers would be. Others say they just couldn't come up with a better name. With nearly $6 billion in revenue in 2001, Apple has proven it isn't anyone's fool.

Related Web site `www.apple.com`

Top Tech Pranks

By Megan Morrone

The Case of the Missing Mouse Ball   When your chosen target steps away from his or her desk, simply unscrew the circular piece of plastic on the underside of the mouse, and remove the ball. They'll never know what hit 'em. If you really want to freak them out, when they get up to complain to tech support, replace the ball. A few hours later, remove the ball again. Repeat the experiment until your co-worker gets hauled off to the loony bin.

 Screwy Shortcuts   When your friend has gone for a coffee break, right-click on one of her shortcuts and choose **Properties**. Delete the information in the window next to the word **Target**. That's the information that tells the computer where to go to find the executable file and open the program.

Replace this information with another target. I always like to use C:\WINDOWS\DEFRAG. If the icon changes with the target, click the **Change Icon** button and browse for the old icon so your foe will never know you've changed a thing.

And now (drumroll, please)... The Best Tech Prank

 Duplicitous Desktop Deception   This trick is my favorite. Russ Pitts tried it on Sarah Lane, and it took her nearly a week to figure it out. Like any good hacker, she just worked around the problem.

Make a screenshot of the desktop:
1. Wait until your target goes to a meeting.
2. Go to the desktop.
3. Press **PrtScn**.
4. Open Microsoft Paint.
5. Paste your desktop pic into the Paint window.
6. Save the image where you'll be able to find it.

Remove those icons from the desktop:
1. Make a new folder on the target's desktop.
2. Move the target's icons into a folder so you can restore them later.
3. Move the folder into the My Documents Folder.

Change the background:
1. Go back to the desktop.
2. Right-click an empty area of the desktop.
3. Choose **Properties**.
4. Click the **Background** tab.
5. Click **Browse**, and find the saved Paint document.
6. Click **Open**.
7. Under **Display**, choose **Stretch**.
8. Click **Apply**.
9. Resize the taskbar so it's invisible.

When your mark returns to the computer, it will look normal but nothing will work. Be sure to return everything to normal after she begs for mercy.

 TIP OF THE DAY   To force the file extension of your choice (and not the application default), type the filename in quotation marks in the Save As dialog box.

 DOWNLOAD OF THE DAY   Another avenue toward hilarity is to make someone think that a video card or monitor has broken. ScreenScrew does just that: rjlsoftware.com/software/entertainment/screenscrew.

TODAY'S FOCUS: Pranks and Hijinks

TELEGRAPH PIONEER DIES

Telegraph inventor Samuel F.B. Morse died in New York on this day in 1872. Morse created the dot-dash code that bears his name to keep track of arriving and departing trains. The scientist and art teacher built the first telegraph model around 1835 using an old artist's canvas stretcher and a homemade battery. Eight years later, Morse convinced Congress to fund the first U.S. telegraph line from Baltimore to Washington, D.C. He transmitted his first successful message, "What hath God wrought?" on May 24, 1844.

Related Web site `morsehistoricsite.org`

More Pranks!

By Evil Morrone

Thanks to Todd from St. Louis for recommending LizardWorks.com, a site with dozens of downloadable pranks. Todd says they're just the thing for driving his little sisters crazy.

Although I was tempted by RudeCDTray, an .exe file that causes your CD tray to open up and give you a raspberry, I was more intrigued by the silent but deadly Swapper. Here's how it works.

Download this small file onto an unsuspecting friend or family member's computer. Double-click the horned mouse icon and your target's right-click will be switched with the left-click. Walk away and watch the magic happen. By the way, Megan made me tell you that you can click on the window in your taskbar to be informed that you've been had.

Incidentally, your antivirus program might identify some of the pranks on this page as viruses. They're not really, but some antivirus companies don't appear to have a sense of humor.

TIP OF THE DAY Here are two commands you can use to shut down Windows 98 and Me in a batch file or shortcut (this trick does NOT work with Windows XP).

The command `runonce.exe  -q` restarts the computer after a 15-second delay. This command is often used by program installers. Or pranksters.

For quicker results, use the command `rundll32.exe shell32.dll,SHExitWindowsEx` *n*, where *n* is one of, or a combination of, the following numbers:

0 Shuts down all running processes, and then logs the user off.

1 Shuts down the system to a point at which it is safe to turn off the power. All file buffers have been flushed to disk, and all running processes have stopped.

2 Shuts down the system and then restarts it.

4 Forces processes to terminate. When this flag is set, Windows does not query running applications to inform them that Windows is shutting down. This can cause the applications to lose data; therefore, you should use this flag only in an emergency.

8 Shuts down the system and turns off the power. The system must support the power-off feature.

Add the numbers together to create different types of shutdown. For example, to restart Windows forcefully, without querying any running programs, use the following command line:

`rundll32.exe shell32.dll,SHExitWindowsEx 6`

Careful. This option can cause programs to lose data.

The `rundll32.exe shell32.dll.SHExitWindowsEx` (*n*) command can be called from the RunOnce Registry key. We'll leave the gnarly implications to your imagination.

DOWNLOAD OF THE DAY Dirty Mouse will make a loved one's mouse act as though it's all gummed up. He'll have all sorts of trouble moving it around the screen! Free from `rjlsoftware.com/software/entertainment/dirty`.

TODAY'S FOCUS: Pranks and Hijinks

2001: A SPACE ODYSSEY PREMIERES

The blockbuster movie based on the science fiction novel by Arthur C. Clarke opened in theaters on this day in 1968. Directed by Stanley Kubrick, *2001: A Space Odyssey* explored the possibility of colonized space and the humanization of machinery. Both the novel writer and the film director collaborated on this legendary project at the same time. Nearly two decades later, the movie was followed by *2010: The Year We Made Contact*. The original flick is still a rental favorite among geeks and space buffs today, even though Clarke's eerie prophecies did not come to pass.

Related Web site   www.palantir.net/2001

Relax, It's Just a Hoax

By Mr. Modem

Be suspicious of emails that warn you of a terrible virus or of some other digital demon—especially if they ask you to forward the message to everybody you know. Don't do it! Odds are it's just a hoax.

Assume such warnings are false, unless you can prove that they are true using a reliable Web-based resource. After you confirm that it is a hoax, notify the person who sent you the warning message so that he can, in turn, notify all the people he alerted. Be sure to send the address of the resource you used to confirm the hoax.

Mr. Modem's Five Flags of Phoniness

A hoax email will display one or more of the following characteristics:

- **Urgent!**—The email will have a great sense of urgency! You'll usually see a lot of exclamation points and capitalization.
- **Tell All Your Friends**—There will always be a request that you share this "important" warning by forwarding the message to everybody in your email address book.
- **This Isn't a Hoax**—The body of the email will contain some form of corroboration, such as a pseudoquote from an executive of a major corporation or from a government agency official.
- **Dire Consequences**—The email text will predict dire consequence if you don't act immediately. The message might inform you that the virus will destroy your hard drive, kill your houseplants, or cause green fuzzy things to grow in your refrigerator.

- **Look to the Past**—Look for a lot of >>>> marks in the left margin. These marks indicate that people suckered by the hoax forwarded the message countless times before it reached you.

Here are some good places to check to see whether a message is a hoax before clicking that forward button:

- HoaxBusters at the Department of Energy: hoaxbusters.ciac.org
- About.com's Urban Legends site: urbanlegends.about.com/science/ urbanlegends/cs/nethoaxes
- Vmyths: vmyths.com
- Symantec AntiVirus Research Center: sarc.com/avcenter/hoax.html
- Urban Legends Reference Pages: snopes.com

(Visit Mr. Modem, a.k.a. Richard A. Sherman, at mrmodem.net.)

TIP OF THE DAY   Hold the Control key while dragging an icon to make a copy of the file instead of moving it.

Press Control when you double-click on a folder to open it in a new window.

Use the Control key and the arrow keys to switch between parts of the address in your Internet Explorer browser window.

DOWNLOAD OF THE DAY   If you want to further mess with someone's mouse, install Mouse Droppings on her PC. As she moves the mouse pointer around the screen, it will deposit black droppings in its path. Ewwwww! rjlsoftware.com/software/ entertainment/droppings.

APRIL 3

TODAY'S FOCUS: Pranks and Hijinks

GARBAGE USED FOR ELECTRICITY

The first large-scale attempt to use garbage as fuel for generating electricity was successfully made on this day in 1972. The Union Electric Company of St. Louis, Missouri, used shredded refuse to fire the boilers in its Meramec Plant. It generated 200,000 watts of power in just the first month.

Related Web site `biodiesel.org`

Twisted List: Top Web Scams According to the FTC

By Martin Sargent

Multilevel Marketing A small but significant fraction of Web scams are multilevel marketing deals. Companies dupe you into becoming a distributor of some sort of diet or beauty product. You're supposed to earn money by receiving commissions on products you sell as well as part of the commissions earned by any friends you convince to sell the products. According to the FTC, such business practices constitute an illegal pyramid scheme.

Credit-Card Cramming Your credit card has been crammed when it's billed for a purchase that you never authorized. Typically, the charges are for Web site services, especially online porn. Most people who are scammed by credit-card cramming have given their credit-card number to a porn site to prove that they're over 18.

If you've ever used your credit card online, be sure to take an extra 10 seconds every month to study your credit-card bill and ensure that no unauthorized charges appear on it.

Web Cramming You get a call from a company saying it will provide your small business with a free Web site for 30 days. If you're happy with the site, you can keep it by paying $30 a month thereafter. Of course, you can cancel any time. In many cases, even if you don't like the site that's created for you, your credit card will continue to get billed.

ISP Scams You get a check in the mail. On the front, it says that you can go ahead and cash it and keep the money, no obligation. But by cashing the check, what you're really doing is signing up for a long-term contract with a shoddy ISP.

Any time you receive a check in the mail, be sure to read the fine print, and expect to come across a trap.

Online Auctions Almost 80% of online fraud pertains to auctions. That's because auction fraud is so easy for crooks to accomplish. Typically, you find an unbelievable deal on an item, score the winning bid, and drop your check in the mail. Weeks go by and you never receive the item you bid on, and your emails to the seller go unanswered.

If you think you've been duped by any of these scams online, call the Federal Trade Commission at 1-800-FTC-HELP.

TIP OF THE DAY Add an Address bar to your Windows toolbar by right-clicking on the toolbar, pointing to **Toolbars**, and selecting **Address**. A box for URLs will appear. To get to a Web site, all you have to do is type in the address and press Enter.

You can move the Address box to the top of your screen by clicking and dragging it to the top of your screen.

DOWNLOAD OF THE DAY Digital Whoopie Cushion is a childish, gross prank. You should be ashamed for even considering it. Free from `zug.com/pranks/zugbugs`.

TODAY'S FOCUS: Pranks and Hijinks

RCA FOUNDED

The Radio Corporation of America made its debut on this day in 1919. The organization was created to protect the U.S. from "foreign interests" when the Navy discovered the British Marconi Company was about to purchase the Alexanderson alternator from General Electric. The Navy pressured GE, AT&T, Westinghouse, and the United Fruit Company to pool their patents in a cartel, and British Marconi sold its U.S. radio interests to RCA. RCA quickly became the largest radio manufacturer in the country. It is now owned by Thomson, the same company that holds the patent to MP3.

Related Web site   `rca.com`

Tax Day is only 10 days away. So, we interrupt this lesson in computer mirth and merriment with a serious look at the...

Top Tax Sites

By Tiffany Bass Bukow

A great way to keep your spirits up for the whole process is to start off with some money funnies to improve your mood. You can find some tax humor at TaxMama, `taxmama.com/ moneyfunnies`. The site also includes articles, tax FAQs, updated news from the IRS, and a weekly newsletter, *Ask TaxMama*.

While you're there, find out whether you're a good candidate for filing online. Read `taxmama.com/Articles/ FilingOnline.html`. If you are, click through to some of these sites.

Online Filing Sites

TaxBrain.com (`taxbrain.com`)   This site has been involved with the tax industry for more than 10 years. Its parent company set up the e-file system for the California Franchise Tax Board. It has a toll-free support number and its rates are quite reasonable. The federal e-file fee is only $4.95. It can even help you get your refund in as little as three days.

H&R Block (`hrblock.com/taxes/doing_my_taxes/ products/otp.html`)   This old favorite walks you through the process of filing your taxes online.

TurboTax (`www.turbotax.intuit.com/welcome/ perm/qcome/welcome.htm`)   This is one of the most popular do-it-yourself Web sites for filing taxes. It's very user friendly.

EStudentTax.com (`estudenttax.com`)   Certainly there are general-purpose sites for filing online, but there are also niche sites that add an interesting twist. Visit this Web site for a student's take on taxes.

Information Web Sites

Perhaps you aren't quite ready to hit the Send button because you're still trying to grapple with the new tax laws and cut a few more dollars from your tax bill. If that's the case, stop by these sites to begin your research.

Quicken.com (`quicken.com/taxes`)   Whether you have questions about your retirement fund or simply want to brush up on the basics, Quicken has information and tools to help you manage your taxes and save money.

Fool.com (`fool.com/taxes/taxcenter`)   Provides a weekly tax article for your perusal, just in case you want to think about taxes 52 weeks a year instead of just one.

MsMoney.com (`msmoney.com/mm/planning/taxes/ taxes_intro.htm`)   And don't forget, MsMoney.com has tax information as well as additional financial and career content that will help you improve your financial health and secure your future.

(Tiffany Bass Bukow is the CEO and founder of MsMoney.com.)

TIP OF THE DAY   Right-click a file, choose **Send To**, and then **3 1/2-Inch Floppy** to send your file straight to diskette.

DOWNLOAD OF THE DAY   When you install Avoid on a victim's computer, you render him incapable of touching the Start button with the mouse pointer. Everyone gets a big laugh (`jlsoftware. com/software/entertainment/avoid`).

TODAY'S FOCUS: Pranks and Hijinks

TEFLON INVENTED

The nonstick coating for which pots and presidents were named was discovered on this day in 1938. The material known as Polytetraflouroethylene resin was created by Roy J. Plunkett for the DuPont Company in the search for a stick-resistant surface for cookware. By the time Plunkett died in the early 1990s, three-quarters of all the cooking pans in America were coated with his invention. Today, Teflon is also used in semiconductors, communications cables, and in clothing.

Related Web site `Teflon.com`

Twisted List: Stupid Games

By Martin Sargent

Feed the Pig (`wackygames.com/games/feedpig` and many other sites) There is something wrong with the person who programmed Feed the Pig. The game starts with an emaciated pig next to a conveyor belt. Food and nonfood items move along the belt, and you drag stuff into the pig's mouth. The object is to overfeed the pig until it explodes. Please do not play Feed the Pig.

Milk the Clock (`bunnygrenade.com`) Feed the Pig is like chess compared to Milk the Clock. In Milk the Clock, you prod a cow with your mouse pointer and bad stuff happens. That's it. There is no point to this game whatsoever.

The Mr. Mouthy Mouth Game (`stupid.com/mouth2.htm`) At least Milk the Clock has some decent animation. Mr. Mouthy Mouth, on the other hand, has absolutely nothing going for it. It's not fun, it requires no skill, and it even hurts your eyes. Please, for the love of Pete, keep the children away from this game.

The Click the Box Game (`stupid.com/games/clickit`) This is the second-stupidest game ever made. You are presented with a grid of check boxes. The object is to click as many of the boxes as you can in 20 seconds. Play a few times and you dramatically increase your chances of getting carpal tunnel syndrome. Wow, a game that's so bad it gives you a disease.

The Mouse Click Game (`stupid.com/games/click.htm`) The worst game ever made is, without a doubt, The Mouse Click Game. All you have to do is click a button as many times as you can in 10 seconds. I defy you to beat my high score of 31. (I played for three hours.)

 TIP OF THE DAY When your Start menu is too full to fit onscreen Windows has two ways of showing you more. The old way is to expand into multiple columns. The new way is to put scroll arrows at the top and bottom of the menu. Many folks hate these new scroll menus.

In Windows XP, turn them off by opening the taskbar and Start Menu Control Panel, clicking the **Start Menu** tab, and then clicking the **Customize** button. If you use a Classic-style Start menu, just uncheck the **Scroll Programs** item in the **Advanced Start Menu Items** box. If you use an XP-style Start menu, click the **Advanced** tab, and *then* uncheck **Scroll Programs** toward the end of the Start menu items list.

DOWNLOAD OF THE DAY Remote Havoc is the mother of all dirty tricks. It gives you total control of a friend's machine. Free from `jokingaround.com/downloads/havoc.asp`.

Like many of our prank programs this week, Remote Havoc might be seen by some antivirus programs as a virus. It's not really.

TODAY'S FOCUS: Accessibility

TRANSCONTINENTAL TELEPHONE SERVICE BEGINS

The first coast-to-coast commercial phone call was placed on this day in 1915. AT&T president Theodore N. Vail made a call from New York to San Francisco by way of Jekyll Island, Georgia. Legend has it the call's off-course routing was because Vail had been sunning himself on the island when Alexander Graham Bell made the first noncommercial transatlantic call earlier that same year. Vail's call cost $20.70 for the first three minutes, and $6.75 for each additional minute—about $360 and $120 in today's dollars, respectively.

Related Web site `att.com`

Assistive Technology for the Blind

By Cynthia Stone

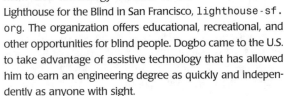

Thanks to specially designed technologies, blind and otherwise visually impaired people have opportunities they haven't had before.

Nicaise Dogbo, who has been blind since childhood, is the director of employment and technology services at the Lighthouse for the Blind in San Francisco, `lighthouse-sf.org`. The organization offers educational, recreational, and other opportunities for blind people. Dogbo came to the U.S. to take advantage of assistive technology that has allowed him to earn an engineering degree as quickly and independently as anyone with sight.

His engineering degree completed, Dogbo now trains others with visual impairments and educates employers and the public about assistive technology.

"You may have a diploma from Harvard, and just because you are a blind person that may automatically prevent them from seeing what other accomplishments you've done in your life," Dogbo said.

Here are some assistive technologies Dogbo and other visually impaired people commonly use:

- Refreshable Braille display terminals output characters in Braille, an advantage for people who are both blind and deaf. The National Institute of Standards and Technology is working on ways to make these displays faster, smaller, and more affordable. Read about their work at `www.itl.nist.gov/div895/isis/projects/brailleproject.html`.
- A Note-Taker is a minicomputer that uses Braille input and output, as well as voice output. Some new Note-Takers feature word-processing and email capabilities and internally synthesized speech: `www.freedomscientific.com`.
- The Voice Mate is a sort of PDA for the visually impaired. It combines several devices in one: talking clock, calculator, note taker, and digital voice recorder: `voice-assistant.com`.
- Closed-circuit TV supplies magnified printed material for people who can no longer read comfortably with glasses. Some manufacturers offer video cameras that transmit magnified images to a television monitor: `nanopac.com/Optelec.htm`.

Adapting assistive technology for the visually impaired is much less expensive for employers today than it was in the past. Whereas companies used to have to invest in expensive hardware, now Mac and Windows-compatible software does the job. But the cost of adaptive tech is still very high and, in many cases, out of reach for those people who need it most.

TIP OF THE DAY Another source for assistive equipment is Infogrip, at `infogrip.com`. It sells a large variety of adaptive technology and alternative computer-access equipment.

DOWNLOAD OF THE DAY Alien Invasion is a Space Invaders-style arcade game designed for players with disabilities. The game can be successfully played with a wide range of standard and adaptive technology controls, including expanded keyboards, head-mouse, and even speech recognition. A large-character option is included for low-vision users. For one or two players, Windows or Mac. Free to try, $15 to buy, from `levelgames.net/aliens.htm`.

APRIL 7

TODAY'S FOCUS: Accessibility

INVENTOR OF EARLY COMPUTER DIES

Frank Baldwin, developer of a mechanical desktop calculating machine, died in New York City on this day in 1925. Baldwin patented the arithmometer in 1875, but lack of money prevented him from ever manufacturing it. In 1912, the New Hartford, Connecticut, native and business partner Jay Monroe perfected a data-processing machine called the Monroe calculator. The apparatus, along with Baldwin's later creations, became standard business machines until the birth of electronic computers.

Related Web site   hpmuseum.org

Here are some more recommendations for devices and Web sites for disabled people, from Jessie Lorenz of the Independent Living Resource (ILRC) in San Francisco.

Devices

ColorTest (aph.org/products/colortes.html) ColorTest is a handheld device designed for people who are blind or color-blind. Scan any object with the wand and it will tell you the color. It senses 150 different shades and vocalizes the colors using a built-in speaker. It also detects patterns, brightness, and contrast.

Franklin Language Master (dyslexic.com/lm.htm) The Language Master is a portable dictionary and thesaurus with full speech capability. It contains more than 130,000 words, 300,000 word definitions, 500,000 thesaurus entries, plus parts of speech, inflections, hyphenation, and related words. The Language Master pronounces every key, function, and display. This text-to-speech device enables the sight-impaired to receive text messages.

Braille Lite 40 (www.freedomscientific.com/fs_products/notetakers_bl40.asp) This device does everything from a word processor to a personal organizer. There is a 40-character Braille display providing space to read documents or entire electronic books. This device delivers Braille access to any Windows application.

VisionKey (eyecan.ca) A portable eye-tracking keyboard that allows people to type with their eyes. Works with most computers.

Sites

AT Network (www.atnet.org) The Assistive Technology Network is dedicated to expanding accessibility of tools, resource, and technology to help increase independence for people living with disabilities.

e-bility (e-bility.com) The place for people with disabilities to find out about relationships, sports and outdoor life, and travel. The site features a complete medical encyclopedia as well as an outlet for purchasing healthcare products.

DisabilityDirect.gov (disabilitydirect.gov) Sponsored by the U.S. Department of Labor's Office of Disability Employment Policy, this site provide resources, services, and information available throughout the Federal government. Go here to find out about civil rights and protections, college and adult education, disability statistics, emergency preparedness, employers' resources, employment, and more.

EnabledOnline (enabledonline.com) This Webzine features extensive editorials, forums for posting messages, resources for teens and kids, and a news and events section. Go to enabledonline.com/text for the text version of the site.

 TIP OF THE DAY Microsoft Narrator is a screen reader that's built into Windows 2000 and XP. To start it, press the Windows key + U any time, even before you log in. To reread any window, press Ctrl+Shift+spacebar. For more shortcuts, see Windows Help. For more information, visit microsoft.com/enable/training/windowsxp/usingnarrator.htm. Microsoft notes that, although Narrator is useful, most users with disabilities will need utility programs with more advanced functionality for daily use.

 DOWNLOAD OF THE DAY If you want your computer to talk with you and you're not yet using Windows 2000 or XP, download Microsoft Agent, free from microsoft.com/msagent. To see what people are doing with Agent, visit the MS Agent Web ring at msagentring.org.

APRIL 8

TODAY'S FOCUS: Accessibility

DOMAIN NAME FEES AXED

On this day in 1998, a federal judge said certain fees charged to register domain names were considered illegal taxes. U.S. District Judge Thomas said official domain registrar Network Solutions had illegally collected almost $50 million to go toward "Internet infrastructure," a fund that was never ratified by Congress. Judge Thomas also rejected claims that Network Solutions was exercising illegal monopoly power. Domain names had previously been jointly registered by Network Solutions and The National Science Foundation, but the NSF bowed out of the partnership a year earlier.

Related Web site `www.icann.org`

Disability and Technology

By Annette M. Hanna

Computers and technology have impacted all of society, but no segment of the population has been more positively affected than people with disabilities. I know, because I have had a disability all my life. I have had to use a wheelchair due to polio I contracted from the vaccine at the age of 7 months.

My first introduction to computers came in 1994 when I was diagnosed with post-polio syndrome. I needed a permanent tracheotomy and vent due to respiratory failure. I came home with little information about my situation, but was determined to learn more. Fortunately, my now husband was a computer buff, and had introduced me to computers. I went kicking and screaming at first, but decided to give the computer a chance.

With days of boredom and trying to deal with my new disability, I decided to learn the computer. I remember the first day I hooked up to the Internet, I was so nervous—I felt like I was jumping into something I knew nothing about.

On the AOL message boards, I found lots of folks who also had post-polio syndrome, trachs, and ventilators. I soon learned that I wasn't the only one in the world with my situation. I learned about the disease, learned about having a trach and vent, but most of all learned that my life wasn't over. I opened myself up to a whole new world.

In the next year, I was able to better cope with my situation and help others who were about to face what I had already experienced.

So, what does technology do for people with disabilities? It gives them the chance to communicate with others when travel is difficult. I don't travel a lot, but the computer gives me a window to the world. The Internet has helped me do research on disability issues, medical info, and network with others in the same situation. With the advent of new technology, such as lightweight digital cameras and art tablets, I have been able to further my interest in photography and art. The computer is a never-ending learning tool.

(Annette is a TechTV viewer whom I met on the message boards at my Web site. She kindly agreed to add her perspective to this week's subject.)

 TIP OF THE DAY MouseKeys allows users who cannot use a mouse to move the pointer with the numeric keypad. In Windows XP, open the Accessibility Options control panel, click the **Mouse** tab, and check the **Use MouseKeys** box.

 DOWNLOAD OF THE DAY Wheels is a 3D action game for power chair training from `rjcooper.com/wheels`.

Try it free seven times, buy it for $29. For Mac and Windows.

TODAY'S FOCUS: Accessibility

SAFETY PIN PATENTED

Years of (minor) bloodshed ended on this day in 1849 when Walter Hunt of New York was awarded a patent for the safety pin. The device found in every sewing kit was created by twisting a piece of wire while Hunt was searching for a way to pay a $15 debt. Hunt didn't think the safety pin would ever catch on, and sold his patent for a mere $400. Some of Hunt's other inventions include a forerunner of the Winchester repeating rifle, a knife sharpener, a sewing machine, and artificial stone.

Related Web site `sewing.org`

Alternative Input Devices

Inventors continue to do great things. Here are some more recent inventions for people with special needs.

Renaissance Mouse (`worklink.net/mice.htm`) Previously called Dr. Mouse or Anir Mouse, Renaissance Mouse is a vertical mouse that puts your hand and arm in a neutral position that's clinically proven to relieve tension and pain in forearm, wrist, and hand. Three-button with scroll feature for PS2 or USB PC, or USB Mac.

"I don't want to do my homework on a computer. I want a computer to do it."

BAT (`worklink.net/products/bat-onehanded.html`) A one-handed, compact input device that replicates all the functions of a full-size keyboard, but with greater efficiency and convenience. The BAT is the ultimate solution for persons with physical or visual impairments and is proven to increase productivity. Available in left-handed, right-handed, or two-handed models for the PC or Mac.

HeadMaster and HeadMasterPlus (`worklink.net/products/headmaster.html`) Allows people who cannot use their hands or arms to operate a personal computer by head movement alone.

Mousamatic (`worklink.net/products/mousamatic.html`) A hands-free device that allows you to move the PC mouse pointer just by moving your head. You can click by pausing on an icon, or by using an external switch (foot switch, sip and puff, simple switch, for example).

DragonDictate (`worklink.net/products/dd.html`) Powerful voice-recognition software that allows extensive hands-free command and control of games and programs—including drawing or painting programs—and allows speech-to-text and text-to-speech.

L&H/Dragon NaturallySpeaking (`worklink.net/products/naturallyspeaking.html`) Command and control your computer by voice with custom voice macros. As you speak at a conversational pace, your words are transcribed immediately onto your computer screen.

Various Split and Tenting Ergonomic Keyboards (`worklink.net/keyboards.htm`) GoldTouch, PerfecTouch, Comfort, Kinesis Maxim, and ErgoLogic ergonomic keyboards allow you to achieve a good center of gravity, and get your body parts into a neutral posture.

Kinesis Contour Keyboard (`worklink.net/products/kinesis.html`) This keyboard is the result of an extensive university study. The designers watched people keyboarding, tabulated the results, threw out all the rules, and then designed and manufactured a revolutionary ergonomic keyboard from the ground up. The Kenesis has a radical look, feels great, and is among our most popular keyboards.

TIP OF THE DAY Microsoft Magnifier makes the screen more readable for people with low vision. It displays a magnified portion of your screen in a separate window. Start Microsoft Magnifier by clicking **Start**, **Programs**, **Accessories**, **Accessibility**. Then select **Microsoft Magnifier**.

If Microsoft Magnifier is not installed on your system, you can add it by going to the Control Panel, selecting **Add/Remove**, and clicking to install the accessibility features.

DOWNLOAD OF THE DAY Battle of the Gods and its nonviolent counterpart, Reign of the Flowerparts, are Space Invaders–type games for people who have difficulty controlling other games. Free from `rjcooper.com/rj's-free-games`.

POLL: Is carpal tunnel syndrome physical or psychological?

74% Physical   26% Psychological

TODAY'S FOCUS: Accessibility

APOLLO 13 DISASTER

Three U.S. astronauts were placed in serious jeopardy on this day in 1970 when an explosion rocked spacecraft Apollo 13. An oxygen tank ruptured less than 10 minutes after an hour-long TV broadcast with the crew, causing the other oxygen tank on board to fail. It was during this incident that Commander James A. Lovell, Jr. uttered the famous words, "Houston, we have a problem." The astronauts managed to escape, but the planned moon landing was canceled. NASA classified the mission as a "successful failure" because the crew was saved.

Related Web site `nssdc.gsfc.nasa.gov/planetary/lunar/apollo13info.html`

APRIL 11

Make Your Web Site Accessible

By Marina Chotzinoff

The Americans with Disabilities Act, which requires businesses to make their facilities accessible to people with disabilities, applies to Web sites as well. Here are some things to consider when designing your site.

Label Your Graphics Vision-impaired and blind users often use screen readers, tools that can read the contents of a page aloud. These readers are stymied by images. This is a particular problem when images are used as navigation buttons.

Always use the ALT tag within any IMG tag to guide people who can't see the images. For example:

```
<IMG SRC="home.gif" ALT="Click here to return
to the home page">
```

Organize and Be Consistent The organization of your site can be crucial to viewers with disabilities. Keep in mind that some browsers allow viewers to skip from link to link with the keys on the keyboard. Put links in an easily accessed location, grouped logically.

Use headers and titles on each page, and try to keep the structure consistent. This way, after viewers have figured out how to navigate your site, they won't be faced with a new challenge on each page.

Don't Get Fancy HTML features, such as frames and tables, can make surfing difficult. If you must use frames, provide a NOFRAMES tag that supplies a version of your site for people who can't use frames. Also, be sure to give a title to each frame and each page called into a frame so users can navigate between the frames.

If you use tables, be sure to keep text in readable chunks. Dividing text between table cells for the sake of a prettier site can lead to pure garble when the browser reads it.

Some scripts, applets, and plug-ins might not be accessible in special browsers. If any information or functionality of your site depends on these features, be sure you provide alternative content or navigation.

Test Your Site Finally, test the accessibility of your site with a tool such as Bobby at `cast.org/bobby`. Enter the URL of the site to test, and Bobby will present you with a list of problem areas. It will even suggest proper syntax and methods for making your site Bobby-approved.

TIP OF THE DAY For more information on making your site accessible, visit these addresses:

WebAIM is aimed at "expanding the Web's potential for people with disabilities." Lots of info at `webaim.org`.

The World Wide Web consortium, W3C, offers its official accessibility guidelines at `w3.org/TR/WCAG20/`.

DOWNLOAD OF THE DAY Get a talking browser, complete with large buttons and keystroke commands for easy navigation. Free for Windows from `weMedia.com`.

FIRST HUMAN IN SPACE

Russian cosmonaut Yuri Gagarin became the first person in space on this day in 1961. The 27-year-old orbited the Earth once in Vostok 1 at an altitude of more than 187 miles and a speed of 18,000 miles an hour. The trip lasted one hour and 48 minutes. Gagarin died at age 34 in a mysterious plane crash during a test flight. Theories surrounding his death range from postulation that Gagarin was drunk while flying, to accusations that the Russian government had poorly organized the test flights that day and was using faulty ground equipment.

Related Web site `russianspaceweb.com`

Disability Resources Online

By Caryn Roberts

Most people with disabilities can benefit from technology, and this includes the Web. Some of the best places to go are online support groups:

- Mobility problems are addressed by many Web sites, but my favorite starting point is `wheelchairjunkie.com`, a peer group of enthusiasts with the same fervor as sports-car rally drivers, moto-cross enthusiasts, and NASCAR participants.
- My particular disability, ataxia, has its own global online support groups at `groups.yahoo.com/group/internaf` and `internaf.org`. Many other disabilities are represented at Yahoo! Groups. A search for "disabilities" at `groups.yahoo.com` turns up nearly 1,000 different groups from all over the world.
- Another great place that provides more information to assist disabled is Half the Planet, at `halftheplanet.org`.
- A disabled person can shop online, which extends their reach to around the world. I've bought everything from pizza to computers, wheelchair gloves to my portable ramp, personal items to gifts for others.

But, even on our trip to visit *The Screen Savers* in San Francisco, we were reminded of how far we need to move as a society. Supposedly ADA-compliant hotel space was inadequate in two of the four motels at which we stayed. The ADA rules are available at the U.S. Department of Justice's Web site, `www.usdoj.gov/crt/ada/adahom1.htm` or call 800-514-0301 (voice), 800-514-0383 (TTY).

Other great resources on the Web include

- Dean Kamen's next generation PowerWheelchair iBOT, `indetech.com/ibot`
- U.S. Government Section 508 Computing Requirements, `www.usdoj.gov/crt/508/508home.html`
- Macromedia Accessibility Help, `macromedia.com/macromedia/accessibility/`
- IBM Accessibility Center, `ibm.com/able`
- University of Washington's DO-IT Program (Disabilities, Opportunities, Internetworking, and Technology), `washington.edu/doit/`
- AbilityHub, `abilityhub.com`

Assistive technology and solutions for people with disabilities wanting to access a computer.

A–Z to DeafBlindness (`deafblind.com`) James Gallagher, a gentleman with deafblindness, created and maintains this site. Incredible.

(Caryn Roberts is a computer programmer and systems analyst. Contact her at `home.earthlink.net/~carynkr`.)

TIP OF THE DAY I've already mentioned RJ Cooper & Associates several times this week. RJ makes products for people with special needs such as learning disabilities, including special software and hardware adaptations for persons with very special needs. He offers a free CD with time-limited versions of all his software for Mac and Windows from `rjcooper.com`.

DOWNLOAD OF THE DAY Levelgames makes arcade games for kids with special needs, including Alien Invasion, Ruby Ridge, and Brickout. For Mac and Windows from `arcess.com`. $15 each, three games for $25.

TODAY'S FOCUS: Accessibility

INVENTOR OF RADAR BORN

Sir Robert Watson-Watt was born in Brechin, Scotland, on this day in 1892. Watson-Watt started as a meteorologist at the Royal Aircraft Factory, and in 1916 proposed the use of cathode-ray oscilloscopes for tracking thunderstorms. In 1923, the British government asked him to develop a counterpart for a German aircraft-spotting "death-ray." On April 2, 1935, the electrical engineer was granted a patent for Radio Detection And Ranging (RADAR). He was knighted for his achievement in 1942.

Related Web site `www.radarpages.co.uk`

Vanilla Sites

By Megan Morrone

When it comes to the Web, we all can use a little accessibility. There are sites that don't have fancy graphics or use Flash, sites that are heavy on the content, light on the fluff. I call them plain-vanilla exceedingly useful sites. And here are some of my favorites.

Music from TV Commercials (`songtitle.info`) If you need to know where the music came from on just about any commercial, check this sim-ple site. By the way, the music from our "Right Here, Right Now" commercial is by Jesus Jones. If you don't know what I'm talking about, turn on TechTV. Right now.

Google/IE (`google.com/ie`) As if Google wasn't simple enough, this page is positively Spartan. It's designed to fit into the left search frame of Internet Explorer, but it's great any time when space matters. Other tiny Googles include `google.com/palm` and `google.com/imode`, versions designed for the tiny displays on PDAs and cell phones. Talk about vanilla.

The Teddy Borg (`draco.mit.edu/teddyborg`) Have you ever wanted to put a networking switch inside a teddy bear? Some students at MIT did. Why? Because they could. And because they thought it would help them meet women. View step-by-step instructions, complete with helpful JPEGS, at their site. We did and built our own Teddy Borg on *The Screen Savers*, `techtv.com/screensavers/showtell/story/0,24330,3375352,00.html`.

We Made Out in a Tree and This Old Guy Sat and Watched Us (`wemadeoutinatreeandthisoldguysatandwatchedus.com`) Okay, not such a vanilla name, but a very vanilla site dedicated to people who abuse the English language. As a former English major myself, it made me laugh until I cried. Don't miss the tech support email.

Free Networks.org (`freenetworks.org`) Looking for some 802.11? FreeNetworks.org is dedicated to people creating autonomous wireless networks all over the world, but mainly in the U.S. Take a look at FreeNetwork WIKI, a collaborative Web site where anyone can add information about wireless networks they know about.

TIP OF THE DAY On most Web pages, you can increase the type size using the View menu. But some pages try to prevent font resizing for aesthetic purposes. You can override these restrictions by following these steps on Microsoft's Internet Explorer:

1. Open the **Tools** menu.
2. Choose **Internet Options**.
3. Select the **Accessibility** box at the bottom of the window.
4. Check **Ignore Font Sizes Specified on Web Pages**.

To change font styles at will, check **Ignore Font Styles Specified on Web Pages**, too.

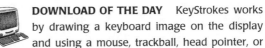**DOWNLOAD OF THE DAY** KeyStrokes works by drawing a keyboard image on the display and using a mouse, trackball, head pointer, or other mouse emulator to type characters into any standard Macintosh application. Free for 15 days, $45 to buy, for Macintosh, from `assistiveware.com`.

TODAY'S FOCUS: Tax Advice

TITANIC SINKS

The "unsinkable" ocean liner went down on this day in 1912 after hitting an iceberg. The ship's distress call was picked up by radio pioneer David Sarnoff. The future NBC founder and RCA president was working as an operator at the world's most powerful radio telegraph station on top of Wannamaker's department store in New York City. Sarnoff exchanged transmissions with the *Titanic* for 72 hours until the vessel sank.

Related Web site `titanic1.org`

Deduct Your PC

Your personal computer might be tax deductible under certain circumstances.

- The business portion of your home computer and peripheral equipment are deductible on Schedule C if you have a sole proprietorship.
- If you buy a computer to use for your job, you can deduct the business portion of the purchase price as a job expense if the computer was purchased as a condition of your employment and for the convenience of your employer.
- If you buy a computer to manage your investments, you can deduct the expense as a miscellaneous itemized deduction.

You may deduct only the portion of the computer related to business, your job, or investments.

Normally, depreciation, whether all at once or over a recovery period, would be reported on Form 4562, `www.irs.gov/pub/irs-pdf/f4562.pdf`, Depreciation and Amortization, Part V. The normal depreciation period is five years. However, if the computer is used more than 50% for business, you also might have an option to expense the business portion in a single year using a section 179 deduction, Form 4562 Parts I and V. Your taxable income must be at least as great as the deduction claimed. Dollar limits and investment limits also apply. For more information on depreciation, refer to Publication 946, `www.irs.gov/pub/irs-pdf/p946.pdf`, How to Depreciate Property.

As always, consult a tax professional or the IRS before claiming any deduction.

Helpful Links
- IRS publication #583—starting a business and keeping records `www.irs.ustreas.gov/prod/forms_pubs/pubs/p583toc.htm`
- IRS publications index `www.irs.ustreas.gov/prod/forms_pubs/pubs/index.htm`

- The Digital Daily—daily tax publication `www.irs.ustreas.gov/prod/cover.html`
- IRS gateway to state tax forms `www.irs.ustreas.gov/prod/forms_pubs/ftaframes.html`

TIP OF THE DAY   Donate your old computer and peripherals to a nonprofit recycling organization and reap a healthy tax deduction. Even if you can't use the stuff, there are thousands of schools, families, and educational programs that can.

Three types of groups will take your computer:

Nonprofit Charitable Programs The Computer Recycling Center `crc.org`) is a good example. Its goal is to keep as much junk out of the landfills as possible. It also reuses parts, and its computers and education program donates systems to schools and community programs. There are locations throughout North America.

For-Profit Companies and Individuals These will take your computer and sell it for as much as possible. There is no tax-deductible receipt.

Local Schools, Churches, and Community Programs These usually can give you a tax-deductible thank-you letter. Sometimes they have levels of machines they will accept and nothing less than those. They might not be capable of taking what they can't use.

Yahoo! maintains a list of charitable computer recycling organizations at `dir.yahoo.com/Business_and_Economy/Business_to_Business/Computers/Services/Disposal/Charitable_Organizations/`.

DOWNLOAD OF THE DAY Get free tax-preparation software right now from `taxact.com`. You can also complete and file your return on the Web for $7.95.

TODAY'S FOCUS: Tax Advice

GENERAL ELECTRIC FORMED

The Thomson-Houston Electric Company merged with Edison General Electric to form the General Electric Company on this day in 1892. Prior to the deal, British Thomas-Houston was one of the largest lighting equipment makers in the world. Today, GE makes everything from light bulbs to aircraft engines.

Related Web site   `ge.com`

Tax Help Online

By Adam Samuels

First Stop: The Catchall Sites Intuit's popular Quicken.com Tax Center, `quicken.com/taxes`, is a one-stop shop for tax advice. If you need help adjusting to the changes this tax season, it can assist you step by step through the filing process. It has advice on tax deductions, mutual funds, and even simplifying taxes for next year. You'll also find information on tax issues as they relate to investing, retirement, and education.

Among the collections of tax-related Web sites, you can't go wrong with the Essential Links Taxes page from Essentix, `el.com/elinks/taxes`. This page is a rich source of tax resources. You can link to a variety of sites and download tax forms, find detailed tax information, or identify books, magazines, and newsletters to assist you. What's more, it has listings to guide you to online newsgroups and tax-related message boards, as well as professional tax preparers.

Log On to the IRS The IRS offers an accessible Web site that's nearly, well, friendly in its presentation. Its Digital Daily page, `www.irs.gov`, offers a warm welcome to visitors, and it directs readers to areas for small businesses, electronic filing services, and more. Don't be shocked if you find yourself smiling.

Crunch the Numbers Financial calculators are definitely one of the Web's killer apps. When it comes to filing your taxes, there's no shortage of tools for crunching the numbers.

H&R Block has a tax outlook calculator, `hrblock.com/taxes/tools/taxcal.html`, to help you see whether there's hope for you this year and for the next 10. The site also offers summary information on tax changes and an office locator if you feel you're in need of some face-to-face assistance.

Have a refund coming your way? Congratulations! In years past, early filers collected an average refund of $1,823. That's money to keep in your account, not in the IRS' coffers. Be sure to use the IRS' W-4 Calculator, `www.irs.gov/faqs/display/0,,i1%3D54%26genericId%3D14807,00.html`, so you, not the government, can keep the interest on that money next year.

Plan for Next Year Ready to start planning for next year? At Microsoft's MoneyCentral (`moneycentral.msn.com/tax/home.asp`), you'll find tools that test your Tax IQ, estimate your taxes, and look for ways to reduce your taxes by finding possible tax deductions.

TIP OF THE DAY You can download tax forms from the IRS site (`www.irs.gov`) and print them using Adobe Acrobat Reader (free from `adobe.com`) but be careful. According to the IRS, forms printed on a laser or inkjet are acceptable, but not on a dot-matrix printer.

Machine-readable forms, including W-2, W-3, 1096, 1098, 1099 series, 5498, and W-2G may not be printed out at home. They must be printed using special paper, special inks, and within precise specifications. You'll have to head to the Post Office for copies of those forms.

DOWNLOAD OF THE DAY Prepare your taxes online (or download the forms for privacy) free at YourPace, `www.yourpace.com/productPage.jsp?category=2:Tax`.

TODAY'S FOCUS: Easter Eggs

FIRST WOMAN TO FLY ACROSS ENGLISH CHANNEL

Harriet Quimby became the first female pilot to cross the English Channel on this day in 1912. The 37-year-old flew in her 50-horsepower monoplane on its maiden voyage between Dover, England, and Calais, France. But her accomplishment did not draw the attention it deserved—the *Titanic* disaster had struck only two days before. Quimby died in an aviation accident less than three months later.

Related Web site `harrietquimby.org`

PC Easter Eggs

An *Easter egg* is an entertaining hidden feature or function within a software application. Easter eggs are created by developers or programmers who want to leave behind a personal calling card in their work. Because Easter eggs are hidden, people often don't know about them, even if they've been working with a particular application for years. In honor of Easter, I've compiled some of my favorite Easter eggs in the next few pages. Enjoy!

Flash 5.0   Goldrush game in Flash 5.0
1. Open Flash 5.
2. Choose **Help**, and then **About**.
3. Click the **Macromedia** logo before the animation stops playing.
4. Click **Thanks**.
5. Play the Goldrush game.

IE 5 Options
1. Open IE5.
2. From the menu, select **Tools**, **Internet Options**.
3. On the **General** tab, choose **Languages**.
4. Click **Add**.
5. Type `ie-ee` and click **OK**.
6. Move **User Defined [ie-ee]** to the TOP of the list.
7. Exit the menu so you can browse in IE5 again.
8. Click the **Search** icon to pull up the side search menu.
9. Laugh at the new options.
10. Select **Previous Searches**.

When you get to the Search menu, click **Customize** to get another egg.

Photoshop 5
1. Hold the Alt key while you open the About Photoshop option.
2. The usual Electric Cat screen appears. But wait!
3. Wait several seconds for the credits to begin scrolling.
4. Press the Alt key to speed them up.
5. While they're speeding, click the big eye once.
6. Keep holding the Alt key and press the Ctrl key.
7. Now, let up on the Alt key.
8. About 60 secret messages will pop up just above the scrolling credits.

TIP OF THE DAY   Our favorite Palm OS Easter egg: You first need to activate the Easter egg in the Palm OS:
1. In the Application Launcher, tap in the upper-right menu and select **System**.
2. Tap on **Prefs**.
3. In the lower-right side of the screen, draw a little clockwise circle. If you do it correctly, a little Easter egg should appear. To remove it, simply draw a counterclockwise circle around the egg.

Now for the fun part.
1. Switch to Memo Pad.
2. Hold down the Scroll down button.
3. While keeping the button pressed, draw a line from the middle of the Graffiti area to the left edge of the case. The line should go between the two silkscreen icons. If you do this correctly, a little car should drive by the screen.

 DOWNLOAD OF THE DAY   Picture fonts are called *dingbats*. Windows comes with one called Wingdings. But why stop there? Visit the Dingbat pages, `www.dingbatpages.com`, for thousands of symbol fonts for Windows. There's also information on the page for Mac users who want to convert the fonts to Macintosh format.

TODAY'S FOCUS: Easter Eggs

ENCRYPTION EXPORT RESTRICTIONS OVERTURNED

A federal judge ruled that laws restricting the export of encryption software were unconstitutional on this day in 1996. A UC Berkeley student sued the U.S. government for prohibiting him from posting his encryption code on the Internet. The government had previously banned the export of strong encryption codes in fear they could be used by terrorists. In the case, the judge ruled that computer code qualifies as "speech" protected by the First Amendment.

Related Web site `csrc.nist.gov`

Excel Easter Eggs

Spreadsheets are not normally considered the most exciting of programs, but there's a long tradition of elaborate Easter eggs in Microsoft Excel. Here's a retrospective.

Excel 95—Hall of Tortured Souls
1. Open a blank worksheet.
2. Select row 95.
3. Press Tab once to move to column B.
4. Select **Help**, then **About Microsoft Excel** from the main menu.
5. Hold down Ctrl+Alt+Shift while you click the **Tech Support** button.
6. A window called Hall of Tortured Souls appears. Use the cursor keys to move around.
7. Go on a quest for pictures of the Excel developers by turning your virtual self around 180 degrees and going down the stairs. Type `excelkfa`, and the wall disappears, revealing a narrow walkway that leads to a quest.

Excel 97—Flight Simulator
1. On a new Worksheet, Press F5.
2. Type **X97:L97** and press Enter.
3. Press the Tab key.
4. Hold Ctrl+Shift.
5. Click the **Chart Wizard** toolbar button.

Use the mouse to fly around. Right-click to move forward and left-click to move in reverse.

Excel 2000—Spy Hunter Clone
1. Open Excel 2000.
2. Choose **File**, **Save As Web Page**, **Publish Sheet**, and **Add Interactivity**.
3. Save to a .htm page on your drive.
4. Load the .htm page with IE. You should have Excel in the middle of the page.
5. Scroll to row 2000, column WC by selecting row 2000 and tabbing so that WC is the active column.
6. Hold down Shift+Ctrl+Alt and click the Office logo in the upper-left corner.

Use the arrow keys to drive, the spacebar to fire, and O to drop oil slicks. When it gets dark, use H for your headlights.

Developer's Credits
1. Open Excel.
2. Create a new spreadsheet.
3. Press F5 (the Go To function).
4. Type **X2000:L2000** in the reference box, and click OK.
5. Press Tab. You should now be at cell M2000.
6. Hold Ctrl+Shift down, and while holding them down click the mouse on Chart Wizard.
7. Exit by pressing Esc.

Unfortunately, Microsoft seems to have put the kibosh on Easter eggs. No one has found one in Excel 2002. Yet.

TIP OF THE DAY   Want more? Here are two great Easter egg sites:

The Easter Egg Archive: `eeggs.com`

Egg Heaven 2000: `eggheaven2000.com`

DOWNLOAD OF THE DAY   One of my favorite puzzle games is Diamond Mine, an online game from `popcap.com`. Your goal is to rearrange jewels to form lines of three or more. It's every bit as addictive as Tetris. Download a copy and prepare to do nothing else for the rest of the day.

Windows: `popcap.com/bejeweled.php`

Mac OS X: `homepage.mac.com/aegidian/jeweltoy`

Palm: `astraware.com/palm/bejeweled`

PocketPC: `astraware.com/ppc/mine`

POLL: Should your tax dollars go to educate fish?

16% Yes   84% No

TODAY'S FOCUS: Easter Eggs

LAST 680X0 CHIP ANNOUNCED

Motorola unveiled its new 68060 microprocessor on this day in 1994. The 32-bit chip was the last successor to the 68040, and was intended more for embedded systems such as networking applications instead of for personal computers. At the time, the 68060 was the highest-performance processor in the family, two to three times faster than the 68040. Apple had already stopped using the classic Motorola chips in its Macintosh models in favor of the PowerPC chips, made jointly by Motorola and IBM.

Related Web site   `www.motorola.com`

APRIL 18

Video Game Easter Eggs

Adventure (Atari 2600)   This might be the Easter egg that started it all. Atari was notorious for downplaying its programmers, so the developer of Adventure, Warren Robinette, added some secret code crediting the development team.

To find it, first you'll need to acquire the bridge, and then find the room that makes the screen flicker even when there is nothing in it. Use the bridge to get to the chamber in the middle of that room. Inside this room, you will see a dot. Take the dot back to the main room. Bringing the dot will make one of the walls disappear. In the new room, you will see the game's credits.

***Star Wars Episode I*: Star Fighter (PS2)**   To view a gallery of images from LucasArts' game Outlaws, start the first mission and quickly turn your ship around. Boost down the canyon. When you see a blue wall, go through it and you will end up in the gallery.

Perfect Dark (N64)   Want to play as a video-game god? Start up a multiplayer game and select a character body you want to play. Then, press up on the directional pad and select a head. The Asian-looking male head is that of Mario's and Link's creator, Shigeru Miyamoto.

Banjo Kazooie (N64)   If you look at the portrait of Bottles the Mole at the beginning of the game, you get an extra jigsaw puzzle game. Solving these puzzles will earn you extra cheats for the game.

Total Annihilation (PC)   You can make your units sing with this egg. Press Enter while in a game and type **#sing** to get your unit's vocal chords working.

Black and White (PC)   After you receive your leashes, attach one to your creature and move your mouse in the following pattern: down, right, up, right, and then down.

It might take a few times to master. After you get it, you will hear the adviser say, "Oooh goody, you've activated a hidden script." A telephone will appear at the end of the longest peninsula. Click to answer the phone a few times, and five more phones will appear. The phone plays messages from Lionhead's development team as well as random answering machine messages.

***Star Wars Episode I*: Battle for Naboo**   One of the coolest Easter eggs ever. Activate the developer's commentary as you play by going to the options screen and then go to **Passcodes**. Enter **Talktome** in the field.

 TIP OF THE DAY   Learn everything you ever wanted to know about your favorite console game, and more, at `gamefaqs.com`.

 DOWNLOAD OF THE DAY   Play Atari 2600 games on your computer with Stella. Free for Mac, Windows, and BeOS from Atariland, `atariland.com/techtv.cfm`.

TODAY'S FOCUS: Easter Eggs

DISCOVERER OF PLUTONIUM BORN

Physicist Glenn Theodore Seaborg was born in Michigan on this day in 1912. Seaborg isolated many of the unstable radioactive "transuranic" elements (elements beyond uranium on the periodic table). The Nobel laureate and his colleagues identified plutonium in 1940. His research was kept hush-hush because of the element's potential for nuclear fission. But plutonium's secret was not kept for long—it was used in the atomic bomb dropped on Nagasaki in 1945.

Related Web site www.lbl.gov/seaborg

How to Find DVD Easter Eggs

By Chris Carle

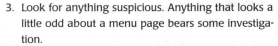

1. Watch the color bars. Often, studios hide their eggs in seldom-watched portions of the DVD, such as the color bar calibration screen.
2. Move around using your arrow buttons. Use the arrow keys on your DVD remote to search for hidden selections in the menus.
3. Look for anything suspicious. Anything that looks a little odd about a menu page bears some investigation.
4. Buy the special edition. You're about 10 times as likely to get eggs out of a special edition, simply because more goes into the making of these DVDs.
5. Search the Web for DVD Easter egg information. Try codes.ign.com, dvdeastereggs.com, and dvdreview.com/html/hidden_features.shtml.

(Chris Carle is the editor-in-chief of IGN Codes and Guides.)

the THX logo just highlighted. Then press 3, wait another second until the screen resets. Then press 8, at which point the documentary will run automatically.

The Matrix—From the disc's main menu, go to the Special Features, and then select The Dream World. Apart from the text menu entries, you will also see a red pill. Select it, and you'll uncover the "What Is Bullet Time?" documentary. Also in the Special Features section, go to Cast & Crew Bios, and then select the Wachowski Brothers. This will bring up another red pill. Select it, and it takes you to a 12-minute documentary called, "What Is Concept?"

Harry Potter and the Sorcerer's Stone—On the Opening screen on Disc two, select Diagon Alley, and tap the bricks until it lets you in. Select the Gringotts sign, press down to select the key symbol, and click to go into Gringotts. You now have money with which to buy a wand. Go to Ollivander's and choose your wand. Third time's the charm. Go back to the main screen and go into the classrooms for lessons. Click the "H" in the middle of the screen. At Fluffy, select the Flute and click. At the keys, select the silver one in the middle with a bent wing. At the bottles, select the round one with the yellow liquid. Select the red stone in the mirror to get to a list of seven deleted scenes.

DOWNLOAD OF THE DAY Windows Media Player can play back DVD on your DVD-ROM—equipped Windows XP machine, but the best DVD playback software for XP is CyberLink PowerDVD XP. Download a limited trial version from www.gocyberlink.com. $49 to buy.

TIP OF THE DAY Here are three of my favorites:

Star Wars: Episode I—Disc one contains a hilarious two-minute gag reel, outtakes, and DVD Credits presentation. This little egg alone is almost worth the price of the set. Click on the Options menu, and then highlight the THX logo. Key 11, and then wait a second or so. The screen then resets with the Lucasfilm logo just above

TODAY'S FOCUS: Easter Eggs

FIRST COMMERCIAL USE OF FORTRAN

The Westinghouse-Bettis nuclear power plant became the first commercial users of the computer language FORTRAN on this day in 1957. According to the story, "Formula Translation" was delivered to programmers at the plant in an unlabeled cardboard box, and without any instructions. When researchers fed the punch cards to their mainframe computer, the program began working right away. FORTRAN was created by IBM's John Backus and was the first widely used high-level computer language.

Related Web site   `fortranlib.com`

Twisted List: Top Five Free Demos

By Megan Morrone

I know I'm always going on and on about the free stuff, but the truth is, I'm all about paying for good software, as long as I can try before I buy. Here are my top five favorite free demos of expensive software.

Paint Shop Pro (`jasc.com`)   I find this graphics program to be a little bit easier to use than Photoshop. This software costs around $100, but you can test a full version for free for 30 days. You might also want to try the Ulead PhotoImpact demo. It's Leo's favorite and just $89 to buy. Free 30-day demo at `www.ulead.com/pi/trial.htm`.

The Coldstone Game Engine for Mac (`www.ambrosiasw.com/games/coldstone`) If you're serious about making your own games for the Mac or PC, you can buy this software for around $50. To get started right away, download the demo for free.

Cool Edit Pro (`syntrillium.com/cep/`) The current version of this music-editing software will run you around $400. The free version has all the features. The only drawbacks are that you can't save your work and you're limited to 30-minute sessions.

Dreamweaver (`macromedia.com/dreamweaver`) The ultimate Web design software costs $300, but you can try it free for 30 days. Well worth it.

Max Payne (`3drealms.com/max/downloads.html`) This violent but exceedingly popular game will take a $50 bite out of your lunch money. If you're not sure you're going to like it, try the demo first. It's a huge download, so if you don't have broadband, beware.

TIP OF THE DAY   When your Windows 98 Start menu is full, you get scrolling arrows on the top and bottom of the menu that allow you to see more of your programs. Personally, I prefer the way Windows 95 handled the too-many-programs-too-little-space conundrum: The Start menu expanded into multiple columns. Here are the instructions for the Registry edit that can take your Windows 98 Start menu all the way back to 1995.

Run REGEDIT (**Start**, **Run**, **REGEDIT**). Find the following key: `HKEY_Local_MACHINE/Software/Microsoft/Windows/CurrentVersion/explorer`. In the Explorer folder, click the **Advanced** folder once to select it. Right-click an unoccupied area in the right pane. Click **New**, **String Value**. In the name box that appears, type **StartMenuScrollPrograms** (all one word), and then press Enter. Right-click the name you just created, and then click **Modify**. In the **Value Data** box, type **FALSE**, and then click **OK**. Exit REGEDIT.

The change should take place immediately. To reverse it, just delete the key you added. Be careful, and remember to back up your Registry before you begin. It's an easy precaution to prevent a hosed PC.

DOWNLOAD OF THE DAY   Looking for Easter graphics for your Web site or greeting cards? Find a bunch at `freegraphics.com/holidayjumps/easter.html`.

TODAY'S FOCUS: Gaming

BORLAND, WORDPERFECT FAIL TO BEAT MICROSOFT OFFICE

Borland International and WordPerfect teamed up to create a suite of office applications to compete with Microsoft Office on this day in 1993. Both companies had struggled against the Seattle-based software giant, and the new partnership didn't solve any problems. Novell purchased both WordPerfect and Borland's Quattro Pro spreadsheet less than a year later, and Corel bought the programs from Novell in 1996.

Related Web site   corel.com

Fast and Smooth Gaming

By Mike Street

For the smoothest 3D gaming, increase the frame rate. Today's high-end video cards can maximize frames-per-second (FPS) without sacrificing visual quality. But if you didn't spend $400 for your video card, you might have to make some sacrifices to get the highest FPS. Here are some in-game settings to play with. Change one at a time to see which gives you the most benefit at the least cost.

- **Color Depth**—Older video cards usually perform poorly rendering in 32-bit color. If your video card has less than 32MB of memory, change your game settings to 16-bit color.
- **Screen Resolution**—High resolutions (for example, 1600×1200) are much more taxing on your video hardware. Try each resolution setting, and find a balance between frame rate and image quality.
- **Transform and Lighting**—If your video card has a hardware T&L engine, enable the **Use T&L Hardware** setting in your 3D games. This frees your CPU for other game computation.
- **Vsync**—A game's frame rate is throttled by your monitor's refresh rate when Vsync is enabled. Turn it off to let your frame rates fly. Reenable Vsync if you see any onscreen tearing artifacts.
- **Double/Triple Frame Buffering**—All current 3D video cards can *double buffer* a scene—one frame is displayed while the next frame is rendered. If you own a newer card, turn on triple buffering, which displays one frame while rendering the next two.
- **Bilinear/Trilinear/Anisotropic Filtering**—Filtering blends adjacent game textures and makes them look realistic when viewed at off angles. Bilinear filtering gives a minor performance hit. Trilinear filtering looks better. Anisotropic looks great but can clobber frame rates.

- **Full-Screen Antialiasing (FSAA)**—Gamers hate jaggies—the "stairstepped" look of straight-edged 3D objects. FSAA cures the jaggies with some fancy math, but it's quite hardware intensive. Experiment with the FSAA settings to balance speed and looks.
- **Fog**—If your system bogs down when many 3D objects are onscreen at once, increase the game's fog setting. You won't see as far in the 3D world, and distant objects might suddenly reveal themselves, but more fog usually helps your FPS remain constant.
- **Shadows**—Generating 3D object shadows is very demanding on your video card and CPU. To help cure your system's hiccuping frame rate, turn off in-game object shadows.

Good luck, and may the fastest machine win!

 TIP OF THE DAY   Upgrading your video drivers often can improve performance and reliability. Check your manufacturer's Web site for the latest version. For help finding that driver, visit drivershq.com.

 DOWNLOAD OF THE DAY   These tiny Windows games won't challenge your video card, but they might tax your vision. Free from www.tinywindowsgames.com/tiny.

POLL: Have video games reduced violent crime?

59% Yes

41% No

TODAY'S FOCUS: Gaming

RECHARGEABLE BATTERY INVENTOR BORN

Raimond Louis Gaston Planté was born in Orthez, France, on this day in 1834. In 1859, the chemist developed the lead-acid accumulator, which provides the large currents required for starting gas and diesel engines. He also invented the first rechargeable battery, which was made using a combination of lead plates and an acid bath. Most of today's car batteries still use this basic technology.

Related Web site rbrc.org

Upgrade Your PC

By Alex "Sharky" Ross

Face it, Bill. PCs are made for playing games. The push toward 2GHz+ processors isn't driven by the need to speed up Excel. When it comes to Office applications, even a 500MHz computer spends most of its time waiting for you. It's only when you start playing complex 3D games that you really tax your hardware. Those 2.2GHz processors with 55 million transistors manufactured on a 0.13-micron process are built to play games, baby. But having a fast CPU isn't where it ends.

If you already own a 1GHz or faster CPU from either AMD or Intel, you're halfway to being able to sample the delights of 3D gaming. But you still need to add one necessary component to your system: a high-end 3D accelerated video card.

You can get a video card that will run all of today's games at more than acceptable frame rates for less than $200. Shop around on pricewatch.com for a card based on the nVidia GeForce 4MX chipset or 8500 LE-based video card from ATI.

If you're the sort for whom only the best will do, look for a card that can take advantage of DirectX 8 pixel and vertex shading effects. For that, you'll pay. The top-of-the-line nVidia GeForce 4 Ti-based cards will run upward of $400. For a little less, you can get one of ATI's excellent Radeon 8500 cards.

Before you buy a card, read the reviews. The following sites keep up with the latest technology and can give you an excellent idea of which cards lead the pack.

HardOCP (hardocp.com) Kyle Bennett's site reviews all kinds of hardware. For the latest on video cards, including which drivers perform the best, click on the **Reviews** link to the left.

AnandTech (anandtech.com) Anand Lal Shimpi founded this site in 1997 when he was still in high school. Don't be fooled by his age—this is one of the most professional hardware review sites online. Regular market updates will keep you up to date on which cards lead the pack.

SharkyExtreme.com (sharkyextreme.com) Check the weekly CPU and RAM prices, as well as video card reviews.

(Alex "Sharky" Ross is the founder of sharkyextreme.com and a columnist for Computer Power User.)

 TIP OF THE DAY In theory, you should be able to get the same performance playing network games with either a wireless or hard-wired network. However, WiFi will slow down as you get farther from the base station. In addition, a limited number of frequencies are available, which means you might see latency increase if you have more than three players sharing the network at the same time.

DOWNLOAD OF THE DAY Play billiards online at Candystand, candystand.com. Practice your shots for real life at www.masterbilliards.com/tips-tricks.htm.

TODAY'S FOCUS: Gaming

IBM KIDS' COMPUTER HITS SHELVES

IBM and Rubbermaid's toy division Little Tikes demonstrated one of the first computers just for children on this day in 1998. The multicolored "Young Explorer" came with a CD-ROM drive, 16MB RAM, a 2GB hard drive, and a whopping $2,399 price tag.

Related Web site `littletikes.com`

Keys to Good Game Design

By American McGee

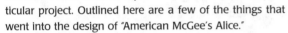

Every game designer approaches his or her job differently. Each design stands alone to address the wants and needs of a particular project. Outlined here are a few of the things that went into the design of "American McGee's Alice."

Story   The idea to make a game based on the fiction of Lewis Carroll was born out of my frustrations with available storytelling action/adventure games on the market. Most seemed to rehash the same story, environments, and gameplay over and over again with only minor details and names changed. It's been space marine versus space monster with space gun since the days of Doom.

"Alice" was a chance to create a product that contained characters, environments, and story elements that were not only fresh and imaginative, but also existed outside the space-marine universe. All we needed to do was add a conflict to drive our story and the player's adventure through Wonderland.

It's important to make the conflict something people can easily understand. In our case, it was simple: Wonderland is being destroyed, and Alice must fight to save it. This conflict naturally grew from the idea that Alice had lost her mind due to the death of her parents. This causes Wonderland, which is inside Alice's head, to suffer.

Gameplay   Without gameplay, we've essentially created a new chapter in Alice's life, but not a game. The interaction with all these new elements must be challenging and entertaining enough to draw people into the fiction and keep them there.

One of the primary goals I had from the beginning of this project was to ensure that even novice players could make their way through Wonderland without too much frustration. Games should be more like toys and less like torture devices.

We came up with the following rules:

1. No jump in the game had to be made perfectly in order to avoid death.
2. No area in the game should kill an aware player without the player understanding why.

Simplicity   Einstein once said, "Make things as simple as possible, but not too simple." This statement is at the heart of many of the decisions that were made on the Alice project. The desire to overload a new game with features and technology can be alluring, but it's usually a trap.

First and foremost, focus on the key elements, story, gameplay, visuals, and sound.

(American McGee is creative director at Carbon6, `carbon6.com`*.)*

 TIP OF THE DAY   Looking for a favorite old game? Many sites preserve abandoned games online.

Try The Underdogs (`theunderdogs.org`) to track down some of the most popular abandonware titles.

The Abandonware Web ring (`abandonwarering.com`) maintains the master list of almost every abandonware site on the Internet.

 DOWNLOAD OF THE DAY   Relive the excitement of the Commodore 64 with the CCS64 emulator for Windows and Unix from `computerbrains.com`.

 Download a Commodore 64 Emulator for Mac from `emulation.net/c64`.

TODAY'S FOCUS: Gaming

FIRST SATELLITE TV SIGNAL

Television signals were relayed by satellite for the first time on this day in 1962. Scientists working for MIT and the U.S. Air Force successfully bounced microwaves off Echo I, a satellite NASA launched two years earlier. The signal was sent from an MIT lab in California and picked up nearly 3,000 miles away in Massachusetts.

Related Web site `howstuffworks.com/satellite-tv.htm`

PainStation

By Rick Lockridge, TechTV
New York Bureau Chief

Cologne, Germany—You think you're pretty tough, but can you handle the PainStation (`www.khm.de/~morawe/painstation/painstation_eng.html`)?

"Come on friend, don't be shy," says a deep voice.

The PainStation is mocking you already.

Standing there in the corner of an old pharmacy building on a nondescript side street, the gleaming 4-foot-tall console's menacing bass can be clearly heard over the chatter going on across the room, where the PainStation's two inventors are warming up with a few turns on the ancient video game, Pong.

"It's really about getting the body involved," Tilman Reiff says with a grin. Reiff is the software guy. His partner, Volcker Morawe, built the console—and the pain-infliction devices. "I was always interested to combine computers and the real world," Morawe says softly.

PainStation is a lot like Pong, but if your opponent knocks the ball past your paddle and hits one of the colored icons behind, you start to pile up punishment points. Lose enough icons and you will be burned, shocked, or whipped by a miniature weed whacker–like device.

For my opponent, Morawe and Reiff handpicked one of their friends who had never played the PainStation before. For the first few moments, neither of us could get the hang of our paddle knobs. My icons were taking a beating, but so were his. And the PainStation was starting to make some ominous noises.

The game heated up. The ball started moving faster. Out of the corner of my eye, I saw a few of my blue icons get hit. Then, all of a sudden, a sharp electrical jolt traveled up my hand and into my forearm. I jumped.

"Ho!" I say, surprised by the severity of the shock. A few seconds later, I felt a searing pain on my palm. Then the whipping started on the other side of my hand.

It seemed like it took forever, but finally the game ended. I'm sure I must have lost, but the score wasn't nearly as important as finishing with my hand still on the table. I felt triumphant. Reiff came over with a Band-Aid. It had "PainStation" imprinted on it.

"You would think that if you produce a game that causes pain, nobody would like to play it," Reiff says. "But people either love it or they hate it, and a lot of them love it."

For now, the two have no plans for mass producing the PainStation. Count yourself lucky.

TIP OF THE DAY   Use the source, Luke. These opensource gaming projects will show you how it's done.

- **FlightGear** (`flightgear.org`)—A cooperative flight simulator development project.
- **Crystal Space** (`crystal.sourceforge.net`)—Free and portable 3D game development kit.
- **QuakeForge** (`www.quakeforge.net/files.php`)—Graphics game engine based on Quake.

DOWNLOAD OF THE DAY   Windows gaming relies on the DirectX library. For best results, download the latest version, free from `microsoft.com/directx`.

TODAY'S FOCUS: Gaming

GUGLIELMO MARCONI BORN

The "father of radio" was born in Bologna, Italy, on this day in 1874. Marconi studied engineering in both Italy and England, and began experimenting at age 20 with radio devices based on the work of Heinrich Herz. In 1898, Marconi transmitted the first wireless telegraph signals across the Atlantic. Two years earlier, he had filed a patent for "improvements for the apparatus of wireless telegraphy," but it was later overturned based on previous work by other scientists, including Nicola Tesla. Marconi won the Nobel Prize for Physics in 1909.

Related Web site   www.marconicalling.com

Gaming and the Mac

By Ryan Vance

The latest Macs sport high-end video cards, much more powerful processors, and lots of RAM. Macintosh comes ready to play out of the box, and Apple hopes that software developers will deliver the games.

So far, so good. Marquee titles such as Black and White, Age of Empires 2, and Return to Castle Wolfenstein are finding their way to the Apple platform. Two of the top Mac publishers are Aspyr Media, www.aspyr.com, and MacPlay, www.macplay.com.

"Mac OS X is built on top of Unix," Mark Dochtermann of MacPlay said. "And because of this, it's got preemptive multitasking and multithreading. It's got all the programming that game developers have come to expect from a modern operating system."

"We're not trying to get every single game that's out there to come out for the Mac," Michael Rogers, president of Aspyr Media, said. "The market doesn't support it, and frankly there aren't always that many good games. So, we try to pick good games that give people value for their money and, of course, things that we think we could make money on."

Mac developers have one big advantage. They don't have to deal with the virtually infinite number of configurations that their PC counterparts face. "Every single Mac that has been shipped has been 3D accelerated and has literally been a self-contained console with a display," Dochtermann said.

"You have one company doing the operating system, and one company designing the hardware," Rogers said. "You know the sound card and all that other stuff has been integrated in. And we have Nvidia and ATI making graphic chips. So, we don't really have to deal with all the different possible configurations."

The Mac gaming market is unlikely to exceed the PC market, but owning a Mac doesn't have to leave you out of the gaming loop.

 TIP OF THE DAY   Apple's specs say that Mac OS X will run in 128MB of RAM, even though they have shipped it on machines with as little as 64MB. So, how much is enough? Mac OS X will run painfully slowly on any machine with less than 128MB. That's the minimum. If you use more than one program at a time, or keep the Classic environment running, 256MB is a more reasonable number. I use 384MB on most of my Macs and that's plenty. My one machine with 640MB doesn't seem particularly faster. Unless you do some pretty memory-intensive stuff, more than 512MB is overkill.

 DOWNLOAD OF THE DAY   The ultimate Asteroids clone runs on Mac, Windows, Linux, and BeOS. Maelstrom is free from devolution.com/~slouken/Maelstrom/binary.html.

TODAY'S FOCUS: Gaming

CHERNOBYL NUCLEAR DISASTER

The worst nuclear accident in history happened in Ukraine on this day in 1986. One of the plant's reactors exploded while workers were conducting safety tests. The Soviet government tried to cover up the details of the accident, but it was later found that employees had failed to follow basic safety rules, and that several fires had released huge quantities of radioactive material into the air. According to a major international conference on Chernobyl, 48 people died from the disaster between 1986 and 1996.

Related Web site   `chernobyl.com`

Online Gaming

By Alison Strahan

You don't have to spend thousands on the latest hardware to play games. There are plenty of wonderful games that will work on even the slowest machine. Here are some online diversions for the whole family.

InkLink (`shockwave.com/sw/content/inklink15`) This Pictionary clone is a really fun and a smart way to connect with people you're not able to visit over the holidays.

Gather in a room where you can join other online players in trying to guess one another's illustrations to win points. When your turn to draw rolls around, a set of rudimentary graphic tools appears along with the clue. I fell into hysterics as I tried to sketch a goat.

Watch out, this game is addictive.

Pogo (`pogo.com`)   Pogo is still going strong as an outlet for gamers of all ages and persuasions. Whether you want to hook up with friends to play cards or perhaps escape your family obligations for a few minutes, just pop into `pogo.com` and play a hand of euchre or hearts.

Try backgammon or dominoes, if you prefer. The atmosphere is generally friendly and forgiving if you're new at a game, although as in all online environments, guard your personal information and don't stand for any nonsense from rude players.

Some games don't even require a computer. (Shocking, but true.)

Family Fun's Game Finder (`family.go.com/ parties/birthday/tool/gamefinder_tlp/?clk= 1011865`)   This site from *Family Fun* magazine offers noncomputer games for every age, occasion, and location. Use the drop-down boxes to choose from indoor or outdoor games, or narrow your choice to games for certain age groups. You also can choose games suitable for various occasions and events, including Christmas, Hanukkah, and Halloween.

After you've selected a game, the site provides step-by-step instructions and a checklist of any objects needed to play the game.

 TIP OF THE DAY   You can't play games with a cluttered desktop. Windows XP's Desktop Cleanup Wizard to the rescue. Open the Display control panel (it's easiest to right-click on the desktop and select **Properties**). Click the **Desktop** tab. Click the **Customize Desktop** button. Click the **Clean Desktop Now** button at the button of the window. A wizard will run to guide you through the steps.

If you're the type that tends to let things go to the dogs, set the cleanup to occur automatically every 60 days. Now if it only were as easy to clean your room.

 DOWNLOAD OF THE DAY   Voice chat while you're gaming with Roger Wilco, free for Windows from `rogerwilco.gamespy.com`.

This program is simple to use and is compatible with almost all sound cards. Because it uses very little bandwidth, Roger Wilco will even work with a 28.8Kbps modem connection or better. You will be limited to 15 minutes chatting per session until you register with the Web site.

TODAY'S FOCUS: Gaming

MOUSE INTRODUCED

The Xerox STAR 8010, the first computer to hit the market equipped with a mouse, was released on this day in 1981. The STAR was the first PC to use a graphical user interface (GUI) and came with a mouse based on the original version developed in 1968 by Stanford Research Institute's Douglas Englebart. The machine took nine years and $50 million to complete and was far from a success—mostly due to its unreasonable $16,500 price tag. The mouse didn't hit mainstream personal computing until 1984, when Apple unveiled its first Macintosh.

Related Web site digibarn.com/collections/systems/xerox-8010

Twisted List: Frog Games

By Martin Sargent

3D Frogman (download.cnet.com/downloads/0-10036-100-903336.html?tag=st.dl.10001-103-1.lst-7-4.903336) The creators of 3D Frogman probably figured they had a surefire hit on their hands by combining the arcade classics Frogger and Pac-Man into one game. But after you play this game for a while, you realize there is no chance of a tabletop version ever showing up in your local Pizza Hut, and there will never be a 3D Frogman spinoff cartoon or breakfast cereal. Some people also claim the game adds spyware to your system, so if that worries you, skip it and move on to No. 4.

Fly Feastin' (www.froggyville.com/games.htm) In Fly Feastin', you sit on a lily pad and try to eat as many flies as possible.

But avoid the bee, which stings your stomach if you swallow it. But at least the bee dies, making the world a little bit safer. A little bit brighter. Kill all bees. President Bush, I implore you, kill all bees. If I have to take it up with Kofi Annan, I will.

Frogapult (www.froggyville.com/games.htm) In Frogapult, you need to catapult a frog onto a lily pad with just the right amount of force to keep the frog from being eaten by a piranha, an alligator, or a swamp bird of indeterminate species. This game is perfect for people who have only one working key on their keyboard, because all you have to do to play is hit a key when the catapult strength meter is in the right place. The argument that video games improve hand-eye coordination is not applicable here. This game improves no part of your mind or body.

Frogger (www.froggyville.com/games.htm) After spending an entire weekend cooped up in my darkened bedroom playing frog games, I've concluded that the best frog game in existence is still Frogger. Evidently, 1982 was the pinnacle of the frog video-game movement.

 TIP OF THE DAY Having a hard time coming up with a really cool name for your online gaming? Try the GameSpy Naminator, gamespy.com/naminator. It randomly generates names guaranteed to strike terror into the heart of your opponents. Or use the L33T version to show how kool you really are. (And the next time you face OutstandingWedgie beware. That's me.)

 DOWNLOAD OF THE DAY Speeding up the computer is not always the problem; sometimes, you have to slow it down. Old DOS-based games tend to fly at blinding speeds on new computers. Enter Mo'Slo, molasses for your PC, free to try and $15 to purchase from hpaa.com/moslo.

POLL: Why do you play video games?

5% Perfect score

2% Score rollover

4% Fame and money

73% Um, for fun?

17% Have no significant other

TODAY'S FOCUS: Customizing Your PC

FIRST TOURIST IN SPACE

Dennis Tito became the first person to pay to go into space on this day in 2001. The 60-year-old American gave the Russian Space Agency $20 million to ride in Soyuz TM to the International Space Station. In the 1960s, Tito helped design missions to Mars, and later worked at NASA's Jet Propulsion Laboratory. But his former employer was not pleased with his vacation plans—Tito was banned from venturing into any U.S. segments of the space station unescorted, and had to promise to pay for anything he might break while in space.

Related Web site space.com/dennistito

APRIL 28

Optimize the Windows XP Media Player

By Mike Street

Download the XP Media Player Bonus Pack (microsoft.com/windows/windowsmedia/download/bonuspack.asp) The bonus pack has extra visualizations and skins, an MP3-to-WMA file converter, a library management wizard, a Media Player tray control, and a utility to import your Media Player playlist into Microsoft Excel. It also comes with a little utility called the Most Recently Used Cleaner PowerToy. This feature enables you to clear out the entries of files you've recently launched with the Windows Media Player. It's a nice feature if you want to preserve your privacy.

Slip into a New Skin Bored with default blue and silver? Give Media Player a different skin and a new look. Click **Skin Chooser** in Media Player's taskbar. Scroll through the list of installed skins (or connect to the Internet and click the **More Skins** button). Select a skin, and then click the **Apply Skin** button.

Conserve Onscreen Real Estate Your monitor is only so big, and media player can take up a lot of room. To save space, click the **Auto Hide Menu Bar** button and the **Hide Taskbar** button.

Tweak Your Equalizer Click the **Show Equalizer** and **Settings**. In the settings area, click the drop-down menu button to change settings group. SRS WOW Effects add deep bass and dynamic range to audio. Adjust the TruBass and WOW Effect sliders to suit your speakers (and your ears). Select **Graphic Equalizer** to set Media Player's 10-band equalizer and balance controls.

Configure Your Player Media player has a wealth of options. Click **Tools** in Media Player's top menu, and then select **Options** from the drop-down list.

In the Options dialog box, click the **Player** tab. If your PC isn't always connected to the Internet, uncheck the boxes beside **Download Codecs Automatically** and **Start Player in Media Guide**. Prefer anonymity? Uncheck the **Allow Internet Sites to Uniquely Identify Your Player** box.

(Mike Street is a freelance writer for TechTV.)

 TIP OF THE DAY For better results when using Windows Media Player to play back Internet audio and video over a slow connection, increase the buffer time. Select **Options** from the **Tools** menu, click the **Performance** tab, and then increase the time for network buffering. The default is five seconds. Try ten seconds. Streaming media will take longer to start, but it is less likely to get interrupted after it does.

 DOWNLOAD OF THE DAY The ultimate Windows skinning program is WindowsBlinds, part of the ObjectDesktop at stardock.com. WindowsBlinds is $19.95. The full ObjectDesktop is $49.95.

POLL: What would you give to go into space?

14% A bodily organ

12% Life savings

49% $39.95 (plus tax)

25% I'm already there, man

TODAY'S FOCUS: Customizing Your PC

ZIPPER PATENTED

Gideon Sundback of Hoboken, New Jersey, patented the "separable fastener" on this day in 1913. Zippers were originally used only on rubber boots—the word *zipper* was coined by B.F. Goodrich in 1923, whose company sold rubber galoshes equipped with the device. Goodrich reportedly came up with the name because he liked the "zipping sound" they made when opening and closing. In 1930, fashion designer Elsa Schiaparelli became the first to use zippers on clothing.

Related Web site   `inventors.about.com/library/weekly/aa082497.htm`

Cool Screensavers

By Megan Morrone

Screensavers were invented to prevent fixed images from getting burned into monitors. That's not really a problem with today's displays, but screensavers are here to stay. Here are some of our favorite freebies—all for Windows.

United Devices Cure for Cancer (ud.com/download) Intel has teamed up with the National Cancer Foundation and the University of Oxford to develop a distributed computing project that helps find a cure for cancer. Distributed computing basically uses your idle CPU cycles for another purpose. In this instance, those cycles are used to test proteins that are possible targets for cancer therapy.

Drempels (geisswerks.com/drempels) This soothing, psychedelic app forms elaborate and colorful patterns as your screensaver. You can also run it straight from your desktop while you work. Press the spacebar to change the pattern. From the maker of the Winamp visualizations plug-in, Geiss.

EPrompter (eprompter.com) If customizing your PC isn't enough of a reason for you to download a screensaver, you might want to try ePrompter. Configure it to check all your different email addresses, and when the screensaver activates, it will display bouncing balls that let you know how many unread emails you have in each of your accounts.

American Flag Screen Saver (risoftsystems.com/store/flag.asp) Show your patriotism on your desktop.

Static TV (isotope244.com/ss.html) If you like TV static, you'll love Static TV. This screensaver turns your computer into a television in need of tuning. It's sure to confuse your co-workers passing by your cube.

Mike Lin's Binary (www.mlin.net/Binary.shtml) You've seen those Matrix screensavers before. They're cool, but do they do DNA sequencing? Binary is a little app developed by programming wunderkind Mike Lin. It will fill your screen with scrolling green ones and zeros or letters of the genetic alphabet (C, G, A, T) to represent DNA sequencing.

DeskSwap (deskswap.com) This little app is a screensaver and a lesson in privacy all rolled up into one. When the DeskSwap screensaver activates, it takes a picture of your desktop. It then shares that picture with everyone else on the DeskSwap network. The creators intended this as a way of showing people how peer-to-peer services such as Napster allow other users to view all your personal files. If you don't care about your privacy and you're into voyeurism, this screensaver is a keeper.

  TIP OF THE DAY   You can never have too many fonts. 1001 Fonts has a font for every need. TrueType and PostScript fonts for both Windows and Macintosh and all free at 1001fonts.com.

 DOWNLOAD OF THE DAY   Change your desktop every 30 minutes using gorgeous photos from Webshots. Free for Windows from webshots.com. Turn on the calendar feature to embed a calendar in the wallpaper.

TODAY'S FOCUS: Customizing Your PC

WWW FREED

The European Organization for Nuclear Research (CERN) announced on this day in 1992 that World Wide Web technology would be free to anyone. The WWW was developed by Tim Berners-Lee (not Al Gore), a British computer scientist at CERN who wrote the first Web client (browser-editor) and server in 1990. Like the technology itself, the first browser was also called WorldWideWeb, but was later renamed Nexus to avoid confusion.

Related Web site   `www.w3.org`

Creating Winamp Skins

By Matthew Stephens

Creating a new look for a program is called *skinning*. The Winamp MP3 player is one popular place for skin artists to express themselves. Hundreds of people have created skins, many of them are available at `winamp.com/skins`. Here's how you can create one of your own.

Skins for Winamp consist of multiple image files. The easiest way to create a new skin is to start with an existing one. Winamp skins are stored in a Skins folder inside the Winamp program folder. Even though skins have the .WSZ file extension, they're really just zip files. Make a copy of one, rename it MYSKIN.ZIP, and then unzip it into a folder with WinZip (`winzip.com`) or a similar program.

Use any drawing program to make a broad, blanket image of how you want the skin to look and feel. This is the largest part of the skin, but also the easiest. I usually start off with the base skin and add detailed buttons and colors later.

Take your base image and make it work with each of the smaller components. Start by creating the buttons as they look when they are clicked.

Now you must make the parts work together as a skin. This is usually done by copying parts of the skin and pasting them over the main skin. I suggest you use a template to make this part easier. We've got one for you at www.deviantart.com/deviation.php?id=189234.

The config files are easy and take little time. Pledit.txt contains the colors for your playlist. Use HEX numbers as you would in HTML. Viscolor.txt is the file that sets the colors for the Visualization panel. It contains 24 lines. Each line is an RGB value followed by a comment. Readme.txt is basically the information that comes up when you select the skin in the setup window.

When your skin is complete, Zip up all the images and rename the Zip file **yourskinname.wsz**. For more information, visit Winamp's own skinning tutorial at `winamp.com/nsdn/winamp2x/dev/skins`.

(Matthew Stephens, `matteo.deviantart.com`, is the co-founder of deviantart.com, an online forum for graphical artists to display their creations for feedback and exposure.)

TIP OF THE DAY   Change the size of your desktop icons in Windows XP by opening the Display control panel, clicking the **Appearance** tab, clicking the **Advanced** button, and selecting **Icon** from the **Item:** list. Choose the size you want on the right, and then click **OK**.

On Mac OS X, select **Show View Options** from the Finder's **View** menu and use the slider to change the icon size on the desktop. To change the size of icons in folders, open a folder first. To make the size apply to all folders, select **Global**.

DOWNLOAD OF THE DAY   Use Internet Explorer Personalizer to customize your browser. Free from `accesscodes.hypermart.net/product01_dl.html`.

MAY 2003

MAY 2003

SUNDAY	MONDAY	TUESDAY	WEDNESDAY	THURSDAY	FRIDAY	SATURDAY
				1 Space Day	**2**	**3**
4	**5**	**6** TechTV cable network launches (1997)	**7**	**8**	**9**	**10**
11 Mother's Day	**12**	**13**	**14** George Lucas born (1944)	**15** E3 Begins (Los Angeles, California)	**16**	**17**
18 Mount St. Helen's eruption (1980)	**19**	**20** International WWW Conference (Budapest, Hungary)	**21** Amelia Earhart flies across Atlantic Ocean (1932)	**22** Unmanned mission to Mars scheduled 2003; Windows 3.0 released (1990)	**23**	**24**
25	**26** *Star Wars* released (1977); Memorial Day	**27**	**28**	**29**	**30**	**31**

TODAY'S FOCUS: Customizing Your PC

BASIC DEBUTS

The BASIC computer language was first run on a computer on this day in 1964. The "Beginner's All-purpose Symbolic Instruction Code" was developed by Dartmouth professors John George Kemeny and Thomas Eugene Kurtz. Because they never patented BASIC, different versions of the languages spread quickly. Today, BASIC's popularity has waned, but it's still the first computer language studied by many aspiring programmers.

Related Web site basicguru.com

One Computer, Multiple Operating Systems

A PC that can start more than one operating system is called a *multiboot system*. Here's how to set up your computer so that it can start Windows 98, Windows XP, or Linux, depending on your mood.

Prepare Your Drive   Start by creating partitions for each operating system. You also might want to create a shared data directory formatted as FAT32 so that all three operating systems can see it. Here's a typical layout for a 30GB hard drive:

Partition	Size	Contents	Format
1	3GB	Windows 98	FAT32
2	3GB	Windows XP	NTFS
3	8GB	Linux	Ext3
4	8GB	Shared Programs	FAT32
5	8GB	Shared Data	FAT32

Be sure to mark the first partition, your C: drive, bootable.

Install Windows   Install your operating systems in this order: Windows 98, Windows XP, and then Linux. XP will automatically install a boot manager if it sees Windows 98 on your drive.

If Windows 98 is already installed on your PC, that's fine—you don't need to reinstall. Just be sure that when you install XP you don't upgrade the 98 installation. Very important: Install XP into its own partition.

Install Linux   Install normally, making sure to put the Linux bootloader in the master boot record. Verify that the Linux boot manager offers the Windows 98 partition as one of its choices; that's where Windows XP put *its* boot manager.

When you're done with the Linux install, cross your fingers and reboot. You should see the Linux boot manager first, with a choice between Linux and Windows. Choose Windows to get a further choice between 98 and XP.

It's normal for this process to take some trial and error, but with any luck you'll be boasting to all your friends about your tri-boot system.

TIP OF THE DAY   Windows stores information about folder customizations in a hidden HMTL file within each folder named FOLDER.HTT. The FOLDER.HTT in the C:\Windows directory is special. It includes instructions for that darn nag screen that warns you each time you try to open the Windows folder.

You could disable the nag by turning off the **View As Web Page** option; or, you could just delete FOLDER.HTT and rid your life of the nagging altogether.

If you can't see FOLDER.HTT, turn on hidden files by opening a folder and selecting **Folder Options** from the **Tools** menu. Click the **View** tab, then click **Show Hidden Files and Folders**. While you're there, uncheck **Hide Extensions for Known File Types**.

If you're really bold, you can edit the FOLDER.HTT file itself by opening it from Notepad. Be sure to make a backup first.

DOWNLOAD OF THE DAY   The best partition manager for Windows is Partition Magic, from powerquest.com. But it's not cheap. Save money with the Ranish Partition Manager from ranish.com. It's free.

MAY 1

TODAY'S FOCUS: Customizing Your Mac

DOMAIN NAME MONOPOLY ENDS

A proposal to end Network Solution's reign as the sole domain name registrar was signed on this day in 1997. The agreement, made in Geneva by the Policy Oversight Committee (iPOC), appointed 28 new registrars and created seven new top-level domain names: `.firm`, `.store`, `.web`, `.arts`, `.rec`, `.info`, and `.nom`.

Related Web site   `www.gtld-mou.org`

MAY

2

Customizing Mac OS X

Use Screen Saver Images As Wallpaper   Mac OS X is infinitely customizable if you know how. Want new wallpaper? Open **System Preferences**, choose the **Desktop** pane, and then drag any image into the well. You also can choose from pictures stored on your hard drive.

My favorite wallpapers come from the built-in screensavers, but first you must copy the images from them. Open the System/Library/Screen Savers folder. You'll see four slideSaver files in there. Ctrl+click on one—I like Forest—and choose **Show Package Contents**. Open the **Contents** folder, and the **Resources** folder inside that. Drag the images inside to your **Pictures** folder. Now you can use them for wallpaper.

Transparent Terminal   Make your Terminal application translucent. Open it up and type the following line:

```
defaults write com.apple.terminal
TerminalOpaqueness '0.75'
```

Use different values instead of 0.75. 1.0 is opaque, and 0 is completely transparent. Or use anything in between.

Or do it the easy way with TinkerTool, a System Preference pane that can change many of your system parameters, including the system font, font-smoothing, and, yes, terminal transparency. Free from `bresink.de/osx`.

Add Channels to iTunes   The iTunes radio tuner comes with several stations, but nowhere near the variety that exists on the Internet. You can add radio stations to iTunes by visiting Shoutcast, at `shoutcast.com`, or Live365, at `live365.com`. Choose one from any of the thousands of stations you see there and it will begin playing in iTunes instantly.

If you find a station you really like, you can save it permanently in iTunes by creating a playlist folder and dragging the radio entry into it.

 Shoutcast, Live365, and many other Internet radio stations download Internet Audio Playlist (.pls) files for each station you listen to. You can save these files into a folder (you'll probably want to give them more descriptive names) and play them directly from the Finder.

More Hints   For many more great Mac OS X customization tips, visit `macosxhints.com` and `osxfaq.com`. Both sites are loaded with OS X information.

 TIP OF THE DAY   You can turn any image into an icon on Mac OS X as simply as cut and paste.

1. Open the **Grab** application (it's in your Utilities folder) and choose **Selection** from the **Capture** menu.
2. Select a 128×128 area of the screen.
3. Select **Copy** from the **Edit** menu to place the image on the Clipboard.
4. Now select any item—a drive, folder, or file—in the Finder.
5. Press Cmd+I to get info on that item.
6. Click the icon in the Get Info box, and press Cmd+V to paste your screen grab onto the icon.

You've changed the icon! To restore the original, select the icon in the Get Info window and choose **Cut** from the **Edit** menu.

DOWNLOAD OF THE DAY   Bring the classic Apple menu back to OS X and make other system tweaks with Haxies. Try them free from `haxies.com`.

TODAY'S FOCUS: Customizing Your PC

EXCEL UNVEILED

Microsoft announced plans for its first spreadsheet program on this day in 1985. Ironically, the program was created for the Macintosh, not for the PC (at the time, Microsoft was one of Apple's largest software suppliers). Excel quickly surpassed Dan Bricklin's VisiCalc in popularity among Mac users. But Excel for the PC wasn't released until nearly two years later, and it didn't catch on the way Microsoft might have hoped. Lotus 1-2-3 was considered the "standard" spreadsheet for many years until the early 1990s, when Excel version 4 was released.

Related Web site `bricklin.com/visicalc.htm`

Windows Tweak Sites

 Windows XP is probably the most customizable version of Windows yet. There are so many ways to personalize your system and optimize your settings that it's hard to know where to start. The following sites might not minimize the confusion, but they will give you a good idea of the options available to users of all versions of Windows.

Windows Registry Guide (`winguides.com/registry`) The System Registry is large and complicated, but it can be tamed in no time at all. Put on your snorkel; it's time to do a little Registry diving with this site.

Windows Support Center (`aumha.org`) Here's a collection of links to end all collections of Windows support links. It's organized, complete, and most of all, helpful. Funny thing, though, it's running on FreeBSD.

AXCEL216's WinDOwS Tricks Secrets Bugs Fixes (`members.aol.com/axcel216`) There's no larger tip resource on the Web. It reads a little like a bottle of Dr. Bronner's Soap, but Axcel knows it all (and then some). Don't be fooled by the `aol.com` URL—if you go here, I can pretty much promise you that you'll learn something new.

Warp2Search (`warp2search.net`) This is currently my favorite "hourly" visit. These people are constantly posting news, downloads, and tips that can directly boost my personal computing experience.

Windows XP Tips (`xtuneup.com`) XP-specific help and home to the XPTuneup application.

XPerience (`xp-erience.org`) Another Windows XP–specific site. News, tips, guides, and downloads with a very clean and easy-to-use user interface.

Windows Annoyances (`Annoyances.org`) This is the granddaddy of Windows customization sites. Annoyances has been helping people cope with Windows since Windows 95.

 TIP OF THE DAY Change the backgrounds in OS X folder windows. Open a folder, click the icon view, and then select **Show View Options** from the **View** menu. Choose **This Window Only**, unless you want to put the same background into all your folders! Click **Picture** and click **Select**.

 To do the same thing in Windows 98, open a folder and right-click on the background. Select **Customize This Folder**, then select **Choose a Background Picture**. Oddly enough, the same option is not available in Windows XP.

 DOWNLOAD OF THE DAY When you're dragging a document to your Recycle Bin or Mac trash, have you ever imagined you were dragging something onto Bill Gates' face? Well, you're in luck. Download Pixture Studio Desktop Icons, thousands of gorgeous icons free from `pixture.com`.

POLL: Where would you spend $10 billion?

46% Unlimited, clean energy

32% A cure for cancer

7% War against terrorism

15% Investment in Microsoft

MAY 3

TODAY'S FOCUS: Customizing Your PC

"I LOVE YOU" VIRUS RELEASED

The worm known as the "Love Letter," "Love Bug," and "I Love You Virus" hit millions of computers on this day in 2000. The Visual Basic Script (VBS) program originated in the Philippines and spread via email, IRC, Windows file sharing, and newsgroups. Virus experts estimate the virus cost U.S. companies nearly $1 billion and infected as many as half the country's computer users.

Related Web site   `getvirushelp.com/iloveyou`

Twisted List: Richest Nerds

By Martin Sargent

Every year, *Forbes Magazine* comes out with its list of the 400 richest Americans (`forbes.com/lists`) and every year, I'm not on it. Here are the richest nerds in America, according to the Forbes 2001 list.

Steve Ballmer Steve Ballmer, CEO of Microsoft, is tenth on the list overall but the fourth-richest tech billionaire (investor Warren Buffet is second, and five of Wal-Mart founder Sam Walton's kids are richer than Ballmer). Last year Ballmer's salary increased to $494,076, but when you factor in all the stocks and other holdings the dude is worth $15.1 billion.

Larry Ellison Oracle CEO Larry Ellison had a tough year. His personal wealth went down 63% to about $21 billion. Aw, poor cocky dude. The main reason his assets sank so much was the demise of the tech sector in the stock market, but also the late release and buggy nature of the software suite 11i.

Larry is using about $60 million of his loot to build a house that will include 6 million pounds of rocks from the Yuba River, seven wells, and a master bath shower that will be built out of 60,000 pounds of stone. Rock on.

Paul Allen With $28.2 billion, my boss, Paul Allen, is third on the list overall and the second richest nerd in America. This despite the fact that so many of the dot-coms he invested in turned out to be serious financial stinkers, such as Pop.com and TheStreet.com. But when you hold as many shares in Microsoft (the company he founded alongside Bill Gates) as Uncle Paul, you can afford to take gutsy risks on companies.

Bill Gates No surprise here—Bill Gates, despite losing more than $7 billion in the dot-com bomb, is still the richest person in America—by a long shot. With $54 billion, he's 38% wealthier than the second richest person, investor Warren Buffet. Gates puts lots of his money to good use—The Bill and Melinda Gates Foundation is worth some $23.5 billion. But you'd think the guy would be able to afford more stylish sweaters. Why does he call Bill Cosby for his hand-me-downs?

TIP OF THE DAY   The toolbar, that useful set of icons found at the top of your Finder window, is easily customized. You can add applications, folders, Web addresses, email addresses, and frequently used documents to it just by dragging their icons into the toolbar when you're in the Finder.

To hide the toolbar, click the toolbar lozenge in the upper-right corner of the window. To further customize the toolbar, press the Shift key when you click the lozenge.

DOWNLOAD OF THE DAY   Add "Move To Folder" and "Copy To Folder" to your right-clicks with copyToXP, a free Registry tweak available from `webattack.com/get/copytox.shtml`.

TODAY'S FOCUS: Online Shopping

PARENTS' INTERNET PROTECTION PLAN INTRODUCED

Vice President Al Gore introduced a policy designed to protect children from "harmful" sites online on this day in 1999. On the presidential campaign trail, Gore proposed the creation of a new "parents' protection page," which was supposed to time, track, and restrict children's Web access. It would also provide safety tips and instructions for reporting online crimes and other potentially dangerous activity. The page was to appear the first time any user accessed the Internet. Fortunately, the idea died a quiet death.

Related Web site eyeontomorrow.com/embracingthechild/pppgore.html

Online Shopping Basics

By Regina Lynn Preciado

Shopping online can save you time and money after you get the hang of it. But for many newbies, the e-commerce jungle can be frustrating and even overwhelming. Let's cut through the thicket.

Four Types of Online Shopping

- **Regular store**—The most prevalent type of virtual store mimics its offline counterpart. The seller offers products at a price; the buyer wanders through, finds what she wants, and buys it.
- **Auctions**—Online auctions have become so popular, some established regular stores have added auction sections. The most famous auction-only site is eBay. Read the new users section to get started, pages.ebay.com/help/basics/n-index.html.
- **Internet innovators**—Priceline (priceline.com) and its ilk turn the commerce model upside down. They offer products from regular vendors, just like regular stores, but invite the customer to set the price, more akin to an auction.
- **Shopbots**—A shopbot scours the Web looking for the items you want at the price you designate while you do other things. When it finds what you're looking for, the program alerts you and gives you the chance to buy. The best known of these is MySimon, at mysimon.com.

Protect Your Privacy Most reputable online stores post their privacy policies in a fairly obvious manner. A privacy policy outlines exactly what the company will and won't do with the information you provide when you place your order. This information includes your email and street addresses, phone numbers, and so on. You should read the privacy policy to be sure you know what you're getting into.

 TIP OF THE DAY To shop America Online, go to AOL keyword: shopping. There are three main ways to shop:

- **Shop by category** This gives you a good overview of products. Companies selling these products are in partnership with AOL.
- **Search by brand** If you know the type of item you're looking for, search by product (type the name of the product in the search box). You'll get a list of products with prices. You can click on each item to get more information, such as a photograph of the item, features, and specifications.
- **Search by store** If you saw something at the mall you wanted to buy but didn't, click on the **A–Z Listing of Stores**. There are lots of stores to choose from, but keep in mind that not all stores will be listed.

 DOWNLOAD OF THE DAY Add a shopping bot to your Internet Explorer toolbar. Edgegain watches while you shop, and then suggests places to find a better deal. Free 7-day trial, $29.95 to buy, from edgegain.com.

POLL: What is the Web best for?		
6% Commerce	2% Activism	
89% Information	3% Altruism	

MAY 5

TODAY'S FOCUS: Online Shopping

FIRST PRACTICAL-STORED COMPUTER DEBUTS

The Electronic Delay Storage Automatic Calculator ran its first computer program on this day in 1949. It was developed by Maurice Wilkes of Cambridge University in England and was the successor to the ENIAC. Although the EDSAC was just as big and bulky as its predecessor, there was an important difference: The ENIAC could perform only one operation at a time and had to be reprogrammed each time it executed a new task, but the EDSAC stored a list of instructions for several calculations. This saved programmers hours of rewiring and made the computer much more practical to use.

Related Web site   www.dcs.warwick.ac.uk/~edsac

MAY 6

Safe Online Shopping

Here are our top tips for safe e-shopping.

Pay with Your Credit Card
If you use a credit card, your transaction is protected by the bank. If unauthorized card use, theft, or loss is reported within two business days, cardholder liability is usually limited to $0.

Never Send Your Card Number via Email   Before you use your credit card online, read the company's privacy and security statements. If you still feel unsure about making an online transaction, most reliable companies have other payment options (phone, fax, and paper mail), but stay away from email—it's like putting your credit-card number on a post card.

Shop with Companies You Know and Trust   Going to the companies you already know can add a great deal of comfort to your online shopping experience. Contact the Better Business Bureau Online (bbbonline.com) for company track records. Check up on computer vendors at resellerratings.com.

Use the Internet to Research Prices   Shopping online can help you narrow choices and locate items that are out of stock at your local stores. Use automated shoppers such as My Simon (mysimon.com), Dealtime (dealtime.com), or Streetprices (streetprices.com) to find the best deals.

Watch Shipping and Handling Charges   When calculating the final cost of a purchase, don't forget shipping and handling charges. Purchasing multiple items can save you money. Be aware of taxes and international costs. Some unscrupulous companies offer very low prices and make their profit on "handling" charges.

Take Advantage of the Online Boom   Many online merchants are more interested in building their customer base than on making a profit. Take advantage of promotions for shopping online. You might even be able to find items below wholesale.

Keep a Record of Your Transaction   Back up your transactions by printing your confirmation order screen or email. These records will serve as a backup just like receipts.

Use Secure Sites   All recent browsers offer built-in encryption to protect your credit-card number and other private information. Before you submit that info, check for a padlock or key in the status bar of your browser. That means encryption is enabled and your transaction is secure.

TIP OF THE DAY   When shopping online, use a credit card, not a debit card. Debit cards withdraw money directly from your checking account, which means it's harder to recover your losses if the sale falls through. In most cases, credit cards offer better fraud protection and lower loss limits than debit cards. Check with your bank for details.

DOWNLOAD OF THE DAY   Copernic Shopper for Windows does comparison shopping on your desktop. Free from www.copernic.com/products/shopper/basic.

TODAY'S FOCUS: Online Shopping

IMAC UNVEILED

Apple showed off its new personal computer on this day in 1998. The original iMac came with a 233MHz PowerPC 750 processor, 4GB hard drive, a 24x CD-ROM, and 32MB RAM. It eliminated the need for a separate tower because the hardware was built into the monitor case. The iMac was also the first computer to come without a floppy drive—a decision that irked many computer users. The funky-colored translucent machines were popular nonetheless—Apple sold 800,000 units just four months after it hit the market.

Related Web site `theimac.com`

Rating Vendors

By Alison Strahan

You've found a great price on a DVD player online, but can you trust the vendor? Spend some time checking up on a company before you seal the deal.

Well-known in the terrestrial world, the Better Business Bureau also operates in cyberspace at `bbbonline.com`. The consumer watchdog group helps track a company's reputation and provides helpful tips to help keep consumers from getting ripped off.

BizRate.com rates stores by categories, such as on-time delivery, customer support, and price. The site asks stores to survey customers when they make a purchase. The stores then provide BizRate.com with customer reviews. Vendors that do not participate in the survey process are rated by BizRate's online research panel.

If you're shopping for computer hardware, be sure to stop by ResellerRatings.com. Opinions on tech vendors abound. Access opinions about 2,233 companies arranged in alphabetical order.

Lots of folks buy everything from plastic reindeer to clarinets on the eBay auction site, `ebay.com`. Making sure an individual seller is reliable is just as important as checking up on an online vendor. When you find a product you're interested in, click the **Seller Rating** link. You'll see an ID card listing all the positive and negative comments about the seller. You can even read comments from other eBay users who bought items from the person in the past.

You have all the resources at your fingertips to make a wise decision before you buy. Do your research to ensure a satisfying shopping experience.

 TIP OF THE DAY Best Shopping Sites

By Chris Pirillo

The other day my electric razor shuffled off its metal coil. What was I to do? Get it online, of course!

First, I decided check Epinions.com to see what razors other people like. The postings pointed me in the direction of a newer model from Braun. Immediately, I was able to compare prices at several online shops.

But I didn't want to shop at just any old store, so I went to ResellerRatings.com (`www.resellerratings.com`) to see what other people had to say about the e-commerce sites selling the shaver. That helped me narrow down the field to a couple big-name stores.

Finally, I checked Amazing-Bargains.com (`www.amazing-bargains.com`) for any coupons, specials, or discounts on the product. I found free shipping and a gift certificate for $10 off.

After shopping around, I found the best price at Amazon.com.

 DOWNLOAD OF THE DAY Put a shopping list on your Palm. Listmaker is free to try $14.95 to buy, `synsolutions.com`. SmartShopper does the same thing for free, `www-users.cs.umn.edu/~cosley/ss`.

POLL: How would you rate your online buying experience?

79% Positive

6% Negative

15% I'm heading to the mall

TODAY'S FOCUS: Online Shopping

FIRST U.S. PHOTOGRAPHY PATENT

Alexander Wolcott received a patent for a picture-taking method on this day in 1840. Wolcott invented a camera that didn't use a lens like later models, but instead came equipped with a large concave mirror that created a positive image on a metal plate. His design allowed for greater light reflection, which substantially decreased exposure time. Earlier that same year, Wolcott opened the "Daguerran Parlor," the first photography studio in the country, and possibly the world.

Related Web site   daguerre.org

MAY 8

Using Priceline to Save on Airfares

By Michael Shapiro

Priceline is an online service that allows you to name the price you're willing to pay for airfare. It can save you money, but it can also cause travel headaches if you're not careful. It's important to be aware of the hidden restrictions and requirements.

What Are Priceline's Restrictions?   You can pick your travel dates, but not travel times. You also might have to make one stopover on domestic flights and up to two connections on international flights. You can't preview your itinerary before deciding whether to take a ticket. If Priceline accepts your bid, it's automatically charged to your credit card. You won't earn frequent flier miles, and tickets can't be changed.

Can You Make More Than One Bid?   Priceline states that you can make only one bid for any itinerary, but if you change the date of your outgoing or returning flight, you can make a new bid. In many cases, if Priceline doesn't accept your bid, you'll be given a chance to raise it. So, it's much smarter to underbid than to overbid. Priceline keeps the full amount of all accepted bids, so if you bid $600 for a round-trip flight to Paris and Priceline can purchase that ticket for $450, Priceline pockets the difference.

Other sites, such as Expedia's Price Matcher, offer similar services. Click the **Flights** tab at expedia.com, and then select **Flight Price Watcher** from the left menu. The service lets travelers bid for flights and hotel rooms.

Hotwire (hotwire.com) can find rock-bottom fares without bidding as long as you're willing to book without knowing the airline or flight time until after you make a purchase. Hotwire is a handy site to use in conjunction with Priceline. Go to Hotwire to gauge airline fares and determine what your maximum bid should be on Priceline. For example, you might get an airfare quote of $329 to Denver from Hotwire, but you might not want to make a purchase if you have a good chance of bidding and getting the flight on Priceline for around $200.

(Visit Michael Shapiro's Web site, Internet Travel Planner, at www.internettravelplanner.com.)

TIP OF THE DAY   Manny, Moe, and Jack might not like to hear it, but you can find car parts online. Head to All-Parts.com, type in the make and model of your vehicle, a description of the part you want, along with your ZIP Code and email address. All-Parts will email you a list of suppliers in your area that carry the part. You can either wait for a supplier to contact you, or simply call yourself.

And yes, the Pep Boys are online, too, at pepboys.com.

DOWNLOAD OF THE DAY   Make a shopping list on your PocketPC; ShoppingList is free from icecomputing.com/download.htm.

TODAY'S FOCUS: Online Shopping

TELEVISION DEEMED "VAST WASTELAND"

On this day in 1961, FCC Chairman Newton Minnow told TV executives their programming was a "vast wasteland," and challenged them to do better. In his famous speech, Minnow criticized the medium for depicting excessive violence and for lacking educational and entertainment value. "When television is good…, nothing is better," he said. "But when television is bad, nothing is worse." Ironically, those words still sound familiar, even more than 40 years later, as policymakers continue to battle over television—and now Internet—content.

Related Web site `museum.tv/archives/etv/M/htmlM/minownewton/minownewton.htm`

Buying Cosmetics Online

By Alison Strahan

When you're shopping online, you have the luxury of comparing prices without having to trudge around all the stores on foot. There are many comparison services online that will help you find the best deals. Just type the name of the product you're after and click **Search**. Some sites list products within categories, such as "Health and Beauty" and "Consumer Electronics."

Being a shallow on-air personality, I decided to compare prices on one of my favorite products, MAC's Lip Glass lip gloss, at mySimon, `mysimon.com`.

Up popped a list of two stores selling the product. StrawberryNet cosmetics had it for $13. It was also listed for $12 at perfumebay.com. The MAC cosmetic site sells the product for $12.50, but it was not included in the mySimon listings. Although StrawberryNet was the most expensive, it offers free standard shipping. The other sites offer shipping for the usual figure of $4.95.

My search brings up three important points:

- Price comparison sites are often sponsored by certain retailers. Listings of sponsors generally come up first, even if they are more expensive. Always scroll through all the pages to find hidden bargains.
- Not all vendors are listed. mySimon missed MAC completely. Perform a search on several sites to try to hit all the possible sources for a product.
- Check shipping and taxes before you seal the deal. Often, a product will seem cheap, but then you get

hit with high shipping and handling charges. Or a product that seems expensive will have a great shipping deal, as I found out in my experiment.

Like mySimon, PriceScan (`pricescan.com`) compares prices for a large range of merchandise, from toys to pet supplies. It also searches vendors that don't have Web sites. Both sites also allow you to search for prescription drug prices.

Finally, if you're in the market for computer hardware, most techies swear by Price Watch, `pricewatch.com`. Prices are presented from least to most expensive, making the search for prices fast, efficient, and easy.

 TIP OF THE DAY Scan print catalogs online, too, at `catalogs.google.com`. Check the list to see whether your favorite catalog is in the searchable database, `catalogs.google.com/catalog_list`. I bet it is.

 DOWNLOAD OF THE DAY Make shopping lists, to-do lists, and elaborate outlines with OmniOutliner, from `omnigroup.com`, for Mac OS X only. Free to try a limited version, $29.95 to buy. I used this program to create this year's Almanac and have nothing but praise for it.

POLL: Whose famous DNA would you buy?

40% Albert Einstein

6% Marilyn Monroe

27% Britney Spears

3% Gary Coleman

24% Martin Sargent

MAY 9

TODAY'S FOCUS: Online Shopping

FIRST SILICON TRANSISTOR

Texas Instruments announced the development of a grown-junction silicon transistor on this day in 1954. Created by a team of scientists led by Dr. Gordon K. Teal, the transistors were made by cutting a rectangular bar of silicon crystal grown from a melt containing impurities (the flawed material conducted currents better than pure silicon). The capability to grow specialized silicon crystals drastically cut the cost of production, and also produced more reliable transistors.

Related Web site `ti.com/corp/docs/company/history/sitrans.shtml`

Designer Outlets

By Jeanette Pavini

It's rare to find high-end designer items that are still in style on the racks in department stores. But there is a way to have your Prada bag or Concord watch and still have money to go to a nice restaurant to show it off.

Online designer outlets have been a hidden secret. The following are just a few examples of designer deals and the sites that bring them to you.

Ashford.com Ashford offers great deals, especially on jewelry and watches. Know the warranties before you buy. Also, Ashford will not accept returns on items that are more than 50% off. Those are final sales, so you better love your purchases.

Nordstrom.com This department store makes life easy when it comes to returns. You can actually return items online to your local store. The store's sales area of the site also has steep discounts on a variety of labels.

BlueFly.com Each deal on Bluefly.com is better than the last. It has a large selection of hot designer items, and there's always a deal of the day.

Outletsonline.com Find real-world outlet stores, and shop in a handful of online outlets. Lists outlet malls all over the U.S. with a list of the stores in each, plus links to online stores when available. A quick way to find out whether a company has opened an outlet online.

A few words to the wise:

* Always know the return policies.
* Save a copy of your order.
* When ordering jewelry, be sure you get a warranty.
* Be sure of what you are getting when you order.

Life's too short not to indulge once in a while; it's just nice to indulge and save money at the same time.

(Jeanette Pavini is a consumer reporter. Visit her Web site at thinksavvy.com.)

 TIP OF THE DAY How much should that car cost? Use these sites to do your research:

StrongNumbers.com (`www.strongnumbers.com`) This site is the blue book for everything. It's organized to analyze 250 auction sites and 2,000 online retailers daily. Assess what you should be paying for a certain product.

Edmonds.com Make the right offer on a car by checking the true values of the vehicle at this Web site.

KBB.com Kelley Blue Book is the trusted source for your car's resale value.

DOWNLOAD OF THE DAY Decode that vehicle identification number with AnalogX's VIN View. Free for Windows from `analogx.com/contents/vinview.htm`. VIN View doesn't work with cars built prior to 1978. You'll need to visit the VIN Library (`autoinsurancetips.com/vin_number.htm`) for more information on older cars and manually decoding your vehicle's VIN.

When you know the VIN, get the vehicle's history from `carfax.com`. $14.99 per car, or $19.99 for unlimited reports for 30 days.

MAY 10

TODAY'S FOCUS: Online Shopping

MACHINE BEATS MAN

The IBM computer Deep Blue defeated world chess champion Garry Kasparov on this day in 1997, marking the first time a computer has ever beaten a human in a one-on-one matchup. The victorious supercomputer, an IBM RS/6000 SP, was composed of 32 processors with an estimated evaluation speed of 200 million moves per second. Kasparov would have taken home $700,000 if he had won, but instead received a $400,000 consolation prize.

Related Web site   `www.research.ibm.com/deepblue`

It's Mother's Day!

By Roy Santos

Mother's Day should be a day when your mom doesn't have to think about anything related to work. What better way to do this than by giving her something indulgent and luxurious?

Saks Sans Snooty Salespeople   One of the better luxury-goods department stores that now has an online presence is Saks Fifth Avenue, at `saks.com`. Here, you can look through many designers of *haute couture* without once hearing, "May I help you?" If your eyes become strained because of all the eye-popping they do from seeing the prices, click on the **Sale** category to find reductions. Be sure to visit the store's special Mother's Day section, where you can buy playful and semi-kitschy items, such as a $385 acrylic bangle and a book on Hollywood moms. But no wire hangers.

The Logo Mom   One of the best places to find couture online is eLuxury, `eluxury.com`. Backed by French fashion conglomerate LVMH, the site houses venerable names such as Louis Vitton, Dior, and Givenchy, as well as newer designers such as John Galliano and Michael Kors.

eLuxury also offers a Mother's Day section for those looking for gift ideas and devotes a section to sale items. You can access both from the front page. You can visit each designer and browse collections in separate sites, but still keep one shopping bag.

Designer Clothes, Gap Prices?   If the sale prices from the stores mentioned still give you the chills, you might warm up to Bluefly, `bluefly.com`. An online Loehmann's, the site stocks merchandise from past seasons and sells it at considerable discounts. For example, we found a black DKNY handbag that normally retails for $49 for a low $29.95. Guess what Mom is getting this year?

(Roy Santos is a TechTV product analyst and a very good son.)

TIP OF THE DAY   Wedding, Bar Mitzvah, Graduation? No matter what the occasion, you can register for gifts at `findgift.com`. Brides and grooms can register for more traditional gifts through Macy's, Tiffany, Bloomingdale's, and many more retailers at `weddingchannel.com`. Or, register for a charitable gift in your name at `charitygift.com/cg?pg=honr`.

Before you register anywhere, you might want to check Consumer Reports ratings for online registries. Free from `Consumerreports.org`.

DOWNLOAD OF THE DAY   Poetry generators take the work out of writing verse this Mother's Day.

Try `jelks.nu/poetry` for random poems on a variety of topics. Does Mom prefer haiku? Crib an idea, or an entire poem, from the Haiku Writer at `familygames.com/features/humor/haiku.html`. If you're looking for more creative input, try Poetry CreatOR 2, from `www-cs-students.stanford.edu/~esincoff/poetry/jpoetry.html`. For the most personal poems of all, try the Personal Poetry Generator, at `www.friedshrimp.com`.

TODAY'S FOCUS: Introduction to Linux

ODOMETER INVENTED

The predecessor of the instrument that tells how far you've driven in your car debuted on this day in 1847. Mormon pioneer William Clayton fixed a set of wooden cog wheels to the hub of a wagon wheel to see how far he had gone each day while crossing the plains from Nauvoo, Illinois, to Salt Lake City, Utah. Previously, distance was judged by tying a rag to the wheel of a wagon and counting the revolutions—a task that was nauseating as well as tedious.

Related Web site   www.howstuffworks.com/odometer.htm

What Is Linux?

Linux is an operating system. It's the program, like Windows XP or Mac OS X, that is the heart of your computer. It can run on a wide variety of hardware, including PCs and Macs.

Linux was written in 1991 by Linus Torvalds while he was a college student at the University of Helsinki in Finland. Linus could have tried to turn Linux into a business, but instead he did a very altruistic thing. He gave it, and all the source code, away.

Linus continues to hold the copyright to the name and supervises the release of new versions of Linux, but anyone who wants to can use Linux for free. And many thousands of people all over the world have contributed to its development, making it one of the most powerful and advanced operating systems you can get today, at any price.

Many different companies distribute versions of Linux. You've probably heard of Red Hat, but there are dozens of others, including Debian, Mandrake, Suse, Slackware, and Yellowdog. Each combines Linus's official Linux kernel with a standard set of Unix-style utilities from the GNU project (gnu.org), and an installer, into something called a distribution. Each distribution, or *distro*, as the Linux geeks call them, has its partisans. I'm a Linux-Mandrake fan, myself.

You can download Linux, but the full distribution is usually a CD worth of software, often much more, so it's best to buy a CD-ROM—especially because you can get one for just a few bucks from companies such as cheapbytes.com and linuxmall.com.

Linux is not quite as user friendly as Mac OS X or Windows; you'll need some technical expertise to install and run it. But it's worth the trouble, and not just because it's free.

Linux is based on Unix, the most reliable operating system in the world. You can run many of the (mostly free) applications developed for Unix on it. If you plan a career in computers, it's good to know something about Unix—most of the Internet runs on it. Plus, Linux is just plain fun to play with.

 TIP OF THE DAY   How do you pronounce Linux? Get the answer straight from the penguin's mouth at www.ssc.com/lj/linuxsay.html.

 DOWNLOAD OF THE DAY   There are two ways to run your Windows programs on Linux. Use Wine, which duplicates the Windows environment so that many Windows programs can run within Linux. Check the Wine Application database to see which programs work and how well, at appdb.codeweavers.com. Download a copy free from winehq.com/download.

If you actually want Windows to run under Linux, you need VMWare. Get a free demo at vmware.com.

POLL: Will you let Microsoft rid you of Linux?

14% Yes   86% No

TODAY'S FOCUS: Introduction to Linux

MAC SYSTEM 7 INTRODUCED

Apple unveiled System 7.0 on this day in 1991. The new and improved version of the OS was the first Macintosh operating system to automatically run multiple applications at the same time. System 7 also introduced color icons, virtual memory, personal file sharing, and balloon help. Upgrading to System 7 required a Motorola 68030 processor and 2MB of RAM.

Related Web site   `www.apple.com`

Why Linux Is Important

By Mark Willey

Everyone these days is talking about Linux. Why?

What is it about Linux that's so new and so important? Well, the truth is, nothing about Linux is new. Unix-like systems have been around for decades. The idea of free software has been around since the first computers. Other venerable open-source operating systems are available.

Linux, however, is the first commercially successful, truly open system. The computer industry has been flirting with the idea of commodity components forever, but has never before come close to what Linux has to offer.

Linux allows users to migrate freely between hardware vendors. How does this help hardware manufacturers? It allows them the freedom to innovate and make design changes that would be more difficult to manage if the operating system that runs on the installed base were proprietary and owned by another company.

The whims of the software house will no longer constrain hardware designers. If hardware designers come up with good technical innovations, Linux developers can adjust to support them. OS companies can't play the hardware manufacturers against one another, and backroom deals aren't possible, because of the open nature of Linux development.

Whether for ego gratification or for profit, the goal is still the same: Software writers want to get their software into the hands of the users.

In a proprietary-OS world, software makers have many barriers to overcome before they reach the user's desktop. It's a tough business to be in if you don't "own" the operating system; it's a little less tough if nobody "owns" the operating system.

Linux doesn't have any undocumented APIs, nor will future revs of the kernel maliciously break your code, because the development process is not shrouded in secrecy. Software makers can truly innovate on the level playing field of Linux.

Linux is a de facto standard that allows any (Linux) application to run on any supported hardware to a degree unheard of before.

Linux will succeed because it brings out the best in the industry. It gives users the freedom to choose any solution that works instead of the meager offering from the company that had the most leverage on a proprietary platform. So, the user is the ultimate winner, and rightly so—the user buys the computers and software!

(Mark Willey is Director of Technical Staff, Penguin Computing, at penguincomputing.com.)

 TIP OF THE DAY   Type `cal` on a Linux/Unix command line, and it displays a calendar (Gregorian) for the current month. Want to display the entire year? No problem. Just type in the year: `cal 2003`. Designate the month for a monthly calendar: `cal 5 2003`. Works in the Mac OS X Terminal, too.

  DOWNLOAD OF THE DAY   Chromium B.S.U. is a space game for Linux, free from `www.reptilelabour.com/software/ chromium/download.htm`. There's a version for Windows, too.

TODAY'S FOCUS: Introduction to Linux

STAR WARS DIRECTOR BORN

George Lucas, famous for his technological achievement in film, was born in Modesto, California, on this day in 1944. The director's first major accomplishment in special effects was in the 1979 blockbuster *Star Wars*. It was the first major film to use the Dolby sound system, and it was the first time many audience members had seen a movie in stereo.

Related Web site `starwars.com`

Prepare for the Penguin

By Tom Merritt

You hear about Linux everywhere these days, but it's not for everyone. If you just want an easy operating system, stick with Windows or Mac OS. If you're curious and want to know what you need to do try Linux, here's how to start:

1. Take an inventory of your system. The key to a successful Linux install is preparation. Know your system inside and out. Most modern Linux installers are deft at automatically detecting your hardware configuration, but if you hit a snag, you'll need to know what's in your box.

2. Get a couple of books. Some may scoff, but a combination of Linux documentation and an independent guide to Linux installs will serve you well. The documentation will guide you through the proper steps and tell you what to expect from your particular distribution of Linux. The independent guide can elaborate and explain a little more about how Linux works.

3. Pick your distribution. For first-timers, we recommend Linux-Mandrake (`linux-mandrake.com`) or Red Hat (`redhat.com`). Both are fairly easy to install.

4. Decide how you're going to boot. If you've got a separate machine that you'll devote to Linux, you don't need to worry about sharing. However, if you're installing Linux on a machine with Windows or another operating system, you'll need to create a partition for Linux before you start. Read the article on multiboot systems from May 1.

(Tom Merritt is Executive Web Producer for TechTV.)

 TIP OF THE DAY Even though Linux very rarely crashes, the applications you run can get hung up. When you need to force an application to quit, launch the terminal and follow these instructions:

1. First, determine the process ID for the program you want to terminate. Type **ps** or **top** to show a list of running processes.

2. Look for the name of your program and the accompanying process ID, or PID. To terminate that process, use the command **kill -9 #**,where # is the PID.

3. For more information, type **man kill** to read the kill manual pages.

 DOWNLOAD OF THE DAY There's a big difference between software that's free and software that's open source. Avantgo and Plucker are good examples. Avantgo is a commercial Web news reader for your Palm. Even if you don't have wireless access on your handheld, you can download all your favorite news and bring it with you to read anywhere. Plucker works in much the same way, but it's open source. That means you won't be bombarded with ads. You won't be asked for your personal information. You can download any Web page, not just the pages that are compatible with Avantgo. You can alter the program any way you want as long as you share the improvements you've made.

Download Plucker free from `plkr.org`.

TODAY'S FOCUS: Introduction to Linux

"CHEAP" CRAY SUPERCOMPUTER DEBUTS

Cray Research, founded by former UNIVAC and Remington Rand scientist Seymour Cray, introduced a supercomputer considerably less expensive than its predecessors on this day in 1990. The Cray EL series was the first low-cost supercomputer line in the company's history. It cost a mere $2.2 million—a bargain in comparison to Cray's other computers, which ranged in price from $5–$23 million.

Related Web site `cray.com`

Installing Linux—A True Story

By Patrick Norton

Let's see here... Linux installation—12-pack of Dr. Pepper. (Check.) Pizza. (Check.) Book to read while install files get copied. (Check.)

Oh yeah. I've also got a Red Hat install disk, my copy of *Sams Teach Yourself Linux*, the MAN and HOWTO pages for my distro (Linux distribution), and my properly prepared system. (Check.) The phone number of a Linux geek is always a plus.

I'm ready to install Linux. (Check.)

In case you didn't pick up on it, my list leans toward the paranoid because of the ignominious 13-hour thrashing I suffered at the hands of the Penguin the first time we met. Today's Linux is a kinder, gentler Linux.

Insert the CD and turn on your machine. The Linux installer should load and you're on your way. Today's graphical Linux installers are all about questions. What language would you like? What keyboard do you have? A two- or a three-button mouse? If you can't answer those questions then stop. You're not allowed to install Linux.

The toughest part usually is getting the graphical user interface, the X Window system, running. If you're lucky, your installer managed to identify your graphics hardware and all you have to do is hit the "test this configuration" button. Worst case? You'll have to manually enter some geeky specs for your monitor and video card. Don't sweat it, just be sure you test the configuration before you go on to the next step.

Now it's time to wait while the files are copied from the CD to the hard drive. Sigh. Pop open the book, break out the snacks, and wait.

When you get the "Installation Is Complete!" message, take the install CD out of the drive and reboot. Congrats. You've installed Linux. Now clean up that mess.

(Patrick Norton is co-host of The Screen Savers.*)*

 TIP OF THE DAY The easiest way to download Linux is to get an ISO image. You can use this file to burn a Linux install CD on your home system. Get a listing of distributions available for download as ISO images from `linuxiso.org`.

Download each ISO file, and then open it in your CD-burning software. Note: You are *not* going to just copy the ISO to the CD. Look for a menu entry in your program that says something like, "Create a CD from an image file." If your program can't handle ISO files, download a copy of Nero from `nero.com`. It's free for 30 days.

After you burn the ISO you will have a CD that is identical to the installer CD. Boot from it and you're on your way to Linux heaven.

 DOWNLOAD OF THE DAY If you like the Windows game IceBreaker, try Jezzball, an open-source clone for Windows and Linux. Free from `mattdm.org/icebreaker`.

TODAY'S FOCUS: Introduction to Linux

FIRST DUAL-PROCESSOR PC

Computer maker Dell announced a personal desktop computer containing two chips on this day in 1995. The Dell Optiplex DGX system featured a pair of Intel Pentium processors, and was intended to provide extra speed and power for high-end programs such as graphic design.

Related Web site `dell.com`

Installing Software in Linux

By Roger Chang

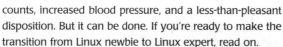

Unlike the simpler Windows and Macintosh, installing software on a Linux machine often means reduced hair follicle counts, increased blood pressure, and a less-than-pleasant disposition. But it can be done. If you're ready to make the transition from Linux newbie to Linux expert, read on.

Software for Linux comes in two forms. Easy and smooth, like a good-quality ice cream, or hard, chunky, and difficult to swallow, such as the coconut-flavored candies no one wants.

Easy Way: Get Binaries If You Can   Precompiled binaries for the distribution you have are about as easy a way to install software as you'll find in the Unix world. You just install and run.

Read the instructions that accompany your binaries. Many Linux binaries require an installer or package manager. For example, in Red Hat and Mandrake the binaries will be in Redhat Package Manager, or RPM form. You can install them from the command line using the rpm application and this magic incantation:

```
rpm -uvh <package-name>
```

In short, an RPM streamlines what would otherwise be a very tedious process.

Hard Way: Use the Source   If you can't get a precompiled binary, you'll have to download the source code and compile the application yourself. Source code will come in an archive with the .tar, .gz, or .tgz extension. Building from source usually involves the following steps, but always read the instructions for specifics:

1. Uncompress the source code:
```
tar zxvf game.tgz
```

2. Change to the source code directory:
```
cd game
```

3. Configure and make the program:
```
./configure
make
make install
```

The make program invokes the C compiler with all the right switches and compiles the source files into a real-live program. Most Linux distributions include C compilers for this reason.

If you're lucky, the compile will proceed without error and you'll have an application. More likely, there will be some missing libraries you'll have to download and install first; all of which might make you ask, "Why bother with Linux?" To which any dyed-in-the-wool Linux lover will reply, "Because it's so much fun."

(Roger Chang is a regular contributor on Call for Help.*)*

TIP OF THE DAY   If you need to become another user, don't log out; use the Unix su command. su, short for substitute user, lets you temporarily become another user by entering **su** and an optional username at the command prompt. If you don't provide a name, su will assume you want to become root. After you enter the appropriate password, you'll be working as another user until you enter the exit command.

su is most often used for assuming the role of root to perform system maintenance.

DOWNLOAD OF THE DAY   You can play Quake III Arena on Linux if you have an accelerated video card and the proper drivers. Download the demo free from `ftp://ftp.idsoftware.com/idstuff/quake3/linux/linuxq3ademo-1.11-6.x86.gz.sh`.

To get it working right, read the Quake III for Linux FAQ at `zerowing.idsoftware.com/linux/q3a/`.

TODAY'S FOCUS: Introduction to Linux

WWW RELEASED

The World Wide Web debuted on computers at The European Organization for Nuclear Research (CERN) in Geneva, Switzerland, on this day in 1991. The concept of the WWW was developed about a year earlier by English computer scientist Tim Berners-Lee, who had built the hypertext system to allow documents to be easily linked to one another. A year later, CERN announced it would make its technology available to the public for free (see April 30 for more details).

Related Web site `www.w3.org`

Linux Web Sites

Linux probably wouldn't exist if the Internet didn't. Linux developers collaborate over the Net, versions of Linux are distributed over the Net, and Linux is best documented on the Net. Here are some of the best Linux sites online.

Linux Online (`www.linux.org`) The first Linux site I ever visited. Probably your first stop, too. Lists all the distributions and where to find them and many other resources.

The GNU Project (`gnu.org`) What we call Linux is really a few megs of Linux kernel bundled with hundreds of megabytes of GNU software.

The Linux Documentation Project (`linuxdoc.org`) This is the ultimate source for Linux documentation. It has lots of amazing resources, including FAQs (frequently asked questions), HOW-TOs (subject-specific help), MAN pages (the manual for individual commands), and guides. Use the search to find the HOW-TO you need when you need it.

SourceForge (`sourceforge.net`) The hub of open source application development. SourceForge is a virtual workspace where developers can collaborate and share their work with users.

Freshmeat (`freshmeat.net`) Catalogs the newest Linux software with a focus on RPMs, binary files for Red Hat and Mandrake.

Linux Newbie (`linuxnewbie.org`) A whole site dedicated to Linux newcomers. Specializing in NHFs, "newbie-nized help files."

The Linux Journal (`linuxjournal.com`) The premiere Linux magazine also runs an excellent site with an article archive, newsletters, news, and more.

ThinkGeek (`thinkgeek.com`) Linux users gotta shop, too. Get your caffeinated mints and geek tools here. You'd look so cool in a "Got Root?" t-shirt.

***The Screen Savers* Linux Superguide** (`techtv.com/screensavers/linux` We've put all our articles on Linux here. We explain the basics and offer lots of tips and tricks for getting started.

TIP OF THE DAY If you happen to forget your Linux root password, you're going to have to change it. Here's how:

1. Start your computer. At the LILO prompt, type **linux single**. Your machine will now start in single-user mode.
2. Type **passwd** and enter the password that you want for your root user. It should then say "All tokens updated successfully."
3. Type **reboot**.

When the machine restarts, you will be able to log in as root with the new password.

DOWNLOAD OF THE DAY OpenOffice is an open source, Microsoft Office-compatible office suite based on Sun's StarOffice version 5. Try it free for many different platforms, including Linux, from `openoffice.org`.

POLL: Which OS is more secure?	
5% Windows 98	8% Free BSD
21% Windows 2000	3% Amiga
8% OS 9	2% AppleDos 3.3
4% BeOS	43% Linux
5% DOS	(your favorite distribution)

TODAY'S FOCUS: Introduction to Linux

FIRST FEMALE HALL OF FAMER

Gertrude Bell Elion became the first woman to be inducted into the Inventor's Hall of Fame on this day in 1991. The chemist and pharmacologist was honored for her research and development of breakthrough leukemia-fighting drugs. The New York native and former teacher also introduced medication to treat gout and herpes, as well as a treatment that blocks the rejection of kidney transplants. In 1988, she was awarded the Nobel Prize in Medicine.

Related Web site `www.leukemia.org`

MAY
18

Twisted List: Penguin Games

By Martin Sargent

The whole Linux phenomenon has spawned bushels of games in which you either guide a penguin toward some goal (typically involving fish) or exterminating penguins. I don't think there are enough games in which you destroy bees. Penguins never hurt anyone, but bees are a national menace. Here are the top five penguin-themed games.

Penguin Bounce (`disney.go.com/games/penguin2/penguin.html`) Admittedly, this isn't the best game you'll play this year, but I said this list is about the five best *penguin* games, which sort of limits my quality control. Penguin Bounce, which you can play in your browser, is sort of like Breakout or Araknoid, in that you control a shield that propels penguins into the air when they strike it. Upon going airborne, the penguins bounce back down toward the shield with ferocious speed. The object is to destroy all the snowflakes before all your penguins drown. It's a hoot.

Peng (`memirsoftware.com/dls.html`) In Peng, swarms of penguins fall from the sky in Galaga fashion, only to land on a chessboard where you must shoot them with a snowball missile launcher. Bombs that drop alongside the penguins help your cause, unless the penguins push them off the chessboard's edge. This game is sort of fun, though inexplicable.

Penguin Shooter (`thesims.ea.com/us/getcool/gamedownload`) In Penguin Shooter, you are once again exterminating, or at least maiming, penguins. When the crazy birds keep jumping up onto an ice floe, you can take aim and fire ice cubes at them, knocking them back into the water.

Penguin Panic (`spikything.com`) Oh dear lord! An iceberg loaded with penguins has floated off to sea. For some reason, penguin common sense breaks down and they start hurling themselves off the ice floe in the middle of the ocean and you, in your cute little tugboat, need to save them. This game is another take on the classic Kaboom.

Tux Racer (`tuxracer.com`) You've probably seen the all-time penguin classic Tux Racer before, but it's so good there's no harm in revisiting it. As Tux, you slide down a ski slope trying to avoid dangers, while eating as much herring as possible. A super-fun game with great graphics and music.

TIP OF THE DAY The X Window System is a great GUI, and, for the most part, you can do everything you need in it. But if X is misbehaving and you need to get to the command prompt, press Ctrl+Alt+Backspace to kill the X session.

DOWNLOAD OF THE DAY MPlayer for Linux is the open-source version of the Windows Media Player. Play back a wide variety of desktop video formats, including Microsoft's ASF and Apple's QuickTime, plus VCD and DVDs. Free for Linux from `mplayerhq.hu`.

TODAY'S FOCUS: Microsoft Internet Explorer

JUSTICE DEPARTMENT SUES MICROSOFT

The United States Justice Department filed suit against Microsoft on this day in 1998. In the largest antitrust case since the breakup of the Baby Bells in the 1980s, the judicial body said the software maker engaged in monopolistic business practices and used its Windows operating system to "crush competition and stifle innovation." Twenty U.S. states followed suit soon after and filed similar suits. After several years of legal battles and unexpected twists (such as the removal of presiding Judge Thomas Penfield Jackson for alleged bias against Microsoft), the DOJ reached a settlement with the Seattle-based company in 2002.

Related Web site `www.usdoj.gov/atr/cases/ms_index.htm`

Internet Explorer Security Settings

By Regina Lynn Preciado

Microsoft's Internet Explorer gives you several ways to protect your computer from malicious Web sites and virus-infected code. For most of us, Internet Explorer's default settings are secure enough. Here's a quick rundown of the security settings you can adjust to suit your browsing style and level of paranoia.

From the **Tools** menu, select **Internet Options**. Click the **Security** tab. You'll see the "zones" across the top, with Internet highlighted and the security level most likely set at Medium (the default).

Your online world is divided into zones. All sites assigned to a particular zone share permissions and restrictions you specify for the entire zone:

- **Internet**—A catchall category containing every site not assigned to any other zone. This is your default, so set a high level of security here, but remember: the higher the security, the less you can do on a site.
- **Local intranet**—Contains addresses you can reach without going outside your LAN or company firewall, such as your internal human resources Web page. Usually very safe, so use the least security here.
- **Trusted sites**—Holds both external and internal sites, but you have to add them individually. Set security low for these sites, too.
- **Restricted sites**—Holds both external and internal sites, but you have to add them individually. Set security highest for these sites.

To restore the original, suggested, settings click the **Default Level** button.

 TIP OF THE DAY Many companies put advertising into Internet Explorer. If your browser says something like "brought to you by Cheesy ISP Inc." or you have a custom logo throbbing at you from the corner of the window, unbrand that browser as follows:

1. Close all browser windows.
2. Go to **Start**, choose **Run**, and type `rundll32 iedkcs32.dll,Clear`.
3. Press Enter.

 DOWNLOAD OF THE DAY Microsoft's Web Accessories add some cool features to Internet Explorer 5:

- **Image List**—Measures image sizes and download time from various connection speeds.
- **Links List**—Tells you all the links on a page.
- **Image Toggler**—Lets you turn images off for greater browsing speed.
- **Zoom In/Zoom Out**—Gets you a closer look at a Web page.
- **Open Frame in New Window**—Does exactly that—lets you load a particular window inside a frame in a new window all to itself.

Download them free from `microsoft.com/windows/ie/previous/webaccess/ie5wa.asp`.

Note: Microsoft says these accessories don't work in IE 6. In fact, some of them seem to, but install at your own risk.

TODAY'S FOCUS: Microsoft Internet Explorer

HP COFOUNDER BORN

Hewlett-Packard cofounder William R. Hewlett was born in Ann Arbor, Michigan, on this day in 1913. The Stanford graduate founded HP in a one-car garage in Silicon Valley in 1939 with his partner, David Packard. The pair's first product was a resistance-capacitance audio oscillator based on a design developed by Hewlett when he was in graduate school. Hewlett resigned as president in 1977 and retired as CEO a year later, but he continued to serve as chairman of HP's executive committee until 1983. In 1987, he was named director emeritus. Hewlett died in January 2001.

Related Web site `www.hewlett.org`

Does P3P Protect Your Privacy?

By Mick Lockey

P3P (Platform for Privacy Preferences) is a relatively new standard currently under development by the consortium that regulates Web-based protocols, the W3C. P3P, which IE 6.0 supports, allows you at least a modicum of control over how some personal information (in the form of cookies) is used by Web sites you browse.

Most reputable e-commerce sites have a privacy policy. They inform you how the information they collect will or won't be used. But who has time to read the privacy policy on each site they visit? P3P is designed to build a bridge between consumers who want their privacy protected while shopping online and Web sites that need users' personal information to complete transactions. A Web site that supports P3P establishes a policy that can be recognized by the browser. The browser can, in turn, automatically enforce the user's privacy preferences.

Here's how the feature works. You establish a "personal" privacy policy through the Internet options menu in IE 6.0. There's a blanket default, but if you select the advanced feature, you can override the default settings.

In browsing tests conducted at TechTV Labs, we encountered intermittent problems when P3P was configured for several types of privacy policies, including blocking all cookies. We experienced the most frustration when we blocked all cookies from all sites. In some browsing sessions, we were unable to download some Web pages. You can also configure P3P to ask whether a cookie can be placed on your hard drive before it's actually placed there. Having the choice to block certain cookies is a welcome feature, but a preponderance of sites seem to require cookies to function. Most users will become so frustrated that they will end up enabling all cookies just so they can surf in peace.

P3P is an attempt to support automated enforcement of user configured privacy policies. It's a great idea, but as currently implemented, it's less than useful and could, in fact, lull users into thinking their privacy is being protected when it isn't.

To read more about the P3P initiative, visit the World Wide Web Consortium at `www.w3.org/P3P`. For an independent assessment of the effectiveness of P3P, visit The Electronic Privacy Information Center at `epic.org/reports/prettypoorprivacy.html`.

(Mick Lockey is a TechTV product analyst.)

TIP OF THE DAY Don't you hate it when you surf to a site and cheesy MIDI music begins blaring from your speakers? Stop the music instantly by hitting the Escape key on your keyboard.

DOWNLOAD OF THE DAY Update your browser to include all the latest security patches. Visit `microsoft.com/windows/ie/downloads/critical`.

POLL: Is privacy dead?

69% Yes

22% No

9% I don't care

FATHER OF SOVIET HYDROGEN BOMB BORN

Physicist and humanitarian Andrei Sakharov was born in Moscow on this day in 1921. Sakharov developed the first atomic bomb in 1953 for the Soviet government. Horrified by his creation, the engineer began to lobby against the proliferation of nuclear arms. In 1957, he wrote a groundbreaking article on the hazards of low-level radiation. Over the next several years, Sakharov continued his humanitarian efforts, and in 1980, the Soviet Union exiled the Nobel Laureate to Gorky, a city about 200 miles from Moscow famous for holding political dissidents. Sakharov died in 1989.

Related Web site   www.wdn.com/asf

IE 6 Versus Netscape 6.2

By Ray Weigel

Microsoft has been winning the browser war for some time, but don't count Netscape out yet. Here's a head-to-head comparison.

Download Speed   Traditionally, Internet Explorer has led the download race, pulling down pages and files faster than Netscape Navigator, but with Navigator's upgrade to version 6.2, it looks like Netscape has finally caught up. Our stopwatch time tests show that Explorer has a negligible edge.

Search Management   Both browsers offer search tabs, but neither lets you choose which engine to search with. Instead, you pick from several preselected choices. Microsoft does provide a larger list of basic engines to choose from (16 versus Netscape's 5) and ultimately offers more preference settings than Netscape.

Feature Integration   Internet Explorer 6.0 and Navigator 6.2 perform the same functions. You can use them to surf the Web and send and receive email, and now you can use them both to IM (instant message) your friends.

For playing Internet media, Internet Explorer uses Windows Media Player, whereas Navigator uses RealPlayer for video and Winamp for audio. Netscape wins in this category because Internet Explorer doesn't include support for the QuickTime format.

Dynamic Content (Java, ActiveX, XML Support)   While previous version of Netscape Navigator had trouble handling too much active content at once, the 6.2 release has little trouble and is easily as capable as IE 6.0. Microsoft still handles dynamic content well, but the lack of Java in the newest version hurts it here.

Security   Microsoft has a flawed P3P implementation. Navigator has adequate cookie control. Neither goes far enough, but there's no clear winner.

Usability   Although the ability to rearrange the toolbars in IE 6.0 definitely is a plus, we like the slick interface of Netscape Navigator 6.2. You also can download or create additional skins, which makes Navigator 6.2 a more customizable browser than IE 6.0.

We also think Navigator's side bar is easier to manage than that of IE. The controls are laid out more coherently, and the content it displays isn't as visually invasive as the content that loads into the Windows toolbar.

Conclusion   The newest update to Navigator has us wondering whether Microsoft should be looking over its shoulder.

 TIP OF THE DAY   If a site is too slow to load, stop and try again; it will often load faster. Press the Esc key, and then press F5 to refresh the page.

 DOWNLOAD OF THE DAY   Booky for Windows is a utility that lets you convert your Internet Explorer Favorites to an Opera Hotlist or a Netscape Bookmarks file. Free from www.yoursurfice.com/Content/Booky/Booky.htm.

POLL: Should you update to IE 6.0?

45% Yes

55% No

MAY 21

TODAY'S FOCUS: Microsoft Internet Explorer

WINDOWS 3.0 UNVEILED

Microsoft announced the debut of Windows 3.0 on this day in 1990. Bill Gates showed off the product at 20 cities around the world simultaneously, via satellite from a theater in New York City. Publicity alone for the new version of the operating system cost Microsoft $10 million. Windows 3.0 sold more than 10 million copies, making it the best-selling system upgrade of the era.

Related Web site   `computerhope.com/win3x.htm`

Local Home Page

Every time you open your Web browser, you have to wait for your system to connect to the Internet and download your home page. Speed things up by loading a home page that's right on your hard drive. Any HTML file on your drive can be a home page, but the easiest way to start is to create a page using your Internet Favorites.

In Internet Explorer, select **Import and Export** from the **File** menu, choose **Next**, and then **Export Favorites**. Select a folder, and then choose **Export to a File or Address**. Save it as **c:\my documents\bookmark.htm**. Now you can use a Web page editor to further customize the file.

Don't have a Web page editor? Don't be so sure. Microsoft Word does a great job with HTML. However, before it can work on your bookmark file, you'll have to add a little bit of HTML. Open bookmark.htm in Notepad and add **<HTML>** to the beginning of the file and **</HTML>** to the end to signal to Word that the file is a bona fide Web page. Now open it with Word.

You can work with the document as you would any word-processing file, adding graphics, changing fonts, entering text, and so on. When you've got the page the way you want it, select **Save As Web Page** from the **File** menu.

Open the file in IE and if it looks right, drag the icon from the address bar to the Home icon in the toolbar and you've made it your new fast, local, home page.

TIP OF THE DAY   To quickly search for a Web page, type a question mark into Internet Explorer's address window, followed by your search term. By default, Microsoft will use the MSN Search engine to find your term on the Web.

Here's how to use a different search engine in the address bar if you're using IE6 in Windows XP:

1. Click the Magnifying Glass icon to open the Search Companion.
2. Click **Change Preferences** and **Change Internet Search Behavior**.
3. Click **Classic Internet Search** and click **OK**.
4. Close and reopen the browser. You'll be using the IE5-style search pane.
5. Select the **Customize** option.
6. On the new window that appears, select **Autosearch Settings**.
7. On the new window that appears, select the search provider you want and how you want IE to act when you search in the address bar.
8. Back on the main Customize Search Settings window, if you want to go back to the IE6-style Search Companion, choose the **Use Search Companion** option. Close and reopen the browser.

It's a little baroque, but you've changed the default address bar search engine.

DOWNLOAD OF THE DAY   Spystop blocks spyware, Web bugs, worms, cookies, advertisements, and scripts. Free to try, $19.95 to buy, from `itcompany.com/spystop.htm`.

TODAY'S FOCUS: Microsoft Internet Explorer

FIRST REMOTE-CONTROL ROBOT

General Electric unveiled the first automated factory machine operated by remote control on this day 1956. The device, nicknamed the "Yes Man," was designed for the Aircraft Nuclear Propulsion Department of the U.S. Air Force. It replaced humans in dangerous manufacturing areas to reduce the risk of employee injury. Three years later, General Electric instituted the technology at its own offices—a robotic arm installed at a GE plant became the first automated device to be used for commercial industry.

Related Web site www.ge.com

Internet Explorer Tip Collection

Command-Line Switches Take control of Internet Explorer with these command-line switches. To activate them, click the **Start** menu, select **Run**, and, in the text box, type `iexplore.exe` followed by a space and one of the following switches:

- **-e**—This starts IE in Explorer mode with the split pane view, so you can browse your computer's directory on the left and look at Web or hard drive content on the right.
- **-channelband**—This opens up IE as a desktop toolbar, with your Favorites displayed.
- **-nohome**—Starts IE without loading any Web page.
- **-new**—Start up a new instance of IE (same as double-clicking the IE icon on your desktop).
- **-slf**—Starts IE and loads your home page from the cache for faster start times (as opposed to updating your home page, as it usually does).
- **-k**—Starts IE in Kiosk mode (full-screen mode meant for demos—press Alt+F4 to exit).

If you use one of these modes frequently, create a shortcut to it. Right-click on the desktop, select **Shortcut** from the **New** menu, and enter the appropriate iexplore command line in the box.

Clear AutoComplete To clear your AutoComplete list:

1. Open Internet Explorer.
2. Click **Tools**, select **Internet Options**, and then click the **Content** tab.
3. Click the **AutoComplete** button.
4. Click the **Clear Forms** and/or **Clear Passwords** buttons.
5. When IE has finished clearing out your passwords and forms, click **OK**.

You can also disable AutoComplete entirely by unchecking the check boxes in the **Use AutoComplete for** section.

Disable Animated GIFs Too many dancing bears on your favorite Web page?

1. Go to **Tools**, **Internet Options**, and click the **Advanced** tab.
2. Under **Multimedia**, uncheck **Play Animations**.
3. If you're tired of long download times for images and you just want get straight to the text, deselect **Show Pictures**.
4. Click **OK** to save your changes.

No More JavaScript Errors Tired of seeing error warnings when you go to pages with buggy JavaScript? Those warnings are useless to anyone but the Webmaster. Turn them off thusly:

1. Click the **Tools** menu and select **Internet Options**.
2. Click the **Advanced** tab.
3. In the window, look for the option **Disable Script Debugging**, and check the box.
4. Find **Display a Notification About Every Script Error** just below, and uncheck the box.
5. Click **OK**.

Open in New Window To open a link in a new window, right-click the link and choose **Open in a New Window**, or just hold down Shift while you click the link.

 DOWNLOAD OF THE DAY Zero Popup claims to kill annoying pop-up windows without human intervention by using artificial intelligence and intelligent agent technologies. It has to be smarter than the pop-ups. Free to try, $20 to buy, from tooto.com.

MAY 23

TODAY'S FOCUS: Microsoft Internet Explorer

HDTV ALLIANCE

Major players in high-definition television agreed to join forces on this day in 1993. AT&T, the David Sarnoff Research Center, General Instruments, MIT, Philips, Thomson, and Zenith told the FCC they would work together to set a much-needed standard for the emerging technology. The "Grand Alliance" was supposed hasten the implementation of digital TV, but testing was repeatedly delayed, and it took four years for the FCC and broadcasters to agree on a plan. The major U.S. networks currently broadcast in both digital and analog in select cities, but a complete switch may still be distant on the horizon.

Related Web site `www.nab.org`

Defeating Web Annoyances

By Megan Morrone

Stop Spyware Many free programs these days are advertising supported. Unfortunately, the ads often come with a hidden support program that keeps track of how often you click them and updates the ads from time to time.

The more paranoid among us further suspect that these hidden programs also might be monitoring your surfing habits and relaying the information back to the home office for marketing purposes. They could be—it's hard to know for sure. But if hidden spyware worries you, here are some Web sites that can help.

Spychecker (`spychecker.com/spychecker.html`) Spychecker is a database of programs known to use spyware, updated daily. With a click of the mouse, you can check to see whether software is spyware, or report your experiences with invasive-free software. Download the program or bookmark the site and enter your query there.

SpywareInfo (`spywareinfo.com`) SpywareInfo keeps you updated on the latest news about suspicious software as well as government surveillance. They also publish the *Spyware Weekly* newsletter.

Clobber Popups Pop-ups are those little advertisements that open new windows over or under your browser. Although some people might argue that these ads help fuel the waning Internet economy, I still think there are better ways to sell products.

Scores of programs will let you get rid of ads, cookies, and other nasty bits that slow down your surfing. These are my favorites:

Pop-Up Stopper (`panicware.com`) Panicware makes a free and pro version of this ad-blocking software. You can set the preferences to general or aggressive pop-up stopping. And if you really do want to see the ad, all you have to do is hold down Ctrl+Shift when you click on the link. I think my favorite feature of this program is that you can make it play a sound every time you kill a pop-up.

Proxomitron (`www.flaaten.dk/prox`) This is my favorite free Web filter because it does so much. It kills pop-up ads, even those really annoying eye-blaster ads that fly across your screen. It also prevents cookies, nosy JavaScript, and the referral information that sites use to detect where you surfed in from. The only thing to watch out for: This download may slow down your surfing, depending on how many items you choose to filter.

 TIP OF THE DAY To type in a new address in IE, press the F6 key or hit Alt+D to select the old address and type in the new. To move between parts of the address, use the Ctrl+ arrow keys.

 DOWNLOAD OF THE DAY Ad-Aware is the ultimate spyware detection and removal utility. Free from `lavasoft.de`.

TODAY'S FOCUS: Microsoft Internet Explorer

FIRST COPYRIGHT LAW

Congress passed the first copyright protection law on this day in 1790. The bill protected copyright holders for 14 years, with a 14-year renewal if the applicant were still alive. Today, a copyright for an individual lasts the person's lifetime plus 50 years, and a copyright for a corporation last 75 years. Copyright law alone didn't always prevent duplication, though. Computer software, while under copyright protection, wasn't subject to patent law until 1981. As a result, it was relatively easy for software makers to create programs similar to those already made by other companies.

Related Web site   `www.loc.gov/copyright`

Twisted List: Internet Fads

By Martin Sargent

The Internet makes super-stars out of the weirdest things. Here are the top three Internet fads in history.

Hampster Dance   Remember the hampster dance? (Yes, *hampster*—not hamster.) If you were online a few years ago, there's a 98% chance you saw the oh-so-lame collection of animated hamster GIFs dancing and swaying to outrageously annoying MIDI music. More than 70 million people logged on to that site, yet it's nearly impossible to find today. I only know of one place, `www.oceanbluepools.com/hamster`, that still hosts the original. If you go to `www.hamsterdance.com` today, you'll find a really slick, interactive version of the hamster dance that has none of the charm of the original. The hampster dance sold out, man.

I Kiss You (`ikissyou.org/mahir/mahirilk.htm`) Mahir was huge. He's the Turkish guy who had the Web site (actually his friend made it as a joke) saying he wanted to kiss you and in so doing promote love and happiness and peace in the world. During the height of the dot-com frenzy, Mahir appeared as the featured guest at gala parties in San Francisco at which he got to kiss lots of women. Now he's talking book and movie deals and hanging with Julia Roberts and Meg Ryan. Mahir proves that anyone can become internationally famous by creating a dorky Web site.

All Your Base Are Belong to Us (`planettribes.com/allyourbase`)   Of all the insane Internet fads, All Your Base Are Belong to Us is by far the most inspired. It all began with a bad English translation of a Japanese video game called Zero Wing.

In A.D. 2101
War was beginning.
Captain: What happen?
Mechanic: Somebody set up us the bomb.
Operator: We get signal.
Captain: What!
Operator: Main screen turn on.
Captain: It's You!!
Cats: How are you gentlemen!!
Cats: All your base are belong to us.

Years later, the translation was discovered and briefly became a hot item on a few gamer message boards. But it wasn't until the song and accompanying Flash animation hit the Net that things really got rolling. View the animation. Relive the fun. All your base *are* belong to us.

TIP OF THE DAY   Here's a quick way to get back to your home page: Press Alt and Home at the same time to take you back home.

DOWNLOAD OF THE DAY   TweakIE controls cookies, backs up important data, and customizes features of IE and Outlook Express. Free to try, $15 to buy, from `http://www.tweakie.com/`.

TODAY'S FOCUS: Digital Photography

ADOBE PRESIDENT KIDNAPPED

Charles Geschke was kidnapped from his company's parking lot in Mountain View, California, on this day in 1992. Mouhannad "Steve" Albukhari and Jack "Rock" Sayeh approached Geschke at gunpoint, blindfolded him with duct tape, and held him for a $650,000 ransom. Geschke spent five days chained and handcuffed in a rented house before the FBI rescued him and captured one of the kidnappers during a ransom drop. The Adobe chief was physically unharmed, but spent the next several months under the protection of bodyguards.

Related Web site   `www.adobe.com`

How Digital Photography Works

By Brett Larsen

Just like film cameras, digital cameras let light in briefly through a lens. Instead of the light hitting a piece of film and creating a chemical reaction, the light hits a chip, creating an electrical reaction. The electrical reaction is turned into digital data, which in turn becomes a photo on your camera's display or computer screen.

There are two types of digital camera image sensors: charge-coupled device (CCD) and complementary metal oxide semiconductor (CMOS). The more common, and higher quality, is the CCD. Each array has millions of sensors, one per pixel, that turn light energy into digital data.

High-end cameras have three chips, each filtered to "see" only one color: red, green, or blue. Each chip picks up the same image, and the combined images create a full-color image.

Most consumer-grade cameras use a single chip. They use a mosaic of red, green, and blue filters on top of the chip, so each pixel "sees" a different color. To create a full-color image, the camera uses *interpolation*, which takes the value of the surrounding pixels to create the missing information and a full-color image.

Once captured, the image data is saved, much the same way you save a document on your computer, so it can be viewed later. The data is often held in a buffer on the camera, and then written onto removable media such as CompactFlash or Smart Media. Depending on how much

of a buffer your camera has and how big a file you've taken, you can snap a few pictures in rapid succession, or only one at a time.

To move the data stored on the camera onto your computer, you either remove the media and use an external media reader with your computer, or you connect your camera directly to your computer via USB or serial (or on some high-end cameras, FireWire). The image data is then transferred to your computer so you can view the files, manipulate them, send them to friends, use them to create Web pages, or even print them out to put in your photo album.

 TIP OF THE DAY   `Digitalphotography.tv` is a great place to learn about taking pictures, see some lovely shots, and find other photographic resources.

Imaging Resource (`imaging-resource.com`) is the ultimate guide to digital cameras, scanners, printers, and other imaging hardware.

The Digital Camera Resource Page (`dcresource.com`) is another trustworthy digital camera review site that includes lots of great photos of each reviewed camera.

 DOWNLOAD OF THE DAY   PIE downloads pictures from your camera, extracts info from images, renames them using date and time, rotates them without loss of quality, and more. Free to try, $19.95 to buy, from `hoju.de/whatis.htm`.

TODAY'S FOCUS: Digital Photography

SCOTCH TAPE INVENTED

Richard Gurley Drew was granted a patent for transparent adhesive tape in St Paul, Minnesota, on this day in 1930. Later that same year, "cellophane tape" was commercially produced by the Minnesota Manufacturing and Mining Company. Later, 3M changed the sticky stuff's name to "Scotch Tape." Today's tape is made with a combination of a film backing with a pressure-sensitive, synthetic adhesive dried in long, high-temperature ovens. A jumbo roll made in 3M's plant is big enough to reach in half-inch strips from Washington, D.C., to Boston, Massachusetts.

Related Web site `3m.com/about3m/student/scotchbrand`

Clean Up Portraits

By Scott Kelby

Anybody can turn regular snapshots into studio-quality photos with the help of these Photoshop techniques.

Remove Dark Circles Under Eyes Choose the Clone Stamp (also known as the Rubber Stamp) tool. In the tool's option bar, change the Blend mode to Lighten and lower the tool's opacity to 50%. Choose a medium-size soft-edge brush. If you're using a Mac, hold down the Option key. PC users will want to hold down the Alt key. Click once just below the area you want to lighten, right below the dark circles. Move over the dark circle areas and paint them away. Because you're in Lighten mode, it will affect only colors (pixels) that are darker than the area you Option/Alt-clicked in, preserving the lighter pixels (and the detail).

Slim and Trim Here's the easy way to lose 10 or 15 pounds without going to the gym. Choose **All** from the **Select** menu. Press Command+T on the Mac or Ctrl+T on the PC to bring up Photoshop's Free Transform command. Grab the left center point and drag it about 1/8-inch or slightly more to

the left to horizontally scale the image in, instantly slimming your subject. Use the Crop tool to recrop the image to size.

Smooth Out the Skin Instantly smooth out the skin and give an overall softer look to the image. Copy the Background layer in the Layers palette. In the Copy layer, apply a Gaussian Blur. Apply a 2-pixel blur to low-res images or a 6-pixel blur for 300ppi high-resolution images. Lower the opacity of the copy layer to 50%. Switch to the Eraser tool, choose a soft-edged brush, and erase the areas that you'd like to have full detail, such as the eyes, eyelids, lips, teeth, jewelry, clothes, and background areas. When it looks about right, merge the two layers by pressing Command+E on the Mac or Ctrl+E on the PC.

Make Eyes Sparkle Enhance or create catchlights in the subject's eyes using the Sharpen tool. Lower the opacity to about 25%. Choose a soft-edged brush approximately the same size as the eyes. Click a few times directly over the eyes to make them sparkle.

(Scott Kelby is editor of Photoshop User *magazine at* `photoshopuser.com`.*)*

TIP OF THE DAY

- Before taking a picture, push the shutter button halfway down to allow the camera to auto-focus and set auto-exposure levels.
- Choose an image resolution that will suit your needs. Low for Web/email shots; high for printing.
- Carry extra batteries. Digital cameras eat up lots of power.

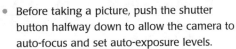

DOWNLOAD OF THE DAY ArcSoft's PhotoFantasyLE allows you to insert your face onto various backgrounds. Free from `www.webattack.com/get/photofantasy.shtml`.

TODAY'S FOCUS: Digital Photography

BIRTH OF COBOL

A two-day meeting that led to the development of the Common Business-Oriented Language kicked off on this day in 1959. COBOL, developed by the U.S. Department of Defense, stems from work begun several years earlier by Grace Murray Hopper.

Related Web site `cobolportal.com`

MAY
28

Making Great Portraits

By Mikkel Aaland

Digital cameras make it easier than ever to take successful portraits. You can instantly show your subject the results on a screen and elicit an immediate response, making the subject more involved in the process. And you can be confident that you've got the right smile and the right look without spending any more time than necessary.

Before You Shoot

- **Get to know the capabilities and limitations of your digital camera**—You will be more confident and your subject will likely pick up on your confidence and relax.
- **Know your camera's lag time**—Many digital cameras have an annoying pause between the time the shutter release is tripped and the moment the shutter actually releases. This is frustrating, but if you are aware of the lag you can anticipate the right moment and improve the odds of getting the shot you want.

- **Know your digital camera's power requirements**—Earlier digital cameras were energy hogs. Newer ones are better. Still, starting with fresh batteries and bringing backups can make a photo shoot go much smoother.
- **Know how many images your camera is capable of recording**—Although the precise number of images you need will vary depending on your subject, it's best if you don't have to stop in the middle of a shoot to erase unwanted shots or switch memory cards.

Shooting Tips

- **Pay attention to the quality of light**—Built-in flashes produce light that can be harsh and unflattering. It's best to mix flash light with ambient light. You can also diffuse the flash with translucent tissue, or, if need be, by placing your finger partially over the flash to cut down the intensity.
- **Use medium-long focal length settings and avoid wide-angle lenses**—Wide-angle lenses tend to distort the face. Longer focal lengths flatten and flatter facial features.
- **Choose your background carefully**—Avoid cluttered or distracting backgrounds. With many digital cameras you don't have the full advantage of selective focus, where the foreground is sharp and the background is blurred.
- **Vary the relative position of the camera to the face**—People with high foreheads, for example, benefit from a slightly lower camera angle. You'll have to experiment to find the most photogenic angle.

(Mikkel Aaland is a professional photographer and author. See his work at `cyberbohemia.com`.)

TIP OF THE DAY   Share your pictures on AOL.

1. Go to You've Got Pictures and click **My Pictures**.
2. Click the tab containing the pictures you want to share.
3. Click the radio button next to the roll or album you want to share.
4. To select individual pictures, click **View Pictures** and place a check mark next to your choices.
5. Click **Share Pictures**. Fill out the email information, and click **Send**.

DOWNLOAD OF THE DAY   B/Works turns your pictures into old-fashioned black-and-white, sepia, or duotone images, free from www. mediachance.com/digicam/bworks.htm.

TODAY'S FOCUS: Digital Photography

FIRST DIGITAL TV TEST

Zenith Electronics and AT&T sent the first long-distance digital television signal from Milwaukee, Wisconsin, to Glenview, Illinois, on this day in 1992. At the time, several companies were racing to develop HDTV technology. A year later, many of those same entities agreed to work together to set a standard for high-definition television (see May 24). However, the transition to digital is still seen by many as painfully slow.

Related Web site `atsc.org`

Online Photo Printing

Digital cameras are great, but my wife keeps asking, "Where are the prints?" You can print them yourself, or use one of these online printing services.

AOL You've Got Pictures You've Got Pictures is a joint venture with Kodak. Bring your rolls of undeveloped film to a participating photo processor. You'll receive prints as usual, but in a few days, the pictures will also be sent to AOL's servers so you can access them online, send them off to friends or family, make photo albums, or order reprints. The price is set by the developer, but the suggested retail is $9.99. You can also upload your own shots into albums you can share with others.

4×6 prints are 49¢, 5×7s cost $1.49, and 8×10s cost $4.49, all plus shipping and handling. AOL also offers mugs, mouse pads, t-shirts, and more.

Ofoto Ofoto is a Kodak company targeted at the digital camera owner. Start by downloading the OfotoNow software, free for Macintosh and Windows. Use the software to copy pictures from your camera, retouch, organize, and upload them to Ofoto. You can also use Ofoto's Web-based interface for uploading. They will develop your roll of film for $3.95 but no prints—they only return the negatives. You can order prints online.

Online storage is free, and you can share your albums with others. 4×6 prints are 49¢ each, 5×7 prints are 99¢ each, and 8×10 prints are $3.99 each, all plus shipping and handling. Ofoto offers many products, as well, including frames and photo greeting cards

Snapfish Snapfish focuses on inexpensive film processing. Send in your film using a prepaid postage coupon that you print from the Internet. Snapfish develops your film for $4.98, including shipping and handling, for a 36-exposure roll and mails you the 4×6 prints. Your images are digitized and stored in an online photo album that you can share. You can also upload pictures and print or share them.

Individual reprints are 49¢ per 4×6 print, 99¢ for 5×7 prints, and $3.99 for 8×10 prints (plus shipping and handling).

For a comprehensive review of other online photo printing services, visit `andromeda.com/people/ddyer/photo/albums.html`.

TIP OF THE DAY EXIF stands for Exchangeable Image File Format, and it's how most modern digital cameras store text information in image files. EXIF tags are used to store information about the camera, when the photo was taken, the camera's settings at that time, and much more. Many programs support EXIF, including OfotoNow, Apple's iPhoto, and Windows XP.

For more information about EXIF, visit `exif.org`.

DOWNLOAD OF THE DAY Extract all the EXIF info from your digital photos with EXIFRead. Free for Windows from `tawbaware.com/exifread.htm`. While you're there, check out his other useful programs for digital photography.

Another free EXIF info viewer is available from `oneilsoftware.hypermart.net/Exif/Exif.html`.

MAY 29

TODAY'S FOCUS: Digital Photography

FIRST NEWSPAPER

The first daily newspaper in the U.S. was published by Benjamin Towne on this day in 1783. *The Pennsylvania Evening Post*, also known as the *Public Advertiser*, was the only paper to be published in Philadelphia during the American Revolution, but it remained in circulation only 17 months. By 1801, there were about 20 daily newspapers in the country, and they existed mainly to provide merchants with information on prices and ship movements. These "mercantile papers" cost about six cents a copy, which was very expensive at the time.

Related Web site `historybuff.com`

Choosing a Digital Camera

By Brett Larsen

The first question I often hear when it comes to digital photography is, "Who needs a digital camera?" I always reply, "Anyone who wants one, really." Not everyone needs a digital camera. If, for example, you take pictures only occasionally or don't currently have a film camera, a digital camera might not be something you need. However, if you're constantly taking photos and are interested in sharing your work with the world (or just your friends), a digital camera is the way to go.

Second question: "Which camera is right for me?" Well, think of your needs. If your intention is only to shoot pictures you'll email, you'll be fine with a 1-megapixel or smaller camera for less than $200. The Olympus D-100 is a good option, as is the Kyocera EZ Digital 1.3, or even the $49 JamCam.

If you want to email photos, post them on the Web, and occasionally make a quick printout that won't be bigger than a 5×7, you'll want to get a 2-megapixel camera. Two great ones are the Canon S110 and the Nikon Coolpix 775. Both are easy to use, take great photos, and are less than $500.

If you're like me, you want it all, including 8×10 and bigger prints. For this, you need a minimum 3-megapixel camera—a 4-megapixel unit if you can afford it. The options in this category are a little pricey. Some add great features, not just a lot of megapixels. My personal favorite in the 4-megapixel category is the $1,700 Olympus E-10, as well as the $999 Canon PowerShot G2.

When deciding on a purchase, think of your budget and what you really want. Buying the latest and greatest is nice, but it will cost you more than you really need to spend. And although the technology of digital cameras isn't making leaps and bounds every month, what was the "best" this year won't be the best next year. Keep that in mind before you fork over $1,000 for the perfect camera.

TIP OF THE DAY Be sure any camera you buy supports the "USB Mass Storage Class" specification. If it does, you'll be able to plug it right into the USB port of your computer—Mac OS X, Windows XP, or Linux—and the camera will be automatically recognized as a hard drive. You generally don't have to install any additional drivers. You can copy your photos right off the camera just as you would any removable storage device.

DOWNLOAD OF THE DAY Ulead's Photo Explorer is an easy way to acquire, view, organize, adjust, and share digital images and video clips. Download a trial version from `ulead.com/pex/trial.htm`. $24.95 to buy.

POLL: How often do you surf while watching TV?

41% Always
31% Sometimes
14% Never
14% When ZDTV's on

TODAY'S FOCUS: Digital Photography

APPLE DUMPS JOBS

Steve Jobs was removed as general manager of the Macintosh unit on this day in 1985. Apple's then-president, John Sculley, made the move after a feud with the computer company's cofounder. Reportedly, Sculley blamed Jobs for the Macintosh's poor market performance—the machine's sales fell far below expectations in its first year. Jobs remained chairman of the board, but he resigned not long after to start another company, NeXT.

Related Web site `apple-history.com`

A Short History of the Netcam

By Martin Sargent

Is the Coffee On? (`www.cl.cam.ac.uk/coffee/qsf/coffee.html`) By most accounts, the first true Netcam was the Trojan Room Coffee Pot Cam in Cambridge, England. The Trojan Room is a computer research lab where, in 1991, about 15 scientists worked. These researchers worked hard and, thus, required a good deal of coffee. Problem was, the lab owned only one coffee maker, and it was way downstairs. Often, a researcher in need of a caffeine fix would journey all the way to the coffee maker, only to find it empty.

Quentin Stafford-Fraser, one of the researchers, pointed a camera at the lab's coffee pot and attached it to a computer equipped with a frame-grabber. Another researcher, Paul Jardetzky, wrote a server program that allowed the grabbed images of the coffee pot to be transferred across the Trojan Room computer network. Meanwhile, Stafford-Fraser wrote a client program that allowed anyone on a network-attached computer to view up-to-date images of the coffee pot. Anyone looking at the images would know whether making a trip to the coffee pot was worth it.

After a few amused journalists heard about and wrote of the Coffee Pot Cam, the researchers made the images of it publicly available on the early World Wide Web. There, it attracted the gaze of hundreds of thousands of curiosity seekers.

Something's Fishy (`home.netscape.com/fishcam/fishcam.html`) The second Netcam ever is the Amazing Netscape Fish Cam. Unlike the Coffee Pot Cam, the Fish Cam has no utility whatsoever. It's simply two cameras that point at a fish-filled aquarium and grab images.

Shockingly, at the height of its popularity, some 90,000 Web surfers per day pointed their browsers toward the Fish Cam. To this day, even in the latest version of Netscape, pressing Ctrl+Alt+F will whisk you directly to the Amazing Fish Cam.

The JenniCam (`Jennicam.org`) When Jennifer Ringley was a 21-year-old economics student at Dickinson College in Pennsylvania, she got a Netcam and decided to keep it on, in her bedroom, 24 hours a day. She wouldn't do anything special or entertaining, but simply live her life as she normally would.

The notion of a publicly lived, private life fascinated and brought out the voyeur in an immense segment of the Internet community. In a short space of time, Jenni was getting more than 100 million hits on her Web site every week.

 TIP OF THE DAY You can save the Earth even if your camera uses disposable batteries. Most work just as well with NiMH rechargeable batteries. MP3 players, too. Many electronics stores carry NiMH batteries and chargers, or buy online at `thomas-distributing.com`.

 DOWNLOAD OF THE DAY MySlideShow creates an autoplay slideshow on your PC. Perfect for burning to CD-ROM and sharing with friends and family. Free to try, $20 to buy, from `anixsoft.com`.

JUNE 2003

June 2003

SUNDAY	MONDAY	TUESDAY	WEDNESDAY	THURSDAY	FRIDAY	SATURDAY
1	**2**	**3**	**4** Henry Ford test drives first auto-mobile (1896)	**5**	**6** George Orwell's *1984* published (1949)	**7** International Math Olympiad (Tokyo, Japan)
8	**9**	**10**	**11** *E.T.: The Extra-Terrestrial* released (1982)	**12**	**13**	**14** Univac I computer debuts (1951); Flag Day
15 Father's Day	**16**	**17**	**18**	**19**	**20**	**21** First day of summer
22	**23** Alan Turing born (1912)	**24**	**25** George Orwell born (1903); Windows 98 released (1998)	**26** Human genome, or DNA, mapped (2000)	**27**	**28** Paul Broca born (1824)
29 Atlantis docks with Mir, orbits Earth (1995)	**30**					

TODAY'S FOCUS: Digital Photography

FIRST MECHANICAL DATA PROCESSOR

U.S. Census takers used the first machine to tabulate population information on this day in 1890. Surveyors used hole punches to record answers on a card, instead of writing responses on paper. The cards were counted by a tabulating machine invented by 29-year-old Herman Hollerith, who some call the world's first statistical engineer. Six years later, the New York native founded the Tabulating Machine Company. After many mergers and management changes, Hollerith's company became part of IBM in 1924.

Related Web site   www-groups.dcs.st-and.ac.uk/~history/Mathematicians/Hollerith.html

Top Five Digital Camera Features

By Chris Pirillo

Here are things to keep in mind when you go shopping for a digital camera.

Digital Zoom   Don't be swayed by those big numbers! Only optical zoom counts. Digital zoom uses interpolation (a.k.a. guesswork) to resample a 640×480 image into a 1600×1200 one—but the results are overly blurry and semipixelated. You can do a better job yourself with your favorite graphics tool.

Removable Digital Media   If the camera doesn't have removable digital media, hold out for one that does. Another thing to keep in mind: data transfer rates. If it uses a serial connection, keep searching for a USB one. Be sure your operating system is supported; if it isn't, don't lose hope. You can also get USB digital media readers (for CompactFlash, Memory Stick, SmartMedia, and so on). I prefer to use my PCMCIA (laptop card) adapter because it transfers the data much faster.

AV Out   If you're into instant gratification, consider getting a device with A/V out, so you can preview the camera's contents instantly on a TV set. This is great when you're using your camera at family gatherings and parties.

Tripod Thread   If you plan to take any low-light shots, be sure to get a camera with a tripod thread on the bottom of it. That'll help keep your camera steady. However, don't spend too much for a tripod unless you plan to use it often.

Never Settle for Second Best   Never, ever settle for second best. Be sure to look at untouched pictures and go with the one that makes what YOU feel is the best image.

If you want great starting points, visit this collection of sites:

- imaging-resource.com
- dpreview.com
- saycheese.com
- megapixel.net
- dcviews.com

TIP OF THE DAY   Windows XP has built-in support for digital photos and other images. Open a folder containing photos and select **Thumbnails** from the **View** menu to see what the images look like. Choose **Filmstrip** for a convenient way to look at your pictures. The buttons on the right under the image enable you to rotate it left or right. In the Picture Tasks bar on the left, you can View as a slideshow, Order prints online, Print pictures, or Copy all the items to a CD.

To display EXIF information, set the View to **Details**. Scroll to the right, and you'll see the date and time the photo was taken and its dimensions. Right-click on the category bar to add other information to the view.

DOWNLOAD OF THE DAY   iView's MediaPro is a Macintosh digital photo organizer with upload, export to Web, archive to CD, and more. Free for three weeks, $65 to buy, from www.iview-multimedia.com/products/mediapro.

TODAY'S FOCUS: Making Your Own CDs

FIRST CORPORATE VENTURE CAPITALIST DIES

General George Doriot, founder of the first non–family-owned venture capital firm in the U.S., died on this day in 1987. The Harvard Business School professor established the American Research and Development Corporation in Boston in 1946. The company was instrumental in funding many of today's technology leaders, including MIT graduate Kenneth Olsen, who founded Digital Equipment Company in 1957. One of Doriet's famous quotes was, "Always consider investing in a grade A entrepreneur with a grade B idea, but never invest in a grade B entrepreneur with a grade A idea."

Related Web site   nvca.org

CD Media

When I was a youth, geeky guys would court gals by giving them a "mix tape," a cassette filled with music that the guy thought would impress the girl with his sensitivity and sincerity. This seldom worked. But you can't keep a good geek down.

These days, geeks make their mixes on CD. It's still just as hopeless, but at least it's a lot easier. Using a computer, you can make a mix CD in less than five minutes.

The process of recording a CD is called *burning*, because the CD recorder's laser heats the surface of the blank to write data onto it. On CD-R discs, the laser changes the reflectivity of the disc by heating a layer of dye. This process is irreversible, so after a CD-R is full, it cannot be written to again.

On CD-RW discs, the laser melts portions of a layer to create bumps and pits. The CD-RW can be melted over and over again, so it can be used many times.

Both CD-R and CD-RW discs can hold 72–80 minutes of music, or 650–700MB of data. You can buy CD-R blanks for as little as 25¢ each. CD-RW discs cost $1 or so each. I generally stick with CD-R discs because they're so inexpensive and work in nearly all CD players.

There's no evidence that name-brand or more expensive CD blanks work better than the cheaper off-brand varieties. And you definitely don't need to buy CD blanks that are labeled for "music." These blanks are no better than any others; they just cost more.

Some folks claim that certain colors of CDs work better or last longer. There's no evidence of that, either. Frankly, the only rule to buying CD media is to use the cheapest disc that works with your recorder.

For a good price on CD and DVD media, try www.cdrecordable.com.

For more information on the CD-R format, visit Andy McFadden's CD-Recordable FAQ at www.cdrfaq.org.

TIP OF THE DAY   You can clean a CD-R just as you would any CD. Use a clean, dry, lint-free cloth and wipe the disc radially, from the center outward. Don't rub it in a circular motion, because the resulting circular scratches are more likely to confuse the CD player's error-correction circuitry.

You can clean a really dirty disc with warm water and dish soap. Stay away from solvents, though, especially with CD-Rs. They can dissolve the lacquer coating.

DOWNLOAD OF THE DAY   One of the best CD-burning applications for Windows is Nero Burning ROM (get it? Nero. Burning. Rome.), free for 30 days, then $50 to purchase, from www.nero.com.

TUESDAY, JUNE 3, 2003

TODAY'S FOCUS: Making Your Own CDs

FIRST SPACEWALK

Edward White made the first U.S. spacewalk on this day in 1965. White flew with Commander James A. McDivitt aboard shuttle Gemini 4 on a four-day mission to study the effects of prolonged space flight. White was attached to the spacecraft by an 8-meter tether during the 23-minute walk. The Americans weren't the first to achieve this feat, however. Soviet cosmonaut Alexei Leonov exited the airlock of Voskhod 2 nearly two and a half months earlier, on March 18 of the same year.

Related Web site   `life.com/Life/space/giantleap/sec4/sec4.html`

Burn CDs in Windows XP

Windows XP's integrated CD burner is powered by the Roxio engine, but it lacks Roxio's Easy CD Creator interface. There is no CD Burner icon on the desktop or in the Start menu. So, where is this promised CD burner? There are two answers, depending on whether you want to burn audio or data CDs.

To Burn Data CDs   Open a folder. Look at the folder options on the left of your screen. You should see an option to Copy All Items to CD or Copy to CD, depending on your folder view. You can also right-click a file or folder and choose **Send To** and then **CD drive**. I appreciate that XP has made it as easy to drop files to a CD as it is a Zip disk. It does not copy the files immediately. Instead, it places them into a repository and waits for further instruction on when and where to burn the CD. Now, place a blank CD into your CD drive or navigate to your CD drive in My Computer, and choose to write the files to a CD.

To Burn Music CDs   The Windows Media Player was always a monstrosity, and now it now includes a new function: CD burning. Select a song in your My Documents folder, and choose **Copy to Audio CD** from the folder options on the left. Surprise! Up pops the Windows Media Player, waiting for you to choose **Copy to CD**. Click the record button, and have a good time.

Limitations of the Incorporated CD Burner   You cannot create bootable CDs with the Windows XP CD burner, nor can you create a CD from an image (such as an .iso file). If you want this functionality, you need to install CD-burning software. As I've mentioned earlier, I'm a fan of Nero, from `nero.com`. It's free for 30 days, and then a mere $49 to buy.

 TIP OF THE DAY   Some software tools, such as Nero, will run only when you're logged in to Windows XP with Administrator rights. But as I've often said, you shouldn't be logged in as Administrator for day-to-day work. Who wants to log out of XP, and then log back in as an Administrator, just to use one app?

Windows XP lets you run any program as any user, including Administrator, with the Run As command. Right-click on Nero's application icon, select **Properties**, and click **Run As**. Choose **Administrator** from the drop-down list, enter the Admin password, and then click **OK**. You'll run the program with all the privileges of the Administrator without logging out.

 DOWNLOAD OF THE DAY   Print CD labels with Label Creator 4000, free from `efrance.fr/survivor`.

TODAY'S FOCUS: Making Your Own CDs

MICROSOFT LICENSES VBA

Microsoft announced it would license Visual Basic for Applications on this day in 1996. The move was designed to help the Seattle-based company compete with Sun's new Java programming language for Internet applications. This version of Visual Basic made it easier to customize Microsoft Office programs and import data between applications. It's used to create custom command buttons, dialog boxes, menus, and more. Today, VBA is the most common programming language used to manipulate other Microsoft applications, including Excel.

Related Web site `msdn.microsoft.com/vba`

Copy Your Home Movies to CD

These days, everyone is talking about recording your own DVDs, but there's an older format called *Video Compact Disc (VCD)* that can put up to 80 minutes of VHS-quality video on a single CD. If you've got a CD burner and the right software, creating VCDs is easy. They're a great way to archive and share video until you buy that DVD burner.

Digitize the Video   Start by getting the video onto your hard drive. To do this, you need a video capture card or, if you have a digital video camera, a 1394 or FireWire port.

You can buy a video capture card for well under $100. ATI's All-in-Wonder is a good choice if you're buying a new video card anyway. ATI also offers the less expensive TV-Wonder video capture card that connects via a USB port. Both are available from `atitech.com`.

Capture your video to hard drive using the best quality possible with a color depth of at least 24 bits per pixel.

Create a VCD   Some capture software can save the resulting video in VCD-compatible MPEG-1 format. If not, save it as an AVI and use the free VCDEasy from `vcdeasy.org` to convert the file to the proper format.

Record a VCD   After you've copied and converted your video, use a VCD-authoring program to burn your VCD. Most CD-burning software supports VCD creation, and some programs even allow you to create menus just like DVDs. Three good choices for burning VCDs are

- Roxio's Easy CD Creator: `roxio.com`
- Ahead's Nero: `nero.com`
- VOB's InstantCD/DVD: `www.vob.de`

VCD video quality is not as good as DVD, but in many cases it's good enough. For best results, play it back on your PC at 640×480 resolution. It will look even better on a TV set; about as good as a VHS tape, in fact.

 TIP OF THE DAY   Nearly all recent DVD players can play VCD discs. For a list of compatible players, visit `vcdhelp.com/dvdplayers.php`. The VCDHelp Web site, `vcdhelp.com`, also offers a wealth of VCD-related information.

 DOWNLOAD OF THE DAY   Windows Media Player can play VCDs with no additional software. Insert the VCD into your CD-ROM or DVD-ROM and use the Media Player to browse to the MPEGAV folder. Open the .dat file to play the VCD.

If you have a VCD with stills and navigation menus, use a software DVD player such as PowerDVD, free to try, $49.95 to buy, from `www.gocyberlink.com`.

 On the Macintosh, you can use QuickTime. Or try MacVCD for Classic and OS X, free to try, $19.95 to buy, from `mireth.com/macvcd.html`.

On Linux, use mtv, free to try, $10 to buy, from `mpegtv.com/download.html`.

TODAY'S FOCUS: Making Your Own CDs

APPLE II RELEASED

The first successful personal computer hit store shelves on this day in 1977. The Apple II featured a color screen, a built-in version of the BASIC computer language, and a $1,298 price tag. It had a CPU speed of 1MHz and 4k of memory. Steve Wozniak built the Apple II's predecessor, the Apple I, several years earlier for his fellow members in the Homebrew Computer Club. In 1976, Woz and Steve Jobs founded Apple Computer in their Cupertino, California, garage (see the April 1 entry).

Related Web site `apple2.org`

Digitally Remaster Your LPs

Here's a great project. Convert all those Frankie Valli 45s into CDs in just four steps:

1. Hook up your stereo to your computer's sound card.
2. Record your old music to the hard drive.
3. Clean up the digital recordings.
4. Burn them to CD.

Connect the stereo to the sound card with a cable from your local electronics store. Look for a stereo cable with RCA jacks on one end and a mini-jack on the other. The RCA connectors go to your amp or receiver. The mini-jack goes into the line-in connector on you computer.

You'll need some sound recording software to capture the music as you play it. When you record, capture the audio as uncompressed WAV files. They take up more space, but there's no loss of quality and WAV files are more easily edited. There are many programs you can use, including

- MusicMatch Jukebox, free from `musicmatch.com`
- SoundForge XP, $59.97 from `sonicfoundry.com`
- Cool Edit 2000, free to try, $69 to buy, from `syntrillium.com`
- AudioTools, free to try, $20 to buy, from `unrelatedinventions.com`
- Audio Cleaning Lab, $24.95 from `magix.net`
- SpinDoctor, part of Roxio's $99 Easy CD Creator Platinum package, `roxio.com`

MusicMatch offers the fewest tools. It can capture your music as an uncompressed WAV file or MP3. It can also record your audio CD.

SoundForge and CoolEdit are primarily sound recording and editing programs. They have the tools you'll need to clean up the pops, clicks, and hiss of analog recordings, but they don't include CD burning. Nevertheless, they'll come in handy.

AudioTools is an inexpensive shareware program that does everything you want. It automatically detects the beginning and end of songs, records to WAV, and has some audio clean-up capabilities. It can even burn your creation to CD. Magix Audio Cleaning Lab offers a similar feature set from a well-known German audio company.

SpinDoctor was designed for this process, too. If Easy CD Creator came with your CD burner, you might already have the program. If not, the upgrade is inexpensive.

Choose your software. Record your music. Clean it up. Burn your CDs. Your favorite songs are ready for another generation of listening pleasure.

 TIP OF THE DAY Do you ever notice a short pause or click between tracks when you burn an audio CD, even if you've turned off the two-second gap? To eliminate the click, select **disc-at-once burning** instead of track-at-once before you click the record button.

 DOWNLOAD OF THE DAY CloneCD is a CD-copying program that works with many copy-protected discs. Free to try, $31.50 to buy, from `elby.ch`.

POLL: Can anyone create an uncrackable code?

16% Yes

84% No

TODAY'S FOCUS: Making Your Own CDs

SEC CREATED

The U.S. Securities and Exchange Commission was created on this day in 1934. The SEC was formed by Franklin D. Roosevelt after the Great Depression to regulate the stock market and restore the public's confidence in investing. The Commission, composed of five members appointed by the president, makes sure companies disclose their financial information to potential investors and oversees the activities of stockbrokers, investment advisors, mutual funds, and public utility holding companies.

Related Web sites `sechistorical.org, www.sec.gov`

Packet Writing

There are two ways to write to CD-R and CD-RW discs. Usually, you'll work in premastering mode, creating a list of files to write to the disc, and then writing them in a batch. But it's often more convenient to write to CD-R/RW media such as a floppy disk, dragging files to the disc icon, and writing them immediately. That's called *packet writing*. All modern CD writers support packet writing, but not all older ones do.

To packet write to a CD-R/RW, you'll need to be running special software in the background all the time—software that tricks the operating system into treating the CD like a hard drive, and then intercepts the write commands to make them work with your burner. Your burner might have come with such a program, such as Adaptec's DirectCD, Prassi's abCD, or Nero's InCD.

When you first insert a blank disc, the software will prompt you to format that disc. The process is very quick because all it's really doing is reserving space on the disc for a table of contents, or TOC. When you're done with the disc—usually when it's full—you can use the software to "close" or "finalize" it, writing the TOC. When the disc is closed, it's just like any other CD-R/RW, but you can no longer add to it.

Until you close a disc, you'll have to be running the packet-writing software to be able to read it because it doesn't have a TOC yet. If you share the unclosed disc with someone else, or try to read it on a normal CD-ROM drive, it won't work without packet-reading software (see below).

 If your burner didn't come with packet-writing software, you can download a free 30-day demo of Instant CD/DVD for Windows from `www.vob.de/us/products/consumer/InstantCD`.

Unfortunately, as I write this, there is no good packet-writing program for Mac OS X.

 TIP OF THE DAY Audio CD player not recognizing your new Phish album? Maybe the data hasn't been entered into CDDB yet. CDDB is a massive database of nearly every audio CD ever recorded. It was created by users like you who uploaded information about their discs. Add to or correct the database through your CD-playing software. For example, in MusicMatch:

1. Click the **Options** menu.
2. Point to **Recorder**, and select **Send Album Info to CDDB**.
3. A window with the CD and track information will open. Click the **Submit to CDDB** button if everything is correct.

Read the submission guidelines first, at `www.gracenote.com/FAQs.html/faqset=subs/page=5`.

DOWNLOAD OF THE DAY If your computer is having trouble reading packet-written discs, download a free reader:

Roxio UDF Reader: `www.roxio.com/en/support/udfwin/udfwinupdates.html`

Nero EasyWriteReader: `nero.com/en/index.html#download`

Instant Read: `www.vobinc.com/us/Downloads.htm`

JUNE
6

TODAY'S FOCUS: Making Your Own CDs

COMPUTER SCIENCE PIONEER DIES

Alan Turing, who made some of the earliest advancements in digital computing, committed suicide on this day in 1954. At age 24, the London native suggested a device that could perform mathematical operations based on a program. The "Turing Machine" became the theoretical model for digital computers in the 1940s. In 1945, Turing developed the ACE computer (Automatic Computing Engine), for the National Physical Laboratory in London. He was also the first to conceptualize artificial intelligence, and believed that some day an abstract computing machine with limitless memory could be programmed to think like humans.

Related Web site   www.turing.org.uk/turing/

Remove CD Scratches

By Roger Chang

When CDs first came out, they were touted as indestructible. Guess we know better now. In fact, CDs scratch very easily.

If the scratch is on the label side, it might be irreparable because the reflective surface and actual data are just under the label. On the other hand, a scratch on the clear side, even a deep one, often can be repaired.

Commercial Scratch Removers   You can spend some money on scratch removers, but do they work? I tried two. First, the SkipDoctor MD from Digital Innovations. SkipDoctor MD is a motorized polisher; it scrubs off the top layer of plastic until the scratches are faint or gone altogether. It worked well on minor scratches but  had a hard time dealing with deeper gashes. Removing deeper scratches takes a bit of time. Even the minor scratches were still visible under close inspection. Although the SkipDoctor MD does work, at $30 it's not cheap.

The next product I tried was Wipe Out!, $15 from Esprit Development. I tested Wipe Out! on three scratched discs. One, an audio disc, was lightly scratched with wear. The two data CDs were deeply scratched with a pocket knife. After repair, all three still played, but with some major hesitation on the data CDs and a skip on the audio CD.

Wipe Out! did much better than the SkipDoctor MD on the larger, deeper scratches, although it ties with SkipDoctor MD on the minor, lighter scratches. The Wipe Out! Solution is pretty toxic stuff and is highly flammable. The SkipDoctor MD uses only distilled water.

Home Remedies   You don't really need to buy a commercial cleaner if the disc is only lightly scratched. You can get good results with any mildly abrasive agent, such as furniture polish or baking soda toothpaste. Just take any lint-free cloth, add some of the abrasive to the afflicted area, and then wipe. Be sure to work radially, from the center of the disc to the rim in a straight line. Never wipe in a circular pattern.

This technique does nothing for the deeper blemishes, though. For that, some people recommend applying a carnauba-based car wax. I tried Turtle Wax and elbow grease but got nothing other than a really shiny CD that still wouldn't play.

 TIP OF THE DAY   Andy McFadden's CD-Recordable FAQ tells you everything you need to know about CD-R/RW, at cdrfaq.org.

 DOWNLOAD OF THE DAY   CD-Mate, CD ripper and burner, is one of the most complete programs out there. Free to try, $29 to buy, from cd-mate.com.

JUNE 7

TODAY'S FOCUS: Geek Vacation Hotspots

"DILBERT" CREATOR BORN

The cartoonist famous for portraying geek life in cubicles is 46 years old today. Scott Adams was born in Windham, New York, on this day in 1957. The former bank and phone company employee originally created Dilbert to use as a visual aide for his business presentations. Today, his comic strip appears in 2,000 newspapers in 65 countries. Adams also owns a restaurant near Silicon Valley and is CEO of his own food company, which makes packaged meals and snacks aimed at the cubicle crowd.

Related Web sites `dilbert.com`, `dilberito.com`

Twisted List: Nerd Vacations

By Martin Sargent

Where does a Dilbert like me go on vacation? Read and learn.

Geek Cruises (`www.geekcruises.com`) Imagine being out to sea with some of the geekiest people in the world. They're on the ship not so much for the sun, white beaches, or tropical drinks, but rather to participate in intense Linux seminars taught by the biggest names in the open-source movement. It's a dream come true.

Take, for example, Linux Lunacy, a seven-day trip through the Eastern Caribbean featuring such luminaries as Richard Stallman, Eric S. Raymond, Jon "maddog" Hall, and Doc Searls. Imagine these dudes at the all-you-can-eat buffets! It must be insane.

It's probably too late to get onboard Linux Lunacy, but you can still get your boarding pass for Mac Mania II, Java Jam III, Perl Whirl '03, or Senior Surf, for older newbies. You know I'll be there.

My Elf Attacks the Orc (`wizards.com/gencon`) About 25,000 role-playing game aficionados converged in Milwaukee, Wisconsin, in August 2002 for the 35th annual Gen Con, the largest science-fiction, fantasy, and gaming convention in the nation. And you better believe it, my 16th-level Drow elf wizard Mezbhul the Grey and I are so ready for Gen Con '03 next August!

If you're into playing Dungeons & Dragons, Call of Cthulhu, and Magic: The Gathering, or if you just like to dress up like a storm trooper or a wood elf, Gen Con should be on your family's vacation short list.

Dave's Silicon Valley Tour (`zanid.com/sv/siliconvalley.html`) Apparently, there are people who travel to Silicon Valley to have their pictures snapped in front of places such as Intel and Hewlett-Packard. Well, at least that's what this guy Dave did. But Dave is not alone. Europeans pay money to be shown around Silicon Valley and other tech hotspots. If you want to join one of these adventures, visit `www.siliconvalley.nl`.

 TIP OF THE DAY Press PrtScrn to capture the screen to your Clipboard; Alt+PrtScrn to capture just the top window.

 On the Mac, press Cmd+Shift+3 to capture the screen to a file, Cmd+Shift+4 to capture a selection. (Use the plus cursor to highlight part of the screen. When you let go of the mouse button, the grayed-out area will be captured.)

 DOWNLOAD OF THE DAY The Quintessential Player is a free music player that does it all, including Autoplay CDs, drag and play MP3s, listen to streaming audio, get music info from the CDDB, and rip CDs. Free from `quinnware.com`.

POLL: What's your Geek Olympic event?

19% Three-Legged Overclocking Race

6% Synchronized Synching

34% Greased Penguin Catch

26% Pizza-Eating Contest

15% Athlon Decathlon

JUNE 8

TODAY'S FOCUS: The Internet

FIRST XEROX PC

Xerox became the first office products company to unveil a personal computer on this day in 1981. The Xerox 820 featured a 4Mhz Z80 CPU, 64Kb RAM, and two 8-inch floppy disk drives. The monitor was capable of displaying 24 lines of 80-character type, but could not display graphics. The system weighed more than 80 pounds and cost $3,000. The 820 also reportedly had a bug that would cause the disk drive to blindly reformat disks and erase users' data.

Related Web site `www.parc.com/company/history/`

Alternative Browsers

By Russ Pitts and Scott Herriott

Just because your computer comes with AOL, Internet Explorer, or Netscape Navigator, you don't have to use them to browse the Web. Here are five alternative Web browsers that run under Windows and Linux.

HotJava (`java.sun.com/products/hotjava`)   A neat Java-based browser from Sun. It's not officially supported under Linux, but it's Java, so it must be good. And, perhaps more importantly, it has a cool name.

Amaya (`www.w3.org/Amaya`)   Amaya is an open-source browser and Web page editor in one from the folks who set the standards for the Web: the World Wide Web Consortium. As such, it's used to demonstrate and test the latest developments in Web protocols. Not much to look at, though.

Xbrowser (`xbrowser.sourceforge.net`)   We just like it because the name has the letter X in it. Also Java-based and open source, and it allows multithreading, so it must be good.

Opera (`opera.com`)   Supposedly the "Fastest Browser on Earth." It *is* fast, has a neat multiple-session feature that remembers where it's been even after shutdown, and is easy to configure. Our favorite feature to date is the capability to forbid Web sites permission to open pop-up windows.

Mozilla (`mozilla.org`)   Topping our list is the king of all open-source browser projects, Mozilla. Originally based on the same source code for Netscape 6.1, this browser is in constant development. It's fast, fun, and hearkens back to the good old days when you had to explain to your mother what a Web browser was.

TIP OF THE DAY   Save your favorite Web sites to your hard drive for those times when you can't get online—like when you're 30,000 feet in the air in a 767.

 In IE 6, surf to the site you want to save. Click **Add to Favorites** under the **Favorites** menu and check the **Make Available Offline** box. Click the **Customize** button and use the wizard to select your settings. You can also use the **Synchronize** item from the **Tools** menu.

To open a synchronized site, select **Work Offline** from the **File** menu, and surf to the site as usual. Remember to uncheck **Work Offline** when you get back online.

 In IE for Mac OS X, surf to the site you want to save and select **Subscribe** from the **Favorites** menu. Then, click the **Customize** button. Click the **Offline** tab to configure the page for download.

 DOWNLOAD OF THE DAY   There are many more browsers than we have room for here. Get a listing of them all on Yahoo!'s browsers page: `dir.yahoo.com/Computers_and_Internet/ Software/Internet/World_Wide_Web/Browsers/`.

POLL: Can the Internet police itself?

64% Yes

36% No

TODAY'S FOCUS: The Internet

CABLE TV DEBUTS

The first television broadcast made via coaxial cable was transmitted on this day in 1936. AT&T, which was granted a patent for the use of coax cable five years earlier, laid the 343-line system that sent a signal from Radio City to the Empire State Building in New York City. That same year, AT&T laid the first experimental coaxial cable between New York and Philadelphia.

Related Web site `cablecenter.org`

Use the Usenet

By Bruce Stewart and Shawn Connally

Some of the best discussions on the Internet happen on Usenet, a collection of text-based message boards. Developed in 1979 by Steve Bellovin at the University of North Carolina, Usenet might seem like an online dinosaur, but it's anything but extinct. This mother of all bulletin boards has been the most successful and important tool in the creation of the "virtual communities" we've all heard so much about. Think of it as thousands upon thousands of separate online discussion groups, spiraling around one another at a dizzying pace.

So, how do you get involved? The Web browser you're using right now probably has everything you need. All that's left is a few configuration tips, some Netiquette hints, and a primer for sorting through the chaos.

Configuring Your Browser Enter the name of a newsgroup into your browser's address bar with `news:` in front of it (for example, `news:rec.humor.funny`) and you'll be prompted through the configuration process. You will need to know the name of your ISP's newsgroup server, typically something like `news.yourisp.com`.

You can also search and read the newsgroups online at `groups.google.com`, but you won't be able to post there. If your ISP doesn't offer newsgroup service, you can subscribe through `supernews.com` for as little as $7.95 a month.

Finding Your Way Around Initially, finding your way around Usenet can be very daunting, and it might not always be obvious where to find a newsgroup on a particular topic.

The newsgroups are arranged in a hierarchical tree structure, which will help you narrow things down a lot once you understand it.

To get started, some of the most common branches are `alt` (alternative), `comp` (computing), `rec` (recreation), `sci`

(science), and `soc` (society). The first part of the name is general (such as "comp"), the second part is more specific (such as "sys," which is short for "system"), and each successive part gets more specific. Some examples of actual newsgroups are `alt.appalachian.literature`, `comp.sys.mac.graphics`, `rec.outdoors.fishing.fly`, `sci.bio.technology`, and `soc.culture.esperanto`.

Usenet Netiquette Some newsgroups are light and humorous, some are very technical, and some tolerate "newbie" questions better than others do. Some are extremely adult. Get to know a newsgroup before jumping in.

Many newsgroups have a FAQ (frequently asked questions) file that gets posted regularly. Read it first. It's also a good idea to read the postings in a newsgroup for a few days before attempting to post your own message, just to get a sense of what's acceptable. When you do post, don't use your real email address, or disguise it. Spambots regularly troll the newsgroups for new addresses to flood.

TIP OF THE DAY Web Resources for Newsgroups

Usenet Help: `sunsite.unc.edu/usenet-i/usenet-help.html`

Searchable List of Usenet FAQs: `www.cis.ohio-state.edu/hypertext/faq/usenet/top.html`

Descriptions of Newsgroups: `sunsite.unc.edu/usenet-i/hier-s/master.html`

Search Newsgroups: `groups.google.com`

DOWNLOAD OF THE DAY Password Agent Lite keeps track of your passwords so you don't have to. Free for Windows from `moonsoftware.com/pwagent.asp`.

TODAY'S FOCUS: The Internet

CYBER STALKER SENTENCED

On this day in 1999, Carl Edward Johnson was sentenced to 37 months in prison for sending death threats via the Internet. The 49-year-old Canadian was convicted of four felony counts of sending threatening email to Microsoft Chairman Bill Gates' personal account, and to two federal judges in Washington state. Johnson had used anonymous remailers and forged email addresses in an attempt to disguise his identity, but the messages were traced and ultimately linked to him.

Related Web site `cybercrime.gov`

FTP: File Transfer Protocol

Usually, when you browse the Web you're using the hypertext transport protocol, or HTTP. But there are other protocols in common use on the Net. SMTP is used to send mail, NNTP serves the newsgroups, and FTP is often used to transfer files.

Like all the rest, FTP is a client/server protocol. An FTP server is used to offer files for downloading; an FTP client is used to download the files.

Client You already have an FTP client on your machine: your browser. Just as an experiment, enter the following line in your browser's address window: `ftp://wuarchive.wustl.edu`.

WUArchive is Washington University's public archive of downloadable files, and you're looking at it as if it were a folder on your hard drive. You can double-click folders to open them, and if you find something you want, you can drag it to your desktop to download it.

Usually, when you're downloading a file from a Web site, the browser is using FTP to do it. Your browser is a fairly primitive FTP client, however. If you run a Web site, or use FTP frequently for other reasons, take a peek at our downloads today for some better choices.

Server Installing and configuring an FTP server is something best left to the expert user. All sorts of security issues rear their ugly heads any time you put a server on your computer. However, if you want to give it a try, you can download a free and powerful shareware FTP server for Windows called Serv-U, from `serv-u.com`. Or, try the free open-source GuildFTPd from `nitrolic.com`.

Mac OS X already has an FTP server installed. To turn it on, open the Sharing System Preference pane and click **Allow FTP Access**. In either case, I strongly suggest thoroughly boning up on network security and the ins and outs of your particular server before you offer your system up to the Internet.

  TIP OF THE DAY Every computer on the Internet has a unique Internet protocol, or IP, address. IP addresses are four bytes long and usually are expressed as a "dotted quad," four numbers in the range 0–256 separated by periods, as in 192.168.0.1.

 In Windows 95/98/Me, open a DOS window and type **winipcfg**. In Windows NT/2K/XP, the command is **ipconfig**. On Mac OS X, open the Network System Preference pane.

 DOWNLOAD OF THE DAY WS_FTP LE is a free FTP client for Windows from www.gabn.net/junodj/ws_ftp32.htm.

I use CuteFTP, free to try, $39.95 to buy, from `cuteftp.com`.

For Mac OS 9, try FTP Client from www.vicomsoft.com/ftp_client/ftp.client.html. Free to try, $30 to own.

Mac OS X users have a good command-line FTP client already. Open the Terminal and type **man   ncftp**. Download the latest version from `ncftp.com`.

TODAY'S FOCUS: The Internet

COMMUNICATIONS DECENCY ACT DEEP-SIXED

A panel of federal judges said no to the Communications Decency Act on this day in 1996. The law made it a crime to transmit indecent material to minors on the Internet. The judges said the bill was unconstitutional and seriously restricted free speech. Later that year, the Supreme Court upheld the previous judges' ruling and struck down the Communications Decency Act altogether.

Related Web site `epic.org/CDA`

The Risks of Internet Gambling

By Avi Rubin

Are online casinos a good bet? Here are some things you should consider before you lay your money down.

Who Holds the Cards? The first and most obvious risk of online gambling is that the house could be crooked, a phony casino set up to loot your money and then disappear. The fancy brick-and-mortar casinos in Las Vegas inspire confidence by sheer physical presence. The pit bosses, security guards, and stacks of cash are enough to convince most people that Vegas casinos are not fly-by-night operations.

Raw Deals There's also the chance that the virtual house will not play by the rules. How do you know that a deck is actually shuffled online? What's to stop the site's software from weighting the hands in the house's favor? In physical casinos, you can see the cards and see the dealer's hands.

Take the Money and Run A basic risk of online gambling is that the house will refuse to pay up. If you win the game, the site can simply refuse to pay. What kind of legal leverage do you have against a seemingly anonymous entity on the Internet that is running out of someone's garage in the Cayman Islands?

Ace in the Hole Who's policing the other players? Think about a poker table at a casino. If you saw players signaling to each other across the table and colluding to beat you, you'd probably take off. Online, however, there is nothing to stop players from sharing information over the phone or via instant messaging to cheat you.

Learn the Law Another risk of gambling online is that it actually might be illegal where you live. There are many legal aspects of online gambling that have yet to be determined in the courts. If you get cheated in an online casino, the authorities will have little sympathy if you were gambling illegally.

Although online gambling may appeal to some people, I'll stick to my occasional exotic trips and free drinks. Besides, ever since I had probability theory in college, I've abandoned games of chance where the odds are against me. I'll stick to predictable and safe bets—such as the stock market.

(Avi Rubin is a principal researcher at AT&T Labs—Research and a member of the board of directors of Usenix, the Advanced Computing Systems Association.)

 TIP OF THE DAY Learn another language with the help of your computer.

 Tell Me More, from Auralog: `www.auralog.com` ($69–$149)

Learn to Speak, from Broderbund: `broderbund.com/SubCategory.asp?CID=152` ($19.99–$49.99)

 DOWNLOAD OF THE DAY Download Accelerator Plus speeds up your Internet downloads by opening several connections at once. A must-have—it really works! Free from `speedbit.com`.

POLL: Did the Net make you do it?

93% No

7% Yes

TODAY'S FOCUS: The Internet

IBM CHALLENGES MICROSOFT

IBM announced it would offer more products and services for the Internet on this day in 1995. The move was designed to help IBM compete with Microsoft—two days earlier, IBM bought Lotus Development Corporation in the biggest computer industry merger of the time. Lotus' assets included its 1-2-3 spreadsheet program and Lotus Notes, which allowed workers on different computers to collaborate on the same document. Microsoft had also announced plans to expand its Web technologies, and was about to release Microsoft Exchange, a collaboration and networking program.

Related Web site   `www.lotus.com`

Be an Internet Broadcaster

Here's a fun project for this weekend. Set up your own Internet radio station in five easy steps.

1. Download and install Winamp from `Winamp.com`. (SHOUTcast works with Mac and Unix, too. Visit the site for instructions.)
2. Download and install the SHOUTcast DSP plug-in and SHOUTcast server from `shoutcast.com`. The plug-in acts as a bridge between the MP3 player and your server so people can hear what you're playing on the Internet.
3. Configure the server. Open the config file and set the maximum number of listeners and the password. You can leave the rest as is.
4. Configure the DSP plug-in to connect to the server.
   1. Open the Winamp preferences window and click the **DSP/Effect** subcategory under the **Plug-Ins** tree.
   2. Click on the **SHOUTcast Source DSP for Winamp** and a configuration box will pop up.
   3. Click the **Output** tab and click the **Connection** button.
   4. Enter the password you selected in step 3. Leave the rest as is.
   5. Click the **Yellowpages** button and enter a Genre.
   6. Finally, click the **Encoder** tab and choose your stream rate.

   Keep bandwidth limitations in mind here. If you have DSL or a cable modem, you're probably limited to 128Kbps upload. That's three users at 40Kbps.

5. Fill your Winamp playlist with MP3s and click **Play**. Go back to the DSP plug-in, click the **Output** tab, and click the **Connect** button. If you see your Winamp player communicating with the server, congratulations: You're on the air. Call Aunt Vera and give her your IP address. She can listen in by opening Winamp, typing Ctrl+L, and then entering the IP address you gave her.

There are some things to keep in mind. Even with a DSL or cable modem connection, you'll be able to serve a maximum of only five 24Kbps streams at a time. You could buy a server time from someone else, but it's going to cost you. And if you're playing music, don't forget the usage and license fees, which are exorbitantly high for Internet broadcasters.

On the other hand, you can use this technique to broadcast over your home network. Or company network. And it sure is a lot of fun to spin the hits, even if only Aunt Vera is listening.

 TIP OF THE DAY   As usual, there's more than one way to do things with a computer. For $6.95 a month, Live365's will do the whole thing for you. That way, a lot more people can listen to your station. Read all about it at `live365.com/broadcast`.

DOWNLOAD OF THE DAY   EmpTemp empties your temp folders, cleans out your cookies, and erases your Internet History. Free from `danish-shareware.dk/soft/emptemp`.

TODAY'S FOCUS: Flag Day

FIRST SCIENTIFIC PRESENTATION ON COMPUTING

Charles Babbage presented the first paper on mechanical computing to the Royal Astronomical Society on this day in 1822. Babbage proposed building a "Difference Engine," a machine capable of calculating equations and printing results. The following year, the British government agreed to fund Babbage's attempt to build the machine. The project was more costly than he had expected, however, and Babbage abandoned his plan for the Difference Engine more than 10 years after it was begun. In 1854, a Swedish engineer succeeded in constructing a Difference Engine based on Babbage's theories.

Related Web site   www.cbi.umn.edu

Celebrate Flag Day

United States flags might be out of stock at your local hardware store today, but they're still available digitally to put on your desktop as a screensaver or wallpaper.

 If you like a little movement in your screensaver, try the American Flag Screen Saver from acez.com/americanflag.htm. It features hundreds of waving flags on a white background or with your desktop as the background.

 Mac users are patriots, too. Download Old Glory from homepage.mac.com/mtrent/FileSharing.html.

 If you're in the market for more than just the flag, I recommend the musical slideshow screensaver from Megascreensavers, megascreensavers.com. It features a series of patriotic images, including Washington crossing the Delaware, Dr. Martin Luther King, Jr. giving his famous "I Have a Dream" speech, and the Constitution. Click on **Settings** if you're in an office environment where you need to mute the sound.

 Show your flag on your desktop, too, today, with Deskflag, from deskflag.com. It's a little waving flag app that runs on top of all your windows. It can also live in the taskbar. To make it wave faster, right-click and choose **DeskFlag Settings**. If you use Windows XP or Windows 2000, you can even make the flag translucent.

 If all the movement is making you jittery, download a beautiful static flag that's perfect for high-res wallpaper for Mac or Windows, from digitalblasphemy.com/dbgallery/5/emblem640.shtml.

It goes without saying, of course, that all of these downloads are 100% free.

 TIP OF THE DAY   Visit these sites honoring the U.S. flag today:

Smithsonian Exhibition of American Flag Magazine Covers from 1942: americanhistory.si.edu/1942

History of the American Flag: www.usflag.org

Flag Etiquette: geocities.com/Heartland/2328/flag1.htm

National Flag Day Foundation: Flagday.org

 DOWNLOAD OF THE DAY   Bring your flag to life with Gareth Hadfield's GT Ripple, a free program for Windows that causes a rippling effect on your desktop, from pnc.com.au/~garethth.

TODAY'S FOCUS: The Internet

FRANKLIN'S ELECTRICITY EXPERIMENT

Benjamin Franklin conducted his famous kite-flying experiment on this day in 1752. To confirm his theory that lightning was a naturally occurring electric current, the inventor attached a key to a kite and flew it during a thunderstorm to see whether lightning would pass through the metal. His experiment led to the discovery of plasma, a stream of electrified air. Today, plasma is used in neon signs, fluorescent bulbs, and flat-panel monitors.

Related Web site   `sln.fi.edu`

Father of the Internet

By Roman Loyola

The Internet has many fathers, not including Al Gore, but the fellow most often awarded that title is Vint Cerf.

As a UCLA graduate student in 1967, Cerf worked with Dr. Robert E. Kahn to develop the host-level protocols of the Advanced Research Projects Agency Network (ARPAnet), a network used by the U.S. military. The work on the ARPAnet eventually led to the Internet we use today.

Over the course of his 25 years watching the Internet evolve, he says the greatest change he's seen is "the emergence of the World Wide Web, for the creativity it's brought, the impact on business, and the possibilities of [global connectivity] and beyond."

Cerf, currently senior vice president at MCI Corp., believes that the biggest change that will occur over the next five years is the Internet's size. "It will rival the telephone network in terms of nodes and the variety of devices hooked up to it," he says.

For more information about the history of the Internet, try these links:

Cerf's Up (`worldcom.com/global/resources/cerfs_up`)   Cerf's personal Web site, with technical documents, frequently asked questions, presentations, and more.

Biography of Dr. Robert E. Kahn (`www.livinginternet.com/?i/ii_kahn.htm`)   Learn more about the co-creator of the Internet.

Internet Archive: ARPAnet (`www.archive.org/arpanet`) Collection of memoranda, interview notes, periodicals, papers, and other materials documenting the development of the ARPAnet for the Department of Defense.

Internet Society (`www.isoc.org`)   Professional membership society that provides leadership in addressing issues that confront the future of the Internet. It's the organizational home for the groups responsible for Internet infrastructure standards.

Internet Architecture Board (`www.iab.org`)   Technical advisory group of the Internet Society. Provides oversight of the architecture for the protocols and procedures used by the Internet.

Global Internet Project (`gip.org`)   International group of senior executives committed to fostering continued growth of the Internet.

Another father…

J.C.R. Licklider (`www.forbes.com/asap/2000/1127/105.html`)   *Forbes Magazine* credits Licklider, an experimental psychologist at Harvard University and MIT, with inventing the Internet.

 TIP OF THE DAY   Decrease the time it takes for your dial-up connection to get through by changing these settings in Windows 98 and Me:

1. Open the Dial-Up Networking folder.
2. Right-click your ISP and select **Properties**.
3. Click the **Server Types** tab.
4. Under **Advanced Options**, uncheck the **Log on to Network** box.
5. Check the box for **Enabled Software Compression**.
6. Under **Allowed Network Protocols**, uncheck **NetBEUI** and **IPX/SPX Compatible**.

DOWNLOAD OF THE DAY   EarthBrowser is a real-time application that displays current weather conditions, combined with satellite images, to give you a pretty impressive view of our little home. Free to try, $19.95 to buy, for Windows and Mac, from `earthbrowser.com`.

POLL: Have you ever fallen for an Internet hoax?

29% Yes   71% No

JUNE 15

TODAY'S FOCUS: Health

FIRST FEMALE ASTRONAUT

Valentina Tereshkova became the first woman in space on this day in 1963. Tereshkova flew aboard the Russian space shuttle Vostok 6 on a joint mission with Vostok 5. Legend has it rocket designer Sergei P. Korolev came up with the idea to train a female astronaut purely as a publicity stunt during the heated space race between Russia and the U.S. Tereshkova, a textile factory worker, was chosen because of her experience as an amateur parachute jumper. Korolev was reportedly unhappy with Tereshkova's performance during the mission and did not let her fly again.

Related Web site `liftoff.msfc.nasa.gov/rsa/rsa.html`

JUNE
16

Childproof Your Computer Area

By Nicole Guilfoyle and Rachel V. Murray

PCs are quickly becoming part of every household, but the personal computer poses hidden threats to infants, toddlers, children, and teens. Here are 10 things you can do to keep your kids safe:

Secure the Computer Room When your baby starts to walk or crawl, you probably won't want your bundle of joy to go near the computer without you. Use a reliable baby gate to block off the computer room.

Buy a Sturdy Desk Choose a heavy desk with locking doors or a rolltop that can conceal your PC from small eyes and hands.

Strap It Down Strap all bookshelves, televisions, and computer monitors to secure them. This prevents them from toppling if a young child climbs them. Use Velcro furniture straps to keep your PC stable on the desk, and secure all decorative items in your office.

Protect the Electric Always cover open outlets with outlet plugs or covers. Safety covers are also available for power strips. Keep all cords out of reach of children. Cord holders help prevent tripping, choking, and strangulation.

Shorten Wires and Cords Shorten all electrical wires using cable ties. This prevents children from chewing through the cord insulation or inadvertently wrapping the cord around their own neck.

Go Hands-Free Get a hands-free headset so you can carry your child even while on the phone.

Playpen in the Office Locate a playpen in your office when you absolutely have to get some work done while keeping an eye on your child.

Monitor Computer Use When your child becomes a little older, instill good computer habits from the beginning. Create a set of rules for computer use and stick to them.

Windows Password Password-protect your PC so a baby's errant keystrokes or a child's curious touch won't harm your files. It will also help prevent unauthorized computer use.

Watch Out for Net Predators Don't fool yourself into thinking filtering software is the answer to your prayers. Talk with your child about the Internet.

(Nicole Guilfoyle is an associate producer with TechTV, and Rachel V. Murray works with Safe & Sound Children, www.safeandsoundchildren.com.)

TIP OF THE DAY If you take vitamins and other dietary supplements, these sites can keep you informed:

InteliHealth (`www.intelihealth.com/IH/ihtIH/WSIHW000/325/7098.html`) Do you even need vitamins?

USDA Nutrient Database for Standard Reference (`www.nal.usda.gov/fnic/cgi-bin/nut_search.pl`) How many vitamins are in your diet?

HolisticHealthPlus.com (`www.holistichealthplus.com/CS.htm`) Compare vitamin prices.

Drugstore.com (`drugstore.com`) Buy online.

DOWNLOAD OF THE DAY They say pets reduce blood pressure and elevate mood. Play with a virtual dog at `virtualpuppy.com`. Cat person? Try `virtualkitty.com` instead.

TODAY'S FOCUS: Health

FIRST MOBILE PHONE SERVICE

The first mobile telephones were installed on this day in 1946. The Southwestern Bell Telephone Company installed car phones in St. Louis, Missouri, for two different customers. Earlier that year, the FCC had granted a license for the system using hardware developed by Bell Labs. But the technology couldn't keep up with demand: The service initially offered just six voice channels, meaning the system could handle only six callers simultaneously, which created a very long waiting list.

Related Web site affordablephones.net/HistoryCellular.htm

Office Exercise

By Laura Burstein

Many of us are stuck at a desk during the workday. Not only is this less fun than, say, walking on a sun-drenched tropical beach, but sitting in front of a computer for long periods of time can damage your body as well as crush your spirit.

More than half a million employees in the U.S. had to take time away from the office due to work-related musculoskeletal disorders (MSDs) in 1999, according to the Bureau of Labor Statistics, stats.bls.gov/iif/peoplebox.htm. But there are ways you can reduce the risk of problems by performing simple exercises at your desk at regular intervals.

Download a free trial version of Office Gym, a program that reminds you when to take breaks from your computer and offers illustrated exercises: download.cnet.com/downloads/0-10050-100-6386152.html?tag=st.dl.10001-103-3.1st-7-11.6386152.

RSI Shield is another download that tracks your use of the mouse and keyboard and forces you to take breaks regularly by actually blocking keyboard input. It also has animated exercises you can do at your desk. The 15-day trial is free; registration for the full version is $39: download.cnet.com/downloads/0-10106-100-6580234.html?tag=st.dl.10001-103-2.1st-7-5.6580234.

Online Options If you're looking for Web-based resources for office exercises, here are a couple of places you can go:

U.S. News Online and InteliHealth's Deskercises (www.usnews.com/usnews/nycu/work/wodesk.htm) This site will teach you desk techniques for "strengthening and stretching your problem areas." Simply choose which area you'd like to work on from the drop-down menu.

British Library (pages.britishlibrary.net/blwww3/deskexercises) This page of desk calisthenics from the British Library focuses on breathing exercises for meditation and relaxation in the workplace. Cute line drawings, too.

Of course, these exercises can't take the place of regular cardiovascular workouts or resistance training, but they can help ease the pain of a long workday sitting in a chair. Now flex those muscles and get moving!

 TIP OF THE DAY Figure out how many calories you burn riding your bike or washing the car with the Activity Calorie Counter at Nutricise, efit.com/calculators.

How many calories have you consumed? See Calories Count's Enhanced Calorie Calculator, caloriescount.com/cgi-bin/Enhanced_calcalc/enhanced_calcalc.cgi.

 Crosstrainer puts it all together with a calorie-counting menu-planner at www.innovativelogic.com/crosstrainer/download.htm. Try it free for 30 days. Pay $39.95 if you decide to keep it.

 DOWNLOAD OF THE DAY Guard against RSI. Every 30 minutes, Stretch Break will remind you to take a break, and show you pictures of recommended stretches. Free for 10 days, $44.95 to buy. Kids' version completely free. Wheelchair and Mac versions available, too; from www.paratec.com.

Typesafe does the same things without the neato pictures, but it's free from businessmetrics.com.

TODAY'S FOCUS: Health

VISICALC DISCONTINUED

Lotus Development Corporation announced it would discontinue VisiCalc on this day in 1985. The enormously successful spreadsheet program, created by Dan Bricklin and Bob Frankston, had been written back in 1979 for the Apple II computer. In 1983, Lotus developed its own spreadsheet program, Lotus 1-2-3, for the PC. At the time, VisiCalc still beat the new program hands-down, with $40 million in annual revenue. A couple of years later, though, the increasing popularity of IBM-compatible computers in the office prompted Lotus to buy VisiCalc's parent company, Software Arts, and dump the old spreadsheet program.

Related Web site The original VisiCalc for DOS was only 27.5KB. You can download it free from `bricklin.com/history/vcexecutable.htm`

Ergonomic Product Tips

By Don Morelli

Computers do not, by themselves, cause injury. It's what we do, how we do it, and for how long that creates the potential for injury. The most common problems related to computer work occur over time, so they can be avoided or reversed if not neglected.

The basic types of injuries associated with computer work include:

* Tendon inflammation
* Tendinitis in the wrist or forearm
* Epicondylitis (tennis elbow)
* Nerve compression
* Carpal tunnel syndrome
* Muscle fatigue
* Backache
* Visual discomfort

No single ergonomic product or rule fits every person, but a few general guidelines apply to most people and work situations.

Chair Your chair should fit your physical dimensions and working style. Focus on the following characteristics:

* Easily operated adjustments for seat height, backrest height, and angle
* Padded and upholstered seat pan and backrest
* Seat pan deep enough to match the length of your thigh, without pinching at the back of the knee
* Adjustable or removable forearm supports
* Rounded seat pan front (that is, waterfall edge)
* Five-legged chair base (for stability)
* Appropriate chair wheels for floor type

Keyboards Standard keyboards are fine for most people. To avoid bad posture habits, learn to touch-type. If you have significantly short or long arms, you might find a modular or alternative keyboard more comfortable than the standard straight, flat keyboard. If you don't input a lot of numbers, consider a keyboard with a separate 10-key. This will allow you to place your mouse or trackball within easy reach.

Mice Your mouse or trackball should fit your hand easily and not force your wrist into any awkward positions.

Monitors Position your display so the top of the screen is no higher than your eyes when seated comfortably. To reduce glare, don't have the display facing a window.

TIP OF THE DAY Many people are turning to yoga as a form of exercise and spiritual guidance. Although online information cannot substitute for personal instruction, here are a couple of great resources where you can learn more about yoga.

The Yoga Research and Education Center (www.yrec.org) offers practical advice on what to look for in a yoga teacher and how to find a center that suits your needs.

Learn more about the principles and history of yoga at Yoga Basics (www.yogabasics.com), a site created by yoga instructor Timothy Burgin.

DOWNLOAD OF THE DAY Download an introduction to yoga, including instructions and photos of poses. Free from Zentrum Publishing, self-realization.com. Check their Web page for several other wellness programs.

JUNE 18

TODAY'S FOCUS: Health

PASCAL BORN

Mathematician Blaise Pascal was born in Clermont, France, on this day in 1623. Blaise's father, a judge in the French tax court, refused to let the future philosopher study mathematics before age 15, and removed all related books from the house. Blaise, however, began to study geometry on his own at age 12. In his late teens, Pascal invented a calculating machine to help his father with his tax computations. He also consulted with Descartes on experiments with the barometer and atmospheric pressure. Pascal died in Paris at age 39 from a stomach growth that spread to his brain.

Related Web site   www.ams.org

AOL Health Resources

America Online has created one of the most complete online guides to health anywhere. AOL members can visit it by entering the keyword "health," but you don't need to be an AOL member to access AOL's health center: You can also visit it on the World Wide Web at aol.com/webcenters/health.

WebMD   AOL recently partnered with WebMD for its health coverage. One of the advantages of AOL's partnership with WebMD is that many of the articles are reviewed by physicians for safety and accuracy. AOL divides its health guide into sections on diseases and conditions, pharmacy and medicines, doctors and insurance, diet and nutrition, fitness and exercise, mental health, pregnancy, and so on.

Pick an Illness   The Diseases and Conditions button leads to a directory of more than 4,000 WebMD condition centers, from Parkinson's to pain management to smoking cessation. Each condition center contains articles, treatment information, newsletters, support groups, and more. Don't know what's wrong? The symptom checker will help you narrow down the possibilities.

Find a Doctor   Under the local health link you'll find a directory of doctors, hospitals, pharmacies, gyms, and spas by geographic location. If you've already entered your ZIP Code, the directory will automatically zero in on health resources close to you.

Design a Personal Exercise Program   Click the Fitness & Exercise button for lots of help staying in shape. Use the AOL Body Mass Index (BMI) calculator to figure out your ideal weight. Calculate your target heart rate, count your calories, or use the dessert wizard to figure out how long you'll have to exercise to burn off that hot fudge sundae.

Check the Alternatives   AOL's Health Center doesn't focus only on traditional medicine. You'll also find lots of information on alternatives such as acupuncture, massage, homeopathy, and yoga.

Join a Support Group   One in four people who go online to get health information also join a support group. Often, the best health information and support comes from other folks in the same boat. Sharing experiences and information with kindred spirits is healing in itself. The AOL Health area is one of the best places to go to find healing help and support.

 TIP OF THE DAY   The Coalition for Access to Affordable Prescription Drugs can save you up to 50% on prescription drugs by mail-ordering them from Canada: unitedhealthalliance.com.

 DOWNLOAD OF THE DAY   Create an exercise plan for yourself and stick with it. Try it for 30 days for free, buy it for $39.95: www.innovativelogic.com/crosstrainer.

POLL: The FDA is

50% Standing in the way of necessary technology

50% Looking out for our best interests

TODAY'S FOCUS: Health

U.S.-RUSSIA NUKE HOTLINE AGREEMENT

The United States and the USSR agreed to establish a "hotline" between Moscow and Washington, D.C., on this day in 1962. The system was designed at the height of the Cold War to prevent the possibility of a nuclear attack. Contrary to popular belief, it is not the big red phone portrayed in many television shows and movies. Instead, the 24-hour-a-day communications link consists of two teletype terminals connected by a wire telegraph circuit and a radiotelegraph circuit. Although the installation of the system was considered an important step in American-Soviet relations, it has never been used.

Related Web site `www.ncs.gov`

Recognizing Quack Weight-Loss Schemes

By Joan Price and Shannon Entin

The Web teems with useful weight-loss information, weight-loss misinformation, and a dogpile of advertisers trying to sell you tomfoolery disguised as the answer to your dreams. Greedy scoundrels feed on your desperation to lose weight, and they know that you'll buy anything that promises to answer your prayers. The sad truth is that most of these products and diets lighten only your wallet.

Here's how to find Web sites that cater to your needs without ripping you off.

Five Signs of a Credible Site

To help you **PILOT** your way through the friendly skies of the World Wide Web's health and fitness information, we've developed a method for evaluating Web site content. This systematic approach helps you quickly weed out the truly useless information and zero in on content that can educate you and help you achieve your health and fitness goals.

- **P**urpose—If the site has a mission statement, read it. If not, read the home page and analyze the site's purpose. Does it inform and educate, or is it designed to persuade, sell, outrage, or entertain?
- **I**nformation—Truly useful Web sites offer valuable information and emphasize facts rather than opinion

and testimonials. If the site is selling anything, ask yourself how that might influence the content.

- **L**inks—The best sites want to inform you and are happy to recommend additional Web sites to further your knowledge in that topic or related topics. The best links are rated or reviewed. Look for links that go beyond the current page and its related companies.
- **O**riginator—Who is responsible for the information? Best bets for sound health and fitness information are consumer-advocacy groups, health-professional organizations, well-known hospitals, and government- and university-sponsored sites. Consider the source.
- **T**imeliness—Depending on the topic you are looking into, the information should not be more than a few years old. Medical information should be more current. Look for sites that update frequently.

(Joan Price and Shannon Entin are the authors of The Complete Idiot's Guide to Online Health and Fitness, *Macmillan Computer Publishing, 1999.)*

TIP OF THE DAY   Identify fitness goals, receive a personalized workout, learn about fitness, and more at FitLinxx, `fitlinxx.com`.

DOWNLOAD OF THE DAY   Keyboard shortcuts save time, keep your hands on the keyboard, and reduce mousing strain. Keyboarding contains 2,900 keyboard shortcuts for Windows 95/98/Me/2000, Access 97 and 2000, Excel 97 and 2000, Outlook 97 and 2000, Word 97 and 2000, and Internet Explorer 4 and 5; free from `camtech2000.net/Pages/Keyboarding.html`.

POLL: Do you believe everything you read online?

3% Yes   97% No

TODAY'S FOCUS: Health

FIRST STORED-MEMORY COMPUTER

The first system to run a program from stored memory was tested on this day in 1948. The machine, developed at Manchester University in England, was based on a cathode-ray tube and proved the theories of mathematician John von Neumann, who had been working on a way to improve Eckert and Mauchly's ENIAC, built at the Moore School a few years earlier. The EDSAC, the commercial descendant of the ENIAC created in 1949 at Cambridge University, used the same principles set forth by this experimental computer (see May 6 entry).

Related Web site `ei.cs.vt.edu/~history/VonNeumann.html`

Essential Health and Fitness Sites

Look for sites that subscribe to the Health on the Net code (HON). It guarantees that all their advice is from medically trained and qualified pros, unless clearly indicated otherwise. It also guarantees your confidentiality and that the site is up-front about sponsorships and financial arrangements. HON (`www.hon.ch`) verifies the site's claim before it can post its seal of approval. All the following sites are HON approved, except for the government agencies.

Non-Commercial Links

Hardin Health Links (`www.lib.uiowa.edu/hardin/md`) The University of Iowa's Hardin Library maintains this voluminous directory of Internet health links. And they're all up to date.

U.S. Dept. of Health and Human Services (`healthfinder.gov`) A portal to health information from the HHS Office of Disease Prevention and Health Promotion. Useful directory of nonprofit and governmental health organizations, online checkups and health news.

MedlinePlus (`www.nlm.nih.gov/medlineplus`) A service of the National Library of Medicine at the National Institutes of Health. Health news and featured site links; dictionaries and directories; useful search engine.

Quackwatch (`www.quackwatch.com`) Dr. Stephen Barrett runs this site as a public service (he's been combating quackery since 1969!). If you wonder about a health claim, check it out here.

Commercial Sites

Dr. Koop (`drkoop.com`) The former U.S. Surgeon General has turned to selling vitamins and pop-ups to stay afloat, but there's still lots of useful information between the ads.

Health A to Z (`healthatoz.com`) "Your family health site." Hundreds of message boards, chats, and expert advice on health, with a focus on wellness.

InteliHealth (`intelihealth.com`) Aetna Insurance's health site aggregates content from Harvard Medical School and the University of Pennsylvania's School of Dental Medicine. There's a useful medical dictionary and drug resource center. Lots of interactive quizzes and calculators.

 TIP OF THE DAY Here are some sites that will help you fight back during allergy season.

The Personal Allergy Profile (`www.allergylearninglab.com/resources/pap/pap.html?id=5500997`): Part of The Allergy Learning Lab. A short quiz you can take to determine what you can do about specific allergies. After you take this quiz, you will be emailed a full report that will include ways to allergy-proof your life and the world around you as much as possible.

Pollen.com (`www.pollen.com`): View the current pollen count for your local area. The graphical layout makes it easy to gauge how hellish the day will be, allergywise.

 DOWNLOAD OF THE DAY Stuck at the computer? Find out what you're missing with WeatherMan, free for 30 days, then $10 to buy, from `homepage.mac.com/deandavis/Download.htm`.

Put the weather in your toolbar with Weatherpop, from `glu.com`. Free and paid versions. Mac OS X only.

 Windows users, put a complete weather station on your desktop with WeatherBug, free from `weatherbug.com`. Careful what email address you give them, unless you want WeatherBug mail forever.

TODAY'S FOCUS: Health

"FATHER OF DIGITAL COMPUTING" BORN

Konrad Zuse was born in Berlin, Germany, on this day in 1910. At age 31, he developed an electromechanical binary calculator named the Z3. Unlike similar machines built at the time, the Z3 did not use vacuum tubes. The German government ordered several of the inventor's calculators during WWII, but they were destroyed by Allied bombing. Zuse later claimed a patent on his machines predated those of any other developer, making him the inventor of the digital computer.

Related Web site `www.zib.de/`

Twisted List: Save the World

By Martin Sargent

Who would have thought that clicking your mouse could save the world? There are dozens of sites that raise money every time you click on one of their advertisers. Here are a few worthy of your mouse finger.

Save the Rain Forests   Any thinking person should be concerned about dwindling rain forests, air pollution, endangered species, and other environmental issues. But few of us have the time or financial resources to really do anything about it.

But at EcologyFund.com (`ecologyfund.com`), you can donate money to environmental crusades simply by clicking on links. As with the other sites I'll show you, by clicking on links you see advertisements, and the companies represented by those advertisements donate money to the cause you clicked, at no cost to you. Admittedly, the money you raise by clicking is a very small sum, like a fraction of a cent. But when lots of people click, it starts to add up.

Another click-to-donate environmental site is `Redjellyfish.com`, a solar-powered Web site where you can save the rain forest *and* feed chimps.

Fight Breast Cancer   Breast cancer is the second-leading cause of cancer-related death in the United States, behind lung cancer. Now you can help to make a difference simply by clicking on ads at The Breast Cancer Site, `thebreastcancersite.com`.

The money generated by your clicking goes toward providing free mammograms to underprivileged women. In 2001, 645 women received mammograms through your clicking.

Other related sites include The Rainforest Site (`therainforestsite.com`), where every click saves 11.4 square feet of endangered rain forest, and the original click-to-donate page, The Hunger Site (`thehungersite.com`), where each click raises enough money to buy one and a half cups of a staple food for hungry people worldwide.

Keep Helping   FreeDonation.com (`freedonation.com`) is a portal leading you toward many more click-to-donate sites on a range of issues, including AIDS, the arts, education, and homelessness.

TIP OF THE DAY   If you're looking for somewhere to volunteer, our Windows expert, Morgan Webb, suggests VolunteerMatch.org. She says it's the best Web site for finding a good place to donate your time and energy.

Simply enter your ZIP Code, and the site will give you a list of volunteer opportunities in your area. Some of the jobs don't even require you to get up from your computer. Organizations need Web designers, typing teachers for the elderly, email buddies, and tons more. Morgan signed up to be an email buddy with an elderly person who is confined to her home. She says it feels pretty good.

DOWNLOAD OF THE DAY   Reduce stress in your life with SereneScreen—the ultimate virtual saltwater aquarium screensaver. Free to try, $21.95 to buy, from `www.serenescreen.com`. Requires 3D accelerated video card.

TODAY'S FOCUS: Computer Networks

TYPEWRITER PATENTED

The first typewriter was patented by Christopher Latham Sholes on this day in 1868. His first model was built around a single telegraph key, in the back of Kleinstauber's machine shop in Milwaukee, Wisconsin. After a series of modifications that included creating separate keys for each letter, Remington and his partners completed the prototype for the first commercial typewriter, marketed in 1873 by the Remington Arms Company. It was the first model to implement the keyboard layout we use today, but could only print capital letters. It featured a wooden spacebar and a vulcanized India-rubber roller.

Related Web site   Test your typing speed: `mrkent.com/kb/kbtest.htm`

Netstat's All That

By Morgan Webb

Netstat is a command-line utility that lists your computer's network connections. The program is useful for tracking the IP address of a friend, for example, or to find your own IP address. It gives you information on all your system's open connections, including local and remote ports and protocols. It can even tell you whether you are infected with a Trojan horse.

To run netstat in any version of Windows, open a DOS or command-line window and type **netstat** followed by one or more of these command-line switches:

- **-a**—Shows you all the open connections on your machine (-a is for all). It will also tell you which remote systems you are connected to, the local port number, the remote port number, and the protocol.
- **-an**—Shows you the same information as above, but with numeric IP addresses instead of the associated name. In other words, it won't do a DNS lookup on the addresses. Handy if you want to find your *own* IP address.
- **-e**—Displays Ethernet statistics. Add s (-es) to subdivide the information by protocol, TCP, UDP, and IP.

For other commands, type **netstat -?**.

You can follow any command with an interval in seconds. Netstat will continue displaying its results, pausing for that interval, until you press Ctrl+C. If you don't enter an interval, netstat will display the information once and exit.

Use **netstat -a** to see whether a Trojan horse application is accessing the network from your computer. Compare the active ports with the list of common Trojans and the ports they use at `doshelp.com/trojanports.htm`.

If there's too much output from netstat to digest, dump the netstat output to a text file by appending > and a filename to the command, as in **netstat -a >logfile.txt**.

(Morgan Webb is the Queen of Windows tips on The Screen Savers.*)*

 TIP OF THE DAY   Windows 95/98/Me users: If you lose your DHCP broadband connection to the Internet, use winipcfg to restore it. Click **Start**, select **Run**, and then enter **winipcfg**. When it opens, press the release and renew buttons in sequence to refresh the address and repopulate your settings. This doesn't work with PPPoE.

In Windows NT/2000/XP, click **Start**, select **Run**, and type **ipconfig /release** to release the connection and **ipconfig /renew** to restart it.

For a GUI version of ipconfig for NT, download wntipcfg, free from `www.microsoft.com/WINDOWS2000/techinfo/reskit/tools/existing/wntipcfg-o.asp`.

 DOWNLOAD OF THE DAY   Make Netstat easier to use with Netmon, a graphical interface for Netstat. Identifies known Trojan activity, too. Free from `adamant.n3.net`.

TODAY'S FOCUS: Computer Networks

AT&T RETURNS TO LOCAL SERVICE

AT&T returned to the local phone market on this day in 1998. A merger with cable giant TCI allowed the long-distance carrier to offer local telephone service for the first time since its historic breakup in 1981. The deal, valued between $32–$55 billion, gave AT&T access to more than 30 million additional homes in the U.S.

Related Web site `www.att.com`

Protect Your Network with NID

By Nir Zuk

Network intrusion detection (NID) is the process of searching network traffic for intrusions and signs of intrusions. These intrusions might be probes for open ports (such as port scans), the presence of Trojans and worms on a network, or an attacker actively trying to break into a network.

Where Firewalls Fail Firewalls are designed to implement an access control policy. This means that they distinguish between good and bad traffic using a preset policy that defines what traffic is good and what traffic is bad. For example, a policy might tell a firewall that HTTP traffic to a Web server is good, while FTP traffic is bad. Firewalls, however, do not look into the traffic they allow. After a firewall has accepted a connection, it will not check that connection for signs of intrusion.

What Can Detect Network Intrusions? Products called *network intrusion detection systems (NIDS)* will look for intrusions on your network and report whenever an intrusion is found.

How an NIDS Works There are several methods for detecting intrusions. The most popular one is signature-based detection, which compares traffic to signatures of well-known intrusion techniques. This process is similar to that used by antivirus products.

Another method gaining popularity is protocol anomaly detection, which compares the actual traffic on the network to the specifications of each protocol (such as HTTP and FTP) and reports anomalies. The idea behind doing so is that many hacking techniques use deviations from protocol specifications, so such a deviation usually means an intrusion attempt. There are many other methods for detecting intrusions, but these are the two most common mechanisms.

What an NIDS Can't Do NIDS products on the market only detect intrusions; they're not in a position to prevent them, because all NIDS products run as sniffers and haven't the capability to drop packets and stop an intrusion before it hits its victim. To prevent attacks, you need an IDP (intrusion detection and prevention) product that, like a firewall, is deployed in the line of packets and can block intrusions as they are detected.

TIP OF THE DAY The definitive open-source intrusion detection program is SNORT, from `snort.org`. You can get a version for Windows and other operating systems free from `snort.org/dl/binaries`. Download and install WinPCap, the Windows packet capture driver first, free from `winpcap.polito.it`. Read the Snort documentation to learn how to configure the program.

DOWNLOAD OF THE DAY For Windows users, the next best thing is NukeNabber, free (and a lot easier to use) from Puppet's Place, `dynamsol.com/puppet/nukenabber.html`.

NukeNabber sets itself up to listen on TCP and UDP ports commonly attacked over the internet. A total of 50 ports can be monitored simultaneously.

POLL: Do you want a WiFi network in your town?

79% Yes

21% No

TODAY'S FOCUS: Computer Networking

FIRST COLOR TV BROADCAST

The Columbia Broadcasting System transmitted the first color television program on this day in 1951. The four-hour, experimental broadcast was sent to CBS affiliates in New York, Boston, Philadelphia, Washington, D.C., and Baltimore, and could not be seen in homes. The first color television available to consumers was advertised in the *New York Times* that same year (but never went on sale). The CBS-Columbia Color Television Receiver, manufactured by Air King, featured a mechanical color spinning wheel mounted in front of a black-and-white cathode-ray tube, and cost $499.95 (nearly $3,500 in today's dollars).

Related Web site `novia.net/~ereitan/Color_Cameras.html`

Home Networking Made Easy

To share Internet access at home, you need to connect your computers into a network. Then, you need to connect that network to the Internet. Let's set up the network first.

CAT5 The least expensive and fastest way to network your home is to string CAT5 Ethernet cable from machine to machine. The cable costs less than 30¢ per foot, and Ethernet adapters for your computers are as little as $15 each. If you shop around, you can create an Ethernet network of three computers for well under $100.

Phone Line If you don't want to string cable, you might be able to use phone-line networking, or PNA 2.0. Each computer will need a nearby phone jack and a special phone-line Ethernet adapter. Cost for a USB PNA adapter is about $50 per computer.

Wireless The easiest way to network a home is also the most expensive: wireless networking using WiFi, a.k.a. 802.11b. WiFi uses 2.4GHz radio signals to connect as many as 50 systems with a range of about 150 feet. You'll need a wireless access point (WAP) for around $100–$200 and WiFi cards or USB dongles for each computer. The dongles are easy to install and cost about $60 each.

The Router Next, connect your new network to the Internet. The best way to do so is with a broadband router that connects to your DSL or cable modem and shares the Internet access out to the rest of the network. Each computer will connect directly to the router. Routers also can come with printer ports for printer sharing. If you're setting up a WiFi network, you can buy a router that doubles as a wireless access point. My favorite brands: Linksys, D-Link, Netgear, and, of course, Apple.

 TIP OF THE DAY To share a printer over a home network, first configure the computer with the printer. In Windows 95/98/Me, turn on Printer and File sharing in the Network control panel. In Windows XP, run the Network Setup Wizard. Then, configure the other systems:

1. Open the Printers control panel.
2. Click **Add a Printer** to start the Printer Wizard.
3. Choose **Network Printer** and click **Next**.
4. Click **Browse**. It may take a minute to continue.
5. You will see a list of the computers on your network. Click the + next to the computer the printer is connected to, and select the printer. Click **OK**.

DOWNLOAD OF THE DAY IP Tools includes 15 utilities for TCP/IP networking in one program, including port scanning, whois, trace route, and more: `ks-soft.net`. Tasty. Free to try, $35 to buy.

TODAY'S FOCUS: Computer Networking

BAR CODE HITS STORES

The Universal Price Code (UPC) made its debut in supermarkets on this day in 1974. The bar code system, also known as the Uniform Price Code, was invented by George J. Laurer in 1973. The first item ever scanned using Laurer's system was a pack of Wrigley gum in a store in Troy, Ohio. The concept predates the current system, however. In 1952, Joseph Woodland and Bernard Silver became the first inventors to patent a bar code that used a series of complex patterns to identify products.

Related Web sites `uccouncil.org, howstuffworks.com/upc.htm`

JUNE
26

Sharing an Internet Connection

By Lon Poole

You share Internet access on a network by adding an Internet gateway, also known as an *Internet router* or a *proxy server*, to your network. This can be software that you install on one of your computers, or a freestanding device that connects directly to your network. Both hardware and software have pros and cons.

A hardware gateway doesn't require you to leave a computer turned on to provide Internet access for the rest of the network. Hardware gateways are generally more reliable, being less susceptible to crashing than a software gateway's computer. But a hardware gateway costs more than gateway software and requires an external modem.

How Does It Work? Like a "mailroom in a box," a gateway receives all outgoing communications from the computers on your network and sends them to sites on the Internet via a single connection. The gateway also receives all incoming communications from the Internet and distributes each communication to the correct computer on your local network. All this rerouting is invisible to you and the computers on your network, as well as to the computers on the Internet.

Most software and hardware gateways also serve as a firewall that provides security for your local network by blocking access for unsolicited Internet traffic. A computer on the Internet can't directly contact your network's computers because it doesn't know your computers' private IP addresses.

Gateway software is available for both Windows and Macintosh computers. All gateway software can handle Internet traffic for both platforms, regardless of the type of computer on which the software has been installed. Most gateway software supports Internet connections via modem as well as ISDN, cable modem, and DSL.

If you have Windows, you already have Internet-sharing software. All you have to do is run the Internet Connection Sharing Wizard. Or see below for a free program that will also do the job.

(Lon Poole has written many books about personal computers, including The Little Network Book, Macworld Mac OS 9 Bible, Using Your IBM PC, *and* Apple II User's Guide.*)*

 TIP OF THE DAY   It's easy to share your Internet connection, but is it legal? Yes, in most cases. You should check your user agreement, but most ISPs allow their customers to share. That's partly because it's nearly impossible to prevent. Don't expect support for more than one computer, however.

DOWNLOAD OF THE DAY   AnalogX's Proxy is a free, lightweight Internet gateway for Windows. Easier to use than ICS, and free from `analogx.com/contents/download/network/proxy.htm`.

POLL: Will the Net be the end of the television networks?

30% Yes

70% No

TODAY'S FOCUS: Computer Networking

COLOR TV DEMONSTRATED

Researchers at Bell Labs gave the first public demonstration of color television in the U.S. on this day in 1929. Mirrors were used to reflect red, blue, and green, which combined to create a tinted picture. To make the most of the limited color spectrum, Bell scientists chose to show images of a watermelon, red roses, and an American flag. Color television sets wouldn't become publicly available until 1951.

Related Web site `tvhistory.tv`

Setting Up a Hardware Router

By Joshua Brentano

Congratulations! You've just brought home a broadband router, and now you're ready to connect your network to the Internet. Let's take a look at what the evening ahead holds in store.

We'll assume you've already got your home network working. If you've been using a hub, connect the uplink port on the hub to a local port on the router; otherwise, connect each computer to the ports on the router.

Now, connect the Internet port, or WAN port, on your router to your cable or DSL modem. Plug in your router and allow it to initialize. Typically, there is a set of lights on the front panel of the router that will show link status. Refer to the instruction manual to decrypt the message of the lights.

If you haven't already, configure each computer on the network to use DHCP to get its IP address from the router. In Windows, that means opening the Network connection and selecting **Obtain an IP Address Automatically**. Reboot if necessary. Reboot anyway—it can't hurt.

Next, configure the router. The exact steps vary depending on the brand you're using, but it will go something like this: Launch a browser on one of your computers and type the address of the router. On Linksys routers, this is 192.168.1.1, but check your documentation to be sure. If you're prompted for a login and password, cheer: You're in communication with your router. Now to get the router in communication with the outside world.

Configure the router just as if you were configuring a computer. In other words, enter the info your ISP gave you. Most ISPs use DHCP, so select **Obtain an IP Address Automatically** or DHCP or the like. Some DHCP servers require a domain and hostname, so enter those if your ISP supplied them. If you have a static IP address, type in all the fiddly little numbers instead.

Now apply the settings, and try to surf the Net. I recommend a visit to `practicallynetworked.com`, the center of all things geeky when it comes to networking. On the other hand, now that you've configured your network all by yourself, you could probably tell them a thing or two!

(Joshua Brentano is an Associate Producer for The Screen Savers.*)*

 TIP OF THE DAY If you have a router, you should check regularly for firmware upgrades to protect yourself against security holes. Here are the sites for the major manufacturers:

Linksys: `linksys.com/download/firmware.asp`

D-Link: `support.dlink.com/downloads`

Firmware upgrades are tricky. Read the instructions carefully and follow them exactly.

  DOWNLOAD OF THE DAY VisualRoute follows your Internet connection from server to server and draws a picture of the route your data is taking, free from `visualware.com`. Full version costs $39.95.

TODAY'S FOCUS: Computer Networking

FIRST SATELLITE CALL

The first telephone conversation over a commercial satellite took place on this day in 1965. The call was made over Early Bird I, the first satellite launched by the Communications Satellite Corporation, a joint venture between international governments and corporations. Under ComSat, NASA would take a satellite system through the research and development stages, and then turn it over to someone else to convert into an operational system. Today, the practice of creating satellites for private business is commonplace. And although satellite phone service is now widely available to consumers, it is still considered unreliable and relatively expensive.

Related Web site `liftoff.msfc.nasa.gov/RealTime/JTrack`

Host Frag Fest

By Patrick Norton

A LAN party isn't just an opportunity to show off your prowess in Quake, it's also a chance for you and your friends and family to get together via networked computers and have a smashing good time.

Want to throw your own LAN party? Read the LAN Party guides at The LANParty Hosting Guide, `lanparty.com/theguide`, and Tweak3D.Net, `tweak3d.net/articles/howtolanparty`. Here are some things to keep in mind:

- Stick to fewer than 20 players for your first LAN party. The networking will be a lot easier to execute—trust me.
- Set up the server early. You don't want to be figuring out how to host a server while 10 friends are waiting. You also don't want to learn how to set up the network on the fly in front of a live audience.
- Be prepared. Everybody you invite should know what games to have loaded and have the proper networking hardware and cables.
- Be sure everybody writes down their home network connections before you blow 'em out to set up that LAN.

 TIP OF THE DAY It's very easy to set up a small network of Macs using an inexpensive Ethernet hub. Connect each computer to the hub, and then turn on file sharing.

Mac OS 9 Open the File Sharing control panel. Name your computer. Give yourself a username and set the password (if you haven't already). Do the same on each machine. To connect to another machine, open the Chooser and select **AppleTalk**. The other machine will pop up. Double-click the machine name and log in with your username and password. The drive will mount on your desktop and you're ready to go.

Mac OS X Open the Sharing System Preference pane. Click **Start** to turn on File Sharing. Your Public folder is now visible. To make files available, copy them to the Public folder. To access a Public folder on another machine, choose **Connect to Server** in the Finder's **Go** menu.

DOWNLOAD OF THE DAY Who owns that Web site? Wonder who belongs to an IP address? Use whois online at `geektools.com/cgi-bin/proxy.cgi`. There are many whois servers on the Net, but Geektools can query them all. Or download their client, free for Mac and Windows from `geektools.com/software.php`.

While you're there, check out the other geek tools, including a listing of the best hotels in the world for high-speed Internet access.

POLL: Who wants WAP?

26% Me

25% Not me

48% Hang up and drive

TODAY'S FOCUS: Computer Networking

MICROSOFT PAYS FOR IBM PATENTS

Microsoft agreed to pay a one-time, multimillion-dollar licensing fee to IBM on this day in 1995. Microsoft's payment covered the use of more than 1,000 IBM patents held on basic software functions, such as the movement of a cursor based on the Tab key. It was the first rift between the two erstwhile partners.

Related Web sites   `www.ibm.com`, `www.microsoft.com`

Twisted List: Biggest Computers in History

By Martin Sargent

Number 5: Univac   The Univac, short for Universal Automatic Computer, was a monster machine. It weighed 16,000 pounds and contained 5,000 vacuum tubes. Despite its size, it ran at only 2.25MHz. Today's gigahertz chips can perform calculations some 26,000 times faster.

The Univac entered history in 1952 when it correctly predicted that Eisenhower would destroy Adlai Stevenson in the presidential election. Despite the prediction, the networks refused to call the election until results trickled in the old-fashioned way.

Number 4: IBM Stretch   During the height of the Cold War in the 1950s, IBM was commissioned to build a computer to analyze results from atomic bomb tests. IBM named it Stretch because it was supposed to be 100 times faster than any previous computer.

Completed in 1961, Stretch was the first commercial computer to use transistors. Although transistors are smaller than vacuum tubes, Stretch was still gargantuan, consuming about 2,500 square feet of floor space.

Number 3: MIT Whirlwind   The MIT Whirlwind was designed to be a flight simulator to train bomber crews. A beast of a machine, Whirlwind contained 4,500 vacuum tubes and ate up 3,100 square feet of floor space. Completed in 1948, Whirlwind was the first computer to use magnetic core memory, the earliest ancestor to the RAM in our computers today.

Number 2: The ENIAC   The ENIAC (electronic numerical integrator and computer) was secretly developed during WWII at the University of Pennsylvania. The goal of the ENIAC was to quickly generate ballistic missile firing tables. The ENIAC was sickeningly large, weighing more than 30 tons and containing 19,000 vacuum tubes.

Number 1: The SAGE   No computer was fatter than the SAGE (semiautomatic ground environment) computer. It contained more than 55,000 vacuum tubes and consumed 1 million watts of power. The vacuum tubes ran so hot it was estimated that if the air conditioning failed, the SAGE would self-destruct in 60 seconds. Despite its size, a decent hand-size calculator of today is more powerful than the SAGE.

Completed in 1958, SAGE linked radar stations in the United States and Canada to detect a nuclear attack. The phone bill required to connect the 23 direction centers that housed SAGE computers was millions of dollars per month.

TIP OF THE DAY   Mac OS X 10.1 and later can share files on a Windows network with no additional software. To connect to a shared folder on a Windows machine, select **Connect to Server** from the Finder's **Go** menu. Then, enter the address of the Windows box as `smb://ServerName/ShareName`.

DOWNLOAD OF THE DAY   My Vital Agent monitors your Internet access and tells you exactly what's happening and how fast. A great tool for detecting bottlenecks in your connection. Free from Lucent at `www.myvitalagent.com`. (Old-timers will recognize this as the next generation of Net.Medic, a shareware program I recommended last year.)

TODAY'S FOCUS: Photo Editing

FIRST HUMANS TO DIE IN SPACE

Three Russian cosmonauts died upon reentry to the atmosphere on this day in 1971. Cosmonauts Georgi Timofeyevich, Vladislav Nikolayevich, and Viktor Ivanovich were killed by pressure changes in the cabin of space shuttle Soyuz 11 after an air valve malfunctioned. The crew of Soyuz 11 had been on a mission to the space station Salyut, where they stayed 23 days and, ironically, had set a new record for duration in space.

Related Web site `liftoff.msfc.nasa.gov/rsa/rsa.html`

Create Neon in Photoshop

By Bert Monroy

Here's how to create a neon sign in Adobe Photoshop:

1. Using the Path tool, create the shape for the letters or symbol you want to be the neon tube.
2. Select the Paintbrush tool. Create a new brush or choose an existing brush that has the size you want the tube to be. Be sure the Spacing is set to 1%.
3. Make a new layer to contain the neon tube. Choose white for the foreground color, and make sure the Paintbrush is selected. In the Path's palette, drag the path for the tube over the Stroke Path icon at the bottom of the palette.
4. Duplicate the layer with the white tube and, with the Lock Transparency selected, fill the duplicate layer with black. Be sure the black filled layer is in back of the white one. Move the black filled tube layer over to simulate a shadow. Reduce its opacity to allow the background to show through.
5. Double-click the layer with the white tube to bring up the Layer Styles dialog box. In the layer styles, set the Fill Opacity in the Blending Options to about 50%. Now add an Inner Glow. You can choose any color you want. Increase the size to simulate the edges of the glass.
6. The Off-State of the neon is now complete. Create a new layer and have it as the selected layer. With the Option (Alt) button pressed, choose **Merge Visible** from the Layer's palette drop-down menu. This will merge all the layers into the selected layer while leaving the original layers intact.
7. Turn off the eye for the completed layer and select the layer with the white tube. In the Layer Styles give it an Outer Glow. Choose a color similar to the color of the neon light.
8. Create a new layer above the white tube layer and stroke the path again, this time with a soft-edged Airbrush tool using the color you want for the light.

Make sure the size of the brush is small enough to be contained within the tube.

9. Make the neon layer a selection by Command (Control)-clicking on it in the layer's palette. Expand the selection to a size that is about three times the size of the tube (**Select**, **Modify**, **Expand**). Feather the resulting selection to a radius that is about half of what the size of the expansion was set to. For example: Expand 20, Feather 10.
10. Create a new layer behind the neon tube and fill the selected area with the color of the neon light. Change the mode to Hard Light in the layer's palette.
11. Turn off the layer with the shadow and your neon's On-State is complete. You can then merge the layers. Note: Do not merge the layer with the Off-State.

(Bert Monroy is a digital artist and author. Visit him at www.bertmonroy.com.)

 TIP OF THE DAY For an incredible variety of free and shareware tools for Windows, visit www.mediachance.com. Their most popular program, Read-DRAW PRO, combines Illustrator-style vector editing with standard bitmap tools and 3D effects into a single, easy-to-use drawing program. Try it free or register it for $49.

 DOWNLOAD OF THE DAY Maya is a 3D animation program that normally sells for thousands of dollars, but you can get a special Maya learning edition free for Windows or Macintosh from alaiswavefront.com/freemaya. The free version has a rather prominent watermark onscreen and can't share files with the paid version, but it's great for learning how to use a powerful tool that's widely used by moviemakers and others.

JULY 2003

SUNDAY	MONDAY	TUESDAY	WEDNESDAY	THURSDAY	FRIDAY	SATURDAY
		1 Gottfried Leibniz born (1646)	**2** Amelia Earhart disappears over Pacific Ocean (1937)	**3**	**4** Independence Day; Pathfinder probe entered Mars' atmosphere (1997)	**5**
6	**7**	**8**	**9** Nikola Tesla born (1856)	**10**	**11**	**12** R. Buckminster Fuller born (1895)
13	**14**	**15**	**16** First manned flight to the moon (1969)	**17**	**18** John Glenn born (1921); Intel incorporated (1968)	**19**
20 Neil Armstrong walks on moon (1969)	**21**	**22** First around-the-world solo flight (1933)	**23**	**24**	**25** First test-tube baby born (1978)	**26**
27	**28**	**29**	**30** Henry Ford born (1863)	**31**		

TODAY'S FOCUS: Photo Editing

GOTTFRIED LEIBNIZ BORN

Mathematician Gottfried Wilhelm von Leibniz was born in Leipzig, Germany, on this day in 1646. Leibniz laid the foundation for differential and integral calculus. He believed doing relatively simple mathematical calculations by hand wasted valuable time, and that a machine could be invented to perform these tasks and ease the burden on scientists. In 1672, Leibniz began work on a device that used gears and rods to add, subtract, multiply, and divide. His "Stepped Reckoner" was one of the earliest known calculators.

Related Web site   vintagecalculators.com

Patriotic Pets

By John Lund

I'm going to teach you how to make a fun patriotic image of your pet for the 4th using Adobe Photoshop. Start with two separate images: a digital picture of an American flag and another digital photo of your pet.

The old adage, "garbage in, garbage out," applies to digital imaging. Be sure the picture of your pet is clear, sharp, and well-lit. I prefer photos that clearly show an animal's eyes, because they express and communicate a lot of emotion.

Open the picture of your pet in Photoshop and perfect the image using the Liquify filter. After you get the facial nuances you want, click **OK**.

Now open the picture of the flag and strip it from its background using the Extract filter. Copy your new selection and paste it over the pet. The flag comes in as a new layer.

Decrease the opacity of the flag photo layer to about 50% so you can see the pet through the flag and make accurate selections.

Use the Pen tool to create selections for the eyes, mouth, and nose. Press Delete, and bring the layer's opacity back up to 100% opacity.

Put the finishing touches on your photo. For example, you can make a few more selections and use the Curves palette to contour the flag to your pet's torso. Or, create a new layer and use the Airbrush tool (with reduced opacity) to paint a shadow below the flag.

Finally, activate the background layer.

Click **Filter**, **Render**, and **Lighting Effects**. Choose the 2:00 Spotlight default. And say hello to your patriotic pet!

(John Lund is a professional photographer and Photoshop artist. His Web site is johnlund.com—visit it for a variety of animal antics.)

TIP OF THE DAY   Using drawing programs such as Photoshop, Paint Shop Pro, and PhotoImpact is much easier if you have a tablet. Tablets connect to your computer just like a mouse (in most cases, you can leave your mouse plugged in) but you'll work much more naturally with a stylus and pad. Look for a pressure-sensitive tablet with a wireless stylus. Smaller 8-inch×8-inch tablets are easier to incorporate into your workspace and cost less, too. I like the Wacom Graphire2. It's less than $100 for Windows or Mac and comes with Photoshop LE. For Mac or Windows, from wacom.com.

DOWNLOAD OF THE DAY   POV-Ray is a freeware ray-tracing program has been around for more than 10 years and is still very popular. Ray-tracing is a technique that creates vividly realistic two-dimensional images by tracing the path of light in the environment. The latest version works on nearly all platforms, including Windows, Mac, and Linux, from povray.org.

TODAY'S FOCUS: Photo Editing

DIGITAL SIGNATURE PROPOSED

The U.S. Commerce Department announced a standard to protect electronic documents from being altered on this day in 1991. The joint project with the National Security Agency created the electronic signature, which was initially intended to reduce paperwork and increase efficiency of government transactions. Electronic signatures were not just for bureaucrats, however: The growth in e-commerce also created the need to verify the identity of consumers. Today, digital signatures enable us to do everything from file our taxes to submit a medical claim.

Related Web site `aspe.hhs.gov/admnsimp/nprm/seclist.htm`

Antiquing Photos in Photoshop

By Bert Monroy

In Photoshop, you can take a picture taken today and make it look like it was taken 100 years ago. Follow these steps from Photoshop master Bert Monroy:

1. Choose a picture you want to antique.
2. Select the entire image (**Select**, **All**) and send it to its own layer (**Layer**, **New**, **Layer via Cut**).
3. Increase the canvas a bit (**Image**, **Canvas Size**) to give yourself about a quarter of an inch on the edges, which you will need later.
4. Select the layer that contains the image, and go to the Hue/Saturation control (**Image**, **Adjust**, **Hue/Saturation**).
5. Choose **Colorize** at the bottom right of the dialog box. This will turn the image into a single hue. To give the image a sepia tone, make the **Hue** setting about **40** and the **Saturation** about **30**.
6. Scan an old photograph that has a lot of damage, such as tears and scratches.
7. Convert the scan to grayscale (**Image**, **Mode**, **Grayscale**).
8. Go to the Levels command (**Image**, **Adjust**, **Levels**).
9. Push the darks (left arrow) and the midtones (center arrow) toward the right to drop out all the details of the photo, leaving the light-colored scratches visible.
10. Using the Move tool, drag the image with the damage onto the first image. This will place it in its own layer, which we will call the *damage layer*.
11. Place the damage layer in Screen mode (Mode setting in the Layer's palette). This will make the scratches appear as if they were on the image.
12. Merge the damage layer with the image layer.
13. With the Lasso tool, make a rough selection where you would like the image to appear torn. Send it to its own layer (**Layer**, **New**, **Layer via Cut**).
14. Rotate the layer with the tear slightly, and move it away from the rest of the image.
15. In a new layer, select a rectangular shape to resemble a piece of tape and fill it with white. Put that layer in Screen mode and reduce the opacity so that it looks like tape.

 TIP OF THE DAY The Wacom site (see yesterday) has some excellent Photoshop tips—they're useful, fun, and well-illustrated: `wacom.com/tips`.

Photoshop's manufacturer, Adobe, also provides excellent online tutorials. They're free from `www.adobe.com/products/tips/photoshop.html`.

 DOWNLOAD OF THE DAY Want to create 3D text for your Web site or presentations? You can animate them, too. Font Magic is free for Windows from `www.mattcawley.com/fontmagic`.

JULY 2

SOURCE CODE NOT FREE SPEECH

On this day in 1998, a U.S. district court ruled encryption software was not protected under the First Amendment. Peter Junger, a law professor at Case Western Reserve University in Ohio, sued to win permission to post encryption programs online for use in his classes. Judge James Gwin said that code did not qualify as "speech" because it wasn't decipherable to the average person. In April 2000, however, that decision was overturned. The Sixth Circuit Court of Appeals ruled encryption was indeed protected because "computer source code is an expressive means for the exchange of information and ideas about computer programming."

Related Web site `www.cdt.org/crypto/`

Add Yourself to a Photo

By Mikkel Aaland

It was one of those situations where old friends were together and someone said, "Hey, let's get a group shot of everyone." I had my digital camera but no tripod. Instead, my wife took a shot with me in it. Then I took another shot with my wife in it, but I left my spot open in the second shot so I could copy and paste myself from one image into the other.

Here's how to do it in Photoshop Elements:

1. Open both digital images, and click on the one with the missing person.
2. Adjust the image levels to make the image look right by clicking the **Enhance** menu, selecting **Brightness/Contrast**, and then selecting **Levels**.
3. Click the picture with the person in it, and press Ctrl+Alt+L. This automatically matches the Levels settings in both images.
4. Now use the Lasso tool to make a loose selection of the missing person. It's okay not to be too precise; in fact, include other areas of the image to help position the pasted selection.
5. Paste the selection into the image missing the person. Photoshop Elements automatically places it into its own layer.
6. From the Layer palette, set the Opacity at 50 percent so you can see part of the underlying image. Use the Move tool to position the selection into place.
7. Now comes the tricky part. Reset the layer Opacity to 100 percent and use the Eraser tool with a Hard Round 19-pixel brush to remove the superfluous

areas around the missing person's head and shoulders. It might help to magnify the image and use a Hard Round 9-pixel brush.
8. Finish with a Soft Round 13-pixel brush, lightly brushing the edges of the pasted selection to make them blend into the background.

Like magic, you've placed yourself in the middle of the picture.

(Mikkel Aaland is the author of Photoshop Elements Solutions. *For more information about Aaland, visit his Web site at www.cyberbohemia.com.)*

TIP OF THE DAY   Photoshop Elements includes a useful Fill Flash command that does a good job of creating a digital fill flash effect, balancing the foreground with the background:

1. Select **Fill Flash** from the **Enhance** menu.
2. Drag the Lighter slider settings until the faces look right.
3. Click **OK**.

DOWNLOAD OF THE DAY   Pixia is the first English version of a very popular Japanese painting program. Free for Windows from `www.ab.wakwak.com/~knight/`.

POLL: Should video-game heroines look more like real women?
44% Yes
56% No

TODAY'S FOCUS: Photo Editing

FIRST PHOTOS FROM MARS

The Sojourner, a robot from the Mars Pathfinder, landed on the surface of Mars and began transmitting images back to Earth on this day in 1997. Pathfinder was launched December 4, 1996, and took exactly seven months to reach the fourth planet from the sun. Pathfinder bounced on Mars' surface about 16 times and rolled over before coming to a complete stop. The images taken from the Red Planet were posted online shortly after they were taken, thus becoming the first photographs of Mars ever published on the Internet.

Related Web site   `mars.jpl.nasa.gov/MPF/`

Online Fireworks

By Kylen Campbell

The Declaration of Independence was signed July 2, 1776. Founding Father, John Adams, predicted the day would henceforth be filled with fireworks, pageantry, and general nuttiness. He was off by a little bit. That celebration came with the public announcement on July 4.

Hence, the yearly celebration of the birthday of the United States of America on this day, and Americans know how to pay tribute and have some fun by blowing up lots and lots of fireworks, even online. And keeping the explosions limited to the Internet variety is a lot safer, too.

Here are some places you can celebrate online.

Boston's Fourth of July (july4th.org)   One of the most famous Fourth of July parties is the bash on the Charles River in Boston, and there's an online view of the goings-on at Boston's Fourth of July. Pictures of last year's fireworks accompany detailed event info (including TV viewing options) and a profile of the Boston Pops Symphony Orchestra.

Larry Crump's Fireworks Page (www.wf.net/ ~lcrump1/index.html) Pomp and circumstance aside, Larry Crump's Fireworks Page takes us behind the scenes of fireworks displays from the pyrotechnicians' point of view.

Pyrotechnics—The Art of Fire (cc.oulu.fi/~kempmp/ pyro.html)   PyroBob, another enthusiast, offers an animation of an exploding shell and resources to get you started. For more serious information, Pyrotechnics—The Art of Fire delves into the physics of fireworks in a detailed manner and offers links to related sites.

Happy Birthday America (usacitylink.com/usa) Happy Birthday America holds fireworks pictures, history, and a speech by some guy named George W. Bush. If you don't want to surf for your fireworks but do want to send a greeting, the Postcard Place has a large selection of appropriate electronic postcards.

Phantom Fireworks (Fireworks.com)   Although we don't recommend setting off your own fireworks, you can see a great show online from this fireworks company. Click the Maximum Load for the best visuals, including a banner that is actually a fireworks show done up in Flash.

National   Council   on   Fireworks   Safety (Fireworksafety.com)   If you gotta blow things up tonight, at least learn how to do it safely. And read the statistics section if you want to know why it might be better to get your pyrotechnics online this year.

(Kylen leaves town on the Fourth but has his own little special celebration. His degree is in American Studies, and he is a freelance writer for numerous publications, including New Media and Axcess.)

DOWNLOAD OF THE DAY   Celebrate the Fourth with fireworks sounds, Sousa marches, wallpapers, screensavers, Web cams, broadcasts, and more at www.kate.net/holidays/ 4thjuly/virtual4th.html. Kate.net celebrates other holidays, too.

JULY 4

TODAY'S FOCUS: Photo Editing

DOLLY THE SHEEP BORN

The first animal ever cloned was born on this day in 1996. The famous ovine was created by Ian Wilmut and other researchers at the Roslin Institute in Edinburgh, Scotland. The scientists cloned Dolly by using genetic material from a mature sheep's udder, which was then inserted into another sheep's unfertilized egg cell.

Related Web site   www.roslin.ac.uk

Create Rain in Photoshop

By Bert Monroy

The effect of rainfall can easily be achieved by the use of a few filters.

1. Start off with the image to which you want to add the rainfall. It's easiest to use an image with sky in it if you're new to Photoshop.
2. Separate the scene in the foreground from the background (if your image has the sky in it, the sky is your background). To separate the two, select the background or foreground. Then, put your selection into its own layer by clicking the **Layer** menu and selecting **New Layer via Copy**.
3. You now have two layers in the image, a foreground layer and a background layer. Create a new layer in between these two layers by going to the **Layer** menu and selecting **New Layer**. Then, move the layer in between the two layers in the Layers palette.
4. Choose black or dark gray for the foreground color and a gloomy blue for the background color. Click the **Filter** menu, point your cursor to **Render**, and select the **Clouds** filter.
5. Select the layer with the foreground images. Using the Hue/Saturation controls, bring down the saturation and lightness to a point where the image looks gloomy.
6. In the Layers palette, create a new layer that rests above the others.
7. Choose **Black** for your foreground color. Fill the new layer with black by clicking the **Edit** menu and selecting **Fill**.
8. Apply the Add Noise filter. Make the mode Monochromatic and give it an amount of about 22 with the distribution set to Gaussian.
9. Apply the Blur More filter to the layer.
10. Using the Levels command, nudge the dark tones (black triangle) and highlight (white triangle) sliders to lessen the amount of noise.
11. Apply a Motion Blur filter at an angle to simulate the directional falling of rain. Give it a small distance, just enough to get streaks.
12. Using the Levels command again, nudge the dark tones (black triangle) and highlight (white triangle) sliders to enhance the look of the falling rain.
13. Finally, put the layer with the rain into Screen mode by going into the Layers palette and selecting **Mode**. This lets the white show through and the black of the layer disappears.

TIP OF THE DAY   Kids deserve good graphics, too. Download free graphics for kids' Web sites from desktopPublishing.com/clipart/kids/kids-babyset-1.html.

Pat's Web Graphics are great, too: www.patswebgraphics.com/kids/kids.html.

CNET's excellent Builder.com site has a great article on building Web sites for kids at builder.cnet.com/webbuilding/pages/Graphics/Kids/.

DOWNLOAD OF THE DAY   Morph one image into another or create QuickTime movies of your morph with MorphX. Free for Mac OS X from www.orcsoftware.com/~martin/Morph.html.

Morpheus does the same thing for Windows—and a lot more. Download the free trial from morpheussoftware.net or pay just $14.95.

TODAY'S FOCUS: Photo Editing

FIRST AIRSHIP CROSSING

The first airship to cross the Atlantic Ocean landed in Roosevelt Field in New York on this day in 1919. The British R-34 was 643 feet long (twice the length of a football field), 92 feet high, and 79 feet in diameter. The dirigible had five 270 hp engines and traveled at an average speed of 62 miles per hour. In January 1921, the ship was badly damaged when it hit the side of a hill. The crew survived, but the ship did not. The remains of the airship were salvaged and sold for scrap.

Related Web site   `www.nms.ac.uk/flight/`

Twisted List: Mindless Web Diversions

By Martin Sargent

When life gets me down, like when I sever a toe while chopping wood, my girlfriend leaves me, and I get stoned by an angry mob all in the same day, I turn to the Internet for a quick pick-me-up. Here are five mindless Web diversions that temporarily make me forget that, this morning, I got trapped under ice.

Black Ribbon (`surface.yugop.com`) I've always enjoyed playing with ribbons. You know, tying them in my hair, adorning the wicker furniture in my condo with bows, etc. But this Web diversion is even more fun! Just drag your mouse across the screen and a trippy black ribbon unfurls in your pointer's wake.

Hungry Rabbit (`esu.lt/andrius/10/go.htm`) Have you ever wanted anything so bad, nothing could stop you from getting it? That's like me and the Ethan Allen Country Crossings collection. And, as for the rabbit, the only thing he wants is your mouse pointer, which he mistakes for a carrot. This is one of the more remarkable interactive animations on the Internet (even better than that ribbon thing).

Nose Pluck (`www.nobodyhere.com/justme/nose.html`) I've never been the kind of guy who enjoys plucking hairs from the nostril. I think it smarts! I mean, ouchies! But nose plucking is a joy on the Internet.

Wallpaper (`www.nobodyhere.com/justme/wallpaper.php3`) I'm constantly redecorating my condo. These days, I'm going with a Victorian theme that's been heavily influenced by what I call a strong "Miami Vice" sensibility. My house is so beautiful that some people say it looks like a room at the Marriott!

Sometimes, I get ideas for new decorating motifs at the site above, which lets you rip off layer after layer of wallpaper, revealing what's underneath.

Hypnotic Flying Images (`titoonic.dk`) Whenever my Bikram yoga class gets cancelled, I need an alternative venue for meditation and solace. I turn to the Internet and methodically click the weird flying cartoons on this site. It brings me closer to moksha.

 TIP OF THE DAY   Photoshop has established a de facto standard for plug-ins that has been adopted by many other graphics programs, including Paint Shop Pro and Ulead's PhotoImpact. For a host of Photoshop-compatible plug-ins (some free), visit `freephotoshop.com`.

DOWNLOAD OF THE DAY   Alienskin makes some of the sweetest Photoshop effects plug-ins on this planet or any other. You can try many of them free at `alienskin.com`. For Windows and Macintosh. Click the link to a particular product then try the Demo or Downloads links to find the freebies.

POLL: Do you trust online storage?

8% Yes   92% No

TODAY'S FOCUS: Microsoft Word

PHILLIPS SCREWDRIVER PATENTED

Henry F. Phillips patented both the screw and the driver that bears his name on this day in 1936. Phillips' system used a fastener with a criss-cross–shaped recess. The X-shaped head allowed the screw to automatically center itself when attached to an object–a trait highly desirable in assembly-line manufacturing. Phillips persuaded the American Screw Company to spend $500,000 to make his screws, and in 1936, General Motors began to use the screws on the Cadillac. By 1940, nearly every American automaker had switched to Phillips screws.

Opening and Saving a Document in Word

By Regina Preciado

A word processor is nothing more than a typewriter with a bunch of fancy features. You use a word processor to write novels, letters, memos, screenplays, and articles. The most popular word processor is Microsoft Word.

Open or Create a Document in Word   When you first open Word, it provides you with a blank document. All you need to do to create your masterpiece is type, pausing frequently to save your work.

To open a new blank document, press Ctrl and N on your keyboard. (Mac users: substitute the Command key whenever I mention the Ctrl key and everything will work the same.) You can have more than one document open at once. Use the Window menu to switch documents.

Save Your Work in Word   If you've worked on a computer for any length of time, you've probably experienced a crash. You don't usually lose *saved* work in a crash, but you *will* lose any work that you haven't saved. Save often while you're working.

Press Ctrl and S at the same time (from now on we'll call that Ctrl+S) to save. The first time you save a document, Word will prompt you to choose a name and a folder in which to store the file. Call your document something logical so you'll be able to find it later. Word will add a file extension (.doc) to the name so that Windows will know that the file is a Word document.

Save As   When you use the File menu to save, you'll also see a menu choice called Save As. Save As enables you to save the document under a new name. That's useful if you want to keep different versions of the same file.

There are many other features in Word, as you'll learn this week. But now you know the two most important.

TIP OF THE DAY   Navigate through your Word document with the keyboard:

- Use the up- and down-arrow keys to move up or down one line.
- Press the Ctrl key and the up- or down-arrow key to move by paragraph.
- Page Up and Page Down keys bring you to the middle of the next page.
- Home goes to the beginning of a sentence.
- End brings you to the end of a sentence.
- Ctrl+Home takes you to the beginning of a document.
- Ctrl+End takes you to the end of a document.

DOWNLOAD OF THE DAY   If you need to open a Word document and you don't have a copy of the program, download the Word viewer, free from Microsoft at `office.microsoft.com/downloads/2000/wd97vwr32.aspx`.

POLL: Would you use a personal lie detector?

51% No

41% Yes

8% Only on my significant other

JULY 7

TODAY'S FOCUS: Microsoft Word

COKE INVENTOR BORN

Caffeine addicts the world over had reason to rejoice when John Styth Pemberton was born in Rome, Georgia, on this day in 1831. The pharmacist invented Coca-Cola in 1885. Its original incarnation was called "French Wine Coca," an alcoholic concoction based on a formula invented in Paris by Angelo Mariani. Later, Pemberton removed the alcohol and added various vegetable extracts to make a new syrup for treating headaches. Coca-Cola was advertised for the first time in an Atlanta newspaper in 1886. Pemberton eventually sold the recipe and manufacturing equipment for the beverage to Asa Candler for $1,200.

Related Web site `coke.com`

Microsoft Word Clip Art

Word isn't just for, well, words. It also does a great job with pictures. It's not a drawing program, but it does make it easy to add illustrations and figures to your document. Word even comes with a large collection of ready-made images called *clip art*.

To add images to your Word document, click **Insert**, select **Picture**, and then click **Clipart**. You can choose from the images that came with Word or insert any other picture from your hard drive. You also can search for art by category or by name.

When you find the clip art you want, click on it and choose **Insert Clip**. The clip will appear in your document with the Picture editing toolbar. The toolbar gives you a variety of options to manipulate the picture so it works for you. You will also notice that a black box surrounds your picture, with black squares around the perimeter. Clicking and dragging these boxes will allow you to resize the graphic. You can drag your clip art to your preferred location within the document.

Text Wrapping The Picture editing toolbar lets you choose how text wraps around your illustration, too. Notice the icon with the dog in front of the Venetian blinds? (Well, that's what it looks like to me.) Click it to see a list of your text wrap choices. It's much easier for you to try this than for me to explain how it works. Personally, I prefer square or tight wrapping, but it also depends on your document and the

kinds of images you choose. Try different settings, and drag the image around in the text to see how the text reacts.

Bonus Tip: Underlines You can make a variety of underlines in Microsoft Word by typing various keys three times and pressing Return. Try these:

* --- Dashes
* ___ Underscores
* ═══ Equal signs
* ### Pound signs
* ~~~ Tildes

Fun!

 TIP OF THE DAY Why does Microsoft Word open a new document with Times New Roman 10-point font every single time? Who uses that font? Change the default font forever. Select **Font** from the **Format** menu. Choose a font and point size you like (my favorite is 12-point Georgia), and then click the **Default** button. Click **OK** to make the change permanent. From now on, your new font will be the starting point in every new document.

DOWNLOAD OF THE DAY Stop hunting and pecking. Teach yourself typing for free with KP Typing Tutor, `fonlow.com/zijianhuang/kp`.

POLL: Should cracking software that you own be illegal?

85% No

15% Yes

TODAY'S FOCUS: Microsoft Word

TESLA BORN

Nikola Tesla (not the heavy-metal rock band) was born in Croatia on this day in 1856. At age 26, Tesla built the first alternating-current induction motor. A year later, he emigrated to the U.S. and sold his patents to George Westinghouse, head of the electric company of the same name. In 1891, the inventor developed the Tesla coil, which is still used today in radios, televisions, and other electronic equipment. Around 1899, Tesla discovered terrestrial stationary waves, which proved his theory that Earth could be used as a conductor of electrical vibrations.

Related Web site `pbs.org/tesla`

Mail Merge

Mail Merge is one of the most useful things you can do with any word processor. With it, you can create a single letter, envelope, or even email message, that you can personalize automatically with the names of many different recipients. You can use it to create sales letters, holiday greetings, party invitations, and more, very quickly. I almost said "and easily." And for a long time that was the problem with mail merge. Only rocket scientists and real-estate sales people could figure it out.

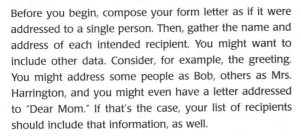

The latest version of Microsoft Word contains a Mail Merge Wizard that simplifies the task considerably. So much so that I can finally recommend it to mere mortals.

Before you begin, compose your form letter as if it were addressed to a single person. Then, gather the name and address of each intended recipient. You might want to include other data. Consider, for example, the greeting. You might address some people as Bob, others as Mrs. Harrington, and you might even have a letter addressed to "Dear Mom." If that's the case, your list of recipients should include that information, as well.

When you have your letter and its intended recipients together, open the Mail Merge Wizard in Word. Choose **Tools**, **Letters and Mailing**, **Mail Merge Wizard**. Walk through the process using your original letter as a starting point.

You'll note that as Word creates your form letter it replaces names and addresses with special fields. Fields that look like this:

<<firstname>>

These are the areas that the merge will fill in to create the custom letter. Word also has some special postal fields used to print bar codes on envelopes to speed your mail.

At the end of the process, check the letters to be sure they all make sense, and then print them. In just a few minutes you can create hundreds of letters, each of which looks personally written.

 TIP OF THE DAY Word's AutoText feature automatically corrects commonly misspelled words. (Try spelling misspell "mispell" for an example.)

If there's something you misspell frequently, add it to AutoCorrect. Select **AutoText** from the **Insert** menu, then click **AutoText** again in the expanding menu. Choose the **AutoCorrect** tab, and add new text to replace. You can also delete the ones you don't want, like the dumb happy face Word insists on filling in for the classic typed smiley :-).

 DOWNLOAD OF THE DAY Keep Word and your other Microsoft Office products up to date. Every few weeks, go to Office update, `office.microsoft.com/ProductUpdates/default.aspx`, and apply any fixes and security patches.

 On the Mac, visit `microsoft.com/mac/download` and check for Office updates.

TODAY'S FOCUS: Microsoft Word

FIRST PRIVATE SATELLITE LAUNCHES

AT&T launched its satellite, Telstar 1, on this day in 1962. The small, 171-pound sphere was the world's first active communications satellite, powered by batteries that were recharged by solar panels. Three hours after launch, Telstar I transmitted a phone call between the chairman of AT&T and Vice President Lyndon Johnson. Later the same day, the satellite sent the first live television signals from the U.S. to Europe. Telstar I stopped working after less than a year in orbit.

Related Web site `www.bell-labs.com`

Print Custom Envelopes

By Greg Melton

If you own Microsoft Office, you can print your own customized envelopes directly from Word. It's relatively easy to do, and it doesn't require anything other than a printer and some envelopes.

In a new Word document, select **Letters and Mailings** from the **Tools** menu, and click **Envelopes and Labels** on the cascading menu.

Enter the delivery instructions in the top form field under Delivery Address. Use a different line for name, street, and city/state/zip code. Enter the return instructions in the bottom form field under Return Address. Use a different line for name, street, and city/state/zip code.

You can change the envelope size and printing options by Click the **Options** button. I always turn on the Delivery Point bar code, as well, because it speeds delivery.

The last step before it's time to start customizing is to click the **Add to Document** button on the Envelopes and Labels dialog box. This feature enables you to add envelopes to your letters so that, when you print the letter, the envelope also is printed out. If you write to one person a lot, you might even want to consider creating a document template with a built-in envelope to save addressing time in the future.

The envelope portion of your document is editable like any other part. You can, for example, change fonts by highlighting all text, and then choosing a font from your Font toolbar.

To insert a picture or clip art onto the envelope, click **Insert**, mouse over **Picture**, and select **From File**. Navigate to where the image you'd like to add is on your hard drive, and then click the **Insert Image** button. Try placing the image on the left side of the envelope to avoid processing problems at the post office.

The final step is to print the envelope. Place an envelope in your printer, and click the **Print** button in Word (or press Ctrl+P for a shortcut).

This might be the hardest part of the whole process. It might take a couple of times before you orient envelopes the correct way in the printer. Keep trying. You'll get it eventually.

TIP OF THE DAY   Return to where you left off. When you reopen a document in Word, press Shift+F5 to jump to the last place you left the cursor.

DOWNLOAD OF THE DAY   Sounds in Microsoft Office are more than mere frippery. They let you know when Office has completed a task, has mail ready for you, and more. Download additional sound cues free from Microsoft, at `office.microsoft.com/downloads/2002/Sounds.aspx`.

JULY 10

TODAY'S FOCUS: Microsoft Word

CP/M CREATOR KILLED

Gary Kildall, developer of the "Control Program for Microcomputers" operating system, died on this day in 1994 after being fatally injured in a bar. Newspaper reports say the 52-year-old was admitted to a community hospital in Monterey, California, the day before with a head wound. Details surrounding his death are vague, and reports on his date of death are conflicting (some say he died July 6). The Seattle native was perhaps most famous for turning down IBM's offer to license CP/M for the PC in 1980. IBM bought Bill Gates' operating system instead for $50,000.

Related Web site `museum.sysun.com/museum/cpm.html`

Macros

By Morgan Webb

You write the same documents every day, make the same file changes, add the same text. Microsoft Word and Excel can handle some simple task customization to make the program work for you.

You can record and use macros to automatically add your official letterhead, add the formal introduction you find yourself using over and over, cut, paste, indent, italicize, format, move, insert, and anything else you can do. And you don't have to know anything about programming. Follow these steps:

1. Open Word. Go to **Tools**, **Macro**, and then select **Record New Macro** from the expansion menu.
2. Type a memorable name for your impending macro.
3. Choose **Keyboard** if you want to assign a shortcut key to your macro, or **Toolbars** if you want a toolbar button. Or just click **OK**.
4. If you chose Keyboard, assign a keyboard shortcut key, and click **Assign** then **Close** to start recording. If you chose Toolbars, drag the new button in the commands column up to a space in your toolbar.
5. When you close these windows, you will have a new little toolbar with commands like a tape deck. Perform the actions you want to record—they can be quite complicated or very simple—and click the stop button when you are finished.

6. Hit your keyboard shortcut or toolbar button to use your new macro over and over and over again. To find out what your macro did, open it by pressing Alt+F8, selecting the macro, and clicking the **Edit** button.

You can probably clean it up a little by deleting duplicate lines. Be careful deleting lines you don't understand, though. You can also combine two macros in the editor by cutting and pasting.

Even macro programmers use the recorder to figure out how to do things. And for nonprogrammers, it's a very powerful way to automate repetitive functions.

TIP OF THE DAY   Keep track of your macros with the Macro Organizer. It will let you move macros from document to document and rename them. To make your macros available to all documents put them in the NORMAL.DOT file. To back up or save macro sets, create new a Word document and copy your macros into it.

To open the Organizer, press Alt+F8 to open the Macro dialog box, then click the **Organizer** button.

DOWNLOAD OF THE DAY   Microsoft offers some supplemental macros free from `office.microsoft.com/downloads/2000/supmacros.aspx`. There's one that periodically reminds you to save your work. Another shows you how to automate communication between Word, Excel, and the Access database.

POLL: Is your PC too noisy?

53% Yes

47% No

JULY 11

TODAY'S FOCUS: Microsoft Word

INVENTOR OF PHOTOGRAPHIC FILM BORN

George Eastman was born in Waterville, New York, on this day in 1854. His interest in photography started when a friend convinced Eastman to take a camera with him on a planned vacation. He took photography lessons and purchased all the current camera equipment for the trip, but he never went. Instead, he started to develop ways to make taking pictures easier. By 1880 he had patented a dry plate that could be saved (instead of exposed right away). His company, Eastman-Kodak, is now one of the largest manufacturers of photographic equipment in the world.

Related Web site   www.kodak.com

Job Hunting

By Marty Nemko

Create Your Résumé from a Template   It's tough to create a résumé from scratch. Search the thousands of model résumés at Rebecca Smith's eResumes & Resources, www.eresumes.com/gallery_rezcat.html. When you find a good fit, cut and paste it into Microsoft Word. Retain the parts of the résumé that fit you, adapt other parts, and plunk in your work history and accomplishments. Voilà! In a few hours, you have an ahead-of-the-pack résumé.

Go Under the Radar   Job seekers are lemmings. Many go after jobs in the obvious industries: high-tech, biotech, and environmental. The fact is, there are hundreds of industries where it's much easier to get hired because few people think of targeting the companies.

Do you know of anyone who aspires for a career in the sheet-metal or mobile-park brokerage industries? Neither do I. Yet, these fields employ thousands of people, the jobs tend to pay well, and there's less competition.

Think About Low-Risk Self-Employment   Never want to be downsized again? Instantly become the president and CEO by starting your own business. Afraid of the risk? There are thousands of high-profit-margin, low-investment businesses you can start.

For example, it costs Starbucks about 15 cents to make your $3 latte. The company's biggest expense is rent. You won't have to pay rent if you buy one or more espresso carts. Strategically place them in office buildings, in hospital lobbies, or across the street from busy Starbucks cafés (with a "Noncorporate Café" sign). Suddenly, you're the president and CEO of the Noncorporate Café Company with branches throughout the metropolitan area.

(Marty Nemko, Ph.D., is the author of Cool Careers for Dummies.*)*

TIP OF THE DAY   Add a work menu to Microsoft Word:

1. Select **Customize** from the **Tools** menu.
2. Go to the **Commands** tab.
3. Click **Built-In Menus** under **Categories**.
4. In the Commands box, click and hold **Work** and drag it onto the Word menu.

Now you can add any documents you use frequently to the Work list just as you would bookmark a Web page. Open the document and select **Add to Work Menu** from the **Work** menu. To remove a document press Ctrl+Alt+- (hyphen), and then go to the **Work** menu and click the document you'd like to take off the list.

   DOWNLOAD OF THE DAY   A new version of Microsoft Office XP Standard costs $479. Unless you plan to use Word, Excel, Outlook, and PowerPoint to their full potential, you might want to consider a free alternative. 602Pro PC Suite is a full Microsoft Office-compatible suite for Windows, free from software602.com.

TODAY'S FOCUS: Microsoft Word

RUBIK'S CUBE INVENTOR BORN

Erno Rubik was born in a hospital air-raid shelter in Budapest, Hungary, on this day in 1944. Rubik studied architecture at the Academy of Applied Arts and Design and became an instructor of interior design. His famous cube was created in 1974 to illustrate the principles of three-dimensional design. In 1979, Rubik convinced the Ideal Toy Corporation to market the cube in the U.S. Today, Rubik's Cube is still one of the best-selling puzzles in history.

Related Web site `www.rubiks.com`

Twisted List: Name Generators

By Martin Sargent

I've gone by many names at various points in my life. Growing up in Compton, my homies called me Daddy Long Legs. My Army buddies called me Cobra T Strike Force. And at Julliard they called me The Man in the Silver Slippers. But thanks to the power of the Internet, I've learned many new names for myself.

The Hobbit Name Generator (`www.chriswetherell.com/hobbit`) I've always wondered what my name would be if I were a furry little Hobbit living in Middle Earth. Well, I need wonder no longer, thanks to this site. According to this mystical Web site, my Hobbit name is Berilac Toadfoot.

Wu-Tang Clan Name Generator (`www.recordstore.com/cgi-bin/wuname/wuname.pl`) I've been trying to gain admittance into the ranks of the fabulous rap conglomerate Wu-Tang Clan for years, but I think they keep snubbing me not because of my lyrical gangstertude, which is tight, but rather on account of my inability to come up with a good Wu-Tang name. Let's change all that with the Wu-Tang name generator. According to this invaluable resource, my Wu-Tang name is Radiophonic Oddity. I can rap with that.

Country Music Name Generator (`mp3.com/rockstarname/rawktell.html?genre=cou&lang=eng`) I was born in a small town, and I have friends in low places. Therefore, I've got the makings of a country music star. All I need now is a good name, and maybe a pickup truck. Let's tackle the name thing first. According to the country music name generator, my name is Grizzly Bear Bodine.

MP3.com hosts many other name generators in loads of music genres, from rap to hip-hop, at `.mp3.com/rockstarname`.

Dungeons & Dragons Name Generator (`www.albans.demon.co.uk/NoFrames/Generate.html`) When I was a kid, I dreamed of finding a portal or dimensional rift that would transport my being into the world of Dungeons & Dragons. But no wizard or elf in the world of Dungeons & Dragons would take me seriously if I showed up as Martin Sargent. According to these guys, my D&D name is Marcker Sawanwasio. Sounds like I'm a ranger!

TIP OF THE DAY If more than one person is working on a Word document, track each person's changes in a unique color with Word's revision tracker. Double-click the TRK in the status bar at the bottom of any Word document to turn on tracking. Double-click it again to turn it off.

When you're done collaborating, you can merge the changes or reject them using the Reviewing toolbar. The toolbar has many other features to help you with tracking. Turn it on in the **Toolbars** section of the **View** menu.

DOWNLOAD OF THE DAY TexNotes goes those little yellow sticky notes one better. It sits in your system tray, ready when you are. Free 30-day trial, and then $15 from `www.gemx.com/texnotes.php`. But I do miss the yellow.

TODAY'S FOCUS: Recreational Computing

FIRST FEMALE U.S. GEOLOGIST BORN

Florence Bascom was born in Williamstown, Massachusetts, on this day in 1862. She was one of the most educated women of her day: She earned three bachelor's degrees, a master's, and a doctorate in her lifetime. Bascom made groundbreaking discoveries by using microscopes in the study of minerals and rocks, and was the first female to be appointed to the U.S. Geological Survey. Bascom taught Geology at Bryn Mawr College in Pennsylvania for more than 30 years, and was the first woman to be elected Fellow of the Geological Society of America. She died in 1945.

Related Web site   www.usgs.gov

Collecting Maps

By David Rumsey

You can travel in time using online maps. On davidrumsey. com, there are more than 6,400 ultra high-resolution map images, and just recently we've added a GIS (geographical information system) browser.

Marking Change with Maps   This new browser enables you to compare old maps of San Francisco and Boston with modern maps and aerial photographs. In time, I plan to add maps of New York, Chicago, Los Angeles, Washington, and Seattle. Figure 1 is an example showing the east end of San Francisco's Golden Gate Park in four views: in 1869 before the park was made (upper right), in 1915 (lower left), and in a modern map (upper left) and aerial photo (lower right). You can see lots of changes.

You can also overlay an old map on top of a modern map to see dramatic changes. You can see that in Figure 2, which overlays an 1852 map of San Francisco Bay (showing the Oakland waterfront shoreline in heavy black lines as it was then) on top of the modern map (showing how the shoreline was massively filled in to create the Oakland container port).

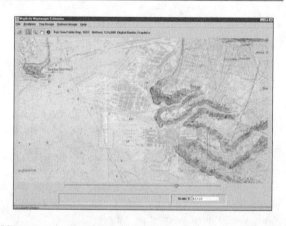

Maps are a remarkable part of the historical record. By putting them online, we can make these rare and fragile documents available to anyone who wants to know more about how time has changed their favorite places.

 TIP OF THE DAY   View incredible satellite images of the Earth online at Terraserver, terraserver.com. Search by city name or longitude and latitude or zoom in on the map. Resolutions as high as one meter.

For aerial photos of even higher resolution, visit GlobeExplorer, globexplorer.com/cfviewer/ viewer.cfm.

 DOWNLOAD OF THE DAY   Create a jigsaw puzzle of your favorite picture or map. All you need is a pair of scissors, a glue stick, a printer (preferably color), some cardboard, and American Greetings Crafts. $15 from broderbund.com/Product. asp?OID=4141205. You can also use it to create buttons, costumes, picture frames, book covers, stencils, bookmarks, labels and stickers, and more.

JULY
14

TODAY'S FOCUS: Recreational Computing

MICROSOFT BREAKS INTO BROADCASTING

MSNBC launched on this day in 1996. The all-news cable network was a $420 million joint venture between Microsoft and the National Broadcasting Company. In the following years, the channel has struggled with declining revenue. Microsoft CEO Steve Ballmer later said in a 2001 interview that if he had another chance to go back and launch MSNBC, he "would not do it again."

Related Web site   `msnbc.com`

Sidewalk Astronomy

By Jane Houston Jones

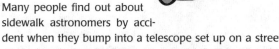

Many people find out about sidewalk astronomers by accident when they bump into a telescope set up on a street corner in a major city. Most are amazed that you can see the moon and planets so clearly from the city.

Buying a Telescope   Sidewalk astronomers and amateur astronomy groups encourage you to test-drive a telescope before you make or buy one. All too often a telescope bought on impulse or received as a gift turns into an expensive hat rack after a couple of frustrating attempts at setup or disappointing attempts at viewing.

Before you buy, look through multiple telescopes at a star party sponsored by an astronomy club. Find groups in your area with *Sky and Telescope Magazine's* guide at `skyandtelescope.com/resources/organizations/default.asp`.

Make a Telescope   My first telescope was amazingly simple to make, and I still use it all the time. The telescopes used by sidewalk astronomers are made with common materials you might find in a dumpster or a trip to the local hardware store.

* Exterior-grade plywood
* A cardboard tube from a construction company
* Leather, paint, glue, screws, nails, and bolts
* Cedar shim shingles
* Cardboard mailing tubes
* Masonite
* 33-1/3 rpm phonograph record
* Primary and secondary mirror

A lot of people make their own mirrors by grinding one piece of glass against another piece with increasingly smaller grades of abrasives between them. But don't worry, you'll be able to find plenty of places that sell finished mirrors.

Here are the steps to making a simple reflecting telescope on a Dobsonian mount, considered one of the simplest mounts available:

1. Buy or grind your own mirror (`users.uniserve.com/~victorp`).
2. Construct your tube and mount (`sfsidewalkastronomers.org/sfsidewalk/cdobplans.htm`).
3. Test and align your mirror.
4. Align the secondary mirror (`tie.jpl.nasa.gov/tie/dobson`).
5. Align the primary mirror (`tie.jpl.nasa.gov/tie/dobson`).
6. Enjoy the universe!

(Jane Houston Jones and her husband Morris "Mojo" Jones are sidewalk astronomers in San Francisco `sfsidewalkastronomers.org`*.)*

 TIP OF THE DAY   Kids' Crafts Sites

Make-stuff.com is the ultimate site for people who like to, well, make stuff. Check the kids' section to learn how to make your own faux play-dough from flour and water. It's safe, nontoxic, and smells like Kool-Aid. You also can make colored macaroni, play putty, and your own crayons with the simple recipes offered up by this site.

AllCrafts.net supplies pages and pages of craft ideas and projects.

The Kids Crafts Bulletin Board, at `wwvisions.com/craftbb/kids.html`, is a bulletin board for parents and teachers to exchange craft ideas.

  DOWNLOAD OF THE DAY   Zoom through the Milky Way, visiting the moon, the sun, or any of the planets. Or, travel outside our galaxy to more than 100,000 stars with Celestia, free from `ennui.shatters.net/celestia`.

TODAY'S FOCUS: Recreational Computing

ATOMIC BOMB TESTED

The first atomic bomb exploded on this day in 1945. The experiment, known as the Trinity Test, took place in the early morning hours at the Alamogordo Air Base, about 125 miles from Albuquerque, New Mexico. The plutonium bomb, nicknamed "Fat Boy," vaporized its steel scaffolding when it was detonated, and created a mushroom cloud 41,000 feet high. The bomb exploded with the energy of 20,000 tons of dynamite and emitted heat three times hotter than the temperature of the sun. It eliminated every sign of plant and animal life within a one-mile radius.

Related Web site `nuclearfiles.org/chron/40/1940s.html`

Horoscopes

By Alison Strahan

Whether or not you believe the movement of the stars and planets influences your personality, investigating your sign online can be a lot of fun.

Portals   Astrology portals are packed with links to sites that give readings ranging from Indian to medieval. AdZe's Astrology Links (`adze.com/links/astrology`) and Yahoo! Astrology (`astrology.yahoo.com/yastro`) are a couple of good ones.

Discover your planetary luck day or choose a place to check your horoscope online from the extensive annotated list at About.com's astrology portal, `astrology.about.com`. Visit the sites while you're in a good mood, though. The fun and friendly New York–based ArtCharts.com talked about my perfectionism and how it limits me (sigh) while the "horror-scope" at Aztec Astrologer (`www.maths.uq.edu.au/~mrb/Aztec`) told me I was born in an unlucky week. It had nothing positive to say at all.

A Dash of Humor   The Zodiac Master, at `thezodiac.com`, dishes out astrology with a dash of humor. Get a Flash-animated overview of your sign. The site informed me in bold letters that I'm a perfectionist. Become more informed about astrology in general by reading about moon signs and sun signs.

Are You and Your Mate Compatible?   Matrix Software (`thenewage.com/new_oracles`) has a beautifully organized site. Generate a horoscope based on your sign and birthday. Check the Friends & Lovers section to find out whether you're really a match, or consult the Oracle with your own questions.

Astrology.com (`horoscopes.astrology.com`) is geared toward women. Generate a free sample report on you and your mate to learn more about your astrological compatibility, or simply check your stars. Watch out: The site encourages you to shell out cash for specialized services such as a "Career Path Report."

 TIP OF THE DAY   Celebrate holidays, birthdays, barbecues, bachelor parties, and more without going through the trouble of writing and mailing dozens of invitations. Use AOL Invitations. Keyword: Invitations.

You must be an AOL member to use Invitations, but you can send invites to anyone with an email account. Guests receive a link to your online invitation where they can RSVP and participate in a message board.

 DOWNLOAD OF THE DAY   Fortune Teller can read your future. Maybe. Choose from classic fortune-telling techniques such as Tarot cards, palm reading, or the crystal ball, or opt for the esoteric, such as I Ching, numerology, or geomancy. Free for Windows from `rkwest.com/fortune.shtml#FTW`.

POLL: When your tech breaks, what do you do first?

50% I fix it myself
2% I bring it to a friend or family member to fix
3% I call tech support
1% I bring it to a repair shop
44% I call *The Screen Savers*

TODAY'S FOCUS: Recreational Computing

STEALTH BOMBER INAUGURAL FLIGHT

The B-2 Stealth bomber made its first successful test flight on this day in 1989. The two-hour mission took place over the California desert, with the plane reaching top speeds of about 200 miles per hour (which is quite slow in comparison to most aircraft). The Stealth project took about 10 years and $22 billion to complete. The Boeing planes were designed to be undetectable to Soviet radar, and cost an estimated $530 million each. Ironically, the Cold War ended that same year.

Related Web site `boeing.com/defense-space/military/b2bomber`

Online Trail Guides

By Nicole Guilfoyle

Attention hikers: Ditch those expensive maps and trail guides. The Net is full of resources for the outdoor enthusiast on a budget.

Before you head out on your next camping trip or weekend getaway, download the trail maps you'll need from the Internet. They're convenient, free, and light. You'll save money, and heavy books won't weigh down your backpack.

Free Trail Maps Trailmonkey (`trailmonkey.com`) boasts a huge collection of free maps of trails for hikers and mountain bikers. The site is easy to navigate and updated often. Large area maps provide an overhead view. Just click on a camera icon to get a detailed map of a particular trail. You can also search for different hiking trails around the world.

Topo, not Gigio Trails.com is another great place to look for hiking paths. Use the trail search to find trails based on location and difficulty. Your results will usually include topographical and area maps. Unfortunately, these maps aren't as detailed as maps from Trailmonkey. However, the site suggests a guidebook appropriate for each trail. You can also get topographical maps of specific areas at `TopoZone.com`.

Most national parks and popular camping areas have hiking maps on their own Web sites. Find these at About.com (`usparks.about.com/travel/cs/maps`) and Yahoo!, `dir.yahoo.com/recreation/outdoors/trails`.

TIP OF THE DAY Hostels are not just for backpackers anymore; they're for anyone who wants to travel the world on a budget.

Hostelling International (`www.hiayh.org/hostels/mapindx.htm`) is an incredible resource for locating hostels within the United States.

Go international at Hostels.com. The guide claims to be the most complete directory in the world, listing thousands of hostels in more than 150 regions.

After you've got a list of possibilities, visit Eurotrip at `eurotrip.com`. Eurotrip posts opinionated reviews of the best (and worst) hostels in Europe. You'll find the lowdown on everything from whether the hostel is well situated to the cleanliness of the bathrooms.

Finally, don't forget to visit an online discussion board to read about the experiences of fellow hostellers. Hostels.com and Eurotrip have message boards where you can find out what a hostel is really like from travelers who have already stayed there.

DOWNLOAD OF THE DAY Everyrule.com's slogan is "Every Rule in the Universe," and it might be right. The site has the rules for everything from chess to go, jai alai to the luge—even TV game show rules are explained here. Everyrule.com also includes etiquette for any occasion, from weddings to tipping at restaurants. Check the Every Other Rules section for a guide to being a guy and how to call "shotgun!"

JULY 17

TODAY'S FOCUS: Recreational Computing

JOHN GLENN BORN

The first astronaut to orbit the Earth was born in Cambridge, Ohio, on this day in 1921. Glenn served in the Naval Aviation Cadet Air program and in the Marine Corps, and flew combat missions in both WWII and Korea. In 1957, Glenn made the first transcontinental flight to average supersonic speed: He flew from Los Angeles to New York in three hours and 23 minutes, setting a new world record. In 1962, he became the first man to orbit the Earth in Friendship 7. In 1998, Glenn returned to space, becoming the oldest astronaut in history.

Related Web site `www.jsc.nasa.gov/Bios/htmlbios/glenn-j.html`

Digital Vacation Photos

By Rick Oldano

Your digital camera is not your grandpa's brownie. These are the things to keep in mind when you take that new-fangled camera on vacation.

Beware of the Dark Most museums don't allow flash photography. Bring a tripod to keep the camera steady in really low light situations.

Digital cameras don't do as well with low light as their film-based brethren. Before you leave home, play with the settings to see how your camera handles low light. If your camera supports it, shoot in manual mode. Try decreasing the shutter speed while increasing the aperture. Remember that you'll get grainier pictures in darker conditions. Of course, the benefit of a digital camera is that you can see right away how your shot came out, so you'll know whether you have what you want before you get home.

Don't Lose Power Turn off the LCD display. It drastically reduces the number of pictures you can take before the batteries die.

If you're lucky, your camera came with rechargeable batteries. If not, consider purchasing a recharger and two sets of batteries. While you're out taking pictures, the spare batteries can be recharging back at the hotel. Be sure you have the proper power adapters for the countries you're visiting, too.

Bring Extra Memory You wouldn't leave home with a single roll of film, but digital cameras come with only one memory card. Unless you're bringing a laptop with you, you'll be limited to the number of pictures you can get on that card, so buy another. The price of flash memory has fallen dramatically. You can get an extra 128MB, enough for more than 100 pictures, for less than $75.

(Rick Oldano is editor-in-chief of Digital Tourist Magazine.*)*

TIP OF THE DAY For help with your next painting project, visit This Old House (`thisoldhouse.com`) and search for "paint."

To figure out how much paint you'll need, use the Benjamin Moore Paint Calculator at `benjaminmoore.com`. For a rough estimate, use All About Home's calculator, `allabouthome.com/calculators/paint.html`.

Now that you know how much paint you need, make an informed choice about what kinds of paint to buy and how to do the job safely, with the help of the National Paint & Coatings Association at `paintinfo.org`.

DOWNLOAD OF THE DAY Don't call it Lego, but it does look a lot like the classic primary-colored building blocks I grew up with. BlockCAD is a free program that lets you design your own Lego-like creations, and you'll never run out of bricks. Free from `user.tninet.se/~hbh828t/proglego.htm`.

TODAY'S FOCUS: Recreational Computing

FIRST PARKING METERS

The first automatic parking meter in the U.S. was installed in Oklahoma City on this day in 1935. The Park-O-Meter was invented by Carl Magee in 1932, but the actual model, dubbed the "Black Maria," was created by H.G. Thuesen and Gerald Hale, who won a design contest sponsored by Magee and city officials. The project was paid for with the nickels collected by the meters.

Related Web site `ionet.net/~luttrell/history.html`

Party Geeky

By Roger Chang

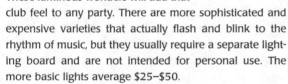

Here are some of your options for the ultimate in high-tech party gizmos:

Multicolored Rotating Light (radioshack.com) These luminous wonders will add that club feel to any party. There are more sophisticated and expensive varieties that actually flash and blink to the rhythm of music, but they usually require a separate lighting board and are not intended for personal use. The more basic lights average $25–$50.

Mirrored Disco Ball (radioshack.com) Although the exact history of the mirror ball remains a mystery, one of the earliest uses on film can be seen in Bogart's *Casablanca*. From '40s swing to '70s disco, the mirror ball adds a touch of ostentatious fun to any get-together. Mirror balls range in price and size but average around $20–$35.

Party Fogger/Smoke Machine (www.cookbrothers.com) (Look in the Electronics category under DJ Lighting.) Like the mirror ball, a smoke machine works best when used in conjunction with specialized dance lighting. They can range anywhere from $80–$200. They also require a bottle of smoke fluid to produce the smoke.

Smoke machines differ slightly from fog machines. Smoke machines fill up a room with smoke, whereas fog machines tend to create a low-level haze (think of a graveyard at night). Be sure you use the less caustic smoke fluid. Some smoke fluid varieties tend to be sticky and leave residue behind that might be hard to get out of furniture. Your best bet would be to use one of these in an open area without furniture.

Karaoke DVD Player (amazon.com) What party would be complete without a karaoke machine? Laugh and deride your friends and family as they try to belt out popular musical tunes. Luckily, many DVD players are capable of playing karaoke discs and even come with the jacks to plug a microphone into. All you need is a microphone and DVD karaoke discs.

Digital Video Projector Use your PC to project DVD movies or video games onto a wall or giant screen. For a dance party light show, use Winamp visualizations. These work great outdoors on a patio or back yard using the side of your house as a screen. Good projectors cost thousands, but you can also rent one for the weekend.

 TIP OF THE DAY Clean up anything well. HowToCleanAnything.com can tell you how to get ink stains out of a white shirt (did you lose that pocket protector again?) or how to clean the fish pond. Use the search engine to solve a particular cleaning problem, and read the top 10 laundry tips for whiter whites and brighter brights.

 DOWNLOAD OF THE DAY Rosemary West's Poetry Generator allows even the most inarticulate individual to spit out poetic prose. Free for Windows from rkwest.com/ed.shtml#POETRY.

POLL: Which political party is more wired?

30% Democratic

59% Republican

11% Reform

JULY 19

TODAY'S FOCUS: Recreational Computing

FIRST LANDING ON MOON

The U.S. beat the USSR to a major milestone in the space race on this day in 1969. Astronauts Neil Armstrong and Edwin "Buzz" Aldrin landed lunar module Eagle in the Sea of Tranquility and walked on the moon's surface for more than two hours. Armstrong's historic first step was televised—the first of any such broadcast in history. To this day, many conspiracy theorists believe the telecast was staged, citing details such as the alleged waving American flag: There is no wind on the moon.

Related Web site www.hq.nasa.gov/office/pao/History/ap11ann/introduction.htm

Read a rebuttal of the moon hoax theory at www.redzero.demon.co.uk/moonhoax.

Twisted List: Useful Web Sites

By Martin Sargent

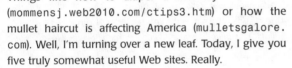

I woke up this morning as if out of a fog and realized that for the past several months I haven't provided one useful bit of information in my lists. It's all been nonsense. Things like how to diaper a monkey (mommensj.web2010.com/ctips3.htm) or how the mullet haircut is affecting America (mulletsgalore.com). Well, I'm turning over a new leaf. Today, I give you five truly somewhat useful Web sites. Really.

Let's say you want to send a text message to anyone who carries a cell phone that's equipped with text messaging. Maybe you want the person to pick up some milk at the store or meet you at the florist later. You can, at onemsg.com. Just type in the phone number, write your message, and within seconds the recipient will be reading your message, no matter which cell phone network he or she is on. Useful, no?

Continuing with the phone theme, ever wish you had a phone number that spells something, like HOT-KISS or BIG-GEEK? Maybe you do. You can find out what your phone number spells, at phonespell.org.

How many times have you wanted to attach an object to another object but didn't know what kind of adhesive to use? The problem is solved, thanks to thistothat.com. You tell the site, for example, you want to attach Styrofoam to metal, and it'll tell you the strongest adhesive to use, as well as the least toxic. A godsend if you're into arts and crafts, like me.

It's a common problem. You want to tell someone a Web address but the URL is like two million characters long. You can assign a shorter, easy-to-remember URL to act as a proxy to that big fat long one with shorterlink.com.

Let's pretend for a minute you want to find some random sound to put on your Web page, in a PowerPoint presentation, or whatever. Now you can find exactly what you're looking for with the nifty search engine FindSounds.com.

TIP OF THE DAY Track movie blunders at movie-mistakes.com. *The Matrix* is the current top mistake-ridden film, with 147 blunders cataloged, but many other big hits make the list. Did you notice that one of the lifeboat passengers in *Titanic* is wearing a digital watch? Neither did I.

DOWNLOAD OF THE DAY Track satellites orbiting the space over your neighborhood with Satscape. Satscape uses user-updated data to accurately map the course and current position of non-classified satellites orbiting the Earth. It renders the information in a 2D or 3D global view. Free for Windows from satscape.co.uk.

POLL: What's your future phone?

16% Finger phone

52% Holographic phone

18% Banana phone

14% Earring phone

TODAY'S FOCUS: Computer Hardware

FIRST ROBOT FATALITY

The first reported death by a robot happened on this day in 1984. A machine in a Jackson, Michigan, auto plant crushed a 34-year-old employee against a safety bar. The worker died from the injuries five days later. The National Institute for Occupational Safety and Health says the incident was "the first documented case of a robot-related fatality in the U.S." However, earlier reports exist of a fatality involving automated machinery in Japan in 1981. A malfunctioning robotic arm allegedly pushed a repairman against a gearwheel-milling machine at a Kawasaki plant.

Related Web site   `www.osha-slc.gov/dts/osta/otm/otm_iv/otm_iv_4.html`

Understanding Overclocking

Overclocking is defined as running a computer's microprocessor at a speed faster than it was intended to go. In some cases, you can get a machine that's as much as 50% faster. But there's a downside, too. You'll void your warranty, you can severely impact your computer's reliability, and, in extreme cases, you can burn the processor to a crisp.

So, why would anyone take the chance? Because it's fun!

To overclock, you need a motherboard you can change the settings on. Although there are two settings that govern processor speed, you can generally only change one:

* **The Bus Speed**—The internal speed of the motherboard. For example, you can often set a normal 66MHz PCI bus to run at 75MHz, 83MHz, or even 100MHz. Some of the latest mobos with a 133MHz bus can run at 150MHz or more—if they don't crash first.
* **The Multiplier**—The processor speed is a multiple of the bus speed. The multiplier determines how fast the processor runs. Every processor we know of today ships "clock locked." That means if you change this setting on the motherboard, the chip will refuse to run.

If you have a machine built by a major manufacturer such as Dell, Gateway, or HP, you won't be able to change the speeds on the motherboard. These machines are not overclockable.

Many other motherboard manufacturers put in features that encourage overclocking. Most newer motherboards let you change clock settings in the BIOS setup program.

On older motherboards, you might have to change physical jumpers on the board itself. Check your manual for details.

Some processors overclock better than others. Overclockers.com's CPU Database lists a wide range of processors, along with information about how fast people have been able to get them to run. Check the database before you even consider overclocking. You might find that you can only get a 5% or 10% increase in speed, which is essentially unnoticeable. Some CPUs can't overclock under any circumstances.

 TIP OF THE DAY   You can overclock some Macintosh computers, too, but it's a little more tricky, and the results are far from mind-boggling.

To overclock a G4, visit `www.xlr8yourmac.com/G4ZONE/G4YIKESOC`.

MacSpeedZone describes how to overclock the iMac Revision A at `macspeedzone.com/articles/html/imachotrod.html`.

For information on other models, see the Clock Chipping Home Page at `homepage.mac.com/schrier/mhz.html`.

 DOWNLOAD OF THE DAY   WCPUID tells you all about your PC's CPU, including its speed. Free from `h-oda.com`.

Monitor your motherboard with the HMonitor, shareware from `hmonitor.com`, or Motherboard Monitor, free from `mbm.livewiredev.com`. Check each program's list of supported hardware to be sure it will work with your machine.

TODAY'S FOCUS: Computer Hardware

BILL GATES HANDS OVER REINS

The founder of Microsoft turned part of his job over to Steve Ballmer, who became president on this day in 1998. Gates had been the company's president and CEO since it was founded in 1975. Gates said Ballmer would take on the day-to-day operations of the software company, while Gates, who remains chairman, took a new position as chief software architect to focus on research and development. Gates and Ballmer's relationship dates back to when they were attending Harvard University. Ballmer was Microsoft's 20th employee.

Related Web site `flamingmailbox.com/maccomedy/movies`

Video Accelerator Terms

 Creating fast 3D graphics is both an art and a science. Following are some definitions for some terms you'll hear gamers and card vendors use.

Antialiasing (AA)—The smoothing of jagged edges along a rendered polygon. Normally, drawing an angled line with square dots results in a stairstep effect called *jaggies*. AA smoothes those jaggies. New high-end video cards can perform AA internally with only modest performance degradation.

MIP maps—Multiple versions of a texture used for scaling purposes. As the distance between the player and an image lengthens, increasingly scaled-down MIP maps are used to achieve a more realistic effect. Likewise, as images become closer, higher-resolution MIP maps are used to increase the detail. MIP maps can be generated by the application or in hardware via the video card itself. MIP is short for the Latin phrase "multum in parvo," which means "many things in a small place."

Filtering is used to smooth the transitions between maps. Three levels of MIP map filtering are commonly used in today's PCs:

- **Bilinear filtering**—The worst-quality filtering. All modern video cards can perform bilinear filtering in hardware with no performance penalty.
- **Trilinear filtering**—Medium-quality filtering. Trilinear filtering helps eliminate the "banding" effect that appears between adjacent MIP map levels.
- **Anisotropic filtering**—The most hardware-intensive of the three forms of texture enhancement, it also provides the best quality. This method of filtering works great with textures incorporating alphanumeric characters. Helps signs and other text remain legible as distances change.

Pixel—A dot on the screen. A 1,024×768 screen has 786,432 pixels.

Texture—A 2D image (usually a bitmap) covering the polygons of a 3D world.

Texel—A textured pixel.

Vertical Sync (V-Sync)—Synchronization of a video card's output with the monitor's refresh rate. Disabling V-Sync allows the video card to render frames as fast as possible. This increases the frame rate at the cost of some visual degradation.

TIP OF THE DAY Tame your BIOS for better video performance:

- Disable System BIOS, Video BIOS, and Video RAM caching.
- Disable Video BIOS Shadowing and all shadowing address ranges.

For more tweaks, read the BIOS optimization guide at `adriansrojakpot.com`.

 DOWNLOAD OF THE DAY Test your video card with benchmark programs from `madonion.com`. 3DMark is widely used to compare video performance. See how your system matches up in the SysOpt.com Benchmarking Database, `sysopt.com/bdatabase.html`.

POLL: What place does a gaming box have in my home?

5% Replaces my PC

64% By my TV

30% None—now get off my lawn, you crazy kids!

TODAY'S FOCUS: Computer Hardware

FIRST COMMERCIAL HDTV BROADCAST

A TV station in Raleigh, North Carolina, broadcast the first high-definition transmission on this day in 1996. The station, WRAL, was granted the first HDTV experimental license a month earlier. About 200 people watched the broadcast from WRAL's studios, but not many others could see it because most television sets were not capable of receiving HDTV signals. Now, several stations in the country's largest markets broadcast in high definition, but the switch has taken longer than expected. The FCC has mandated that all television stations in the U.S. broadcast entirely in digital by the year 2006.

Related Web site `wral-hd.com`

FireWire

FireWire was first developed by Apple as a speedy way of connecting devices to computers. It boasts an impressive maximum throughput of 400Mbps, or roughly 50MB per second, and works with a wide variety of computers and peripherals.

Because Apple used to charge people to use the trademarked name "FireWire," there has been some confusion over what to call it. The Institute of Electrical and Electronics Engineers (IEEE) approved it as an industry standard in 1995, awarding it the name IEEE 1394 High Performance Serial Bus. Many PC manufacturers call it IEEE 1394. Some call it HPSB. And when Sony began equipping its camcorders with FireWire, it called the technology iLink.

But whether it's called FireWire, IEEE 1394, HPSB, or iLink, it's all the same technology, and devices and cables designed for any will work with all.

FireWire is used in areas where lots of data needs to be transported quickly. In slower applications, USB 1.x is more common. The two are similar. Both are serial connections: Bits of data are transferred one at a time, which makes the cabling simpler and more reliable.

Both are plug and play: Devices can be added while the computer is on and the computer will automatically recognize them. They also can be removed without powering down or rebooting. And in both cases, a single connector can handle many devices. A USB connection has a theoretical limit of 125 devices; FireWire can connect with up to 63. In both cases, because all the devices share the bandwidth, the realistic maximum is much lower.

FireWire is a flexible, fast, and powerful solution that makes it easy to connect peripherals to a computer. All Macs come equipped with FireWire these days and, in my opinion, all PCs should, as well.

Tomorrow we'll talk about USB 2.0, a newly emerging standard that's aimed squarely at FireWire.

 TIP OF THE DAY If you can keep your PC cool, it will run more reliably and last longer. The Heatsink Guide (`heatsink-guide.com/maxtemp.htm`) lists the maximum temperatures for a wide variety of processors, but it's best to stay well below the maximum. I recommend operating your CPU below 130 degrees Fahrenheit. The temperature inside your case should be under 120 degrees.

To get help with cooling, visit the reviews of CPU coolers at [H]ard|OCP, `hardocp.com/reviews.html?cat=NiwsLCws`.

 DOWNLOAD OF THE DAY The Intel Application Accelerator enables faster delivery of data from the hard drive to the processor and other system-level hardware. Requires a Pentium III or 4 processor and an Intel 8xx series chipset. Free for Windows from `appsr.cps.intel.com/scripts-df/Product_Filter.asp?ProductID=663`.

JULY 23

TODAY'S FOCUS: Computer Hardware

AMELIA EARHART BORN

The first woman to fly a plane solo across the Atlantic Ocean was born in Atchison, Kansas, on this day in 1897. In 1920, Earhart bought her first plane, a prototype of a Kinner plane she named the "Canary." Shortly after, she set the record for the highest altitude achieved by a woman: 14,000 feet. She made her historic trans-Atlantic flight on June 23, 1928 from Halifax, Nova Scotia, to Burry Port, South Wales. Earhart went missing on a flight from New Guinea to Howland Island in the Pacific Ocean on July 2, 1937, and was never found.

Related Web site   `ellensplace.net/eae_intr.html`

USB 2.0

All computers sold these days come with USB: USB 1.1, that is. That's fine for most current applications, but the USB Implementers Forum, `usb.org`, has been worried for some time that FireWire would steal USB's thunder, so it announced an update to USB v 2.0 several years ago. We're just now starting to see 2.0-equipped computers and peripherals.

To get USB 2.0 on your old computer, you'll have to buy an upgrade card. They're very inexpensive—less than $20 in many cases. Your old 1.1 cables and hubs should work. Computer manufacturers should be shipping new USB 2.0 capable machines any day now, and many USB 2.0 peripherals are already in the pipeline.

What will you get with version 2.0? In a word: speed. It's much faster even than FireWire with a top speed of 480Mbps, 40 times faster than the existing USB.

The increased bandwidth of USB 2.0 opens the door for PC peripherals with more functionality, including faster broadband Internet connections, higher-resolution video conferencing cameras, next-generation printers and scanners, and fast external storage units.

Most importantly, USB drives can finally live up to their potential. Drives and burners that connected via USB 1.1 were limited to a throughput of less than 1MB of data per second. That's very slow for a hard drive. Too slow, even, for anything more than a 4x CD burner. USB 2.0 should allow you to connect external devices that are every bit as fast as internal devices.

TIP OF THE DAY   In theory, USB 1.1 and 2.0 cables cannot reach farther than five meters. It's possible to extend this distance with extenders. In our informal tests we've been able to connect to a Netcam via a 17-meter cable with no loss of quality but a noticeable increase in the length of time the image takes to get to the computer. That's the problem with longer cables: Reflections inside the cables slow the data down, and eventually attenuate it to the point where it doesn't get there at all.

For more taxing USB devices, more expensive products exist that can really extend the range of USB. One example is QVS's Active Repeater extension cable, from `www.qvs.com/usb/usbrptr.asp`. These cables boast effective operation at up to 80 feet.

The best, and most expensive, option is using a product such as Icron's $270 USB Ranger, which uses Ethernet to increase USB's range to 100 meters. `www.icron.com/prod_usbr100400.html`.

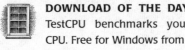

DOWNLOAD OF THE DAY TestCPU benchmarks your CPU. Free for Windows from `testcpu.webz.cz`. Try his school project, a Web-based benchmarking system that compares your CPU with the rest of the world. Smart kid!

JULY
24

TODAY'S FOCUS: Computer Hardware

FIRST TEST-TUBE BABY BORN

The first human conceived out of the womb was born on this day in 1978. Louise Brown was delivered by Caesarean section in Oldham, Great Britain, to parents Gilbert John and Lesley Brown. Physicians Patrick Steptoe, Robert Edwards, and Barry Bavister developed the in-vitro fertilization technique by which an egg taken from a woman's ovary is fertilized with the father's sperm in a test tube, and then returned to the mother's womb to grow.

Related Web site   www.sivb.org

Wireless Audio/Video

By Greg Melton

A wireless audio/video sender and receiver is an extremely practical device to have around the house. With these little gadgets, you can send audio and video wirelessly throughout your home from one room to another, up to 300 feet away.

The practical uses of a wireless A/V sender and receiver are almost endless. These devices connect to any line-in or line-out RCA jack. What electronics device doesn't come equipped with RCA jacks these days? If it doesn't come with an RCA jack, you can always buy additional adapters at your local electronics store.

If you use one in conjunction with a video camera, you could have a baby monitor set up in any room of the house in a matter of minutes. Pick up an adapter with an eighth-inch stereo mini-jack at one end and two RCA plugs at the other and you can broadcast audio or video from your computer to a stereo or TV.

These devices also make it easy to distribute the same signal from a VCR, DVD player, or satellite receiver to another TV. This means you can watch the same program or movie on a different TV in your house without having to purchase a separate VCR, DVD player, or satellite receiver.

These devices send and receive audio and video signals using either the 900MHz or 2.4GHz spectrum. The higher frequency travels farther, but both frequencies are used by other common household devices such as cell phones, portable phones, and WiFi networking. That can cause interference, so pick a frequency that's least populous. You'll also want to have a clear line of sight between the transmitter and receiver. Anything in between can degrade the signal.

Some popular products in this category:

- CamPro, $99 from AV Com Wireless: www.avcomwireless.com/pages/campro.html
- Leapfrog, $100 from Terk: www.terk.com/multiroom/product/wavemaster.html
- 2.4GHz Wireless Room-to-Room Audio/Video Sender, $99 from Radio Shack: radioshack.com
- WAVECOM Second Room, $99 from RF-Link: rflinktech.com/prod/prodindex.html

 TIP OF THE DAY   One keyboard, one mouse, one monitor, many computers. That's what a KVM switch can do for you. For about $99, the Belkin Omniview SOHO 2-port KVM switch with audio, PS/2, and USB allows you to share a keyboard, mouse, monitor, and speakers among multiple computers. With the proper connectors, you can even combine a Mac and a PC. We use 'em on TV all the time: catalog.belkin.com/IWCatSectionView.process?Section_Id=56.

 DOWNLOAD OF THE DAY   If you've got the hardware, nVidia has the demos. These incredible programs look amazing when run on a PC equipped with high-end video cards. Download ChameleonMark to test shaders. Wolfman for volumetric fur. Squid for Vertex Processing. Tidepool for bump maps. Real eye candy, free for Windows from nvidia.com/view.asp?PAGE=power_demos. Check the Demo archives for even more fun.

JULY 25

TODAY'S FOCUS: Computer Hardware

WORM CREATOR INDICTED

On this day in 1989, a federal grand jury indicted Robert Morris, Jr. for releasing an experimental Internet worm. The 24-year-old Cornell graduate student wrote a self-replicating, self-propagating program that infected thousands of computers, including those at NASA, UC Berkeley, Wright Patterson Air Force Base, MIT, and others. Morris was the first person to be prosecuted under the Computer Fraud and Abuse Act of 1986, and was found guilty in 1990 of federal computer tampering. Morris was fined more than $10,000 and was sentenced to three years' probation and 400 hours of community service.

Related Web site `netsecurity.about.com/library/blworm.htm`

High-Tech Emergency Kit

By Greg Melton

Here's a list of high-tech gadgets that would complement any emergency kit in the event of an earthquake, flood, hurricane, tornado, or anything else Mother Nature throws your way.

FreeCharge (`freeplay.net`) It's handy to have this portable human-powered cell-phone battery charger when disaster strikes. Just wind the FreeCharge for 45 seconds and your cell phone will have 4 to 5 minutes of talk time or several hours of standby time. This would allow you to call for help if your phone lines ever go down.

Sun Quest Sun Tap Combo (`sunstar-intl.com`) Be prepared for a blackout with a versatile flashlight/lantern and AM/FM Radio with 10-channel weather band that is solar powered. The Sun Tap Combo also features a hand crank to charge its internal batteries—which never need to be replaced—if it ever runs out of juice. It also features a siren and red LED flashers and plugs into conventional wall outlets and cigarette lighters. It retails for $59.95.

Esbit Pocket Stove (`www.adventuresports.com/asap/product/mpi/esbit.htm`) Imagine a portable stove that fits in your pocket. The Esbit stove uses tiny cubes that burn for 10 to 15 minutes at a time; it's perfect for cooking or boiling water. The Esbit cubes also provide a great source of kindling for fires.

Katadyn Pocket Filter (`www.katadyn.net/katadyn_pocket.html`) Filter bacteria, microorganisms, even nuclear waste, from any untreated water supply. The Katadyn Pocket Filter retails for $199 and can process 13,000 gallons of water on a single filter.

TIP OF THE DAY Keeping your PC cool is key to keeping it running. For high-end hobbyists with bucks to spare, there's nothing like a water-cooled system.

Upgrade an existing PC with InfiniPro's AquaCool kit, $78 from `infinipro.com`. Includes waterblocks for the processor and chipset, a pump, tubing, clips, and mounting hardware. It doesn't include the all-important radiator and fan, which cost an extra $54.

Or, buy a ready-made water-cooled case. Koolance's PC2-C Mid-Tower Case is $199 from `koolance.com`. It looks good, too. A top module houses three fans and a temperature monitor, and the system uses two pumps as a failsafe. Comes with a CPU block, add blocks for your chipset ($23), graphics accelerator ($23), and your hard drive ($34). A power supply is optional.

Added bonus: Water-cooled computers are quieter, too.

DOWNLOAD OF THE DAY Inventory and test your PC's hardware with HardInfo. 30-day free trial, $79 to buy, from `usro.net/products/hardinfo/`.

POLL: Is cyber-rage a crime?

46% Yes   54% No

TODAY'S FOCUS: Computer Hardware

ATLANTIC CABLE LAID

The Atlantic telegraph cable line was successfully completed on this day in 1866. The *Great Eastern*, a former passenger ship captained by James Anderson, spent 11 days dropping cable from Valencia, Ireland, to Heart's Content, Trinity Bay, Newfoundland. The cable stretched nearly 2,000 miles and was laid as deep as two miles under the ocean in some places. This was a replacement of an older cable laid in 1858. Four British and American ships had spliced a telegraph cable and completed the job in one day. Although the original cable worked, the signal was weak, and service was quickly abandoned.

Related Web site `atlantic-cable.com`

Twisted List: Things to Do with an Old Computer

By Megan Morrone

Got a new computer? Here are five good things you can do with the old one.

Donate It (`heartsandminds.org/links/computers.htm`) Your shiny new PC might make your old box look dull to you, but chances are you won't have trouble finding a new home for it.

Dedicate It to a Distributed Computing Project (`setiathome.ssl.berkeley.edu`, `members.ud.com/download/gold`) You can participate in distributed computing projects such as SETI@home, and United Devices Cure for Cancer. Just download the software and donate your unused CPU cycles for a greater good.

Install Linux (`linux.org`) I know you. You've wanted to go open-source for a while, but you're afraid of blowing your computer into a million smoldering pieces. If you're getting rid of it anyway, what's the risk?

Create Art (`applefritter.com`) I'm a huge fan of art made of trash. My favorite old computer art project is definitely the Macquarium.

Throw It off a Cliff (`techtv.com/screensavers/showtell/story/0,24330,3337045,00.html`) This is definitely the least productive way to get rid of an old computer, but I can also say personally that it is the most satisfying. Don't forget to clean up the parts afterward.

TIP OF THE DAY If you watch TV, you've probably seen those advertisements hawking refillable ink cartridges. These kits offer a great alternative to high-priced cartridges, but they're not for everyone. Refilling an ink cartridge can be a very messy job if you're not careful.

Most kits come with ink, gloves, syringes for injecting ink, and any necessary additional hardware, plus detailed instructions. Kits run from $20 to $60, depending on the printer type and number of possible refills.

You might void your printer's warranty if you use refilled ink cartridges. If it's okay to refill, use only the ink recommended by your printer's manufacturer. Some brands may leak and cause major printer damage.

Before you refill any ink cartridge, check for wear on the cartridge head. In that case, refilling the cartridge will not make it work; you'll need to buy a new one.

Be sure to cover your work surface with a towel or a piece of plastic wrap before you remove the contents of the kit. This way, if you spill ink, it will not damage anything. If you follow the instructions, everything should be fine.

We recommend that you reuse your ink cartridge no more than two times, and stick with brand-name kits for best results.

DOWNLOAD OF THE DAY Benchmark, survey, test your hardware with the ultimate all-in-one tool, SiSoft's Sandra. Free to try, but for access to all the tools, register for $29 from `www.sisoftware.demon.co.uk/sandra`.

JULY 27

TODAY'S FOCUS: Email

FINGERPRINTS USED FOR ID

Fingerprints were first recorded for identification purposes on this day in 1858. Sir William Herschel, Chief Magistrate of the Hooghly district in Jungipoor, India, took the palm print of a native with whom he was signing a contract. From then on, the magistrate required palm prints, and eventually, prints of the index and middle fingers, on every signed agreement. It was originally used, however, as a scare tactic to get locals to honor their word. It wasn't until later that Herschel discovered the "signatures" could be used to identify specific people.

Related Web site `www.fingerprints.demon.nl`

Microsoft Outlook Email Tips

By Bill Dyszel

Move Your Older Messages to an Archive File for Safekeeping

1. Choose **Tools**, **Options**, **Other**.
2. Click the **Autoarchive** button.
3. Set the autoarchive frequency and check the box to activate autoarchiving.

Find Your Archive File Fast

1. Right-click the icon for the module you want to find.
2. Choose **Properties**.
3. Click the **Autoarchive** tab. The name of your archive file is listed there. Note: Outlook archive files have *.pst extensions.

Open an Archive File

1. Choose **File**, **Open**, **Personal Folders File**.
2. Pick the archive file you want to look at.
3. When you open a Personal Folder in Outlook, you have to open the Folder List. Just choose **View**, **Folder List**.

Create Extra Personal Folders

You can create special collections of Outlook items that you can use and reuse for testing or as special applications. Just choose **File**, **New**, **Personal Folder**.

Use Date Shortcuts

Anytime you need to enter a date in Outlook, take the shortcut. If you're setting an appointment for this Thursday at noon, type **thu noon** and press Tab. Outlook will figure out what you mean and translate it into a normal date.

Flag Messages

Flag important messages when you don't have time to give them your attention immediately.

1. Right-click the message.
2. Choose **Flag for Follow-up**.
3. Enter a due date in the Flag dialog box. This makes a reminder pop up when you're ready to respond to the message you flagged.

Set Up Views

The Outlook View menu contains powerful tools for managing messages, tasks, and other items. If you flag messages regularly, use the Flagged for Seven Days view to see what's next on your agenda.

 TIP OF THE DAY To set up Outlook for multiple users in Windows XP, open the Mail control panel and click **Show Profiles**. Click **Add** to create a new profile, give it a name, and then input your email account settings. (If you don't have settings right away, don't worry; you can add them later.) Click **Prompt for a Profile to Be Used**, and Outlook will ask for the name of the user each time you start it.

 DOWNLOAD OF THE DAY Searching for a quick and easy way to clean up forwarded email? EmailStripper will remove the unnecessary formatting characters that make forwarded email hard to read. Free for Windows from `papercut.biz/emailStripper.htm`.

POLL: Have you ever regretted pressing the Send button?

73% Yes   27% No

JULY 28

TODAY'S FOCUS: Email

NASA CREATED

The National Aeronautics and Space Administration was established on this day in 1958. The agency was signed into law by President Eisenhower to direct U.S. space policy during the Cold War. Almost a year earlier, the USSR launched the first satellite, Sputnik 1, a milestone that was considered a humiliating defeat to the U.S. government. NASA, which officially went into operations in October 1958, absorbed the earlier National Advisory Committee for Aeronautics, its 8,000 employees, five research labs, and an annual budget of $100 million. Today, NASA's yearly budget is about $14 billion.

Related Web site   `history.nasa.gov`

Fighting Spam

By Tom Geller

If you've been on the Internet for more than a week, you've surely gotten unsolicited bulk email, commonly known as spam. If you're like most people, you grumble, delete it, and wish you could stop it from filling your inbox every day.

Unfortunately, there's no magic bullet to keep spam out of your mailbox. Even the best filters let some spam through, and spammers continually invent new methods to get past filters.

No matter what you do, act responsibly. Don't complain about spam unless you're sure the email is from someone you don't know and haven't explicitly given permission to send you email. Don't exaggerate, don't make threats you can't fulfill, and don't be rude. The truth is sufficient, and will set your mailbox free. Instead, prevent spam from being sent in the first place. Here are five ways you can help eliminate spam.

Learn How Spam Works and What Its Effects Are   Read the primers at the Coalition Against Unsolicited Commercial Email (CAUCE) (`www.cauce.org/about/ problem.shtml`), This Is True (`thisistrue.com/spam. html`), and the SpamCon Foundation (`spamcon.org/ about`).

Track Spammers Down   Spammers usually put a fake address in the "From" field. You must dig a little deeper to bring the guilty to justice. SpamCon tells you how at `spamcon.org/recipients/spam-response/ contact-spammerisp.shtml`.

React Effectively   If you just hit Delete, you're guaranteed to get more junk from the same spammer. Complaints often get them kicked off their Internet service provider (ISP). Statistics reports help governments develop antispam policies, and private lawsuits cripple spammers' ability to operate.

Take Part in Community Antispam Efforts   Several discussion groups help track individual spammers and devise ways to stop their activities. See the list of groups here at `spamcon.org/directories/discussions. shtml`.

Join an Antispam Organization   It's only through cooperation that we can lick this problem. Join SpamCon to learn what else you can do. Join CAUCE as well, it fights for good antispam laws and guards against bad ones.

(Tom Geller is the executive director of the SpamCon Foundation.)

TIP OF THE DAY   Whenever I have to give out an email address on the Web, I use my Spamcop address. For $30 a year, Spamcop offers Web-based email service with high-quality spam filtering. If any spam does get through, you can use the Spamcop reporting service to turn the spammer in.

Pass your mail through Spamcop.net or have your Spamcop mail forwarded to your regular account. Well worth the money. `spamcop.net`.

DOWNLOAD OF THE DAY   SpamWeasel is a sophisticated mail filter that flags spam in your mailbox. Free from `mailgate.com/ products/spamweas/sw_feat.asp`.

JULY 29

TODAY'S FOCUS: Email

FIRST ROVER LANDS ON MOON

Apollo 15 deposited the first vehicle on the moon's surface on this day in 1971. The small car, dubbed the "Lunar Roving Vehicle," was battery powered and could travel up to 11 miles per hour. Astronauts David Scott and James Irwin assembled the battery powered rover while on the moon's surface, and drove a total of 17 miles in three separate excursions. They collected 168 pounds of moon rocks and conducted other studies on the lunar surface. The astronauts of Apollo 15 stayed on the moon for three days, longer than any previous crew.

Related Web site   `www.nasm.si.edu/apollo/AS15/a15.htm`

Email Filtering

Email filters or rules help you control spam, flag important messages, and keep your mail organized by parceling it out into different folders. Here's how to use the rules feature in Outlook Express:

1. Go to **Tools**, **Message Rules**, **Mail**, and then choose **New**.
2. All mail rules are based on the same principle: If a certain condition is met, take a particular action. Set the condition in Section 1. For example, if you choose **Where the From Line Contains People**, Outlook Express will select each email from a designated person or group.
3. In Section 2, you assign Outlook Express an action. Check **Move It to the Specified Folder**, and choose a folder. Outlook Express will automatically place all email from the chosen person in the designated folder.
4. The Section 3 spells out each step of your rule. Any text that is underlined can have more detail and can be edited. Click the text that says **Contains People**. A pop-up window appears. You can either type the email address in the top field or click on the address book to select one or more addresses. Click **OK** when you have finished. You will see that the underlined text now contains the email address you specified.
5. Next, click the text **Specified Folder**. A window will pop up that contains all your existing Outlook Express folders. You may either select a folder or create a new one.
6. Finally, give the rule a name so that you can manage it in the future. You will see your new rule with a check in front of it and a description of what the rule does at the bottom. Anytime you want to change the rule, just select it and choose **Modify**.

 TIP OF THE DAY   Famous 3D IMPersona allows users of MSN Messenger to add characters and speech to instant messages. You can choose from a selection of 3D floating heads, including President Bush and Queen Elizabeth. Free from `www.impersona.com`.

DOWNLOAD OF THE DAY   CrazyTalk is a facial-animation tool that gives you the power to create talking animated images from a single photograph, complete with emotions. Attach your mug to email and really scare your friends. Free to try, $39.95 to buy, from `reallusion.com`.

Facemail can also give email a personal face, just not yours. Choose from a roster of "virtual people" (including one very creepy clown) that will "speak" your email messages directly to friends and family. Free from `lifefx.com`.

POLL: Should the law guarantee email delivery?
49% Yes
51% No

JULY
30

TODAY'S FOCUS: Email

U.S. PATENT OFFICE OPENS

The first patent office in America opened its doors on this day in 1890. The first patent was granted to Samuel Hopkins of Vermont for a method of making potash and pearlash—the boiled and filtered ash residue of hardwood trees. His concoctions were used to make glass, gunpowder, soap, and more. The potassium compounds are now mined and used mainly in fertilizer. Today, more than four million patents are in force. The U.S. Patent Office currently employs more than 5,000 people and occupies more than 1,400,000 square feet of office space.

Related Web site www.uspto.gov

Understanding Email Headers

By Megan Morrone

Every email message contains two types of headers. You're probably familiar with the simple headers that contain the most basic information (To:, From:, and Subject:). If you want to know more, you'll have to view the extended headers.

View the Headers   Different email clients reveal the full headers in different ways. Open your message, and then follow the process for your particular program.

- In Outlook Express, select **Properties** from the **File** menu and click the **Details** tab.
- In Outlook, select **Options** from the **View** menu. The Extended headers are visible in the Internet Headers box. To see them more easily select the text, copy it, and paste it into Notepad.
- In Netscape Mail, select **Headers** from the **View** menu and **Select All**.
- In Eudora, select **Options** from the **Tools** menu. Click **Fonts & Display**. Check the **Show All Headers** box. Or, just click the BLAH button on your toolbar. Honest.

What Email Headers Mean   Here are the most common fields in the email header:

`Return-Path: <megan@techtv.com>`

The sender's address.

`Received: from <server X> by <serverY> with ESMTP id <Z> <date time>`

This is the good stuff. One of these blocks is added each time your mail is handed off from server to server. Read it as: Server Y received message id Z from server X at <date time>. The blocks are listed in reverse order, so in the first Received: block Server X is your ISPs mail server and Server Y is somewhere on the Internet. You can examine the times to see how long it took for your mail to travel the Net. The server indicated in the last Received: block is, in theory, the place from which the mail originated. Unfortunately, if the mail is spam, the originating server is almost always forged.

X-Sender or X-Mailer or X-Anything

These are optional extended headers. Programs can add all sorts of stuff here, and it's sometimes revealing to read what's in there. For example, occasionally the X-Mailer header will actually identify a known bulk mailer.

`Mime-Version: 1.0`

MIME stands for Multipurpose Internet Mail Extensions. It lets you exchange audio, video, images, and other attachments via email.

`Content-type: text/plain; charset=us-ascii`

The MIME type of the message and any attachments. This is a plain text message using the U.S. character set.

TIP OF THE DAY   To rebuild Outlook Express's databases on Macintosh, hold down the Option key when you launch it.

DOWNLOAD OF THE DAY   Eudora is one of the oldest and most popular email programs. It's free for Windows and Macintosh from Eudora.com.

JULY 31

August 2003

SUNDAY	MONDAY	TUESDAY	WEDNESDAY	THURSDAY	FRIDAY	SATURDAY
					1	**2** PC pioneer Philip Don Estridge died in plane crash (1985)
3	**4**	**5** Neil Armstrong born (1930)	**6** Atomic bomb dropped on Hiroshima, Japan (1945)	**7**	**8**	**9** Netscape initial IPO (1995)
10	**11** Steve Wozniak born (1950)	**12**	**13**	**14**	**15**	**16** International Olympiad in Informatics (University of Wisconsin)
17	**18**	**19** Orville Wright born (1871)	**20**	**21**	**22**	**23** George Cuvier born (1769)
24/31 August 24 – Windows 95 released (1995)	**25**	**26**	**27** Mariner II space probe launched (1962)	**28**	**29**	**30**

TODAY'S FOCUS: Email

SQUIRREL TAKES DOWN NASDAQ

Trading on the NASDAQ was halted on this day in 1994 when a squirrel caused a power outage. The 34-minute interruption started when the furry creature chewed on a power line near the stock exchange's computer center in Trumbull, Connecticut. To make matters worse, the temporary backup system failed, causing the third NASDAQ system crash in a month. This wasn't the first time an overzealous rodent had caused problems for the tech-heavy exchange: A similar squirrel incident occurred in 1987.

Related Web site   `nasdaq.com`

Outlook Stationery

By Bill Dyszel

It's always nice to send personalized greetings to friends, loved ones, and business colleagues. If you've waited too long to send one via snail mail (or if you're too cheap to spring for cards, as I am), you can fill the bill with colorful Outlook stationery and a quick mass email.

Get Premade Stationery   The easiest way to create email stationery is to download an online package from one of the scads of Web sites that specialize in email stationery. My favorite site at the moment is CloudEight Stationery at `thundercloud.net`, but there are hundreds of other good sources. Thundercloud.net offers all sorts of stationery, some for a price and some free. Using prepackaged stationery saves time but limits your options because someone else's idea of attractive stationery might not be the same as yours.

Make Your Own   You can design your own stationery for Outlook by creating an HTML page in your favorite editor, and then placing that page and any embedded images in the folder that contains all your other Outlook stationery. That's usually `c:\program files\ common files\microsoft shared\stationery`.

It's easiest to start by modifying the HTML in an existing stationery file. Open the stationery folder, right-click one of the htm files—`sunflower.htm` will do—then choose **Open With** and select an appropriate Web page editor. Microsoft FrontPage is great if you have it; Word will do fine. You can use Notepad as a last resort, but you'd better be up on your HTML.

Steal Someone Else's Custom Stationery   If somebody sends you email on stationery that you find especially attractive and you want to use it yourself, just open the message and choose **Save Stationery** from the **File** menu.

(Bill Dyszel is the author of Microsoft Outlook for Dummies *and a regular guest on* The Screen Savers.*)*

TIP OF THE DAY   Add an automatic signature to your email.

- In Outlook Express, select **Options** from the **Tools** menu and click the **Signatures** tab.
- In Outlook, select **Options** from the **Tools** menu, click the **Mail Format** tab, and then click the **Signatures** button.

 In Mail for Mac OS X, open Preferences and select the Signatures pane.

You can have as many signatures as you want, but select one to be the default signature.

 DOWNLOAD OF THE DAY   David Harris's Pegasus Mail is one of the best free email applications for Windows and DOS. Harris practically invented email filtering more than 10 years ago and continues to lead the way with a fast and powerful program. Download it free from `pmail.com`.

POLL: Should you be forced to have an email address?

11% Yes

89% No

TODAY'S FOCUS: Email

TELEPHONE INNOVATOR BORN

Elisha Gray was born in Barnesville, Ohio, on this day in 1835. The scientist created the first electronic musical device, albeit by accident, when he invented the basic single-note oscillator (a self-vibrating electromagnetic circuit). Gray also invented a telegraph printer and many communications devices. Gray could have been known as the inventor of the telephone, but Alexander Graham Bell beat him to the patent office by just a few hours. Gray fought a long legal battle with Bell over the years, but failed to gain legal recognition for his work on the telephone.

Related Web site ohiobio.org/egray.htm

Get Your Email Anywhere

By Martin Sargent and Roger Chang

Here are four ways for you email addicts to collect your mail on the road. Just promise us you won't use them when you're riding a ski lift or sitting in church or something.

Listen to Your Email (j2.com, phone. yahoo.com) Email-by-phone, from j2 Global Communications, is good medicine for email junkies. It lets you access email from any phone in the world. Call a toll-free number, input your j2 account and PIN numbers, and a computerized voice reads your email. You can respond by leaving j2 a voice message that'll appear in your recipient's email inbox in the form of an audio attachment. After a $15, one-time activation fee, you pay $12.50 per month for 30 minutes of use, plus 10 cents for each additional minute.

If you already have a Yahoo! Mail account, you can have your email read to you over the phone for $4.95 a month.

Is That Email in Your Pocket? (pocketmail.com) The PocketMail service works with two devices: the $99 PocketMail Composer and the $149 BackFlip for the Palm. On the back of each is a snap-out acoustic coupler. You receive and send email by holding the acoustic coupler to the receiver of any phone on which you've dialed the toll-free PocketMail number.

You'll pay $15 a month for the service. Messages are limited to 4,000 characters and must be sent to your dedicated PocketMail email address. That means you'll have to forward mail from your other accounts before you hit the road.

BlackBerry (blackberry.net) The best on-the-go email system is the BlackBerry, a pager that features an alphanumeric keyboard, manufactured by RIM. It comes with organizer software that can sync with your PC. The BlackBerry is always connected to the wireless network. It beeps or vibrates when a new message arrives.

BlackBerry devices sell for $399 to $499 and the service costs $20 to $40 a month. Wireless service is limited to North America.

 TIP OF THE DAY To attach a file to an email in Outlook or Outlook Express, click the paperclip icon, choose the file, and click **OK**. Repeat to attach additional files.

Remember to let the recipient know you'll be sending an attached file—it's dangerous to open unexpected attachments. And try to keep the total file size below 1MB. If the files are bigger than that, consider sending them over a period of a few days. Or, use a service such as Whalemail (whalemail.com) to handle the transfer.

DOWNLOAD OF THE DAY AOL2POP lets you use Outlook, Outlook Express, Eudora, Pegasus, and Netscape Mail with any AOL account. Free to try, $20 to buy, from aol2pop.com.

TODAY'S FOCUS: Email

NUCLEAR SUB GOES TO NORTH POLE

The world's first nuclear submarine left for the North Pole on this day in 1958. The *USS Nautilus* dove at Point Barrow, Alaska, and traveled nearly 1,000 miles at a depth of about 500 feet under an arctic ice cap. The *Nautilus* was built by the U.S. Navy and took its maiden voyage in 1952. It was 319 feet long and displaced more than 4,000 tons submerged. The uranium-powered reactor enabled *Nautilus* to travel faster than 20 knots underwater. The submarine traveled nearly 500,000 miles in its career and was decommissioned in 1980.

Related Web site   www.ussnautilus.org

Twisted List: Things You Should Never Download

By Martin Sargent

Here are three pieces of software that you should avoid downloading because they will either infest your system with spyware, change your system settings without your explicit permission, or are just plain stupid.

Go!Zilla (gozilla.com)   Go!Zilla is a good download manager. It's free because it's supported by ads. You can see the ads, but what you can't see are the applets that communicate with Radiate, the company that distributes Go!Zilla. These applets tell Radiate what ads you look at so they can send you more of the same—it's sort of a directed advertising approach. If you don't want your Internet habits monitored, Go!elsewhere.

BonziBuddy (bonzi.com)   BonziBuddy is a purple monkey that bugs you as you search the Web, carrying on about this and that and making a general nuisance of himself. Worse, he's almost impossible to uninstall. BonziBuddy will drive you bonkers. Stay away.

GoHip (gohip.com)   GoHip is one of those stupid browser extensions that nobody really needs. When you install it, it makes GoHip.com your start page and attaches an advertisement for itself to your email. And its uninstaller doesn't work. After thousands of complaints, the company finally posted a removal utility. Don't GoHip, but if you do, GoHere: www.gohip.com/remove_browser_enhancement.html.

TIP OF THE DAY   Archive your Web-based email before your host deletes it. Download the mail into Outlook Express, where you can keep it forever. Outlook Express syncs directly with Hotmail, as well as other Web-based email providers that support the POP3 standard, such as Yahoo! Mail.

Configuring Outlook Express for Hotmail is easy—wonder whether that's because they're both Microsoft products. Nah. Just create a new email account and use your Hotmail address. Outlook Express will recognize it and fill in the fields appropriately. Use your full Hotmail address as your login name. OE will create a new set of folders for the Hotmail mail.

Configuring OE for Yahoo! Mail is only a little more complicated. Set up a new Internet mail account. In the Email Servers Name section, set the incoming mail server to pop.mail.yahoo.com and the Outgoing mail server to smtp.mail.yahoo.com. Use just your account name, without the @yahoo.com, as your logon name.

You might want to create a Yahoo! mail folder and set a new mail rule directing all Yahoo! email to this folder. This will make archiving much easier if your local mail folder is in use by another account.

Now download your Web-based email to Outlook Express, and feel the power.

DOWNLOAD OF THE DAY   IncrediMail turns email into a multimedia event. Free from incredimail.com.

POLL: Are you drowning in email?

54% Yes

46% No

TODAY'S FOCUS: Pocket PC and Windows CE

DEATH OF COMBUSTIBLE ENGINE INVENTOR

Jean-Joseph Étienne Lenoir died on this day in 1900. He was born in Luxembourg on January 12, 1822. The Belgian innovator was known for building the world's first commercially successful internal-combustion engine, which was used on cars and boats. He was awarded the first patent for his work in 1860. Lenoir's other inventions include a railway telegraph, but he died impoverished.

Related Web site `inventors.about.com/library/inventors/blcar.htm`

Why I Switched

By Leo Laporte

I was a devoted Palm user for years. I bought the first Palm, back when they were still called Pilots. I bought a Palm VII the day it came out. And just one year ago I bought a Sony Clié, which I still consider the best of the Palm OS devices. I spent close to $1,000 on that Clié. I added a 128MB memory stick, bought QuickOffice, FastCPU, and Linksoft's Secret. I even spent $90 on Scorepad, a program for scoring baseball games. I used it to record Barry Bonds's record-breaking 71st and 72nd home runs at Pac Bell Park. The Clié went everywhere with me.

Then, Dale Coffing of PocketPCPassion.com gave me an HP Jornada 565. Dale's a great evangelist for Pocket PC (not a surprise, he's a minister in real life) and he knew I was still not a member of the flock.

There's an old saying that it takes Microsoft three versions to get it right. Pocket PC 2002 is a classic third-generation Microsoft product. For one thing, Microsoft clamped down on the hardware specs. Pocket PC 2002 devices come with only one type of processor, not three, and nearly identical capabilities across all the manufacturers. That's good. It simplified software development, and it made it easier for consumers, who no longer had to figure out which processor they had before installing software. The new Pocket PC handhelds have the best screens of any PDA. They come with a great software bundle out of the box, and third-party developers have really stepped up to fill the gaps.

I even was able to find a baseball scoring program, KforCE, from `rakonza.com`. So, this year when Barry breaks the record, I'll be there in the stands, Pocket PC in hand.

As usual, Microsoft has hit another home run, just when they were about to strike out.

TIP OF THE DAY Conserve power in Pocket PC to keep your handheld running longer.

1. Mute the sound. Click the **Speaker** icon and select **Off**.
2. Dim the backlight. Press and hold the **Calendar** button, and then select **Low Power**. You can permanently dim the screen by opening the **Backlight** item in the **Settings** folder. To turn off the backlight any time, press and hold the **Power** button. To turn off the display when you don't need it press and hold the **LED** button.
3. Open the Power Preferences and lower the Auto-suspend time to 30 seconds. Check **Turn Off Display When System Cannot Auto-Suspend**. Uncheck **Keep Power for CF Card**.
4. Open the **Sounds & Notifications** item in **Settings**. Click the **Notifications** tab and turn off the **Flash Light** item.
5. Avoid using the CF card if you can; it eats power.

DOWNLOAD OF THE DAY Every version of Windows has to have its PowerToys. Download the Pocket PC PowerToys free from `microsoft.com/mobile/pocketpc/downloads/powertoys.asp`.

TODAY'S FOCUS: Pocket PC and Windows CE

NEIL ARMSTRONG BORN

The first man to walk on the moon was born in Wapakoneta, Ohio, on this day in 1930. Neil Alden Armstrong uttered his famous quote, "One small step for man, one giant leap for mankind" in 1969 when he set foot on the lunar surface. Armstrong was also the first U.S. astronaut to orbit the Earth in 1966 aboard Gemini 8. The former Navy pilot served in the Korean War and was a test pilot.

Related Web site `astronauthalloffame.com`

Power Up Pocket PC

By Dale Coffing

These are a few great programs and accessories for Pocket PC.

WriteShield (`times2tech.com/ws.htm`) Improves viewing by reducing glare and fingerprints on screen, plus it shields the screen from scratches. WriteShield is easy to install and bubble-free, and it lasts for months. I haven't replaced mine since it was installed about four months ago.

Pocket PC 2002 Connection Wizard (`microsoft.com/mobile/pocketpc/downloads/connwiz.asp`) This free download walks you through the intricacies of setting up a connection for your Pocket PC using dial-up, wireless, or wired access.

StorageTools for Pocket PC (`softwinter.com`) If you use a storage card, you need StorageTools. This $15 product formats, scans, and defragments storage cards in your Pocket PC. Defragmenting your card can improve performance several times over. Try the free download before you buy.

T2TNet (PPC 2000) (`www.pocketpcpassion.com`) This free download makes the File Explorer's network file-sharing much more effective. Instead of just being able to access a shared network folder and then copy or move selected files to your Pocket PC, you can now execute file swaps in place.

Microsoft Transcriber 1.5 (`www.microsoft.com/mobile/pocketpc/downloads/transcriber.asp`) Pocket PC 2000 users can download a free Transcriber handwriting recognition tool. Pocket PC 2002 users already have it.

(Dale Coffing is the Webmaster of Pocket PC Passion, www.pocketpcpassion.com.)

TIP OF THE DAY The memory on your Pocket PC device is used for both programs and data. Maximize the amount of available RAM with these tips.

1. Delete unneeded samples and templates.
2. Remove programs you don't use. Select **Remove Programs** in **Settings**.
3. Don't sync more data than you need. Open ActiveSync on your desktop, and then go through your sync settings by right-clicking each item in your sync list and selecting **Settings**. Here are a few ways you can save memory:
   - **Calendar:** Sync only as many weeks as you need.
   - **Contacts:** Use categories to reduce the number of contacts you keep on your handheld.
   - **Tasks:** Sync only uncompleted tasks.
   - **Favorites:** Don't sync these at all unless you use the browser on your PDA.
   - **Inbox:** Reduce the number of lines you keep and the number of days you copy. Don't sync file attachments.
   - **Files:** Sync only the files you'll be working on right now. Don't sync files at all if you don't want to copy work from your desktop.
4. Careful with your AvantGo, Zagat, and Vindigo settings. These programs can eat a lot of memory. Only take as much information with you as you'll use.

DOWNLOAD OF THE DAY Keep your passwords and other private information safe with eWallet for Pocket PCs, Palms, Handheld PCs, and others. Free to try, $19.95 to buy. Bundle the desktop and PDA versions for $29.95, from `iliumsoft.com`.

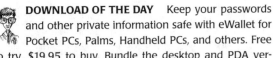

POLL: Would you read an e-book?

63% Yes   37% No

AUGUST 5

ATOMIC BOMB DROPPED

World War II drew near to its close on this day in 1945 when the U.S. dropped a nuclear weapon on Hiroshima, Japan. The experimental uranium bomb, nicknamed "Little Boy," was dropped from an altitude of 2,000 feet by the Enola Gay, an American B-29 bomber. The bomb exploded with the energy of 15,000 tons of dynamite. About 80,000 people were killed instantly, and an estimated 100,000 more died later from radiation or injuries. Three days later, the larger of the two U.S. nuclear bombs, dubbed "Fat Man," was dropped on the city of Nagasaki, killing 150,000 people.

Related Web site `www.city.hiroshima.jp/index-E.html`

Pocket Hoops

By Lisa Picarille

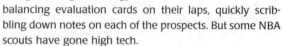

The life of an NBA scout involves watching 20 to 30 college games a year. These scouts sit in crowded college and high-school gymnasiums balancing evaluation cards on their laps, quickly scribbling down notes on each of the prospects. But some NBA scouts have gone high tech.

The Los Angeles Lakers and the Philadelphia 76ers have starting equipping their teams of scouts with Pocket Hoops, a software program from Los Angeles-based Infinite Mobility, that runs on Pocket PC handheld devices (www.infinitemobility.com/pockethoops.htm).

Jonathan Schreiber, chief executive of Infinite Mobility, got together with the Lakers in 1999 to develop the Pocket Hoops software. University of Connecticut basketball coach Jim Calhoun is an investor in the company.

With Pocket Hoops, scouts have a database of all top college teams, and all their players, at their fingertips. Scouts can chart shots, assess players on quickness and effort, and record comments, without missing a key play.

When the game is over, the scout's assessments are sent via modem to the team rather than via U.S. mail. This allows the pro team's front office to study a potential draft choice's charts 24 hours a day.

Mitch Kupchak, general manager of the defending world-champion Lakers, said his team of six scouts is using Pocket Hoops with great results. "The big advantage is that in the past, scouts have cards to fill out during the game. Then they would put the cards in the mail to us in L.A. and then we would put them on clipboards in alphabetical order and sometime they ended up sitting on my desk for days or weeks."

Although Kupchak was hesitant to say that the technology helped them make better draft choices, he does claim that it's a much more efficient way to accumulate, store, and move data.

Infinite Mobility charges about $15,000—plus $1,200 per scout—for the handheld devices, training, and program customization. Teams also pay $130 for monthly service, which includes tech support.

 TIP OF THE DAY   Skin your Pocket PC 2002 with themes from PocketPCThemes.com. There are thousands of beautiful themes to choose from. Download your favorite, then copy the .tsk file to the Windows or My Documents folder on your Pocket PC. Click **Settings** in your Pocket PC's **Start** menu, click the **Today** item, and select your new theme.

DOWNLOAD OF THE DAY   Add Flash to Pocket PC 2002 with the Macromedia Flash Player, free from `macromedia.com/software/flashplayer/pocketpc`.

To play Windows Media files from within Pocket Internet Explorer, download the free Windows Media Player control from `microsoft.com/windows/windowsmedia/create/embedppc.asp`.

AUGUST 6

TODAY'S FOCUS: Pocket PC and Windows CE

FIRST PHOTO OF EARTH

The first satellite to take pictures of Earth launched from Cape Canaveral on this day in 1959. The Explorer VI transmitted the images while orbiting at a speed of about 18,000 miles per hour. Explorer VI was also at the center of another mission during its time in space. The U.S. Air Force used it as a target to test air-launched ballistic missiles. A test missile dubbed "The Bold Orion" passed within four miles of the Explorer VI satellite, the closest an experimental ballistic missile had ever come to reaching its target.

Related Web site `spaceline.org`

GPS in the Palm of Your Hand

If you're looking to put a small digital map that plots your location via GPS on your handheld device, you've got a couple of options. Both choices download map info from your desktop or notebook PC to the handheld device, although you can only carry as many maps as the handheld's memory can hold. We'd recommend carrying extra

batteries, or a 12-volt power adapter, because the connection between a CE device and the GPS unit can suck down lots of power.

If you already own the GPS receiver, try the TeleType GPS US from `www.teletype.com`. This $95 program tracks your location on full-color maps you download from your PC to the PDA. The program requires NMEA output from your GPS and a serial cable connection, so check the manual and find that cable before you whip out the credit card. TeleType also sells a GPS receiver that fits into the CF slot of your Pocket PC.

If you don't already own a GPS device, and you have a Palm device, you might consider DeLorme's EarthMate Road Warrior Edition, around $200 from `delorme.com`. It includes DeLorme's EarthMate GPS receiver—a small, yellow, battery-powered GPS device—DeLorme's Street Atlas USA Deluxe, the Solus software for Palm OS that downloads maps and communicates with the EarthMate, and the appropriate cable.

You'll have to build your own bundle for Pocket PC. The EarthMate GPS receiver is $129.95, DeLorme's XMap Handheld Street Atlas is $39.95, and the right cable will set you back another $20.

The EarthMate setup is fairly painless, but it doesn't offer as many features as the TeleType software, such as the address search. That could be an issue if you don't plan in advance. If you're especially interested in using the GPS off road while hiking (or raging in your 4×4), you should check out DeLorme's Topo maps. Its new 3D TopoQuads are actually USGS 7.5-minute quadrangle maps.

 TIP OF THE DAY Keep track of how much time you've got left on your battery with PowerTime for Windows CE 2.0. PowerTime keeps stats on your Pocket PC's past power performance to give you the most accurate estimate of exactly how many minutes you have left. Free from `sixxac.com`.

DOWNLOAD OF THE DAY Share data between Pocket PC and Palm devices with these programs:

- **Peacemaker Pro**, $14.95 (`conduits.com`)—Sends business cards, appointments, tasks, memos, and files to Palms and other infrared-equipped devices. A freeware version is available, but it only sends contacts.
- **SyncTalk**, $49.95 (`synctalk.com`)—Transfers business cards, appointments, and files between any PDA or laptop. A copy of the program must be installed on each device with which you wish to communicate.

AUGUST 7

TODAY'S FOCUS: Pocket PC and Windows CE

NIXON RESIGNS

Surveillance technology helped spur the resignation of President Richard Nixon on this day in 1974. Nearly two years earlier, burglars were caught breaking into the Democratic Presidential campaign headquarters at the Watergate Hotel in Washington, D.C., to adjust bugging equipment they had previously installed. President Nixon, a Republican, was soon linked to the break-in and other alleged incidents of spying, bribery, and sabotage. A month before Nixon stepped down, Congress had voted to invoke the first article of impeachment. But "Tricky Dick" beat them to the punch, becoming the first U.S. president to resign from office.

Related Web site `www.washingtonpost.com/wp-srv/national/longterm/watergate/`

Hantulla's Hot Handheld Tips

By Dan Hantulla

Change a few settings on your palm-size or handheld PC and you convert your handheld companion into a pocket powerhouse.

Synchronize Your Clocks Synchronize both your desktop and handheld computer's clock with the atomic clock for up-to-the-millisecond accuracy. In Windows XP, open the Date and Time control panel, click the **Internet Time** tab, and check **Automatically Synchronize with an Internet Time Server**. Then:

1. Open Windows CE's ActiveSync window.
2. Select **Tools**.
3. Select **Options**.
4. Be sure the **Synchronize Mobile Device Clock Upon Connection** check box is selected.

Faster Phone Entries If you enter phone numbers with the same area code, you can cut a third of the time by setting your home area code.

1. In the Contacts application, select **Tools**.
2. Select Options.
3. Enter your local area code in the second field.

Now, when you start a new contact and tap on any phone-number entry field, it will automatically populate the area code for you.

Daily Agenda Automation The daily agenda view is one of the most powerful features of the Windows CE Calendar. In one glance, you can view your schedule and active tasks for the day. Although few people know about this view at all, even fewer know that you can make it appear automatically on top of all your applications, first thing in the morning.

1. In the Calendar application, select **Tools**.

2. Select **Options**.
3. Check the **Show Daily Agenda Each Day** option.

The system will turn on at midnight and load the calendar in Agenda view.

Pocket PC 2002 has an even better agenda display called *Today*. To get the Today screen to automatically pop up after an hour of inactivity, open Today in the Settings folder and click the **Items** tab. Check **Display Today Screen** and set the time for one hour.

TIP OF THE DAY Pocket PC works best with Windows—no surprise because it's a stripped-down Windows version itself—but it's possible to sync it with a Macintosh thanks to a new product called PocketMac. $69.95 from `Pocketmac.net`.

I've been using the beta version with Microsoft Entourage and it works well, but to avoid duplicate entries it's best if you don't try to sync your Pocket PC with both a Mac and a Windows machine.

DOWNLOAD OF THE DAY Watch MPEG movies on your Pocket PC with PocketTV. For every Windows-powered PDA using Win CE 2.0 or higher. Free from `mpegtv.com`.

POLL: Where should you not use a mobile phone?

28% Car

6% Restaurant

41% Theater

4% Restroom

12% Anywhere

8% Cell phones belong everywhere

AUGUST

8

TODAY'S FOCUS: Pocket PC and Windows CE

ESCALATOR PATENTED

Nathan Ames of Saugus, Massachusetts, patented a "moving stairway" on this day in 1859. The next day, his invention was up and running for the public to try. Legend has it that confused users riding the machine thought they were going the wrong way, and kept running in the opposite direction trying to get to the other side. When the power went out and the contraption stopped, the people on the escalator weren't sure what to do. Thinking they were stranded, passengers called on a rescue team to help them down.

Related Web site `eesf.org`

Pocket PC Sites

Microsoft PocketPC (`microsoft.com/pocketpc`) The mothership for all things Pocket PC. Click the **Downloads** link to see the newest stuff, including patches and security updates. The Support page has a search engine for finding the exact answer to your problem. Join Club Pocket PC for a newsletter and other benefits.

Handango (`Handango.com`) This is the premiere commercial download site for all handhelds. If it exists for Pocket PC, Handango will have a link. I always check the bestsellers to see whether there's a killer app I'm missing.

PocketPC Passion (`www.pocketpcpassion.com`) Dale Coffing, minister by day, evangelizes the Pocket PC by night. And he does a devil of a good job of it. Dale converted me—watch out; he might convert you, too.

pocketpcsoft (`pocketpcsoft.net`) Thousands of links to software and news for Pocket PC users. Graphically simple, content rich.

PocketPC 4 You (`ppc4you.com`) Another great resource for downloads, themes, applications, e-books.

PocketPC Themes (`Pocketpcthemes.com`) Take advantage of that gorgeous screen by downloading color wallpaper from this site. Thousands to choose from, and the FAQs will help you install them or create wallpaper of your own.

Pocket Movies (`Pocketmovies.net`) Finally, a handheld with enough oomph to show video. Show off your Pocket PC by putting short films, trailers, even commercials onboard. I could just keep watching the *Matrix* trailer forever.

Puzzle Express (`puzzleexpress.com`) If you like solitaire, crosswords, and word games, you'll find a bunch here. For Windows as well as Pocket PC and Windows CE.

PocketRocketFX.com (`pocketrocketfx.com`) A great source for entertainment on your Pocket PC. Download movie trailers, TV commercials, music videos, flash games, e-books, themes, skins, and lots more.

MobiGeeks (`mobigeeks.com/e`) I don't know about you, but whenever anything new comes out for Pocket PC, I wonder, "What would the French think?" Now you can find out at Mobigeeks. A great site for information about handhelds of all kinds, but Pocket PC-focused.

PDA Gold (`pdagold.com`) Lots of information on Pocket PC and Windows CE devices. The very active message board is a good place to discuss the latest news and get your questions answered. Go to the links section for dozens of other great Pocket PC sites.

TIP OF THE DAY Animate your Today screen on Pocket PC with Animated Today. Put moving desktops and simple Flash applications on your screen. Requires the Macromedia Flash Player for Pocket PC. Free for 14 days, $14.95 to buy, from `gigabytesol.com`. Get more animated themes from `pocketpcthemes.com`. I like the Devil Fish myself.

 DOWNLOAD OF THE DAY Want your daily dose of Garfield on your Palm? Ready to watch Andy Griffith on your Pocket PC? Put up-to-the-minute news, music, comics, and multimedia on your PDA every time you sync with Mazingo. Text-only content is free, premium service costs $4.95/month, from `mazingo.net`.

TODAY'S FOCUS: Pocket PC and Windows CE

SMITHSONIAN FOUNDED

The Smithsonian Institution, named for British scientist James Smithson, was founded in Washington, D.C. on this day in 1846. The original building, dubbed "The Castle," was designed by architect James Renwick, Jr. and completed in 1855. Today, the Smithsonian is the world's largest museum complex. It's composed of 16 galleries and museums and houses more than 142 million objects. One of the most comprehensive collections of technology is in the National Air and Space Museum, which displays such famous artifacts as Charles Lindbergh's "The Spirit of St. Louis" and "Sputnik 1," the first artificial satellite to go into orbit.

Related Web site `smithsonian.org`

Twisted List: Online Clocks

By Martin Sargent

I think it was in college when I first got interested in horology. But after I started playing around on the Internet, my interest in the study of timekeeping became an obsession. Here are the five most titillating online clocks.

TimeTicker (`timeticker.com`) TimeTicker tells you the exact time in any country in the world. Lots of sites do the same thing, but TimeTicker does it with lots of bells, ticks, and voices and has a flashy interface. It makes it fun to find out what time it is in Burundi right now. In no time, you'll have wasted hours at the site, in Senegalese time.

Decimal Time (`decimaltime.org`) Our current system of telling time is based on multiples of 12 and 60, dating back to the sexagesimal system used by the ancient Babylonians. According to the weirdos at Decimal Time, it's high time we change to a decimal time system. In a decimal time system, you would only have 10 "hours" in the day. So, *The Screen Savers* would start at something like 7.2 Eastern. "Hey, meet me at the Tully's Tap Room at 6.23 o'clock!" It just makes so much more sense than our current antiquated system of keeping time.

The Death Clock (`deathclock.com`) The Death Clock is creepy. You type in the date of your birth and it tells you when you are scheduled to die. How many seconds you have left to breathe. How much time you have left to do something constructive with your ever-diminishing life.

The Human Clock (`yugop.com/ver3/stuff/03/fla.html`) The Human Clock is so cool I wish I could have it on the wall in my kitchen or on the dashboard of my car. The clock is constantly redrawn by a graphical representation of human hands.

TIP OF THE DAY Download maps of more than 500 cities worldwide from `microsoft.com/pocketstreets/mapdownload/MapDownload_EN.html`.

You must have Pocket Streets 2002 to use the maps. Pocket Streets 2002 is bundled with Microsoft's 2002 mapping products, Microsoft Expedia Streets and Trips, AutoRoute, and MapPoint.

DOWNLOAD OF THE DAY Download audio books, radio shows, audio newspapers and more from `Audible.com`. Choose from over 4,500 books and 14,000 other programs. Play the audio back on your Macintosh or Windows desktop, or put it on an Audible-compatible player and take it with you.

Works with all Pocket PC models, Handspring Visor with AudibleAdvisor Springboard Module, the Rio500, Rio600, and Rio800 MP3 players, Iomega's HipZip, the Digisette Duo-Aria MP3 player, Franklin's eBookman PDA, and Audible's own Otis player.

I listen to Audible books on my Pocket PC every day as I commute.

TODAY'S FOCUS: Privacy

APPLE INVENTOR BORN

Steve Wozniak was born in Sunnyvale, California, on this day in 1950. The Apple Computer co-founder and the creator of the Apple I was interested in electronics from an early age: He received a ham radio license when he was in sixth grade. In 1976, Woz worked for Hewlett-Packard designing chips for calculators. Shortly after, he designed the first Apple Computer, the Apple I, to show to fellow members of the Homebrew Computer Club. Three marriages and three children later, Woz still lives in Silicon Valley and regularly donates computer equipment to local schools.

Related Web site `woz.org`

Using Public Connections Safely

By Greg Melton

When you use the Internet in a public place, you might leave behind critical data that could allow someone to access your accounts. Here are some things to do before and after you use a shared computer.

Disable AutoComplete Forms and Passwords The first thing you should do before logging on to check your email or bank account at a public computer is to turn off AutoComplete Forms and Passwords. This way, your account logins and passwords won't stick around after you've logged off the computer.

To turn off AutoComplete in Internet Explorer, follow these directions:

1. Open Internet Explorer.
2. Choose **Tools**, and then **Internet Options**.
3. Select the **Content** tab.
4. Click the **AutoComplete** button.
5. Be sure all the check marks are removed next to the text labeled Web Addresses, Forms, User Names and Passwords on Forms.
6. Click both the **Clear Forms** and **Clear Passwords** buttons.
7. Click **OK**, and then click **OK** again to save your changes.

Cookies, Temp File, and History The next step to covering your tracks on the Internet needs to occur *after* you've ended your Internet session. This involves clearing the cookies, cache, and history folders.

Cookies store your passwords and other information about the Web sites you visit. The pages you visit are stored in a *cache*, where they remain until deleted. *History*

records every Web address you've ever visited during a set period of time. Clearing these three settings isn't hard. In fact, they all appear on the same tab in the Internet Options dialog box. To clear these settings, follow these instructions:

1. Open Internet Explorer.
2. Choose **Tools**, and then **Internet Options**. You should now be on the General tab.
3. Under Temporary Internet files, click the **Delete Cookies** button, and then click the **Delete Files** button to erase the entire temp folder.
4. Next, under History, click **Delete History**.
5. Click **OK**.

 TIP OF THE DAY DoubleClick and other online advertising agencies keep track of which banner ads you've seen and clicked as you travel across the Internet. To stop the snoops, opt out. Visit `networkadvertising.org` and click the **Opt-Out** button. Check the boxes to replace your unique identifier cookie with a generic opt-out cookie. Opt out again any time you delete your cookies, reinstall your system, or move to a new machine.

 DOWNLOAD OF THE DAY Kill the cache, clear history, and empty the Recycle Bin automatically with Privacy Eraser, from `privacyeraser.com`. Free to try, $24.95 to buy.

POLL: What's more important?

62% Protecting privacy at work

38% Saving money

AUGUST 11

TODAY'S FOCUS: Privacy

FIRST PC

IBM announced its first personal computer on this day in 1981. The new PC was powered by a 4.77MHz Intel 8088 microprocessor—the only 16-bit chip with an 8-bit bus available at the time. The system came with 64kb of RAM, a floppy drive, monochrome graphics, and the Microsoft PC DOS 1.0 operating system. It cost $3,000 (almost $6,000 in today's dollars). IBM's machine was a success: The company sold 136,000 units in the first year and a half.

Related Web site `www.ibm.com`

Toss Your Cookies

By Megan Morrone

Cookies are preference files that Web sites store on your hard drive for retrieval the next time you visit. Many sites store your login information in a cookie so you don't have to type it in every time you visit. Cookies also can be used by advertising sites to customize the ads they deliver to your page. There are limits on what sites can do with cookies; for example, only the site that set the cookie can read it. Still, many folks are wary of cookies. Here's how to show those cookies who's the boss.

Clobber 'em Open your browser, select **Internet Options** from the **Tools** menu, click the **General** tab, and then click the **Delete Cookies** button. Warning: This will delete all the information every site has stored about you, including login information. If you don't remember all the passwords you've used, don't click this button. Use a selective cookie deletion utility such as CookieWall, below.

Stop 'em Internet Explorer 6.0 or higher has built-in cookie management:

1. Choose **Tools**.
2. Select **Internet Options**.
3. Click the **Privacy** tab.
4. Adjust the privacy thermometer to low, medium, or high.

Weed 'em There are hundreds of programs that will help you manage cookies. I like CookieWall, free from `analogx.com/contents/download/network/cookie.htm`.

TIP OF THE DAY Windows XP, 2000, and NT have a built-in service called Messenger that can be used to spam you. Kevin Rose, on our staff, discovered this problem and the fix.

Messenger is supposed to be used by system administrators to warn users of any change in network status. But anyone who knows your Internet address can use it to spam you, or even worse, to flood your computer with messages, making it unusable.

You're probably saying to yourself, "No one knows my IP address. I'm safe." Not true. You and your hidden messenger service can easily be detected by running a simple port scan. The messenger service is part of the NetBIOS service that runs on TCP port 139. To detect potential targets, the spammer will look for IP addresses with port 139 open. You can block such attacks with any firewall, including the one built into Windows XP, or you can disable the Messenger service entirely if you don't need it.

To permanently disable the messenger service in XP:

1. Open the Performance and Maintenance control panel and go to Administrative Tools.
2. Double-click on **Services**, and then scroll to **Messenger**.
3. Double-click **Messenger** and click **Stop** to stop the service.
4. Open the Properties and change the startup type to **Disable**.

DOWNLOAD OF THE DAY FilterGate removes pop-ups and banner ads, kills cookies, referrers, and Web bugs, and stops adult content. Free to try, $24.95 to buy, from `filtergate.com`.

AUGUST 12

TODAY'S FOCUS: Privacy

PAY PHONE PATENTED

William Gray of Hartford, Connecticut, received a patent for a coin-operated telephone on this day in 1889. In 1888, so the story goes, Gray asked workers at a nearby factory to use the phone to call the doctor because his wife was ill. He was denied and told the phone was not available for public use. Eventually, he was allowed to make the call, but his experience made him determined to develop a public phone. Gray, with the help of Amos Whitney, designed the first working pay phone, which was installed in the Hartford Bank.

Related Web site   `www.payphone-directory.org/`

Protecting Your Privacy Online

The Staff of *CyberCrime*

The amount of information available on the Internet is enormous. More than likely, some of that information is about you. And you have been the primary source of what other people know about you.

Although you can't completely prevent personal information from proliferating all over the Internet, there are steps you can take to minimize the amount of information out there.

Newsgroups   Newsgroups live forever, and they're a primary source of email addresses for spammers. If you want to include a return address in your postings, create a special email account on Yahoo! Mail or Hotmail just for that purpose. And disguise your email address so that spam robots can't extract it from your message. Use something such as myname at techtv dot com.

Personal Web Pages   Many people have personal Web pages that list details about their jobs and interests, email addresses, even their families. But putting private information on the Web is no different than broadcasting it on TV. Consider who might be reading your page.

Web Browsing   Whenever you visit a Web site, the site logs your unique Internet address. If you volunteer personal information, the site can connect that info with your IP address. Read the site's privacy and security statements before volunteering any personal information. And look for a policy that is verified by a third party such as TRUSTe.

 TIP OF THE DAY   Windows Media Player creates a unique identifier so that the servers streaming audio or video to your computer can monitor the connection and maintain high-quality playback. Unfortunately, a flaw in the player makes it possible for Web sites to track your media requests. Although a site wouldn't be able to gain your personal information, it would be possible for the site to create a profile of your media use from the data.

Turn off the unique identifier to protect your privacy:

1. Choose **Options** from your **Tools** menu.
2. Click the **Player** tab and look at the Internet Settings.
3. Uncheck the **Allow Internet Sites to Uniquely Identify Your Player** check box, and click **Apply**.

The next time you request streaming audio or video, Windows Media Player will generate a random identifier.

 DOWNLOAD OF THE DAY   Anonymize your surfing with GhostSurf. By routing your information through anonymous hubs around the world, GhostSurf makes it impossible for Web sites to see who you are or from where you come. GhostSurf blocks personal information from being sent by your browser, and lets you see everything that is sent—in real-time. Free to try, $19.95 to buy, from `tenebril.com/products/ghostsurf`.

POLL: Is biometrics bogus?

55% Yes

45% No

AUGUST 13

ELECTRIC METER PATENTED

On this day in 1888, Oliver B. Shallenberger of Rochester, Pennsylvania, was granted a patent for the electric meter. Westinghouse's chief electrician came up with the concept while working on an AC lamp. A spring fell out while Shallenberger and his assistant were working on the lamp, and began to rotate in the lamp's electrical field. The inventor used the phenomenon as the basis for the meter. Shallenberger had a working model within three weeks, and more than 120,000 Shallenberger meters were sold over the next 10 years.

Related Web site `watthourmeters.com`

How Encryption Works

Encryption is the process of turning data into a form that can be read only by its owner or intended recipient. Modern encryption mathematically modifies the data by scrambling it with an encryption key.

The key itself is one vulnerability of encryption. If two parties are to exchange data, they must exchange a key first, and if that key is intercepted, the encryption can be broken. This problem was solved by Whitfield Diffie and Martin Hellman in 1976 when they invented public key cryptography.

Public key crypto uses two keys. One, the public key, is used to encrypt the data. A second, the private key, is used to decrypt the data. It doesn't matter who knows the public key, because it can be used only to encrypt.

Without access to the private key, snoops have only two ways of cracking the code. They either have to discover your password or use brute-force computation to try every possible key until one works.

And when I say brute, I mean it. A 30-bit key has roughly one billion possible combinations (2 to the 30th). A supercomputer that can try one billion keys a second could crack the code in less than a second. Increase the key length to 128 bits, the standard for secure Web sites, and the same computer will need more time than the Earth has existed to break a single message.

That's why I recommend using an encryption technology that uses keys at least 128 bits long.

TIP OF THE DAY If you want to know more about encryption, here are three good books to get you started:

- *The Code Breakers*, by David Kahn (Scribner, 1996) ISBN: 0684831309. The classic history of crypto. More than 1,000 pages long.
- *The Code Book*, by Simon Singh (Anchor Books, 2000) ISBN: 0385495323. This one's a little easier going, and lots of fun to read. I have to thank an anonymous fan in Tom's River, New Jersey, for introducing me to this book. He gave me his copy in return for an autograph.
- *Cryptonomicon*, by Neal Stephenson (Harper Perennial, 2000) ISBN: 0380788624. One of the greatest novels about cryptography ever written.

DOWNLOAD OF THE DAY Deleting a file on most operating systems doesn't erase the data—it just releases the space for another file to use. Until the space is actually occupied, your old data is still there for anyone to read. To really delete a file, you need a file-deletion utility such as Tolvanen's Eraser. Eraser not only deletes files, it overwrites them several times. Think of it as a paper shredder for your PC. Free from `/tolvanen.com/eraser`.

PANAMA CANAL OPENS

The largest man-made waterway went into operation on this day in 1914. The series of locks, channels, and artificial lakes was built by the U.S. to join the Atlantic and Pacific Oceans. Previously, ships had to sail around Cape Horn, at the southern tip of South America. The U.S. and Panamanian governments fought over control of the canal for many years. In 1903, the "Canal Zone" became U.S. territory. Control of the waterways, however, were returned to Panama on December 31, 1999.

Related Web site   `www.pancanal.com`

Wireless Cameras

By Avi Rubin

We've all seen the pop-up ads for the X10 wireless camera. This camera transmits captured images over the air waves at 2.4GHz. Because it requires no cables, it can be put just about anywhere. A receiver can be connected to a computer anywhere within range, and the images will be stored on the PC's hard drive.

There are many uses for such a technology. Some people install the cameras to watch their little babies in their cribs. Others keep tabs on the babysitter or nanny. Businesses use them as security cameras, and still others use them in less reputable ways to catch a sneak peek of unknowing neighbors.

Stolen Glances   Although the camera and the receiver can communicate with ease over a certain range, there is nothing to prevent someone with another receiver from picking up the signal as well. Such eavesdropping is utterly undetectable, and by using an external antenna, the range of signal interception can be dramatically increased.

Most people assume that if they use such a camera, others cannot access the images—just like with a cordless phone, where people tend to forget that their airborne conversation can easily be tapped.

Solution?   If you use X10 cameras, your security options are limited. Your best protection is to assume that anyone driving by can see the images captured by your cam, so don't use it to record your romantic escapades. If you're worried that someone is spying on you with a hidden X10 camera, get an X10 receiver and scan the channels for a signal emanating from your area.

And remember, whenever you use any wireless device, there's a good chance someone could be intercepting the signal without your knowledge.

(Avi Rubin is a principal researcher at AT&T Labs - Research and a member of the board of directors of USENIX, the Advanced Computing Systems Association. `avirubin.com`*.)*

 TIP OF THE DAY   The best way to protect your information is with a strong password. Never use words you can find in the dictionary, or the names of friends, family, or pets. Don't use your username as the basis for a password or, for that matter, use the word "password" itself. The best passwords don't make any sense. Use a combination of at least eight uppercase and lowercase letters, numbers, and symbols (*, #, !, +, etc.). And, for heaven's sake, don't write your password on a sticky note glued to your monitor.

 DOWNLOAD OF THE DAY   KeySpy records everything typed on a computer and logs all Web sites visited and all programs launched. You can choose to have the log encrypted or even emailed to you at another location. Free from `keyspy.net`.

AUGUST 15

TODAY'S FOCUS: Privacy

XEROX FINED

Xerox was ordered to shell out $25.6 million on this day in 1978. The electronics giant was charged with preventing Smith-Corona from competing in the photocopier market. Xerox was the first to commercialize xerography, and it held all the patents for the technology. But the FCC put a halt to its monopolistic tactics and ordered the company to make its practices available to competitors.

Related Web site `smithcorona.com/About_Smith_Corona/Mission.cfm`

Steganography with MP3s

By Joshua Brentano

Steganography is not the dinosaur with the big plates on its back; it's a way of hiding files within other files. You can create a secret document, insert it into a photo, and post it on the Internet. The photo still looks the same, but it is hiding a document inside. Someone who knows about the hidden file can decode the picture and retrieve the information.

But that sounds too sedate; let's do something more extreme. We're going to hide a secret document in an MP3. The MP3 still works and sounds the same, but it carries a passenger. You can then take that MP3, copy it to your portable MP3 player, and nobody will know you're smuggling a secret file.

The program we found to do this is a command-line application called MP3Stego, `www.cl.cam.ac.uk/~fapp2/steganography/mp3stego`. It includes two DOS applications: encode and decode.

To encode, you must start with a WAV file (name it musicfile.wav for this example) and, of course, your secret message in a text file (we'll call it secret.txt).

1. Copy the audio and text files to the directory where you installed MP3Stego.
2. Open a command prompt by typing **command** in the **Run** menu. Press Enter.
3. Navigate through DOS to the MP3Stego directory.
4. Type **encode -E secret.txt musicfile.wav musicfile.mp3** (it might take a minute or two to compress).

You can now copy that musicfile.mp3 to your portable player and take it to its destination. To decode it, use the command **decode -X musicfile.mp3**.

 TIP OF THE DAY For many of us, the most sensitive data on our computers is our financial data. Password protect your Quicken or Money file to keep prying eyes out.

Quicken 2002:

1. Go to the **File** menu and click **Passwords**.
2. Choose to protect a file or transaction.
3. Type a password in the new password and confirm password boxes, and click **OK**.

Money 2002:

1. Go to the **File** menu and click **Login Lockbox**.
2. Type your new password and confirm it. Click **OK**.
3. If you have an MSN Passport, you can use it for additional Web-supported password protection.

DOWNLOAD OF THE DAY Spytech SpyAgent Professional is a powerful monitoring solution with tons of features and configuration options. SpyAgent Professional records keystrokes, windows opened, applications run, passwords used, Internet connections, Web sites visited, and even captures screenshots that can be displayed in a slideshow. It can also be configured to send a log file to a specified email address every few minutes. The trial download features 30-minute limits on monitoring sessions. Free to try, $49.95 to buy, from `spytech-web.com`.

TODAY'S FOCUS: Privacy

CRUISE CONTROL INVENTOR BORN

Road trips became a lot more bearable thanks to Ralph R. Teetor, who was born in Hagerstown, Indiana, on this day in 1890. The mechanical engineer, blinded at age five, built an automobile with his cousin when he was 12 years old. While working for the Perfect Circle Corporation, Teetor was inspired to build cruise control after riding in a car with his lawyer, who would slow down while talking and speed up while listening. Teetor was so annoyed by the lawyer's inconsistent driving that he became determined to build a speed-control device. Cruise control debuted in 1958 on select Chrysler cars.

Related Web site `www.howstuffworks.com/cruise-control.htm`

Twisted List: Web Wisdom

By Megan Morrone

Everything I know I learned from a blog. I'm not kidding. Look what I learned this week.

The Earth Could Get Hit By an Asteroid at Any Moment (`robots.cnn.com/2002/TECH/space/03/19/asteroid.blindside`) While browsing a Weblog called Little Green Footballs (`littlegreenfootballs.com/weblog`), I found a link to a CNN story about a space boulder that passed a mere 288,000 miles from Earth. Nobody noticed, because it was in our blind spot. Great. I didn't even know we had a blind spot.

Spam Radio (`spamradio.com`) What's the only thing better than spam? Spam Radio, of course. I learned about it from kade, a regular contributor to the collaborative Weblog called Memepool, `memepool.com`. Spam Radio is pretty much what you'd expect, a streaming Webcast of a computer voice reading spam emails aloud. This site isn't appropriate for anyone under the age of 18. But then again, neither is most of the spam that I get in my inbox.

You Are Where You Live (`cluster2.claritas.com/YAWYL`) MetaFilter (`www.metafilter.com`) is a Weblog of the Slashdot genre, where anyone can post a link to a story or useful Web site. On Monday, a user named MidasMulligan posted a link to a disturbing site called You Are Where You Live. Simply enter your ZIP Code and you can find out exactly what kind of person you are—at least according to the people who target you for junk mail.

 TIP OF THE DAY **Q:** I'm running a firewall, but after visiting a link about Windows tweaks, I got a pop-up that showed me all the contents of my C:\ directory with no alarm. How did this happen? —Russ from Apex, North Carolina

A: We fell for the same joke at `www.hacker-spider.de`. Click the **Security Check** link and prepare to be shocked.

Fortunately, you haven't revealed anything. You're the only one seeing the directory listing. It's no different from typing C:\ into your browser's Address bar and clicking Go.

The trick is accomplished using simple HTML like so:

`<IFRAME src="C:\">`

It's completely harmless.

 DOWNLOAD OF THE DAY Tracks Eraser Pro is a privacy cleaner that can cover your Internet tracks and other activity on your computer. Erase the browser cache, selected cookies, history, typed URLs, auto-complete memory, and index.dat from your browser, Windows temp folders, run history, search history, open/save history, recent documents, and more. Includes a secure delete, home page protection, and more. Free to try, $19.95–$29.95 to buy, from `acesoft.net`.

POLL: Who should carry implanted ID chips?

12% Kids

29% Bad guys

16% Everybody

43% Nobody

TODAY'S FOCUS: DVD

FIRST PARACHUTE JUMPER DIES

André-Jacques Garnerin died on this day in 1823. The French balloon pilot was the first person to make a successful parachute jump. In October 1797, he lept from a hot-air balloon 3,000 feet above the ground in Paris. His white canvas parachute was 23 feet in diameter and had a basket attached. Although he survived the jump, Garnerin shook back and forth violently during the descent. The physicist Lalande suggested creating an opening in the top of the parachute to improve air flow. Garnerin died while preparing balloon equipment when a beam struck his head.

Related Web site `uspa.org`

What Is DVD?

By Jim Taylor

DVD is an increasingly widespread and popular optical storage technology used for audio, video, and computer data.

A DVD disc is the same physical size as a CD, but it reads faster and has a much higher storage capacity. Often called a *convergence medium*, because it encompasses both home entertainment and information storage, DVD is expected to replace the audio CD, videotape, laserdisc, CD-ROM, and even video-game cartridges.

DVD has support from all major electronics companies, all major computer hardware companies, and all major movie and music studios. With this unprecedented level of support, DVD has become the most successful consumer electronics product of all time within only a few years of its introduction.

DVD-Video Versus DVD-ROM It's important to understand the difference between DVD-Video and DVD-ROM. DVD-Video (often simply called DVD) holds video programs and is played in a DVD player hooked up to a TV. DVD-ROM holds computer data and is read by a DVD-ROM drive hooked up to a computer. The difference is similar to that between audio CD and CD-ROM.

Most computers with DVD-ROM drives can also play DVD-Video discs, CDs, and CD-ROMS. DVD-ROM also includes recordable variations (DVD-R, DVD-RAM, DVD-RW, and DVD+RW). A super-high-fidelity DVD-Audio format is available, but not yet widely supported.

DVD-ROM drives are steadily replacing CD-ROM drives in computers. Many forecasters expect manufacturers to stop making CD-ROM drives in the next year or do. If you're thinking about buying a new computer, you might want to consider getting one with a DVD drive, because all DVD drives can read CDs.

(Jim Taylor created the Internet DVD FAQ, dvddemystified.com, and serves as Technical Director for the DVD Association.)

TIP OF THE DAY In the market for a DVD video player? Look for one that's easy to use. If you have to read a 900-page operating manual before you watch a movie, pick another model. Check out the remote: Most DVD players are primarily operated with the remote. It should be clearly laid out with easy-to-read labels and functional buttons.

You don't have to spend big bucks, either. Why pay $500 when you can get a very good DVD player for less than $100? Unless you're a videophile with a progressive scan TV and high-end surround-sound audio system, the least expensive DVD player will look just as good as the most expensive.

DOWNLOAD OF THE DAY Click n Design creates DVD and CD labels and inserts, free to try, 14.95 to buy, from stompinc.com.

TODAY'S FOCUS: DVD

ELECTRONIC TV INVENTOR BORN

Philo Taylor Farnsworth, co-inventor of the electronic television, was born in a log cabin near Beaver, Utah, on this day in 1906. Farnsworth formed the idea of creating images using electrons when he was just 14 years old. In 1927, he succeeded in transmitting an electronic picture. But Vladimir Zworykin, an engineer with Westinghouse, had applied for a patent four years earlier, and later developed a camera tube called an *Iconoscope*. After many legal battles, Farnsworth was named the true inventor of television, but RCA quickly snatched up his patents when they expired. Farnsworth died March 11, 1971.

Related Web site   `philo75.com`

Playing DVDs on Your PC

If you want to use your computer's DVD player to watch movies, you'll need to install a DVD decoder. Decoders come in two flavors: hardware and software. The type you should use depends on your system and needs.

Hardware Decoders   Hardware decoders are best for older PCs and people who want to play back their DVDs on their home entertainment systems.

A hardware DVD decoder is a card that you install in your PCI slot. The card does all the work of decoding the DVD, instead of on your CPU, which is why they're a good solution for older PCs. Our favorite hardware decoder is Sigma Design's REALmagic Hollywood Plus, around $79 from `www.buyrealmagic.com`.

If you have a PC with a 500MHz Pentium II processor or slower, you'll almost always get better video playback if you use a hardware decoder.

Hardware decoders often have the video and audio connectors needed for playing movies back on your TV, too. If you don't already have video out of your PC, a decoder is probably your best choice, no matter how fast your processor.

Software Decoders   Software decoders are best for people with fast computers and high-end video cards who plan to watch their DVD movies on their computer monitors.

Software decoders rely on your computer's CPU to do all the work, but with today's gigahertz-plus computers and added support from your video card, that's not a problem. And believe it or not, software-only playback usually looks better on a computer monitor.

Our favorite software decoder is Cyberlink's PowerDVD, from `www.gocyberlink.com`. You can download a trial version, or buy the full version for $49.95.

TIP OF THE DAY   **Q:** I'd like to play DVDs from my laptop and broadcast the picture and sound through my TV. Can you tell me how to do this? —Jeff from Madison, Indiana

A: If your laptop comes equipped with an S-Video or composite (RCA) output jack, you can easily configure it to play DVDs on your TV. You'll need an appropriate cable. Many computers come with these, or you can pick one up at Radio Shack. You'll also have to configure your laptop to pass the display through to the video-out jacks. Check your manual for information on "video mirroring."

DOWNLOAD OF THE DAY   Smartripper makes back-up copies of your DVDs onto hard drive. The most complete program on the market, free for Windows from `doom9.net`.

POLL: Is copying a DVD terrorism?

3% Yes

97% No

AUGUST 19

TODAY'S FOCUS: DVD

FIRST CANINE COSMONAUTS

The first animals to survive a trip to space landed safely back on Earth on this day in 1960. A day before, the Soviets launched Sputnik 5 with several plants and animals on board, including 40 mice, two rats, and two dogs. The dogs were named Belka and Strelka, Russian for "Squirrel" and "Arrow." Sputnik 5 orbited the Earth 18 times and was brought down with the creatures unharmed. This wasn't the first time the USSR had sent animals into space, however. The first animal to orbit the Earth was a dog named Laika, who died in space aboard Sputnik 2 in 1957.

Related Web site   `liftoff.msfc.nasa.gov/rsa/rsa.html`

DVD Recordable Formats

DVD-RAM   DVD-RAM is available only in rewritable formats. Discs can be rewritten up to 100,000 times. DVD-RAM discs can be easily identified by their cartridge enclosures that protect the media surface from dust, fingerprints, and scratches. Two cartridge types exist for the DVD-RAM format. Type 1 DVD-RAM features a nonremovable cartridge, whereas Type 2 allows the protective cartridge to be removed for playback in a standard DVD-ROM drive. Of all rewritable types of DVD media, DVD-RAM is the least compatible with set-top DVD players and older DVD-ROM drives.

DVD-RW   Pioneer developed the DVD-RW format to give consumers a medium to record DVDs for home use. DVD-RW was the first consumer format available that offered compatibility with a majority of set-top DVD players. Introduced initially as a write-once technology (DVD-R), Pioneer quickly added a rewritable media type, and thus DVD-RW was born.

DVD-RW can match the 2x recording speed of DVD-RAM when using DVD-R (write once) media. DVD-RW (rewritable) uses phase-changing materials similar to those found in CD-RW media, and it suffers a similar performance hit, limiting it to 1x recording. You will often see blank DVD-RW media (-R or -RW) listed with a (G) attached to the end. DVD-RW comes in two media types: Authoring (A) and General Use (G). DVD-RW for Authoring requires expensive recording equipment and is intended for professional use. The rest of us will stick to using General Use media because both the recorders and blank media are far less expensive.

DVD+RW (DVD "plus" RW)   Developed by the DVD+RW Alliance that includes Sony, Hewlett-Packard, and Philips Electronics, DVD+RW is an upcoming format that shares many characteristics with DVD-RW. However, DVD+RW has a few key differences that its proponents say will provide even better compatibility with set-top players than DVD-RW media. In our early tests, that claim seems to be borne out.

At 2.4x record speed, DVD+RW is slightly faster than DVD-RW, but faster drives will likely ship in both formats.

 TIP OF THE DAY   DVD recording speed terminology differs significantly from CD speed ratings.

- A CD recorder burning at 1x is recording data at 150KBps.
- A DVD recorder burning at 1x is recording data at 11.08Mbps.

That means a 1x DVD recorder is roughly as fast as a 9x CD recorder. At 2x DVD recording speeds, a 4.7GB disc takes about 30 minutes to fill.

 DOWNLOAD OF THE DAY   DVD2SVCD contains all the software you need to convert your DVDs into VCD format for burning on to CD-ROMs. Free from `doom9.net`.

TODAY'S FOCUS: DVD

ADDING MACHINE PATENTED

On this day in 1888, William Seward Burroughs was granted a patent for the first adding machine to be successfully marketed in the U.S. The St. Louis, Missouri, native conceived of the idea for an accurate calculating machine when he was a bank clerk in New York. In 1882, poor health forced Burroughs to leave his job, and he began creating prototypes for his machine. A year after making his patent application in 1885, Burroughs created his own company, the American Arithmometer Corporation of St. Louis, with an authorized capitalization of $100,000.

Related Web site `www.hpmuseum.org/prehp.htm`

DVD Authoring

By Bill Elias

It wasn't so long ago that VHS replaced Super 8 as the medium of choice for capturing home movies of special events and celebrations. Fast-forward to 2003, and VHS is dying a slow death. Pocket-sized digital video recorders have replaced the bulky old VHS versions. Today, the home auteur downloads digital video directly to a PC to edit out the boring parts. The easiest way to archive and share such cinema vérité is now available through home DVD authoring. Below are two options for budding Cecil B. DeMilles.

 Apple iDVD2 (`apple.com/idvd`) With fully customizable interfaces and drag-and-drop usability, it's hard to beat Apple's newest version of its iDVD software. For Macintosh users who already own a requisite SuperDrive, this application is at the top of the heap. The $20 price tag is also hard to beat, although it comes with hefty hardware requirements. Pro users who need more advanced features, such as chapter encoding, should look at Apple's high-end DVD Studio Pro for $999.

 Ulead DVD MovieFactory (`ulead.com`) Receiving equally high review marks, but designed for Windows, is Ulead's DVD MovieFactory. The $50 application gives you functions for editing captured video clips, the ability to organize those clips in a customizable DVD interface, and the ability to burn the results to a DVD or video CD. 30-day free trial available.

TIP OF THE DAY   DVD-authoring tips, by Joe Stefan

- **Know what device you're targeting**—Be sure you burn to a DVD media type supported by your target DVD player.
- **Be sure your player supports the audio type you've selected**—Although most newly released DVD players support MPEG-1 Layer II audio, older players support only PCM. PCM is many times larger and can sometimes cause your project to exceed the space available on your target media.
- **Use DVD-RW or DVD+RW discs to preview your DVD**—The prices of DVD-R discs are dropping every week, but they're still too expensive to be considered throwaways.
- **Buy better-quality DVD blanks**—Typically, the lower the cost of the blank DVD media you purchase, the greater the chances of slight imperfections on the media surface, which can cause skips, pauses, or other problems.
- **Buy a CD/DVD printer**—For the best-looking discs and to eliminate any chance of wobble, invest in an inexpensive CD/DVD printer and use white printable media. These printers print directly to the discs using ink-jet technology and can be purchased for less than $400.

(Joe Stefan is President of DVDCre8, dvdcreate.com.)

 DOWNLOAD OF THE DAY   Dazzle's DVD Complete is a complete DVD authoring solution; it even prints the labels. Free to try, $99 to buy, from `dazzle.com/products/dvdcomplete.html`.

AUGUST 21

TODAY'S FOCUS: DVD

FIRST SUPERCOMPUTER

The Control Data Corporation introduced the CDC 6600 on this day in 1964. The machine was designed by Seymour Cray and is considered to be the first supercomputer in history. It had a clock speed of 100 nanoseconds—the fastest at the time—and was one of the first systems to use Freon refrigerant cooling. It also was the first commercial computer to use a cathode-ray tube (CRT) console. The solid-state system had 65,000 60-bit words of memory and supported the FORTRAN 66 compiler. The 6600 sold for $7 million, about $40.5 million in today's dollars.

Related Web site `www.nersc.gov/~deboni/Computer.history/cdc_6600.html`

DVD Audio Formats

When you think of DVDs, you usually think of the two or more hours of visual entertainment. But there's another component of the movie experience that's often overlooked: audio. Enhanced audio completes your movie experience, and DVDs now include audio options that can make you feel like you're in a movie theater.

Pick up a DVD movie, and you'll notice references to "Dolby Digital Surround Sound," "5.1 audio," and "DTS." What do these terms mean? We'll explain them and tell you how you can take advantage of them.

Surround Sound   Surround sound is often referred to as "5.1." Modern surround-sound systems use five speakers, plus a subwoofer for low-frequency sounds:

- A center speaker plays most of the dialogue.
- Right and left front speakers play the music and sound effects.
- Left and right surround-sound speakers, usually positioned at the rear or alongside the viewer, play ambient sounds.

Dolby Digital   Dolby Digital is a lossy encoding scheme created by Dolby Laboratories.

To use Dolby Digital sound, you need a DVD that is recorded using Dolby Digital, a DVD player that decodes Dolby Digital, and a Dolby Digital-ready receiver.

DTS Digital Surround   DTS digital surround was created by DTS Technology. Like Dolby Digital, DTS is a lossy encoding scheme that can support up to 5.1 channels of sound. Some enthusiasts prefer it because it's not as compressed as Dolby Digital.

DVD-Audio   If you've visited your local music store lately, you might have noticed the new DVD-Audio discs. DVD-Audio discs include interactive multimedia features and support for 5.1 surround sound, although DVD-Audio discs also support stereo setups.

Not all DVD players can play DVD-Audio discs. The player must be specifically labeled as supporting DVD-Audio to play DVD-Audio discs. You also need a receiver that can accept a multichannel input from the DVD-Audio player.

 TIP OF THE DAY   No consumer DVD recorder can copy DVD videos; nor would it make sense to, because the cost of blank discs approaches the cost of the actual video. On the other hand, there's great interest in copying DVDs to hard drives, CDs, and even sharing them over the Internet. The movie industry says that's illegal under U.S. law, although proponents claim that personal copying of a DVD you own is protected. The courts will have to decide this one, but to learn more about the ins and outs of DVD copying, visit `doom9.net` and `flexion.org`.

DOWNLOAD OF THE DAY   Ulead's PictureShow can burn slide shows onto DVD (and CD). Send the DVD to friends, and they can watch on most DVD players. Free to try, $29.95 to buy, from `Ulead.com`.

TODAY'S FOCUS: DVD

DEC FOUNDED

The Digital Equipment Corporation went into operation on this day in 1957. The company was founded by MIT engineers Kenneth Olsen and Harlan Anderson in an old woollen mill in Massachusetts. In 1960, DEC developed the first interactive computer, the PDP-1 (Programmed Data Processor). Three years later, the PDP-5 was unveiled, dubbed the first "mini-computer." DEC was acquired by Compaq in 1998.

Related Web site `www.compaq.com`

DVD Sites

By Roger Chang

DVD has been one of the most quickly adopted pieces of consumer technology in recent history. Just head down to the local video rental store to see its influence.

Hailed as the next big thing in consumer video, the influence of DVD is often compared to the way audio CDs changed the way music is distributed. It offers higher visual and aural fidelity over its magnetic tape–based predecessor, it's infinitely more durable than videotape, and it's physically and fiscally more manageable than laserdisc.

Like most consumer electronics, there are several things the buyer needs to understand about DVD: what it is, how it works, and why DVD does and doesn't do certain things. To help you along with the quest of understanding DVD, we have provided links to some very good explanations of DVD technology.

How DVD Players Work (`www.howstuffworks.com/dvd.htm`) This is a great site on understanding how DVD works. It offers explanations, complete with graphics and analogies on the mysterious workings of DVDs.

DVD Benchmarks (`hometheaterhifi.com/volume_7_3/dvd-benchmark-introduction-9-2000.html`) See how different DVD players stack up. This is the site for the true videophile. It explains what makes a good-quality DVD player and DVD disc, and the site gives a modest comparison among the more popular DVD players available.

DVD Region Code Enhancement (`www.flexion.org/video/DVDLingo/RCE/`) See how region code enhancement might prevent you from watching certain DVDs.

DVD Demystified (`Dvddemystified.com`) The DVD FAQ by Jim Taylor. Everything you ever wanted to know about the DVD format, and then some. This is the authoritative source.

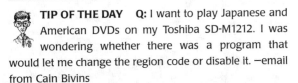

TIP OF THE DAY **Q:** I want to play Japanese and American DVDs on my Toshiba SD-M1212. I was wondering whether there was a program that would let me change the region code or disable it. —email from Cain Bivins

A: Region codes exist to preserve the box office for movies that will be released in international markets after the DVD video ships in the domestic market. Each DVD player is assigned a code for the region in which it's sold. The player will refuse to play discs from other regions. This means that discs bought in one country might not play on players bought in another country.

There's nothing you can do to change the region code of a DVD video player without hacking the hardware. This is not a simple undertaking and might be illegal. Read more at `codefreedvd.com`.

However, you might be able to unlock the region code when playing DVDs back on your computer. Read on.

DOWNLOAD OF THE DAY DVD Genie lets you modify the region codes and other hidden settings in many popular DVD player programs including Cinemaster, PowerDVD, and WinDVD. Free for Windows from `inmatrix.com`.

POLL: Does tech accuracy matter in the movies?

80% Yes

20% No

TODAY'S FOCUS: DVD

WINDOWS 95 RELEASED

Microsoft's new operating system went on sale on this day in 1995. Some buyers lined up the night before outside computer stores across the country to buy what some have called the most publicized software release in history (until Windows XP, that is). The 32-bit system featured a completely redesigned user interface and allowed full preemptive multitasking, networking, and more. The upgrade cost $70–$90. System requirements were 4MB RAM, 35MB hard drive space, and DOS 5.0 or higher (although Win 95 came with MS-DOS 7.0). Microsoft sold more than 1 million copies of Windows 95 within four days of its release.

Related Web site members.fortunecity.com/pcmuseum/windows.htm

Twisted List: Lame Online Games

By Martin Sargent

Last week was a long, strange week. Here's what happened on just three of those strange days.

Sunday Sunday morning I was feeling pretty depressed and decided to go to church, to get a little guidance in my life. But the deacon refused to let me in the door on account of the glazed ham incident I was at the center of at a recent church potluck. So, I went home and spent all afternoon releasing air pockets in virtual perpetual bubble wrap (www.urban75.com/Mag/bubble.html). When you break a bubble, it just comes back, unlike that ham.

Monday Monday after work I decided to read my viewer mail to see whether there were any nice notes about my performance on the show. Thought it might perk me up. But here's the first email I got:

"Martin, are you a botard? Every time you come on *The Screen Savers*, I turn the channel to that guy who sells knives on QVC. Next time there's an earthquake in San Francisco, please don't stand in a doorway."

Well, that didn't brighten my day at all, so I started playing the Reflex Tester game (www.stupid.com/games/reflex.htm) to get out of my funk. The object of the game is to click a button in as little time as possible after a square changes color. My record is .27 seconds. You cannot beat that, because I am far quicker than you.

Tuesday My Dungeons & Dragons club called and told me they didn't need my eighth-level elf around this week—last week I set off two booby traps and mistakenly blew a poison dart into our wizard's neck—so I ended up spending the entire night as I've spent so many other nights, sitting at my computer and spanking this monkey (massaar.homestead.com/files/flamjam.swf). Poor little monkey.

TIP OF THE DAY Improve DVD playback on the Mac. Turn off unnecessary extensions that can cause the DVD to pause or jump. Disable AirPort, LaserWriter, file sharing, location manager, multiple users, remote access, TCP/IP, USB printer sharing, Web sharing, and applications running in the background.

DOWNLOAD OF THE DAY Some call it the killer app for DVD players. Netflix rents DVD movies, as many as you want, three at a time, for $20 a month. Keep the movie as long as you want, there are no late fees, and when you're done, put it in the prepaid mailer and Netflix will send you the next movie on your wish list. I know people who bought DVD players so they could subscribe to this service. Netflix.com.

TODAY'S FOCUS: Wireless Networking

TV TUBE PATENTED

Howard Weinhart of New Jersey received a patent for a miniature television tube on this day in 1925. His "electric discharge device" was about two inches high, a half inch in diameter, and operated on a single dry cell. The patent was assigned to Western Electric Company, who dubbed it a "peanut tube," but the term wasn't new. Peanut tubes had been used since the early 1920s for transistor radios, mostly in home-brew models. Various peanut tubes are still around today—some eager vendors even sell them online for more than $40 each.

Related Web site   www.electron-valve.com/

WiFi Basics

By Matt Peterson

Wireless Ethernet equipment is marketed under two names: 802.11b or WiFi. The official IEEE standards name is 802.11b, whereas WiFi is a product interoperability testing organization at weca.net.

All 802.11b networks include at least two components: a client network adapter and an access point. APs function as radio frequency transmitters, which broadcast out an attached wired Ethernet connection. Think of Ethernet as "in," Wireless "out."

802.11b uses an Ethernet protocol that runs at 11Mbps. Both 802.11 and 802.11b run in the 2.4GHz bandwidth and are cross compatible. That's the same 2.4GHz bandwidth that cordless phones and many other consumer devices run on.

Matt's top five 802.11b tips:

- Use all available security options. Turn on WEP (Wired Equivalent Privacy). Use MAC address filtering (which only allows a limited set of NICs to connect to the AP). Turn off "broadcast mode."
- Always use SSL/SSH "end-to-end" security for sensitive data, such as online banking.
- Attach your access point(s) on an outside untrusted network segment, such as a DMZ. Do not attach them to internal corporate networks, unless you want the world to drive by and sniff your private data.
- Experiment placing your AP in different locations. The closest hub/switch might not be the ideal location for coverage.
- Stay current with firmware versions; each ups security and reliability.

Using 128-bit WEP and a password is no guarantee of privacy. For true security, use VPN or IPSec to encapsulate and encrypt all traffic. For the details on WEP security issues, visit www.isaac.cs.berkeley.edu/isaac/wep-faq.html or www.cs.umd.edu/~waa/wireless.html, and read tomorrow's article.

(Matt Peterson is the founder of the Bay Area Wireless Users Group, www.bawug.org.)

 TIP OF THE DAY   If you've got two AirPort-equipped Macs that you'd like to connect, you don't need to invest in Apple's AirPort base station. Instead, you can elect to use the software base station option.

Open the AirPort control panel. Click on **Software Base station**, and configure your network. You'll need to give it a name, a channel on which the two machines will communicate, and a password to keep out other nearby users. Go to the other machine and open its AirPort control panel. Select the newly set-up machine as your station, and you're ready.

This trick works with PCs using WiFi, too.

 DOWNLOAD OF THE DAY   Wardriving is looking for open WiFi (a.k.a. 802.11b) networks on the road. Use Netstumbler. Free for Windows from netstumbler.com.

Pocket PC users can download Mini Stumbler from the same site. In both cases, you'll need a system with a working WiFi card, of course.

TODAY'S FOCUS: Wireless Networking

FIRST WIRE NEWS REPORT

The first news dispatch sent by commercial telegraph was received by the *New York Sun* on this day in 1858. The message, an announcement that Britain and France had signed a peace treaty with China, was sent via the transatlantic telegraph cable, completed a little more than a week earlier. The cable quickly deteriorated, however, and service was stopped after just three weeks.

Related Web site `www.atlantic-cable.com/`

WiFi Security

By Avi Rubin

Wireless networking has taken off, due in large part to the availability of the 802.11 standard. Although another standard, Bluetooth, is also gaining in popularity, the longer range and higher speeds achieved by 802.11 make it the protocol of choice for wireless LANs. Office buildings, conferences, and even many residences now offer 802.11 connectivity.

The PC cards that are most often used in these networks provide a security protocol called *wired equivalent privacy (WEP)*. WEP is easy to administer. The device using the 802.11 card is configured with a key, which in practice usually consists of a password or a key derived from a password. The same key is deployed on all devices, including the access points. The idea is to protect the wireless communication from devices that do not know the key.

WEP uses RC4 IV cryptographic methods improperly, and our attack exploits this design failure. With our implementation, and with the permission of the network administrator, we were able to recover the 128-bit secret key used in a production network with a passive attack.

The attack was described in a recent paper I wrote with Adam Stubblefield and John Ioannidis (`www.cs.rice.edu/~astubble/wep/`). Our paper describes the attack, how we implemented it, and some optimizations to make the attack more efficient. We conclude that 802.11 WEP is totally insecure, and we provide some recommendations.

The impact of this attack has been great. Many government and corporate organizations have reported to us that they are adding IPSec and other VPN technologies on top of their wireless networks. Others are moving their 802.11 outside their firewall. Some even told us that they have completely disabled their wireless networks for now.

The work has received widespread media attention and was featured on CNN and TechTV, and in the *New York Times* and many other print media. It has fundamentally changed the way people view wireless LAN security.

(Avi Rubin is a principal researcher at AT&T Labs and author of White Hat Security Arsenal (Addison-Wesley 2001). Visit him online at `avirubin.com`.)

TIP OF THE DAY If you don't know the name of the local WiFi network you're logging into, try using the name ANY. In most cases, that will log you into any available network.

DOWNLOAD OF THE DAY MacStumbler is a Mac OS X version of yesterday's download, Netstumbler. If you have an AirPort card installed, you can use it to find any nearby WiFi network, Apple or PC. MacStumbler will tell you how strong the signal is and how it's protected. Free from `homepage.mac.com/macstumbler`.

POLL: If you use your neighbor's WiFi connection, you are...

34% Stealing
48% Sharing
18% What's WiFi?

TODAY'S FOCUS: Wireless Networking

FIRST RADIO BROADCAST FROM AIRPLANE

The first radio transmission to be sent from a flying airplane was made on this day in 1910. The message was sent from J.A. McCurdy in his Curtiss plane to Harry M. Horton during an air meet over the Sheepshead Bay race track in New York. The demonstration was reportedly witnessed by several members of the media and thousands of spectators. Although other pilots had previously attempted similar experiments, this event is recognized as the first official transmission of a wireless telegraph message from a plane in the U.S.

Related Web site www.pbs.org/kcet/chasingthesun

Wireless ISPs Q&A

By Greg Melton

Q: My mom lives in a town where wireless Internet service is being offered. What are the pros and cons of this type of service? —Kevin from Las Vegas, Nevada

A: Wireless Internet service providers (WISPs) run the gamut from small local operations such as Colorado River Internet (www.laughlin.net/wireless) to national giants such as Sprint, www.sprintbroadband.com. Using the 802.11b wireless standard, WISPs use high-powered transmitters and transceivers that send data over radio waves along the 2.4GHz spectrum.

The average installation requires an antenna or transceiver, cabling, and either a modem or a special wireless PC card. Because there's no hardware standard among WISPs yet, setups will vary depending on the provider.

You can expect to hear the term *fixed wireless* associated with this type of service. This means that all data is delivered wirelessly from an access point to a transceiver located on your roof and then routed to a stationary computer in your home. With a fixed wireless connection, you won't be able to walk around your home with a laptop and wirelessly connect to the Internet unless you have additional hardware.

For this type of service to work correctly, there must be a near line of sight between transmitter and transceiver. Depending on the provider, you can expect access points to be spread out every few miles.

Monthly rates are equal to or less than the amount of money you'd spend on a DSL or cable modem connection. Colorado River Internet charges $20 a month, and Sprint charges $49 a month for what appears to be the same type of service.

Advertised speeds vary between WISPs, but, on average, most are comparable to that of a DSL provider. Typically, both upload and download speeds fall between 500Kbps and 1,000Kbps.

The future of WISPs has been placed in some doubt by Sprint's recent decision to close its wireless broadband service to new customers. The company says it's too expensive to provide the service today, but it hopes future advances will make it viable in the future. Meanwhile, many small ISPs continue to push the future with wireless broadband.

TIP OF THE DAY Years ago, hobos used to leave cryptic chalk marks on houses where you could bum a meal or a place to sleep. Now geeks are doing the same thing with WiFi. Learn the signs at warchalking.org.

DOWNLOAD OF THE DAY If you frequently change network settings on your laptop, moving from the office, to the road, to home, you need Netswitcher. Maintain multiple sets of network settings, and apply them without rebooting in many cases. Free to try, $5 to buy, from netswitcher.com.

AUGUST 27

TODAY'S FOCUS: Wireless Networking

FIRST U.S. OIL WELL

Prospectors found a new source of "black gold" on this day in 1859. Edwin Laurentine Drake and his company struck oil at a depth of nearly 70 feet in Titusville, Pennsylvania, after many failed attempts. His success was due to new drilling equipment he had invented that could penetrate the rocky terrain. Drake's hole became the first successful oil well in the U.S. and started the world's first oil boom. Today, the site of Drake's well is a museum.

Related Web site www.rigzone.com

The Future of WiFi

It's a weird little alphabet, but in the world of 802.11 the letter "b" comes before "a" and "g." The 802.11 spec originally referred to a wireless networking system that uses the Ethernet protocol and runs at 2Mbps. As the 802.11 spec grew, the IEEE added letters.

802.11b (also called WiFi) uses an Ethernet protocol that runs at 11Mpbs. Both 802.11 and 802.11b run in the 2.4GHz bandwidth and are cross compatible. That's the same 2.4GHz bandwidth that cordless phones and many other consumer devices run on.

802.11a supports 54Mbps in the 5GHz band for asynchronous transfer mode (ATM) networks. 802.11a is also known as WiFi 5. Vendors such as Actiontec (www.actiontec.com), D-Link (www.dlink.com), Proxim (www.proxim.com), and Intel (www.intel.com) are either already shipping WiFi 5 products or planning to ship them soon.

802.11g promises 54Mbps in the 2.4GHz band. Better yet, it should be backward compatible with existing WiFi (802.11b) products. 802.11g products should be appearing Any Day Now.

Is it time to upgrade to 802.11a or 802.11g? Not yet. 802.11a is not compatible with any existing hardware and looks to be an interim technology. Unless you need the extra bandwidth, I'd wait for 802.11g. But don't be the first on your block to buy that, either; wait to see whether it lives up to its hype and is really compatible with 802.11b. Meanwhile, 802.11a is here now, gets the job done, and is getting less expensive to implement all the time.

Helpful 802.11 links:

- SearchNetworking's definition of 802.11: searchnetworking.techtarget.com/ sDefinition/0,,sid7_gci341007,00.html
- 801.11 Planet: www.80211-planet.com
- IEEE 802 Standards Committee: www.ieee802.org
- Download a copy of the IEEE spec: standards.ieee.org/getieee802

TIP OF THE DAY   Having trouble with your network connection? Use ping to test it. Most computers come with a ping program. In Windows, open a command prompt. In Mac OS X, use the Terminal program. To test your network, first ping the IP address of your router (if you have one). On my system, I type **ping 198.162.1.1**.

If the router responds, you know your hardware and internal network is working. Next, ping the IP address of a box outside your network. I use Yahoo! because they're always up: **ping 66.218.71.113**. If that works, you know the problem must be with the DNS settings or server. Try pinging by name: **ping yahoo.com**. If *that* works, kwitcherbellyachin'; everything's fine!

DOWNLOAD OF THE DAY   Learn Java and have fun doing it. Robocode is a free download from IBM's alphaWorks team, robocode.alphaworks.ibm.com. Program your robot to beat robots from other programmers around the world. May the best coder win!

TODAY'S FOCUS: Wireless Networking

AUTO INNOVATOR BORN

Charles F. Kettering was born in Detroit, Michigan, on this day in 1876. Kettering was known mostly for his work in the auto industry, but he held more than 200 patents, including one for the invention of the electric cash register. In 1909, Kettering and Edward A. Deeds founded Delco (Dayton Engineering Laboratories Company). There, he developed many ways to improve cars, including lighting and ignition systems, lacquer finishes, antilock fuels, and leaded gasoline. He is perhaps best known, however, for inventing the electric starter, which was first used on the 1912 Cadillac. Kettering died in 1958.

Related Web site `kettering.org`

Bluetooth

By Martin Sargent

As the story goes, Harald Bluetooth was a Viking king who united tribes and was known for his bridge-building projects, not to mention his blue teeth. Harald's namesake is Bluetooth technology, which lets you exchange data between computing devices. It's basically a wireless technology that synchronizes computers, PDAs, cameras, and cell phones within a range of 30 or more feet.

Analysts expect this technology to be huge. Research firm Dataquest predicts that by 2004, a billion Bluetooth-enabled devices will be on the market. I find it hard to believe that there will be one Bluetooth device for every six people on Earth, but that's their prediction.

One such device is the proposed tri-mode phone that operates like a cordless landline phone in your home with normal home phone rates, a wireless handset when you're out and about, and a free walkie-talkie when you come within range of another Bluetooth-enabled phone.

Of course, if you need to be within 30 feet of another Bluetooth phone for the devices to detect one another, I'm thinking you could just raise your voice a little. I'm sure the engineers will figure something out.

As many analysts have pointed out, Bluetooth is not really needed on PCs. 802.11 operates at 10 times the speed of Bluetooth and costs less. Bluetooth won't hit its stride until it starts to operate in gadgets and appliances—not PCs. We're still waiting.

TIP OF THE DAY Windows XP can synchronize your computer's internal clock with an Internet time server, keeping your system accurate to within a second or two of the atomic clock.

To turn on synchronization, open the Date and Time control panel. Click the **Internet Time** tab, select the time server you want to use, and place a check mark next to the text that reads **Automatically Synchronize with an Internet Time Server**. Your time display will automatically be synchronized once a week.

If you want it to sync more often, or if you're using an older version of Windows, I recommend Dimension4, free from `thinkman.com/dimension4`.

Mac OS 9 and X can do the same thing. In X, Open the Date & Time pane in the System Preferences, click the **Network Time** tab, and then check the box that says **Use a Network Time Server**. The Mac will synchronize whenever your clock is off by more than a few seconds.

DOWNLOAD OF THE DAY Tweak your system like crazy. TweakAll uses a plug-in architecture to be infinitely extensible. Free for Windows, from `codeforge.co.uk`.

POLL: Would you trust your secrets to a wireless network?

24% Yes

76% No

AUGUST 29

TODAY'S FOCUS: Wireless Networking

IBM ENDS WINDOWS FIGHT

IBM said it wouldn't oppose Microsoft's attempt to trademark the name "Windows" on this day in 1994. The terms "windows" and "windowing" had become slang in the software industry for adjusting the layout on a computer monitor to view different programs simultaneously. More than a year earlier, the U.S. Patent and Trademark Office rejected Microsoft's attempt to register the trademark, but reversed its decision a few months later.

Related Web site   www.uspto.gov

The Next Generation of Cell Phones

By Dave Roos

In tech circles, it's practically a given that high-speed, Web-enabled mobile devices will one day become an integral part of our lives, both for work and play. The questions are how fast these devices will be and how soon they will arrive. Enter 3G, or third-generation wireless technology.

What Is 3G?   3G is not an existing product or platform. It's a technological movement calling for the expansion of the current radio spectrum to bolster faster download speeds and greater accessibility for wireless, Web-enabled devices. The technology that will enable this expansion is called wide code division multiple access, or W-CDMA.

3G promoters promise "always on" mobile Web devices with bit rates as fast as 2Mbps by the year 2005. Currently, Web-enabled cell phones and PDAs operate anywhere from 9.6Kbps to 14.4Kbps. If 3G lives up to its hype, mobile access to video on demand (VOD) and other multimedia file applications could be greatly increased.

In the summer of 1999, several large telecom companies, including AT&T Wireless Services, British Telecom, and Nokia, joined in a "3G alliance" to collectively lobby for construction of the infrastructure necessary to support 3G's dreams of lightning-fast bandwidth.

This lobbying process includes the purchase of extremely expensive radio spectrum from the FCC and other similar regulatory communication commissions across the globe. Recently, five U.K. telecom operators paid the British government upward of 22 billion pounds for the required spectrum licenses to run 3G. Meanwhile, in the U.S., the FCC is still trying to figure out whether there is any spectrum available to sell in the first place.

Not everyone believes that a push for immediate 3G implementation is necessary for increased download speeds and accessibility. So-called "2.5G" advocates believe that we can increase wireless download speeds to accommodate high-speed multimedia applications without having to expand the current spectrum. Clearly, 2.5G would be cheaper and easier to implement, but even its highest available download speeds would come nowhere close to the 2Mbps fantasies of 3G futurists.

TIP OF THE DAY   Q: I'm worried. While messing around on my Windows XP Home system, I found a phantom user account named "Account unknown." Have I been hacked? —Tim from Louisville, Kentucky

A: No, Tim. You've found a bug in the Windows XP Home Edition installer. The account is created during the install and it's supposed to be deleted. Microsoft explains in more detail at support.microsoft.com/default.aspx?scid=kb;en-us;Q312131. You can ignore it, or contact your vendor for a fix.

DOWNLOAD OF THE DAY   Windows XP comes with a built-in VPN client for connecting securely to company networks. Apple hasn't added PPTP VPN to OS X, yet. Until it does, download PiePants from Rob the Dude. Silly name, great program. Free from homepage.mac.com/robthedude/PiePants.

TODAY'S FOCUS: Wireless Networking

MOVIE CAMERA PATENTED

Thomas Edison patented the first motion picture camera on this day in 1897. Edison had created the device nearly six years earlier and opened the world's first motion picture studio in 1893. But the patent wasn't approved until this day. His kinetographic camera used photographic film that moved several frames per second past a camera lens, creating the illusion of motion. Edison's pictures could not be seen by large audiences, however; images were viewed through the peephole of a device called a *kinetoscope*.

Related Web site `tomedison.org`

Fantasy Football

By Corey Roberts

The week before the NFL season starts is known as "draft week" to millions of football fans. Fantasy football team owners across the country get together, at home or online, to draft their teams for the upcoming season. More than 30 million people participate in this fantasy sport.

Pick a Team If you and your friends are looking to make a fantasy football league this season, you have a couple options:

Use an online league management tool, such as those provided by Fantasy Football (`sportsline.com/u/fantasy/football`), or RealTime Fantasy Sports (`www.rtsports.com`). Download customized statistics from a stat service, such as Allstar Stats (`allstarstats.com`) or Total Quality Stats (`tqstats.com`).

If you're looking to become involved in a fantasy football league by yourself, there are a few different types of games available:

Match your fantasy team against a different owner's team each week in head-to-head games. Set up your own game at Yahoo! or Stats, `www.stats.com`. In salary cap games, your goal is to assemble the best fantasy football team possible while staying below a set salary cap. Play this type of game at CBS SportsLine.com (`sportsline.com`), or NFL.com. Find pick-'em games at Lycos, `fantasy.lycos.com`. Just pick the winners of each game throughout the NFL season.

The key to becoming a champion in fantasy football is staying on top of your team and what's going on in the NFL. There are some Web sites that specialize in providing up-to-the-minute NFL news and notes specifically for fantasy sports players. My favorites are RotoWire (`www.rotowire.com`) and The Sporting News (`sportingnews.com`).

(Corey Roberts is a project manager at STATS, Inc.)

 TIP OF THE DAY WinPopUp sends messages to other people on your network, identified by their login user name. The recipient of your message needs to have WinPopUp running, too. In Windows 95/98/Me, click **Start**, **Run**, and type `winpopup`.

There's no WinPopUp on Windows XP, but you can download an even more functional clone called LanTalk XP from `lantalk.com`. Free to try, $14.95 to buy.

DOWNLOAD OF THE DAY I've been holding out on you. Here it is the end of August and I haven't even told you about the best download for Mac ever. I'm such a tease. Watson was written by Dan Wood to teach himself OS X programming. Along with LaunchBar (see January 20), it's one of the two must-have shareware applications for OS X.

So, what's it do? Watson grabs information from the Internet. To use the in-vogue term, it "scrapes the Web." Track packages, look up movie times, find phone numbers, search eBay auctions, get weather reports, recipes, and dictionary definitions. Watson has 16 plug-ins, with many more to come. Try it free, buy it for $29. From `www.karelia.com/watson`.

AUGUST
31

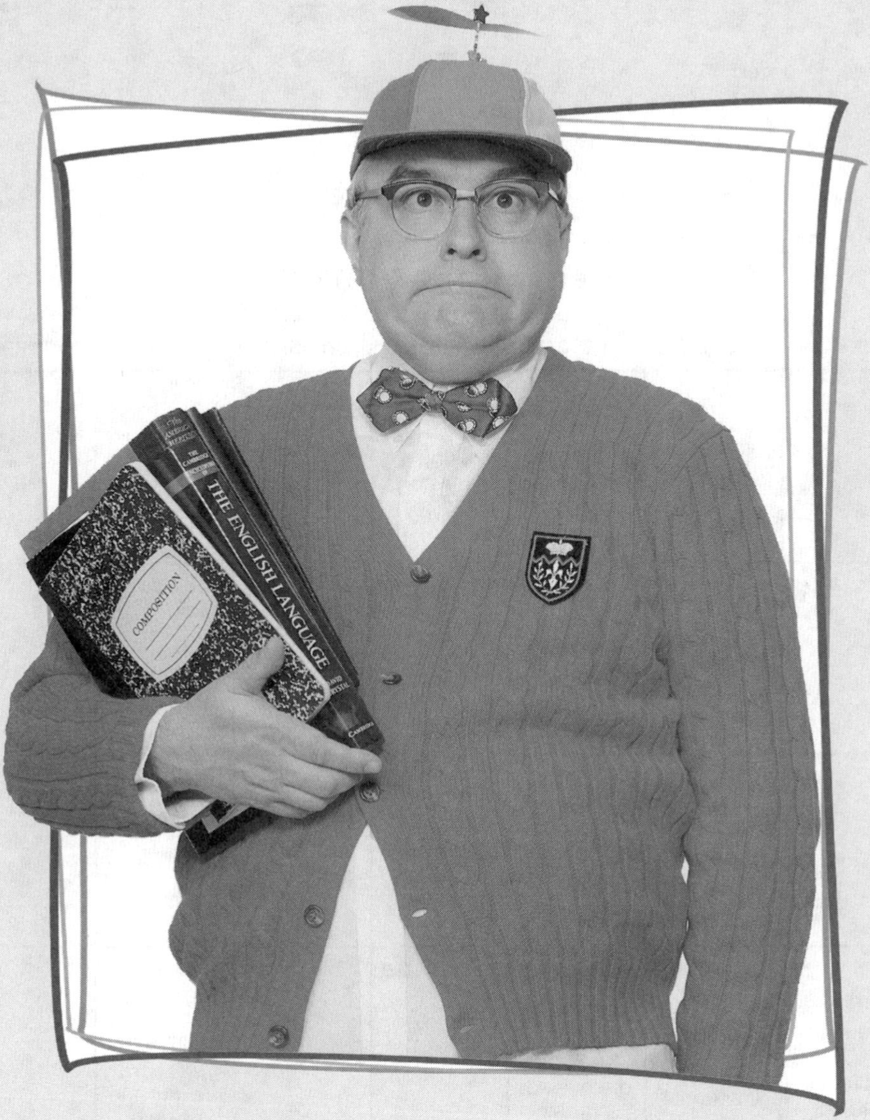

SEPTEMBER 2003

SEPTEMBER 2003

SUNDAY	MONDAY	TUESDAY	WEDNESDAY	THURSDAY	FRIDAY	SATURDAY
	1 Labor Day; *Titanic* wreck located (1985)	**2** Andrew Grove born (1936)	**3** Viking II lands on Mars (1976)	**4**	**5**	**6**
7	**8** *Star Trek* premiered on TV (1966)	**9** David Packard born (1912)	**10**	**11** Patriot Day— 2-year anniversary of World Trade Center and Pentagon ter- rorist attacks	**12**	**13**
14	**15** Laura Burstein's birthday	**16**	**17** Citizenship Day	**18**	**19**	**20**
21 J.R.R. Tolkien's *The Hobbit* published (1937)	**22** OCEANS 2003 (San Diego, California)	**23** First day of autumn; Neptune discovered (1846)	**24**	**25**	**26** U.S. and others sign nuclear weapons testing ban (1996)	**27**
28	**29** Seybold, San Francisco, California	**30**				

TODAY'S FOCUS: Back to School

GRAMOPHONE PATENTED

Emile Berliner applied for a patent for the gramophone on this day in 1887. The German-born inventor had earlier developed a microphone that improved upon the transmitter in Alexander Graham Bell's new telephone. American Bell Telephone Company bought the rights to his microphone patent for $50,000 and hired Berliner as a researcher. In 1884, he resigned from his position to work at home, where he invented the predecessor to the record player. Incidentally, Berliner's trademark was a picture of a dog listening to "his master's voice" playing from a gramophone. RCA later adopted the logo and still uses it today.

Related Web site   `memory.loc.gov/ammem/berlhtml/berlhome.html`

Classroom Connect

By Dave Roos

On any given day, in average middle-school classrooms across the country, students are taking field trips to Africa, Australia, the Amazon, and remote Pacific islands. No permission slips required. No potty breaks. No brown-bag peanut butter and jelly sandwiches getting soggy on the bus. These students are being led on exotic virtual explorations by long-distance bicyclist Dan Buettner and a team of entertaining, educational experts from Classroom Connect.

From Bikes to Tykes   Buettner began his career as a world record-breaking cyclist, completing a mind-boggling (and thigh-busting) 15,500-mile route down the Pacific coast from Alaska to Argentina. After tackling similar treks across Africa and Russia, Buettner was approached by Classroom Connect, an online curriculum resource, to lead worldwide Webcast expeditions to teach children about indigenous cultures and endangered natural resources.

With three kids of his own, Buettner understands the importance of teaching children about the larger world around them. During his international quests, Buettner and his cohorts not only stream video through the Web site, but also get the kids at home involved through interactive polls and projects. The students are often asked to influence the next step of the quest, and their advice is dutifully followed.

Next stop: ColumbusQuest: a journey following Columbus's route through the Bahamas to Cuba. Classrooms and individual students are invited to participate at quest.classroom.com. While you're there, visit previous quests to Australia, Central America, the Amazon, and Greece.

 TIP OF THE DAY   One of every eight school-age children needs special help in school. Most have learning disabilities that affect their ability to use written or spoken language. Your computer can help. Practice skills with the Fast ForWord family of programs from `scientificlearning.com` and Earobics from `earobics.com`.

Two of the best parent resource sites are Weird Kids (`weirdkids.com`) and the Texas Center for Autism Research & Treatment, at `www.tcart.org`.

 DOWNLOAD OF THE DAY   ChemLab simulates a real-world chemistry lab, complete with equipment: beakers, Erlenmeyer and Florence flasks, test tubes, graduated cylinders, burettes, eye droppers, pipettes, watch glasses, filtering flasks with Buchner funnels, Bunsen burners, balances, a distillation setup, hot plate and magnetic stirrer, stirring rods, an evaporation dish, a calorimeter, conductivity meter, potentiometer, spectrophotometer, and even more.

You'll complete different labs using the common lab interface. It's perfect for long-distance learning or just plain old fun on your PC. Standard version, $24.99. Pro edition, $129.99, from `modelscience.com/products.html`.

POLL: Should schools use open-source operating systems?

83% Yes   17% No

SEPTEMBER 1

TODAY'S FOCUS: Back to School

GREGORIAN CALENDAR BEGINS

England and its colonies switched from the Julian calendar to the Gregorian calendar on this day in 1752. The change was designed to make date calculations closer to the actual length of time it takes for the Earth to complete an orbit around the sun. Eleven days were dropped, so the following day was September 14, not September 3. Other European countries had adopted the "new" system nearly two centuries earlier in 1582. The Gregorian Calendar introduced leap year days and is the same calendar system we follow today.

Related Web site `timeanddate.com`

Back-to-School Computer

Want to send your student back to school with a shiny new computer? Here's your shopping list.

Processor Don't overspend on the processor. No matter what your kid says, anything over 1GHz will do just fine. Put the money you save toward a larger monitor, more RAM, a faster hard drive, or a graphics tablet. Save even more by buying a processor from AMD instead of Intel.

Memory Get a minimum of 256MB of RAM. And if your student is using Windows XP or Mac OS X, you can even go as high as 512MB. More RAM means junior can do more things at once, and faster, too.

Storage Don't skimp here. Get at least 30GB and a 7200 RPM drive for speed. Keep backups in mind, too: A CD burner is an inexpensive way to protect those papers and presentations. If you want to be a nice parent, include a DVD-ROM for movie night.

Ports Add an Ethernet card if the school has a network, and if your student is going to do any video editing, add FireWire, too. If the school offers wireless networking, consider a WiFi card, especially in a notebook.

Extras Don't forget a good speaker system, an inkjet printer if the school doesn't offer networked printing, and a UPS so Junior's term paper doesn't bite the dust when the power goes out.

Desktop or Notebook? A desktop PC is a great choice in situations where flexibility and upgradability are paramount and desk space is not an issue.

Notebooks are better for cramped dorm rooms, and it's handy to be able to tote them to class or the library. But keep in mind that they're also easily stolen. Don't buy a notebook unless your student is responsible enough to protect it.

TIP OF THE DAY It's never too late to go back to school. SoYouWanna.com teaches you how to do everything from get a pilot's license to fake an appreciation for art.

DOWNLOAD OF THE DAY Adobe's Portable Document File format, PDF, is a perfect way to hand in reports and presentations. You don't have to buy Adobe's expensive PDF distiller to make PDF files, though.

Mac OS X users can create PDF documents just by choosing Print Preview in any application and selecting Save as PDF. For Mac OS 9, download Jim Walker's Print2PDF from `jwwalker.com`. Free to try, $20 to buy.

Windows users can download EasyPDF from `visagesoft.com`. The software is free for two weeks, $30 to buy.

In a pinch, you can use Adobe's online PDF creator at `cpdf.adobe.com`. The first five documents are free.

TODAY'S FOCUS: Back to School

FIRST ELECTRIC TRAIN

The first train in the U.S. to run on electricity took its first journey on this day in 1931. The Lackawanna Railroad was developed to run from Hoboken to Montclair, New Jersey, to help cut down on air pollution around the New York area. The trains ran connected to overhead wires and were nicknamed the "wickerliners" because the cabins were equipped with wicker seats. Thomas Edison operated the first train to leave Hoboken Terminal at the railroad's inauguration.

Related Web site `rrhistorical.com`

Be a Better Girl Geek

By Megan Morrone

Start early.

I started skiing when I was five years old. I was fearless, and when I fell down, I didn't have that far to fall. For those who don't start skiing until they're grown up, it's not that easy. The same goes for getting involved in tech. It's never too late to get involved in technology, but if you grow up with it, it will be that much easier.

Never Ask for Help Computers and technology might seem difficult, but the truth is, they're mostly logical. If you click around long enough, you're bound to figure it out. If your natural tendency is to ask your boyfriend, husband, or IT person before you try to solve the problem yourself, you will never learn anything.

Always Ask for Help I am a woman; therefore, I contradict myself. If you find yourself in over your head, there's nothing wrong with asking for help. Geeks are helpful by nature. They're used to having people give them glazed-over looks when trying to explain what root access means. If you truly want to know, they're more than willing to help. Unless, of course, they're one of those grumpy IT guys who get off on being smarter than you are.

Read Science Fiction In space, there's not only no gravity, there's also no inequality. Women of science fiction are a powerful bunch who fight against evil right next to men. Read science fiction for tips on being a female geek.

Don't Fake It There's nothing wrong with having little or no interest in technology. There's no shame in it. The shame comes in pretending to be someone you're not. This applies to males or females, but I think it's more important for us gals to remember because we're often watched more closely. If I remember one piece of advice that Leo and Patrick gave me when I started on *The Screen Savers*, it was "Don't fake it." Geeks are smart. If you try to talk about something you don't understand, they'll see right through you.

TIP OF THE DAY No matter what Barbie says, math isn't hard. Get some help online at Math Forum@Drexel (`mathforum.org`), a learning hub with resources, activities, math help, and a community for students, teachers, and people just interested in math.

DOWNLOAD OF THE DAY Windows still has the same calculator that shipped with version 3.1. Upgrade it with a free high-precision calculator from `twopaths.com/calculator`. The Windows PowerToys calculator is pretty buff, too. Free from `microsoft.com/windowsxp/pro/downloads/powertoys.asp`.

Apple's not much better. That's why I use WCalc, free for OS X from `homepage.mac.com/memoryhole/wcalc/wcalc.html`.

POLL: Should education be for sale?
16% Yes
84% No

SEPTEMBER 3

TODAY'S FOCUS: Back to School

FIRST TRANSCONTINENTAL TV BROADCAST

The first coast-to-coast television broadcast in the U.S. took place on this day in 1951. President Harry Truman delivered an address from San Francisco during a conference to discuss a peace treaty between the United Nations and Japan. The transmission of the president's speech was the first using AT&T's newly laid transcontinental coaxial cable. The line was buried underground across 12 states. The telecommunications company had worked on the line for nearly two decades.

Related Web site `home.att.net/~long-lines/microwave.html`

Protect Your Kids Online

My wife always says there's no substitute for parental supervision. Of course, she's talking about me, but it applies to the kids, too.

The Internet is a boon for children, bringing the whole world into their living rooms, but it also has its dark side. Keep an eye on your kids when they're online. It's best to keep the computer in a communal area where there will always be others around to help and supervise.

Set the rules in advance, and be sure your kids can talk with you if they have a problem. Discuss things such as where they can and cannot go online, what kinds of activities are allowed, what kinds of information they can disclose, and what things they should never reveal.

Online searches for "Little Women" don't always turn up Louisa May Alcott novels. It's best to use search engines geared for children, such as Ask Jeeves for Kids (ajkids.com) and Yahooligans (yahooligans.com). Everyone's favorite search engine, Google, can be configured to leave out the adult stuff by clicking the preferences link on the front page and turning on Safe Search Filtering.

Pornographic spam might be one of the biggest problems facing parents today. Even if your child has his or her own email address, it's only a matter of time before the spam begins creeping in. I filter all my kids' mail through

`spamcop.net`. For $30 a year, it does a great job of keeping their inbox clean. You also can use your email program's filter rules to delete mail that's not specifically addressed to your kids. This won't eliminate all spam, but it will get rid of most of it. Check their mail from time to time to make sure no bad stuff is leaking through.

If your children are on AOL, you can block mail from all but known addresses, and also set it to reject photos and other attachments. It's a good idea for each child to have his or her own screen name so that you can set parental controls appropriately. On AOL, the keyword is "parental controls."

To learn more about protecting your kids online, visit these Web sites:

- SafeKids: `safekids.com`
- Wired Kids: `wiredkids.org`
- GetNetWise: `getnetwise.org`
- NetMom: `netmom.com`

TIP OF THE DAY The U.S. Consumer Product Safety Commission estimates that 191,000 children were treated in emergency rooms for toy-related injuries in 2000. Select toys that are safe for your kids; visit the CPSC kid safety Web site, `cpsc.gov/kids/kidsafety`. ToySafety.net has more rules of thumb for parents to follow, including a comprehensive list of shopping tips: `toysafety.net`.

DOWNLOAD OF THE DAY StarCalc creates star maps from any location at any point in history. Know what you're looking at in the night sky. Download StarCalc free from `www.relex.ru/~zalex/files_eng.htm`.

TV RATINGS PIONEER BORN

Arthur Charles Nielsen was born in Chicago, Illinois, on this day in 1897. He was instrumental in creating a system for gauging and analyzing television viewing habits. Today, a television program's success is still based on its Nielsen ratings. Advertising revenue, the show's position in a network's lineup, and the cast's salary are all heavily influenced by these numbers. (Tell me about it.) Incidentally, Nielsen was also an avid tennis player and was inducted into the International Tennis Hall of Fame in 1971. He died June 1, 1981.

Related Web sites   www.nielsenmedia.com, www.nielsen-netratings.com

Paper Airplanes Take Off

By Roger Chang

Even the lowly paper airplane can fly high tech, thanks to paper airplane software. Here are three programs you and your kids will love, starting with Paper Airplane Factory from Little Bits Multimedia at littlebitsmultimedia.com.

This program is perfect for first-time paper aviators. Print out a template of the plane you want to create, and follow along with onscreen instructions. The free version has some options and features disabled, but other than that, it's extremely easy to use. A fully functional version of the program can be purchased for $10.

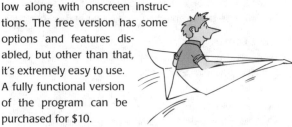

If you want more advanced designs, take a look at The Greatest Paper Airplanes, from KittyHawk Software, khs.com. The demo version only allows you to try out standard Darts designs, those old-fashioned paper airplane models just like you made back in school. The full version is $20 for Mac and PC.

KittyHawk also makes Paper Air Force, which focuses on creating paper models of actual planes. After hours of real-life cutting and pasting, I was able to construct a reasonable paper facsimile of an F-86 Sabre. Although I have yet to build up the courage to fly my creation, the product does claim that each model is capable of being flown after being built.

This title is designed for more advanced builders, as glue and precise cutting are involved. Overall, I recommend this as the ultimate paper airplane program. It's like having two toys in one: both a model plane kit and a paper airplane program. Paper Air Force is $25 for Mac and PC.

  TIP OF THE DAY   Add page numbers in Microsoft Word. Select **Page Numbers** from the **Insert** menu.

 DOWNLOAD OF THE DAY   Use your Palm to keep the kids entertained. (It's better than the back of your hand.)

The Sorting Hat (freewarepalm.com/misc/sortinghat.shtml)   What house would your child be in at Hogwarts? Find out by entering his or her initials into this Palm app. I'm in Gryffindor. Yes!

Palm Reader (www.peanutpress.com)   Download children's e-books to your Palm, and you'll never be without a story to read to the kiddies. Turn on the backlight at bedtime to capture that comforting reading-under-the-covers-with-a-flashlight feel. One of my favorite new e-books is *A Handful of Beans* from inebooks.com.

HowLongToGo (rubens.org.uk/howlong)   This tiny app is for curious kids, answering questions about how many days until his or her birthday, Christmas, or any other longed-for event. The only thing that would make this application better is if it answered the question, "Are we there yet?" The £5 shareware fee is voluntary—all the cash goes to buying books for kids in Frieth, Buckinghamshire, in the United Kingdom.

TODAY'S FOCUS: Back to School

RADAR DEVELOPER BORN

Ernst Weber was born in Vienna, Austria, on this day in 1901. After graduating with degrees in both engineering and physics, Weber worked for the Siemens-Schukert company in Austria and Germany designing more energy-efficient industrial machines. In 1930, he moved to New York and became a professor at the Polytechnic Institute of Brooklyn. Much of Weber's work revolved around microwaves, an integral part of RADAR. Weber was granted more than 30 patents for microwave-related technology. In 1945, he founded the Microwave Research Center at the Polytechnic Institute. Weber died February 15, 1996.

Related Web site `www.poly.edu/research/wri.cfm`

Homework Helper Sites

By Martin Sargent

Here are five cool sites that'll help you with your school assignments. But if you use any of them to plagiarize stuff, I'll hunt you down and give you a fat lip.

Big Chalk (bigchalk.com) With more than 100,000 links, it provides resources for students at every grade level, elementary school through high school. Each link leads to a large selection of subtopics. Select a subject and age group to browse hundreds of resources, or search for selections that match your keyword.

BJ Pinchbeck's Homework Helper (bjpinchbeck.com) BJ Pinchbeck (his friends call him "Beege") is 16 years old. He sort of looks like Harry Potter. In 1996, with the help of his dad, this homework wizard started building a collection of helpful homework links. Today, his collection includes more than 700 links for everything from math to gym class.

Multnomah County Library (multcolib.org/homework) The librarians in Multnomah County, Oregon, do an amazing job of bringing together homework resources. Tap into this no-frills topical guide for sites on everything from animals to social issues. The library also provides helpful advice on evaluating Web sites and using search engines.

Jiskha Homework Help (jishka.com) Don't ask me what a jiskha is, but go ahead and ask your homework questions here. The homework help forums are a wonderful resource, as are all the articles covering an extensive range of subjects.

AOL@SCHOOL (school.aol.com) You don't need an AOL account to use the company's stellar homework site. Choose your grade and subject, and you'll receive a list of helpful resources. Yahoo!'s Yahooligans division also offers an extensive directory of sites you can use to research your projects at yahooligans.com/School_Bell.

 TIP OF THE DAY These are some of the more useful (and lesser-known) keyboard shortcuts in Microsoft Excel. For the complete list, press F1 to open the Office Assistant, and then type **keyboard shortcuts**.

Select Entries:
- Select the column: Ctrl+spacebar
- Select the row: Shift+spacebar
- Select all: Ctrl+A

Working with Numbers:
- View cell values versus view cell formulas: Ctrl+single left quotation mark
- Recalculate all sheets in a workbook: F9
- Recalculate a worksheet: Shift+F9
- Enter the date: Ctrl+semicolon
- Enter the time Ctrl+colon
- Fill the selected range with contents of current cell: Ctrl+Enter
- Show the Go To dialog box: F5
- Open the Format Cells dialog box Ctrl+1

 DOWNLOAD OF THE DAY Don't tell Palm, but their Desktop software makes an excellent free PIM, even if you don't own a Palm. For Windows and Macintosh from palm.com/support/downloads.

POLL: Who knows more about tech?

94% Students   6% Teachers

TODAY'S FOCUS: Back to School

DAVID PACKARD BORN

The second half of Hewlett-Packard was born in Pueblo, Colorado, on this day in 1912. Packard and fellow Stanford University graduate, William Hewlett, founded their famous electronics company in a garage in Palo Alto, California, in 1939. Packard was appointed deputy defense secretary by President Richard Nixon in 1968. Three years later, Packard resigned and returned to HP as chairman of the board, a position he held until 1993. But he continued to advise the White House on defense issues until the 1980s. Packard died March 26, 1996.

Related Web site `www.packard.org`

Twisted List: Things You Can Only Learn Online
By Martin Sargent

You might not know that I've studied at universities on four continents, lived with indigenous tribes in the Amazon basin, and consulted for the Russian space program. I have acquired much knowledge, much wisdom. But it wasn't until I first logged on to the World Wide Web that I really started to learn about the truly important subjects of the universe.

How to Diaper a Monkey (`mommensj.web2010.com/ctips3.htm`)   While meditating for a year with a Nepalese guru, I learned much, but one piece of knowledge my master never imparted on me was how to diaper a monkey. It wasn't until I visited the Web site of Sherry Freeman and her pet monkey, Sammy, that I learned that while diapering a monkey, you should keep its tail between your knees. Also, you don't need to cut a piece out of the diaper for the tail, you just need to fold around the tail.

The Frito Files (`fritolay.com/faq.html`)   I've always got my hand in a bag of corn chips—chili cheese-flavored, please—but I really didn't know anything about the subtler aspects of snacking until I visited the FAQ file on the Frito-Lay Web site. I just want to know, what does "the more potato, potato chip" on the Ruffles package mean?

How to Build a Space Habitat (`clubs.yahoo.com/clubs/howtobuildaspacehabitat`)   I belong to more than 380 Yahoo! clubs, but the club that has taught me the most is my How to Build a Space Habitat club. All my buddies in the club believe that our future is in space, so we need to start building. And boy, I can't wait to get off this planet. Things have got to be better up there, in my cozy little space habitat. Note to Lt. Commander Sol Expanse: I totally disagree with your theory of cylinder instability (I lectured on this during my tenure in the Russian space program), but we can talk about it at tonight's meeting.

TIP OF THE DAY   My worst day in school, ever, was frog dissection day. I can still remember the feeling of cold linoleum on my cheek as I woke up on the floor. Wish they'd had NetFrog, a virtual dissection online at `teach.virginia.edu/go/frog`. Catch me, I'm feeling light-headed again.

DOWNLOAD OF THE DAY   Kids are so much more sophisticated today. In my youth, we used to disrupt class by making rude noises with our armpits. Today's kids do it digitally with Random Burper, free for Windows from `rjlsoftware.com/software/entertainment/burp`. Excuse me.

SEPTEMBER 7

TODAY'S FOCUS: Advanced Linux

AOL TAKES OVER COMPUSERVE

America Online acquired struggling online service provider CompuServe on this day in 1997. The deal made AOL's subscriber base six times larger than that of MSN, its closest competitor.

Related Web site `www.aol.com`

Software Sharing and Open Source

By Jon "maddog" Hall

A lot of people think that freely distributed open-source software is something totally GNU, but this is not the case. About 300 years ago (well, okay, it was more like 1969), I was a student at Drexel University in Philadelphia, trying to learn how to program a PDP computer.

Unfortunately, the amount of software available to run on these machines was sparse, but DECUS, the Digital Equipment User's society, was willing to collect contributions of software and distribute them at the cost of copying on paper tape.

At the same time, Ken Thompson and Dennis Ritchie were inventing Unix at AT&T Bell Labs. Unix really started to flourish when it escaped to the universities and coders started sharing software. Eventually, a user and technical group called USENIX grew out of this sharing. Source code was often redistributed at USENIX meetings.

In 1975, microcomputer-focused magazines such as *Byte*, *Kilobaud*, and *Dr. Dobb's Journal* started to spring up. Again, to help people know how to program these wee beasties, source code was written and shared through these magazines and bulletin-board systems.

In 1984, Richard Stallman started the Free Software Foundation to encourage the creation of free software and with the goal of creating an entire open-source operating system called *GNU*.

Finally, in 1991, a young university student named Linus Torvalds decided that he wanted a powerful operating system that could be distributed easily, and that he was going to give it away. Linus and a band of intrepid programmers made what most people call *Linux*.

Today, there are more than 250,000 people working on more than 25,000 projects on a site called SourceForge, `sourceforge.net`. With the aid of low-cost hardware, high-speed networking, and the energy of volunteers, computer science moves forward.

(Jon "maddog" Hall is the executive director of Linux International, `li.org`.)

TIP OF THE DAY In many ways, Richard Stallman and the GNU project are as responsible for Linux as Linus Torvalds and his volunteer programmers. The vast majority of the software you get with a Linux distribution comes from the GNU folks. And the GNU software license, the GPL, is the basis for most Linux software licenses. So, it's no wonder Stallman wants the world to call Linux GNU/Linux instead. And in a more fair universe, it would be.

We don't want to confuse anyone, though, so we refer to it as plain-old Linux throughout this book. But let's not forget the other half of Linux, the folks at the GNU project who have donated so much time to keep software free. Read more about them at `gnu.org`.

DOWNLOAD OF THE DAY Gentoo is the "build-it-yourself" Linux distribution. Download a small base installation, and then add the components you want automatically. Free for x86, PowerPC, Sparc, and Sparc64 systems from `gentoo.org`.

POLL: Is now a good time to get into tech?

81% Yes

19% No

TODAY'S FOCUS: Advanced Linux

FIRST COMPUTER BUG

The first discovery of a live computer bug was made on this day in 1945. Computer programmer Grace Murray Hopper found a moth in Relay #70, Panel F, of the Harvard University Mark II Aiken Relay Calculator. Hopper and her assistants removed the critter with a pair of tweezers, and computer operations were resumed. The insect was put on display at the Naval Museum in Dahlgren, Virginia, and is now at the National Museum of American History in the Smithsonian Institution.

Related Web site `www.lewhill.com/firstcomputerbug.html`

Building the Linux Kernel

Compiling your own kernel is a major rite of passage for any aspiring Linux wizard, and it's easier than you might think. Start by reading up on the process in Brian Ward's Linux Kernel HOWTO: `www.linux.org/docs/ldp/howto/Kernel-HOWTO.html`.

The latest version of the kernel source code is kept at the Linux Kernel Archives, `kernel.org`. After you download and unpack the sources, you're ready to configure them for compiling.

If you're in X, type **`make xconfig`** to pop up a graphical interface to the configuration process. On the command line, use **`make menuconfig`** instead. Step through all the settings in the Kernel configuration dialog box. In most cases, the defaults are fine.

- Be sure to select the proper processor. Compiling for the right processor can speed Linux up considerably.
- Enable loadable module support and turn on the kernel loader module. It automatically loads support for hardware on demand—very handy.
- Include support for all the file systems you'll be using.
- You'll almost certainly load sound-card support as a module.
- Leave Kernel hacking off. You're doing enough hacking for now.

After you've worked through all the settings, save and exit. You're ready to move on to the compilation phase. Type the following command. Your system will spend some time churning on the last bit. That's the actual compilation process.

```
make dep; make clean ; make bzImage
```

After you've completed the compile, configure the modules:

```
make modules ; make modules_install
```

If everything went well, you're ready to copy the files to their rightful places and restart.

There are many more details in the HOWTO. I strongly suggest you read it before you attempt this yourself. I've had to leave a lot out for brevity's sake.

Some might say that arcana like this keep Linux from being a mainstream operating system. Perhaps, but there's no other OS in the world that gives you access to its source code, let alone letting you rebuild it to suit yourself. That's one of the things that makes Linux so exciting for true geeks. Want to take the rite of passage yourself? Go for it. It's a wonderful feeling when Linux boots up on a kernel you've just built.

 TIP OF THE DAY   Learn what a kernel is, how it works, and how the Linux kernel got to be the way it is. Read the Linux Kernel Book at `kernelbook.sourceforge.net`.

 DOWNLOAD OF THE DAY   Looking for a Linux with a built-in stateful inspection firewall and hardened Linux kernel? Who isn't? Astaro is a high-security Linux distro, free from `astaro.com`.

SEPTEMBER 9

TODAY'S FOCUS: Advanced Linux

FIRST PLANETARIUM

The first planetarium in the U.S. opened to the public on this day in 1930. The Adler Planetarium in Chicago, Illinois, was founded by Max Adler, a senior officer and shareholder in Sears, Roebuck and Company. His planetarium was modeled after the work of German engineer Walther Bauersfeld, who in 1923 had developed an optical projection device that created the illusion of a night sky. Bauersfeld's machine projected light onto the inner surface of a dome in a hemispherical-shaped room. Today's planetariums are still based on the same scientific principles.

Related Web site www.adlerplanetarium.org

The Unix Shell

Unix users have a choice of a graphical interface, such as Windows or Mac, and a command line, such as DOS. For many tasks, the command line is faster and easier.

Just as in DOS, the Unix command line is really a program called a *command shell*. The shell accepts input from the user and acts on it. In Linux, the default shell is bash. In Mac OS X it's csh, pronounced "sea shell."

Both shells support a variety of commands. For example, ls is used to display a directory listing, cp to copy a file, mv to move or rename a file, and so on. You type these commands at the shell prompt, typically the percent sign:

```
% ls
```

One of the real strengths of Unix is that you can use the output of one program as the input of another. Unix gurus use the pipe character, |, to create commands like this:

```
% cat somefile.txt | grep "screen savers" | wc -l
```

This command counts the number of appearances of "screen savers" in the file somefile.txt by piping the output of cat into grep to search for the text, and then counting the number of lines grep outputs. Enter this line in the shell and it will respond with the line count:

```
% 6
```

You can also string multiple commands together in a text file to create very powerful shell scripts, something like DOS's BAT files on steroids.

Most shells offer many of the features of real programming languages such as if/then statements, loops, variables, and more.

There's a whole lot more you can do with shell scripts. For more information, read any good Unix reference or the man pages for your particular shell: % man bash for Linux, % man csh for Mac OS X.

TIP OF THE DAY Linux distributions are huge. A single install CD is often more than 600MB. A multi-CD distribution might weigh in at several gigabytes. Even if you have a fast connection to the Internet, it makes more sense to buy a CD.

You can get most Linux distributions for just a few dollars per disc from one of the following vendors. All of them return a portion of the profits to the distribution's creator.

- Best Linux CDs.com: bestlinuxcds.com
- Cheap*Bytes: cheapbytes.com
- Linux Central: linuxcentral.com
- Linux Mall: LinuxMall.com
- Tux CDs: tuxcds.com

DOWNLOAD OF THE DAY Many open-source purists prefer the Debian distribution of GNU/Linux, because it's a noncommercial operation maintained entirely by volunteers. Debian also has a reputation as a very robust and secure build, but it's not the easiest to install. Download a copy free from debian.org.

TODAY'S FOCUS: Advanced Linux

AMERICA REACHES OUT

Millions of people in the U.S. and around the world expressed grief, donated money, and followed news updates online when disaster struck on this day in 2001. News sites, chat rooms, and message boards were flooded after terrorists flew commercial jetliners into the World Trade Center in New York City and into the Pentagon in Washington, D.C. An online survivors' database was available almost immediately following the attacks. This was the most large-scale use of the Web in relation to a single event. More than $1.5 billion in private donations were made in response to 9/11, much of it contributed online.

Related Web sites   `libertyunites.org, networkforgood.org`

Linux Window Managers: KDE and Gnome

Linux's GUI is based on the X Window System, but you need to run something on top of X to provide the user interface. That's called a *window manager*. There are dozens of window managers for Linux. Here we look the two most popular.

KDE   KDE is the default choice for most new users. It's mature, powerful, and extremely stable. Moreover, it has that familiar Windows look and feel. The biggest problem with KDE is its large memory requirements. Don't try to use it with less than 128MB of RAM.

KDE is based on a GUI library called QT. The original QT license was not GPL, and that worried some vendors like Red Hat and Debian so much that they declined to distribute it. These groups promoted development of a fully open manager called Gnome.

Gnome   Gnome is based on the GTK libraries first created for Gimp and is 100% pure GPL. The conflict is yesterday's news now, because the QT libraries have been GPLd and KDE is now pure, too, but Gnome lives on.

Technically, Gnome is not a window manager, it's an architecture. The Gnome window manager is Sawfish, but most people call the Gnome/Sawfish combination simply Gnome.

Gnome's chief strength is the huge number of toys and geegaws and widgets written for it. The GTK libraries are very popular with developers, so a great many GUI apps are written for Gnome. The good news is that Gnome widgets will usually run in KDE, and vice versa.

TIP OF THE DAY   Macs have aliases. Windows has shortcuts. Unix uses links. They all mean the same thing. They're pointers to files that can be used as if they were the file itself.

To create a link in Unix-like operating systems, including OS X and Linux, use the `ln` command. The first parameter is the original file, the second the name of the link. So, to make a link to /etc/fstab called "file system table" type

```
ln /etc/fstab "file system table"
```

By default, `ln` makes hard links, but if you want to create a link for a folder, you'll have to make a symbolic link using the `-s` parameter:

```
ln -s origfolder fauxfolder
```

To remove a link, just delete it:

```
rm fauxfolder
```

The original remains.

DOWNLOAD OF THE DAY   Learn all about gravity, momentum, and stuff with Spaced Penguin, a free online game from `bigideafun.com/penguins/arcade/spaced_penguin/info.htm`. But watch out, it's addictive.

POLL: What kind of computers should the government use?

25% Windows

13% Mac

43% Linux

19% Other

SEPTEMBER 11

TODAY'S FOCUS: Advanced Linux

NETSCAPE INTRODUCED

Mosaic Communications unveiled a new Web browser called Mosaic Netscape at a trade show in Atlanta on this day in 1994. Netscape Navigator 1.0 shipped the following December. It was the dominant browser until Microsoft's Internet Explorer gained ground in the late '90s. AOL acquired Netscape for $4.2 billion in stock in November, 1998. In 2002, Netscape sued Microsoft for alleged monopolistic practices, saying Bill Gates and company quashed competition.

Related Web site   `www.netscape.com`

MP3 on Linux

By Chris DiBona

Whether you're playing or encoding MP3s (or both at once), you'll probably find that Linux is the smoothest platform out there for digital music.

Encoding   There are any number of programs that are terrific at converting your CD collection to MP3s. I recommend Grip (`www.nostatic.org/grip`), a very powerful and simple-to-operate little program by Mike Oliphant.

Grip has a convenient setting that allows it to start encoding the moment you pop a CD into the drive. It will eject the CD when it's done ripping, which makes short work of encoding a collection. For the more advanced user, Grip will even fill a SQL database with song information that can be used by a number of playback applications.

Playback   Many Linux users will agree that XMMS, from `xmms.org`, is far and away the best choice for playing back MP3s and other sound files under Linux. XMMS is a highly configurable and expandable player that sounds and looks great. Check out some of the plug-ins, too.

Linux and Portable MP3 Players   You don't have to give up your portable MP3 player with Linux, either. Through Linux's USB support or via a PC Card adapter, a user can easily move songs from a laptop or desktop to the player. There are a few caveats, however. A few players will take songs only from their own file-transfer software, which is usually Windows only. Also, it might be difficult to upgrade a player's firmware using Linux.

Ogg Vorbis   MP3 has several troubling patent issues for the open-source developer. In response to these issues, several developers created the open Ogg Vorbis format, `vorbis.com`. An Ogg file is not unlike an MP3 file in that it has a compressed audio stream inside it. Among its advantages is multichannel support, which can't be done in MP3 files. Some say that, given identical file sizes, Ogg files have superior sound quality.

That said, Ogg is still immature. Only one portable music player that I know of—Iomega's HipZip—can play Ogg files, but the format is definitely worth watching.

(Chris DiBona works for OSDN. His personal home page can be found at DiBona.com.)

TIP OF THE DAY   *Daemons* are Linux processes that run the entire time the machine is on. As with Windows boxes, these background servers pose a security risk.

Check `/etc/inetd.conf` and your system's rc/init scripts to see what's running. Services you should consider removing include imapd, talkd, popd, rusersd, shell, login, netstat, and systat. Replace FTP and Telnet with secure versions. Turn off SMTP, DNS, and NFS. In general, if you don't know what a service does, or you're not using it, disable it.

DOWNLOAD OF THE DAY   Use GKrellM to graphically monitor system resources and activity in X. Download a free copy from `freshmeat.net/projects/gkrellm`.

TODAY'S FOCUS: Advanced Linux

FIRST DIESEL CAR

The first diesel automobiles in the U.S. were unveiled on this day in 1977. General Motors' Oldsmobile 88 and 98 models were the first cars to feature the new engine. The device was first conceived in 1893 by German inventor Rudolph Diesel. Diesel's creation compressed air (rather than an air-fuel mixture) to a very high pressure, thus creating a higher compression ratio and, in turn, greater fuel efficiency. Although diesel is more efficient, it also gives off higher emissions than today's unleaded gasolines.

Related Web site `www.dieselnet.com`

Linux for Windows Users

Believe it or not, you can run a PC without using Microsoft products. The alternative is Linux. Now, admittedly Linux isn't as polished, doesn't work with as many devices, and is not as universal as Windows. But on the other hand, it's free, it's very reliable, and Linux users can be every bit as productive as Windows users, maybe even more so.

Getting Started   The key to having a good experience with the Linux install is preparation. Check to see whether your current hardware is compatible with your Linux distribution. Visit the Web site of the Linux distribution for a hardware compatibility list. Keep an eye out for Linux drivers for your video card, printer, and USB devices.

I recommend installing Red Hat or Linux-Mandrake. Both have excellent installers and are most widely supported. (Mandrake *is* Red Hat with some additional software and configuration tweaks.)

Linux is easiest to install on a dedicated machine. If you're going to take the plunge, go all the way: Delete Windows and use Linux exclusively.

Choose KDE as your desktop environment. It's the most like Windows, so you'll be least disoriented. It comes with configuration tools such as KPPP that will make it much easier to get online.

Linux Software   After your operating system is installed and running, it's time to find the software you need. For graphics it's The GIMP, a handy and powerful open-source image editor that's every bit as powerful as Photoshop. And a lot cheaper. It's free, in fact.

You'll need an office suite, too. KDE comes with KOffice, so give that a try. Other good candidates include the free OpenOffice (`openoffice.org`), Sun's StarOffice, $75

from `staroffice.com`, and gobe's gobeProductive, $125 from `gobe.com`. All of them will read and write Microsoft Office file formats so you can collaborate with your Windows-addled brethren.

If there's a Windows program you can't duplicate in Linux, you might be able to run it using Wine (`winehq.org`), a Windows emulator that also comes with Linux.

In fact, that might be the hardest thing to get used to in switching from Windows to Linux: Linux comes with everything you need for next to nothing. The only price you pay is the effort of learning a new way of doing things. But I promise that effort is worthwhile.

 TIP OF THE DAY   The biggest problem Windows users have with Linux is installing software. FreshRPMS.net makes it easy to install a program by creating ready-to-run builds of popular programs for Red Hat and Mandrake users.

DOWNLOAD OF THE DAY   Xearth puts the world on your desktop. Free.

 Windows: `hewgill.com/xearth`

 Mac: `www.dtek.chalmers.se/~d2linjo/mac_xearth.html`

 Unix: `www.cs.colorado.edu/~tuna/xearth`

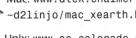

POLL: Will Linux kill the Mac?

27% Yes

73% No

TYPEWRITER RIBBON PATENTED

The first typewriter ribbon was patented by George Anderson of Memphis, Tennessee, on this day in 1886. Although the first typewriter was developed by Christopher Sholes and his associates nearly 20 years earlier, the concept of the ribbon hadn't yet been introduced. Instead, carbon paper was used to create letters on paper. The first commercially produced typewriter ribbon (essentially long, thin strips of carbon paper) was made by L.H. Rogers & Company. The ribbon was sold in cardboard boxes or cans of various design, which are considered collectors' items today.

Related Web site `mytypewriter.com`

Keep Tabs on Your Linux Box

By Woody Hughes

Ever wondered what's going on inside your Linux machine? With all the different services running at any given time, you might feel overwhelmed. Here are three tips to help you spy on your inner penguin.

Run Top Execute top from the command line to watch processes that currently run on your machine. If your machine gets bogged down, run top and take a look at what's eating the CPU cycles. It could be a runaway Netscape process or some other little devil that's causing your machine to run in low gear.

Keep Backups of Important config Files Keeping backups should be second nature for any Linux user. Config files, such as those located in the /etc directory, should have a backup in case things go wrong. Text editors, such as joe, automatically create a backup of whatever file you're editing. Joe then appends a tilde (~) to the file that you just edited. In this way, joe has created a backup file for you, in case you forget to create it yourself. A routine backup of the entire /etc directory is a good idea.

Is there a specific place to back up your important data? Not really, but backing up on a totally separate hard drive or partition is always a good idea.

Access Maintenance Mode Maintenance mode, or Single-User mode, allows a person to work in an environment where maintenance without interruption can be a reality. To access Maintenance mode, type **init 1** at the command line, or reboot, and when your LILO boot loader prompt appears, type **single** or **<label> single**, where <label> is the name of the kernel image that you assigned in your /etc/lilo.conf file. After pressing the Enter key, your machine will promptly boot into Maintenance mode.

(Woody Hughes is a former editor at Maximum Linux Magazine *and is a regular contributor to* The Screen Savers.*)*

TIP OF THE DAY Samba lets a Linux box provide file and print services to Windows machines using SMB and CIFS. If you don't already have a copy (and you most likely do), you can get the latest version free from `samba.org`.

You configure Samba using SWAT, the Samba Web Administration Tool, which comes with Samba. To access SWAT, launch Netscape and enter **localhost:901** in the address bar. Log in as root and proceed to configure your system. SWAT's online help will lead the way.

DOWNLOAD OF THE DAY Everybuddy is an X-based all-in-one messaging client for Linux. Supports AIM, ICQ, MSN, Yahoo! and Jabber. Free from `www.everybuddy.com`.

TODAY'S FOCUS: Advanced Web Design

PENICILLIN DISCOVERED

One of the most important medical breakthroughs in history occurred on this day in 1928. Sir Alexander Fleming, a Scottish bacteriologist, discovered a type of mold that could kill Staphylococcus, a dangerous bacterium. Sources argue just how the mold, named *Penicillium notatum*, found its way into Fleming's petri dish. Some say the Staph sample was contaminated by moldy bread. Others say a mold spore drifted in from a mycology lab downstairs. Regardless, the development of penicillin cured many previously fatal diseases, including syphilis, gangrene, and tuberculosis. Fleming won the Nobel Prize for physiology in 1945 and is considered the father of modern antibiotics.

Related Web site `cellsalive.com/pen.htm`

Make an Imagemap

By Marina Chotzinoff

You've probably heard the term *imagemap* tossed about, and you've undoubtedly clicked on more than a few. Imagemaps are simply Web page images you can click. Different parts of the image can link to different pages.

So, how do these imagemaps work?

The image is placed in your Web page as any other image would be, except the image tag references a map that contains a list of coordinates for the clickable regions in the image. Each region is associated with a URL that the browser will go to when the region is clicked. Here's an example:

```
<IMG SRC="doggie.gif" USEMAP="#doggiemap"
BORDER=0>

<MAP NAME="doggiemap">
  <AREA SHAPE=POLY
  COORDS="29,71,  65,48,  44,36,  87,36"
  HREF="hats.html"
  ALT="hats">

  <AREA SHAPE=RECT
  COORDS="102,4,  156,116"
  HREF="coats.html"
  ALT="coat">

  <AREA CIRCLE=RECT
  COORDS="12,117,  69"
  HREF="collars.html"
  ALT="collars">
</MAP>
```

We start with a normal image tag, with one extra parameter, USEMAP. That points to the following MAP block, named `doggiemap`. This block can live anywhere on the page, even at the bottom.

The MAP defines three clickable regions, as described by the three AREA tags. The regions are a polygon (POLY), rectangle (RECT), and a CIRCLE. Polygons are described by a succession of point pairs, one pair for each vertex of the polygon. Rectangles have two coordinate pairs describing the upper-left and lower-right corners of the box. Circles are defined by a coordinate pair describing the center point and a single number describing the radius of the circle in pixels. I've added some extra spacing so you can see the coordinate groupings.

Then comes the URL to go when clicked. We've also included an ALT tag for each region. The ALT tag is a good idea because the user can see what's going to happen before she clicks.

It's simpler than it looks, but trust me: You don't want to make an imagemap by hand. Measuring all those coordinates is exactly what a computer was made to do. Most high-end Web design software, such as Dreamweaver and FrontPage, has imagemap support built in. Or you can use shareware. We've got a good recommendation below.

TIP OF THE DAY You can download free trial versions of most of the top Web design programs. Use them to create all your imagemaps, and then uninstall. My favorite is Macromedia Dreamweaver for Macintosh and Windows, from `dreamweaver.com`. But watch out, after you try Dreamweaver, you might find it hard to give up.

DOWNLOAD OF THE DAY CoffeeCup's Image Mapper makes it easy to create imagemaps. Try it free or buy it for $20 from `coffeecup.com/mapper`.

SEPTEMBER 15

TODAY'S FOCUS: Advanced Web Design

"RABBIT EAR" INVENTOR BORN

Early television viewers (and those of us today who refuse to pay for cable) are indebted to Marvin P. Middlemark, born in Old Westbury, New York, on this day in 1919. The self-made millionaire developed the "rabbit ear" TV antenna, along with many other patents for consumer electronics between 1956 and 1968. Other inventions included a water-powered potato peeler and rejuvenating tennis ball machine. Middlemark died in 1989, leaving behind a bizarre collection of belongings, including stained-glass windows of Marilyn Monroe and Albert Einstein and 1,000 pairs of woollen gloves.

Related Web site   antennaweb.org

Add a Message Board to Your Site

There are two ways to add a message board to your Web site. You can do it yourself or have someone else do it for you. To do it yourself, you need a Web host that supports CGI and a programming language such as Perl, and you'll need some strong Unix skills, or the willingness to learn them.

Here are four free Perl-based message-board programs that have stood the test of time. Each of them has its own fervent partisans.

- vBulletin: vbulletin.org
- phpBB: phpbb.com
- Ikonboard: ikonboard.com
- Discus: discusware.com

After looking at all four, and installing two, I chose to go with a commercial product called UBB.Threads from infopop.com for my site, leoville.com, and I'm very happy with it.

Infopop also hosts message boards, and that's the easy way to do it. For between $30 and $40 a month, Infopop will run the message board for you. You run it as you want to, but you never have to worry about the technical side. Bravenet (bravenet.com) does something similar for free, but you'll have to put up with banner ads. Both services link seamlessly from your site.

Online communities can drive traffic to your site and keep it there, but it's not as easy as installing the software and waiting for people to move in. Making a great online community takes time, energy, and a willingness to get involved. But providing a place for people to gather can be one of the most satisfying things you can do with your Web page.

TIP OF THE DAY   The best way to password-protect a site is to use Apache's .htaccess files. You'll need Telnet access to your host and some familiarity with Apache config files. Read all about it at javascriptkit.com/howto/htaccess.shtml.

The next best way is with a CGI script. If your host offers CGI access and a language such as Perl or Python, it's fairly simple to write one of these, or download a program from Matt's Script Archive, scriptarchive.com. Last time I looked, Matt had more than 100 Perl password scripts.

Finally, the easiest—and least secure—way to protect a page is with a little JavaScript. If you're not worried about getting hacked, JavaScript is the way to go. JavaScript Kit has several good JavaScript password programs you can cut and paste into your code, at javascriptkit.com/script/cutindex6.shtml.

DOWNLOAD OF THE DAY   Webpad is a handy little program for editing HTML. Free to try, $19 to buy, from dzsoft.com.

POLL: Do subliminal Web ads scare you?

46% No

34% Yes

20% Too frightened to answer

TODAY'S FOCUS: Advanced Web Design

VAPOR LAMP PATENTED

The predecessor to the fluorescent lamp was patented on this day in 1901. Peter Cooper Hewitt improved upon Edison's incandescent bulb by developing a glass lamp chamber that was illuminated by gas, usually mercury vapor. Hewitt's early lamp was much more energy efficient than previous bulbs, and therefore less expensive to operate. However, it produced only a strange blue-green light, making it impractical for everyday use. The vapor lamp was widely used by photographers and moviemakers, however, who used only black-and-white film at the time.

Related Web site   www.howstuffworks.com/fluorescent-lamp.htm

Putting Sound on Your Web Page

Before you put audio files onto your Web site, consider download time, tonal quality, and your server's capabilities. And be sure you know what the file formats are. These are the most common audio formats.

MIDI   Pronounced "middy," MIDI is an acronym for musical instrument digital interface, a standard adopted by the electronic music industry for controlling devices that emit music.

MIDI music files are the most compact because they contain only the score for the music, not the music itself. The computer is responsible for synthesizing the music from the score. Depending on the quality of a computer's MIDI synthesizer, MIDI music ranges from teeth-gratingly annoying to merely cheesy.

WAV   WAV is the de facto sound file format for Windows, and thus for the Web. WAV files are actual sound recordings and can range in sound from CD quality to hissy warbling, depending on how the original was recorded. WAV files are not compressed, so all but the shortest sounds are too big for Web delivery.

MP3   MP3 sounds as good as WAV, but it's about 1/11 the size, thanks to compression. They're still pretty big for Web pages unless you know all your users will have broadband connections.

RealAudio   A highly compressed audio format designed to transfer quickly online. RealAudio files can either be downloaded entirely before playing, or streamed; that is, played back as they download. Quality varies depending on file size.

You can use a variety of HTML or JavaScript commands to embed any of these sounds into your Web page. The basic techniques include

- Linking to sound files using the `<a href="file">` tag.
- Autoplaying sound files using the `<meta>` tag.
- Embedding sound files using the `<Embed>` tag (Netscape specific)
- Adding background sound using the `<bgsound>` tag (IE specific)
- Adding sound via JavaScript

Check out Project Cool's Audio Zone, www.devx.com/projectcool/developer/audioz, for the specifics of using each of these techniques.

To further confuse matters, the World Wide Web Consortium is encouraging Webmasters to use the new `<object>` tag for embedding multimedia into Web pages. Read all about it at www.w3.org/TR/html4/struct/objects.html.

 TIP OF THE DAY   Lissa Explains It All was started by an 11-year-old girl to provide HTML help to kids who want to make their own Web sites. The site's not just for kids, though. Lissa Explains It All is a fine resource for beginning Web authors of all ages: lissaexplains.com.

 DOWNLOAD OF THE DAY   Crescendo is a streaming MIDI and MP3 player for Web sites. To download the Crescendo player, visit any Crescendo-enabled site (try tuxjunction.net if you like swing) and the player will download automatically. To add Crescendo to your site, visit the Crescendo-nator, liveupdate.com/addmusic/addmusic.html.

SEPTEMBER 17

TODAY'S FOCUS: Advanced Web Design

AIR FORCE FOUNDED

The United States Air Force was established as a separate entity on this day in 1947. Previously, the aviation division was part of the Army. The decision went into effect after months of negotiations by Congress and members of the armed forces. The previous July, President Truman had signed National Security Act of 1947, which called for an independent Air Force for "offensive and defensive air operations" and placed the Army, Navy, and Air Force on equal grounds under the Secretary of Defense. Today, the Air Force has more than 350,000 full-time, active personnel.

Related Web site `www.af.mil`

XML

By Charles Goldfarb

By now, everyone familiar with the Web knows that it's undergoing a radical change that is introducing wonderful services for users and amazing new opportunities for Web site developers and businesses.

The HyperText Markup Language (HTML) made the Web the world's library. Now its sibling, the Extensible Markup Language (XML), is making the Web the world's commercial and financial hub.

In the process, the Web is becoming much more than a static library. Increasingly, users are accessing the Web for Web pages that aren't actually on the shelves. Instead, the pages are generated dynamically from information available to the Web server. That information can come from databases on the Web server, from the site owner's enterprise databases, or even from other Web sites.

And that dynamic information needn't be served up raw. It can be analyzed, extracted, sorted, styled, and customized to create a personalized Web experience for the end user. To coin a phrase, Web pages are evolving into Web services.

For this kind of power and flexibility, XML is the markup language of choice. You can see why by comparing XML and HTML. Both are based on the Standard Generalized Markup Language (SGML), but look at the difference:

In HTML:
```
<p>P266 Laptop<br>Friendly Computer
Shop<br>$1438
```

In XML:
```
<product><model>P266
Laptop</model><dealer>Friendly Computer
Shop</dealer><price>>$1438</price></product>
```

Both of these might look the same in your browser, but the XML data is "smart" data. HTML tells how the data should look, but XML tells you what it means.

With XML, your browser knows there is a product, and it knows the model, dealer, and price. From a group of these, it can show you the cheapest product or closest dealer without going back to the server.

With that kind of flexibility, it's no wonder that we're starting to see a new Web of smart, structured information. It's a semantic Web in which computers understand the meaning of the data they share.

(Charles F. Goldfarb invented SGML, the basis of HTML. To find out more about XML, visit `xmlhandbook.com`*.)*

 TIP OF THE DAY   Using the HTML <meta> tag on your Web site can help search engines properly categorize you.

Use `<meta    name="keywords"    content="my keywords">` to list keywords for your site and `<meta name="description" content="my site description">` to define a site description.

Read   the   details   at   Search   Engine   Watch, `searchenginewatch.com/webmasters/meta.html`.

 DOWNLOAD OF THE DAY   Kurt Grigg offers many free and very cool DHTML applications you can paste into your Web pages at `www.btinternet.com/~kurt.grigg/javascript`. Try Silly Clock and Morph Spin. Wild.

POLL: Is the spirit of the Web dead?

49% Yes   51% No

TODAY'S FOCUS: Advanced Web Design

FIRST E-BOOK

The first Internet-only story by a major, bestselling author was made available for download on this day in 1993. Stephen King's short story, an excerpt from *Nightmares and Dreamscapes*, sold for $5 a copy. Users had to email an online bookstore to download the work. King's book was available in stores the following month. In March 2000, the horror writer broke ground again when he published his first online novella, *Riding the Bullet*. The book was downloadable to e-book devices, Palm-based PDAs, or PCs.

Related Web site `www.stephenking.com`

Set Up Your Own Spycam

All you need to give people all over the world a peep into your so-called life is a computer with a camera, a Net connection, a Web page, and some software.

If image quality is not paramount, get an inexpensive USB Webcam. They're easy to install, and they cost less than $100. You can also use your camcorder if you've got a way to get the video into the computer, either a video capture card or a FireWire connector. The camcorder will give you much better images.

Before the world can watch your mug on the Net, you need to snag some server space. If you've already got a Web page, you're set. Otherwise, set up a page at one of the free Web hosts or with your ISP. You'll need FTP access to the site for uploading your images. And if your spycam site gets popular, be prepared for big-time bandwidth use.

Create a Web page on the site with a link to the local Webcam image. If you want the page to refresh every time there's a new image, use the following tag in the header:

```
<meta http-equiv="Refresh" content="30">
```

This command will cause most browsers to reload the page every 30 seconds.

Your spycam software should have FTP capability built-in. Configure it to upload an image at regular intervals—every 30 seconds is pretty typical. If you have lots of bandwidth and your users are interested in your *every* move, you can send a picture even more often. Change the `meta` tag to reflect the new interval. Some programs have additional features, such as time lapse and moving images. In most cases, they'll create the appropriate HTML for you.

You'll also want to add a witty caption to the image, plus the date and time. The program will update those automatically.

That's it. Turn it on and start showing the world the essence of you, at 30-second intervals. But make sure you make your bed first.

 TIP OF THE DAY Users can copy any image from any Web page just by right-clicking on it and selecting **Save Image As**. To protect the images on your site, disable right-clicking using JavaScript. Copy the code from `javascript.internet.com/page-details/protect-images.html` and paste it into your Web page. Users can get around the code by disabling JavaScript, but it's good enough to stop casual copying.

For a more robust solution, try digital watermarks from companies such as Digimarc, `digimarc.com`.

 DOWNLOAD OF THE DAY The best Webcam software for Windows is WebCam32 from Surveyorcorp, `surveyorcorp.com`. Try it free for 10 days, buy it for $39.95. It's what I used to capture this shot while I was writing this book.

210 days down - 155 to go

Arthur Cam - Mon Jul 01, 2002 - 09:01:43 PDT

SEPTEMBER 19

TODAY'S FOCUS: Advanced Web Design

ELECTRIC RANGE PATENTED

The "electroheater" was patented by George B. Simpson of Washington, D.C., on this day in 1859. Simpson's invention worked by passing electricity through wire coils to generate heat. Over the decades, the device was modified and refined by various other people. General Electric unveiled its first commercial model, the Calrod Electric Range, in 1928.

Related Web site www.ge.com

Twisted List: Lights, Camera, Web Site

By Martin Sargent

Don't let a complete lack of talent stand between you and international fame. All you need is a digital camera, server space, and a brilliantly simple idea, and you, too, can be a Web original! The following Web projects are living proof that a novel idea mixed with a lot of love can result in online magic.

How to Blend In (www. deanandnigel.co.uk) Dean and Nigel are two cheeky blokes with an unnatural talent for imitating everyday folk (the wigs and glasses don't hurt). The page takes a wee bit of time to load, but the payoff is tremendous.

Phone Bashing (www.phonebashing.com) Once again, the Brits take the cake when it comes to sociopolitical commentary in the form of hilarious destruction. Watch video clips of men in cell-phone costumes stealing mobile phones and smashing them to bits. Remarkably, no one shoots them.

Postal Experiments (improbable.com/airchives/ paperair/volume6/v6i4/postal-6-4.html) Question: What happens when you send an unwrapped wheel of rancid cheese through the trusty U.S. Postal Service? Answer: It arrives safely, and in a protective plastic bag.

Shopping 2001 (lightning.prohosting.com/ ~receipts/shopping2001) Formerly known as Derek's Big Web site of Wal-Mart Purchase Receipts, this site chronicles the mundane and strangely telling purchases of one Derek from Fargo.

The T.W.I.N.K.I.E.S. Project (www.twinkiesproject. com) A true Internet "classic," this site tests the limits of everyone's favorite genetically engineered alien puff pastry from Pluto.

Way Too Personal Ad Responses (www.waytoopersonal. com/responses.shtml) Placing a personal ad is like picking up guys in a bus station bar. Comb through the questionable responses one woman received to her innocent plea for companionship.

TheSpark.com Christian Rudder, editor-in-chief of TheSpark.com, is the unofficial king of online tomfoolery. So far, Christian's pseudoscientific exploits include the original Stinkyfeet Diaries, Stinkymeat 1 and 2, The Fat Project, and the devious but delightful Date My Sister Project.

The Couch (www.romansempire.com/couch/) TechTV's own Roman Loyola, Web producer for *The Screen Savers*, created this photo retrospective while working for *MacUser*, a company that sounds suspiciously like a walk-in clinic for people addicted to McDonald's cheeseburgers. It doesn't get much simpler or more entertaining than assembling photos of co-workers sitting on a couch. Or does it? It's hard to say.

 TIP OF THE DAY There are many ways to add chat to your Web site. I've seen everything from Flash-based chat servers to massive CGI programs. The easiest way is to set up a Java-based chat room through a provider such as Bravenet. Like all of Bravenet's services, the chat is ad supported and free to Webmasters and users. Check it out at bravenet.com/samples/chat.php.

 DOWNLOAD OF THE DAY The best spycam software for the Mac is Oculus. It runs on OS 9 and X and comes with special effects, clock, and weather plug-ins. Try free, buy for $20, from intlweb.com.

POLL: Should the government control the Web?

11% Yes   89% No

TODAY'S FOCUS: Advanced Web Design

AOL OFFERS ONLINE ACCESS

America Online said it would provide Internet access to its 500,000 subscribers on this day in 1993, becoming one of the first online services to do so. AOL began in 1985 as Quantum Computer Services, an Internet bulletin board system. Founder and CEO Steve Case changed the company's name to America Online in 1989. Four years after it announced it would offer Internet access, the company's subscriber base soared to nearly 10 million. Today, AOL has well over 30 million members.

Related Web site   `www.aol.com`

Twisted List: Top Five Hobby Sites

By Martin Sargent

Surfing the Web has become a major hobby for many an American. Here are the top five hobby and lifestyle sites, according to Jupiter Media Metrix. One will put a smile on your lips in the face of adversity, one could help you impress a date, and yet another could make you rich. These sites could change your life.

Chin Up, Kiddo (quickinspirations.com)   Quick Inspirations says, "Our site is chock-full of bite-sized entertainment that is guaranteed to put a smile on your face and a spring in your step." It works. I remember when my girlfriend dumped me, I lost my job, and got trapped under ice all in the same day. But later I went to Quick Inspirations and looked at a picture of a bird sitting on a pier and it really helped me put everything in perspective. Thanks, Quick Inspirations!

Eat More Food (foodtv.com)   *The Iron Chef, The Essence of Emeril, East Meets West*—if you're lucky enough to receive FoodTV on your local cable and have an interest in cooking and eating then you're probably familiar with these show titles. But even if you don't get the station, you can take advantage of the culinary wisdom the network imparts by logging on to the Web site.

Trace Your Roots (ancestry.com, rootsweb.com) The two most popular genealogy sites, according to a recent study, are RootsWeb.com and Ancestry.com. Actually, the two sites are in cahoots. At either site, you can search for the names of relatives, but the main goal of the two sites is to connect genealogists across the Web. So, if you upload your family tree, another genealogist might find a link between your tree and his, greatly expanding both of your trees.

Free Money (foundmoney.com)   Here's how it works: You type your name into the search box and the site tells you whether any money is owed to you through inheritances, refunds, and the like. But it tells you how to get the money only if you pay the $20 membership fee. Be careful, because many other people in the land might share the same name as you, and the free search cannot differentiate among like names.

TIP OF THE DAY   Add a guest book to your Web site. Microsoft's FrontPage has built-in guest book capabilities, but you have to use a Web host running the FrontPage extensions. Get a free guest book that works on any site, anywhere, from `theguest-book.com`. Don't want the banner ads? You'll have to pay. `Guestbook.mycomputer.com` charges $59/year for an ad-free guest book.

DOWNLOAD OF THE DAY   Create thumbnails of your images suitable for the Web with Easy Thumbnails, free for Windows from `fookes.com/ezthumbs`.

SEPTEMBER 21

TODAY'S FOCUS: Computer Projects

FIRST AMERICAN CAR UNVEILED

The first automobile built in the U.S. was taken for a spin on this day in 1893. Bicycle makers Charles and Frank Duryea showed off their creation on the streets of Springfield, Massachusetts. Two years after the inaugural test drive, Frank Duryea won the first American Automobile Race in Chicago.

Related Web site   `www.hfmgv.org`

Paint Your Computer

By Bobby Kinstle

Nearly all plastics found in computers are polycarbonate or lexan. Paints for polycarbonates will not stick to lexan, but lexan paint will stick to both materials. My favorite lexan paint is Pactra, made by Testors. I also like to use Faskolor, from Parma International, with my airbrush. Don't buy a paint made for metal: It will often melt plastic parts.

Most plastics are cast in molds coated with a waxy release agent that allows easy removal of the casting. Before you begin to paint, remove any residual release agent so that your paint will stick.

I prefer to spraypaint or airbrush plastic, being careful not to make water-based paints too thin. Lay the parts flat on cardboard or plastic. Spray back and forth over parts about 8–12 inches away from the pieces, using smooth and even strokes (closer with an airbrush). Start before reaching the part and follow through past the end. Repeat until you've applied two to five thin coats. New coats can be applied before an old coat is completely dry.

Plastic paints take about three days to fully polymerize. Be careful handling parts, and wait for the paint to fully dry. Your patience will pay off.

Protect your new creation with a coat of acrylic spray enamel, available in glossy or matte finishes. Consider applying a clear lacquer coat to high-wear areas such as your laptop. Lacquer is a lot of work.

Apply five to seven coats, waiting for each to dry before reapplying. Wet sand with a 1,500–2,000 grit sandpaper, recoat, and hand polish to a new-car shine. Get a high shine using automotive carnauba wax (but don't plan on touching the surface afterward). Never use a silicone wax on your work (or your car, for that matter).

Feel free to experiment with your own techniques. Some of my biggest mistakes end up looking great afterward. There will always be small imperfections, but only you will notice.

(Bobby Kinstle's customized cases can be viewed online at Applefritter.com.)

TIP OF THE DAY   **Q:** I've accumulated a small collection of 2.5-inch laptop hard drives. Do you know whether there are adapters that will allow me to install them into desktop computers? —Kevin via email

A: Notebooks use 2.5-inch IDE drives with special connectors that carry both data and power. You'll need to purchase an adapter to connect to the desktop's IDE cable and a power tail. The drive also will need a special mount to fit into the 3.5-inch drive bays on your PC. TechCraft has the adapters and mounting kits at `www.computerplug.com/access_mountingTech.htm`.

DOWNLOAD OF THE DAY   Manage your aquarium with Maquarium from Everyday Software. Free to try, $12 to buy, from `everydaysoftware.net/maquarium`.

For Windows, try Aquarium Manager, free from `fishlinkcentral.com`, or the more up-to-date (and more expensive) Marine Fish and Mini-Reef Support Program, from `micromarinesoftware.com`.

TODAY'S FOCUS: Computer Projects

NEPTUNE DISCOVERED

The second farthest planet in our solar system was spotted on this day in 1846. German astronomer Johan G. Galle found the celestial body after only an hour of searching. Before 1845, Uranus was thought to be the farthest planet from the sun. But Cambridge mathematician, John Adams, hypothesized that another planet was causing Uranus' irregular orbit. Another astronomer, Urbain LeVerrier, published a similar theory, and went on to determine the approximate size and shape of Neptune. LeVerrier then asked Galle to search for the planet, which was only one degree off from LeVerrier's calculations.

Related Web site `solarsystem.nasa.gov`

Climb Your Family Tree

By Frederick S. Sherman

People who are interested in genealogy happily spend their time trying to identify their ancestors and learn about the places and conditions in which those ancestors lived. Modern computers and software effectively keep track of what they have learned and where they learned it. And with the Internet and email, it's easy to share this hobby with others who are interested in the same families, places, and events all over the world.

Here are some tips for those of you just getting started:

Start at the Beginning Visit Cyndi's List, `cyndislist.com`. This site has more than 126,700 links to sites for genealogists. Click on **Are you new to genealogy?** to get a list of Web sites to get you started. The National Genealogical Society, `ngsgenealogy.org`, is also perfect for beginners. Select **Learning Center** and then **Getting Started**.

After you know some interesting tidbit about your family tree, find out whether anybody else knows the same fact at RootsWeb, `rootsweb.com`. The RootsWeb mailing list is the perfect place to find surnames or to locate places (usually counties in the United States).

Free Databases The Internet provides extensive databases for locating ancestors, but these help only if you already know enough to recognize your ancestor when you see a record containing his or her name. Here are three free sites:

- FamilySearch (`familysearch.com`) has been built up over the decades, partly by extraction from official Latter Day Saints or government records, and partly by collecting information sent in by members of the church.

- The American Family Immigration History Center (`ellisislandrecords.org`) offers access to records generated during the arrival of immigrants and others who entered the United States through Ellis Island between 1892 and 1924. Successful use of these records requires some prior knowledge of name changes adopted by your immigrant ancestors.

- The Bureau of Land Management's General Land Office Records site (`glorecords.blm.gov`) presents information about land patents issued to individuals by the U.S. government between 1820 and 1908. It's mostly for the Western states, but goes as far east as Ohio and Alabama.

(Rick Sherman is the director of research for the California Genealogical Society.)

 TIP OF THE DAY Turn your family tree into a coffee-table book at `mypublisher.com`. $29.95 for a 10-page book, $3 for each additional page. We received our book just three days after placing our order, and it's beautiful.

 DOWNLOAD OF THE DAY Ancestry Family Tree genealogy software supports photos, generates HTML for creating Web pages, and prints reports in multiple formats. Free. Includes one-week access to ancestry.com's database. `aft.ancestry.com`.

POLL: Should NASA subsidize itself with advertising?

68% Yes

32% No

TODAY'S FOCUS: Computer Projects

FIRST NUCLEAR AIRCRAFT CARRIER

The first nuclear-powered aircraft carrier was launched in Newport, Virginia, on this day in 1960. The *USS Enterprise* held 86 planes and nearly 5,800 crew members, making it the largest warship in the world. The ship was 1,120 feet long, 250 feet wide, and was powered by eight nuclear reactors. Because it did not need to carry its own fuel, there was more room on board for aviation fuel and weapons. Three years after its maiden voyage, *Enterprise* and other nuclear vessels made a nonstop voyage around the world to demonstrate the benefits of nuclear power.

Related Web site `www02.clf.navy.mil/enterprise`

Landscape Design

By Diana Rathbone

Most of us can't afford to hire a professional landscape designer, but it's hard to visualize what you'll need for a major project. Software is a great tool for do-it-yourself gardeners, letting you experiment with different designs and plants before you begin to work.

Don't Start from Scratch Computer-savvy designers will enjoy creating a schematic design of a house and garden. The rest of us will probably prefer to choose from the selection of ready-made houses provided in a software package.

While using Sierra Home's Complete 3D LandDesigner, I chose a Cape Cod cottage to represent my San Francisco Victorian, rather than deal with the program's confusing wizard.

Save yourself some headaches by restricting surrounding structures to the area of the house you want to work with.

Simplify the design process by scanning a photo of the area you'd like to landscape into the software. By using a picture of the shady side of my house, I got a better idea of how the area would actually look with each of my changes, and I was able to get started right away.

Get Help Choosing Plants CD garden encyclopedias provide a good description and picture of each plant. You can sort the plants into categories. By choosing "shade lovers," I was able to develop a list of plants that will thrive when planted at the side of my house.

I did find, however, that the Sunset Garden book is more inclusive and easier to navigate than the CDs.

Web Sites Use the Internet to look up plants and landscaping advice:

- BBC Online: Gardening (`www.bbc.co.uk/lifestyle/gardening`) has a great description of how to make a flower bed.
- Garden Design (`nzdesigns.co.nz/garden`) is a New Zealand site with lovely photos and excellent step-by-step instructions for garden design.
- Michael Weishan's World of Gardening (`garden-worksonline.com`) has extremely practical advice about all gardening matters, including design.

(Diana Rathbone is a garden columnist for the San Francisco Chronicle.*)*

 TIP OF THE DAY Autumn doesn't mean it's time to give up gardening. Suite101 has a host of autumn gardening tips at `www.suite101.com/subjectheadings/contents.cfm/10156`. So does the About.com Gardening section, `gardening.about.com/cs/msub114`.

Get ready for holiday decorating with pots of Euphorbia pulcherrima, more commonly known as the humble poinsettia. Find everything you need to know about making this plant thrive at The Poinsettia Pages, `www.urbanext.uiuc.edu/poinsettia`.

 DOWNLOAD OF THE DAY Design Your Own Railroad helps you plan your railroad layout before you begin to build it. HO, N, Z, O, OO, S, or G scale. Free for Macintosh and DOS from `www.abracadata.com/0201Free.shtml`.

 Windows users get CATrain, free from `membres.lycos.fr/catrain`.

TODAY'S FOCUS: Computer Projects

FIRST AMERICAN NEWSPAPER

The first newspaper in the British colonies was published by Benjamin Harris in Boston, Massachusetts, on this day in 1690. *Publick Ocurrences, Both Foreign and Domestic* was printed on three pages of 6-inch×10-inch paper, and first sold at the London-Coffee-House. The periodical was considered so offensive by the government, it was banned after its first edition. In particular, officials bristled at the way Indian allies had treated French captives during the French and Indian War. Harris was a former publisher of Whig books, and had fled England with his family four years earlier for publishing objectionable political material.

Related Web site `www.historybuff.com`

Science Projects for Kids

By Michelle Von Wald

Do you remember grade school, when you could design experiments that exploded in order to learn more about science? Well, don't despair. You can re-create those carefree, budding scientist days with these super-cool science project kits you can buy online.

Cat-A-Pults (`www.exploratoriumstore.com/catapults.html`) For only $40, you can create a complex chain reaction involving a foam cat flying through the air. This toy was invented by an MIT artist known for starting large-scale chain reactions.

Flying Things (`shop.store.yahoo.com/explo/flyingthings.html`) Learn how to build devices that twirl, spin, and glide through the air. Discover more about the atmosphere that surrounds our planet and about the role of air pressure in keeping planes (both paper and 747s) aloft. It's only $12.99.

Dark Shadows (`shop.store.yahoo.com/explo/darkshadows.html`) Measure the diameter of the Earth using a shadow. Kids learn about optics and astronomy, including why the moon changes shape over the course of a month. It's only $12.99.

Outrageous Ooze (`www.exploratoriumstore.com/outrageousooze.html`) Ever wonder how plastics are made? Create exploragoo, polyester used in clothing, and fake-it-til-you-make-it jewels. It's $15.95.

Sparks & Zaps Totally Shocking (`www.exploratoriumstore.com/sparksandzaps.html`) Discover the science behind static. It's fun and will only set you back $15.95.

Build & Erupt Your Own Volcano (`www.exploratoriumstore.com/buileryourow.html`) Everything is included. All you need is water to make your own exciting volcano and eruption. This kit costs $13.50.

Soccer Robot (`www.exploratoriumstore.com/soccerrobot.html`) If you don't have anybody to play soccer with, don't worry. You can build a partner for only $45.90.

Fog Blaster (`store.yahoo.com/explo/fogblaster.html`) Mimic a tornado, hurricane, or other naturally occurring vortices to create and shoot fog rings up to 14 feet. It's only $24.95.

Rocket Car (`www.exploratoriumstore.com/rocketcar.html`) Make your own rocket fuel to send your rocket into the air. Why not, it's only $22.50?

Flashin' Bracelets (`www.mpgwear.com/station/index.html`) For $15, you can wear a groovy-looking bracelet that looks like Doppler Radar.

TIP OF THE DAY The Internet can even teach you how to juggle. In fact, many geeks, including our own Laura Burstein, like to toss the Indian clubs between bouts with the computer. You can, too. Learn how at The Juggling and Unicycle Site, `juggler.ca`.

For more inspiration, view photos from the latest World Juggling Day at the International Jugglers' Association Web site, `juggle.org`. If you're diligent, you could be there next year.

DOWNLOAD OF THE DAY Download 300 quizzes in science for middle- and high-school students. Free for Windows from `the-planet-mars.com/freeware/download.html`.

POLL: Would you donate your brain to science?

47% Yes   53% No

TODAY'S FOCUS: Computer Projects

FIRST TELEVISED PRESIDENTIAL DEBATE

The first televised United States presidential debate was broadcast across the country on this day in 1960. Democratic Massachusetts Senator John F. Kennedy faced off with his opponent, Republican Vice President Richard Nixon, at WBBM-TV in Chicago. Studies later showed that four million voters made up their minds about the election while watching the telecast: Three million of them voted for Kennedy.

Related Web site `www.jfklibrary.org/history_day_2000_resources.html`

Teddy Borg

By Yoshi DeHerrera

Would you like to put a router inside a teddy bear? Who wouldn't?

We started by visiting the Teddy Borg project for inspiration: `draco.mit.edu/teddyborg`. Here's my shopping list:

- Teddy bear (get one big enough to hold the rest of the stuff, and be sure he's fireproof: It gets pretty hot with all those electrical components inside)
- Switch, hub, or router
- RJ-45 wall jack connectors
- CAT5 cable
- Wire 26awg
- Shrink-wrap tubing or electrical tape
- Soldering iron and solder
- X-acto knife (scalpel)
- Superglue
- Thread and needle (suture)
- Wire cutters
- Perforated blank circuit board
- CAT5 cable tester
- Soldering stand
- Plenty of candy

Open up the teddy by finding the seam where he is sewn together. Cut the seam, and pull out all the stuffing (save for later). Turn it inside out. Now open up the switch. We used a Linksys broadband router. Desolder the power connector and LED that will be relocated to the eyes. Use the wire to resolder them so they will reach.

Graft the RJ-45 connectors, LEDs, and power connector to the teddy. I used a small length of CAT5 wire attached to the RJ-45 wall connector as extensions.

Cut out the eyes to accept the LEDs. Glue the LEDs into the eyes with superglue (careful—I got stuck to the bear for a few terrifying minutes).

Install the switch in the teddy and use the saved stuffing to fill him back up. About two hours of work, and it's alive! Mwahahahaha.

CAUTION: Teddy Borg is a fire hazard. We don't use ours for real, and neither should you.

(Yoshi gets paid to do stuff like this on The Screen Savers.*)*

TIP OF THE DAY Put your family on your desktop by making custom wallpaper. First, open a painting program; Microsoft Paint comes with every version of Windows and will do just fine. Set the image size to your screen size. Press Ctrl+E and enter the height and width. Be sure the pixel units are selected.

Now open your family photos, copy them, and paste them into your wallpaper image to create a montage. When you have it just as you want it, save the file as a 24-bit bitmap in your Windows directory. Remember the filename!

To select your new wallpaper, open the Display Properties control panel, click the **Desktop** tab, and choose your file in the Background window. Nice job!

DOWNLOAD OF THE DAY Put a potted plant on your computer desktop with DeskSoft's DesktopPlant. Choose from an azalea, maple tree, cactus, or philodendron, or grow all four. But be sure to water and fertilize your plant or it'll croak. Your plant will also die within 30 days if you don't buy the software. Talk about blackmail. $10 per plant at `www.desksoft.com/DesktopPlant.htm`.

TODAY'S FOCUS: Computer Projects

FIRST PASSENGER TRAIN

The first locomotive to regularly transport people and freight began service on this day in 1825. The train, dubbed "Locomotion No. 1," was operated by the Stockton & Darlington line and traveled 21 miles from Shildon to Stockton in County Durham, England. The steam engine pulled 34 wagons and one passenger coach. The railway service was the brainchild of George Stephenson, who was the first to establish a regular timetable for his train service.

Related Web site   `www.trainweb.com`

Computer Construction Secrets

Building your own PC probably won't save you any money, but you can pick exactly the parts you want, and you'll learn a whole lot about how computers work. Here are a few tips to get you started.

Shopping To save money, buy all your parts online—I use `pricewatch.com` to find the best price—except the case. Shipping costs make it smarter to buy that at a local store.

Workspace   Find a table or bench that is well-lit and free of clutter. If you have to commandeer the kitchen table, so be it, but be sure you won't have to move everything for dinner. Look for a space you can occupy for a day or two without interruption.

The parts you'll handle are very sensitive to static electricity. If static is a problem in your area, purchase a grounding wrist strap at your local electronics store. Spraying carpet with a diluted mixture of fabric softener and water (1 part softener to 10 parts water is about right) will also cut static.

The Right Tools   As for tools, we all have our favorites. I use a small Craftsman power screwdriver. Roger prefers a manual screwdriver with interchangeable bits, and Patrick actually spent a few paychecks on a set of extreme screwdrivers. All you absolutely need is a Phillips screwdriver, although a "small-part-grabbing-device" or a screwdriver with a magnetized tip might save you a few scraped knuckles.

Avoid Shorts   A common pitfall when installing motherboards is using too many screw mounts in the case. Be very careful to match the mounts with the motherboard's screw holes. If you have an extra mount touching the motherboard, it could short-circuit and destroy it.

Don't Panic   It's rare that your new PC will work right the first time. That's okay. Go through the system and double-check your work. The number one reason a home-built PC won't boot is improper drive connections. Be sure your CPU and memory are snug in place, too. And you did remember to connect the keyboard, didn't you?

TIP OF THE DAY   Make temporary tattoos with the Inkjet Temporary Tattoo Kit from Papilio. It includes 8 tattoo sheets, 8 sheets of nonstick paper, special adhesive, and foam pads for $16.95. `papilio.com/inkjet_tattoo.htm`

Or try Temporary Tattoo Paper from Bel Decal. It includes 5 sheets of water slide tattoo paper, plus 5 sheets of adhesive, for $19.95. `beldecal.com/tattoo_paper.cfm`

DOWNLOAD OF THE DAY   My son Henry loves mazes. Now I never run out with Mazecreator. Create mazes from any image, free from `mazecreator.com`. Or visit `freemazes.com` for onscreen mazes of amazing complexity.

POLL: Whom would you like to design your next computer?

12% Arthur C. Clarke

25% Isaac Asimov

14% William Gibson

48% Dr. Seuss

TODAY'S FOCUS: Computer Projects

FATHER OF SUPERCOMPUTING BORN

Seymour Cray, founder of the Cray Computer Company, was born in Chippewa Falls, Wisconsin, on this day in 1925. In the 1950s, the electrical engineer worked on UNIVAC, the first commercial digital computer. In 1972, he founded Cray Research. The company's first system, the Cray 1, was installed at Los Alamos National Laboratory for $8.8 million. The machine performed 160 million floating-point operations per second and had a one million-word memory. Cray died in a car accident in October 1996.

Related Web site www.cray.com

Twisted List: Saddest Online Museums

By Martin Sargent

The Internet is rife with wonderful online museums that are a precious resource for scholars of every stripe. But here are five online museums that are of no legitimate benefit to anyone.

Toilet Seat Museum (unusualmuseums.org/toilet) Barney Smith has decorated more than 600 toilet seats over the past 30 years. One appears to be devoted to Montel Williams. Another features the Pyramids at Giza. Yet another is an ode to the Kennedy Space Center. His garage has long served as his toilet seat museum, and now he's taken his commodious collection online.

Toilet Paper Museum (nobodys-perfect.com/vtpm) Barney Smith's museum is like the Guggenheim compared to The Virtual Toilet Paper Museum. The museum curator has actually posted photos of every brand of toilet paper imaginable, as well as artworks that depict or incorporate toilet paper.

Lucky for us, the museum is expanding. According to the curator: "We've been expending considerable time, effort, and expense scouring the darkest corners of the globe to locate and acquire wondrous specimens as have rarely been seen by mankind." Hooray.

Toaster Museum (toaster.org) Did you know that the word *toast* comes from the Latin Torrere, which means to scorch or burn? Or that the ancient Egyptians started toasting their leavened bread not because it's a delicious morning treat, but rather because it lasts longer if cooked? You would have if you'd spent any time at The Cyber Toaster Museum! Lots of pictures of toasters from throughout the 20th century.

Becky's Bananas (beckymartz.com) Becky's online museum specializes in banana stickers, of which she has amassed hundreds, but also includes her collection of 72 different broccoli bands and 102 asparagus bands. She recently met with 18 other banana sticker collectors at a mini-convention in Munich, Germany. That's all I care to say about this troubling matter.

Navel Lint (feargod.net/fluff.html) Graham Barker has been collecting his own navel fluff for over two decades. It's all on display in his online museum. I apologize for bringing this to your attention.

TIP OF THE DAY Why wait for the *Sunday Times* when you can get your crossword puzzle fix online?

- Yahoo! Games provides a new crossword daily, as well as an archive of puzzles from the last two weeks: games.yahoo.com/games/login?game=Crossword
- MSNBC has a free daily crossword at msnbc.com/comics
- *The New York Times* charges $3.95 a month to play current puzzles, but the archived puzzles are free: nytimes.com/pages/crosswords

DOWNLOAD OF THE DAY Curling is Scotland's number one sport. Or something like that. Play it online at Virtual Curling, www.electricscotland.com/games/Curling.html. Hit the Escape key when the virtual bagpipes get to be too much.

Sandboard Slalom takes you shredding down the slopes at www.sandbox.com/swsandboard/pub-doc/home.jsp.

SEPTEMBER
28

TODAY'S FOCUS: Storage

SOLAR AIRPLANE INVENTOR BORN

Paul Beattie MacCready was born in New Haven, Connecticut, on this day in 1925. The Yale graduate developed sailplanes and other glider technology during the 1940s. In 1977, the physicist's "Gossamer Condor" made the first sustained, man-powered flight. Two years later, he led a team that created the "Gossamer Albatross," the first human-powered plane to cross the English Channel. In 1980, MacCready turned his attention toward photovoltaic cells and built the "Gossamer Penguin," the first solar-powered plane to make a successful flight. A year later, his "Solar Challenger" flew 163 miles at an altitude of 11,000 feet.

Related Web site   `members.aol.com/maccready`

Adding a Second Hard Drive

By Greg Melton

If your current hard drive is running out of space due to all those music downloads, or if you'd like a quick and painless way of performing weekly data backups, you might want to consider installing a second hard drive.

The process involves opening your computer's case, designating a master/slave, mounting a new drive, running a partition program, and then formatting the new drive to complete the process.

Open the Case   Before you open the case on your computer, be sure it's unplugged from the wall. Only after you've unplugged should you open it up. Consult your manual if you need help.

Check to make sure you have an extra space in which to insert the new hard drive, an extra connector on the IDE cable, and a free power supply adapter.

Configure the Jumpers   When using more than one hard drive on a computer, one of the drives must be designated a master and the other a slave. It's unpleasant terminology, I know, but that's what they're called. Fortunately, hard disks don't have feelings. Your computer boots from the master drive. Your new drive will be the slave.

Take a look at the top of the drive. On it, you should see a diagram showing how to configure the drive as the slave. Use tweezers to move the jumpers to the proper positions.

Mount the Drive   To install the new drive in your box:
1. Place the drive into an available drive bay.
2. Attach the drive with two screws on each side.
3. Connect the power tail to the back of the hard drive.
4. Connect the IDE ribbon cable to the back of the hard drive. Place the red wire closest to the power connector.

Partition   Before you use the drive, you will have to partition and format it. In Windows XP, log in as administrator and open the Computer Management tool in the Administrative Tools control panel. Click **Disk Management**. Your new drive should show up as Disk 1. Right-click it and select **New Logical Drive**. The New Partition Wizard will walk you through the rest of the process. The first time you open the new drive, Windows will offer to format it for you.

 TIP OF THE DAY   Move all your data from the old hard drive to the new one, or copy your stuff to a new PC with Aloha Bob's PC Relocator. Funny name, great product. $39.99, from `alohabob.com`.

 DOWNLOAD OF THE DAY   Drive Rescue helps you find and restore deleted or lost data. Free for Windows from `home.arcor.de/christian_grau/rescue`.

POLL: How often should you upgrade your computer?

1% Never

44% I follow Moore's law, about every 18 months

33% When it dies

22% When a snappy new product comes out

SEPTEMBER 29

TODAY'S FOCUS: Storage

FIRST MAN-MADE FIBER

Rayon was patented by William H. Walker, Arthur D. Little, and Harry S. Mork of Massachusetts on this day in 1902. The method for "making of cellulose esters" was developed to be used as an inexpensive replacement for silk. The fabric was originally called Viscose, but in 1924, the textile industry changed its name to "rayon" after the French word for "ray," a reference to the fabric's shiny quality. Although rayon is man-made, it's not truly synthetic: It's primarily made from wood pulp.

Related Web site `www.fabriclink.com/History.html`

Adding an External Hard Disk

By Greg Melton

Advanced computer users who need extra storage space can always add an extra hard drive, but cracking the computer case might be a little daunting to some. You might not have the space inside, either. Fortunately, there are many external storage solutions to choose from.

On Windows and Macintosh, external storage devices are plug and play: All you need to do is plug the device into the designated port on your computer, and the OS should automatically load the drivers required to operate it. If a new peripheral doesn't just plug and play, installing the software that comes with the device will usually automatically install the drivers.

Port Choices These days you have three choices for connecting external hard drives: USB 1.1, USB 2.0, and FireWire.

USB 1.1 is a standard that all computers come with, and it makes connecting new devices super easy. But it's slow, topping out at 1.5 megabytes per second.

USB 2.0 uses the same connectors as USB but is 40 times faster. This is a huge increase in the amount of data that you can move back and forth—but don't get too excited yet. You won't be able to take advantage of the speed increase USB 2.0 offers if your computer has the old USB chipset, and most still do. Luckily, USB 2.0 is backward compatible, which means you can still plug USB 2.0

devices into your current USB system, but you'll need to add a USB 2.0 adapter card before being able to take advantage of the speed increase.

FireWire or IEEE 1394 is an even better choice for hard drives. It's extremely fast at 50 megabytes per second. If your computer isn't equipped with a FireWire port, you can install a FireWire card on your machine. These have come down in price drastically over the last year and can be found anywhere from $40–$60.

 TIP OF THE DAY   Q: I always get static electricity in the area around my computer. How can I stop this? —Tim in Atlanta, Georgia

A: Carpeting is the big culprit here. Mix 1 part fabric softener with 10 parts water in a spray bottle. Spray the solution on the carpeting in your computer area. This should stop the static electricity.

By the way, if you ever open up your computer to remove or add components, you should always ground yourself with a static strap. This will prevent you from zapping sensitive components.

DOWNLOAD OF THE DAY WinBench measures the performance of a PC's graphics, disk, and video subsystems. Free from `etestinglabs.com/benchmarks/winbench/winbench.asp`.

POLL: Which would you rather lose?

12% Your wallet

88% Your cell phone

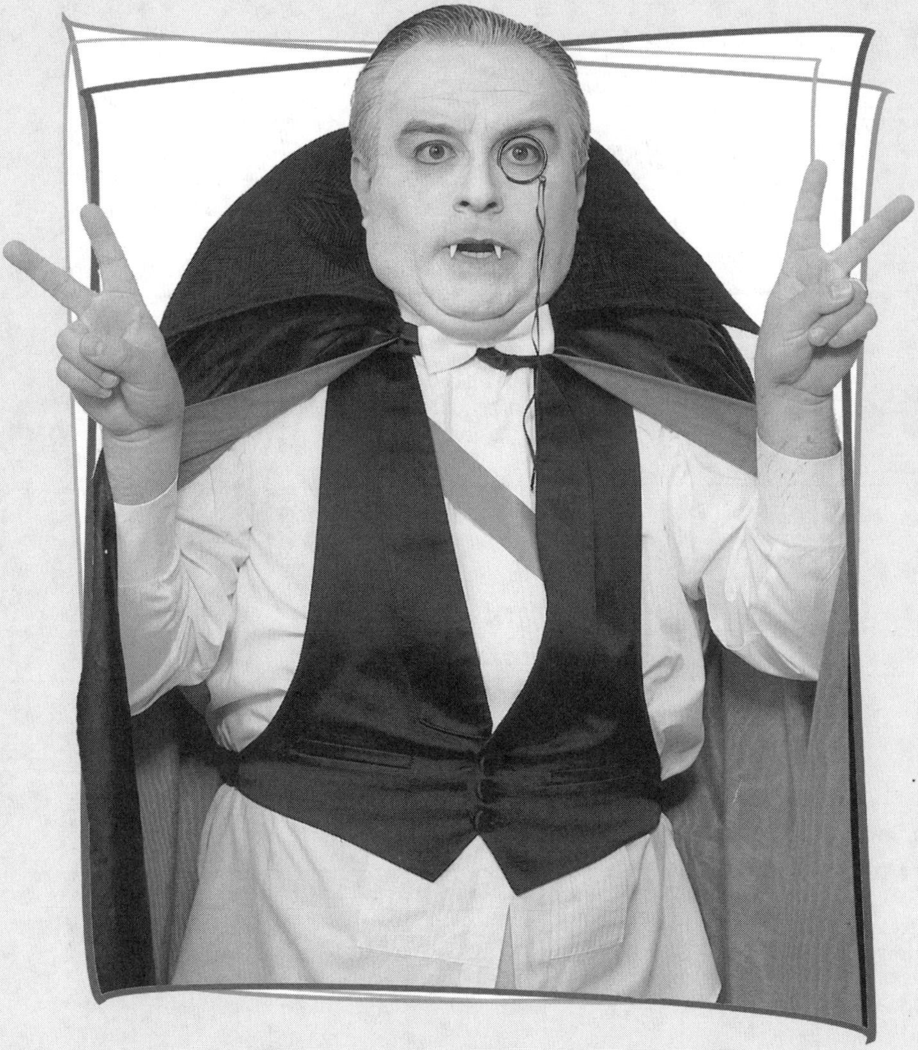

OCTOBER 2003

OCTOBER 2003

SUNDAY	MONDAY	TUESDAY	WEDNESDAY	THURSDAY	FRIDAY	SATURDAY
			1 First mass-produced automobile introduced (1908)	**2**	**3**	**4** Soviet Sputnik satellite launched (1957)
5	**6**	**7** Film rating system adopted by Motion Picture Association (1968)	**8**	**9**	**10**	**11** Albert Einstein writes about possibility of nuclear weapons (1939)
12	**13** Columbus Day	**14** Chuck Yeager travels faster than the speed of sound (1947)	**15**	**16** Sweetest Day; Boss Day	**17**	**18**
19 Intel introduces the Pentium processor (1992)	**20**	**21** Thomas Edison invents incandescent electric light (1879)	**22**	**23** Michael Crichton born (1942)	**24** Gene Roddenberry died (1991)	**25**
26 Daylight Saving Time ends	**27**	**28** Bill Gates born (1955)	**29**	**30** *War of the Worlds* radio broadcast causes panic (1938)	**31** Halloween	

TODAY'S FOCUS: Breast Cancer Awareness Month

CD PLAYER DEBUTS

The first compact disc player was unveiled in Japan on this day in 1982. The Sony CDP-101 was the first model to hit the market and was a collaboration of four companies, including Sony, CBS/Sony, Philips, and Polygram. The first CDs were touted as being infinitely durable and virtually indestructible (myths that were later proved wrong). Sony's original prototype, the Goronta, was designed to play the disc vertically. However, researchers decided to make the tray sit horizontally in the first commercial model. The CDC-101 cost 168,000 yen—almost $1,400.

Related Web site   www.sony.com

Breast Cancer Awareness Month

By Megan Morrone

One in every eight women in the United States will develop breast cancer. October is Breast Cancer Awareness month. Here are some online resources and ways you can participate.

Add a Pink Ribbon to Your Desktop
One way of showing support is by adding an image of a pink ribbon to your Web site or desktop. Choose from 25 different images at the Pink Ribbon Library, www.geocities. com/SoHo/2703/pink_ rib_lib.html.

Download an e-Book   Bryan H. Joyce and Dave Burns have collected short stories and poems from around the world to generate funds for cancer research. You can download the book, *Painting with Shadows*, for free, and the authors encourage you to donate money to your local Cancer charity in return: www.paintingwithshadows. co.uk.

Don't Forget Your Breast Exam   If you tend to forget your annual clinical breast exam or mammogram, the National Alliance of Breast Cancer Organizations (NABCO) can help. Enter your name and email address to get reminders sent right to your inbox. They'll keep your information strictly confidential: www.nabco.org/ reminder/emr_enter.phtml.

For an excellent collection of Breast Cancer resources, including prevention and treatment information, visit the Women's Health Center at ivillagehealth.com.

TIP OF THE DAY   I confess: I have fat fingers. And I can't help hitting the Caps Lock key ALL THE TIME. Shoot. Did it again. Who needs Caps Lock, anyway? Here's how to disable the thing entirely.

If you have a Microsoft keyboard, it probably came with the IntelliType software. That adds a tab to your Keyboard control panel that lets you assign functions to the extra keys on top. But it also lets you reassign or disable other keys, including Caps Lock.

Otherwise, download *PC Magazine's* ZDKeyMap, a marvelous little program for all versions of Windows that puts a very complete keyboard remapping tab into your Keyboard control panel. Free from downloads-zdnet. com.com/3000-2094-5934950.html?tag=lst-4-2.

If you don't mind hacking your system, you can remap the keyboard in Mac OS 9 with Resedit. There's a step-by-step description at ResExcellence, resexcellence.com/hack_html_ 99/09-11-98.shtml. Or download KeySwapper, free to try, $5 shareware fee, from northcoast.com/ ~jvholder/keyswapdesc.html.

There's a System Preference pane that will do the same thing on Mac OS X. uControl was originally for Unix geeks who want to put the control key where the Caps Lock key is, but it can do other things, too. A pretty neat hack, and free to boot, from gnufoo.org/macosx.

DOWNLOAD OF THE DAY   Donate your spare CPU cycles to finding a cure for cancer with Pioneer. Free for Windows from ComputeAgainstCancer.org.

OCTOBER 1

TODAY'S FOCUS: Storage

NAVIGATION PIONEER BORN

Charles Stark Draper was born in Windsor, Missouri, on this day in 1901. A licensed pilot, Draper received a master's degree in engineering and a doctorate in physics from MIT. "Doc" later founded the Instrumentation Laboratory at the institute, where he built navigational equipment based on the study of gyroscopes. Among his inventions were a system used for aiming guns aboard U.S. Navy ships, and guidance systems for various missiles. Draper also designed the navigational system used on the Apollo missions, including Apollo 13, whose instruments helped return the astronauts home safely.

Related Web site   draper.com

External Storage Options

An external drive is a great backup solution. Here are some of our picks for external storage on PC and Mac. Prices were current when we went to press, but check pricewatch.com for current street prices.

Hard Drives

LaCie FireWire (lacie.com)   These bad boys operate at 7,200 RPM and range anywhere from $179 for the 40GB model on up to $399 for the 160GB model. They are perfect for a traveling MP3 collection or for someone who works with digital video on the go.

Fantom USB 2.0 hard drives   Clunkier-looking than the LaCies, but compatible with any computer that has USB. 80GB 5400 RPM for $219; 160GB 7200 RPM for $429. Works with USB 1.1 and 2.0, but 2.0 is much faster.

CD-RW Drives

SmartDisk VST FireWire Portable CD-R/W (smartdisk. com) $249.95 for the 16×10×24 model and features a headphone jack on the front of the drive. Outstrips any USB 1.1 CD-R/W by a factor of four.

LaCie USB 2.0 CD-RW (lacie.com)   This is a perfect solution for having a mobile burn station with you at all times. Expect to pay $169 for the 16×10×40 model and $199 for the 40×12×48 model. Pay the extra $30. Again, works with USB 1.1 but only at 4x.

DVD-RW Drives

LaCie DVD-RW FireWire or USB 2.0 (Lacie.com)   The drive of the year. Add DVD recording capability to any computer. Includes 4.7GB of data storage and burns DVDs at 2x, CDs at 8x. The drive is a little pricey at $489, but prices should fall fast.

Solid State

USB Drive (usbdrive.com)   Indestructible portable disk that looks like a highlighter pen with a USB connector on one end. It fits on a keychain and is capable of holding 16MB to 1GB of data. Works driverless with Mac, Windows, and Linux versions supporting the USB Mass Storage class. Prices start at $35 for the 16MB model. If I had $899, I'd buy the 1GB model. Cool.

TIP OF THE DAY   **Q:** I just bought a 40GB hard drive. When I installed Windows, the install says that there are only 38GB on the drive. What happened to the 2GB? —Jose, Guaynabo, Puerto Rico

A: That's perfectly normal, Jose. Your drive manufacturer measures drive sizes before formatting. 40GB is the raw capacity of the drive, but formatting eats up some space. Windows is telling you how much space is left *after* formatting; roughly 5% less.

To avoid disappointment in the future, be sure to look at the formatted capacity when buying a drive.

DOWNLOAD OF THE DAY   Test RAM thoroughly with GoldMemory, from www. goldmemory.cz. Free to try, $24 to buy. Runs in DOS to avoid interactions with Windows (as all good memory testers should).

OCTOBER 2

TODAY'S FOCUS: Storage

VACUUM CLEANER PATENTED

Housework became a lot easier on this day in 1899 when John S. Thurman of St. Louis, Missouri, patented the motor-driven vacuum cleaner. His "pneumatic carpet renovator" was a large, gasoline-powered system. Previously, vacuuming devices resembled large bellows that would suck up dirt. They didn't work very well, and often had to be operated by two people. Thurman pulled his contraption door to door on a horse-drawn carriage, and offered vacuuming services for $4 per visit—nearly $100 in today's dollars. By 1906, Thurman was selling built-in central vacuum systems for homes and offices.

Related Web site   `www.howstuffworks.com/vacuum-cleaner.htm`

Drive Problems

It's a good idea to check your hard drive for bad sectors from time to time. In Windows, open My Computer and right-click on your hard drive. Select **Properties** from the pop-up menu and click the **Tools** tab. Click the **Error-Checking** button. Check both boxes and click **Start**.

On the Mac, run Disk First Aid (Mac OS 9) or Disk Utility (Mac OS X).

Both the Windows and Mac utilities offer minimal error checking. It's a good idea to buy a more functional program, such as Norton Systemworks for Windows from Symantec or Micromat's TechTool Pro for Macintosh.

Disk utilities do two things: They check your file system to make sure it's in working order, and they check your hard drive for bad sectors. A *sector* is the smallest unit of data storage on a hard drive. If one is bad, the program either will try to recover it or move the data off it and keep it from being used again.

All hard drives have bad sectors, but the number of bad sectors shouldn't increase dramatically. If you notice that sectors continually fail on your system it's likely that the entire drive is about to fail. Back it up and start shopping for a new one.

Fortunately, hard drives are cheaper, faster, bigger, and more reliable every year, so it's likely that your new drive will be much better than the old one.

TIP OF THE DAY   Rumor has it that the QWERTY keyboard layout we all know and love was designed intentionally to be inefficient, to keep typists from jamming early typewriters. Type faster with the Dvorak keyboard layout.

 To switch in Windows 95/98/Me, open the Keyboard control panel, choose the **Language** tab, and click **Properties**. Choose **United States - Dvorak**. Your computer might ask you for the Windows Install Disk.

In Windows XP, open the Regional and Language Options control panel. Click the **Languages** tab and click **Details**. Click the **Add** button to add the Dvorak keyboard layout.

 In Mac OS X, open the International system preference pane, click the **Keyboard Menu** tab, and select one of the Dvorak layouts. A keyboard menu will appear letting you choose from different layouts.

Confused by the old keycaps? Print out a page with the Dvorak keyboard on it from `www.mwbrooks.com/dvorak/dvorkeys.pdf`, or buy keycap stickers or a whole new keyboard from Kinesis (`kinesis-ergo.com`), Fentek industries (`fentek-ind.com/dvorak.htm`), or Hooleon.com (`hooleon.com/prod-dvo.htm`).

 DOWNLOAD OF THE DAY   Learn (or relearn) to type Dvorak style with Zippy Type, free for Mac OS 7.5 and later, from `strout.net/macsoft/zippy-type`.

 For a list of Windows-compatible programs visit MW Brooks, `www.mwbrooks.com/dvorak/training.html#tutors`.

 Learn online at `www.karelia.com/abcd`.

OCTOBER 3

TODAY'S FOCUS: Storage

SPUTNIK LAUNCHED

The Soviets became the first nation to launch an artificial satellite into space on this day in 1957. Sputnik 1 was about the size of a basketball and weighed 183 pounds. It traveled 18,000 miles per hour and completed one orbit of the Earth in about an hour and a half. The event threw the U.S. government into a panic: The Americans hoped to launch a satellite before the USSR. The success of Sputnik 1 is regarded as the beginning of the U.S.-Soviet space race, a tit-for-tat competition between the two nations that lasted until the Cold War ended around 1989.

Related Web site `www.hq.nasa.gov/office/pao/History/sputnik/`

Warning Signs

By John Christopher

Whether you're ready to face it or not, the day will come when your hard drive will simply give up the ghost. These tips can help prevent the loss of your precious data.

Back Up, Back Up, Back Up Okay. There, we said it. If you value your data, take the time to back up your critical files. Do it right now, because Murphy's Law—anything that can go wrong, will—rings doubly true when it comes to computers. My customers spend thousands of dollars recovering lost data—data they would have if they'd been making backups.

Don't Ignore Warning Signs If your hard drive emits unusual noises, turn it off immediately. This symptom typically indicates a head crash that can destroy your data. Hard drives spin fast, at 7,200 to 15,000 revolutions per minute. Extensive damage can occur quickly. If you don't have a backup and you need to recover data, you should contact a professional data recovery service immediately because this situation demands work in a clean room environment.

Here are some noises to be wary of:

* Whining
* Rattling ball bearings
* Repetitive clicking that doesn't stop
* Banging
* Grinding like a knife sharpener
* Raygun-like sounds

Use Utilities Wisely Disk utilities can provide excellent preventive maintenance by fixing directory corruption problems. But they can also render data unrecoverable in the event of extreme corruption. Always save an "undo" file (a record of the changes the utility has made to your drive) in case it doesn't correct your problem. Symantec's Norton Utilities software in the Mac or PC flavor is capable of creating an undo file that you can save to a floppy disk.

(John Christopher is a data-recovery engineer for DriveSavers in Novato, California: `Drivesavers.com`.*)*

 TIP OF THE DAY It happens all the time. You install a new driver that's supposed to make your system work better, and instead it crashes the computer. Windows XP's driver rollback will let you go back to an earlier, happier time.

1. Right-click **My Computer** and select **Properties**.
2. Click the **Hardware** tab.
3. Click the **Device Manager** button.
4. Locate the device you'd like to roll back, and double-click it to bring up its properties.
5. Click the **Driver** tab.
6. Click the button labeled **Roll Back Driver**.

 DOWNLOAD OF THE DAY Today's hard drives are SMART. SMART stands for self-monitoring, analysis and reporting technology, and it helps hard drives predict their own demise. To find out what your SMART hard drive is doing, download SMART Indicator for Windows, free for noncommercial use from `adenix.net/smart`.

TODAY'S FOCUS: Women and Computing

TUPPERWARE CREATOR DIES

Earl Silas Tupper died in Costa Rica on this day in 1983. Tupper worked at DuPont in 1937, where he developed a new form of polyethylene made from the waste products of refined oil. In 1938, he left DuPont and started his own company, where he made bowls, plates, and other kitchenware. He also developed a special airtight lid for his containers. At first, Tupperware did not sell well because plastic was considered inferior. But a woman named Brownie Wise suggested demonstrating Tupper's products in homes instead of in stores—hence, the birth of Tupperware parties. Tupper sold his company in 1958 for $16 million.

Related Web site `tupperware.com`

List: Women and Computing

By Megan Morrone

Women have been coding right beside men even before the first computers were invented. Here's a list of my favorite women role models in the woolly world of computer programming.

Ada Lovelace (1815–1852) (`www.cs.yale.edu/homes/tap/ada-lovelace.html`) No list of important women in computing is complete without Ada Lovelace. A century before the first computer was built, Lovelace envisioned simple programming concepts based on the work of Charles Babbage.

Grace Hopper (1906–1992) (`www.sdsc.edu/ScienceWomen/hopper.html`) Hopper was also an early female programmer. As a rear admiral in the U.S. Navy, she worked on the Mark I and helped devise the Univac I. During her work creating the COBOL language, she invented the compiler, a critical advance in computer programming.

Evelyn Boyd Granville (1924–) Granville is known more for her work as a mathematician than as a programmer, but she did develop programs for the IBM 650 during the 1950s.

Frances "Betty" Snyder Holberton Holberton also worked on the ENIAC, the world's first electronic digital computer. She also helped create the COBOL and the FORTRAN languages.

Adele Goldstine Goldstine wasn't officially a programmer, but she did write the manual for the ENIAC. So, if you hate computer manuals, don't blame Goldstine. She was only doing her job.

 TIP OF THE DAY Microsoft is a cagey customer. It eliminated several old Windows favorites in Windows XP—or did it? They're not in the Start menu, but here's how to resurrect those Windows classics.

In all cases, open the **Start** menu and click **Run**, then type the word in quotes into the window and press Enter.

- Windows Briefcase: `syncapp`
- Netmeeting: `conf`
- System Configuration Utility: `msconfig`
- Windows Media Player 6: `mplayer2`
- Desktop Themes: `themes`

If you don't have a Run command in your Start menu (those boys in Redmond are really diabolical, aren't they?), open the Taskbar and Start Menu Properties control panel, click the **Start Menu** tab, click the **Customize** button, click the **Advanced** tab, do the hokey pokey, and spin yourself around, and then check **Run command** in the Start menu items window.

Actually, the hokey pokey is optional.

 DOWNLOAD OF THE DAY Virtual CD copies CDs to the hard drive so you don't have to keep them in your CD-ROM drive. Great for playing games on laptops or keeping your favorite audio CDs handy. Download a 30-day free trial from `www.virtualcd-online.com`. Buy it for $39.95.

POLL: Is a female virus-writer a breakthrough for women?

25% Yes   75% No

TODAY'S FOCUS: More Windows

XEROGRAPHY PATENTED

The process for duplicating documents was patented by Chester Floyd Carlson on this day in 1942. Carlson was fed up with trying to copy complicated patent drawings while he was working for an electronics firm. After four years of experimentation, he made the first copy on October 22, 1938. His machines weren't successful, however, until 1947, when the Haloid Company in New York licensed the technique. The company later changed its name to Xerox, and is now one of the largest copy-machine manufacturers in the world.

Related Web site `xerox.com`

Windows Basics

By Regina Preciado

Windows Is an Operating System A computer without an operating system is like a car without a dashboard. No matter how powerful the engine, you can't drive without the dashboard. Likewise, you can't do any work on your computer without an operating system.

The OS

- Manages invisible activities, such as assigning memory to software so you can use more than one program at a time
- Allows programs (such as Microsoft Word) to communicate with your hardware (such as your hard drive)
- Lets you interact with different programs through mouse clicks and keyboard strokes
- Organizes and stores your files for future use

You've probably heard of a few other operating systems, such as the Mac OS, Unix, and Linux. Each of these performs the same essential role, albeit in different ways.

Windows Is a Series of Mixed Metaphors We've already used one metaphor to describe an OS: the car dashboard. Windows itself comes with several built-in analogies to help you understand how it works.

- **Windows**—The term *windows* refers to the boxes that appear on your screen when you work with the computer. Each box contains a separate task. You can organize your work by organizing the windows, just like the pieces of paper on your desk.
- **File Cabinet**—You store your work in documents or files. Windows organizes these files inside folders, which can be nested. Folders are also sometimes called *directories*—they're the same thing.

You can organize this files-within-folders scheme as it suits you. You can make one folder called Stuff and save all your files in it. (Windows does this for you, providing you with a default My Documents folder.)

- **Menu**—Many of the windows you open in Windows contain a series of menus. Menus are a great way to learn what a program can do, because most of the program's commands appear somewhere in there. Unfortunately, as of this writing you still can't order lunch from Windows' menus.

TIP OF THE DAY Change your user picture in Windows XP. Click the **Start** button, and then click the picture at the top of the **Start** menu. Choose from the existing images or click the **Browse for More Pictures** link to use any picture from your hard drive. The picture will be scaled to fit. Square images work the best.

DOWNLOAD OF THE DAY Download a free program to expand your Zip files. StuffIt Expander can't create Zip files, but it's a very simple way to expand them. I often recommend it to novices. Free for Mac, Windows, Linux, and Solaris, from `stuffit.com/expander`.

UltimateZip is a full-featured zipping program that's comparable in every way to WinZip. Free from `ultimatezip.com`.

TODAY'S FOCUS: More Windows

FIRST RADIO NETWORK

Two radio stations teamed up on this day in 1922 to create the country's first radio "network." WGY in Schenectady, New York, and WJZ in Newark, New Jersey, were connected by a landline to broadcast the fourth game of the World Series, played at the New York Polo Grounds. Grantland Rice did the play-by-play. The New York Giants beat the New York Yankees 4–3 and went on to win the pennant.

Related Web site `www.baseball-reference.com`

Advanced Searching in XP

Windows XP comes with powerful search capabilities that help you find anything on your hard drive. And with today's massive hard drives, that's a good thing.

To start the search engine, press F3 or select **Search** from the **Start** menu. The Search Companion will open up in a pane on the left of your window. Some default searches are pre-configured, including searches for media files, Office doc-uments, and network and people searching. For now, click **All Files and Folders**.

Here, you can search by filename or part of a filename, or by the contents of the file (this works only with text and Microsoft Office files). You also can choose the areas to be searched. Don't cast your net too widely—it really slows down the search. Choose **My Documents**, for example, if you know what you're looking for is in there. Searching My Computer searches everything.

To narrow the search to a specific date, click the button next to **When Was It Modified**. Use the modify date to search only for files you recently worked on or to search for old versions you no longer want.

The file size option is a handy way to find the biggest disk wasters. Just do a search with all fields blank and set file size to a suitable large level. Try searching for files that are at least 100,000KB (that's 100MB). You might be surprised by the number of huge files you're harboring. Be sure to

search My Computer, not just the Desktop. I found 30. I was able to get rid of 10 of them, saving more than 1GB of disk space.

Click the **More Advanced Options** button for some added settings. The most useful is the search by file type. You can find old MP3s, delete ancient Word documents, and more by using this setting in conjunction with the others.

Finally, go back to your starting point and click **Change Preferences**. Here you can turn off the search doggie or choose a different character. There are 10 annoying char-acters to choose from.

 TIP OF THE DAY If there's a search you perform often, you can save it by selecting **Save Search** from the **File** menu. You'll create a .fnd file, which you can double-click to re-create the search.

 DOWNLOAD OF THE DAY Whether you want to tweak your Windows Registry, clean up your hard drive, or increase your multimedia and game performance, Customizer XP's integrated suite of programs can get your system running at peak per-formance levels. Free for 10 days, $25 to buy, from `tweaknow.com`.

POLL: Is profit-free piracy permissible?

64% Yes

23% No

13% Fuhgedaboutdit

OCTOBER 7

TODAY'S FOCUS: More Windows

PERM INVENTED

The first "permanent wave" for hair was demonstrated on this day in 1906. German hairdresser Karl Ludwig Nessler showed off his invention in his beauty salon in London to a group of fellow hairstylists. The wave was created by soaking hair with an alkaline solution and rolling it with hot metal rods. Unfortunately, the process took about five hours and was very expensive. Later, it was discovered that subjecting hair to a perm too often would cause it to break off. During the early 1940s, Nessler moved to the U.S. and opened salons across the country, including New York, Chicago, and Philadelphia.

Related Web site salonchannel.com/

Top Five Help Questions

Here are the answers to the top five questions we get at TechTV.

1. My taskbar disappeared. How do I get it back? Usually, the taskbar has disappeared because you accidentally shrank it. Here's how to get it back:

1. Press Ctrl+Esc.
2. Press Alt+space.
3. Press S.
4. Use the up arrow to resize the taskbar.

2. How do I turn off CD AutoPlay?

1. Right-click **My Computer** and select **Properties**.
2. Click the **Device Manager** tab and double-click the CD-ROM branch.
3. Double-click the CD-ROM driver entry.
4. On the **Settings** tab, uncheck the **Auto Insert Notification** box.

To suspend AutoPlay just this once, hold down the Shift key while inserting a CD.

3. How can I turn off that annoying modem sound?

1. Right-click **My Computer** and select **Properties** again. Go back to the **Device Manager** tab.
2. Click **Modem** to show the modem you have.
3. Double-click your modem to bring up its properties.
4. Turn off the sound.

4. How do I disable the startup sound?

1. Open the Control Panel.
2. Click **Sound Speech and Audio Devices**.
3. Click **Change the Sound Scheme**.

4. Scroll down in the Program Events window and highlight **Start Windows**.
5. Choose **(None)** from the sound name drop-down menu and click **OK**.

Turn off all sounds by selecting the **No Sounds** Sound scheme.

5. How do I turn off Recycle Bin confirmation? What if your garbage asked you, "Are you sure?" every time you took it to the curb? So, why should Windows?

1. Right-click the **Recycle Bin** and choose **Properties**.
2. In the **Global** tab feature of the Recycle Bin properties, uncheck **Display Delete Confirmation Dialog Box**.

 TIP OF THE DAY One of Windows XP's coolest new features is its album thumbnail generator. Let's say you just finished ripping Britney Spears' new CD and you want the cover to be displayed on the folder where all the MP3s are stored. Just download the album cover art from CDNow.com or Amazon. Try finding an image with a size about 200×200 pixels. Save it inside the MP3 folder with the name `folder.jpg`.

Use the Thumbnails view in your My Music folder, and the album art should appear on the folder containing Britney's LP. (Do they still call them LPs?)

 DOWNLOAD OF THE DAY Searching for *le mot juste*? LangToLang makes it easy to translate any word on a Web page. Install the LangToLang Internet Explorer extension for the language you want. When you get to a word you need translated, select it, right-click on it, and LangToLang will translate it automatically. Free for Windows Internet Explorer from langtolang.com.

TODAY'S FOCUS: More Windows

HOOVER DAM DELIVERS ENERGY

The first generator at Boulder Dam began transmitting electricity to Los Angeles on this day in 1936. The complex, later known as the Hoover Dam, took five years to build and was, at the time, the biggest of its kind. Its concrete walls are about 730 feet high and weigh nearly 7 million tons. Today, the Hoover Dam is still one of the largest hydroelectric installations in the world. The power plant's 17 main turbines generate more than 4 billion kilowatt-hours a year, which is enough to provide electricity for 1.3 million people.

Related Web site `www.hooverdam.usbr.gov`

Turn Off XP Uglies

By Morgan Webb

Ugly No. 1: Crash Reporting Anytime an application crashes, XP asks you whether you want to send a bug report to Microsoft. I don't believe Microsoft is really going to sift through all those reports, and the pop-ups are intrusive. Fortunately, they are easy to turn off:

1. Right-click on **My Computer**.
2. Select **Properties**.
3. Click **Advanced**.
4. Choose **Error Reporting**.
5. Check the box to disable error reporting.

Ugly No. 2: Candy-Apple Interface I don't want an interface that shouts, "I'm easy!" I want something bland and sedate. Fortunately, inside that brassy XP exterior beats a heart of solid gray. Right-click the Desktop, select **Properties**, and choose the **Windows Classic** theme. Boring is beautiful.

Ugly No. 3: Automatic Updates I am very good about updating software on my own, and I do not want my computer to download things automatically under any circumstances.

1. Right-click **My Computer**.
2. Select **Properties**.
3. Click the **Automatic Updates** tab.
4. Click the radio button that best suits your need for control, or uncheck **Keep Windows Updated** to never update again.

Leo says this is a bad idea. I never listen to Leo when it comes to matters of esthetics. Have you seen those shirts he wears?

Ugly No. 4: Stupid Yellow Highlights The highlights on newly installed programs really bother me for some reason. Fortunately for me and the bulging vein in my forehead, they are simple to turn off.

1. Right-click the **Start** button and choose **Properties**.
2. Click **Customize** and choose the **Advanced** tab.
3. Uncheck **Highlight Newly Installed Programs**.

TIP OF THE DAY Windows XP comes with a new set of sounds that will surely add pizzazz to the way you work in Windows. But there's one problem: You need to actually turn on the Windows default sound scheme before you'll be able to hear them.

To turn on the Windows XP default sound scheme, follow these steps:

1. Open the Control Panel.
2. Click the **Sounds, Speech, and Audio Devices** icon.
3. Click **Change the Sound Scheme**.
4. Select the Windows Default from the pull-down scheme menu and click **Apply**. Windows will ask you whether you want to save the previous sound scheme. Because there wasn't a sound scheme already loaded, just choose **No**.

DOWNLOAD OF THE DAY Put everything on your computer at your fingertips with KeyLaunch. Press the ScrollLock key, then enter the first few letters of any program or file, hit Enter, and it launches. You'll wonder how you ever lived without it. Free to try, $12 to buy, from `software.xfx.net/utilities/kl`.

TODAY'S FOCUS: More Windows

FIRST LAUNDRY DETERGENT

The first synthetic detergent was introduced to consumers on this day in 1933. Procter & Gamble's "Dreft" used man-made surfactants. Lye-based soap had been used for many years to clean clothes, but it did not work effectively in hard water. Procter and Gamble developed special two-part molecules that could pull grease out of clothes and suspend the dirt until it could be washed away. The introduction of the detergent sparked a revolution in synthetic home-cleaning products and inspired a new radio program: the soap opera.

Related Web site   `www.pg.com`

Speed Up Startup

Oddly enough, the most common complaint about Windows is that it starts too slowly. What's the matter with you people? It's as if you actually want to go to work.

Windows XP speeds up the startup considerably. If you haven't upgraded, that's one good reason to do so. There are some other things you can do, no matter what version of Windows you use.

The biggest improvement in boot time comes when you eliminate programs from the startup process. Some installers stuff icons directly into the Startup folder. These automatically launch every time Windows boots. Microsoft Office and RealAudio are both guilty of this crime. Drag stuff you don't need out of the Startup folder. That includes Microsoft Office and Findfast, both unnecessary on today's fast machines.

Some applications offer a "load on startup" feature. Try to shut off these "quick launch" or startup features in each of the programs' settings. Sometimes you can even do it by right-clicking on the icon in the system tray.

If you can't turn off a program that starts on boot any other way, you can generally shut the door on it with the System Configuration Manager. Select **Run** from the **Start** menu and type `msconfig`. Click the **Startup** tab, and you'll see a check box list of all the applications that start with Windows. Uncheck the box next to the programs you don't want to start.

You should also reduce the number of fonts you have installed. They all get loaded at startup, and I bet you don't use more than a handful. Move the rest out of the Fonts folder. You can always put them back later.

Some BIOS settings also affect startup time. Open your BIOS setup and be sure you do a quick memory check, disable the splash screen, stop the floppy seek, boot first from the hard drive, and say no to Plug and Play OS. All these settings can shave precious seconds off that boot time and get you to work quicker. Me, I'm going fishin'.

TIP OF THE DAY   If there are programs you use all the time, you can keep them in the Windows XP Start menu by "pinning" them there. Right-click on the program in the menu (if it's not there yet, run it once), and then select **Pin to Start** menu. You can pin as many programs as your menu has room for. To unpin, right-click again and select **Unpin**.

DOWNLOAD OF THE DAY   *PC Magazine*'s TrayManager lets you consolidate your system tray icons. Free from download.com.com/ 3000-2094-5943070.html.

POLL: Do you read the fine print?

12% Yes

71% No

16% I can't see it

TODAY'S FOCUS: More Windows

CRYPTOGRAPHY BREAKTHROUGH

A 100-digit number was factored for the first time on this day in 1988. The 100-digit breakthrough was made by a world-wide cooperative of 400 computers linked via the Internet. It took less than a month to accomplish the task. This kind of factoring is key to cracking modern encryption, which uses large numbers that are the products of two primes. Today, factoring 100-digit numbers is considered easy and 200-digit numbers next to impossible.

Related Web site   rsasecurity.com/rsalabs/challenges/factoring

The Windows Registry

Most of the tweak toys we recommend in this book—TweakUI, TweakAll, XSetup, and the rest—are really just interfaces to the Windows Registry. Anything these programs can do, you can do by hand with the Registry Editor, if you know where to look and what to do. It's just easier to do it with the GUI tools. Safer, too. But for your edification and amusement, today we'll delve a little into the guts of the Registry. Please, keep your hands and arms inside the vehicle at all times.

The Registry is not a single file, even though we speak of it that way. It's a pair of binary files, SYSTEM.DAT and USER.DAT, that store all Windows settings. You can edit the Registry using the built-in Registry Editor. Invoke it by selecting **Run** from the **Start** menu, typing **regedit**, and hitting Enter.

Regedit gives you an Explorer-like view into the Registry. In the left pane are the folders, called HKEYs. For the most part, user changes to the Registry occur in HKEY_LOCAL_MACHINE. Open that key and you'll see more keys. Click **SOFTWARE**, **Microsoft**, **Windows**, **CurrentVersion**. Now we're in the heart of the beast. Click the **Run** key. In the right pane you'll see a series of subkeys; some of these will look familiar. These are programs that get started when Windows first runs. Deleting a key here will keep that program from starting. But let's not mess with anything right now. Close Regedit and breathe a sigh of relief.

I don't think there's anyone, even at Microsoft, who knows everything the Registry can do. The closest thing to a Registry guru out there is John Woram, who wrote the classic *The Windows 98 Registry*. Unfortunately, he hasn't published a sequel for Windows XP, but many of the techniques he mentions there are still applicable. I highly recommend the book and his Web page, woram.com, for more information on the Windows Registry.

 TIP OF THE DAY   Windows XP System Restore can bring your system back to life.
Before you modify the Registry, set a restore point:

1. Open the System Restore Wizard. It's in the **Accessories/System Tools** folder on your **Start** menu.
2. Select **Create a Restore Point** and click the **Next** button.
3. Name your new restore point.
4. Click **Create**.

To restore, open the System Restore and select **Restore My System to an Earlier Time**. You'll see a list of previous restore points. Go back as far as you need to.

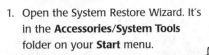 **DOWNLOAD OF THE DAY**   Do you hate that annoying bar of color beneath your icons in Windows 95/98/Me? Want your desktop wallpaper to shine through? Make the icon label disappear with Simply Transparent. Free from jonathangrimes.com.

OCTOBER 11

TODAY'S FOCUS: More Windows

DIGITAL MILLENNIUM COPYRIGHT ACT PASSED

Congress approved a bill requiring new protection for copyrighted material on the Internet on this day in 1998. The law had far-reaching implications for the entertainment industry, and for computer-users worldwide. One of the results was a crackdown on peer-to-peer file sharing. Napster, the free music-swapping site, became a poster child of sorts in the battle between consumers, who wanted to exchange free files, and the recording industry, who wanted its share of royalties. There are still many, however, who do not agree with the DMCA, as evident by the numerous peer-to-peer clients still active today.

Related Web site `www.loc.gov/copyright/legislation/dmca.pdf`

Nine More Things You Didn't Know About Windows XP

By Chris Pirillo

1. Internet Explorer now has built-in support for Google (as long as you're using the search assistant).
2. They finally updated the card backs in Solitaire. Considering how many people play it on a regular basis, it's a notable improvement.
3. Go directly to the Start Menu properties by right-clicking on the **Start** button. Switch to the "classic" Start menu if the new one annoys you. The **Highlight Newly Installed Programs** feature is nice for download maniacs.
4. Microsoft's marketing campaign is a bit misleading; you can't play DVD movies without purchasing a third-party decoder first. Although MP3s can be played out of the box, ripping music into this audio format is possible only through additional software.
5. Even with XP's built-in Internet Connection Firewall features, I still recommend Tiny Personal Firewall (free from `tinysoftware.com`).
6. The Windows Help system has a wealth of new features. In one swoop, you can perform queries against the local database as well as the Microsoft Knowledge Base.
7. I thought it was rather shortsighted that XP doesn't allow you to associate WMA sounds to your events. I mean, they're shoving the format down your throat

in every other application; why not here, too? At least the default system sounds have received a much-needed upgrade.

8. When was the last time you forgot your password? Uh, don't forget it for Windows XP until you create a password recovery disk. Under Related Tasks in the User Accounts Control Panel applet, click **Prevent a Forgotten Password**.
9. The Kodak Imaging Application that came with other versions of Windows has been replaced by the Windows Picture and Fax Viewer. It has a few built-in options, but you can't easily view the image at its full size. Although this replacement is good enough, I miss the Kodak app already.

 TIP OF THE DAY   The boot disk is back, baby. To make a boot floppy in Windows XP, insert a floppy disk, right-click the Floppy drive icon, select **Format**, and then place a check mark in **Create an MS-DOS Startup Disk**. A boot floppy is a must for when your system won't start. Don't expect to access NTFS drives with it, though.

 DOWNLOAD OF THE DAY   Microsoft did not include the Java Virtual Machine in Windows XP. If you need Java for a Web page, download it free from `www.microsoft.com/java/vm/dl_vm40.htm`.

POLL: Is Internet access a human right?

73% No

27% Yes

TODAY'S FOCUS: Graphics

LONG-DISTANCE SIGN LANGUAGE

A breakthrough was made for the hearing impaired on this day in 1940. Two deaf women communicated in sign language via two-way television for the first time. The demonstration took place in two locations: at the New York World's Fair and at a television station eight miles away. Providing reliable access to television for the deaf took nearly four decades, however. Closed captioning was developed in the 1970s and officially began service in 1980. Today, the FCC requires captioning on virtually all broadcast television programming in the U.S.

Related Web site `www.nidcd.nih.gov`

Graphics File Formats

By Alison Strahan

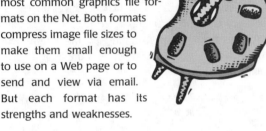

You've probably heard the terms *GIF* and *JPEG*. They're the two most common graphics file formats on the Net. Both formats compress image file sizes to make them small enough to use on a Web page or to send and view via email. But each format has its strengths and weaknesses.

Use JPEG for

* Photos
* Detailed artwork
* Graphics with millions of colors that blend into one another

Use GIF for

* Graphics with solid areas of color
* Line drawings
* Logos
* Transparent graphics designed to have a background the same as the page's
* Animation

JPEG stands for Joint Photographic Experts Group. It uses a lossy compression scheme that removes data that the eye can't see to reduce file size.

Because you will lose data when you save an image as a JPEG, you should not open and resave JPEGs. Losing data with each save will degrade the image quality. Always work with a copy so that you can go back to your raw image if you want to make more changes.

GIF stands for graphics interchange format. CompuServe developed the format for its online ventures. You'll often see it referred to as CompuServe GIF.

GIFs save space by restricting you to 256 colors or fewer (unlike JPEGs, which allow millions). If you look closely at a GIF image, you might see a bunch of dots in certain areas. This is due to *dithering*. Because GIFs only work with a certain number of colors, they shift the dots around from the colors they have to create (to fake) the colors they don't have.

It's not a good idea to save an image in one format and then again in another. Keep originals of your images so you can go back to make changes without crunching previously compressed images.

 TIP OF THE DAY   Matching the resolution of your input and output devices is fundamental in digital-imaging. Why scan an image at 600dpi if your ink-jet printer can't produce images any finer than 200dpi? An image destined only for the Web doesn't need to be any higher resolution than 75dpi. Make it higher, and you're inflating file size without increasing quality.

 DOWNLOAD OF THE DAY   iPhoto is the ultimate application for digital photography. Plug in your camera and iPhoto downloads the images, organizes them, and lets you share them with others. Free for Mac OS X from `www.apple.com/iphoto`.

Windows and Mac OS 9 users can get similar capabilities with OfotoNow, a free program from Kodak's Ofoto photo printing service, `ofoto.com/DownloadClient30.jsp`.

TODAY'S FOCUS: Graphics

SOUND BARRIER BROKEN

U.S. Air Force Captain Chuck Yeager became the first person to fly faster than the speed of sound on this day in 1947. Yeager's experimental rocket plane, the X-1, was lifted by a B-29 bomber to an altitude of 25,000 feet above the Mojave Desert in California. Upon release, "Glamorous Glennis" shot up to 40,000 feet and surpassed Mach 1, breaking the sound barrier at an airspeed of nearly 700 miles per hour.

Related Web site   www.chuckyeager.com

Photoshop Techniques

By Scott Kelby

Quick Zoom   Zoom in

- On a Mac, press Command++ (plus symbol).
- On a PC, press Ctrl++.

Zoom out

- On a Mac, press Command+- (minus symbol).
- On a PC, press Ctrl+- (minus).

Layer Opacity Shortcut   To change the opacity of your active layer, switch to the Move tool (by pressing the letter "v"), and then simply type in the desired amount of opacity (82 percent, 65 percent, 25 percent). If you want a round number (such as 20 percent, 30 percent, 40 percent) just input the first number (that is, 2 for 20 percent, 3 for 30 percent, and so on).

Repeating Filters   To reapply the last filter you used, using the exact same settings, on a Mac press Command+F and on a PC press Ctrl+F.

Resetting Your Default Colors   To quickly reset Photoshop's foreground and background colors to their default settings (black foreground, white background), just press the letter "d."

Handy Views   To view your Photoshop document at its full 100% size, double-click the Magnifying Glass tool in the toolbar.

To have your Photoshop document "Fit in Window" (displaying the entire document as large as possible in your monitor window), double-click the Grabber Hand tool in the toolbar.

Tight Cropping Web Graphics   Want to crop your Web graphics as tightly as possible? Photoshop 6.0 can do it for you automatically. Just choose **Trim** from the **Image** menu, and it will crop your Web graphic as tightly as possible for the smallest possible file size.

(Scott Kelby is editor of Photoshop User *magazine.)*

 TIP OF THE DAY   You can't use a traditional flatbed scanner to scan film negatives or slides. Flatbed scanners bounce light off an image and into the scanner's sensor. To capture an image from negatives or slides, the scanner must pass the light *through* the film into the sensor.

You can buy adapters for flatbeds that use mirrors to bounce the light around, but the results are generally mediocre. The most effective way to scan slides and negatives is with a film scanner. Film scanner prices haven't dropped as quickly as flatbed prices, but they're still much less expensive than they used to be. Our two favorites are the Nikon Coolscan 4000 and the Polaroid SprintScan 4000.

 DOWNLOAD OF THE DAY   Web pages look different on different monitors because of the different screen resolutions. Because you have no idea what visitors to your site will be using to view your page, you need to make your site look good in all resolutions. Size-O-Matic lets you test your page at any screen resolution, free from downloads-zdnet.com. com/3000-2383-904767.html.

POLL: Should Net-movies be eligible for Oscars?

29% No

53% Yes

17% Only the Pamela Anderson/ Tommy Lee variety

TODAY'S FOCUS: Graphics

FIRST PAGER

The first radio paging service began on this day in 1950. Aircall of New York City transmitted the first page to a doctor who was golfing 25 miles away. The pocket radio receiver weighed six ounces, and subscribers could hear their call numbers repeated in numerical sequence on the air at least once per minute. Today, text pagers have replaced the audio pager, but doctors can still be found on a golf course from time to time.

Related Web site   www.telecomweb.com/wirelessdata

3D Character Modeling

By Mark Swain

Here's a simple method you can use at home to create 3D models. All you need is two drawings or a couple of snapshots of your subject, one from the front and one from the side.

The most important aspect of modeling using this method is to get all the key features lined up. If you're hand-drawing the character, it's best to draw the front view first, and then draw ruler lines at the key features, such as the eyes, nose, chin, and any other feature. Next, draw in the key features of the side view using the ruler lines as a guide. If the drawings do not line up, the 3D character will tend to look a little off.

You also can use snapshots of real subjects. Here are a few tips for preparing a front and side view of a subject's head:

1. Using a makeup pencil, place a series of dots in a gridlike pattern on the subject's face.
2. With a camera on a tripod and your subject on a swivel chair, take a front picture.
3. Turn the subject 90 degrees and snap the side picture.
4. Line up both images in Photoshop using the dots as a guide.

When the front and side view pictures are completed, they can be loaded in as a background image in many 3D computer graphics programs. With the images loaded, start with a primitive object, such as a sphere. It's really simple to push and pull the point on the sphere to start filling in the shape of the character. When the character is blocked in, you begin the process of cutting and adding the details to the primitive shapes. Modeling takes time, but it's surprising how fast the 3D character starts to take shape.

TIP OF THE DAY   Three-point lighting is a technique used to light subjects in traditional photography and film. The principles of three-point lighting apply very well to 3D animation:

- **Key light**—The key light is the primary light source in your scene. The key light should be placed above and to the right or left of the camera.
- **Fill light**—The key light tends to create very dark shadows. It's the job of the fill light to lighten these shadows and to simulate other sources of illumination in the scene.
- **Back light**—The job of the back light is to bring out the silhouette of the subject. The back light helps separate the subject from the background; this directs the viewer's eye toward the subject.

DOWNLOAD OF THE DAY   DVGarage offers great tutorials in 3D animation. Download the 3D Toolkit for Mac and Windows, too. Free for 30 days, from www.dvgarage.com.

OCTOBER 15

TODAY'S FOCUS: Graphics

INTEL 386 UNVEILED

Intel introduced its first 32-bit microprocessor on this day in 1985. The Intel 386 operated at a speed of 16MHz and could access 4GB of physical memory. The chip consisted of 275,000 transistors—more than 100 times as many as Intel's first chip. It was also Intel's first multitasking processor.

Related Web site `intel.com/intel/intelis/museum/exhibit/hist_micro`

3D Posing and Staging

By Donovan Keith

Animation at its most basic level is a series of poses shown over a given length of time. To make your animation more convincing, there are some basic guidelines that should be followed when posing your characters.

Strike a Pose When posing characters for animation, start by analyzing what you want to convey with the pose. Is your character happy or sad? What's your character thinking? Is your character very confident or shy? All these questions should factor into how you pose your character.

The easiest way to come up with a pose is for you to get into the mindset of your character and show through body language what it is you're feeling. After you have done this, just look into a mirror for reference. Put your character into this pose, adjusting for any differences in body type. Then, try to exaggerate this pose to really get the idea across.

Keep these things in mind when posing a character:

- **Balance**—The character should look balanced. Weight should be pretty evenly distributed throughout the pose.
- **Symmetry**—Many poses will have a very rough symmetry, but they should not have an exact symmetry. For example, If your character is resting its hands on its hips, one hand should be higher than the other hand, and the hips should be rotated slightly.
- **Exaggeration**—The key to really believable animation is to actually make unbelievably exaggerated poses.

Stage Too Your character might be posed beautifully, but if it's staged improperly, it won't have nearly as strong an impact on the viewer. Ideally, the camera should be positioned so that the pose would be clearly defined if the character were silhouetted. The viewer's eyes should be directed to the most important part of the character's pose. Try moving the camera to different positions and see how it affects how the pose looks. Also, you will need to make decisions about whether to have one continuous moving shot for your animation or a series of cuts to different angles.

Keeping posing and staging in mind will add greatly to your character animations.

(Donovan Keith is a student and teacher of 3D animation. Learn more about Donovan and his work at `bentplug.com`*.)*

 TIP OF THE DAY At 3D Buzz, you'll find reviews of graphics programs, lists of plug-ins, 3D-related job openings, loads of tutorials, and prefabricated models that you can incorporate into your own 3D projects: `3dbuzz.com`.

 DOWNLOAD OF THE DAY Download a watermarked version of Cinema 4D, a top 3D animation package, free for Windows and Macintosh from `maxon.net`.

POLL: Have you called in sick to see a movie?

18% Yes

61% No

21% I'm unemployed. Movies are my job.

TODAY'S FOCUS: Graphics

FIRST AFRICAN-AMERICAN FEMALE ASTRONAUT BORN

Mae C. Jemison was born in Decatur, Alabama, on this day in 1956. Jemison earned a Bachelor of Science degree in Chemical Engineering from Stanford University in 1977, and graduated from Cornell Medical School four years later. In 1987, NASA chose her to participate in astronaut training. In 1992, she served as a Science Mission Specialist aboard the space shuttle Endeavor. During the eight-day mission, she conducted research on bone loss and space sickness. Dr. Jemison left NASA in 1993 and now leads various humanitarian efforts.

Related Web site `maejemison.com`

Simple Photo Fixes

By Mikkel Aaland

Most digital-imaging software titles have similar capabilities. Today, I'll use Adobe Photoshop Elements to demonstrate simple photo fixes.

Eliminate Red-Eye Red-eye is such a common problem in color images that Photoshop Elements includes an easy-to-use tool devoted to fixing the problem. Here are the steps:

1. Select the Red-Eye Brush tool from the toolbar.
2. Choose a brush from the pop-up palette on the options bar. I chose a Soft Round 65-pixel brush, but the brush you choose will depend on the specifics of your particular image.
3. Click **Default Colors** on the options bar and specify black as the replacement color.
4. Select **First Click** from the **Sampling** pop-up menu, and specify a Tolerance of 30 percent.
5. Click on the red area of the eye to specify the color for removal.
6. Drag over the eye until the red is replaced with black. If the replacement black is too light, use the Burn tool to darken the pupil.

If a person's face is pink, sometimes the Red-Eye Brush doesn't work as well. To reduce this problem, use the Lasso tool to select the red-eye area, and then apply the Red-Eye Brush tool.

Use Digital Fill Flash It's common to take a picture of a person against a bright background. However, if you don't use a fill flash or specifically expose for the skin tones, a face will turn into a silhouette.

Photoshop Elements includes a useful Fill Flash command that does a good job of creating a digital fill flash effect, balancing the foreground with the background.

1. Select **Fill Flash** from the **Enhance** menu.
2. Drag the **Lighter** slider settings until the faces look right, and click **OK**.

It's that easy.

You can get more helpful hints and see examples of my work at `cyberbohemia.com`.

(Mikkel Aaland is the author of Photoshop Elements Solutions.*)*

TIP OF THE DAY Apple's iPhoto can create slideshows from your pictures and export them to a QuickTime movie you can share with others, even Windows users. First, create the slideshow. Then, use the Export option in the Share section to turn your slideshow into a QuickTime movie. The resulting movie will have no transition effects or music. To add those, convert the movie to DV format and open it in iMovie.

DOWNLOAD OF THE DAY Milkdrop is a Winamp visualization plug-in that uses "iterative image-based rendering techniques" to synchronize spectacular 3D graphics with your music. Free from `geisswerks.com`.

OCTOBER 17

THOMAS EDISON DIES

One of the most influential and prolific inventors in history died in New Jersey on this day in 1931. Thomas Alva Edison was granted more than 1,000 patents over the course of his life, including one for the first incandescent lightbulb. Henry Ford convinced the inventor's son to capture Edison's last breath in a test tube. Several years later, the tube was given to the Edison Institute in Michigan, which Ford founded in 1929. The test tube is still in the same building, now known as the Henry Ford Museum.

Related Web site `roadsideamerica.com/attract/MIDEAbreath.html`

3D Software

By Mark Swain

If you plan to get into computer graphics full time then consider selecting a package that the studios use. Maya, Softimage, LightWave, 3D Studio Max, and Houdini are among the top choices. Most companies offer student discounts for these pricey titles. Also use your local schools as a resource.

Maya (`aliaswavefront.com`) Most film studios use Maya, and it's slowly working itself into the games market as well. It's powerful at NURBS modeling, character animation, and dynamics. Maya's scriptable environment, mel, allows users to create new tools and user interfaces.

Softimage 3D/XSI (`softimage.com`) Softimage is still responsible for most of the character animation seen in big-budget Hollywood movies. In the last few years, Softimage has fallen behind a few of the other packages, but it seems to be coming back strong with its new version, called XSI.

Lightwave 3D (`newtek.com`) Excellent package, used in many television shows, commercials, and video games. It has a powerful modeler and rendering engine.

Inspire 3D (`newtek.com`) If you can't afford Lightwave, try Inspire. It's basically the same package, minus a few features such as rendering animation. You can generate only stills. Still, it's an excellent learning tool.

3D Studio Max (`discreet.com`) This package just keeps getting better each year. Discreet improved the interface on the newest version. The character studio plug-in gives you excellent character animation tools.

Houdini (`sidefx.com`) The original procedural 3D graphics package, excellent for dynamic simulations, particles, and various special effects. It presents a steep learning curve, but after they get the package, most users never go back.

Electric Image (`electricimage.com`) Electric Image used to run only on the Macintosh but has been used extensively in several films. It has an extremely fast render engine.

Rhinoceros (`rhino3d.com`) An excellent NURBS modeling system. Used in both entertainment and product design companies.

Caligari: trueSpace (`caligari.com`) Caligari has been around forever. Its trueSpace software has loads of new features and is relatively low priced.

Animation:Master (`www.hash.com`) This package uses an innovative model method called Hash-Spines, which allows for excellent organic/character modeling. Many short films have used this program over the years.

(Mark Swain is a professional animator with a well-known movie studio and is a regular guest on The Screen Savers.*)*

TIP OF THE DAY These are the 3D sites Mark recommends:
* www.flay.com
* www.3dlinks.com www.3dlinks.com/
* www.highend3D.com www.highend3D.com/
* www.vfxpro.com
* www.3dcafe.com

 DOWNLOAD OF THE DAY iTunes comes with built-in visualizations to go with your music (press Cmd+T to see the fun) and you can add more. Try iGoom for iTunes, free from `goom.sourceforge.net`.

  You can download versions of the goom visualizer for Winamp, WMP, and XMMS there, too.

TODAY'S FOCUS: Graphics

DOW JONES PLUMMETS

The Dow Jones Industrial Average suffered one of the biggest crashes of all time on this day in 1987. The U.S. stock index fell nearly 23%, or 508 points, on "Black Monday." Many experts blamed rising interest rates, as well as steep trade and budget deficits. Some tried to pin the fall on the Dow's computerized trading system. The 1987 crash held the record for the largest one-day point drop in history until September 17, 2001. Affected in part by the widespread deflation of the tech sector, the Dow dropped 684.33 points, or 7.1%.

Related Web site `www.djindexes.com`

Twisted List: Online Comics

By Megan Morrone

You can read the Sunday funnies online, too. Here are my top five favorite online comic strips:

Keenspace (keenspace.com) Keenspace offers free hosting to would-be comic artists. Browse the Keenspace Line-Up to see a hoard of amateur artists.

Compu-toon (comicspage.com/computoon) Comic Charles Boyce chronicles the way people interact with technology in a simpler way than most cartoonists I've seen. Think of Compu-toon as Dilbert without the sarcastic edge. It's syndicated by the *Chicago Tribune*, but you can read it online here.

User Friendly (userfriendly.org) True geeks already know User Friendly. If you've never heard of it, don't be ashamed. Just go here right now. I mean it. If you've already seen it, maybe you'll be interested in reading why the artist thinks geeks are funny. If you've seen that too, I'm sorry. I have nothing else to offer you.

Dork Tower (www.dorktower.com) I promise that I liked this cartoon even before Carson the muskrat fell in love with me. I would link to the Dork Tower strips that were about me, but I can't find them now.

Linux Lass (geekculture.com/joyoftech/ joyarchives/240.html) The coolest comic ever. The Linux Lass is a former librarian who was miraculously transformed into an open-source freedom fighter. To find out how, read how she was compiled.

TIP OF THE DAY Save Web pages in a form you can email to others using Microsoft's Web Archive format.

 In Internet Explorer 6 for Windows, choose **Save As** from the **File** menu, and select **Web Archive** as the file type. The entire page will be saved, graphics and all, in a single file with the .mht extension. You can email this file to friends and the links will still work.

Office XP can create Web archive files, too, as can Office 2000, with a simple download from office. microsoft.com/Downloads/2000/webarchive.aspx.

 Internet Explorer for the Mac also supports a Web archive format, and it's even more flexible. Click the **Options** button to save sound, movies, and linked pages, too. Unfortunately, the file formats are not cross platform—you can't send these files to your Windows-using friends. But then, they can't send you their Web archives either.

 DOWNLOAD OF THE DAY Adobe offers free tryouts of most of its products, including Photoshop, Photoshop essentials, Illustrator, and After Effects. For Windows and Mac from www.adobe.com/products/tryadobe/main.html.

POLL: Is your system fast enough for you?

0% Yes

33% No

0% Maybe when it's light speed

67% Not even then

TODAY'S FOCUS: Computer Programming

FIRST AUTOMATED POST OFFICE

The first mechanically operated post office went into service on this day in 1960. The $20 million experimental system, installed at the Corliss Street station in Providence, Rhode Island, sorted mail electronically at a rate of 18,000 pieces per hour. That same year, a four-cent commemorative stamp was issued in honor of the automated post office. Today, the United States Postal Service delivers more than 200 billion pieces of mail a year to 135 million addresses. The USPS is the largest investor in Optical Character Reader technology, and estimates that about 80% of handwritten letters are "read" by computer.

Related Web site `www.usps.gov`

What Is Computer Programming?

Humans program computers by giving them specific, step-by-step instructions. One program can contain many of these instructions: Windows XP, for example, contains more than 50 million lines of code.

The instructions themselves are written in a language designed to be expressive enough for humans to use, and concrete enough for computers to act upon. The list of human-readable instructions that make up a computer program is called its *source code*, but computers can't understand source code. Before a program can be run, it must be translated—we call it *compiled* or interpreted—into a string of ones and zeros called *machine language*.

The closest thing to machine code that humans use is assembly language. Each assembly instruction translates directly into a single machine-level instruction, but the assembly instructions are a little easier for humans to understand. Assembly language is used when efficiency is more important than ease of programming.

More often, programmers use high-level languages such as BASIC, C, Java, JavaScript, and Perl. Each has its own unique syntax and is designed with different goals in mind. But ultimately, every programming language does the same thing: It acts as a bridge between the wishes of a human and the actions of a machine.

 TIP OF THE DAY   JavaScript isn't Java. Despite the similarities in their names, they are very different things.

Java is a compiled programming language from Sun Microsystems that has a unique write once, compile once, run everywhere philosophy. Java programs are compiled to run on the Java Virtual Machine (JVM), not machine language. Hardware and operating system vendors are responsible for writing JVMs that work in their environment. In theory, a Java program should work anywhere there's a JVM without any modifications.

JavaScript is an interpreted browser scripting language created specifically for Web pages by Netscape Communications. Its original name, LiveScript, was changed to JavaScript by the folks in marketing to take advantage of Java's success, but in truth the similarities end there. JavaScript is widely used on the Web for simple programming tasks.

 DOWNLOAD OF THE DAY   Get the Java programming language from the company that invented it. Download the Java 2 Platform compiler and tools, free for Windows, Linux, and Solaris from `java.sun.com/j2se`. There's no fancy programming environment—it's strictly command line, but the price is right.

To get a taste of what it's like to use a fancy integrated development environment (IDE), download a 30-day trial of Metrowerks CodeWarrior for Java. The compiler works on many platforms, but the trial version's for Windows only, from `metrowerks.com/desktop/java/trial`.

TODAY'S FOCUS: Computer Programming

NOBEL PRIZE FOUNDER BORN

Alfred Bernhard Nobel was born in Stockholm, Sweden, on this day in 1833. The chemist patented dynamite in 1867 and invented smokeless gunpowder a decade later. Over the course of his life, Nobel was awarded a total of 355 patents. Upon his death in 1896, Nobel left most of his estate to a fund for annual prizes in physics, chemistry, physiology or medicine, literature, and peace. The first Nobel Prize was awarded in 1901.

Related Web site www.nobel.se

Advice to Young Programmers

By Ryan Staake

Start Out Small Don't expect to start out making a masterpiece that will rival commercial programs. Wait until you have a solid knowledge of the language you are learning before you start writing large applications.

Plan Out Your Programs If you are planning on releasing a program to the public, sketch out your program's planned interface. This can save a lot of time and give you a physical blueprint when you actually sit down and start writing code.

Learn with Your Friends If you have a friend who is also into computers and programming, compare what you know about the language and how you use it. Being able to ask each other questions will let both of you learn much more about programming than you would from learning independently.

Use the Internet to Your Advantage The Internet houses tons of resources to help you increase your knowledge of programming. I would suggest using developer and programming Web sites, IRC, and Hotline.

Learn As Much About Technology As Possible Reading technology magazines or watching technology-based shows will teach you more and more about the many facets of technology.

Write Your Code Clearly Try to keep your code as clean and understandable as possible without downgrading the quality of your program. Putting comments in your code can also be very helpful.

Know Your Weaknesses If you're not able to create good, clean graphics and interfaces for your applications, don't. Ask someone else to help you. A bad interface is one of the main things that will turn users away from your programs.

Don't Get Discouraged You will probably see some programs that make you think, "I could never do that." Keep in mind that most programs are written by adults with a vast knowledge of programming. If you keep at it, you will be able to write programs like the pros.

(Ryan is a high-school student and the president of Melonsoft, melonsoft.com.)

TIP OF THE DAY Stagecast is a great way for kids to create their own games and learn programming basics. Download a free version for Windows and Mac from stagecast.com.

DOWNLOAD OF THE DAY To learn to program C, you need a compiler. Linux and Mac OS X already come with C compilers. Here are some Windows compilers you can download free:

- Borland makes a copy of its powerful C compiler for Windows available for free, at borland.com/bcppbuilder/freecompiler.
- DJGPP is a free compiler for DOS, from delorie.com/djgpp.
- LCC-Win32 works on Windows, free from www.cs.virginia.edu/~lcc-win32/.
- Many books on Microsoft C++ come with a student version of the compiler, as well.

POLL: Can women program as well as men?

70% Yes   30% No

TODAY'S FOCUS: Computer Programming

GENETICS PIONEER BORN

George Wells Beadle was born in Wahoo, Nebraska, on this day in 1903. Beadle graduated from the University of Nebraska in 1926 and began studying hybrid wheat, corn, and fruit flies. This research eventually helped lead Beadle to found the study of biochemical genetics. In 1958, Beadle shared the Nobel Prize for Physiology or Medicine for his work in genetic research.

Related Web site   www.wahoo.ne.us

Visual Basic

By John Smiley

Visual Basic is more than a programming language—it's a software development package that permits you to create Microsoft Windows applications or programs. It's currently estimated that programmers use Visual Basic for 70% of all Windows development.

No other development package allows you to create a Windows application as quickly. It's fun, as well. I've successfully taught thousands of people to write Microsoft Windows programs using VB. Anyone can learn to create a Windows program of their own using Visual Basic. That isn't true of every language.

Creating a VB program takes two main steps. First, you design the Graphical User Interface (GUI) using a toolbox containing a variety of built-in objects or controls (buttons, text boxes, check boxes, and so on). By itself, the GUI doesn't do much, although it does include some built-in functionality. For example, if you use a mouse to click on a check box, an 'x' appears in it. You don't have to tell it to do that.

After you design the GUI, you write code to enable the program to do what's intended. You write code in VB using the English-like BASIC language. The code is generally associated with a control and an event: for example, the clicking of a check box.

The fun begins when you decide what code to write and what control and event to associate it with. In a matter of minutes, you can design and code a beautiful working VB program.

(John Smiley is author of many books on VB, including Learn to Program with Visual Basic 6 *from Active Path. Visit his Web site at* johnsmiley.com.)

 TIP OF THE DAY   Windows 98, 2000, and XP ship with a built-in program engine called the Windows Scripting Host (WSH). Windows 95 users can download a copy free from msdn.microsoft.com/scripting.

The host is designed to support several programming languages, including Visual Basic for Applications, VBScript, and JScript, Microsoft's version of JavaScript. You can use Notepad or any text editor—I prefer Notetab from notetab.com. To create a script in one of the supported languages, save it with the appropriate extension, and then double-click the file and WSH will run it. To learn more about creating Windows scripts, visit msdn.microsoft.com/scripting.

WSH is a useful tool, but it's also the vehicle many viruses use to infect Windows machines. If you don't intend to write Windows scripts, you should disable VBS files. Open an Explorer window, select **Folder Options** from the **Tools** menu, click the **File Types** tab, and then delete the entry for VBScript. This prevents VBS files from being run when you double-click them.

 DOWNLOAD OF THE DAY   Microsoft offers a version of Visual Basic 5 for free download at msdn.microsoft.com/vbasic/downloads/tools/cce. Many books on Visual Basic also come with a limited edition of VB.

TODAY'S FOCUS: Computer Programming

LINUX GETS WORDPERFECT

Corel announced it would make a version of its WordPerfect word processing software for the Linux operating system on this day in 1998. The partnership seemed logical, because Corel's products had been struggling against the market dominance of Microsoft Word, and Linux, the free, open-source operating system, was partly growing in popularity out of protest against Windows. Corel later followed with an entire software suite for Linux, which included the Quattro Pro spreadsheet, Presentations presentation software, and Corel Central personal information manager.

Related Web site `linux.corel.com`

Promoting Python

Choosing a programming language for work is easy: You use what the boss requires. These days, that's almost always C++, unless you have the misfortune to be working for a COBOL nut. But if you just want to write programs for yourself, for the fun of it, you have plenty of other great choices.

People who use Windows exclusively often start programming with Microsoft Visual Basic. VB is a modern programming language with nice features for Rapid Application Development, but it has one drawback in my opinion: It works only with Windows.

I'd like to propose another choice: a language that's great for beginners but has all the power professionals crave. This language runs on Windows, Macintosh, and most Unix flavors, including Linux. In fact, it comes with most Linux distributions. Better yet, people who start with this language will have a much easier time stepping up to professional languages such as C++. Best of all, it's free. The language is called Python, and the real question is why it isn't much better known.

Professional programmers use Python for rapid prototyping, Web page scripting, and even production code. The Red Hat installer is written in Python. NASA has standardized on it for its Integrated Planning System and at Mission Control in Houston. Yahoo! Groups was originally implemented in Python. Four11 uses it, as does Infoseek. It's the scripting language for Caligari's trueSpace. And on and on.

Python is an interpreted language (technically, it compiles to byte code, which is then interpreted). That means it's really useful for trying out ideas because you get instant feedback. But it also supports modular development. And it's object oriented, with support for classes, inheritance, encapsulation, and all the other buzzwords modern programmers require. Python code is clean and readable, and its syntax encourages good programming habits without weighing the programmer down with fussy punctuation requirements.

You'll find plenty of good Python information on the Web, and there are many good Python books in stores. Python has an excellent online tutorial, and it's easy to dive in. And because Python is free, there's nothing to stop you from downloading it right now and giving it a try. You can thank me later.

 TIP OF THE DAY You can search thousands of programming books for just the right answer with Safari Tech Books Online. A real boon to programmers. Free two-week trial. $9.99/month to join, from `search.safaribooksonline.com`.

  DOWNLOAD OF THE DAY Download Python free for every platform under the sun from `python.org`. Try a good Python tutorial for nonprogrammers at `hetland.org/python/instant-hacking.php`.

POLL: Is open source un-American?
9% Yes
82% No
9% "I am not now and never have been..."

TODAY'S FOCUS: Computer Programming

EIGHT-HOUR WORK DAY MANDATED

The Fair Labor Standards Act of 1938 was passed into law on this day in 1940. The FLSA established a 40-hour work week and set minimum wage, overtime compensation, and child labor laws. The FLSA didn't apply to employees of the U.S. Federal Government, however, until 1974. Even today, many salaried employees are exempt from these laws: Tech workers pulling all-nighters are perhaps the most famous examples.

Related Web site   `www.dol.gov`

Understanding CGI

Web servers are simple programs that do one thing well: serve up Web pages. Ask them to add 2+2, validate a credit-card number, or display a counter, and they'll draw a blank. That's why the Common Gateway Interface was created.

CGI is an easy way to extend the capabilities of Web servers. A Web designer can use CGI to call on external programs to do things the servers can't. For example, we're going to use CGI to call a Perl program that will update a counter on the page.

We'll use Server-Side Includes (SSI) to embed the output of the CGI script into the HTML page, so all our Perl program will have to do is open a text file on the server with the current count, add one to it, save the file back, and return the updated count to the Web server. The server will embed the count back into our Web page. We can do all that in just a few lines of code. Start with the Perl program:

```
#!/usr/bin/perl -w
use strict;
my $counter;

# open the count file with read/write access
open (COUNT, "+<count.txt");

# lock it, read it, then increment the count
flock(COUNT, 2);
$counter=<COUNT>;
$counter++;

# store the newly incremented count back in
the count file
seek(COUNT, 0, 0);
print(COUNT $counter);
truncate(COUNT, tell(COUNT));
close (COUNT);

# send the new count to the web page using the
print command
print "Content-type: text/html\n\n";
print $counter;
```

Create a Web page to test the script called test.shtml and containing the line

```
This page has been viewed <!--#include
virtual="/cgi-bin/counter.pl"-- > times.
```

Also create a count.txt file: a plain text file with the number 0 in it, our starting count.

Upload counter.pl and count.txt to your CGI directory, usually /cgi-bin. Upload test.shtml to your normal Web directory. Make counter.pl executable, make count.txt world read and writable, and then point your browser to test.shtml. If you see a number after the word "viewed" and it increments each time you reload the page, bingo: You've done it.

Congratulations. Getting this simple CGI script to run is a good first step to creating your own, more complex, CGI scripts. Good luck, and happy scripting.

 TIP OF THE DAY   Perl is so powerful it can even modify every HTML file on your Web site in a single line. Try that, Superman.

Let's say you've decided to rename your pictures directory to images. Now you're faced with going through hundreds of HTML files. Or, you can just type the following line at the command prompt:

```
perl -i '.bak' -pe 's$pictures/$images/$g' *.html
```

In seconds, the job's done. Thanks, Perl.

DOWNLOAD OF THE DAY   Mac OS X and Linux distros come with Perl already installed. Download a copy for Windows, free from activestate.com/Products/ActivePerl.

OCTOBER 24

TODAY'S FOCUS: Computer Programming

FIRST FEMALE FBI AGENTS

The first women were admitted into the Federal Bureau of Investigation for training on this day in 1972. Susan Lynn Roley and Joanne Pierce graduated from the 14-week course with a group of 45 men. Previously, women worked for the FBI, but not as agents. In 1948, 30% of FBI employees were women, but they worked as secretaries, file clerks, and in other similar positions. Much of the blame goes to J. Edgar Hoover, who refused to let women serve in federal law enforcement. When he died May 12, 1972, the FBI announced it would accept female recruits almost immediately.

Related Web site `www.fbi.gov`

Security Mistakes Programmers Make

By Matt Conover

In my job as a security analyst, I'm always looking for flaws in programs that can give a malicious user a way to crack into a machine. You'd be surprised how many I find. When searching for possible holes in a program, I use several methods:

- If the source code is available, I look for problems there.
- If not, I usually look at the network traffic the program generates. I try to determine whether the traffic is encrypted, and if so, whether the encryption looks weak.
- I try to see whether it creates any temporary files with predictable names, if it's using a weak seed for random-number generation.
- I try sending long strings where it's expecting short strings.
- I send garbage or numbers where it's expecting letters.

Basically, I try to think of scenarios or means of attack that the developer didn't anticipate.

One of the most common program errors is buffer overflow. The Code Red and Nimda worms exploited a buffer overflow in Microsoft's Internet Information Server. As an example, here's a bit of code that can suffer a buffer overflow error:

```
void setusername(char *input)
{
  char username[16];
  ...
  strcpy(username, input);
}
```

The problem is that the `username` variable can hold only 16 bytes. If a malicious user passes in 32 bytes, he or she will be overwriting the `username` variable by 16 bytes, corrupting the stack. If the extra bytes are cleverly coded, they can actually be executed from the stack, giving the attacker control of the machine.

Basically, these problems stem from the developer's assumption that people will use his or her product the way the developer intended, forgetting, however, that there are malicious people in the world who don't always do as they are supposed to. Every programmer should keep that in mind.

(Matt Conover was a founding member of w00w00 (www.`w00w00.org`) the world's largest nonprofit security team. He holds a senior-level position at a security company in the San Francisco Bay Area and is an undergraduate at Utah State University.)

TIP OF THE DAY Learn the ins and outs of Web security from Lincoln Stein's WWW Security FAQ at `www.w3.org/Security/Faq`. Pay close attention to the CGI section.

DOWNLOAD OF THE DAY The best Perl programming editor for Windows is DZSoft's Perl Editor. Free to try, $49 to buy, from `dzsoft.com`.

There's no better text editor for Perl and HTML than BBEdit Pro. Download the Lite version free, and then pay $79 to upgrade to Pro, from `barebones.com`.

OCTOBER 25

TODAY'S FOCUS: Computer Programming

FIRST ANIMAL-HUMAN HEART TRANSPLANT

Doctors transplanted the heart of a baboon into a human baby on this day in 1984. "Baby Fae" was born prematurely nearly two weeks earlier with a malformation of the heart. Dr. Leonard Bailey performed the transplant at the Loma Linda University Medical Center in California. The operation appeared to be successful at first, but Baby Fae's immune system rejected the new organ. She died three weeks later.

Related Web site `www.llu.edu/llumc/index.html`

Hacking Ain't Cracking

By Geoff Nunberg

There's a Gresham's Law of meanings: The bad ones drive out the good ones. Senile used to mean just "old," but that meaning disappeared when the word acquired a sense of mental defectiveness. A junket was originally just a party, before it got associated with trips taken at public expense.

Or take the word hack, as in "hack writer." That was originally a shortening of hackney, which referred to a horse that was easy to ride. The word came from the Hackney area of London, where horses were raised in the Middle Ages. Then it came to refer to a horse kept for hire, and then to anyone who hires himself out to do menial or servile jobs.

These uses of hack had only an indirect influence on the way computer programmers started using hack and hacker in the 1960s. Probably these new senses owed as much to the use of hack to mean "chop," as in tennis hacker and golf hacker. But like the older senses of hack, the programmer's hack started out as a positive term—part of the cult language that grew up among programmers at places such as MIT and Carnegie Mellon. When you hear a programmer say, "She can really hack," it's in the same appreciative tone that a jazz musician uses when she says, "He can really blow."

In recent years, though, hacker has gone down the same steep road that hack and hackney did a couple of hundred years ago. The process started early on. Already in the 1960s, engineering students were using hack to refer to an ingenious prank, which might involve a computer-system break-in. And when break-ins began to make headlines in the 1980s, the press naturally took the term to describe the perpetrators. Today, that's the only sense of the word most people know.

A lot of programmers get indignant about this use of the word. They want people to reserve hacker as a term of praise, and suggest the word crackers as a name for people who do malicious break-ins. I appreciate their point, but there's no possibility the process will be reversed—no more than hackney is going to go back to meaning a horse that's easy to ride.

(Geoff Nunberg is a professor of linguistics at Stanford.)

 TIP OF THE DAY Hack your TiVo with back-door codes from `tivonews.com/features/backdoors.shtml`. Teach it to skip through commercials 30 seconds at a time, turn on advanced wish lists, and more.

DOWNLOAD OF THE DAY One of the best development environments ever designed is free for Mac OS X. The Macintosh Developer's Tools can be downloaded, after registration, from `connect.apple.com`. Works with C, Objective C, C++, Perl, and Applescript.

TODAY'S FOCUS: Online Auctions

SEWING-MACHINE INVENTOR BORN

Isaac Merrit Singer was born in Pittstown, New York, on this day in 1811. The traveling machinist designed his first sewing machine while working in a Boston machine shop in 1850. In 1863, Singer and his business partner, Edward Clark, incorporated the Singer Manufacturing Company. The company became the most successful sewing-machine manufacturer in the world, and many of his basic designs are still used today.

Related Web site `www.ismacs.net`

Selling Your Items on eBay

By Sue Rabeaux and Laura Burstein

An online auction site such as eBay can be a great place to sell your wares to a vast customer base without ever leaving your computer.

To start, set up an eBay seller's account and place a valid credit card on file. If you don't have a credit card (or don't want to use one), you must be ID Verified.

If possible, buy a few things on eBay before you start selling. This will help you establish some positive feedback before you begin to sell.

Get to know the competition before putting anything up for sale. Look for items similar to yours and take note of the categories in which they're listed, their titles, starting bids, item descriptions, and final closing prices. This will help you determine how to list your items.

Provide as much information as possible in the item description. Disclose any shipping or insurance costs. Use HTML or formatting to spruce up your listings, but don't go overboard.

Products with photos always sell better than those without them. You can upload one free photo per listing to the eBay server, or you can link to photos on your own Web site.

Decide which payment options you're willing to accept, such as eBay Payments, PayPal, money orders, or checks. If you choose to use PayPal, you must also set up a separate PayPal account. There is a nominal charge to use electronic payment services.

You'll be notified by email when the auction closes. After the buyer completes the checkout process, you will receive an email confirmation with the buyer's shipping address. If he or she pays with eBay Payments or PayPal, you'll receive a confirmation email from the electronic payment service. If the buyer pays by money order or check, wait until you've received payment before shipping.

Don't forget to leave feedback on the buyer's profile after the item's been sent.

 TIP OF THE DAY Any profit you make in an online auction is treated like ordinary income. And that means you've got taxes.

If you sell any big-ticket items, and owe at least $1,000 in taxes, you're supposed to file quarterly estimated tax returns, because this income is not subject to withholding. If you're making substantial profits from auctions, you'll need to file a Schedule C and the SE form because the IRS considers your auction sales a business.

If you're not sure whether your eBay auctions are a hobby or a business, read IRS Publication 334, `www.irs.gov/forms_pubs/pubs/p334toc.htm`.

 DOWNLOAD OF THE DAY AuctionWatch Sales Manager helps you launch auctions simultaneously on eBay, Amazon, and Yahoo!. Various fee schedules from `auctionwatch.com`.

POLL: Should auction sites be responsible for the sins of the seller?

23% Yes

77% No

TODAY'S FOCUS: Online Auctions

BILL GATES' BIRTHDAY

Microsoft's founder and chairman was born in Seattle, Washington, on this day in 1955. William H. Gates, a Harvard Business School dropout, started the small company in 1975 with his childhood friend, Paul Allen.

Related Web site `microsoft.com/billgates`

Buying on eBay

By Laura Burstein and Sue Rabeaux

Online auction sites such as eBay can be a great resource for finding bargains and rare items not available in stores. Here are a few tips to help you become a savvy bidder.

Set Up Your Account   Register for eBay and create a user ID. If you also plan to sell, you might want to choose a name that identifies the items you plan to offer. You'll receive a confirmation email from eBay shortly after signing up. Follow the instructions in the message to complete your registration.

Go Shopping   There are several ways to shop on eBay. To find items by category, click the **Browse** button and choose the descriptions that best fit what you're looking for. Use the search feature to find more specific items. For a basic search, simply type keywords into the search box on the main page. Smart Search allows you to narrow your criteria based on price, location, category, etc. The advanced search allows you to specify exact phrases, exclude keywords, and use wildcards.

How to Bid   Research the item and the seller before you place a bid. Read the feedback in the seller's profile and contact him or her if you have any questions about the product. Also read the listing carefully see whether there are additional shipping or insurance costs, and what forms of payment the seller accepts.

Sometimes a seller will offer multiple quantities of the same item in his or her listing. This is called a *dutch auction*.

If you like what you see, decide the maximum price you're willing to pay. When you set your maximum bid, eBay will automatically increase your bid up to the maximum amount when others bid on the same item. This is called *proxy bidding*. You'll receive an update email from eBay every time you're outbid.

If you don't want to bid right away, keep track of the item by clicking **Watch This Item**. The status of the auction will be visible on the "My eBay" page, and you'll also receive a daily email update for all the items you're watching.

After the Auction   You'll be notified by email when the auction closes if you've won. If the seller accepts electronic payments, click the **Checkout** or **Pay Now** buttons to complete the transaction. When sending payment, include your complete shipping address, auction number, and the name of the item, as well as any special instructions.

Inspect your item when it arrives. If there are any problems, contact the seller immediately. Finally, leave feedback for the seller after the transaction is complete.

 TIP OF THE DAY   Internet Explorer for Mac OS X has a built-in auction manager. IE will track your auctions, notify you when the bid changes and more. Select **Auction Manager** from the **Tools** menu for more information.

 DOWNLOAD OF THE DAY   Track your auctions in Windows with Auction Trakker, free to try, do I hear $39.95 to buy? timbercreeksoftware.com

POLL: Will you spy for eBay?

9% Yes

72% No

19% Who wants to know?

OCTOBER 28

TODAY'S FOCUS: Online Auctions

INTERNET CREATED

The first connection to the precursor to the Internet was made on this day in 1969. Charley Kline sent the first data packets on ARPAnet from UCLA while trying to connect to Stanford Research Institute. By the end of the year, a total of four sites were up and running: UCLA, Stanford, UC Santa Barbara, and the University of Utah.

Related Web site `www.arpa.gov`

Uncle Griff Allays Your eBay Fears

Q: Does eBay offer any product guarantee or insurance for what I buy?

A: Because eBay never handles the merchandise, we cannot guarantee product description accuracy. However, we have recently introduced a buyer insurance program. If you receive an item and it's not as the seller described, and the seller refuses to take the item back, you may submit a claim per the instructions on our site. We then examine the claim and send it to our underwriters, Lloyds of London, for processing. They then may award the claim amount to you. This program is good for any item that sells between $25 and $200.

Q: What recourse do I have if I don't receive the product?

A: You can use the eBay Insurance Program to file a claim for items that sold for a price between $25 and $200. Buyers can also file mail fraud complaints and send a report of the incident to our fraud department. The best protection is to research all sellers before you bid on their items.

eBay provides a wonderful tool called *Feedback* for just this purpose. Every eBay user can leave and receive comments from other users in their individual Feedback files. These files are public record and are open for all to see. Bidders can then check a seller's feedback history to determine whether that seller is honest and easy to deal with.

Q: How do you track and deal with people who bid on their own items or are involved in fraud?

A: We have a special investigations department called *SafeHarbor* that is staffed with eBay customer support representatives. They determine who is abusing the site, based on reports of site abuse that our users send to us.

Our users are the official "watchdogs" of the site. eBay users are very protective of their neighborhood and do not appreciate shady activity. When they uncover something suspicious, they let us know. No less-than-honorable seller gets away with any chicanery for very long.

We suspend sellers who bid on their own items or who engage in fraud.

Q: What other features does eBay offer, such as chat or feedback, that help you learn the auction process and communicate with others?

A: We provide more than 30 different message boards for users; many are category specific. Users can ask other users questions about procedure, eBay navigation, how to list images, and so on, and get real hands-on expert advice from other users.

(Jim "Uncle Griff" Griffith is eBay's official ambassador. Visit him online at unclegriff.com.)

 TIP OF THE DAY   Know what it's worth before you bid. Visit Kovels' online price guide for collectibles, at `kovels.com/catalog.shtml`.

 DOWNLOAD OF THE DAY   Keep track of all that stuff you've bought online with Collectify's MyStuff. Try free for 30-days, $99 if you keep it, from `www.collectify.com`.

POLL: Is the spirit of the Web dead?

49% Yes

51% No

TODAY'S FOCUS: Online Auctions

TIME CLOCK INVENTED

Employees could no longer fudge on their workday when the first U.S. patent for a time clock was issued on this day in 1894. Daniel M. Cooper of Rochester, New York, developed the "Workman's Time Recorder" to keep track of laborers' hours. The terms "clocking in" and "clocking out" were coined when the invention, nicknamed the "Rochester," was first put into use.

Don't Get Ripped Off

By Jack Karp

Here's some advice on how you can protect yourself when bidding online.

Find Out How the Auction Works Some auction sites, such as eBay and Amazon.com, verify user IDs, insure sales, and prevent shilling (in which sellers or their friends bid on an item to drive up the price). Some auction sites don't. Read the rules and instructions on each auction site before you bid.

Do Your Homework Know exactly what you're bidding on. Find out its worth and whether or not it comes with a warranty, the seller's return policy, whether there are shipping charges, and the terms and conditions of the sale. Get a definite delivery date and ask the seller to insure the shipment. Print out and keep item descriptions and photos to document any claims the seller made.

Check Out the Seller Find out what other buyers have to say about the seller. Don't buy from someone with a bad track record. Also, keep in mind that glowing recommendations can be false, having been planted by the seller or his friends.

Get Contact Information Having the name, street address, and phone number of the seller can make it a lot easier to check up on that seller or follow up if there are problems. Don't deal with a seller who won't give you that information. Also, be cautious of addresses with P.O. boxes.

Be Wary of Certain Sales Be careful when bidding on expensive collectibles. Remember that you won't be able to examine them or have them appraised until after you've already paid for and received them. Many consumer protection laws don't apply to private sales or foreign sellers.

Use a Credit Card Paying with a credit card actually protects both the buyer and the seller. Buyers can dispute charges if an item is never delivered, and sellers don't have to worry about receiving bad checks.

Think About Insurance Many auction sites, including eBay and Amazon.com, insure buyers for up to a certain amount of money in case something goes wrong.

Consider Using an Escrow Service An escrow service can hold a buyer's payment and then forward it to the seller when the buyer receives the item. Although there's a small fee, sellers may find escrow services to be cheaper than using credit cards.

Report Fraud If you get conned, let the auction site and law enforcement agents know. The seller might be conning other buyers, and that person can't be stopped if no one knows what she's doing.

TIP OF THE DAY Search hundreds of auctions at once with BidFind, bidfind.com.

DOWNLOAD OF THE DAY BidderBlock prevents bad bidders from taking part in your auctions. Works with eBay. Free from hammertap.com.

POLL: Are you afraid to eBay?

38% Yes

62% No

OCTOBER 30

TODAY'S FOCUS: Halloween

LAST MULTICS MACHINE

After 18 years of service, the last computer to run the Multics operating system was shut down on this day in 2000 at the Laboratory for Computer Science at MIT. Multics was a mainframe timesharing system developed in the mid-1960s by MIT, Bell Labs, and General Electric. When Bell Labs dropped out of the Multics project in 1969, several of its programmers went on to create a substitute, playfully called *Unix*.

Related Web site `multicians.org`

Spooky Sites for Tonight

Halloween Screensaver (free-halloween-screensavers.com) Download this cool Halloween screensaver. It's a big ol' haunted house, all spooky-looking, with some pumpkin-headed ghosts that float across your screen.

Jack-o-Lantern (jack-o-lantern.com)   Jack-o-Lantern gives you a wealth of creative ideas on the old carving-a-pumpkin ritual. There are so many more ways to make ol' Jack than the usual triangle eyes, triangle nose, and gap-toothed grin.

Virtual Haunted House (www.geocities.com/Area51/Keep/8477/index-18.html) What's better for Halloween than a scary haunted house? We love the spirit behind this nonfrightening and cheesy Virtual Haunted House, even if the execution leaves a bit to be desired.

Haunted America (www.hauntedamerica.com) Ghost stories are another staple of Halloween. There's something about this time of year that makes you much more susceptible to these spooky tales. Haunted America is a repository of ghost stories collected from around the nation. Browse by state, read stories, and even submit your own.

International Ghost Hunters Society (www.ghostweb.com) International Ghost Hunters Society isn't quite as catchy as "Ghostbusters," but it will have to do when you have a real spook or poltergeist that needs getting rid of. No word on whether the society has those cool laser guns and ghost traps or whether they drive a hearse.

Corpses for Sale (www.distefano.com) Not for the squeamish, Corpses for Sale will sell you, well, a corpse—or a really realistic-looking fake one, anyway. The site brags that even a foot away you couldn't tell the difference from the real thing, except for the smell. Now isn't that just a pleasant thought?

Moonlight Manor (www.jade-leaves.com/moonpalace/moonlightmanor/) We can't quite make heads or tails of this, but Moonlight Manor wins the award as the coolest virtual haunted house we've seen on the Net. It's a Myst-type point-and-click game played entirely on your favorite Web browser.

 TIP OF THE DAY It's not too late to send a spooky Halloween card with the help of these online greeting card sites.

Blue Mountain (www.bluemountain.com/eng/halloween) This widely used greeting card site lets you choose from several animated and musical graphics.

Hallmark.com (www.hallmark.com/hmk/Website/Shopping/sh_eg_home.jsp) This Web site has a more sophisticated selection of virtual greetings, most of which use Flash animation.

AmericanGreetings.com (www.americangreetings.com) There are several Halloween cards to choose from here.

 DOWNLOAD OF THE DAY Me On A Pumpkin is a wonderful program that can take any picture and turn it into a stencil suitable for a fancy pumpkin carving. There's no free download for the program—I guess they figure since you'll use it only once a year they'd better get your money up front. It's only $20 for Windows from meonapumpkin.com. You can download some cool stencils for free, though, from meonapumpkin.com/freestuff.

NOVEMBER 2003

NOVEMBER 2003

SUNDAY	MONDAY	TUESDAY	WEDNESDAY	THURSDAY	FRIDAY	SATURDAY
						1 U.S. explodes the first hydrogen bomb (1952)
2	**3** Soviets send first dog into space (1957)	**4**	**5** Nintendo releases the GameCube (2001)	**6**	**7**	**8** Microsoft releases the Xbox (2001)
9 Carl Edward Sagan born (1934)	**10** First nonoperator-assisted long-distance call (1951)	**11** Kurt Vonnegut, Jr. born (1922); Veterans' Day	**12**	**13**	**14** Apollo 12 launched (1969)	**15**
16	**17** Comdex Fall, Las Vegas, Nevada	**18**	**19**	**20** Windows 1.0 released (1985)	**21** MacExpo (London); phonograph invented by Thomas Edison (1877)	**22**
23/30	**24** Darwin's *Origin of Species* published (1859)	**25** Dynamite invented (1867)	**26**	**27** Thanksgiving Day	**28** U.S. Mariner 4 completes first mission to Mars (1964)	**29** Leo Laporte's birthday

ARTIFICIAL INSEMINATION SUCCESS

The first animal in the U.S. to be conceived by artificial impregnation was shown off to the public on this day in 1939. Dr. Gregory Pincus of Clark University fertilized an egg he had removed from a female rabbit's ovary. The egg was then transferred to the womb of a second rabbit, where the embryo matured until delivery. The rabbit was put on display at the New York Academy of Medicine. Dr. Pincus later went on to help develop the birth control pill in the early 1950s.

Related Web site   www.plannedparenthood.org

Auction Sniping

By Beth Rimbey and Nicole Guilfoyle

Online auctions are full of fierce competition as people place their bids, hoping to be the final winner. What many bidders don't know is that there are people lying in wait to snatch up the prize at the last second. Sniping, the act of placing last-second bids, has become rampant in the online auction world.

There are ways to protect yourself from the guile of the auction sniper. Amazon Auctions, for example, automatically extends an auction every time a new bid is placed at the last minute to ensure that the highest bidder wins. Yahoo! and eBay both offer auctions with hard closes and automatic extensions, but you'll need to do your research to find out which type of auction you're participating in.

But what if you don't want to restrict yourself to auctions with automatic extensions? Some say if you don't beat 'em, join 'em. "The best thing to do is learn how to snipe. Learning how to snipe isn't difficult, it's not illegal, it's not immoral, everyone can do it and everyone should," says freelance high-tech columnist Dennis L. Prince.

If you're determined to become an auction sniper, software and the Net can help. Programs such as Cricket Jr (cricketsniper.com) and Merlin AuctionMagic (merlinsoftware.com) can be programmed to automatically execute bids seconds before the clock stops ticking.

If you don't want to pay for software, or you worry your Internet connection is too slow to execute bids fast enough, Prince recommends turning to the Net. "There's also a Web site called esnipe at esnipe.com that's a

Web-based sniping tool," says Prince, "The sniping actually takes place on their server as opposed to these other programs, which you download to your PC."

As the ethical debate rages on, online auctions are sure to heat up. Look for more technology to change the face of online auctions in the future.

(Beth Rimbey is a reporter for TechTV, and Nicole Guilfoyle is a Web producer for Call for Help.)

TIP OF THE DAY   Buy what you need and benefit the needy at these charitable auction sites:

- Goodwill: www.shopgoodwill.com
- MissionFish: missionfish.com
- WebCharity: webcharity.com
- Yahoo Charity Auctions: auctions.yahoo.com/phtml/auc/us/charity/charity.html

 DOWNLOAD OF THE DAY   Automatically make those last-second bids with iSnipeIt for Windows. Free to try, $33.95, no, make that $34.95 to buy, from isnipeit.com.

Want a free tool? Try HammerSnipe PowerTool, free from HammerTap.com. Uses its own sniping server to guarantee the bids get in on time.

POLL: Would you use a single-use credit card?

66% Yes

34% No

NOVEMBER 1

TODAY'S FOCUS: Online Auctions

FIRST INTERNET WORM

The first known Internet worm escaped into the wild on this day in 1988. The "Morris Worm," written by 23-year-old Cornell doctoral student Robert Tappan Morris, Jr., infected more than 6,000 computers in just a few hours. The worm took advantage of a bug in the Unix fingerd and sendmail programs. Although it didn't alter any files or cause any physical damage, the worm spread more rapidly than the author had intended. Morris was fined $10,050 and ordered to complete 400 hours of community service. The event also spurred the formation of the Computer Emergency Response Team (CERT).

Related Web site www.cert.org

Auction Tips

By David Spark

1. Promotional Tool Even if you already have an e-commerce site, an auction can do wonders for Web traffic. Take a few notable items out of your storeroom and put them up for auction. Choose unusual items. The goal is to garner some recognition, interest, and ideally some press. On your auction page, include a link back to your store.

2. Alternative Spellings All searches are conducted in your item's description field. So, obviously, you'll want to include as many descriptive keywords as you can. In addition, consider alternative spellings of your product. For example, selling a Game Boy? Write it as one word ("Gameboy") and two words ("Game Boy").

3. Don't Waste Real Estate On eBay, the description field allows for a maximum of 45 characters. Avoid wasting precious real estate with Crazy Eddie terminology such as "awesome" and "wow!" Nobody's searching for an "awesome Game Boy."

4. Keep Pictures Small Use JPEGs instead of GIFs. Edit your picture. Make it look good. Don't doctor it up. Keep it small. Your max for all pictures combined should be 50K. Give visitors the option to click through for larger and alternative images on your site.

5. Keep Pages Small This goes hand-in-hand with keeping pictures small. If visitors have to wait for your page to load, they'll go place a bid at one of your competitors' sites.

6. Give Background For collectibles, give some background; people will pay for a good story. But keep it short. Ideally, write in bullet points. No essays.

7. Make It Easy to Read Browse through some of the auctions on eBay. What do most of them have in common? They're hideous to look at! You can do better.

8. End Your Auction on a Weekend Start your auction so it closes late on a Saturday or Sunday. That way, you'll get maximum bids: Web traffic is highest on the weekend, and most bidding happens during an auction's last 48 hours.

9. Avoid Reserve Pricing Reserve-pricing figures are kept hidden from bidders. Most people are hesitant about participating in reserve auctions, so dump the reserve price. You'll be surprised at how many more bids you'll get.

 TIP OF THE DAY If you're worried about selling your stuff yourself, use a trading assistant: an eBay veteran who will do the selling for you for a fee. Terms are negotiable: ebay.com/tradingassistants.

  DOWNLOAD OF THE DAY Auction Tender for Mac OS 9, X, and Windows keeps track of your customers, prints packing slips, and generates ads and email templates. Free to try, $14.95 to buy, from colourfull.com/ATver30.htm.

TODAY'S FOCUS: Macintosh

FIRST VIRUS CREATED

The first computer virus was written as an experiment on this day in 1983. Len Adleman designed the virus to prove to security experts that such a thing was possible. The virus took eight hours to develop and was implanted into a Unix VAX 11/750 system. A total of five experiments were performed, including a demonstration at a security seminar on November 10. The famous virus never escaped into the wild, however. Adleman is credited with coining the term "computer virus," and is the "A" in RSA Security, a world-renowned data security firm.

Related Web site www.rsasecurity.com

Living Mac in a PC World

These days we few, we proud, we Mac users live in a world where Windows users get the first pick of all the good software. Or at least it seems that way. It's certainly true for gaming and productivity apps. Macintosh holds its own in Web design and multimedia, although there are some strange gaps. One wonders why there are no good CAD programs on the Mac.

Yet, for most tasks, it's possible to use a Macintosh and get the job done. All new Macs come with AppleWorks, an excellent all-in-one office suite. For power users, there's Microsoft Office. The latest version of Office, Office.X, is in many ways superior to the Windows version. And both AppleWorks and Office can read and write Microsoft Office for Windows files. That means your Windows-saddled co-workers don't even have to know you're using a Mac.

Macintosh computers can read and write disks formatted by Windows, so physically moving files back and forth is easy. Mac OS X can coexist on Windows networks with no additional software, sharing file servers, printers, and other network resources automatically.

When it comes to the most popular use for any computer, email and the Internet, Macs are very nearly equal to Windows. Some sites won't work on a Mac, but they're getting fewer. After all, who wants to leave millions of users out in the cold?

In one way, Macintosh has stolen a lead on Windows. Mac OS X is based on Unix and can use the thousands of applications designed for Unix. Windows can't.

As far as I'm concerned, a computer is a computer. I'm a noncombatant in the operating system wars. I use Windows and Macintosh and have found something to love in both of them. But if you prefer one over the other, you should be able to choose it, confident that you'll be able to get the job done.

Unless there's a specific Windows application you have to run, or a piece of Windows hardware you just have to have, feel free to choose Macintosh. After all, it's the only computer that smiles at you when you turn it on.

 TIP OF THE DAY MacLinkPlus Pro for the Mac can read and write most PC file formats. $99 from www.dataviz.com/products/maclinkplus.

 DOWNLOAD OF THE DAY Convert Windows TrueType fonts to Macintosh format with TT Converter, free for Classic from ngenious.com/signaturefactory/ttconverter.htm.

POLL: Did Apple do the right thing in ending licensing?

41% Yes, clones hurt Apple and the Macintosh.

59% No, Mac clones were good for the Mac market.

NOVEMBER 3

TODAY'S FOCUS: Macintosh

KING TUT'S TOMB DISCOVERED

The entrance to the tomb of King Tutankhamen was discovered in the Valley of the Kings in Egypt on this day in 1922. The excavation, led by British archaeologist Howard Carter, uncovered several thousand objects and the 3,000-year-old mummified body of the "boy king." Perhaps as mysterious as the tomb itself is the myth of the "mummy's curse." Carter's financial backer, Lord Carnarvon, died suddenly a few months after Tut's sarcophagus was opened. By 1929, 11 people connected with the discovery of the tomb had died early and of unnatural causes.

Related Web sites `www.emuseum.gov.eg`, `www.nationalgeographic.com/egypt/`

OS X's Built-In Firewall

Mac OS X comes with an industrial-strength firewall called *ipfw*. Like many other applications hidden in OS X, ipfw is part of Darwin, the FreeBSD Unix foundation upon which OS X is built. While OS X is generally secure as shipped, the firewall is not enabled. If you use your Macintosh on the Internet, it should be.

You can configure ipfw by hand, but it's tricky. A misconfigured firewall is worse than no firewall at all. It's safest to download a front end to ipfw. Two good shareware choices are available:

- Brian R. Hill's BrickHouse, $25 from `personal-pages.tds.net/~brian_hill`
- Glu's Impasse: $10 from `glu.com/products/impasse`

Pick one or the other—they don't coexist well. I'll use BrickHouse as an example, because that's what I use.

When you run BrickHouse, it will walk you through a series of choices about the kind of protection you want. In general, it's best to block all incoming and outgoing traffic except for the services you know you want, such as HTTP (for the Web) and FTP (for file transfer). Based on your decisions, BrickHouse will create a configuration script for ipfw and install a startup script that turns on ipfw each time you boot.

If you want to understand what ipfw is doing, I recommend an excellent discussion of BSD security and ipfw on the FreeBSD Web site, `www.freebsd.org/handbook/firewalls.html`. Keep in mind that OS X does things a little differently than FreeBSD, so some of the instructions

don't apply. You can also read the manual by opening the Terminal application and typing `man ipfw`.

When you have your firewall running, check it by visiting ShieldsUp at grc.com. With ipfw running, ShieldsUp should give you a clean bill of health, assuring you that your system is fully secure. You won't need to run BrickHouse again unless you want to change your configuration.

 TIP OF THE DAY If you use Apple's AirPort wireless networking (or any 802.11b or WiFi network), be sure to secure it by turning on WEP encryption and requiring a password to log on to your network. Open the AirPort Admin Utility, select your base station, and then select **Configure Base Station** from the **File** menu.

 DOWNLOAD OF THE DAY GPG, the GNU Privacy Guard, is a set of strong encryptions tools that are open-source replacements for PGP (Pretty Good Privacy). Available free from gnupg.org.

 For Mac OS X, install the command-line GNU Privacy Guard using fink or download the installer from macgpg.sourceforge.net. Use GPGKeys for a graphical interface and GPG DropThing to easily encrypt files.

To combine GPG with Entourage, download EntourageGPG from software.simonster.com/entourageGPG.php.

All programs are open source and free.

TODAY'S FOCUS: Macintosh

INDUSTRIAL DESIGN PIONEER BORN

Raymond Fernand Loewy was born in Paris on this day in 1893. The "Father of Streamlining" was responsible for the refinement of many modern machines and consumer products. Loewy moved to the U.S. in 1919 and began redesigning radios, toothbrushes, refrigerators, and more. He also designed several models of Studebaker cars, and numerous trains and buses. In the 1970s, Loewy helped NASA design the experimental space station Skylab. The inventor and engineer is also known for creating the logos for the U.S. Post Office and Air Force One. Loewy died in Monaco at age 92.

Related Web site   `www.raymondloewyfoundation.com`

Mac OS X Tips

Hack into Darwin   Enter the single-user shell by pressing Command+S on boot. You'll be at a BSD command prompt. Here are some things you can do:

Check your disk: Type

`fsck -y`

Change your root password: Type

`/sbin/mount -uw /`
`/sbin/SystemStarter`

When the prompt returns after a minute or so, type

`passwd root`

to change the root password. Works with any username.

Type **reboot** when you're done.

Keep People from Hacking into Darwin   If you *don't* want people changing your root password, download Apple's Open Firmware, free from `apple.com/downloads/macosx/apple/openfirmwarepassword.html`.

Make Linux Users Jealous   Watch your machine start up in all its geeky glory by pressing Command+V on boot for a verbose startup.

Snoop Inside Applications   Control-click on an application and select **Show Package Contents** to browse inside. The Resources folder often contains interesting pictures and icons. Check the OS X screensavers for some great images you can use as wallpaper.

Reset Passwords   Here's another way to change your admin password:
1. Insert your Mac OS X CD.
2. Restart while holding the C key.

3. When the installer appears, go to the **Installer** menu.
4. Choose **Reset Password**.

Software Update   You should run software update regularly to make sure your system is up to date, but if there are some updates you never want to install (such as all those different language versions or printer drivers for printers you don't own), you can turn them off. Open **Software Update**, click Update Now, and then select Make Inactive from the **Update** menu.

TIP OF THE DAY   OS X Keyboard Tricks

Click and hold on an icon in the dock to get a pop-up menu of things you can do with that icon. Press the Option key to see additional options.

Command+Tab switches between applications. Keep your finger on Command and tap H to hide the application or Q to quit it. Command+Shift reverses direction.

Option+Command+clicking on an application in the Dock will select that application and hide all others.

Command+Option+A opens the Application folder.

Option+ any sound key brings up the Sound System Preference pane.

Option+ any display brightness key brings up the Displays pane.

If you hold down Option when you use scrollbars, it will scroll pages instead of lines.

DOWNLOAD OF THE DAY   Get your friends to say, "How'd you do that?" with Transparent Dock. Makes the Mac OS X dock transparent; your icons will float on air. Free from `homepage.mac.com/kfkel`.

NOVEMBER 5

TODAY'S FOCUS: Macintosh

NEW YORK'S FIRST FLASHING SIGN

The biggest electric flashing sign of its day was installed on *The New York Times* building on this day in 1928. The sign covered all four sides of the building and used more than 14,000 light bulbs. Although impressive at the time, it was only a flicker in comparison to the signs of New York City today. Times Square now boasts some of the largest illuminated signs in the world. The eight-story NASDAQ MarketSite Tower, for example, measures 10,800 square feet and consists of 8,200 modules, which are divided into eight screens made up of more than 18 million LEDs.

Related Web site   `timessquarebid.org`

Mac to PC and Back

Macs don't come with floppy disk drives anymore, so you no longer can share files with your Windows friends on floppy. But there are many other ways to exchange files between a PC and Macintosh.

Ethernet Connection   To network your Mac and PC, you'll need an Ethernet card for your PC, a single CAT5 crossover cable (or a pair of normal cables and a hub), and some software. All recent Macs come already equipped with Ethernet.

If you're using OS 9, you'll need to download either Thursby Software's Dave, from `www.thursby.com/products/dave.html`, or PC Maclan from Miramar Systems, `www.miramarsys.com/products`.

Mac OS X-equipped Macs should be able to see the Windows network without additional software. Check out our tip on June 29.

Removable Media   Macs can read and write PC-formatted disks with no additional help. So, use a PC-formatted Zip, Jaz, Orb, or other removable disk to swap files. Be sure to use PC-style file extensions in all your filenames.

I use a small USB drive to transfer files back and forth. This solid-state device fits in my pocket and can hold anywhere from 16MB to 1GB. The smaller sizes are very inexpensive. Look for a USB drive that adheres to the USB Mass Storage class specification. It will work with nearly any computer without drivers. CD-R/W and DVD-RW work fine, too.

MacDrive   If you need to get the PC to read a Mac disk, MacDrive 5 makes any Mac-formatted floppy, Zip, Jaz, SyQuest, CD-ROM, CD-R, or hard drive act like a normal PC disk. It will even allow you to format disks in the Mac format directly from Windows. It also preserves long filenames and even indicates Mac files with a special icon. The program is free to try for five days or $49.95 if you decide to keep it.

TIP OF THE DAY   The latest Macs come with pretty good video cards, but older versions of Mac OS X are not designed to take advantage of them. Upgrade to Mac OS X 10.2, a.k.a. Jaguar, for the best performance on machines with GeForce and Radeon video cards.

DOWNLOAD OF THE DAY   Refight World War II from the air with WarBirds III. Download and play the single-player version for free, or pay to go online and join hundreds of other flying aces in bombing runs, dogfights, and more. For Mac and Windows, from `www.ient.com/warbirds`. Check the site for free weekend play times.

POLL: What operating system should the government use?

25% Windows

13% Mac

43% Linux

19% Other

PENTIUM BUG REVEALED

A floating-point bug in Intel's first Pentium chip was announced in the *Electrical Engineering Times* on this day in 1994. Intel spokespeople admitted they had known about the problem for some time, but claimed they didn't consider it serious enough to mention. The bug, although rare, caused mathematical errors while performing high-precision computations. More notably, however, it created an outrage among computer users when Intel said it would replace flawed chips only if users could prove they used the computer to make these complicated calculations. After considerable pressure, the company eventually agreed to replace all chips upon request.

Related Web site `www.intel.com`

The Mac OS X Web Server

Mac OS X comes with the most popular Web server software in the world: Apache. Turning your machine into a Web host is easy. Open the Sharing preference pane and click the **Start** button under **Web Sharing**. Apache is now running.

Open your browser and enter the URL `localhost`. The default Apache Web page will show up. Where's it coming from? Deep within your system: /Library/Webserver/ Documents. You could build a Web site there, but there's another location that's much better.

Take a look at your home directory. Notice a Sites folder in there? That's where your personal Web site should go. In fact, a temporary Web site is already in there. Go back to your browser and enter the URL `localhost/ ~yourname`. Replace *yourname* with your username. The page that loads is the index.html file inside the Sites folder.

To create a new Web site, replace index.html with your own custom creation. If you're on a network, other people can see your site, too. Replace `localhost` with your IP address in the URL above, and they'll be able to surf there from anywhere on the Internet.

That does raise an important security issue. When you turn on Apache, you are opening up access to your system. Apache is very secure, but it's always best to be careful. Turn off the server when you're not using it.

TIP OF THE DAY In Mac OS X (and all Unix-based operating systems), each user's personal files are located in his or her home directory. On OS X, the default location of home is /Users/yourlogin. You can change the location of your home directory with the NetInfo Manager.

Open NetInfo Manager—it's in the Utilities folder. Click the Users section in the middle pane, and then choose a user in the right pane. Scroll down in the lower window until you see the home property. To the right is the path to home. You can change that by clicking the padlock in the lower-left corner and entering the Administrator password.

DOWNLOAD OF THE DAY To change your picture on the Mac OS X login screen, open the Login pane in System Preferences. Click the **Login Window** tab. Be sure **Automatically Login** is unchecked. Click the **List of Users with Accounts on This Computer** radio button.

Now open the Users preference pane. From the list, select your username. Click the **Identity** tab. You can drag any picture, even from the hard drive, to the Login Picture: window to make it your login picture.

TODAY'S FOCUS: Macintosh

ELECTRIC PLUG PATENTED

The precursor to the modern plug was patented on this day in 1904. Originally, electricity was used only for lighting purposes. Houses were wired only with light sockets for screw-in bulbs. Harvey Hubbell II invented an adapter with two holes that mounted onto a light-bulb socket. A separate device, called a "separable attachment-plug," was equipped with two prongs that matched the holes. The outlets were later hard-wired directly to the circuitry of a building. Hubbell's two-prong plugs were the same basic design and shape as the electric plugs still used in the U.S. today.

Related Web site `www.hubbell-ltg.com/`

Dr. Mac's Top Five Speed-Up Tips

By Bob LeVitus

Here are some of my favorite tips for speeding up your Mac's performance and your productivity when running OS X.

1. More RAM makes OS X faster. How much is enough? Apple claims OS X will run on 128MB of RAM, and it will, but if you plan to use any programs with it, you'll want more—at least 256MB.

2. Using up the RAM in your Mac will still slow things down. If you're experiencing virtual memory "pageouts," you need more RAM.

To monitor virtual memory, open the Terminal application in your Utilities folder. Type **top** followed by a carriage return. Look for the number of pageouts: It's the last statistic in the first paragraph of information. Zero pageouts is good. More than a few, and you need more memory. Press **q** when you're done with top.

3. Don't quit programs if you think you'll use them again before you log out, reboot, or shut down. Because OS X doesn't crash very often and rarely needs to be restarted, you can save a lot of time each day by not quitting a program you expect to use again. I usually have between 10 and 20 programs running at any given time. In fact, I have 10 programs in my Login Items system preference panel that start up automatically when I log in. They remain open until I log out.

4. Keeping your hands off the mouse will make you more productive. Learn and use keyboard shortcuts instead of menus.

5. The Mac OS X Finder is slow; avoid it if you can. Because I like to keep my hands off the mouse, my favorite tool for avoiding the Finder is LaunchBar, a $20 shareware program that lets you open any item on any mounted volume by typing a few letters of its name. Or, you can use a more visual (and more mouse-intensive) Finder substitute such as DragThing or DropDrawers. Try all three, but adopt one or more to increase your productivity.

All the programs mentioned here (and more) can be found at `VersionTracker.com`.

(Bob "Dr. Mac" LeVitus is a columnist and resident tipster at `OSXFAQ.com`.)

 TIP OF THE DAY   Not much can crash OS X. In fact, I know of only two things that can: buggy drivers and hardware problems. If your system is crashing, check the RAM. Download Gauge Pro, a Classic application, free from `macupdate.com/info.php/id/4512`.

 DOWNLOAD OF THE DAY   TinkerTool is an easy way to tweak many of Mac OS X user interface settings. Download a copy free from `bresink.de/osx`.

TODAY'S FOCUS: Macintosh

VIRUS DISCOVERER BORN

The man who discovered viruses was born on this day in 1864. Russian microbiologist Dmitri Ivanovski made the discovery in 1890 while studying a mysterious disease that was killing tobacco crops. Ivanovski realized that an organism found in sap could transfer diseases between plants.

Related Web site `library.thinkquest.org/23054/basics/page3.html`

Three Things You Didn't Know About Apple

By Martin Sargent

Think you know everything about the Apple Computer story? We'll see about that.

Jobs in Space When Steve Jobs was chairman of the board at Apple Computer during the mid-1980s, he really didn't have all that much to do. So, with his usual arrogance, Jobs tried to convince NASA to let him ride along on the next voyage of the space shuttle. NASA said no, which turned out to be a very good thing for Jobs: The shuttle that he would have ridden on was the Challenger, which tragically blew up two minutes into its flight, killing all seven crew members.

The Magic Bus To get the money needed to make the original Apple I circuit board, Steve Jobs had to sell his red-and-white Volkswagen Bus for $1,500. Jobs was something of a hippie, even spending a lot of time at a commune in Oregon called the All One Farm. Fellow Apple brainchild Steve Wozniak contributed by selling an HP 65 programmable calculator for $250.

Speaking of the cars of Apple, Wozniak's father once found $250,000 worth of uncashed checks littering his son's vehicle like Big Mac wrappers. Woz's father is quoted as saying, "A person like him shouldn't have that much money."

The Third Founder We've all heard that there was a fifth Beatle, and there was also a third founder of Apple: a painfully unlucky man named Ron Wayne. Wayne, who created the original Apple logo of Sir Isaac Newton sitting under a tree, was given 10% of the company stock when he, Jobs, and Wozniak founded the company. But that 10% share also made him responsible for 10% of any debts the company incurred. Wayne got scared that the Apple wasn't going anywhere, so he sold his share of the company for $500 and reportedly bought a coin shop.

 TIP OF THE DAY Winter's here, and winter driving can be dangerous. Use your computer to stay safe.

Test your knowledge of winter road safety at `www.mtq. gouv.qc.ca/etat_routes/jeu_en.htm`. Take the French version for a real challenge.

The Federal Emergency Management Agency (FEMA) publishes a Winter Driving Fact Sheet full of excellent tips on how to prepare for and deal with emergency road conditions: `www.fema.gov/hazards/winterstorms/ winterf.shtm`.

FEMA also provides wire updates on potential emergency situations and weather forecast maps for the next six to ten days on its Storm Watch page: `www.fema.gov/ storm/winter.shtm`.

Check the Federal Highway Administration's National Traffic and Road Closure page for links to current highway information, lane closures, and weather conditions: `www.fhwa.dot.gov/trafficinfo/#WEAT`.

 DOWNLOAD OF THE DAY Keep track of hundreds of news sites in the Mac OS X Dock. MacReporter gets the headlines so you can scan them, and then fetches the article if you want to read it. Free to try, $12 to buy, from `inferiis.com/mac/ macreporter`.

POLL: Which OS do you want at work?

42% Windows

35% Mac

23% Linux

NOVEMBER 9

FIRST MOTORCYCLE

The first motorbike of sorts made its debut on this day in 1885. The Gottlieb Daimler Reitwagen, or "riding car," was built as an experiment to test the company's new engine: The one-cylinder was capable of 0.5hp at 700rpm. The motorcycle's frame and wheels were made of wood, and power was transferred from the engine to the gears by a leather belt. The contraption could reach a top speed of 12 kilometers per hour. A year later, Daimler used the same engine to power its first motorized carriage.

Related Web site www.daimlerchrysler.com

Upgrading Your Computer

By Rich Fisco

New PCs cost as little as a few hundred dollars and are orders of magnitude faster than a machine that's just a few years old. But if you can't bear to part with that old beast, here are the upgrades to consider, in order of bang for your buck.

RAM Although many people think a faster processor will give them the biggest performance boost, memory is a better place to start. Adding RAM to any Windows system with less than 128MB will speed things up. If you run multiple applications, you need 256MB or more.

Hard Drive Hard drive upgrades are usually done for more space, but you can get a performance improvement in the deal as well. A hard disk's rotational speed is key. Old IDE drives spin at 5,400rpm or less, whereas the fastest rotate at 7,200rpm. Hard drive prices have plummeted. You might be surprised at how much you can get for less than $100.

Video Card If you're not into today's fast-moving, 3D shoot-'em-up games, a graphics card upgrade is a waste of money; 2D performance for applications such as a word processor, home finance programs, and email is fast enough with just about any card. 3D performance in games, on the other hand, is where you can find even the most powerful system brought to its knees. If this happens to you, consider one of the new 3D accelerators based on the Nvidia GeForce 4 or ATI Radeon 8500 chipsets.

CPU The upgrade least likely to make a difference is your CPU. Check companies such as PowerLeap (powerleap.com) and Evergreen Technologies (evertech.com) to see what upgrades will work with your system. Keep this in mind, though: If a new CPU costs more than $100, it makes more sense to get a whole new machine.

(Rich Fisco is technical director at PC Magazine Labs.)

TIP OF THE DAY **Q:** Can I use 133MHz RAM on a motherboard with a bus speed of 100MHz? — Jeremy, Las Vegas, Nevada

A: Yes. The speed rating on the RAM is the maximum it can tolerate. It will run at a slower rate just fine. The opposite doesn't apply, however. It's unlikely that PC-100 RAM will work reliably on a 133MHz motherboard.

DOWNLOAD OF THE DAY Make 2003 like 2001…

The HALemulator from Galatoire Games adds the look, feel, and sound of Stanley Kubrick's creepy talking computer HAL-9000 to your desktop. Free for Mac Classic from galatoire.com/software.

PC users can get HAL toys, too, from tbid.com/toybox/pg/hal9000.html.

POLL: Would you want a vibrating mouse?
47% Yes
34% No
19% Zzzzzzzzzz

NOVEMBER 10

TODAY'S FOCUS: Veterans Day

TELESCOPE PATENTED

An important telescope design was patented by Alvan Clark of Cambridge, Massachusetts, on this day in 1851. Clark was a portrait painter and avid amateur astronomer. With the help of his two sons, Clark began developing small lenses and mirrors for telescopes. Alvan Clark & Sons became one of the largest telescope lens manufacturers during the 1800s. Their 40-inch lens at the Yerkes Observatory at the University of Chicago is still the largest working refractor in the world today.

Related Web site `astro.uchicago.edu/yerkes`

Veterans' Sites

By Alison Strahan

Armistice Day marked the end of World War I at the 11th hour of the 11th day of the 11th month in 1918. Now known as Veterans Day, the holiday commemorates the soldiers from all the wars of the twentieth century.

Veterans of Foreign Wars (`www.vfw.org/amesm/origins.shtml`) The VFW is the oldest American veterans organization, and has advocated for benefits and assistance for veterans returning home. Read a description of the history of Veterans Day, originally Armistice Day. Suggestions for helping out servicemen and women include instructions on how to donate a phone card or adopt a unit.

The American Legion (`legion.org`) The American Legion is a community-service organization for America's wartime veterans. The site includes resources and downloads for teachers and schools to learn more about Veterans Day. You can also send a Veterans Day-inspired e-card to friends or family serving in the military.

Vets Day (`www.umkc.edu/imc/vetsday.htm`) This site has many great project ideas for kids to learn more about Veterans Day and honor the vets. One suggestion is to start a class project of writing to hospitalized veterans to let them know they aren't forgotten.

U.S. Department of Veterans Affairs (`www.va.gov/vetsday`) Naturally, the VA has its own Veterans Day page, with a history of the day, a FAQ, patriotic fact sheet, and links to several excellent educational sites, including the Army's History of Korea and the White House Lessons of Liberty.

Veterans History Project (`www.loc.gov/folklife/vets`) The best way to learn about how our veterans served America is through their own voices. The dramatic Veterans History Project at the U.S. Library of Congress will touch you and fill you with pride in our country.

TIP OF THE DAY Windows XP and 2000 use a DNS cache to save look-up time (most modern operating systems do) but the Microsoft implementation is flawed. After a page gets a DNS error for any reason, even if it's just that the DNS server was busy for a moment, the entire domain will be inaccessible until you restart Windows.

To permanently fix this problem, download a Registry patch from John Navas's Cable Modem/DSL Tuning Guide, at `cable-dsl.home.att.net`. When you get there, search for "reduce DNS errors" and download the INF file. Right-click it and select **Install** from the pop-up menu. You can delete the file after you install the patches.

DOWNLOAD OF THE DAY Origin Systems has released the classic Ultima IV as freeware. Originally released in 1985, Ultima IV: The Quest of the Avatar was truly innovative in its emphasis on ethics and the consequences of your actions. Download the complete package free for DOS from `uo.warcry.com/index.php/content/ultima4`.

NOVEMBER 11

TODAY'S FOCUS: Advanced Hardware Hacking

FIRST LOBOTOMY

The first modern brain surgery to "cure" mental illness was performed on this day in 1935. Egas Moniz first used the procedure on a human at Santa Marta Hospital in Lisbon, Portugal. Moniz drilled two holes into a mental patient's skull and injected pure alcohol into the frontal lobes, thereby killing the brain's emotional nerve center. The operation was based on previous work done by Yale University scientist Carlyle Jacobsen, who had experimented with the technique on chimpanzees. Moniz was awarded a Nobel Prize in Physiology or Medicine for his work in 1949. Lobotomies are almost never used anymore, and are considered by many to be inhumane.

Related Web site   www.psych.org

How Does a Surge Suppressor Work?

By Bill Manning

Imagine that a bolt of lightning just hit a transformer near your house, sending nearly 6,000 volts into your AC lines. Your computer and electronic equipment were built to handle a peak surge voltage of roughly 300–500 volts. A good surge suppressor reduces that massive voltage to let through the same safe level of power your equipment was receiving before the lightning strike.

Surge suppressors reduce surges by absorbing, filtering, and diverting the current:

* Filters isolate surges from the protected load.
* Suppressors divert the surge from protected loads.
* Surges are clamped or limited to a peak voltage, and the energy from the excess voltage is absorbed.

Each of these methods has shortcomings that prevent them from being completely effective alone.

Combine Your Surge Suppressor Methods   Metal oxide varistors (MOVs) are the most common component of choice to suppress surges/spikes. These devices typically achieve full clamping at 300 volts or more. However, an MOV by itself will let through a wide variety of common surges without attenuation.

When MOVs are used in combination with circuits, which filter and divert surges, they achieve the most effective protection. Surge-protection products that incorporate MOVs and across-the-line capacitors or LC filtering networks will attenuate a surge better than MOV-only products.

A surge suppressor with a balanced design will always exhibit superior performance to a "hardware store"-type surge suppressor.

Essential Surge Suppressor Features   Make sure your surge suppressor incorporates the following:

* **Let-Through Voltage**—Less than or equal to 300 volts.
* **Building Wiring Fault Indicator**—Diagnoses any problems with your outlet and wiring. If the surge suppressor isn't plugged into a properly wired outlet, it won't provide the necessary protection. Without this indicator, you might not know until it's too late.
* **Protection Working Indicator**—Lets you know if the surge suppressor is working properly. If it isn't lit, the unit has been damaged and should be replaced.
* **Thermal and Fast-Acting Fuses**—Your surge suppressor should incorporate these fuses into its construction. In the event of a massive surge, the fuses will blow, disconnecting your equipment from the utility to prevent further damage.

TIP OF THE DAY   Master obscure computer networking topics, such as priority queuing, HSRP, and IP access lists, with the help of celebrities such as Don King, Gary Coleman, and Anna Nicole Smith at routergod.com. Sure beats CCIE night school.

DOWNLOAD OF THE DAY   Give your computer that "fresh-tested" feeling with Fresh Diagnose. Analyze, inventory, and benchmark your system, free for Windows from freshdevices.com.

TODAY'S FOCUS: Advanced Hardware Hacking

FIRST MAN-MADE SNOW

Scientists created the first man-made storm on this day in 1946. Vincent Joseph Schaefer, a researcher at General Electric, dropped several pounds of dry-ice pellets from an airplane into a cloud over Mount Greylock, Massachusetts, and caused snow to fall. Previously, Schaefer had used a home freezer in the GE lab to create miniature clouds, and discovered that dry ice (frozen carbon dioxide) created precipitation. Schaefer later led a team that cut out a giant GE logo in a cloud during a demonstration. His weather modification techniques were known as the first example of "cloud seeding."

Related Web sites `www.nws.noaa.gov/`, `www.ametsoc.org`

Tweak Your Monitor

Many factors can affect the appearance of your monitor, ranging from adjustments to stray magnetic fields. Here are some tips that will help your display look its best.

Place your monitor away from strong magnetic sources, and not in direct sunlight or bright light.

Adjust the size of the displayed image on the monitor. Start by adjusting it to fit the edges of the screen—on curved screens, your image should not extend all the way to the front bezel. Use a square grid to be sure the aspect ratio is accurate: Adjust the screen until both sides of a square in the grid are equal.

Adjust brightness and contrast. It's easiest to do this with a monitor testing utility such as Displaymate or our DOWNLOAD OF THE DAY.

Common Monitor Controls

Contrast/Brightness   Use the contrast control to adjust the difference in brightness between the light and dark areas of the screen. Use the brightness control to dim or brighten the monitor screen.

Zoom   This control will stretch the monitor's screen both horizontally and vertically at the same time. Use this control if you have a black frame around your screen.

H-Position   The H stands for horizontal. This allows you to move the entire contents of the screen left or right.

V-Position   The V stands for vertical. This allows you to move the entire contents of the screen up or down.

Pincushion/Balance   Corrects the distortion of horizontal and vertical lines, which tend to bend inward toward the center of the display.

Keystone/Trapezoid   Corrects the distortion when vertical lines are straight but not parallel with each other.

Color Temperature/RGB   Adjusts red, green, and blue levels of a monitor. Think of this set of controls in the same way you'd adjust the RGB values on a TV.

Degauss   Removes magnetism from a monitor. The Earth's magnetic force or a magnet placed too close to a monitor can cause a picture to become fuzzy and distorted. Degaussing works by realigning the magnetic fields inside a CRT monitor.

 TIP OF THE DAY   For a wealth of information on choosing and testing a monitor, visit `displaymate.com`. Displaymate also makes excellent display calibration software: $69 for Windows from `displaymate.com/enduser`. But read on for a similar product that's free.

 DOWNLOAD OF THE DAY   Calibrate your monitor with Nokia Monitor Test. Works with all makes of monitor, free from `freepctech.com/rode/004.shtml`. After you launch the program, click the buttons in the middle for different tests. Click the button with the scholar's cap for help.

POLL: Have you bonded with your PC?

66% Yes

34% No

NOVEMBER 13

TODAY'S FOCUS: Advanced Hardware Hacking

FIRST BLOOD TRANSFUSION

The first recorded blood transfusion was made on this day in 1665. Oxford physician Richard Lower, in a gruesome experiment, drained the blood of one dog to another dog, whose own blood was simultaneously being drained. The first canine was drained to death, and the second one survived. Two years later, French physician Jean-Baptiste Denis reported the first successful blood transfusion to a human from a sheep. In 1795, Dr. Philip Syng Physick performed a human-to-human blood exchange in Philadelphia.

Related Web site `www.redcross.org/donate/give/`

Motherboards

By Roger Chang and Roman Loyola

The motherboard, or main board, is the skeleton of your computer. It provides the structure for all the components—processor, hard drive, RAM, and peripherals—and lets them work together as the computer you know. Let's take a tour of your mobo.

CPU   The easiest chip to identify is the largest chip on the motherboard. That's the central processor. It might be hidden by a fan or heat sink, or both.

Chipset   The chipset is also referred to as the bridge chips, the logic chips, or the glue chips. One or two chips, sometimes also covered by a fan and labeled Intel, VIA, SIS, or ALI. The chipset contains controllers for the memory, the PCI bus, and your peripheral cards, among other things.

RAM Chips   Look for one or two small circuit boards inserted vertically or at a slight angle into the motherboard. The angled boards are SIMMs; the vertical boards are DIMMs. You'll have one or the other. You might have additional empty sockets; that's where you'll add RAM.

Slots   There are a variety of slots:

- The old-style ISA slots are being phased out, and you might not have any, or you might have one or two at the edge of your board. These are black and about four inches long.
- PCI slots are the current industry standard. You'll have three to five of these, some of them with cards inserted. PCI slots are white and about three inches long.
- You might find an additional brown slot near the center of the board. That's the AGP slot, used only by video cards.

 TIP OF THE DAY   The Basic Input/Output System, or BIOS, is a set of software instructions stored on an EEPROM (Electronically Erasable Programmable Read-only Memory) on your motherboard. It's the first program that runs when you start up your machine, and it controls key functions of the motherboard hardware.

Like most other things in your system, the BIOS can be upgraded. This isn't something to do just for fun, but if you're having trouble  with your hardware, or you want to upgrade the capabilities of your motherboard, check the mobo manufacturer's site for BIOS updates.

Warning: Follow their instructions to the letter. A failed BIOS update can turn your computer into a doorstop. I know: There's one holding my door open right now.

 DOWNLOAD OF THE DAY   X-Setup, from X-Teq, helps you completely customize your Windows interface to increase productivity—or you can use it just for fun. Try changing the name of your Start menu or your Recycle Bin. Free for Windows from `xteq.com`.

POLL: Whom do you want to win the chip wars?

16% Intel

69% AMD

1% National Semiconductor

14% Frito-Lay

TODAY'S FOCUS: Advanced Hardware Hacking

FIRST MICROPROCESSOR

The Intel 4004 was unveiled on this day in 1971. Although integrated circuits had been used in computers before, large numbers of ICs were needed to power a single digital device. Intel was asked to create a design for a new line of calculators built by Busicom, a Japanese company. Busicom had requested a dozen silicon chips, but Intel engineer Ted Hoff and company put all the calculators' main functions onto a single new chip, the 4004, ushering in the era of the CPU, the central processing unit.

Related Web site `www.intel.com/intel/intelis/museum/exhibit/hist_micro/index.htm`

RAM Cram

Without random access memory, or RAM, your computer wouldn't operate. Every program it runs, including the operating system, every bit of data it crunches, is stored in RAM on its way into and out of the CPU.

Don't confuse RAM with your hard disk. Both are forms of memory, but RAM is short-term memory that sits between your hard drive and the microprocessor. When you turn your computer off or reboot it, the contents of RAM are cleared. If you want anything to survive, you'll need to save it to long-term memory, such as your hard disk drive. To avoid confusion, we reserve the word *memory* for RAM and call hard-drive space *storage*.

In most modern personal computers, RAM comes on small circuit boards with silicon memory chips soldered on to one or both sides. These boards are called *memory modules*, or sticks. Older RAM comes on SIMMs (single inline memory modules), newer RAM on DIMMs (dual inline memory modules). These sticks of RAM are seated into slots on the motherboard where the CPU can get at it. Data travels to and from RAM along a route called the *data bus*.

Most RAM is synchronous; that is, it reads and writes data at the speed of the computer's bus. Some RAM is DDR, or double-data rate. This memory doubles its effective throughput by executing two read or write cycles for each bus cycle.

There is no easier or more inexpensive way to give your system a performance boost than by increasing its RAM. This is especially true if you're running modern operating systems such as Windows XP or Mac OS X.

 TIP OF THE DAY **Q:** My motherboard's DIMM slots are taken up by two sticks of 64MB each. Is there any reason why I can't just upgrade to the largest size DIMMs available? —Steve from St. Petersburg, Florida, via email

A: Before you go out and buy a mega-DIMM, you need to check the limitations of your motherboard. Your manual or the manufacturer's Web site should have that information.

Another way to find out what kind of RAM your system uses is to visit memory vendors `crucial.com` or `kingston.com`. Both sites will help you figure out what you need. But remember, the one true and final authority on what kind of RAM your system can take is your motherboard manual.

 DOWNLOAD OF THE DAY Test your memory with DocMemory from Simmtester, a manufacturer of hardware RAM testers. Install on a self-booting floppy, and then run all night to really exercise your RAM. Free from `simmtester.com/page/products/demos.asp`.

POLL: Will you upgrade your RAM just because it's cheap?

74% Yes

26% No

TODAY'S FOCUS: Advanced Hardware Hacking

LIFE PRESERVER PATENTED

The first known life preserver was patented on this day in 1841. Napoleon E. Guerin of New York City developed "a jacket, waistcoat or coat composed of any kind of tissue in which is introduced a quantity of rasped or grated cork." Cork was chosen because of its buoyancy and insulating properties. Within a few years, the U.S. government recognized the need for increased safety laws on the ever-more crowded waterways, and issued regulations for the manufacturing of life preservers.

Related Web site `uscgboating.org`

Sites I Look at First Thing in the Morning

By Martin Sargent

I Hate Bees (`stingshield.com/!ahbtitl.htm`) The first thing I do every day, and probably the most important thing all day, is to look at this map of the Africanized killer bee distribution in the Southwest to track how close the bees have gotten to San Francisco. I do a lot of my killer bee research at Sting Shield Insect Veil. The guys behind the site are true unsung heroes.

Asteroid Threat (`neo.jpl.nasa.gov/neo/pha.html`) After looking at the killer bee map, I always check NASA's current asteroid impact risk charts to ensure that no asteroids could smash into Earth today. There are currently 444 known potentially hazardous asteroids. I might not be coming to work tomorrow, and I might do a lot of things tonight that I've always wanted to do.

Good Morning Smileys (`www.justsaywow.com/morning.htm`) When the killer bee and asteroid data sets get me down in the morning, there's one thing that always cheers me up. "The Good Morning Smileys" song. It's sung to the tune of the theme from *The Benny Hill Show*!

"Good Morning" in 250 Languages (`elite.net/~runner/jennifers/gmorning.htm`) I always come into the office in the morning all cheery thanks to the "Good Morning Smileys" song. I greet all my co-workers every day with a new way of saying good morning. I learn how to say good morning in other languages using a site called Good Morning in 250 Languages.

People always look forward to me walking in the office door. "Mayad-ayad nga agahon, Cat!" That's the Aklanon language of the Philippines. "Dila mshvidobisa, Patrick!" That's how people say it in the Republic of Georgia. "Wasiz'otya nyabo, Morgan!" That's Ugandan.

Daily Affirmations (`orindaben.com/dbaffirm/affirm.cfm`) And finally, before I leave the house every day, I need to say my daily affirmations, all of which I found at this site. Here are a few:

- I am increasingly magnetic to money, prosperity, and abundance.
- I know exactly what to do to evolve my body, and I do it.
- I sense the angelic presences in flowers and plants.
- I choose to buy and eat food with high vibration.

TIP OF THE DAY If you can find a part number or read a BIOS ID string on the screen, you can identify your motherboard. Usually, a Google search will do the trick, but if that doesn't work, try the BIOS numbers page at `wimsbios.com`.

DOWNLOAD OF THE DAY Chameleon Clock takes the place of the system clock. It will synchronize the time with atomic clock servers and can launch applications at a predetermined time. Hundreds of different digit sets can be downloaded free. Free to try, $15 to buy, from `softshape.com/cham`.

POLL: Would you clone your pet?

67% No

33% Yes

HONDA FOUNDER BORN

Soichiro Honda was born in Iwata Gun, Japan, on this day in 1906. He began his career as an auto mechanic as a teenager, and opened his own repair shop at age 22. In the mid-1930s, the former race-car driver ventured into piston-ring manufacturing. Soon after, his company began building motorcycles. In 1963, Honda unveiled its first sports car and light truck. Soichiro Honda retired in 1973 and was appointed a "supreme adviser." He died August 5, 1991. Today, the Honda empire includes car, motorcycle, and equipment manufacturing divisions, as well as the Acura automobile brand.

Related Web site `www.honda.com`

The World According to Blog

By David Roos

Web - log (Web'log) n. An often-updated site that points to articles elsewhere on the Web, often with comments, and to onsite articles. See also: blog, Web journal, online diary. (courtesy of `Weblogs.com`).

To *blog* is to engage in the pursuit of what one extremely popular blogger, Lance Arthur at `glassdog.com`, calls PIPA: Personally Identified Public Anonymity, "the ability to announce your feelings, emotions, opinions, and far-out unreasoned theories to an unknowing public as yourself, but you are, in fact, no one."

As a blogger, you are not entirely anonymous, because it is your blog with your name and your email address on it. However, posting a highly opinionated blog is not the same as standing on a street corner and slinging insults at passersby. For starters, there's much less punching.

Of course, not all bloggers are raving lunatics looking for a safe way to rant. Bloggery can also be a powerful ampli-fier of otherwise small voices.

As an example: Noah Grey, blogger-in-residence at NoahGrey.com, is a self-professed agoraphobic, manic-depressive living at home who hasn't had a face-to-face friend in more than four years. People read Noah's daily posts and send him comments. Readers are drawn to Noah's blog because they are drawn to Noah, or at least the version of Noah cloaked and magnified by PIPA. His posted insights are rich, and his blog design is richer. Noah has even created his own, free blogging software

called Greymatter. Noah's fame, it would seem, is well-deserved.

Blogs encourage surfing in its purest form. Well-stocked and updated blogs are swelled with links, and many of the links are to other blogs about some guy, which in turn link to other blogs about some girl, and other blogs about some other dude, ad infinitum. What the blog community sometimes lacks in well-conceived content it more than makes up in sheer depth. Try as you might, you will never dig to the bottom of the blog pile. There's always another link, and always another geeky, hipster blog to suck you in to a life as uninteresting as your own, and therefore—in that voyeuristic Web way—incredibly interesting.

 TIP OF THE DAY MIT Media Lab's blogdex attempts to make sense of the blog universe by collecting links from blog sites and ranking them to give you an instantaneous look at Internet fashion from democratic means. Or something. `blogdex.media.mit.edu`.

 DOWNLOAD OF THE DAY Blog makes it easy to create and maintain a blog. You'll need your own server space, but it works with Tripod and other free hosts. Free from `cyberian.tripod.com/Blog.htm`.

POLL: Can the nerds declare victory?

75% Yes

25% No

TODAY'S FOCUS: Blogging

X-RAY BREAKTHROUGH

The first "fluoro-record reflector camera" was announced on this day in 1950. The camera, made by the Fairchild Camera and Instrument Corp. of Jamaica, New York, was the first piece of modern X-ray equipment to be introduced for medical purposes. The device could make X-ray pictures in one-sixth of the time previously required, and was used for gastrointestinal surveys. X-rays were first discovered around 1885 by German physicist Wilhelm Conrad Roentgen. He was awarded the first Nobel Prize in physics in 1901 for his work, but the scientist refused to patent any of his inventions.

Related Web site `www.xray.hmc.psu.edu/rci/centennial.html`

Express Yourself

By Evan Williams

Blogger is a service that helps people publish their thoughts on the Web. Essentially a hosted Web-publishing tool, Blogger helps people of all skill levels create and maintain Weblogs, or "blogs."

How Blogs Work Blogger allows anyone to create and easily maintain a blog on an ongoing basis. The key is that blogs are quick and easy to publish. Have a thought, and you can post it on your Web page in a matter of seconds. This changes the dynamic of publishing a Web site. It makes your site more alive and current.

Read a Blog The best way to learn about blogs is to visit some. The Blogger home page always lists the most recently updated Blogger-powered blogs. There are tens of thousands all over the Web.

My five favorite blogs (some contain adult content):

- **b-may** (`b-may.com`)—Bryan Mason worked at the Olympics in Salt Lake City and blogged interesting incidents in a funny style.
- **Scripting News** (`scripting.com`)—One of the oldest and most widely read blogs on the Web. Whether you agree with him or not, Dave Winer, software developer/journalist, is rarely boring.
- **The EGR Weblog** (`www.rageboy.com/blogger.html`)—Co-author of *The Cluetrain Manifesto* and author of *Gonzo Marketing*, Chris Locke/RageBoy rips it up on his blog.

- **SATN** (`satn.org`)—This new blog is a collaborative work between two brilliant computer scientists/pioneers, Bob Frankston and David P. Reed, with help from Dan Bricklin.
- **Lightning Field** (`lightningfield.com`)—A completely different kind of blog by professional journalist and amateur photographer David Gallagher. It's mostly a photojournal with beautiful pictures from New York and elsewhere he has traveled.

(Evan Williams is the co-creator of Blogger and CEO of Pyra Labs. He publishes his personal blog at `evhead.com`.)

TIP OF THE DAY Setting up your own blog is free and easy with Blogger.com. Just register, choose to use Blogger's free hosting service, pick a template, and start writing: `Blogger.com`.

DOWNLOAD OF THE DAY Want instantaneous notification when a blog has been updated? Use BlogToaster for MSN Messenger. Create a new contact named `toaster@zaks.demon.co.uk`. Start a chat session, enter **add leoville.com/blog** and press **Enter**. Repeat with all the URLs of the Weblogs you want to be notified about. Enter **list** to see the list of URLs you've registered. When BlogToaster picks up a change from `weblogs.com` of a URL you've registered, it'll send you a message.

NOVEMBER 18

TODAY'S FOCUS: Blogging

FIRST AUTOMATED TOLL BOOTH

The first automatic toll-collection machine went into service at the Union Toll Plaza on New Jersey's Garden State Parkway on this day in 1954. Motorists were required to pay 25 cents to drive on the road, which they dropped into a wire mesh hopper. The first toll road in the U.S. was the Pennsylvania Turnpike, which opened in 1940. Today, "FasTrak" systems are rapidly replacing traditional toll booths: Drivers with special transponders attached to their windshields can drive through designated lanes and have their tolls electronically charged to a prepaid account.

Related Web site   `http://www.aaroads.com/kick-off/highway.html`

Installing Movable Type

I use Movable Type for my blog, `leoville.com/blog`. It's server-side software, which means you have to put a copy on your Web server. Your host must support CGI and Perl, and you have to know, or learn, a little about how Unix works. For a fee, Ben and Mena will install MT for you, but you can do it yourself if you follow the documentation carefully. Here are some of the things to keep in mind as you go.

Before uploading the files, you'll need to create a folder for your blog. I suggest creating it at the root level of your Web site with a good descriptive name. This is where users will point their browsers to read your blog, so the name matters. I used "mt," but wish I'd used "blog." The MT data, docs, styles.css file, and images will go inside this folder. I also make an archives folder for old blog pages: keeping things straight is easier.

The remainder of your files will go into a directory in your cgi-bin folder. It's very important that only executables go in here. If you put an HTML or image file in the cgi-bin directory, your server won't serve it; it'll try to execute it. In other words, keep content out of cgi-bin, and that includes the style sheet, styles.css.

There's another little pitfall here that the documentation touches on but I'd like to underscore. Tell your FTP client explicitly to upload everything but the contents of the images folder as ASCII. The images must be uploaded as binary files. Some FTP clients don't do a good job of automatically choosing the right format.

After you've uploaded everything, change the file permissions as instructed by the docs. I use CuteFTP, which has a chmod built in. MT won't run unless the permissions are set properly.

You might need to add a few Perl modules. I had to add quite a few. Finally, run MT's automatic configuration utility. If it doesn't work right off the bat, recheck the file permissions and be sure you put everything where it belongs.

Don't forget to delete the installation program, mt-load.cgi, as soon as you're finished with it. Leaving it on the system is a security no-no.

TIP OF THE DAY   For a huge list of active blogs, visit `weblogs.com`. Run by the folks at Scripting news, creators of Radio, Weblogs is a list of blogs that have just been updated. A great way to find new blogs to read.

DOWNLOAD OF THE DAY   Download your own copy of Benjamin and Mena Trott's superb blogging software, Movable Type, free from `movabletype.org`.

POLL: Which method of marriage proposal is acceptable?

3% Blog

4% Email

1% Chat room

7% Instant Message

7% Tattoo

15% All the above

62% None of the above

NOVEMBER 19

TODAY'S FOCUS: Blogging

WINDOWS 1.0 SHIPS

The first version of the Windows operating system hit store shelves on this day in 1985. It was a long time coming, however: Microsoft had first announced the premiere version of Windows at the Plaza Hotel in New York City two years earlier. Bill Gates had originally named the OS *Interface Manager*, but a marketing executive convinced him that *Windows* was more user friendly. Although the first version of Windows was successful, the operating system didn't truly dominate the personal computer market until 1991: Windows 3.1 sold more than one million copies within the first two months of release and widely replaced DOS among PC users.

Related Web site `inventors.about.com/library/weekly/aa080499.htm`

Weblogs of the Rich and Famous

On the Web, everybody's a celebrity, and every celebrity is just one of us. Here's a chance to see what the famous are really like. Guess what? They're just as dull as the rest of us.

Wil Wheaton Dot Net (`wilwheaton.net`) *Star Trek* space cadet, sorry ensign, turned Web boy. Wesley, we hardly knew ye.

Bill's Space (`williamshatner.com/billspace`) I think Bill's given up and decided that he is, indeed, Captain Kirk. At least he doesn't sing. Hope you sold that Priceline stock in time, Cap'n.

The Grey Book: Notes from Ian McKellen (`mckellen.com/cinema/lotr/journal.htm`) McKellen's journal during the shooting of *The Lord of the Rings*. One blog to rule them all…

Al's Journal (`alroker.com/journal.cfm`) *Today Show* weatherman and bon vivant, Al Roker, journal. Watch for low-flying planes and barbecue sauce.

Anna Kournikova's Journal (`kournikova.com/journal`) The tennis star, not the virus, posts every few months on such scintillating topics as "My foot injury" and "My stomach's getting bigger." Wonder whether the virus has a blog?

RuPaul's Weblog (`www.rupaul.com/weblog.shtml`) Drag queen RuPaul turns out to be a real person. This is an actual Weblog with regular postings about real things. And he looks good in pants. Who knew?

Melanie Griffith: First Peek (`melaniegriffith.com`) A blog only Danielle Steele could love. From the first strains of harp music and Melanie asking you to "Please sign my guest book," you'll know you've entered another world. Click around just to hear Melanie talk.

And my favorite of the bunch…

Jeff Bridges's blog (`www.jeffbridges.com`) Jeff draws his blog using a Wacom tablet and Painter Classic on his Macintosh. Nicky, his Webmaster, uses Dreamweaver to turn the drawings into Web pages. The result is incredible.

 TIP OF THE DAY Pitas was one of the first blog hosts. Hosts your blog for free with an address such as *yourname*`.pitas.com`. Sign up at `pitas.com`.

  DOWNLOAD OF THE DAY Radio Userland is blog software that thinks differently. You do everything locally on your computer, and Radio Userland updates your remote blog site automatically in the background. Lots of nice features, especially for folks who like to comb through the news for their blog links. Try it free for 30 days, then pay $39.95 for the software and a year's worth of hosting. For Windows and Mac, from `http://radio.userland.com/`.

POLL: Whom would you like to see in space next?

6% n*sync's Lance Bass
1% Leszek Czarnecki
5% Lori B. Garver
35% Leo and Pat
33% Megan and Morgan
19% Martin and Bat Boy

TODAY'S FOCUS: Blogging

EDISON DEMONSTRATES PHONOGRAPH

Thomas Edison announced the invention of his "talking machine" on this day in 1877. Edison discovered the technology a few years earlier while working on a way to record telephone conversations. While experimenting with a stylus on a tinfoil cylinder, Edison was able to play back a recording of "Mary Had a Little Lamb." Edison stopped work on the phonograph in 1878 to improve his incandescent light bulb. But he later returned to the device, this time implementing the wax-cylinder technique developed by Charles Tainter. Although the phonograph was originally used for dictation, Edison's National Phonograph Company eventually released a series of musical and theatrical recordings beginning in 1906.

Related Web site archervalerie.com/edison.html

Things I've Learned on Blogs

By Megan Morrone

Make Your Own Arcade Game (arcadecontrols.com) While surfing Memepool this week (memepool.com), I learned that playing with the arcade emulator Mame on your PC isn't enough. If you're a true fan, you'll create your own stand-up arcade cabinet for your PC. Everything you need to know is at Build Your Own Arcade Controls.

The Flo Control Project (quantumpicture.com/Flo_Control/flo_control.htm) Have you ever wanted to keep your cat from bringing in mice, voles, or other little varmints? The folks at Quantum Picture have figured out how. The Flo Control System also keeps your cat from inviting friends over. Thanks to the folks at MetaFilter (metafilter.com) for pointing me toward this site.

Really Cheap People (www.philly.com/mld/inquirer/2925523.htm) Before I read this article, I thought my husband was cheap. Now I know that in comparison to the other freaks in the world, he's a big spender. You can find links to this bizarre story as well as many other strange-but-true stories at The Obscure Store & Reading Room, obscurestore.com.

Mathematical Lego Structures (lipsons.pwp.blueyonder.co.uk/mathlego.htm) Math is easy. Lego is hard. Andrew Lipson builds mathematical structures such as Klein bottles and moebius strips, with Lego. He uses a computer to generate the design, but the model is entirely made with toy building bricks, and to make it doubly hard, he has to do it only with bricks he already owns. No borrowing allowed. Strangely beautiful. Or maybe just strange.

TouchGraph Google (lipsons.pwp.blueyonder.co.uk/mathlego.htm) You can make a graph out of anything. Like the interrelationships between sites on Google. TouchGraph hosts an interactive graph that demonstrates how sites are interrelated. Follow the links to explore the universe. You have to try it to understand it. And even then you might not.

Friday Five (fridayfive.org) Bloggers are desperate for content. Every Friday, a blogger named Heather posts five inane questions and challenges blogs all over the world to answer them. Questions such as "What is your favorite writing pen?" and "What have you lost recently?" And, strangely enough, people answer them. You'll find Friday Five answers all over the Web. Oh, okay. It's the Pilot Varsity disposable fountain pen... and my mind.

 TIP OF THE DAY Search blogs (and news sites) with daypop.com. They also make some fun lists, such as the top Amazon wish items and a Top 40 that lists the top topics blogs are linking to.

 DOWNLOAD OF THE DAY One of the first blogger programs was written by Noah Grey to run his own blog. The current version is free, open-source, and available for download from noahgrey.com/greysoft.

TODAY'S FOCUS: Blogging

MICROSOFT LICENSES APPLE DESIGN

Microsoft struck a deal with Apple to license the Macintosh's "look and feel" on this day in 1985. Windows used many of the same design elements as the Mac user interface, which Steve Jobs modeled after the Xerox Alto, the first computer to use a graphical user interface. When Microsoft released Windows 3.0 a few years later, Apple sued Microsoft for copyright infringement, because the original deal applied only to Windows 1.0, not subsequent versions. But the courts ruled that Microsoft's use of Mac interface elements did not violate Apple's copyrights. The lawsuit was dismissed in 1991.

Related Web site `apple-history.com`

Brendan's Realm

brendansrealm.com Brendan B. Johnson is a true American hero.

A mild-mannered Bell South programmer by day, by night (and perhaps during coffee breaks), Brendan transforms into the Webmaster of Brendan's Realm, a collection of Brendan-owned, Brendan-created, Brendan-programmed sites that epitomize all that is upstanding and honorable on the do-it-yourself Web.

Nobody pays Brendan to run these sites. Brendan has few banner ads and even fewer corporate sponsors. Brendan answers to no one but Brendan (well, and Bell South), and that's why Brendan B. Johnson is a Web original.

The jewel in Brendan's online crown is The Nitpickers Site (`nitpickers.com`), a community forum dedicated to the popular geek pastime of sapping all the fun out of a movie by pointing out each and every minute editing glitch and plot flaw until all that's left are a car chase and a fart joke. It's a fabulous Internet idea, and unlike the rest of Brendan's numerous Web projects, it has garnered a considerable following.

Brendan's other Web ventures are compelling in an intangible geeky way, but have yet to draw much of a crowd. Brendan's kind of a film freak, so the majority of the sites in his "realm" are flick-related. These include The Movie Quotes Site (`moviequotes.com`), Movie Minutia (`movieminutia.com`), and the newsy Movie Cosmos (`moviecosmos.com`).

You can't help rooting for a guy like Brendan: full of ideas, entrepreneurial moxie, and bushels of useless information. In our opinion, the tech world needs far more Brendans.

Sure, Brendan has an icicle's chance in Yuma of making one red cent from his online labor of love, but that's the price you pay for being a Web original. God bless you, Brendan B. Johnson, and keep reaching for the stars!

(For those of you keeping score at home, we used the word "Brendan" 20 times. A new world record!)

 TIP OF THE DAY Megan's favorite blogging software is LiveJournal. You can update it from the Web or download software to update locally. The only catch is that you have to be invited to participate. Get to know one of the bloggers, and then ask nicely. Free from `livejournal.com`.

 DOWNLOAD OF THE DAY Martin's favorite blogging software is DeadJournal, LiveJournal's evil twin. No need for an invite here, just sign up and start kvetching at `deadjournal.com`. Careful, the front page has mild profanity. There's worse inside.

Works with all the LiveJournal clients for Mac, Windows, and PDAs from `livejournal.com/downloads`. You just have to set the server to `www.deadjournal.com` instead of `www.livejournal.com`.

POLL: Would you pay for Google?

16% Yes

84% No

NOVEMBER 22

TODAY'S FOCUS: Blogging

PENCIL SHARPENER PATENTED

A U.S. patent was issued to John Lee Love of Fall River, Massachusetts, for a pencil sharpener on this day in 1897. Previously, writers and artists had to whittle a pencil point to sharpness with a pocketknife. Love's invention was similar to the devices we still use today. The pencil was inserted into a hole in a cylindrical case, and then rotated by hand. Internal gears turned a sharpening blade around the writing instrument, and the shavings were caught within the case.

Related Web site   howstuffworks.com/question465.htm

Best Internet Games

By Ray Weigel

Store-bought games are getting more and more expensive. If you want to try before you buy, you have to download a demo, which takes more time than most gamers have.

Luckily, a lot of rebel game designers care less about their profit margins than about creating cool games that people love to play. You can find their games for low prices on the Internet. Some are even free.

These games may lack the awesome 3D graphics and Dolby Surround sound sported by many of today's blockbuster hits, but they excel where most store-bought games fall short: gameplay.

Betrayal at Krondor (www.sierra.com/demos/ preview/1,1690,104,00.html) Sierra.com describes this game best: Betrayal at Krondor is an original story based on the best-selling *Riftwar* novels by Raymond E. Feist, and the game is the first serious attempt to present an interactive fantasy story divided into chapters like a book. The gameplay within each chapter is nonlinear; you must determine your goal and accomplish it before you can see the rest of the story."

Sub Space (www.fileplanet.com/index. asp?search=subspace&file=48611&download=1) A top-down, 2D, massively multiplayer shoot-'em-up space game, Sub Space is a cross between Asteroids and Doom. Players zap each other with heavy laser cannons.

Nethack (www.win.tue.nl/games/roguelike/ nethack) Every true old-school gamer remembers playing Rogue, an RPG adventure game built entirely out of ASCII characters. These days, people are playing Nethack, a free, downloadable, Rogue-like game that pulls you back into the ASCII dungeons of your youth to uncover the mystical Amulet of Yendor.

MafiaMob (www.mafiamob.com) You are cordially invited to join "the family" in Mafia Mob. Interact with other family members, work your way up through the ranks, and maybe someday you, too, can become a Don. For a yearly $19.95 subscription fee, you can put a hit out, bribe political officials, and hire strongmen to do your dirty work.

Graal Online (www.graalonline.com/index_2001. html) Although the massively multiplayer Graal Online costs a small fee to play, you can download the classic version for free. The game reminds me of early Zelda games or the Game Boy Pokémon games, with your little character exploring a fantasy world. The difference is that this world is inhabited by many people, much like you, who interact with one another instead of playing against the computer. It's a very fun game.

 TIP OF THE DAY Diaryland is another blog-hosting service. Use any browser to update and maintain your blog, and no banner ads or pop-ups. No graphics either, unless you pay a little extra. Otherwise, free from diaryland.com.

 DOWNLOAD OF THE DAY Add a local weather report to your blog (or Web site) with weatherpixie, free from weatherpixie.com.

NOVEMBER 23

TODAY'S FOCUS: Cooking

PORN RULED LEGAL IN LIBRARIES

On this day in 1998, a federal judge said public libraries could not block adult-oriented Web sites. U.S. District Judge Leonie Brinkema struck down Virginia's Loudoun County Public Library's policy to install X-Stop, a brand of filtering software, on every computer with an Internet connection. Although library officials claimed such material was "harmful to minors," Judge Brinkema said the implementation of such technology was unconstitutional. This was the first court case in the U.S. to apply First Amendment principles to the Internet in public libraries.

Related Web site   `www.8e6technologies.com`

Cooking Gadgets

By Michelle Von Wald

Take the brainwork out of your next meal with these high-tech kitchen helpers.

Polder Thermal Timer Cooking Probe (`surlatable.com`) Take away any guesswork when deciding whether your meat is done. Preprogram this thermometer to the desired temperature, and it will beep to let you know it's done. The probe is inserted into your food and the LCD display stays on the stove, so you don't have to burn your eyelashes by constantly opening the oven. It's worth the $30 for this alone.

Maverick's Remote Check Wireless Thermometer (`appliances.com`) Perfect for grilling, this thermometer lets you monitor food from up to 100 feet away. It has two probes so you can monitor different meats at the same time. It beeps when food reaches the desired temperature. Spend the $50 and relax at the pool while grilling dinner.

Bar B Fork Pro (`surlatable.com`) Stick a fork in it, it's done. This electronic food probe thermometer checks readiness and doneness of food instantly. You'll never overcook again. It's simple, quick, and easy to use. Just insert into food, press the button for five seconds, and read. Perfect meat costs only $21.

Capresso C3000 (`capresso.com`) At $2,345, this is the Ferrari of espresso machines. The C3000 froths hot milk in your cup, then grinds beans, tamps, and brews your coffee in less than 50 seconds. Now that's service. This machine does everything but buy the coffee and walk the dog.

ToastControl Digital (`www.krups.com`) Krups has done it again. This toaster not only looks good, with a sleek chrome finish, but you can program it with your personal toasting preferences. It also offers a "Countdown to Toast" feature that displays the time remaining until toasting is complete. For just $50, you can have perfect toast every time.

KitchenCalc Pro (`calculated.com/products/8304.html`) This handy converter is perfect for those of us who need a little help translating grams to ounces or scaling down that recipe yield from 12 dozen cookies to only two. It also converts volume, weight, and temperature, and it can perform regular math calculations. Bonus: It also doubles as a kitchen timer and costs only $40.

Make life simpler with these high-tech kitchen gadgets.

TIP OF THE DAY   Looking for the recipe for a sidecar? TheVirtualBar has everything you'd ever want to know about adult beverages. It also has recipes, games, tips, and much, much more: `Virtualbar.com`.

DOWNLOAD OF THE DAY   ERMster is the Napster of recipe programs. Share your recipe with others, and search other folks' recipes online. Chat room included. Free from `foryourinfotech.com`. Requires the ERM cookbook, free to try, $15 to buy, from `foryourinfotech.com`.

BENZ INVENTOR BORN

Karl (Friedrich) Benz, who developed the cars that bear his name, was born in Germany on this day in 1844. The mechanical engineer completed his first project in 1879—a two-stroke engine that took him two years to build. In 1885, he designed and built the world's first practical automobile powered by an internal-combustion engine. Benz was granted several patents for the car, and opened a factory soon after. Unlike many other auto pioneers, Benz designed the entire car, not just the engine. In July 1886, he introduced the first commercial Benz automobiles, which were made available to the public two years later.

Related Web site   www.mercedes-benz.com

Cooking Advice from the Wired Chef

By Philip Ferrato

Web sites that deal with cooking, entertaining, and nutrition abound. As households sign on for faster Internet services, these sites will become more a part of our daily lives. Three of the best:

Epicurious.com (epicurious.com) Epicurious puts the combined resources of Conde Nast's *Gourmet* and *Bon Appetit* magazines (as well as Epicurious TV) together to create a site with great depth. The Epicurious database includes more than 10,000 recipes and extensive how-to knowledge: A search for "brownies" delivers 56 results. One of my favorite sections is the online version of *Food Lovers Companion*, the superb culinary dictionary.

***Cuisine* magazine** (cuisineathome.com)   This is a great site. Simple and clearly illustrated, the recipes are straightforward and emphasize quality ingredients. It also has a valuable tips section. Most importantly, while the recipes are current and stylish, the site is oriented toward cooking and entertaining at home.

The New York Times (www.nytimes.com)   It's not a cooking site, but within it you will find the results of decades of unmatched food journalism in the paper's "Living" section. Look here for up-to-date articles on food and style, as well as organized cooking lessons and videos. You have to register to read the content, but there's no charge.

Computers are not going to cook for you, even if your refrigerator does start talking to the dishwasher. But the synthesis of high speeds, dropping prices on peripherals, and corporate investment in well-considered Web sites will make your computer just as valuable in the kitchen as great cookware.

Helpful low-tech hint: Print out your recipes in large type (the better to read from afar) and put them in a vertical stand-up presentation binder with clear plastic slip sheets. This eliminates running to read the screen in another room, pesto sauce on the keyboard, and a slew of food-stained 3×5 cards.

(Philip Ferrato is the executive chef at Wired *magazine in San Francisco.)*

 TIP OF THE DAY   Have you ever wondered what's inside a Hostess Twinkie, PayDay candy bar, or Chevy's chips and salsa? Author Todd Wilbur has collected some of the most sought-after fast-food recipes in a book and accompanying Web site called Top Secret Recipes, topsecretrecipes.com.

DOWNLOAD OF THE DAY   Turn your $2,000 computer into a $5 kitchen timer with MDStopWatch, free for Windows from microdimensions.co.uk/pcstopwatch.html.

POLL: Has technology increased your workload?

57% Yes

43% No

NOVEMBER 25

TODAY'S FOCUS: Cooking

FRANCE LAUNCHES SATELLITE

France became the third country to send an artificial satellite into space on this day in 1965. A rocket called Diamant was launched from Algeria with Astérix, a 92-pound satellite named after Astérix le Gaulois, a well-known French comic book superhero. France founded the Centre National d'Études Spatiales (CNES) in 1961, when the U.S. and Russia were already well-engrossed in the international space race. Over the next few years, France conducted many high-atmosphere tests, including test flights for a rat named Hector and Félicette the cat.

Related Web site   www.cnes.fr

Shop Online for Tomorrow's Feast

By Alison Strahan

Thanksgiving is serious business. Take a little time to do some research, so you can prepare a feast that fits your sense of the occasion. The first step to planning Thanksgiving dinner is to choose what you're going to cook. Here's how to find your turkey or vegetarian alternative.

Vegetarian Turkey   If you're a vegetarian who enjoys the turkey tradition, but not the meat, there's a new curd, I mean, bird, on the block. Tofurkey is a 100% vegan roast with soy drumettes, stuffing, gravy, and wishbones from tofurkey.com. The Tofurkey meal serves four and costs $26.95. But shipping is a steep $28 if you buy online. I suggest using the site's list of retail stores to find a shop in your neighborhood that carries Tofurkey, so you can pick one up for yourself. (Watch the Tofurkey videos for some fun while you shop.)

Organic Turkey   People who prefer poultry should read the down-to-earth tips on choosing a fresh, frozen, organic, or kosher turkey at The Reluctant Gourmet, reluctantgourmet.com/turkey_tips.htm. The USDA can also help explain how turkeys are bred, and it supplies guidelines for organic turkey, www.fsis.usda.gov/OA/pubs/farmfreeze.htm.

Finding an organic turkey can sometimes be difficult. If you're having trouble, visit your local health-food store or farmer's market. You'll also have access to organic or free-range turkeys if you join a co-op or community-supported agriculture program, www.prairienet.org/co-op/directory.

Order Meals Online   Carnivores around the United States can have turkeys, ham, or entire Thanksgiving meals delivered from Omaha Steaks (omahasteaks.com), or Hickory Farms (hickoryfarms.com).

And yes, there is a National Turkey Federation, at eatturkey.org. It actually has some pretty good information on everything from thawing and roasting to the best way to determine when the bird is cooked—and an all-star lineup of virtual chefs to help you with your bird.

TIP OF THE DAY   Try Nonnie Laporte's Thanksgiving stuffing this year:

1 bag Pepperidge Farm bread crumbs	1 stick butter
1 cup orange juice	2 eggs, beaten
1 onion, diced	1/2 cup parmesan cheese, grated
1 bunch celery, diced	1/2 cup apple sauce
1 bunch parsley, chopped	1 pound pork sausage

Sautée onion, celery, parsley in butter.

Add sausage and cook until browned.

Add bread crumbs, orange juice, eggs, cheese, and apple sauce; salt and pepper to taste.

Buon appetito!

 DOWNLOAD OF THE DAY   Kids Domain has various fun freeware and shareware screensavers and desktop themes for kids. One even bounces turkeys and pumpkins all over the screen! kidsdomain.com/holiday/thanks/pc/screensaver.html

If you'd rather deck out your desktop with Disney, Looney Tunes, Norman Rockwell, or Precious Moments Thanksgiving themes, find all the links at About.com's Thanksgiving desktop themes roundup, shareware.about.com/cs/thanksgiving2

TODAY'S FOCUS: Thanksgiving

CELSIUS BORN

The inventor of the temperature scale that bears his name was born in Uppsala, Sweden, on this day in 1701. In 1740, Anders Celsius invented the first tool for measuring the brightness of stars. Later, he invented the centigrade scale for measuring temperature. Originally, however, Celsius' scale was inverted, meaning, zero degrees was the boiling point for water, and 100 degrees was the freezing point. When the centigrade scale was reversed, it was renamed in the inventor's honor. Today, the Celsius scale is the standard for determining temperature nearly everywhere in the world. The only notable exception is in the U.S., where Fahrenheit is used.

Related Web site `www.astro.uu.se/history/Celsius_eng.html`

Turkey Tips

By Alison Strahan

Stuck for a new way to present your Thanksgiving turkey? Have a hankering to freshen up your mashed potatoes and squash? Here are my recipe choices to ensure your Thanksgiving meal is delicious and mouthwatering.

Everything but the Bird (`eat.epicurious.com/bonappetit/menus/index.ssf/?/bonappetit/menus/meatlessthanks.html`) Epicurious, the premier gourmet presence on the Web, has generous Thanksgiving recipe offerings for vegetarians. It provides four complete menus, ranging from a Mediterranean-inspired meal to a Mexican menu. The pumpkin roll cake with toffee cream filling and caramel sauce looks delicious.

The site also has menus from some of America's finest chefs. Each menu is inspired by the customs and produce of different states. For example, Charlie Trotter's Midwestern Thanksgiving includes peppercorn and thyme-roasted goose, whereas Jasper White's New England menu features lobster soup and roast Vermont turkey.

The First Thanksgiving (`www.geocities.com/NapaValley/6312/indian.html`) Try out Native American recipes at Adam Starchild's site. Recipes include mouthwatering chestnut cakes and a solid-sounding maple beer. This Native American chef gets my vote—he's written an entire cookbook devoted to the banana.

Butterball (`Butterball.com`) If you're having trouble figuring out how long to thaw or cook your turkey, get some help from Butterball. Aside from these handy turkey preparation tips, you can call and talk with a live person. Check out the Butterball Talk-Line top ten. Or use the turkey calculator to figure out how big a bird you'll need.

Kids' Stuff (`childfun.com/menus/thanks.shtml`) Get the kids into the kitchen to help. ChildFun.com has creative craft ideas and recipes, including a turkey made from an apple and toothpicks that you can use as a centerpiece.

Talk Turkey (`holidayinsights.com/tday/turkey.htm`) Take the turkey trivia exam, and then get on to more serious stuff: Turkey safety.

Safe Turkey (`securityworld.com/library/health/turkeysafety.html`) Turkeys are dangerous. I'll never forget how Uncle Bill broke his toe by dropping a frozen 20-pound bird on it. Seriously, there are some things you need to know about food safety when it comes to turkeys, and those paranoids at Security World know it all. Read it here, but don't share the info at the dinner table, please.

 TIP OF THE DAY The Red Kitchen is a collaborative blog full of recipes and kitchen tips from a number of contributors. The submissions are all on recipe cards, just like Mom makes, and include feedback from other visitors: `theredkitchen.net`.

 DOWNLOAD OF THE DAY CookWarerecipe software is a full-featured program that helps you manage all your recipes. From the magazine *Cooking Light*. You can download each month's recipes (Mastercook version available, too). Free after registration for Mac and Windows, from `cookn.com`.

NOVEMBER 27

TODAY'S FOCUS: Cooking

CHILDREN'S INTERNET PROTECTION ACT SIGNED

President Bill Clinton signed the Children's Internet Protection Act (CIPA) into law on this day in 1998. CIPA required schools and libraries that received certain types of federal funding to adopt an "Internet Safety Policy." This included the use of filtering technology and monitoring children's Internet use by school and library staff.

Related Web sites `www.ifea.net/cipa.html`, `www.ala.org/cipa`

Mastercook, Not Dead Yet

I've got bad news and I've got good news. The best cooking software out there, Mastercook, was discontinued by its publisher, Sierra Home. That's the bad news. The hopeful news is that a discount software company called ValuSoft has acquired the title. The good news is that they're selling it online at `valusoft.com` for as little as $9.99.

I've used Mastercook for years on both Windows and Mac, and I love it. It's been around so long that thousands of recipes are available online in Mastercook format. Even if there weren't, Mastercook does a tolerably good job of importing files in a variety of other formats.

Other great Mastercook features include

- **Scaling**—Say a recipe makes only 4 servings, but you're having a dinner party for 12. No need to fuss with tripling the recipe and making a mistake with the measurements. Mastercook lets you enter the number of servings and scales the measurements for you automatically.
- **No-Shopping-Required Meals**—Plug in ingredients you have in the fridge, and it shows you your recipe options.
- **Create Shopping Lists**—You can make a shopping list as you go for ingredients you don't have. You can even organize the list by supermarket section: produce, bakery, etc.
- **Add Your Own Recipes**—Mastercook lets you add your own favorite recipes to its files. You can design and print customized recipe cards and cookbooks. There's even a spell checker.

- **Nutrition Analysis**—Makes it easy to watch what you eat because all recipes include nutrition information. The Mastercook Suite also breaks down the nutrition information for each ingredient.
- **Yield and Equivalent Guide**—Mastercook Suite helps with age-old questions, such as how many cups are in a quart.

The Mastercook Web site, `mastercook.com`, is a shadow of its former glorious self, but there's still a message board where Mastercook supporters share recipes and reminisce about better days. One of the message-board moderators has started her own independent site at `mc6help.tripod.com`.

Long live Mastercook!

TIP OF THE DAY   It's fun to cook for your pet.

- Get tips for feeding dogs and cats as well as recipes online at `howtoadvice.com/PetFood`.
- Doggie Connection has an extensive list of recipes just for dogs at `doggieconnection.net/recipe`.
- If you have a pet bird or want to attract wild birds for your yard, try these recipes for bird treats from `coco.essortment.com/birdtreats_rgzk.htm`.

Always check with your veterinarian before beginning a new feeding plan for your pet. Also be aware that pets might develop food allergies or need additional supplementation in addition to regular meals.

"Bone" appétit!

 DOWNLOAD OF THE DAY   It's the day after Thanksgiving, time to put up the holiday lights. Holiday lights for the Mac and PC get festive in a twinkling, and they're free from `tigertech.com`. Pay $19.95 to get a bigger variety of decorations.

TODAY'S FOCUS: Cooking

NUCLEAR TESTING GOES UNDERGROUND

The first underground nuclear explosion occurred on this day in 1951. A nuclear bomb was detonated in a 17-foot-deep pit at "Frenchman Flat" in the Nevada desert. Previously, nuclear bombs had been dropped from planes or exploded from towers. This test was commissioned to determine how nuclear weapons would perform below ground level. The bomb had the explosive power of 1.2 kilotons of TNT—much smaller than the bombs dropped on Hiroshima and Nagasaki in 1945. Since then, the U.S. government has conducted more than 800 underground nuclear tests at the Nevada test site.

Related Web site www.nv.doe.gov/nts

Giving Thanks by Giving

By Alison Strahan

One way to give thanks for all we have is to help those who have less. Here are some ways you can lend a helping hand to your community.

Food left over from the Thanksgiving feast? America's Second Harvest operates more than 200 food banks nationwide and in Puerto Rico. Use the drop-down menu to find a food bank in your area and drop off some holiday cheer: www.secondharvest.org/foodbanks/foodbanks.html.

New York residents can contact City Harvest (www.cityharvest.org), a charity devoted to feeding the hungry. City Harvest collects dried, canned, and prepared food from restaurants, bakeries, and individuals. It distributes the donations to various charities, which pass them on to people in need. So, cook up an extra batch of greens or mashed potatoes and send them over!

The California Association of Food Banks (www.cafoodbanks.org) has a user-friendly site where you can search for food banks throughout the Golden State. It also suggests other means of donating time, money, or services. Perhaps you have a unique skill, such as Web design or photography, and could assist the organization.

At Idealist.org (www.idealist.org), you'll find volunteer opportunities and internships all over the world. Search by country, state, or area of focus. Read inspiring articles that will motivate you to volunteer or take the lead and create your own organization to help your community. The site also suggests ways to get the whole family involved in volunteering.

VolunteerMatch (www.volunteermatch.org) can help you find volunteer opportunities in your city. Search for positions in areas that interest you. Check the specific search boxes to find organizations that welcome help from children, teens, and seniors.

 TIP OF THE DAY Commercial beauty products can enhance the way you look and feel, but the cost soon adds up. Here are a few ways you can pamper yourself at home and save money by using natural ingredients.

Grandma's Drugstore (azwebsuites.com/grand.html) This e-book contains natural recipes for face, hair, and body.

Pioneer Thinking (www.pioneerthinking.com/chfacials.html) This is another source for homemade facials. This site has step-by-step instructions for making masks and scrubs for nearly every skin type.

About.com (beauty.about.com/cs/maskrecipes) You can find more food-based facial mask recipes at this Web site. Here you'll find everything from an ancient Egyptian mixture to "Prune porridge."

 DOWNLOAD OF THE DAY Now You're Cooking is a cookbook program that comes with thousands of recipes, meal planning tips, nutrition advice, and more. Free for 60 days, $19–$43 depending on version, from ffts.com.

POLL: Should the Web be freshness dated?

89% Yes

11% No

NOVEMBER 29

TODAY'S FOCUS: Cooking

MASON JAR PATENTED

One of the most famous food-preserving containers was patented by John Landis Mason on this day in 1858. Mason's design featured a shoulder-seal jar with a zinc screw cap. In 1869, Mason added a flat top seal that fit between the jar and the lid, which preserved food even more effectively.

Related Web site `mcclungmuseum.utk.edu/objectmo/ob-9808.htm`

The Science of Cooking

By Blanche Shaheen

Although the quality of ingredients is important, some chefs claim that understanding the science behind cooking can open doors to better dishes.

"Food is chemistry," said chef Marco Ilaria, who teaches at the California Culinary Academy in San Francisco. To illustrate his point, the chef walks through the scientific steps necessary to make a perfect béarnaise sauce. Ilaria emulsifies a mixture of melted butter and egg yolks. Emulsification requires the combination of two liquids that are normally unmixable, joining them to create a harmonious sauce or dressing.

"You have to cook the egg yolks just long enough to make the butter separate," Ilaria said. "In this way, you separate the molecules of the butter. Otherwise, you'll have scrambled eggs in a heartbeat."

An even temperature is key. Emulsification requires like temperatures and like consistencies.

The scientific process is called *agitation*. The energy from whisking ingredients over an even temperature causes the molecules to interact without bonding. This, in turn, prevents curdling. Finally, he adds a seasoning of vinegar, shallots, and tarragon.

"The acid that's in the shallot reduction is going to help make it so the butter and the eggs don't cling to the palate, and leaves a cleaner feeling in the mouth," Ilaria said.

In a different demonstration, chef instructor Jake Ference, also of the culinary academy, shows the importance of hydrogen bonding in making a successful fondant.

Fondant is a smooth icing made of sugar, water, and flavorings that is used in classical pastry.

"The sugar will be totally dissolved in a process that interferes with the crystallization of sugar molecules," Ference said.

He boils sugar and water together over an even temperature so he can control the crystallization process. The aim is to keep the sugar molecules separate from the hydrogen ions in the water. The sugar crystals become microscopic, and the human tongue cannot distinguish them.

Corn syrup is the interfering agent that prevents further crystallization. After the liquid boils into a jellylike stage, it's ready to be agitated. Ference pours the liquid onto a cool marble board and smears the solution until it forms the thick smooth paste: a perfect fondant.

Before you turn your kitchen into a chemistry lab, the chef has some important advice. "Once you know what makes you happy and you enjoy what you're doing, whether you take a chemistry class or you simply read books, you're going to become pretty good at what you do," Ference said.

Understanding cooking science is a step in the right direction.

TIP OF THE DAY Recipe Source is a search engine dedicated to cooking. Search for a recipe by name, or use the advanced search to search for ingredients. Categories for baby food, pet food, camping, and more. Even medieval and humorous recipes: `www.recipesource.com`.

DOWNLOAD OF THE DAY Accuchef is YACB— yet another cookbook program. Free to try 60 times, then $19.95 to buy: `accuchef.com`.

NOVEMBER
30

DECEMBER 2003

SUNDAY	MONDAY	TUESDAY	WEDNESDAY	THURSDAY	FRIDAY	SATURDAY
	1 World AIDS Day	**2** First controlled nuclear chain reaction demonstrated (1942)	**3** First successful human heart transplant (1967)	**4**	**5**	**6** First sound recording made (1877)
7 Pearl Harbor attacked (1941)	**8**	**9** Windows 2.0 released	**10** Nobel Prizes awarded	**11**	**12**	**13**
14 DNA created in test tube (1967)	**15**	**16** Arthur C. Clarke born (1917)	**17** Orville and Wilbur Wright make first flight (1903)	**18** Steven Spielberg born (1946)	**19** Benjamin Franklin began publishing *Poor Richard's Almanac* (1732)	**20**
21 Radium discovered (1898)	**22** First day of winter	**23** First transistor created (1947)	**24** Christmas Eve	**25** Christmas Day	**26**	**27** Johannes Kepler born (1571)
28	**29**	**30**	**31** New Year's Eve			

TODAY'S FOCUS: Our Geek Gift Guide

CHUNNEL COMPLETED

The first stage of the passageway that connects England and France underneath the English Channel was completed on this day in 1990. Diggers from the two nations met midway and shook hands in what would later become the service tunnel. The idea for a cross-channel tunnel was first imagined during the reign of Napoleon, but no attempt was made to conquer the 31-mile long stretch until 1987. Eurostar train service began in the chunnel in 1994. Trains can travel up to 186mph, drastically faster than the ferries previously used.

Related Web site   eurostar.com

Gifting the Geek

Finding the right geeky gift can be challenging. Luckily, you have us. Here are some things to keep in mind:

- **Newbie and Non-Techie Shoppers**—Rely on the "sure things." Affordable peripherals, such as scanners, printers, speakers, or joysticks, are great gifts. Look at software that lets you do creative things or be productive at home. Books that teach new skills are very helpful.
- **Shoppers with Technical Savvy**—Remember, you're shopping for someone else. You need to know the specifications of your recipient's computer if you want to give a hard drive, CD-ROM, or DVD drive. Graphics cards and CPUs especially need the specification match. Belarc has a profiler that you can use to find out the specifications of a computer: Belarc.com.
- **Research the Product**—Be sure to read the product reviews on TechTV, www.techtv.com/products. Other magazines, such as *PC Magazine* (pcmag.com) and *Macworld* (macworld.com), can help. You can also check user review sites, such as Epinions (epinions.com) and the Usenet newsgroups (groups.google.com). Don't forget to look at the manufacturer's Web site for specifications.

Other factors to consider:

- **Name Brand vs. Generic**—You know what you're getting with a name brand, but you can save some cash with a generic product.

- **OEM vs. Retail**—This not only affects the price, but the type of support you get.
- **MSRP vs. Street**—Plan appropriately, or you can end up going over budget.

If you still end up not getting the right gift, you'll be glad you saved the receipt. If you buy software, be sure it still has the shrink-wrap or a seal to show it has never been opened. Some stores won't take software back if they think it's been opened.

TIP OF THE DAY   He's making a list, he's checking it twice. Better make sure your name is in the correct column. Email Santa and tell him what a good little boy or girl you've been, emailsanta.com. I'm sure he'll believe you.

Come Christmas Eve you can watch Santa's progress, thanks to the North American Air Defense Command. We'll, they've got to do something now that the Cold War's over: noradsanta.org.

DOWNLOAD OF THE DAY   Start the countdown tonight with this animated Advent calendar, from rooneydesign.com/advntcal.html.

POLL: What's the ultimate geek gift?

25% The Death Star
46% The Enterprise
13% Robby the Robot
16% A Black Hole

TODAY'S FOCUS: Our Geek Gift Guide

FIRST NUCLEAR EXPERIMENT

Dr. Enrico Fermi of Columbia University set off the first controlled nuclear chain reaction while conducting tests for the U.S. government on this day in 1942. The experiment was carried out at a reactor built on an old squash court at the University of Chicago. A year earlier, President Franklin Delano Roosevelt had authorized the Manhattan Engineering District, nicknamed the "Manhattan Project," to develop an atomic bomb.

Related Web site atomicmuseum.com

Geek Library Recommendations: Culture

Electronics aren't the only things geeks like. For the next four days we'll give you some of our recommendations for books that belong in every geek's library.

Today: the Geek Culture.

***The Soul of a New Machine*, by Tracy Kidder** In 1978, Massachusetts-based Data General Corporation was the third-largest seller of minicomputers—computers that were not quite as powerful or expensive as IBM's industry-dominant mainframes. Data General's bread and butter, the Eclipse, was beginning to show its age by the mid-'70s, so the company embarked on a two-year effort to create a new, 32-bit successor.

Journalist Tracy Kidder joined the design team in its earliest days, and in this classic book, follows the ups and downs of creating a new machine, from drawing board to delivery. No one has ever done a better job of describing the pressure-cooker environment of computer design, and even though these events took place 20 years ago, the story is retold in Silicon Valley every day.

***Hacker Crackdown*, by Bruce Sterling** *Hacker Crackdown* looks at electronic freedom in a period when the Internet was in its infancy. With insight and amazing lucidity, the book explores the history and effects of electronic freedom. Each step is placed within a sociological and political context. From senators and law enforcement to anarchists and corporate officials, the book covers those who shaped today's Internet. *Hacker Crackdown* makes an excellent read, even for the most technophobic reader.

To further the cause of electronic freedom, the entire book has been put on the Web at www.lysator.liu.se/etexts/hacker.

***The Cuckoo's Egg*, by Clifford Stoll** Author Clifford Stoll gives a first-person account of stumbling across a KGB-backed spy ring while tracking a 75-cent accounting error on his mainframe. In the course of a year, Stoll managed to track, identify, and eventually expose an international espionage ring, all from a computer.

What's cool about the book is that a geek does all of it, not some 007-style super spy. Just an individual who, through tenacity and a computer, managed to keep sensitive material from being leaked. It's a story geeks would be happy to tell their children.

TIP OF THE DAY Geeks like movies, too. Any of these would make a great gift, but DVD only, please. VHS is so last century.

The Matrix	*Lord of the Rings*
Blade Runner	*2001: A Space Odyssey*
WarGames	Any *Star Wars* movie
Forbidden Planet	Any *Star Trek* movie

Revenge of the Nerds I, II, III, IV
(yes, they actually made that many)

If you want to avoid looks of disgust, do *not* give your geek:

Hackers	*The Net*	*Blowfish*
Takedown	*You've Got Mail*	

Or, just forget the whole thing and give her a Netflix subscription, Netflix.com.

 DOWNLOAD OF THE DAY It wouldn't be Christmas without it. Elf Bowling, from nstorm.com.

TODAY'S FOCUS: Our Geek Gift Guide

FIRST SUCCESSFUL ARTIFICIAL HEART

Barney C. Clark, a 61-year-old dentist from Utah, was implanted with the first permanent artificial heart on this day in 1982. Dr. William DeVries performed the procedure at the University of Utah Medical Center in Salt Lake City. The mechanical heart, known as the Jarvik-7, was invented by Robert Jarvik in 1970. Clark lived for 112 days with the artificial organ, but he soon died from an infection related to the tubes that connected the heart to the air-driven pumping machinery.

Related Web site   `www.americanheart.org`

Geek Library Picks: Reference Works

The Little Mac Book, by Robin Williams In a better world, every computer book would be as simple, precise, and fun as Robin Williams' *The Little Mac Book*, the classic introduction to the finer points of fairer OS.

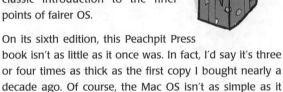

On its sixth edition, this Peachpit Press book isn't as little as it once was. In fact, I'd say it's three or four times as thick as the first copy I bought nearly a decade ago. Of course, the Mac OS isn't as simple as it once was, either.

Ms. Williams still does a spectacular job of educating the newbie into the basics, then the finer points, of the OS. (Heck, I still keep it around and I've been using the Mac OS forever.)

Practical Unix and Internet Security, by Simson Garfinkel and Gene Spafford For nearly 10 years, Unix system administrators have turned to this book for guidance to the principles of security, internally and externally. Written in 1991 and extensively updated in 1996, it's still the classic. As Cliff Stoll says, "Buy this book and save on aspirin."

The Art of Computer Programming, by Donald E. Knuth Here's a geek library recommendation: three books I own but have never read. Nor have many others (unless forced to by demonic computer science professors). Even Bill Gates says "Send me a résumé if you can read the whole thing."

But nearly all hardcore programmers know of it, and many proudly display it. This three-book set is the bible of computer-programming algorithms—the methods for solving problems.

The first book covers the mathematical foundations of computer science and information structures, such as lists, trees, memory allocation, and garbage collection. Book two tackles the thorny (and most important) issue of creating random numbers plus arithmetic algorithms. Book three is all about searching and sorting. Knuth has been writing book four for about 20 years. He'll publish it one of these days.

Despite the dense subject matter, Knuth writes with clarity and humor. You might not read these three all the way through, but you'll find plenty of interesting material worth dipping into.

TIP OF THE DAY   Save yourself the greeting-card frenzy this year. Email animated holiday cards from these sites:

- American Greetings: `americangreetings.com`
- MSN Greeting Cards (formerly EGreetings): `greetingcards.msn.com`
- Blue Mountain: `free.bluemountain.com`
- Amazon.com: `amazon.com/exec/obidos/tg/browse/-/225945`
- Hallmark.com: `hallmark.com`
- Yahoo! Greetings: `greetings.yahoo.com`

  DOWNLOAD OF THE DAY If you didn't get an Intellivision under the tree 20 years ago, you can get one on your PC today. Download an emulator, free from `bliss.retrogames.com`, or buy a CD with 30 licensed games, from `intellivisionlives.com`.

TODAY'S FOCUS: Our Geek Gift Guide

ELECTRIC CAR DEBUTS

The first electric vehicle to be mass-produced was released on this day in 1996. The EV1, manufactured by General Motors, could not be purchased, only leased. Today's EV1 GEN II features a 137-horsepower, 3-phase AC induction motor, a 26-valve–regulated high-capacity lead-acid (PbA) battery pack, and a driving range of 55 to 95 miles on one charge. Hybrid cars, which run on a combination of electricity and gasoline, are also showing up on the mass market. Honda and Toyota both currently offer such fuel-efficient models. But with price tags that hover around the $20,000 mark, their popularity has yet to skyrocket.

Related Web site   www.gm.com

Geek Library Picks: Sci Fi

***Childhood's End*, by Arthur C. Clarke**
Clarke is the science-fiction author that scientists read. He focuses on the science first, and the fiction second. Both aspects are masterfully intertwined in his 1953 novel, *Childhood's End*. The world is about to annihilate  itself with war and technology, and it's descending into chaos. Suddenly, aliens calling themselves the Overlords appear and begin a campaign of mandatory "improvements." The apparently benevolent race forces an end to war, poverty, and disease—but to what purpose?

***Cryptonomicon*, by Neal Stephenson**   What can you say about a bestselling novel written using BeOS, that includes a Perl script in it, and has its own Web site? That it's a must-read for geeks everywhere.

Stephenson earned his cyberpunk laurels with the seminal *Snow Crash*. *Cryptonomicon* represents a huge leap forward in Stephenson's writing. Not science fiction precisely, the story jumps back and forth between World War II crypto specialists and modern-day computer whizzes, but the cyperpunk sensibility shines through in Stephenson's love of mathematics and technology.

One more thing to like about *Cryptonomicon*: The encryption technology woven throughout the book is considered good enough to be classified as munitions by the United States government.

***I, Robot*, by Isaac Asimov**   *I, Robot* is a collection of Asimov's short stories on robots, the first of which was published in 1940. As a collection, they represent the more memorable subjects encountered in the career of Susan Calvin, the first "robopsychologist" for U.S. Robotics, the largest manufacturer of cybernetics in Asimov's fictional world. Calvin served as Asimov's base for exploring the moral side of cybernetics.

To paraphrase a thesis I found online, Asimov's stories take robot building out of the hands of blasphemers and into the hands of engineers. No small feat, especially when you consider the three laws of robotics. Don't know 'em? Then go track down a copy.

TIP OF THE DAY   These two Windows XP Power Toys can help you create inexpensive gifts with heart:

- **Slide Show CD** (download.microsoft.com/download/whistler/Install/2/WXP/EN-US/SlideshowPowertoySetup.exe)—Make them something they'll really appreciate for less than a buck. You can burn your favorite pictures onto a CD that plays automatically. Label kits, with the needed software and special paper, are available at your local computer or stationery store and add a nice professional finish.
- **Web Page Slide Show** (download.microsoft.com/download/whistler/Install/2/WXP/EN-US/HtmlgenPowertoySetup.exe)—Put it at a URL that you only send to family and friends. You can send out a thoughtful gift with just an email.

 DOWNLOAD OF THE DAY   Picozip does everything WinZip does, and for five bucks less. Download the demo version from picozip.com.

TODAY'S FOCUS: Our Geek Gift Guide

FIRST PREFAB SHIP

The *USS Michigan* was launched at Erie, Pennsylvania, on this day in 1843. The vessel was the first prefabricated ship to be assembled in the U.S. and was the nation's first steam-powered, iron-hulled warship. The ship was built in Pittsburgh, and then reassembled in Erie. It patrolled the waters of the Great Lakes during the Civil War and helped protect against Confederate sympathizers in Canada. The ship was renamed the *USS Wolverine* when the Navy began planning a new *USS Michigan*. Today, the name belongs to SSBN 727, a Trident-class nuclear-powered submarine.

Related Web site `www.michigan.navy.mil`

Geek Library Recommendations: Science

Chaos: Making a New Science, by James Gleick

By Tom Merritt

I picked up this book at a time in my life when I felt everything was subjective and there could be no definitive answers. Gleick's book proved to me that I wasn't far wrong.

"Where chaos begins, classical science stops," Gleick states in the prolog. *Chaos* opened my mind to the wonders of strange attractors, the butterfly effect, and the Mandelbrot set. This is an important book for clearing up misunderstandings over what people sometimes claim are mystical truths proved by physics.

***Six Easy Pieces*, by Richard Feynman**   Richard Feynman was a brilliant theoretical physicist who worked on the Manhattan Project during World War II and won the Nobel prize in 1965 for his work on quantum electrodynamics.

Shortly before his death in 1988, Feynman once again made news by discovering the cause of the space shuttle Challenger explosion. He was also well-known for translating Mayan hieroglyphs and playing bongos. But Richard Feynman's most lasting legacy may well be his work as a teacher.

Feynman was a professor at CalTech, and these are six of his brilliant lectures on physics given to CalTech freshmen and sophomores in the early '60s. The lectures are available in book, cassette, and CD. Anyone who has studied and enjoyed high school–level physics will love these lectures, delivered in Feynman's trademark Brooklyn accent with his puckish sense of humor. They're probably all any educated person needs to know about modern physics.

***One, Two, Three... Infinity*, by George Gamow**   Originally published in 1947 and revised in 1961, this classic has been reissued by Dover. Gamow was a Russian-born nuclear physicist, best known in scientific circles for his work on the big bang. No other author I know can make the mysteries of number theory, special relativity, and quarks so accessible.

TIP OF THE DAY   The holidays remind me of friends and family who live far away. I'm also prompted to remember the people I haven't really kept in touch with over the year. If you're in a similar situation, assuage some guilt and connect with those you care about by creating a holiday newsletter in Microsoft Word.

Open Word and select **New** from the **File** menu. Go to the **Publications** tab and double-click the **Newsletter Wizard** template. It will walk you through the process of setting up your newsletter. Now get writing! Oh, and one last tip: Try to get it in the mail before April.

 DOWNLOAD OF THE DAY   Go sledding without getting snow down the back of your neck, with Sketchy. For PC and Mac from `kewlbox.com/games/game.cfm?gameId=61`. There's an online version, too.

TODAY'S FOCUS: Our Geek Gift Guide

COMMERCIAL ELECTRIC SERVICE BEGINS

The first commercial carrier of electricity began sending energy to customers on this day in 1922. General Electric's Utica Gas and Electric Company plant in Utica, New York, was built using transmitters, power lines, and receivers. The overhead electric line system could carry both power and telephone signals, and one line could carry numerous frequencies simultaneously. The plant was later taken over by The Central New York Power Corp. but is no longer in operation today.

Related Web site `www.eia.doe.gov`

Geek Gadgets

Some great gifts *we'd* like to see under the tree. Starting with the budget busters.

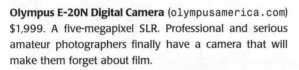

Samsung 54-Inch Plasma HDTV (www.samsungusa.com) $20,000. This isn't a TV—it's a movie screen that fits in your living room.

Olympus E-20N Digital Camera (olympusamerica.com) $1,999. A five-megapixel SLR. Professional and serious amateur photographers finally have a camera that will make them forget about film.

RoboScout Personal Robot (www.sharperimage.com) $899. Who needs help when you can get a robot?

Under $300

Microsoft Xbox (xbox.com) $199. Microsoft's first entry into the game console market is a winner. It's the most powerful game console ever, and it has the games to back it up.

Lego MindStorm Invention Set (mindstorms.lego.com) You don't have to be a scientific genius to build a robot with this Lego set.

TiVo (www.tivo.com) Record your favorite shows on a hard drive. Pause and replay live TV. This baby will change the way you watch TV. Honest. Requires monthly service fee of $10.

Under $50

Belly Lights (www.gammagarb.com) $7–$14. Light up the holidays with this body jewelry that runs on small button batteries. Flashing LEDs on top of the battery container are activated with a twist of the button. Fun for parties during the holidays and for New Year's Eve.

Kensington FlyLight (www.kensington.com/products/pro_c1438.html) $19. This light plugs into your USB port and provides a little extra light on plane flights and in dark places. It comes in platinum or black, and the light is available in red or white.

The Lap Wrap (www.thelapwrap.com) $29–$39. Customizable covers for your laptop available in more than 40 designs. Monogramming also available for an extra fee. Cover attaches to laptop with Velcro and laptop can be used while cover is attached. Helps protect your laptop.

TIP OF THE DAY A magazine subscription is always appreciated. For the general-interest enthusiast, *PC Magazine*, *Maximum PC*, *Linux Journal*, or *MacWorld*, depending on platform of choice, is a good start. The scientifically inclined might like *Scientific American* or *Popular Science*, and the aspiring digerati flock to *Wired*. For the programmer, there's nothing like *Dr. Dobb's Journal*. Its slogan: Running light without overbyte.

Subscribe to these and more online, at magazinecity.net.

 DOWNLOAD OF THE DAY In the simplest terms, fractals are geometric shapes repeated over and over again at smaller and smaller scales. Fractals can be found in nature, on a screensaver, or on the wall of a college kid's dorm room. Fractals are mathematical art.

Fract-o-rama is a free open-source fractal generator from fractorama.com.

POLL: Do you buy CPUs by performance or by clock speed?

84% Performance

16% Clock speed

DECEMBER 6

TODAY'S FOCUS: Our Geek Gift Guide

RIAA SUES NAPSTER

The Recording Industry Association of America filed suit against Napster on this day in 1999 for alleged music piracy. The RIAA claimed swapping copyrighted material online was a form of theft. After much heated debate within the music industry, Napster was taken offline in response to the allegations. Despite efforts to reinvent itself as a pay-for-download site that conforms to industry standards, Napster has yet to relaunch. The company filed for bankruptcy in 2002, and sold some of its assets to global music giant Bertelsmann. But other peer-to-peer music sites still continue to thrive online today, much to the RIAA's chagrin.

Related Web sites `napster.com`, `riaa.org`

Twisted List: Lamest Gifts for Geeks

By Martin Sargent

Holy Surfing (`stupid.com/Merchant2/merchant.mv?Screen=PROD&Store_Code=store&Product_Code=STIS`) Not long ago, the Vatican named Saint Isadore the patron saint of the Internet. Now you can have your very own Saint Isadore plastic figurine to keep watch over your Internet-connected machine, hopefully warding off evil viruses and hackers and keeping you from straying into the dark and wicked corners of the Web.

You've Got Zen! (`stupid.com/Merchant2/merchant.mv?Screen=PROD&Store_Code=store&Product_Code=BUDA`) If you prefer Eastern religions, get yourself a Laptop Buddha. The portly little mystic sage sits atop your computer working away at a laptop and washing your machine in good Karma.

Computer Voodoo (`stupid.com/Merchant2/merchant.mv?Screen=PROD&Store_Code=store&Product_Code=VOOD1`) If Buddhism doesn't do it for you either, try Voodoo! The computer voodoo doll is a pincushion shaped like a computer that you can pierce with sharp objects in an attempt to take vengeance upon your computer for it crashing, deleting your files, or causing any other manner of misery in your life.

Circuit-Board Coasters (`stupid.com/Merchant2/merchant.mv?Screen=PROD&Store_Code=store&Product_Code=COAS`) God forbid your coffee mug creates an unsightly ring on that particleboard computer desk it took you all night to assemble. What nerd wouldn't relish a set of computer-component coasters made from real circuit boards? And when the boys come over to play some Dungeons & Dragons, won't they be excited to place their Jolt colas on what might have been the circuit board controlling a Soviet missile silo rather than directly on the basement card table?

For Professional Nerds (`cybercal.com/ComputerDragon.html`, `cybercal.com/CyberWizard.html`) Most social psychologists would consider computer addicts who are also hooked on Dungeons & Dragons to exist deep within the realm of nerd. The ideal gift? A pewter figurine of either a dragon or wizard using a PC. That's geek times two!

Welcome! You're a Dork! (`cybercal.com/weldotmat.html`) If you're ever heading out on a blind date and you get to the person's house and they have a Wel.com doormat, run like the wind.

TIP OF THE DAY Give the gift of software without annoying nag screens, from `nonags.com`. But don't forget to pay your shareware fees anyway. Visit the Association of Shareware Professionals to find out why (and download some great programs), `asp-shareware.org`.

DOWNLOAD OF THE DAY Terragen is a 3D terrain generator. You can create or generate a landscape, and then render it with valleys, mountains, sunlight, clouds, and water. When you're done, export the image as a BMP to use with another 3D-rendering application, a Web page, or anything else that accepts bitmap images. Free from `www.planetside.co.uk/terragen`.

DECEMBER 7

TODAY'S FOCUS: MP3

COAX CABLE PATENTED

A patent was issued for coaxial cable on this day in 1931. The "concentric conducting system" allowed thousands of telephone conversations to be carried simultaneously on long-distance circuits. A coaxial cable consists of a center wire surrounded by an insulating material. A grounded shield of coiled wire encompasses the insulation, which minimizes interference from radio frequencies and electricity. Coax has been used to wire computer networks and is still widely used in homes for cable television.

Related Web site `www.tvinsite.com`

A Brief History of Audio Formats:
The Analog Age

By Charlie Amter

Here is a brief history of audio formats past, and a peek into how we might listen to music in the 21st century.

The Phonograph In the early 19th century, it was all but impossible to imagine what great changes were in store for the world of audio. Although the first successful recording device was developed in 1855, it wasn't until Thomas Edison's phonograph (invented in 1877) and Emile Berliner's Gramophone (patented in 1887) that the phonograph started to come into its own.

The proliferation of electricity and the jazz age both helped turn the phonograph into one of the most celebrated inventions of the modern era. That is, until radio came along.

Radio It's hard to imagine a world without radio, but the technology has been around only since the 1920s. Radio was originally developed for military use during World War I, but the gramophone industry helped spur demand for recorded music delivered over the air. When the Radio Corporation of America (RCA) acquired the Victor Talking Machine Company in 1929, the modern era of the music industry was born.

The 8-Track Few audio formats evoke more nostalgia than the doomed 8-track. Invented in the early 1960s by William Powell Lear, and heavily marketed and used in the '70s, the 8-track was the premier portable audio format for almost 15 years.

The Cassette Tape The cassette as we know it didn't come into the average home until the late 1970s. Cassettes outlasted 8-tracks because they were more compact and sounded better, thanks to the efforts of Dolby Laboratories. The debut of Sony's Walkman in 1979 was the final nail in the 8-track's coffin; cassette tape sales soared into the '80s.

Tomorrow: The appearance of digital music formats.

TIP OF THE DAY Apple's iPod MP3 player holds a lot of music: 5GB or 10GB, depending on the model. That's several thousand songs. To keep you from using it for mass piracy purposes, Apple designs the iPod to work with only one computer at a time. If you connect it to another Mac, iTunes will erase all the songs on the iPod and replace them with *its* library. Turn off iTunes' automatic updates and use a third-party utility instead. Two of my favorites are Xpod, free from `bitcom.ch`, and PodMaster 1000, $8 shareware from `homepage.mac.com/calvert/iplod`.

DOWNLOAD OF THE DAY PsychicMP3 isn't really psychic, but it might seem that way. It correctly names your MP3s by looking them up online. Free from `psychicmp3.com`.

POLL: Where do you stand on the online music sharing debate?

96% I should be able to share my MP3 without consequence

4% Share an MP3, go to jail

COMPUTER "BUG" DISCOVERER BORN

Admiral Grace Hopper was born in New York City on this day in 1906. She was the first woman to achieve the rank of rear admiral in the U.S. Navy, and was an early proponent of using COBOL as a standard programming language. She was a programmer on the Mark I, the world's first large-scale digital computer. Hopper is also credited with finding the first reported computer "bug." Although the term had been used for years to describe glitches and problems, Hopper found an actual moth in one of the relay panels in the Mark II case. She died January 1, 1992.

Related Web site   `gracehopper.org/gmh.html`

A Brief History of Audio Formats: The Dawn of Digital

By Charlie Amter

The great sea change in music recording and listening began when the first digital formats emerged in the 1980s.

The Compact Disc   Developed by Philips and Sony in Japan, the audio CD as we know it came out in 1982. The CD was highly touted and slow to catch on. However, the sound quality and portability of CDs outweighed the cost for most consumers, and the CD was the medium of choice by the end of the '80s.

Digital Audio Tapes (DAT)   Introduced in 1987 for the studio market, digital audio tapes quickly became de rigueur in professional recording industry circles. Although DATs never fully caught on in the consumer market because of the high cost of DAT players, they remain a mainstay of the pro-audio world because of their low price and enhanced digital storage capabilities.

MiniDisc   Marketed exclusively by Sony, MiniDiscs have captured a small, but devoted, segment of the consumer market since 1998. Fans of the MiniDisc swear by its size, recording capability, and durability. Although very popular abroad, the MiniDisc has never taken off in the United States.

MP3   Invented in 1989 in Erlangen, Germany, MP3 has quickly come to symbolize a paradigm shift in the way many people access their music. The home computer revolution, along with the Internet, has allowed millions of Net-connected music fans to take advantage of the latest audio medium.

In 1997, the format truly realized its potential, thanks to a man named Tomislav Uzelac, who created the AMP MP3 playback engine. The first MP3 player was invented just in time for the Napster revolution in the form of 1998's Winamp, widely regarded as the first free, consumer-ready MP3 player.

The 21st Century and Beyond   If the past is any indication of how you will listen to music in 20 years, expect the unexpected. The future of music no doubt involves convenience, and some form of the celestial jukebox. Access to every song ever recorded will be at your fingertips—or more likely your vocal chords, as voice-recognition technology will likely become seamlessly integrated into our music-selection process.

TIP OF THE DAY   The volume of MP3s is not always consistent. If you have a large collection, the variations can be significant. Normalize the volume level of your MP3 with mp3Trim, free for Windows from `logiccell.com/~mp3trim`.

DOWNLOAD OF THE DAY   Rename your files based on their ID3 tags with MP3 PrettyNamer from Don't Panic Software. Free for Mac OS 9 and X from `homepage.mac.com/wille/`.

POLL: Will the Web die?

84% Never
1% In one year
2% In five years
8% In ten years
5% Already dead

TODAY'S FOCUS: MP3s

FIRST NOBEL LAUREATES

The first Nobel prizes were awarded on this day in 1901. The prestigious awards were established by Alfred Nobel, the inventor of gunpowder. When Nobel's brother Ludvig died in 1888, a French newspaper mistakenly attributed the invention of the explosive material to the deceased. The article referred to the late Nobel as a "merchant of death." Alfred was reportedly so shaken by the insult, he was determined to change his legacy.

Related Web site   `www.nobel.se`

Build Your Own MP3 Player

Why spend hundreds of dollars for a hard drive-based MP3 player when you can build one yourself for less than $20?

To gather together the hardware, try eBay or garage sales, or raid your parts closet. You'll need at least a 486 DX100 class system. That's enough processor for playback, but older systems had surprisingly puny hard drives. Put a 16-bit SCSI card into the box and scrounge up a SCSI hard drive to get around the IDE limitations of the old 486 BIOS.

Believe it or not, the best operating system for a dedicated MP3 player is DOS. Unlike Windows or Linux, DOS systems can be turned off without a lengthy shutdown process. And if all you're doing is playing back MP3s, DOS's lack of a GUI and inability to multitask won't be liabilities.

Save the hard drive for your MP3s: make a DOS boot disk with the appropriate drivers and a DOS MP3 player such as DAMP (www.damp-mp3.co.uk) or MPXPlay (geocities.com/mpxplay). Both are free and surprisingly functional. DAMP even supports visualizations. With a boot disk, you can just turn on the machine and it will start the MP3 player within 30 seconds. No need to wait for a GUI to start up.

Naturally, you'll need a sound card. A Sound Blaster 16 will do fine. You can get the DOS drivers from `creative.com`. Forget buying speakers for this beast; they'd set you back much more than the entire system. Instead, hook it up to your stereo.

You'll still need a monitor and keyboard to control the player, although both DOS MP3 players support LCD displays and control via the serial port, which means if you're handy with hardware you could cobble together a simple interface more suitable for the stereo rack than the computer desk.

TIP OF THE DAY   Q: How can I modify the MP3s I have ripped? —Justin from Corona, California

A: In general, it's best to edit the file as a WAV before you convert it to MP3, if possible. The problem with most MP3 editors is that they convert the MP3 to WAV for editing and then recompress to MP3, causing an inevitable loss of quality. Look for an editor that works "in place" or "without conversion."

My favorite is Audacity, free for Mac, Windows, and Linux, from `audacity.sourceforge.net`. You'll need to download the MP3 plug-in, as well.

DOWNLOAD OF THE DAY   MP3 Rage is the definitive collection of tools for MP3 enthusiasts. You can edit ID3 tags, play MP3 files, catalog, organize, rename, find, and change thousands of MP3 files and their ID3 tags quickly and painlessly. It also has a clean, powerful, and easy-to-use interface. For Mac OS 9 and X. Free to try, $24.95 to buy, from `www.chaoticsoftware.com`.

TODAY'S FOCUS: MP3s

LAUGHING GAS USED ON DENTAL PATIENTS

The first dental anaesthetic was used by Dr. John M. Riggs for a tooth extraction on this day in 1884. Riggs administered nitrous oxide (better known as "laughing gas") to Dr. Horace Wells, who had seen the substance used in a demonstration in Hartford, Connecticut. Wells was so impressed by nitrous oxide's capability to dull pain, he decided to try it himself. He convinced Riggs, his colleague, to perform the operation. A recent study found that the gas works by interfering with a receptor in certain brain cells, which in turn slows down the brain's excitatory activity.

Related Web site   www.ada.org

Store Your MP3s Online

There's only one problem with MP3s: There's only so much space on your hard drive. One way to prevent the invariable storage overflow is to store your MP3s online.

Several sites specialize in doing this. One of the most popular is MyPlay.com. It offers three gigs of space in your music "locker." Setting up an account is quick and painless, and the site has a variety of tracks and DJ mixes you can populate your locker with. MyPlay.com is blessedly free of ads and pop-ups for now, but be sure you edit your options if you don't want email from the service.

The only drawback to online MP3 storage is that you'll have to upload your songs before you can listen to them, and that's going to take a while: 170 hours for 3GB on a dial-up modem. Because MyPlay.com doesn't offer batch uploads, you're going to have to do it one song at a time. Ouch.

Other music and data storage sites include

* Xdrive: xdrive.com
* Epitonic's Blackbox: epitonic.com/blackbox
* MyMP3.com: my.mp3.com

The advantages of online MP3 storage are twofold: It's a way to back up your collection, and you can access your music anywhere you can get online. The disadvantage is the amount of time it takes to get your music uploaded.

TIP OF THE DAY   I connect my MP3 player to the car's stereo with an inexpensive cassette adapter. The adapter adds a little hiss, but it's more than adequate for the suboptimal listening environment of an AMC Pacer.

On the other hand, if you don't like the wires, try the iRock! 300W Wireless Music Adapter by First International Digital, about $29 at our local computer store. The 300W runs on a pair of AAA batteries, is about the size of a stopwatch, and packs its FM antenna into the 7-inch tail that plugs into your CD or MP3 player. It broadcasts on 88.1, 88.3, 88.5, and 88.7 FM.

It's a radio transmitter, so it's prone to all the ills radio can suffer, including static and interference. It's sort of like listening to well-worn vinyl LPs, if you're old enough to remember that. But, if you hate the wires or you're stuck in a rental car without a cassette deck, the iRock! is the answer. From First International Digital at myirock.com/players/irock300w.htm.

 DOWNLOAD OF THE DAY   CDex is an excellent free CD ripper: Turn your music collection into MP3s. Uses CDDB and the LAME encoder. Free from surf.to/cdex.

POLL: Would you risk jail for MP3s?

42% Yes

58% No

DECEMBER
11

TODAY'S FOCUS: MP3s

FIRST TRANSATLANTIC WIRELESS MESSAGE

Guglielmo Marconi sent the first wireless transmission from West Cornwall on England's west coast to Newfoundland, Canada, on this day in 1901. Marconi was in Newfoundland when he heard the message, which was three dots Morse code, representing the letter S. Unappreciated in his native Italy, Marconi had received funding from the British government to conduct his communications experiments. Marconi was awarded the Nobel Prize in Physics in 1909.

Related Web site `www.marconicalling.com`

CBR Versus VBR

Q: My friend says that VBR MP3s are better. I've always encoded my MP3s with CBR, and I always thought that was better. Who's right? —email from Chad in Minnesota

A: Depends on what *better* means. Let me explain. VBR and CBR are two different ways to apply MP3 compression to audio. VBR stands for variable bit rate; CBR stands for constant bit rate.

To understand the difference, you need to understand how MP3 works. MP3 data is encoded at a specific bit rate; that is, a specific number of bits of data per second of audio: The higher the bit rate, the better the audio quality. You can set most MP3 encoders to encode data at anywhere between 8Kbps and 320Kbps.

Now here's the key point. The more complex the audio source material is, the higher the bit rate that will be needed to encode it well. A simpler passage can get by with a lower bit rate.

When MP3s are recorded with CBR, the rate chosen is a compromise. It might be too low to accurately encode a very busy passage, and it might be saving more data than necessary for a simpler passage. VBR optimizes the bit rate and file size every second as it encodes, to create the best possible audio without wasting disk space.

So, if you're looking for optimal quality and file size, VBR is, indeed, better. But CBR does have some advantages. For one, you'll know exactly how big the file will be. A 128Kbps recording will take exactly 128 kilobits of disk space per second of audio. Furthermore, some portable

MP3 players cannot play back VBR recordings, so CBR is better if you want to maximize compatibility.

In general, though, if your MP3 encoder and players support VBR, it's best to use it. Set the bit rate to a high value to start, and be sure to allow plenty of headroom for those complex passages.

TIP OF THE DAY The MP3 format allows room for more than music. You can add information about the track, including artist, album title, track title, genre, and more. This information is stored in something called *tags*. The original tag standard, ID3v1, was fairly limited. The new standard, ID3v2, allows you to include nearly anything in a tag, including lyrics and album art.

Most MP3 players and recorders will allow you to modify your tags, or you can use a standalone tag editor for more control. To know more about the ID3 standard and what it can do, visit `id3.org`.

 DOWNLOAD OF THE DAY Tagmaster helps you control the ID3 tags in your MP3s. Free from `analogx.com/contents/download/audio/tagm.htm`. (See January 14 for more tag editors for Windows and Mac.)

POLL: Which chip-maker do you trust?

56% AMD

32% Intel

1% Transmeta

11% No one

DECEMBER

12

TODAY'S FOCUS: MP3s

AIRBAG PROPONENT DIES

Allen Kent Breed died on this day in 1999. The American inventor developed a small electromechanical sensor, which consisted of a tiny metal ball that was held snugly in place in a tube by magnets. A sudden movement would jerk the ball free, which would then complete an electrical circuit. His devices were first used by the military, but Breed later realized they could be used for airbag triggers in car crashes. He was instrumental in convincing Congress and the car companies that airbags should be installed in all new cars. Breed was inducted into the Automotive Hall of Fame in 1999.

Related Web site   `www.breedtech.com`

Ogg Vorbis

If you've been hanging in the digital audio underground for the last few years, you've probably heard of Ogg Vorbis. This is the odd moniker for an audio compression format much akin to MP3, MPEG-4 audio (AAC and TwinVQ), and PAC. It provides high-quality audio (44.1KHz to 48KHz, 16+ bit, polyphonic) at a fraction of the original file size (bit rates from 128Kbps to 350Kbps using the Ogg Vorbis encoder).

The buzz around Ogg Vorbis, besides the fact that it sounds good, is that the format is open source. It's totally patent- and royalty-free for private, public, commercial, and nonprofit consumption, and it's open for developers to continue its evolution. The format itself is called Vorbis, whereas Ogg refers to the Ogg Project, `xiph.org/ogg`, a multimedia open-source initiative in which Vorbis, `vorbis.com`, is the primary effort.

Using FreeRip MP3 from `mgshareware.com`, we've encoded tracks into Vorbis (.ogg files) and have listened to them using a free plug-in for Winamp. Vorbis files sound excellent and have many modern features, such as surround channels and streaming capabilities. Because it belongs to everyone, the format will continue to evolve.

   For an excellent Ogg Vorbis encoder, player, and editor that works in Windows, Mac, and Linux, download Audacity, free from `audacity.sourceforge.net`.

 For a CD-ripping program that encodes in Ogg Vorbis format, try CD-DA X-Tractor, free for Windows from `xtractor.sourceforge.net`.

TIP OF THE DAY   Even within the MP3 specification, there are a number of different encoders your software can use. The original encoder was created by the inventor of the MP3 format, Fraunhofer, and it's still generally considered the best. But software vendors must pay a license fee to Fraunhofer for the use of the technology. That doesn't sit well with small developers and open-source proponents.

That's why the LAME project was started. LAME, which stands for, LAME Ain't an MP3 Encoder, is, in fact, an MP3 encoder. It's open source and is being used more and more widely in MP3 software, including some well-known commercial products. I don't exactly have golden ears, but as far as I can tell, LAME-encoded MP3s sound every bit as good as Fraunhofer-encoded songs. And given the amount of energy being put into the LAME project, I bet it starts sounding even better soon.

For more information about LAME, visit `mp3dev.org/mp3`.

 DOWNLOAD OF THE DAY   Sonique is another music player for Windows that looks great and plays back most digital music formats including Windows media files, OGG, MOD, CDs and MP3. Free for Windows from `sonique.lycos.com`.

POLL: Are cell phones a scapegoat for bad driving?

59% Yes

41% No

DECEMBER 13

TODAY'S FOCUS: Online Clubs

LAST MOON WALK

Apollo 17 departed from the lunar surface on this day in 1972. Commander Eugene A. Cernan was the last man to walk on the moon. Cernan says the last words spoken as the two-man crew was preparing to depart were, "Okay, let's get this mother out of here." But according to the official NASA transcript, Cernan only said, "Now, let's get off." Although there have been no return visits to the moon since, there are rumors that the Chinese government hopes to put humans on the moon in the next few years.

Related Web site   www.genecernan.com

Twisted List: Online Clubs You Should Never Join

By Martin Sargent

Yahoo! Groups are fabulous online communities where you can meet, chat with, and share files with people who share your interests. But here are five clubs that are so sad that if you join them, you really ought to do so anonymously.

The Condiment Packets Club (groups.yahoo.com/ groups/condimentpackets)   The three proud members of the Condiment Packets Club meet online to discuss the rewarding pastime of visiting fast food restaurants to grab as many ketchup, mustard, and relish packets as possible. The club president has even scanned hundreds of condiment packets onto his Web site. If you want to meet exciting people who share your love of hot sauce and honey, join The Condiments Packet Club today.

The World of Mayonnaise (groups.yahoo.com/group/ theworldofmayonnaise)   The three mighty members of The Condiments Packet Club must always be on their guard, for Yahoo! Groups also hosts a fearsome rival gang known as The World of Mayonnaise. According to a message from the founder, the club is "A general egg-based food dressing forum of utter exquisite joy!" I'll take two packets.

The Duct Tape Club (groups.yahoo.com/group/ ducttapeclub)   Even more disturbing than the various tribes of condiment fetishists are the duct-tape enthusiasts. Over 1,000 Netizens belong to one of 41 distinct duct tape groups at Yahoo!.

The We Hate Shauna Club (groups.yahoo.com/ group/wehateshauna)   The We Hate Shauna Club was formed to talk smack about Shauna. Shauna is hated by the members of the club because she calls the club's Dungeon Master, Jayson, and interrupts their games of Advanced Dungeons & Dragons. According to one club member, "There we are almost getting into an adventure, and Shauna calls. No big surprise anymore, but I hope she gets the message soon. WE HATE SHAUNA!!!"

Apparently, no club members ever have a problem with other girls calling them and interrupting whatever they're doing.

The Saddest Club of All (groups.yahoo.com/group/ MartinSargentFans)   The most depressing Yahoo! club, bar none, is Martin Sargent Fans. The club's namesake, Martin Sargent, asks you to join to feel misery alongside him. Only one person has posted a message in the club since May 11, and that person is clearly insane. Woe is Martin.

TIP OF THE DAY   Spread Christmas cheer with Project Santa. It's Space Defender in a sleigh. I particularly enjoy the weirdly flat music track. Play online at projectsanta.com. Requires Flash.

DOWNLOAD OF THE DAY   Total Recorder can capture streaming audio from any site and save it to disc for later playback. Schedule recordings like a VCR, too. Free to try, $11 to register for unlimited recording, from highcriteria.com.

POLL: Should PC makers be responsible for protecting copyright?

5% Yes   95% No

TODAY'S FOCUS: Notebook Computers

BILL OF RIGHTS RATIFIED

The first 10 amendments of the U.S. Constitution became law on this day in 1791. The amendments were influenced by the English Bill of Rights of 1689, as well as Virginia's Declaration of Rights, written by George Mason in 1776. The First Amendment has often been invoked in the evolution of technology from sharing music files, to encryption, to online message boards.

Related Web site `www.archives.gov`

Notebook Buyer's Guide

By Hahn Choi

Price is the biggest determining factor for most people when buying a notebook computer, but keep in mind that notebooks are inherently difficult to upgrade, so it's a good idea to spend more initially rather than outliving the usefulness of your notebook too quickly. Upgrades such as more memory and bigger hard-drive size should be considered from the outset.

Things to remember:

- **Processor Speed**—A 900MHz processor can do everything that a 1.8GHz processor can and draws less power.
- **Display**—Go with resolutions as low as 1,024×768. A 14-inch versus a larger 15-inch display will save some money, too. A 14-inch display may suit your needs as much as a 15-inch display. Always buy the active matrix or TFT display. They're brighter, crisper, and more legible.
  SVGA displays have a resolution of 800×600 and are found in 12-inch or smaller displays.
  XGA displays have a resolution of 1,024×768 and are found in 12-inch or larger displays.
  SXGA+ displays have a resolution of 1,400×1,050 and are found in 14-inch or larger displays.
  UXGA displays have a resolution of 1,600×1,200 and are found in 15-inch or larger displays.
  For 12.1-inch (measured diagonally) displays, get XGA over SVGA. With larger displays, get the best resolution you can afford.
- **Memory**—Buy memory online from a third-party source. Manufacturers charge a premium for branded RAM.

- **Hard Drive**—A 48GB hard drive is significantly more expensive than a 30GB drive. Go for the smaller option and spend the savings on a CD-R/RW drive, which can provide limitless storage.
- **Input**—Try the keyboard and pointing device before you buy. Designers often sacrifice comfort for size.

Finding a suitable notebook computer ultimately means sacrificing certain features, and setting your priorities. No machine has it all. But it's worth it for the portability.

TIP OF THE DAY To extend battery life on your notebook, turn off extensions you're not using. Disable auto-insert notification on PCs. Turn off WiFi cards. Use the energy-saving control panel to shut down the drives when idle. Don't set the timer to too small an amount, however: Spinning the drives back up takes extra juice. Turn your display off when not in use.

To increase battery capacity, charge and drain a brand new battery three times before you put it to work. Same if you haven't used the battery in a long while. This fully activates the battery chemicals.

 DOWNLOAD OF THE DAY Turn your notebook into a DJ workstation with Virtual Turntables by Carrot Innovations. Modeled after Panasonic CD-decks, the robust interface comes complete with mouse-controlled jog dials, BPM matching, and crossfader. This program is free to try, $42 to keep, from `carrotinnovations.com`.

POLL: Have computer prices hit rock bottom?

26% Yes

74% No

TODAY'S FOCUS: Notebook Computers

FEMALE ANTHROPOLOGY PIONEER BORN

Margaret Mead was born in Philadelphia, Pennsylvania, on this day in 1901. Mead made her mark on the scientific community in 1928 with the publication of her book, *Coming of Age in Samoa*. The work discussed how stages of human development could be influenced by cultural expectations. Its lively writing and controversial subject matter propelled it onto the bestseller lists. Throughout her career, Mead published 20 books, received 28 honorary doctorates, and served as the president of both the American Anthropological Association and the American Association for the Advancement of Science. She died in 1978.

Related Web site   `www.mead2001.org`

Types of Notebook

By Hahn Choi

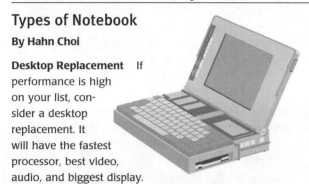

Desktop Replacement   If performance is high on your list, consider a desktop replacement. It will have the fastest processor, best video, audio, and biggest display. Desktop replacements typically include three drives: optical drive (DVD, CD-RW, CD-ROM, DVD/CD-RW), floppy drive, and hard drive. With these machines, you'll find 14-inch or 15-inch displays and full-size keyboards.

Desktop replacements come with all the legacy ports and typically include two PCMCIA slots for additional devices. They usually weigh more than 7 pounds.

Thin-and-Lights   Thin-and-lights can be found with processing performance comparable to desktop replacements, but have only a hard drive and an optical drive. Floppy drives are available through a USB-based device or as a swappable drive replacing the optical drive. Thin-and-lights include all the legacy ports and at least one PCMCIA slot, and usually tout full-size keyboards.

Display sizes are typically 13 inches or 14 inches, but some are beginning to show up with 15-inch screens. Thin-and-lights typically fall between 4 pounds and 7 pounds, blending portability with performance.

Ultraportable   Ultraportables have slower processors, usually less than 1GHz. Notebooks in this class provide only the hard drive. Other drives are external. Many ultraportables do not include legacy ports and rely on external port replicators or docking stations.

Displays are typically 12 inches or smaller and graphics performance is essentially 2D, although they may claim 3D. They weigh less than 4 pounds and often have smaller keyboards.

Subnotebooks   Subnotebooks are typically less than 3 pounds and have displays of less than 11 inches. Keyboards are smaller as well, and the performance isn't as good as on an ultraportable. This form factor is much more common in Asia.

TIP OF THE DAY   Increase your battery life by up to 10 hours with an external battery. Electrovaya has created an 11 3/4-inch by 8 3/4-inch by 3/8-inch slab called the *PowerPad* that pledges to keep users mobile all day long.

In our informal tests with the PowerPad 160, we were able to operate for more than 10 hours before we got tired of computing. In short, PowerPad outlasted us even with power-hungry 802.11b hardware in constant use.

Electrovaya claims the $500 PowerPad 160 will supply power for 12 to 16 hours depending on the notebook, whereas the $400 120 version can keep you mobile for 8 to 12 hours.

DOWNLOAD OF THE DAY   The icon on the Windows taskbar only identifies the percentage of battery power remaining at any given time. Utilities such as Power Center go a few steps further, tracking the way you work and judging how many minutes of power you have left. Free from `www.zdnet.com/downloads/stories/info/0,10615,38604,00.html`.

DECEMBER

16

TODAY'S FOCUS: Notebook Computers

FIRST FLIGHT

The Wright Brothers made the first sustained flight at Kitty Hawk, North Carolina, on this day in 1903. This year marks the 100th anniversary that Orville and Wilbur flew the original "Wright Flyer" for a total of 12 seconds and a distance of 120 feet. The siblings made numerous other test flights following their first success, but they were capable of flying in a straight line for only very short durations. Within a couple of years, however, the aviation pioneers were able to stay aloft for more than half an hour. Their 1905 Wright Flyer was considered the world's first "practical" airplane.

Related Web sites   `www.firstflightcentennial.org`, `www.first-to-fly.com`

Notebook Security

More laptops are getting ripped off than ever before, literally thousands a day. Keep your portable safe.

Laptop Antitheft Software   Most of these programs automatically send the computer's IP address and other information to an online service every time the computer logs on to the Internet. When a computer is stolen, the service tracks down the physical location of the computer using this information. The antitheft service usually works in conjunction with law enforcement to retrieve your laptop. Here are the most popular products currently available:

- **zTrace** (`ztrace.com`)—An invisible software security application that traces the location of missing laptops for recovery. If the laptop is reported missing, the zTrace recovery team identifies the computer's exact physical location.
- **Lucira** (`lucira.com`)—Uses two methods to pinpoint a laptop's location, and then automatically transmits that information to the police. It also encrypts, sends, and destroys sensitive data on command.
- **The CyberAngel** (`sentryinc.com`)—This program will automatically transmit the calling location ID— whether it be a telephone or a network connection— when the password entry system is violated. Using public databases, the service identifies the street address where the stolen laptop is being used.
- **ComputracePlus** (`computrace.com`)—Built for corporate users, this program contacts an online monitoring center on a regular basis with IP address and phone number.

Tips on How to Protect Your Laptop
- **Laptop Theft, Know Before You Go** (`corporatetravelsafety.com/laptoptheft.html`)—Travel safety consultant Kevin Coffey offers

these tips on keeping your laptop computer safe when on the road.

- **Tips for Preventing Laptop Computer Theft** (`mpdc.dc.gov/info/consumer/laptop_theft.shtm`)—Guidelines on how to keep your computer safe, from the Washington, D.C., police department.
- **Laptop Theft** (`rr.sans.org/homeoffice/laptop_theft.php`)—The SANS Institute examines methods and scams used to steal laptops.

TIP OF THE DAY   Register your notebook's serial number. If it's stolen, law enforcement can get it back to you.

- **Stolen Computer Registry** (`stolencomputers.org`)—Formed by an industry consortium in 1992 to foil hardware theft and foster confidence in the purchase of used computers. The Registry does not charge for its services.
- **theRegistry** (`pcid.com`)—An independently run database of computer systems, household and business items, and other assorted property that increases the odds of getting back an item that was lost or stolen. Charges $21.95 to register a laptop.

 DOWNLOAD OF THE DAY   Back up your email before you take it on the road with Outlook Express Backup. Free to try, $29.95 to keep, from `genie-soft.com`.

POLL: Do Windows XP security updates make you feel more secure?

24% Yes

35% No

41% I don't use Windows XP

DECEMBER 17

TODAY'S FOCUS: Notebook Computers

ELECTRON DISCOVERER BORN

The man who first identified electrons was born on this day in 1856. Sir Joseph John Thomson experimented with *cathode rays*: electrical currents inside glass vacuum tubes. In 1887, he hypothesized that the mysterious rays were streams of particles much smaller than atoms. He suggested that the particles, which he called "corpuscles," might make up all the matter in atoms. His discovery of the electron was considered a major breakthrough in the study of atomic structure. The English scientist was awarded the Nobel Prize for Physics in 1906, and was knighted two years later.

Related Web site   `www.aip.org`

Budget Notebooks

By Hahn Choi

Buying a notebook is like buying a car, so be prepared to spend a little more than you think, because this is an investment that must serve your needs for at least the next two years. Many major manufacturers now offer notebooks for less than $1,000. Don't be entranced by the price alone; consider what you might be giving up. Here's an overview of what you'll see in the value notebook market and what to look for before you buy.

Performance   Today, sub-$1,000 notebooks come with Intel Celeron or AMD Duron processors running at 1GHz or higher. Don't put too much emphasis on processors, because all processors manufactured in the last year or so perform well with most applications.

The cheapest performance boost comes from additional memory. Sub-$1,000 notebooks come with 128MB, but jumping to 256MB can show a significant performance improvement. With Microsoft Windows XP, 256MB is our recommended minimum.

Graphics performance is one of the most significant differences in value notebooks. Don't expect stellar 3D performance or game-playable frame rates. Generally, these graphics systems will perform 2D well and offer dual display support, but shy away from the 3D capabilities found in more expensive systems.

Display   Even sub-$1,000 notebooks are shipping with 14-inch displays with a native resolution of at least 1,024×768. To us, that's a solid combination.

Storage   Because notebooks are inherently difficult to upgrade, get the most storage possible. Windows XP, which ships on most notebooks, takes around 1GB alone. Add in your favorite applications, perhaps digital music and pictures, and you'll consume more hard drive space than you ever imagined. A year ago, 10GB was considered a good size, but times are changing, and we recommend 15GB minimum. Even the cheapest notebooks can be found with 20GB drives.

TIP OF THE DAY   Add WiFi capability to your notebook and you can get online wirelessly at work and home, as well as in coffee shops, airports, and many other locations.

For the Macintosh, the choice is a no-brainer; all new Macs come AirPort-ready with built-in antennas. Apple's $99 AirPort card is the obvious choice.

There are many choices for Windows users, but TechTV's Labs like 3Com's Wireless LAN card with XJACK because the antenna retracts when not in use. 3Com's card delivers a strong, high-speed connection even in low-signal areas. It also comes with the best WiFi software, WLAN Launcher. $89 from `3com.com/products/en_US/detail.jsp?tab=features&pathtype=purchase&sku=3CRWE62092A`.

DOWNLOAD OF THE DAY   Add the Nutshell toolbar to your browser to search Google, Amazon, Dictionary.com, the IMDB, and Daypop. All-in-one and free for Windows from `torrez.org/projects/nutshell`.

TODAY'S FOCUS: Notebook Computers

EARLY PC UNVEILED

The Altair 8800, considered by many to be the first microcomputer, went on sale on this day in 1975. The machine, sold by MITS of Albuquerque, New Mexico, came with 256 bytes of memory and cost $395 as a do-it-yourself kit, or $495 pre-assembled. Within three months, 4,000 people had ordered the kit, including Bill Gates, then a student at Harvard University. He and his friend Paul Allen wrote programs for the Altair using the BASIC programming language. Their success prompted the duo to start their own software company, called Micro-Soft—and the rest is history.

Related Web site `Virtual Altair Museum exo.com/~wts/wts10005.HTM`

Apple's Notebooks

Let's not leave Apple out of this notebook extravaganza. I own both a Powerbook and an iBook and consider them among the best notebooks ever made. As I write this, Apple's current 14.1-inch iBook is powered by a 700MHz G3 processor, features a 30GB hard drive, a combo DVD/CD-RW drive, and an improved ATI RADEON graphics adapter with 16MB of VRAM, all for a surprisingly affordable $1,800. Entry-level iBooks cost $1,200.

iBooks come equipped with every port you'll ever need. On the left edge of the computer are two USB ports, a single FireWire port, a 56K modem, an Ethernet jack, and a video-out jack. On the iBook's right side, you'll find a power jack for the small, folding AC adapter and the combo optical drive.

Weighing in at nearly six pounds—a pound heavier than the smaller versions—the 14-incher does claim to have added an hour more battery power per charge. That would be an astonishing six hours. We ran a couple of tests with energy saver off and were able to get only four hours of battery life out of our iBook.

On the high end, there's Apple's mouth-watering Titanium PowerBook G4. The current version sports an 800MHz G4 processor, a 1MB L3 cache, and a widescreen 15.2-inch display with a native resolution of 1,280×854 pixels. Apple delivers another first: a DVI connector on a laptop.

Add a $150 DVI-to-ADC converter and you can plug into any of Apple's LCD monitors, including the high-end, 23-inch Apple Cinema HD Display.

One problem continues to plague the Titanium PowerBook: Spare change and pens in laptop bags and metal watch bands that come in contact with the computers tend to mar the machines' finish. The problem is so well-known, threads have been started on Apple's message boards, and a paint "fix" has been created called TiPaint, at `TiPaint.com`.

Both notebooks, like all new Macs, ship with Mac OS X as the default operating system. Users still have the option to boot up in OS 9 if they prefer. In addition, Appleworks, iTunes2, iMovie2, and iPhoto come standard.

TIP OF THE DAY Get your desktop and notebook to talk together to share files and email with Laplink Gold. $139.95 from `laplink.com`. Add a $50 USB networking cable for even easier connections.

GoToMyPC offers online file transfer and remote access to your PC from anywhere on the Net for $14.95/month from `gotomypc.com`.

DOWNLOAD OF THE DAY Expand the Windows clipboard to hold up to 200 entries at one time. Yankee Clipper Plus is free and easy from `yankee-clipper.net`.

TODAY'S FOCUS: Notebook Computers

FIRST NUCLEAR ELECTRICITY

On this day in 1951, the EBR-1 turbine at the Argonne National Laboratory became the first nuclear reactor to generate electricity. The energy output was unimpressive: The reactor lit only four 200-watt light bulbs, but it marked the beginning of the domestic nuclear power industry. Later, the reactor, also known as Chicago Pile-4, proved itself as a breeder reactor, meaning it simply produced more nuclear energy than it consumed. In 1953, the reactor successfully converted uranium into plutonium, which can be used in the creation of nuclear weapons. Today, the EBR-1 is a registered National Historic Landmark.

Related Web site `www.anl.gov`

Laptop DVD to TV

Q: I'd like to play DVDs from my laptop and broadcast the picture and sound through my TV. Can you tell me how to do this? —Jeff from Madison, Indiana

A: If your laptop comes equipped with a TV video-out port, you can easily configure it to play DVDs on your TV. The only issue might be getting the connectors to match. Many notebooks come with custom adapters that ultimately output composite video. A simple RCA-to-RCA connector will work here.

If your computer has S-video out but your TV doesn't have S-video in, you'll need to get an S-video to Composite connector. Instructions on how to wire an S-video to composite connector are online at `hut.fi/Misc/Electronics/circuits/svideo2cvideo.html`. To convert the signal to RF (ick), add an RCA-to-RF adapter. Needless to say, the best quality will be achieved by an S-video-to-S-video connection.

To get the video to come up on the TV you'll have to select the external port. Check your notebook's Display control panel for an appropriate setting. While you're there, change your laptop's screen resolution to either 800×600 or 640×480. This will ensure that your TV displays the full laptop desktop without losing any of the picture.

If it doesn't, you're faced with converting the RGB signal from the monitor port into the NTSC signal your television craves. This is going to require a scan converter, something like the $100 Pocket Scan Converter from AITech (`aitech.com/psc1106-details.htm`), but at that price you're much better off just buying a $100 DVD video player. It'll look a lot better, too.

So, now that we have the video portion of our DVD displaying through a TV monitor, it's time to connect the audio. To do this, you're going to need to get one 1/8-inch stereo mini-jack to two phono plugs adapter.

Be sure that the volume control isn't muted on your laptop, fire up the DVD, grab a bowl of popcorn, and you should be ready to go.

TIP OF THE DAY   Extreme heat, jostling, vibration, and moisture can damage your notebook or the drive inside. That's why it's crucial to back up before you travel. Invest in a padded bag designed for your laptop. Although, it might be easier to throw everything into a purse, your laptop will have no protection from jostling.

 DOWNLOAD OF THE DAY UltimateZip does everything WinZip does, for free. No banner ads, either. Download a copy from `ultimatezip.com`.

POLL: Is the HP/Compaq merger good for consumers?

23% Yes

39% No

37% I couldn't care less.

TODAY'S FOCUS: Cats

FUEL CELL INVENTOR BORN

Francis Thomas Bacon was born in Billericay, Essex, England, on this day in 1904. The engineer developed the first practical hydrogen-oxygen fuel cells, which convert air and fuel directly into electricity. The idea was conceived nearly a century earlier by Sir William Grove, but it was never seriously pursued. In the early 1940s, Bacon proposed using this type of fuel cell in submarines. Later, his creation was used in the U.S. Apollo space vehicles.

Related Web site `www.usfcc.com`

Twisted List: I Love Cats

By Martin Sargent

It's estimated that better than 50% of the Internet is composed of Web pages devoted to people's cats. There are so many cat-related Web sites that there's even a feline search directory, I-Love-Cats.com. During the Internet boom of the late 1990s, the directory was valued at more than $4 billion. Here are some of the worst.

My Cat Hates You (`www.mycathatesyou.com`) The idea behind this site is that people send in pictures of their cats in bad moods and state why their cat hates you, the person looking at its picture on the Web site. That's okay: I hate your cat.

CliffyB's Cat Scan (`www.cat-scan.com`) Cat Scan is an old favorite of the easily amused. Cat owners use their flatbed scanners to scan their cat and email the picture to the site's Webmaster. As you can imagine, the Webmaster has gotten tons of hate mail charging him with animal cruelty. He's posted all that mail on the site. At least he didn't put cats in the paper feeder of his laser printer.

Grey and Black's Litter Box Cam (`litterboxcam.com`) If you're lucky, when you log on to this site, you'll get to see a cat go into its litter box and do its business. Nowadays, ever since Jenni got kind of heavy, it's actually more tantalizing than the Jenni Cam.

How to Toilet Train Your Cat (`karawynn.net/mishacat/toilet.shtml`) You don't even need a litter box if you toilet train your cat. This site tells you how. According to the site, the most important thing to do is to always remember to put the toilet seat down, just as if you were toilet training the woman you're dating.

Even if you do manage to toilet train your cat, it's not a good idea to install a Webcam in your bathroom.

TIP OF THE DAY How can you back up your laptop if you don't have a built-in CD burner?

1. Connect it to your desktop via the network or with a crossover cable and copy the data over. Pros: inexpensive, as little as $10 for the cable. Cons: Network setup is tricky.
2. Upload it to offline storage. Pros: inexpensive and convenient, backup is available anywhere. Cons: slooooooow.
3. Buy an external drive, parallel port, USB, or FireWire. Pros: fast and easy. Cons: expensive. Apricorn's EZ-Gig, for example, starts at $249 for a 10GB drive.

 DOWNLOAD OF THE DAY If you try to run a downloaded application and it complains that you need MSVBVM60.DLL or the like, don't fret. The developer didn't include a needed Visual Basic file in the package.

Microsoft offers all the VB runtime files free on its site, but go ahead and try to find them. Fortunately, Simtel.net has links to them all at `simtel.net/vbrun.php`.

TODAY'S FOCUS: Your New PC

ROLLER COASTER PATENTED

The first U.S. patent for a "switchback railway" was issued to La Marcus Thompson on this day in 1885. A year earlier, Thompson had opened the 600-foot ride at Coney Island in New York. It could go only six miles per hour, but it was so popular that the inventor recouped his $1,600 investment in three weeks. Today, there are more than 1,400 roller coasters worldwide.

Related Web site `rcdb.com`

Part One: It Arrives

It's finally here. Four boxes, two delivery trucks, and one big bill later your new computer has arrived. Now what? Even if this isn't your first computer, there are some things you can do now to make ownership much easier down the road.

Unhand That Knife   No doubt you're tempted to tear right into all the boxes, raining plastic bags and Styrofoam peanuts all over the living room. It's a pain to be patient, but it pays to unpack your new PC methodically. And it's sure a lot easier to clean up afterward.

Start by organizing the paperwork with three large envelopes. Label them "Documentation," "Registration/Receipts," and "Software." As you unpack, file away all the little pieces of paper and CDs that tumble out. These are easy to lose, but very important. Make a note of the contents of each box on the outside of the Registration/Receipts folder. You'll want an inventory in case anything is missing.

Save the packing materials in case you need to ship anything back. You can recycle the boxes after a few months.

If It Feels Good, Do It   Before you actually begin setting up the computer, spend some time thinking about where to put it.

Choose a chair that allows you to plant both feet firmly on the ground, with your thighs parallel to the floor. Find a height that allows your elbows to be at right angles when your hands are resting on the keyboard. You should be neither reaching up nor down to type. Some experts believe that a wrist rest is important for support. Others prefer ergonomic keyboards. Do what feels best to you.

Your monitor should be at arm's length with the top of the screen at eye level so that you don't have to crane your neck to see. Position it so that direct light doesn't fall on the screen. Your desk light should be positioned so that it illuminates your work but doesn't cause glare on the monitor. If you spend a lot of time typing in text, invest in a copy stand that can hold papers at eye level.

No matter how well you've designed your space, it's important to take regular breaks. Ergonomists recommend a 15-minute break every two hours. Get up and stretch, paying special attention to your wrists and neck. Don't forget to blink your eyes, too. When you're staring into a monitor, your eyes blink less and remain at a single focal distance. Look out the window to give those focusing muscles a stretch.

One last tip from my favorite eye doctor: Rub your palms together briskly for about 10 seconds to warm them up, and then gently press the balls of your hands into your eyes. The warmth and darkness are a wonderful break.

POLL: Which gaming console will you buy?

13% Sony PS2

34% Microsoft Xbox

43% Nintendo GameCube

9% None

TODAY'S FOCUS: Your New PC

FIRST TRANS-WORLD NONSTOP FLIGHT

The experimental aircraft Voyager became the first plane to fly nonstop around the world on one tank of fuel on this day in 1986. Pilots Dick Rutan and Jeana Yeager landed at Edwards Air Force Base less than nine days and four minutes after takeoff. Voyager had just five gallons of fuel left in its tank after the 26,366-mile journey. The plane had a wingspan of 111 feet and was made of layers of carbon-fiber tape and paper impregnated with epoxy resin.

Related Web site `www.dickrutan.com`

Turn It On

Now it's time to set up your computer. Inside the Documentation folder should be assembly instructions. Many computers today come with large posters with easy-to-follow instructions. In most cases, installation will involve nothing more than connecting the keyboard, mouse, and monitor to the central processing unit and plugging the computer and monitor into the wall. And now for the moment of truth: Turn the computer on.

If everything seems to be working right, and smoke doesn't come pouring out of the box, you're ready to take the next step.

Name, Rank, and Serial Number Computer companies want to get to know you. They want your email address and your mailing address. They want to know how much money you make and what kinds of things you spend that money on. It's not that they want to become best buddies. All that information is worth big bucks to the marketing department. And your relationship begins the moment you turn on your computer.

I'll tell you the same thing I tell my kids. When a stranger asks you for personal information, clam up. And if you have to, it's okay to lie. Computer companies have an obligation to support the hardware and software they sell you. You have no obligation to give up your privacy in return.

You can usually ignore hardware companies' registration cards entirely. Because the hardware itself is tangible proof of ownership, you can almost always get it serviced without registering.

Software's a little different. Software piracy is so rampant that most companies require proof of ownership before they'll give you support. Often, you'll have to register online when you install the software. Apple requires you to fill out a registration form the very first time you turn on your computer.

If you can't avoid registration, give as few personal details as possible. If registration requires an email address, don't use your main address. That's a sure way to encourage junk email. I recommend creating an address on one of the free Web-based email sites such as Yahoo! Mail (`mail.yahoo.com`) or Hotmail (`hotmail.com`) just for this purpose.

No matter what, save all the registration cards and serial numbers, just in case you need them later. I make a habit of writing software serial numbers directly on the install CD or on the inside front cover of the manual so I won't lose track of them.

If you purchased a CD-recorder, here's a chance to break it in. Make copies of all your master discs and file the originals away somewhere safe. Some discs are protected and will not copy properly, but most will. It's your right to make a single backup copy for archival purposes: Use it.

> **POLL: Which Simpsons' character's philosophy do you live by?**
>
> 31% Lisa: "I think, therefore I am."
>
> 17% Bart: "I terrorize, therefore I am."
>
> 6% Marge: "I worry, therefore I am."
>
> 46% Homer: "I burp, therefore I am."

FIRST RADIO PROGRAM

Radio entertainment was born on this day in 1906. Professor Reginald Fessenden broadcast a poetry reading, a violin solo, and a speech from Brant Rock, Massachusetts, to promote his new alternator-transmitter system. The Canadian inventor used a 429-foot-high antenna and an alternator driven by a steam engine to send the signal, and asked listeners to contact him with feedback on the clarity of the broadcast. A few days earlier, Fessenden had demonstrated the system to AT&T executives, in hopes they would buy the rights to his patents. But the company refused, noting it was not yet refined enough for commercial telephone service.

Related Web site `www.science-tech.nmstc.ca`

Power Protection

There's one piece of hardware many people forget: a surge suppressor. I know you want to play with your new computer right now, but if it's not plugged into a surge suppressor, do yourself a favor and run down to the computer store and pick one up.

Your computer is very sensitive to fluctuations in power. Line noise, power spikes, brownouts, and sudden jolts from lightning and the like, can easily damage the delicate hardware inside the PC. A good surge suppresser is insurance against such catastrophes. It filters the noise and traps the surges before they can get inside the computer.

Be sure to pass everything that comes from the wall and into the computer through the suppressor. That includes power cords, modem cables, and Ethernet cables. Lightning's most common route into your computer is through the phone line, so be sure the suppressor you buy has connectors for modems or Ethernet cables, and use them.

Look for a suppressor that is UL 1449 rated and has a clamping voltage of 400 volts or less with a response time of 10 nanoseconds or less. It should also come with insurance that pays off if your computer is damaged while the suppressor is in service. My favorite brands are APC, Panamax, and Tripplite. A good suppressor should be between $50 and $100.

The same companies also make uninterruptible power supplies, or UPSs. These devices have all the features of a good surge suppressor but also contain batteries. They're useful if you live in an area with frequent brownouts or blackouts. When the power goes down, the UPS will switch to battery power, giving you a few minutes to save your work and shut down normally. Unless your UPS comes with a diesel generator and outdoor gas tank, however, don't expect to continue working. Buy a UPS that provides enough wattage to keep your entire system up just long enough to shut down normally. APC has a wattage calculator on their site at `apcc.com/template/size/apc`. Be prepared to spend from $150 to $500 for a UPS.

Even if you have a surge suppressor or UPS, it's a good idea to disconnect your computer during electrical storms. If lightning is headed your way, shut down, disconnect your computer from the wall, unplug your modem or other Internet connection, and hide under the bed.

Safe Computing It's not enough to protect your hardware; protect yourself, too. I began this book with the seven keys to computer security. Now's a good time to reread them.

POLL: Is tech support an oxymoron?

52% Yes

12% No

36% Can't answer, still on hold

SIR ISAAC NEWTON BORN

One of the most influential scientists in history was born in Woolsthorpe, England, on this day in 1642. Newton formulated the three laws of motion, which is the basis of modern physics: Every object in motion tends to stay in motion; force is equal to mass times acceleration; and, for every action, there is an equal and opposite reaction. Newton's *Philosophiae Naturalis Principia Mathematica*, published in 1687, is one of the most famous scientific works to date.

Related Web site   `www.newtonproject.ic.ac.uk`

Going Online

We've spent enough time preparing your computer—now it's finally time to use it. Your very first task is to get online. A computer that isn't connected to the Internet is nothing more than a souped-up calculator.

Most systems these days come with software that makes it simple to sign up for an online service. On the Macintosh, run the Internet Wizard. In Windows, click **Explore the Internet**. It's okay to use the preinstalled ISPs to get online right away, but be careful about long-term commitments. As you become more sophisticated, you might well decide that there are better ways of getting Internet access. It's nice to have the flexibility to switch.

New users and people who want a little handholding on the Information Superhighway might want to choose an online service such as America Online or its sister service, CompuServe. Online services are full service providers. They're the easiest to set up, and after you're online they manage your experience to keep it from being too confusing or overwhelming.

If you're an experienced user, you'll want an Internet service provider. ISPs are more like utilities; they'll hook you up to the Net, but it's up to you to figure out how to use it. ISPs come in a wide array of prices. There are even free services such as NetZero.com.

Choosing an ISP   The most important thing to look for in an Internet service provider is a local access number. You'll be spending many hours online each month. If it's a long-distance call to your ISP, that means many dollars down the drain. To find a provider with phone numbers in your area use the ISP search engine at `thelist.com`, or check the Yellow Pages under "Internet Access."

After you have a list of local ISPs, ask around. The best way to judge an ISP is to talk with their customers. Ask whether it's easy to get through: Too many busy signals means an ISP has too few modems. Ask what kind of throughput users get. If access slows noticeably during the early evening, the ISP doesn't have enough bandwidth to supply all its users. If you're not an expert user, you'll also want to know how current customers rate the ISP's tech support. This is especially true if you use a Macintosh. Many ISPs who can handle Windows problems fine are lost at sea when it comes to the Mac.

If you travel, you might look for an ISP with a national or even international presence. Big ISPs, such as EarthLink and AT&T WorldNet, offer dial-up numbers nearly everywhere. CompuServe and AOL have the best selection of overseas access points. ISPs range in price from $5–$25 per month, with most costing around $20/month for unlimited access.

POLL: Is there anything on your hard drive that you don't want anyone at all to see?

77% Yes

23% No

TODAY'S FOCUS: Your New PC

CHARLES BABBAGE BORN

Charles Babbage was born in London, England, on this day in 1791. He was a noted mathematician who, in 1821, invented the Difference Engine, sometimes called the first automatic calculator. Babbage is known as the "Father of Computing" based on the design of his Analytical machine, which was intended to be a general symbol manipulator. Babbage was given funding by the British government to complete his invention, but none of his machines were ever built.

Related Web site `www.cbi.umn.edu`

Broadband

As Web sites get fatter and the Internet carries more audio and video, you might begin to feel the need for more speed than a modem can give you. That's why more and more people are turning to high-speed access, or broadband.

The most common broadband connections today are cable modems and DSL. These services can be anywhere from 2 to 100 times faster than modems, depending on your provider, but they're available only in limited geographic areas. Call your local cable company to see whether it offers cable modem access. You can find a DSL provider online with the DSL Reports search engine, `dslreports.com`, or call your phone company. High-speed access usually requires an installation fee of around $100–$150 and will cost $40–$50 per month.

If you don't have access to cable or DSL connections you can still get high-speed access via satellite. DirecPC (`www.direcpc.com`) and Starband (`starband.com`) both offer two-way satellite Internet access.

Your First Download One of the most important reasons to get online is to get support. As Internet access becomes ubiquitous, more and more companies are moving their support operations to the Web. It's often easier, faster, and more effective to use email for tech support than a phone call. Many companies put extensive information about their products online. And you'll also use the Web to download bug fixes and updates.

In fact, that's your next assignment. Before you play that new game, update your software. Start with your operating system. In Microsoft Windows, use the Windows Update command on the Start menu. Macintosh users will find Software Update in System Preferences under the Apple menu. Update your OS before you do anything else. After you've updated your system, it will automatically check for updates every time you're online. It's a good idea to keep your operating system up to date, both to make your system more reliable and to maintain security.

Next, update your antivirus software. Most antivirus programs have an automatic update function that will download the definitions for newly invented bugs. Use it. An out-of-date antivirus is worse than useless; it provides you with a false sense of security. Update your antivirus weekly to keep your system protected from infection.

Finally, it's a good idea to check for software and hardware updates. Even though your computer is new, there will likely be some updates available for it. Use the system inventory you made earlier to find out what hardware and software you have installed, then visit the manufacturers' Web sites to check for updates. Bookmark these sites for future reference, as well.

Windows users can also keep track of updates automatically at `catchup.com`. For updates on Macintosh programs, use `versiontracker.com`.

POLL: Should the human genome be open source?

18% No

70% Yes

12% Only if it has a GUI

TODAY'S FOCUS: Your New PC

DARWIN BEGINS HISTORIC VOYAGE

The *HMS Beagle* set sail from Plymouth Harbor on its round-the-globe voyage on this day in 1831. The vessel carried Charles Darwin, who used his natural observations and collections to write the celebrated work, *Origin of Species*. Legend has it the ship was supposed to have set sail the day before, but after-Christmas hangovers afflicted the majority of the *Beagle*'s crew. The trip around the globe took nearly five years. Darwin collected an amazing variety of natural artifacts and published an entertaining account of his trip, in *The Voyage of the* Beagle.

Related Web site   www.aboutdarwin.com

Break Your System

If your computer is going to break down, it will usually do it in the first few months. Now is the time to break your computer, while it's still under warranty. I normally recommend turning off your computer when you're not using it to save energy, but for the next few months leave it on. Run it hard. Play games with it. Use all the peripheral devices as much as you can. Really stress your computer. If it survives for the first few months, chances are it will be reliable for years to come.

Getting to Know Your New Computer   If you've followed all my recommendations up to this point, you've done more to ensure a happy computing experience than 99% of computer users out there. Pat yourself on the back. Now comes the hard part: using your new PC.

Take a look at your computer. You are facing the most complex piece of equipment you've ever owned—perhaps the most complex device ever created by humankind. On your desk sits more computing power than existed on the entire planet 30 years ago. The main microprocessor alone contains the equivalent of 20 million transistors. The programs on your hard drive represent millions of programmer hours. The biggest geek alive couldn't hope to understand every detail of what's going on inside that giant brain. And you've got a life. So relax.

You can no more expect to master your computer in one day than you could expect to pick up a violin for the first time and play a jig. Start slow. Pick one program that interests you and learn to use that. Just that. Don't be tempted to try to learn all the programs that came with your computer at once—that will just end up confusing and frustrating you.

I just bought a new computer for my wife. It's her first. She's interested in email, so I'm teaching her how to use Outlook Express. Just Outlook Express. For some folks, a word processor is the best place to start. Introduce your kids to the computer with a game. Your first activity should be something you really want to do—something you've been aching to try. That way, you'll be motivated to get past the inevitable frustration that comes with first using a computer.

By mastering one program, you're mastering the most important computer skill: understanding how the computer thinks. When you can think in computer, every other program will come naturally to you. The overwhelming complexity of it all will begin to make sense, and you'll be well on your way to mastering the entire system.

POLL: If they proved cell phones boil your brain, would you still use them?

37% Yes

63% No

TODAY'S FOCUS: Your New PC

FIRST MOVIE HOUSE OPENS

The Lumière brothers opened the world's first movie theater on this day in 1895. Auguste and Louis showed 10 short films in a basement room of the Grand Café on the Boulevard des Capucines in Paris, including *Leaving the Lumière Factory*, the first film made using the Cinematograph. It was a movie of workers leaving the family factory. They built what came to be known as the Lumière camera, which both shot and projected moving pictures. The Institut Lumière has preserved much of the family's work, and continues to keep their legacy alive today.

Related site   institut-lumiere.org

We Are Not Alone

You're not on your own in this journey. There are many ways to get help, starting with the built-in help. On Windows machines, press F1 any time you want to know how to do something. On the Mac, check the Help menu. Online computer help can vary in quality. It's often incomplete, sometimes incomprehensible. But more and more companies are taking the time to create help files that are really, well, helpful.

If you're the type of person who learns better from another human being, you can find help at a local computer user group. Apple keeps an online list of such groups at apple.com/usergroups. The Association of PC Users Groups has a locator at cdb.apcug.org/loclist.asp. Your local community college will also offer helpful courses.

A trip to the bookstore will reveal a bewildering range of computer books, but I have three favorites for beginners. From Peachpit Press, I recommend *The Little PC Book* by Larry Magid and *The Little Mac Book* by Robin Williams. These are the friendliest, most useful introductions to computers ever written. If you're the type that wants to understand the inner workings of computers, try *How Computers Work* by Ron White, published by Que.

The World Wide Web is also a wonderful resource for better understanding your new plastic pal, starting with our own site, techtv.com. The Yahoo! Internet directory is another great resource. Check their technical support page, dir.yahoo.com/Computers_and_Internet/Technical_Guides_and_Support, for a long list of help sites.

It's Not Your Fault   There's one last thing I want you to know: It's not your fault.

It's very common for computer users to blame themselves when something goes wrong. You might even get some reinforcement for this belief from frazzled computer support technicians. Well, it ain't so.

When your computer doesn't make sense, when it does something strange, when it won't work right at all, it's not because you're dumb, it's because it was poorly designed. We all feel dumb sometimes when faced with technology. Why else would a computer book series "for Dummies" be such a hit? But you're not dumb. It's just that the hardware, software, and manuals have been designed by people who already understand computers intimately. Computer wizards have long ago forgotten what it's like not to speak the language. And frankly, some of them like to perpetuate the myth of their superiority by intentionally confusing naïve users. Don't fall for it. You can figure this out. You will figure it out. And you're in for one of the most exciting, and satisfying, journeys of your life. Have fun!

POLL: Are lawyers ruining high tech?

83% Yes

7% No

10% I respectfully decline to comment

TODAY'S FOCUS: Troubleshooting

INTEL FOUNDER DUBBED MAN OF THE YEAR

The prestigious "Man of the Year" title, granted annually by *Time* Magazine, was given to Andrew S. Grove on this day in 1997. Grove was born in Budapest, Hungary, in 1936, and graduated from the City College of New York in 1960 with a Bachelor of Chemical Engineering. He received his Ph.D. from UC Berkeley in 1963. In 1968, he helped found Intel, the world's largest manufacturer of microchips. Grove holds several patents on semiconductor devices and technology, and has an impressive list of honorary awards and degrees.

Related Web site `intel.com/pressroom/kits/bios/grove.htm`

Laptop Troubleshooting Tips

By Mike Nadelman

Spilled Beverages on Keyboard
Immediately unplug the laptop from the AC adapter, turn it off, and flip it upside down. Shake out any liquid, and then remove the battery.

If the spill is just water, wait a day, and leave it in a warm place to dry. If it is any other liquid, take it to a repair shop as soon as possible to have the keyboard either washed out or replaced.

Dim Image Onscreen   Laptop screens have backlight (a small florescent bulb) or an inverter power supply that lights the LCD from behind. Try the brightness and contrast controls to improve the image temporarily. Replacing the bulb usually costs less than $300. Be warned: Some manufacturers might want to charge $700–$1,500 for a whole new screen.

Battery Won't Hold Charge   Although there are several possibilities, a bad battery or charging circuit are the most likely. It could also be a faulty AC adapter or the connection between the AC adapter and the laptop. To learn more about your laptop battery, visit Fedco Electronics (`www.fedcoelectronics.com/quality6.tmpl`).

(Mike Nadelman has owned his own computer repair business since 1982, Advanced Computer Solutions, www.computer-repair.com.)

TIP OF THE DAY   Is it cheaper to build or to buy? We sent intrepid producer David Prager out on a shopping expedition, and here's what he learned.

Dell 1.4GHz Pentium 4 system: $824 complete   After scouring the Web for many hours, I managed to find some of the least-expensive prices for individual parts in Dell's list of specs on the package deal above. My Dell-equivalent system came out to $919, not including the full warranty or the year of free Internet service.

Sony Vaio Digital Studio PC: $1,200 complete   After another round of rigorous searching, my do-it-yourself price (without tax and shipping) came to $1,515. This total doesn't include a full warranty or Internet service, either.

The big guys get volume discount deals you and I can't hope to compete with. They'll always beat us on price. But what's the price tag on the knowledge you earn, and the confidence you gain on building your own PC from scratch?

DOWNLOAD OF THE DAY EzVoice turns your computer and modem into a telephone answering machine. Free for Windows from `internetsoftsolution.com`.

POLL: Can cyber romance be cheating?
75% Yes
25% No

TUESDAY, DECEMBER 30, 2003

TODAY'S FOCUS: Troubleshooting

KIBOSH ON ENCRYPTION

The U.S. Commerce Department announced a new policy for exporting encryption devices on this day in 1996. The new policy limited the strength of encryption and ordered all products shipped overseas to have a built-in "key" that would allow law enforcement officials with court orders to break the code. The policy stated that 56-bit encryption keys would be issued on a case-by-case basis, a decision that wreaked havoc within the software industry. Lobbyists said the new rules were a shift in President Clinton's policy, who had signed an executive order allowing companies to sell more powerful encryption just two months earlier.

Related Web site `www.doc.gov`

Top Five Troubleshooting Steps

By Kate Botello, TechTV

Try these tips before you call your geeky friends:

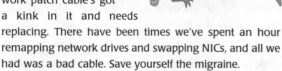

1. Wiggle the Cables I can't tell you enough how often a "broken" monitor or mouse cable has just come loose, or a network patch cable's got a kink in it and needs replacing. There have been times we've spent an hour remapping network drives and swapping NICs, and all we had was a bad cable. Save yourself the migraine.

2. Reboot If you're having hardware problems, do a reboot: "warm" first (Start, Run, Restart), and then "cold" (turn it off, count to five, turn it back on). Yes, do both.

3. Identify the Source When was the last time your computer worked right? What's changed between now and then? Identify all changes you've made to your machine to see whether they've been the cause of your sorrows.

4. Ask Around One thing all computers have in common is that they break. Your problem is undoubtedly more universal than you think. Check message boards about your equipment. Read the FAQs from the manufacturer. You might find that the most recent batch of video cards it sent out caused hundreds of machines to smell like boiling artichokes. Of course, you can always call tech support. Before you do that, however, be sure you've made note of the following:

- What changed before the errors occurred
- The exact error message you get
- The probable catalysts for the error message (what you think causes it)
- How you get the error to "go away"
- Your user license number
- The troubleshooting steps you've taken so far (be honest)

5. Take a Cleansing Breath, and Reinstall First, reinstall the errant program. If that doesn't work, fully uninstall the program, and then reinstall. Next, reinstall the OS right on top of itself. Often, that will correct corrupted or missing files. Last, count your losses, back up your data, reformat, and start over.

TIP OF THE DAY If Windows 98 won't boot, or crashes frequently, one of the system files could be damaged. Try replacing it with the System File Checker. Look for the System Information utility in the Accessories/System Tools menu. Select **System File Checker** from the **Tools** menu. Windows XP automatically checks and fixes its system files so you don't have to.

 DOWNLOAD OF THE DAY Lemon Rising is a fast-paced single-player shareware game for Mac OS X. Fight the evil lemons: download Lemon Rising, free from homepage.mac.com/slipstream2001/aboutlemon.html.

POLL: Do you spend more time inside since you got a computer?

19% No   81% Yes

DECEMBER
30

NOBEL TWO-TIMER

Marie Curie became the first person to receive a second Nobel Prize on this day in 1911. She was awarded the prize for chemistry for isolating the element of metallic radium. Curie, who was also the first female Laureate, had previously received a prize for physics along with her husband, Pierre, for their discovery of radioactivity and the elements of polonium and radium. The element Curium, which was discovered by Glenn Seaborg in 1944, was named in the couple's honor.

Related Web site mariecurie.org

Looking Ahead to 2004

Well, that's it. Another year done. I hope you've had as much fun reading these pages as I've had writing them. In the past 365 days, you and I have downloaded and installed more than 500 programs, surfed to countless Web sites, and stayed up late looking for just the right tip or trick. I've learned a lot in the process, and I've become even more excited about the direction that computing is taking.

In the past year, computers have become easier to use and more friendly. For the first time in my memory, they've become more reliable, too. Computers running Windows XP, Linux, or Mac OS X hardly ever crash. And they do more of what real people want them to do. Forget spreadsheets and mail merge: Our computers help us make music, take pictures, edit movies, and, yes, even write books.

In 2004, technology will become more about getting the job done and less about fiddling with the hardware. For years, we've focused on megahertz and megabytes, bandwidth and interrupts, but no more. We've finally got computers that are more than powerful enough, and programs that do what we want them to do with a minimum of fussing. Now it's time to start focusing on the fun stuff: Using technology to express ourselves.

In 2004, digital devices will come in a variety of shapes and sizes. They won't be just "computers" any more. They'll be Web pads, PDAs, and communicators. Each of us will own many computers, but they won't look like computers. The beige box on our desk isn't going away, but its importance will be eclipsed by a variety of digital devices that each do one thing well.

Internet access will be ubiquitous and inexpensive. Most of our devices will get online in one way or another, and they'll all be able to communicate with one another. The notion of using a computer that can't get online will seem ludicrous.

There are some things that 2004 will not bring us. Voice and handwriting recognition are still years away. The lowly keyboard and mouse, *Star Trek* notwithstanding, will be here for some time to come. Microsoft's promise of complete online security will not come to pass, and its failure will weaken the company's hold on the desktop. We'll still have to worry about hackers and viruses, but we'll be better equipped to do so, and less likely to panic when faced with the bad guys.

Most importantly, 2004 will be the year people everywhere begin to use and embrace digital technology. It will be the year you assert your mastery over the machine and begin to use it as a tool to complete your life.

It's going to be a great year.

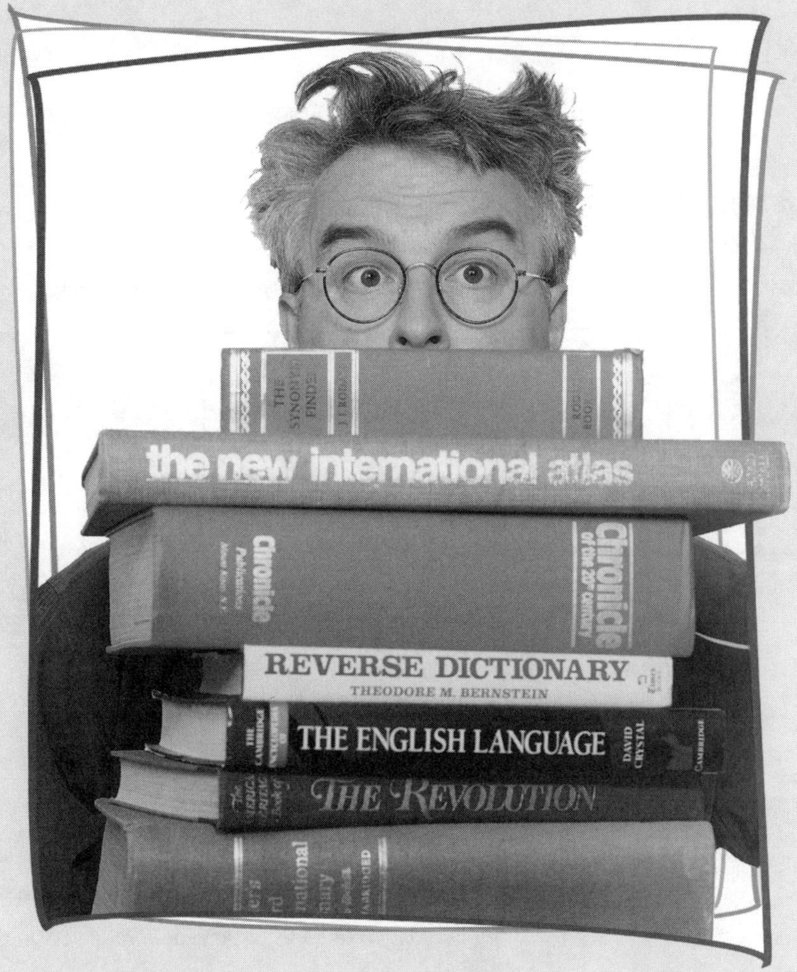

FACTS AND FIGURES

COMPUTER HARDWARE AND SOFTWARE

Lots of Beige Boxes

Total number of PCs in use, worldwide (millions):

Year	Units (millions)
1995	229
2000	530
2001	603
2007 (projected)	1150

Source: Computer Industry Almanac, Inc. (www.c-i-a.com)

Selling Beige Boxes, Domestic Edition

United States PC sales (millions of units):

Source: IDC (www.idc.com)

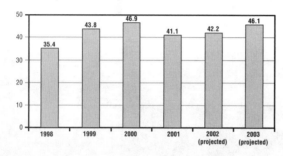

Selling Beige Boxes, Global Edition

Worldwide PC sales (millions of units):

Source: IDC (www.idc.com)

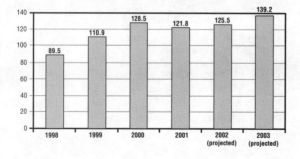

Selling Beige Boxes, by Manufacturer

Worldwide market share of top five PC vendors in 2001:

Rank	Manufacturer	Market Share
1	Dell	13.3%
2	Compaq	11.1%
3	Hewlett-Packard	7.2%
4	IBM	6.4%
5	NEC	3.8%

Source: Gartner Dataquest (www.gartner.com)

PCs Around the World

Total number of PCs in use by country, year-end 2001 (millions):

Source: Computer Industry Almanac, Inc. (www.c-i-a.com)

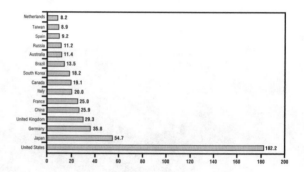

European Vacation

Percent of Europeans who do not use a computer: 53.3%

Source: European Commission Eurobarometer (www.gesis.org/en/data_service/eurobarometer/)

There's No Place Like Home

Home PCs as percent of total PCs in use, by region:

Region (projected)	1995	2000	2001	2007
United States	35.2%	43.5%	45.1%	52.3%
Western Europe	39.2%	48.5%	49.9%	52.9%
Asia-Pacific	29.3%	35.8%	38.3%	53.9%

Source: Computer Industry Almanac, Inc. (www.c-i-a.com)

Proliferating Peripherals

Fastest-growing computer product categories, Q4 2001 versus Q4 2000:

Peripheral	Year-Over-Year Growth
LCD monitors	+261.7%
External hard drives	+182.0%
Memory cards	+142.9%
Network access points	+128.3%

Source: NPDTechworld (www.npdtechworld.com)

Boys School

Gender breakdown of students earning undergraduate degrees in computer science:

Source: U.S. Department of Education (www.ed.gov)

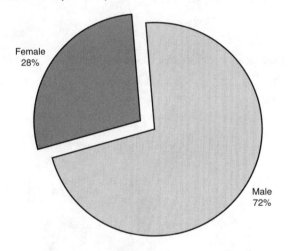

Female
28%

Male
72%

The 90/20 Rule

Total number of commands available in Microsoft Word for the Mac, Version 6: 642

Number of commands accounting for 90% of use: 20

Source: OWL: A Recommended System for Organization-Wide Learning, MITRE (www.mitre.org/technology/)

Software Piracy

Global revenues lost to software piracy (2000): $11.75 billion

Percent of software that is pirated globally (2000): 37%

Percent of software that is pirated in the U.S. (2000): 24% (lowest in the world)

Top 10 countries for software piracy (2000):

Rank	Country	Piracy Rate
1	Vietnam	97%
2	China	94%
3	Indonesia	89%
4	Ukraine	89%
5	Russia	88%
6	Lebanon	83%
7	Pakistan	83%
8	Bolivia	81%
9	Qatar	81%
10	Bahrain	80%

Source: Sixth Annual BSA Global Software Piracy Study, Business Software Association (www.bsa.org)

THE INTERNET

Online Population Explosion, Part 1

Number of Internet users worldwide, in millions:

Source: NUA (www.nua.com)

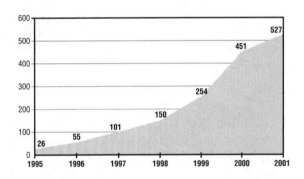

Online Population Explosion, Part 2

Looking forward, the projected number of Internet users worldwide, in millions:

Year	Users (Millions)
2004	945
2007	1460

Source: Computer Industry Almanac, Inc. (www.c-i-a.com)

It's a Small World

Number of Internet users by country, March, 2002 (in millions):

Country	Number of Users
Argentina	2.0
Australia	5.0
Austria	2.7
Bahrain	0.1
Belarus	0.1
Belgium	2.7
Brazil	6.1
Bulgaria	0.5
Canada	14.2
Chile	1.8
China	33.7
Colombia	0.7
Croatia	0.3
Cuba	0.1
Czech Republic	2.2
Denmark	1.6
Djibouti	0.1
Egypt	0.4
Estonia	0.4
Finland	2.0
France	11.0
Germany	26.0
Greece	1.3
Hong Kong	3.9
Hungary	0.7
Iceland	0.1
India	5.0
Ireland	1.0
Israel	1.2
Italy	11.0
Japan	22.0
Jordan	0.1
Kuwait	0.1
Lebanon	0.4
Libya	0.1
Lithuania	0.3
Malaysia	2.0
Mexico	2.3
Morocco	0.1
Netherlands	6.8
New Zealand	1.3
Norway	2.2
Oman	0.1
Philippines	2.0
Poland	4.9
Portugal	3.0
Qatar	0.1
Romania	0.6
Russia	7.5
Saudi Arabia	0.3
Singapore	1.3
Slovakia	0.7
Slovenia	0.4
South Africa	1.5
South Korea	16.7
Spain	7.0

Country	Number of Users
Sri Lanka	0.1
Sudan	0.1
Sweden	4.5
Switzerland	3.4
Syria	0.1
Taiwan	6.4
Thailand	4.6
Tunisia	0.1
Turkey	3.7
Ukraine	0.7
United Arab Emirates	0.9
United Kingdom	33.0
United States	149.0
Vietnam	0.1
Venezuela	1.2
Yemen	0.1

Various sources, as compiled by CyberAtlas (www.cyberatlas.internet.com)

Parlez-Vous Anglais?

Percent of Internet users worldwide, by language (as of March, 2002):

Source: Global Reach (www.glreach.com/globstats/)

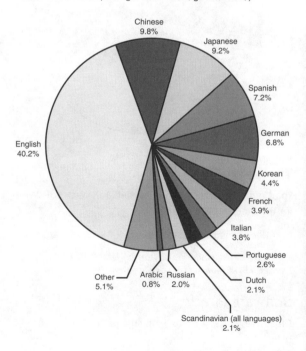

- Chinese 9.8%
- Japanese 9.2%
- Spanish 7.2%
- German 6.8%
- English 40.2%
- Korean 4.4%
- French 3.9%
- Italian 3.8%
- Portuguese 2.6%
- Dutch 2.1%
- Scandinavian (all languages) 2.1%
- Russian 2.0%
- Arabic 0.8%
- Other 5.1%

Internet Capacity

Estimated U.S. Internet traffic per day (2001): 20,000 terabits

Projected amount of U.S. Internet traffic per day in 2006: 1.5 million terabits

Number of broadband switches and routers required to move U.S. Internet traffic in 2001: 40,000

Source: Insight Research (www.insight-corp.com)

Master of Your Domain

Percent of Web servers by domain (June, 2002):

Domain	Description	Percent
.com	Commercial	51.2%
.de	Germany	6.6%
.net	Network	6.5%
.org	Nonprofit organization	5.8%
.uk	United Kingdom	3.6%
.nl	Netherlands	2.2%
.jp	Japan	1.9%
.dk	Denmark	1.9%
.pl	Poland	1.8%
.ru	Russian Federation	1.5%
.it	Italy	1.1%
.edu	Educational	1.1%
.ch	Switzerland	1.0%
.br	Brazil	1.0%

Source: Security Space (www.securityspace.com)

Home Sweet Home, Part 1

Number of users worldwide with Internet access from home (Q4 2001): 498 million

Source: Nielsen/NetRatings (www.nielsen-netratings.com)

Home Sweet Home, Part 2

Percent of U.S. homes with Internet access (July, 2001): 58%

Source: Nielsen/NetRatings (www.nielsen-netratings.com)

How We Connect

U.S. Internet subscribers by access type (Q3 2001):

Source: Telecommunications Reports International (www.tr.com)

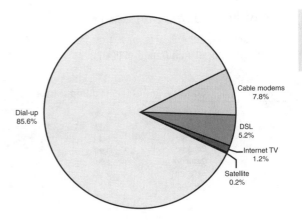

Dial-up 85.6%
Cable modems 7.8%
DSL 5.2%
Internet TV 1.2%
Satellite 0.2%

Broadband Connections, Part 1

Total number of U.S. broadband (cable and DSL) subscribers, Q1 2002: 11.8 million

Total number of U.S. broadband subscribers, Q1 2001: 6.6 million

One-year increase: 5.2 million

Source: Leichtman Research Group, Inc. (www.leichtmanresearch.com)

Broadband Connections, Part 2

Top 10 broadband cities, as of April 2002:

Rank	Market	Subscribers (000s)	Year-Over-Year Growth
1	New York	2,780	+70.5%
2	Los Angeles	1,766	+87.9%
3	Boston	1,120	+48.4%
4	San Francisco	1,110	+21.0%
5	Philadelphia	785	+69.9%
6	Seattle	691	+22.3%
7	Dallas	623	+12.8%
8	Chicago	555	+13.9%
9	Washington, DC	532	+153.2%
10	Atlanta	517	+87.7%

Source: Nielsen/NetRatings (www.nielsen-netratings.com)

Broadband Connections, Part 3

Top 10 countries for DSL use, based on number of DSL lines per 100 population (January, 2002):

Rank	Country	DSL Lines per 100 Population
1	South Korea	10.95
2	Hong Kong	5.56
3	Taiwan	4.83
4	Canada	3.73
5	Denmark	2.85
6	Belgium	2.76
7	Germany	2.23
8	Sweden	2.18
9	Finland	1.66
10	United States	1.59

*Source: Point-Topic (*www.point-topic.com*)*

Broadband Connections, Part 4

Projected number of U.S. broadband Internet subscribers in 2005 (millions):

*Source: The Yankee Group (*www.yankeegroup.com*)*

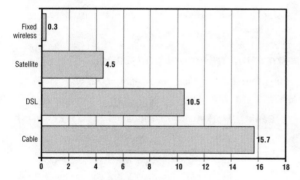

Dial-Up to Broadband, Part 1

How switching from dial-up to broadband changes Internet use:

Activity	Change
Page views	+130%
Pages per person	+55%
Sessions	+25%
Time spent online per person	+23%

*Source: J.D. Power and Associates (*www.jdpa.com*)*

Dial-Up to Broadband, Part 2

Satisfaction of dial-up Internet subscribers with the quality of their Internet service:

*Source: Parks Associates (*www.parksassociates.com*)*

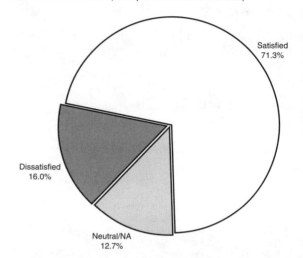

Dial-Up to Broadband, Part 3

Interest in moving from dial-up to broadband access in the next year:

*Source: Jupiter Media Metrix, Inc. (*www.jmm.com*)*

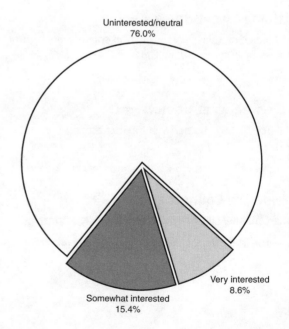

Wireless Connections

Percent of Internet users projected to connect via wireless access, by region:

Source: Computer Industry Almanac, Inc. (www.c-i-a.com)

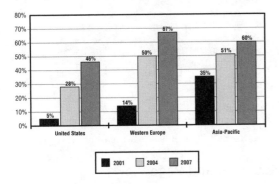

| | 2001 | 2004 | 2007 |

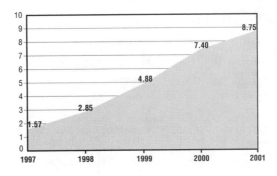

Adults Only

Number of adult Web sites (2001): 74,000

Source: Web Characterization Project, Online Computer Library Center (wcp.oclc.org)

Why *Not* to Go Online

Biggest reasons given for not using the Internet (among those who don't intend to go online):

Reason	Percent
No need for it	40%
Don't have a computer	33%
Not interested in it	25%
Don't know how to use it	16%
Cost (general)	12%
Not enough time to use it	8%
Not able/too old	7%
Don't know how to get it	3%
Current PC/terminal can't access Web	2%
Content not of interest/use/relevant	2%
Not my choice/decision at work	2%
Content not in my language	1%
Cost for ISP/subscription/access	1%
Cost—local telephone and toll service charges	1%
All other responses	4%
Unsure	2%

Source: Ipsos-Reid (www.ipsos-reid.com). Multiple answers allowed.

Lots of Sites

Number of sites on the Web (millions):

Source: Web Characterization Project, Online Computer Library Center (wcp.oclc.org)

Just Another Manic (Online) Monday

Internet use by day of week:

Source: StatMarket (www.statmarket.com)

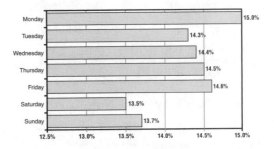

Who Does What, International Edition

Internet activities among users aged 16+, for selected non-U.S. countries, for the six months ending Q1 2002:

Country	Email	Chat	Instant Messaging	A/V Content	Internet Radio
Australia	90%	23%	30%	40%	20%
Brazil	75%	41%	42%	35%	40%
Denmark	89%	20%	13%	27%	23%
France	80%	27%	26%	27%	20%
Germany	83%	25%	18%	24%	18%
Hong Kong	84%	28%	26%	34%	38%
Italy	79%	20%	16%	25%	19%
Netherlands	90%	21%	29%	30%	17%
Spain	82%	38%	43%	32%	23%
Sweden	88%	19%	32%	29%	25%
Switzerland	89%	21%	24%	22%	13%
U.K.	90%	16%	35%	41%	21%

Source: Nielsen/NetRatings (www.nielsen-netratings.com)

Who's Online

Age Group	Percent of Total
18–29	28%
30–39	23%
40–49	23%
50–64	24%
65+	5%

Percent of adult population online. *Numbers rounded up to nearest percentage.

U.S. online population by gender (March 2002):

Gender	Percent of Total
Women	51%
Men	49%

U.S. online population by race/ethnicity (March 2002):

Group	Percent of Total
White	76%
Black	12%
Hispanic	9%

U.S. online population by education (March 2002):

Age Group	Percent of Total
High school or less	37%
Some college	31%
College graduate/post graduate	32%

U.S. online population by income (March, 2002):

Age Group	Percent of Total People at This Income
$25,000 or less	18%
$25,001–$50,000	25%
$50,0001 and over	46%

Source: Harris Interactive Inc. (www.harrisinteractive.com)

It's a Man's Man's World

Internet audiences by gender, by country (June, 2001):

Country	Male	Female
Australia	51.6%	48.4%
Austria	58.1%	41.9%
Belgium	60.6%	39.4%
Brazil	59.7%	40.3%
Canada	49.0%	51.0%
Denmark	55.9%	44.1%
Finland	53.9%	46.1%
France	61.9%	38.1%
Germany	63.4%	36.6%
Hong Kong	56.6%	43.4%
Ireland	54.8%	45.2%

Country	Male	Female
Israel	57.1%	42.9%
Italy	60.9%	39.9%
Japan	58.4%	41.6%
Mexico	54.0%	46.0%
Netherlands	59.8%	40.2%
New Zealand	52.5%	47.5%
Norway	58.0%	42.0%
Singapore	56.5%	43.5%
South Korea	54.3%	45.7%
Spain	60.9%	39.1%
Sweden	54.8%	45.2%
Switzerland	58.7%	41.3%
Taiwan	55.8%	44.2%
United Kingdom	57.2%	42.8%

Source: Nielsen/NetRatings (www.nielsen-netratings.com)

Sessions and Page Views

Average activity for a Web user in January, 2002:

Activity	Data
Number of online sessions per month	36
Page views per month	1,299
Page views per session	36
Time spent online per month	19 hours, 57 minutes, 56 seconds
Time spent online per session	33 minutes, 5 seconds
Duration of each page view	55 seconds

Source: Nielsen/NetRatings (www.nielsen-netratings.com)

What Kids Want

Medium that kids (aged 8–17) would choose if they could have only one:

Source: Knowledge Networks/SRI (www.statisticalresearch.com)

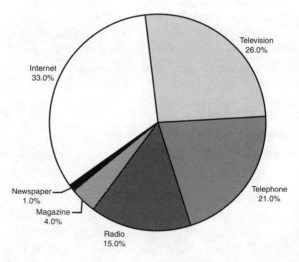

Television 26.0%
Internet 33.0%
Telephone 21.0%
Radio 15.0%
Magazine 4.0%
Newspaper 1.0%

Teenagers Online, Part 1

Percent of teens using specific technologies:

Technology Use	Percent
Have cell phones	34%
Go online at home	78%
Think the Internet is "cool"	90%

Source: Teenage Research Unlimited (www.teenresearch.com)

Teenagers Online, Part 2

Number of teenagers who go online at least once a month: 17 million

Source: Fulcrum Analytics (www.fulcrumanalytics.com)

Teenagers Online, Part 3

Top 10 U.S. cities for teens (aged 12–17) online:

Rank	City	Hours/Week Online
1	Pittsburgh	15.8
2	New York	14.9
3	Cleveland	14.8
4	San Diego	14.4
5	Miami-Ft. Lauderdale	14.1
6	Hartford & New Haven	13.4
7	Los Angeles	13.3
8	Detroit	13.1
9	Philadelphia	12.9
10	Milwaukee	12.8

Source: America Online/Digital Marketing Services (www.dmsdallas.com)

Teenagers Online, Part 4

What teenagers do online:

Source: America Online/Digital Marketing Services (www.dmsdallas.com)

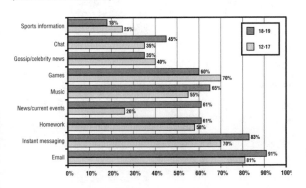

Teenagers Online, Part 5

Percent of teenage girls sexually harassed while using Internet chat rooms: 30%

Source: Girl Scout Research Institute (www.girlscouts.org/about/ResearchInstitute/GSRIMain.htm)

Sexaholics Online

Percent of male Internet users who are compulsive cybersex addicts: 6.5%

Amount of time each week cybersex addicts engage in cybersex activities: 5.7 hours

Source: MSNBC/San Jose Marital and Sexuality Center (www.sex-centre.com)

Doctors Online

Percent of physicians who work in practices with Web sites: 42%

Percent of Internet-connected doctors who use email to communicate with patients: 13%

Source: Harris Interactive, Inc. (www.harrisinteractive.com)

Patients Online

As of January, 2002, number of U.S. Internet users (dubbed "cyberchondriacs") who have gone online for information about health-related topics: 110 million

Most visited health-related sites:

Type of Site	Percent of Users Who Visit
Medical journals	45%
Commercial health sites	44%
Academic or research institutions	43%

Percent of users by education level visiting health-related sites:

Source: Harris Interactive, Inc. (www.harrisinteractive.com)

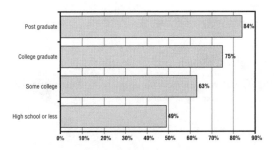

Job Hunters Online

Top 10 career-oriented sites, Q4 2001:

Rank	Site	Audience Reach
1	Hotjobs.com	8.6%
2	Monster.com	6.7%
3	Jobsonline.com	3.1%
4	Careerbuilder.com	2.5%
5	Headhunter.net	1.5%
6	Net-Temps.com	1.0%
7	Usjobboard.com	0.9%
8	Homeemployed.com	0.9%
9	Salary.com	0.8%
10	Flipdog.com	0.8%

Source: Jupiter Media Metrix, Inc. (www.jmm.com)

Employers Online

Percent of companies using the Internet for recruiting, by sector (2002):

Sector	Percent of Companies
Healthcare	100%
Manufacturing	98%
High tech	95%
Consumer	92%
Transportation	92%
Wholesale	91%
Natural resources	88%
Financial	87%
Utilities	84%

Source: iLogos Research (www.ilogos.com)

Schools Online

Percent of public-school classrooms with Internet access (2000): 77%

Source: Internet Access in U.S. Public Schools and Classrooms: 1994-2000, National Center for Educational Studies (nces.ed.gov/pubs2001/ InternetAccess/)

Our Government Online, Part 1

Percent of adult Internet users who visited a local, state, or federal government Web site in 2001: 55%

Percent of adult Internet users who conducted business with a government Web site in 2001: 21%

Source: National Technology Readiness Survey, Rockbridge Associates, Inc. (www.rockresearch.com)

Our Government Online, Part 2

Features of state and federal Web sites (2001):

Feature	Percent
Access to publications	93%
Databases	54%
Privacy and security policies	28%
Disability access	27%
Fully executable services	25%
Foreign languages	6%

Source: Global Government Survey, Taubman Center for Public Policy at Brown University/World Markets Research Centre (www.wmrc.com)

Newspapers Online

Percent of adults in immediate market visiting local newspaper Web sites (in 2001):

Newspaper Site	Percent of Market
Washington Post	40.2%
Omaha World-Herald	27.4%
San Antonio Express-News (MySanAntonio.com)	27.0%
Charlotte Observer	26.6%
Hartford Courant	26.1%
Minneapolis Star-Tribune	25.5%
Orlando Sentinel	25.2%
Sacramento Bee	24.8%
Daily Oklahoman (NewsOk.com)	24.0%
Kansas City Star	23.5%
New Orleans Picayune	23.4%
Ann Arbor News	23.4%
Raleigh News & Observer	23.0%
Lexington Herald Leader	23.0%
Atlanta Journal-Constitution	22.4%
Virginian Pilot (Norfolk)	22.3%
Houston Chronicle	21.9%
Seattle Times	21.8%
San Diego Union-Tribune	21.4%
St. Louis Post-Dispatch	20.8%
Jackson Clarion Ledger	20.8%
Des Moines Register	20.7%
Arizona Republic (Phoenix)	20.6%
Buffalo News	20.4%

Source: The Media Audit (www.themediaaudit.com)

TV News Online

Only six local TV station Web sites in the U.S. attract more users than competing newspaper sites (including two stations that partner with local newspapers):

Station	Market	URL	Percent of Market
KENS	San Antonio, TX	MySanAntonio.com	27.0%
KWTV	Oklahoma City, OK	NewsOk.com	24.0%
WISC	Madison, WI	Channel3000.com	22.2%
WRAL	Raleigh, NC	WRAL.com	20.0%
KCRG	Cedar Rapids, IA	KCRG.com	16.4%
WXII	Greensboro, NC	ThePiedmontChannel.com	8.6%

Source: The Media Audit (www.themediaaudit.com)

More Net, Less TV?, Part 1

The effect of the Internet on traditional media use:

Source: Scarborough Research (www.scarborough.com)

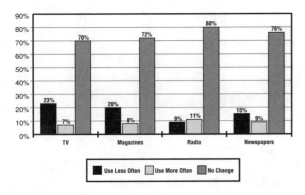

More Net, Less TV?, Part 2

If you had to choose between giving up all the televisions in your home or giving up your Internet access at home, which would you rather give up first?

Source: Arbitron/Edison Media Research (www.edisonresearch.com)

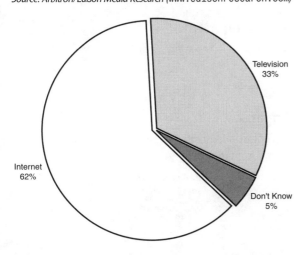

More Net, Less TV?, Part 3

Percent of U.S. consumers who use the Internet at the same time they're watching TV: 11%

Source: Knowledge Networks/SRI (www.statisticalresearch.com)

If It's Online, It Must Be Free

How consumers feel about fees for downloading online content:

Type of Content	Oppose	Neutral	Support	No Opinion
Information (driving directions, news stories, financial reports, health articles, etc.)	77%	11%	4%	9%
Pictures	66%	17%	7%	10%
Sound files (non-music, such as WAV format files)	60%	17%	7%	15%
Audio files (MP3, WMA, etc.)	51%	20%	17%	13%
Games	50%	24%	16%	10%
Video clips or movies	48%	25%	16%	12%
Computer software	43%	25%	22%	10%
Electronic books	40%	25%	21%	14%

Source: Consumer Electronics Association (www.ce.org)

Instant Messaging, Part 1

Number of at-home users using one of the four major instant messaging networks (AOL Instant Messenger, ICQ, MSN/Windows Messenger, Yahoo! Messenger) in May, 2001: 41 million

Number of office workers using one of the four major instant messaging networks in May, 2001: 12.6 million

Source: Nielsen/NetRatings (www.nielsen-netratings.com)

Instant Messaging, Part 2

Market share of the four major instant messaging networks (May, 2001—some users subscribe to more than one network):

Rank	Network	Share
1	AOL Instant Messenger (AIM)	53.4%
2	MSN/Windows Messenger	38.0%
3	Yahoo! Messenger	30.0%
4	ICQ	8.8%

Source: Nielsen/NetRatings (www.nielsen-netratings.com)

Email (At Work)

Percent of employees who spend more than one hour per day managing their email: 24%

Percent of internal business emails that contain unsolicited messages: 34%

Percent of business email that requires immediate attention: 27%

Source: Newsweek

Slacking Off...

Percent of U.S. workers who admit to personal Web surfing during work hours (2001): 60.7%

Percent of U.S. workers who send personal email from work (2001): 58.1%

Source: The UCLA Internet Report 2001: Surveying the Digital Future, UCLA Center for Communication Policy (www.ccp.ucla.edu)

...Or Not

Percent of workers who believe that Internet access at work makes them somewhat or much more productive: 60.9%

Source: The UCLA Internet Report 2001: Surveying the Digital Future, UCLA Center for Communication Policy (www.ccp.ucla.edu)

Losing Productivity

The various ways using the Internet at work makes employees *less* productive:

How Made Less Productive	Percent
Spend time on the Internet unrelated to work	33.2%
Spend too much time on work email	13.8%
Too much time spent on personal messaging/chatting	13.8%
Difficult to convey complex ideas remotely	6.9%
Connection is too slow	5.4%
Not familiar enough with the technology	4.0%
Hard to resist responding to personal email	3.5%
Very distracting	3.5%
Other	16.0%

Source: The UCLA Internet Report 2001: Surveying the Digital Future, UCLA Center for Communication Policy (www.ccp.ucla.edu)

Abusing the Privilege

Number of companies who say that employees have abused their Internet access privileges by downloading pornography or pirated software: 78%

Source: Computer Security Institute (www.gocsi.com)

Big Brother Is Watching...

Percent of all U.S. companies using some form of surveillance to spy on their employees: 78%

Type of surveillance employed:

Source: American Management Association (www.amanet.org)

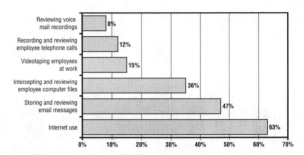

...And Laying Down the Law

Percent of companies that have disciplined employees for inappropriate use: 60%

Percent of companies that have terminated employees for Internet abuse: 30%

Source: Center for Internet Studies (www.virtual-addiction.com)

Work from Home

Number of remote and mobile workers in the U.S.: 78 million

Source: In-Stat/MDR (www.instat.com)

Spam, Part 1

Percent of Internet users who say that unsolicited email (spam) is a problem: 44%

Source: Pew Internet and American Life Project (www.pewinternet.org)

Spam, Part 2

Percent of U.S. Internet users who automatically delete email from unrecognized senders without opening it: 52%

Source: Quris (www.quris.com)

Spam, Part 3

Number of junk email messages received by the average Internet user in 2001: 700

Total number of spam messages received in 2001: 206 billion

Source: Jupiter Media Metrix (www.jmm.com)

Spam, Part 4

Global cost of spam (2000): $8.6 billion

Source: European Union (europa.eu.int/ISPO/ecommerce/issues/spam.html)

Virus Attacks, Part 1

Biggest computer virus of all time (as of June 2002): Klez.H

Number two: SirCam

Source: MessageLabs (www.messagelabs.com)

Virus Attacks, Part 2

Rate of virus infection in North America (2001): 113 infections per 1,000 computers

Source: ICSA Labs (www.icsalabs.com)

Hack Attacks

Percent of U.S. businesses and government agencies suffering hacker attacks within the past year: 90%

Total damage caused by said attacks: $455 million

Average cost per attack: $204,181

Source: 2002 Computer Crime and Security Survey, Computer Security Institute/Federal Bureau of Investigation (www.gocsi.com)

Searching, Part 1

Methods used by Web users to find specific sites:

Source: eMarketer (www.emarketer.com)

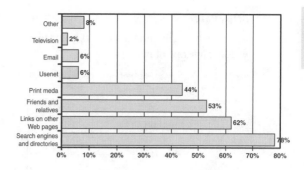

Searching, Part 2

Average number of minutes spent per visitor of each search site in the month of February, 2002:

Source: Jupiter Media Metrix, Inc. (www.jmm.com)

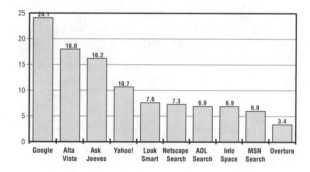

Searching, Part 3

Most popular search engines (March, 2002):

Source: Jupiter Media Metrix, Inc. (www.jmm.com)

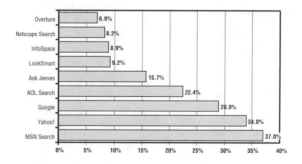

Searching, Part 4

Size of major search engines and directories indexes as of December, 2001 (millions of pages):

Source: Search Engine Watch (www.searchenginewatch.com)

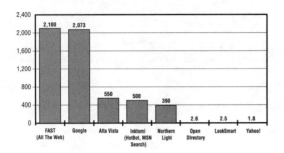

Searching, Part 5

Freshness of search engine indexes, based on newest and oldest pages found (April, 2002):

Search Engine	Newest Page Found	Oldest Page Found
Google	1 day	68 days
MSN Search (Inktomi)	1 day	80 days
HotBot (Inktomi)	1 day	136 days
AltaVista	12 days	51 days
AllTheWeb	16 days	191 days
Teoma	54 days	167 days
NLResearch	49 days	187 days
WiseNut	247 days	286 days

Source: Search Engine Showdown (www.searchengineshowdown.com/stats/)

Browser Wars

Browser use, as a percent of total Web users (as of June, 2002):

Browser	Percent
Internet Explorer 5	53.0%
Internet Explorer 6	37.0%
Netscape 4	3.7%
Internet Explorer 4	3.1%
Gecko (incl. Netscape 6)	1.2%
Opera	0.8%
Internet Explorer 2	0.1%
Internet Explorer 3	0.1%
Netscape 3	0.1%
Other	1.4%

Source: Browser News (www.upsdell.com/BrowserNews/stat.htm)

ISP Wars

Top 10 U.S. Internet service providers, based on numbers of subscribers during the first quarter 2002 (in millions):

Rank	ISP	Subscribers
1	America Online	26.1
2	MSN	7.7
3	United Online (NetZero & Juno Online)	5.2
4	EarthLink	4.9
5	SBC/Prodigy	3.3
6	CompuServe	3.0
7	Road Runner	2.4
8	AT&T Broadband	1.4
9	AT&T WorldNet	1.4
10	Verizon	1.4

Source: ISP Planet (www.isp-planet/research/rankings/)

Server Wars

Market share of major Web servers (May, 2002):

Server	Market Share
Apache	63.7%
Microsoft	27.4%
iPlanet	1.5%
Zeus	1.3%

Source: Netcraft Web Server Survey (www.netcraft.com/survey/)

Tool Wars

Use of Web authoring tools, as a percent of all Web pages examined (June, 2002):

Source: Security Space (www.securityspace.com)

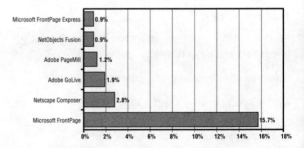

Site Wars, Part 1

Top 10 visited Web properties, based on millions of unique visitors (February, 2002) (includes all sites owned by the parent company):

Rank	Site	Visitors (Worldwide)
1	Microsoft Corp.	246.3
2	Yahoo! Inc.	218.4
3	AOL Time Warner	172.1
4	Terra Lycos	143.7
5	Google, Inc.	97.7
6	CNET Networks, Inc.	73.9
7	Amazon.com, Inc.	69.4
8	Primedia, Inc.	67.6
9	InfoSpace, Inc.	62.2
10	RealNetworks, Inc.	57.4

Source: comScore (www.comscore.com)

Site Wars, Part 2

Top 10 most linked-to Web sites (June, 2002), as a percent of all Web pages examined:

Rank	Site	Percent of Total
1	www.microsoft.com	5.2%
2	www.adobe.com	2.9%
3	www.geocities.com	2.6%
4	www.amazon.com	1.6%
5	www.google.com	1.3%
6	www.macromedia.com	1.3%
7	www.yahoo.com	1.2%
8	members.aol.com	1.2%
9	www.netscape.com	1.0%
10	home.netscape.com	1.0%

Source: Security Space (www.securityspace.com)

ONLINE ADVERTISING

It Depends on Whom You Ask

Size of online advertising market in 2001: $2.5 billion (CMRi)

Size of online advertising market in 2001: $5.7 billion (Jupiter Media Metrix, Inc.)

Size of online advertising market in 2001: $7.2 billion (Interactive Advertising Bureau)

Size of online advertising market in 2001: $7.9 billion (GartnerG2)

Projected change in online advertising expenditures 2001–2002: +11% (eMarketer)

Projected change in online advertising expenditures 2001–2002: −13% (Lehman Brothers)

Projected change in online advertising expenditures 2001–2002: +19% (Jupiter Media Metrix, Inc.)

Projected change in online advertising expenditures 2001–2002: +44% (GartnerG2)

The Big Get Bigger

Top 10 sites for online advertising revenue, 2001 (in millions):

Rank	Site	Ad Revenue
1	Yahoo!	$344.0
2	AOL.com	$319.9
3	Excite	$126.8
4	Lycos	$111.0
5	Netscape	$108.0
6	AltaVista	$77.5
7	WebCrawler	$57.4
8	ESPN.com	$44.1
9	MSN	$33.6
10	Weather.com	$31.8

Source: CMRi (www.adnettrackus.com)

The Size Is the Thing

Most popular online ad sizes, based on billions of paid online impressions (January, 2002):

Size	Impressions (billions)
Banners	35.4
Small formats (squares, rectangles, and skyscrapers)	23.7
Combined large ads (bars and buttons)	5.6
Skyscrapers	3.1
Squares and rectangles	2.5

Source: Jupiter Media Metrix, Inc. (www.jmm.com)

ONLINE SHOPPING

Put It in Perspective

Online retail sales as a percent of total U.S. retail sales (for the year 2000): 0.8%

Source: U.S. Department of Commerce (www.doc.gov)

But It's Growing

Estimated online spending in 2001: $51.3 billion

Increase from 2000: 21%

Projected increase for 2002: 41% (to $72.1 billion)

Source: The Boston Consulting Group (www.bcg.com)

It's a Fourth-Quarter Business

Estimated U.S. retail e-commerce sales by quarter (billions):

Source: U.S. Department of Commerce (www.doc.gov)

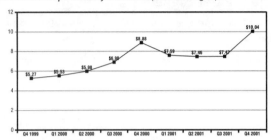

Lots of Shoppers

Projected number of online shoppers in 2002: 223.4 million (77% of total online population)

Source: eMarketer (www.emarketer.com)

Do It, Baby, One More Time

Percent of total online revenues generated by repeat purchasers in 2001: 53%

In 2000: 40%

Source: The Boston Consulting Group (www.bcg.com)

It's Not a Guy Thing Anymore

Percent of online holiday orders by gender:

Source: BizRate (www.bizrate.com)

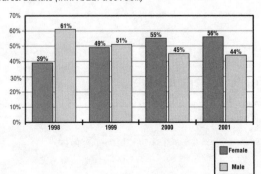

Shop Till Your Mouse Drops

Comparing Internet "power shoppers" (the one-third of online shoppers who buy twice as much as the other two-thirds) with regular shoppers:

Activity	Power Shoppers	All Others
Average age	38	55
Average annual income	$67,000	$34,000
Online spending last 12 months	$1200	$480
Online spending next 12 months	$1660	$680
Overall satisfaction with Internet shopping (on a scale of 1–10)	8.8	6.8
Percentage who desire free shipping for products costing less than $25	30%	68%
Percentage who find banner ads annoying	55%	75%
Percentage who have more than one email address	90%	70%
Percentage who enjoy email marketing	75%	42%
Percentage who enjoy email newsletters	90%	70%
Percentage who prefer email delivery of coupons and other offers	70%	45%

Source: iCustomer Observer, Valentine Radford (www.valrad.com)

Top Shopping Categories, Small-Ticket Items

Revenues generated by online sales in December 2001, for small-ticket items:

Source: Forrester Online Retail Index, Forrester Research, Inc. (www.forrester.com/NRF/)

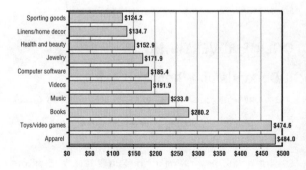

Top Shopping Categories, Big-Ticket Items

Revenues generated by online sales in December 2001, for large-ticket items:

Source: Forrester Online Retail Index, Forrester Research, Inc. (www.forrester.com/NRF/)

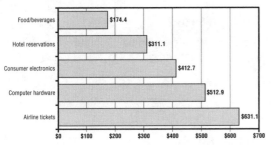

When to Shop

Peak shopping weeks for specific online shopping categories/types of merchants during the 2001 holiday season:

Category	Peak Week
Computer hardware	Week ending November 11
Consumer electronics	Week ending December 2
Shopping aggregators	Week ending December 2
Toys and games	Week ending December 9
Apparel	Week ending December 9
Value-oriented sites	Week ending December 9
Home and garden	Week ending December 16
Books	Week ending December 16
Music	Week ending December 16
Video	Week ending December 16
Specialty gifts	Week ending December 23

Source: Nielsen/NetRatings (www.nielsen-netratings.com)

Where We Shop

Top 10 holiday season shopping sites (2001):

Rank	Site	Unique Visitors (Five-Week Average) (000s)
1	eBay.com	4,515
2	Amazon.com	2,519
3	MyPoints.com	2,016
4	BizRate.com	683
5	Half.com	660
6	McAfee.com	652
7	Columbia House sites	598
8	eShop.com	588
9	AmericanGreetings.com	563
10	ToysRUs	515

Source: Jupiter Media Metrix, Inc. (www.jmm.com)

How We Shop

How the Internet is used for shopping:

Source: NPD Online Research (www.npdor.com)

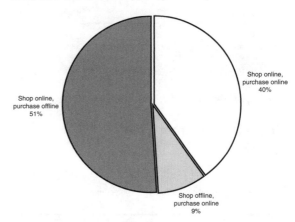

Why We Buy

Common influences on online purchases:

Source: Vividence (www.vividence.com)

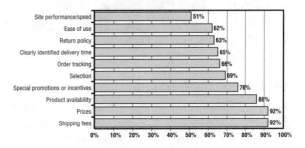

Customer (Dis)Satisfaction, Part 1

Reasons for abandoning online shopping cart without completing order:

Source: Vividence (www.vividence.com)

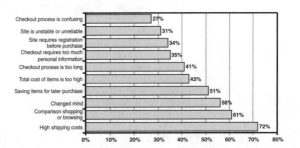

Customer (Dis)Satisfaction, Part 2

Amount of time taken by online retailers to respond to online customer service inquiries:

Time Frame	Percent
Within 6 hours	30%
6–24 hours	18%
1–3 days	18%
Longer than 3 days—or no response at all	33%

Source: Jupiter Media Metrix, Inc. (www.jmm.com)

Whom Do You Trust?, Part 1

Types of online sites and services that users trust with their personal information:

Source: Jupiter Media Metrix, Inc. (www.jmm.com)

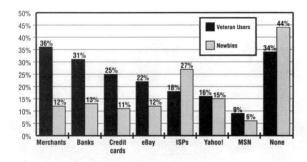

Whom Do You Trust?, Part 2

Percent of Internet users who are very concerned about the security of their bank and brokerage account numbers when executing online transactions: 86%

Source: GartnerG2 (www.gartnerg2.com)

It's a Fraud, Part 1

Number of complaints received by the Internet Fraud Complaint Center in 2001: 49,711

Most common complaint: Online auction fraud (43% of all complaints)

Most common single fraud: Nigerian Letter Scam

Source: Internet Fraud Complaint Center (www.ifccfbi.gov)

It's a Fraud, Part 2

Amount of online credit card fraud in 2001: $700 million

Online fraud as a percent of total online sales: 1.14%

Source: GartnerG2 (www.gartnerg2.com)

Turning a Profit

Percent of retailers reporting profits from their online operations in 2001: 56%

In 2000: 43%

Source: The Boston Consulting Group (www.bcg.com)

ONLINE MUSIC

We All Do It

Percent of Americans (aged 12 or over) who have downloaded music from online file-sharing services: 19%

Translated into numbers of users: 40 million

Percent of each age group who've downloaded music:

Source: Ipsos-Reid (www.ipsos-reid.com)

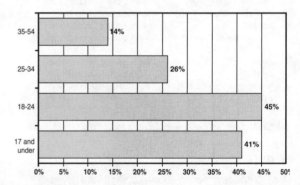

Men Do It More

Percent of males who've downloaded music files from the Internet: 25%

Percent of females who've downloaded music files from the Internet: 14%

Source: Ipsos-Reid (www.ipsos-reid.com)

Youth Is Served

Average number of MP3 files stored on home computers, by age (as of April, 2002):

*Source: Parks Associates (*www.parksassociates.com*)*

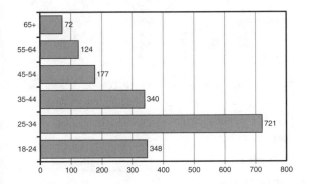

It's Big on Campus

Percent of U.S. college students who have downloaded music from the Internet: 75%

Percent of U.S. college students who purchase music on CD: 79%

*Source: Greenfield Online/YouthStream Media (*www.greenfieldcentral.com*)*

Why They Download

Percent of college downloaders who listen to downloaded music on their PCs: 72%

Percent of college downloaders who use downloaded music to sample music before they buy: 66%

Percent of college downloaders who use downloaded music to burn custom CDs: 35%

*Source: Greenfield Online/YouthStream Media (*www.greenfieldcentral.com*)*

They Won't Pay for It

Likelihood of paying for online music if no free material were available:

*Source: Ipsos-Reid (*www.ipsos-reid.com*)*

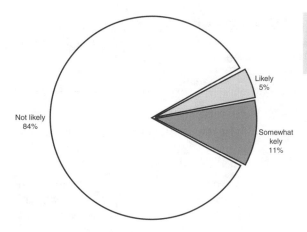

Burn, Baby, Burn

Percent of all Americans who own a PC-based CD burner: 24%

Percent of file-sharers who own a PC-based CD burner: 53%

*Source: Ipsos-Reid (*www.ipsos-reid.com*)*

Effect of Downloading on CD Sales

Percent of file downloaders who report that their CD purchases have stayed the same or increased since they've been downloading music from the Internet: 81%

*Source: Ipsos-Reid (*www.ipsos-reid.com*)*

Multimedia Formats

Users (in millions) of the three major multimedia formats, as of April, 2002:

*Source: Nielsen/NetRatings (*www.nielsen-netratings.com*)*

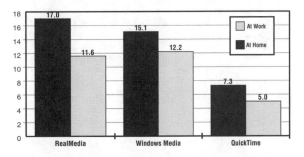

Digital Music Players

Sales of portable digital music players (both solid-state and CD-based), in millions (projected):

2002	2006
7.2	30

Source: In-Stat/MDR (www.instat.com)

It's Not Just Music

Estimated number of full-length movies illegally downloaded from the Internet every day: Between 400,000 and 600,000

Number of Internet users who have tried to illegally download movies from the Internet: 10 million

Number of Internet users who have *successfully* downloaded complete copies of movies from the Internet: 2 million

Source: Viant (www.viant.com)

PDAS

Sales, Sales, Sales, Part 1

Personal digital assistant (PDA) sales in the United States, by type (millions of units):

Source: Computer Industry Almanac, Inc. (www.c-i-a.com)

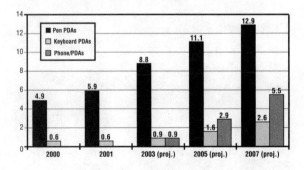

Sales, Sales, Sales, Part 2

Worldwide PDA sales, by manufacturer, in 2001 (millions):

Manufacturer	Unit Shipments
Palm	5.0
Handspring	1.6
Compaq	1.2
Hewlett-Packard	0.7
Casio	0.5
All others	3.9

Source: Gartner Dataquest (www.gartner.com)

Why to Buy

Reasons for purchasing one PDA over another:

Reason	Percent
It's a brand I trust	31.0%
It has the latest technology	19.5%
Product had the features I wanted	12.9%
Recommended by a friend or relative	10.3%
The brand is a good value for the money	10.0%

Source: NPD Online Research (www.npdor.com)

Who Buys

Percent of PDA purchases who are males between the ages of 25 and 54: 70%

Source: NPD Online Research (www.npdor.com)

TELEPHONY

They're Everywhere

Number of Americans who owned a cellular telephone in 1994: 16 million

Number of Americans who owned a cellular telephone in 2000: 110 million

Source: U.S. Census Bureau (www.census.gov)

Amazing Growth

Estimated number of cellular subscribers, worldwide (millions):

Source: CTIA's Semi-Annual Wireless Industry Survey, December 2001. Used with permission of the Cellular Telecommunications & Internet Association (www.wow-com.com/industry/stats/)

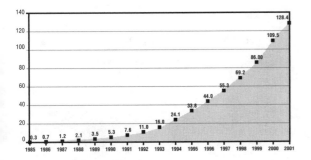

Billions and Billions...

Projected number of cellular telephones in use worldwide by the end of 2006: 1.9 billion

Source: Strategy Analytics (www.strategyanalytics.com)

Sales, Sales, Sales

Number of mobile phones sold worldwide in 2001: 506 million units

Source: Gartner Dataquest (www.gartner.com)

Don't Need Both

Percent of U.S. households that have replaced traditional landline service with cellular service: 1.7%

Projected number of homes that will give up their traditional landline service over the next five years: 2.3 million

Source: Forrester Research, Inc. (www.forrester.com)

It's Getting Cheaper

Average monthly U.S. cell phone bill in 1990: $80.90

Average monthly U.S. cell phone bill in 2001: $47.37

Source: CTIA's Semi-Annual Wireless Industry Survey, December 2001. Used with permission of the Cellular Telecommunications & Internet Association (www.wow-com.com/industry/stats/)

Prepaid Cellular

Percent of European cell phone users with prepaid service: 60%

Percent of U.S. cell phone users with prepaid service: 11%

Source: Sixth Annual Report and Analysis of Competitive Market Conditions with Respect to Commercial Mobile Services, Federal Communications Commission, 2001 (www.fcc.gov)

Get an M-Life

On a scale of 1 to 6, interest in specific 3G applications (among current U.S. Internet users/mobile phone owners interested in 3G):

Source: TNS Intersearch (www.intersearch.tnsofres.com)

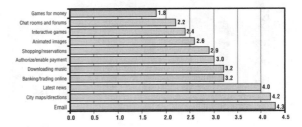

TELEVISION

Digital Sales

Factory-to-dealer sales of digital television (DTV) products in 2001: 1.46 million

Total number of DTV products sold since introduction in 1998: 2.5 million

Projected sales of DTV products in 2006: 10.5 million

Source: Consumer Electronics Association (www.ce.org)

Digital in the Home

Projected number of homes worldwide with DTV in 2008 (projected): 374 million

Source: Strategy Analytics (www.strategyanalytics.com)

Interactive in the Home

Number of homes worldwide with access to digital interactive television (iTV) services (2001): 38 million

Distribution of worldwide iTV audience:

Region	Percent of Total
Western Europe	62%
North America	18%
Asia-Pacific	10%
Latin America	1%

Source: Strategy Analytics (www.strategyanalytics.com)

Interactive Activities

Most desired activities for iTV, by age group:

Source: TNS Intersearch (www.intersearch.tnsofres.com)

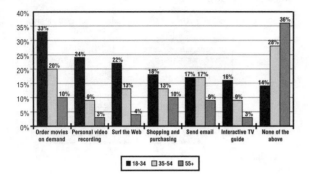

PLAYING GAMES

Video Games

Video Game sales by genre (2001):

Source: Interactive Digital Software Association (www.idsa.com)

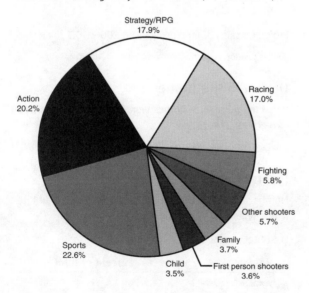

PC Games

Computer game sales by genre (2001):

Source: Interactive Digital Software Association (www.idsa.com)

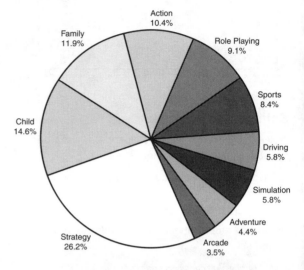

Bigger Than Basketball—or Football

Number of computer and video games sold in 2001: 225 million

Number of NHL tickets sold in 2000/2001 season: 20.3 million

Number of NBA tickets sold in 2000/2001 season: 19.9 million

Number of NFL tickets sold in 2000 season: 15.8 million

Source: Interactive Digital Software Association (www.idsa.com)

OTHER CONSUMER ELECTRONICS

DVD, Part 1

Percent of U.S. households with DVD player (2001): 25%

Source: Consumer Electronics Association (www.ce.org)

DVD, Part 2

Manufacturer-to-dealer sales of DVD players in 2001: 12.7 million units

Source: Consumer Electronics Association (www.ce.org)

VCR

Manufacturer-to-dealer sales of VCRs in 2001: 14.9 million units

Source: Consumer Electronics Association (www.ce.org)

Movies

Amount of money spent on buying and renting movies on video (2001): $16.8 billion

Amount of money spent on movie tickets (2001): $8.1 billion

Source: Ernst & Young/DVD Entertainment Group (www.dvdinformation.com)

Digital Photography, Part 1

Manufacturer-to-dealer sales of digital cameras in 2001: 5.4 million units

Source: Consumer Electronics Association (www.ce.org)

Digital Photography, Part 2

Sales of digital cameras as a percent of total camera unit sales (2000): 21%

Source: 2001 Worldwide Digital Camera Forecast Summary, InfoTrends Research Group, Inc., September 2001 (www.infotrends-rgi.com)

Digital Photography, Part 3

Average purchase price for a digital camera in the U.S.: $280

Largest digital camera makers: Sony, Olympus, Kodak, Hewlett-Packard, and Fuji

Source: 2001 Worldwide Digital Camera Forecast Summary, InfoTrends Research Group, Inc., September 2001 (www.infotrends-rgi.com)

Automotive Technology

Interest in high-tech features in cars:

Feature	Percent Interested
Built-in advanced theft deterrent systems	30%
Built-in road condition sensors to detect hazards	22%
Remote ability to start and warm up the car	17%
Global positioning navigation system	12%
Satellite radio with hundreds of stations	9%
Built-in voice control telephone system	9%

Feature	Percent Interested
Internet email inbound and outbound	6%
Full Internet connectivity	6%
Internet music downloading	5%

Source: Greenfield Online (www.greenfieldcentral.com)

Top Consumer Electronics Manufacturers

Ranked by revenues, the top five consumer electronics manufacturers, worldwide, in 2001:

Rank	Manufacturer
1	Matsushita
2	Sony
3	Philips Electronics
4	LG Electronics
5	Thomson Multimedia

Source: Hoover's Online (www.hoovers.com)

Top Appliance Manufacturers

Ranked by revenues, the top five appliance manufacturers, worldwide, in 2001:

Rank	Manufacturer
1	Electrolux AB
2	Whirlpool
3	Toshiba
4	GE Appliances
5	Maytag

Source: Hoover's Online (www.hoovers.com)

Top Consumer Electronics and Appliance Retailers

Ranked by revenues, the top five consumer electronics and appliance retailers in the U.S., in 2001:

Rank	Retailer
1	Best Buy
2	Circuit City
3	METRO AG
4	Dixons Group
5	RadioShack

Source: Hoover's Online (www.hoovers.com)

BIOTECHNOLOGY

It's Big Business

Number of biotechnology companies in the U.S. (2000): 1,273

Market capitalization of U.S. biotechnology companies (2000): $353.3 billion

Revenues generated by U.S. biotechnology companies (2000): $22.3 billion

Yearly research spending by U.S. biotechnology industry: $10 billion

*Source: Biotechnology Industry Organization (*www.bio.org*)*

It's Good Business

Number of people (worldwide) who have been helped by biotech medicines: 250 million

*Source: Biotechnology Industry Organization (*www.bio.org*)*

There's More Coming

Number of biotechnology drug products and vaccines approved by the FDA (2000): 117

Number of biotech drug products and vaccines currently in clinical trials: More than 350

*Source: Biotechnology Industry Organization (*www.bio.org*)*

What They Do

Biotech products currently on the market: Home pregnancy tests, diagnostic tests that keep the blood supply safe from the AIDS virus, biopesticides that reduce dependence on conventional chemical pesticides, enzymes found in most laundry detergents, and various biotech-enhanced foods—including papaya, soybeans, and corn

Diseases targeted by in-development biotech products and vaccines: various cancers, Alzheimer's disease, heart disease, diabetes, AIDS, and arthritis

*Source: Biotechnology Industry Organization (*www.bio.org*)*

LEO'S LITTLE BLACK BOOK

ANTIVIRUS AND SECURITY

Command Software Systems
1061 E. Indiantown Road, Suite 500
Jupiter, Florida
33477

561-575-3200

www.commandsoftware.com

F-Secure, Inc.
675 N. First Street, 5th Floor
San Jose, California
95112

408-938-6700

www.f-secure.com

McAfee.com
535 Oakmead Parkway
Sunnyvale, California
94085

408-992-8100

www.mcafee.com

Symantec Corporation
20330 Stevens Creek Blvd.
Cupertino, California
95014

408-517-8000

www.symantec.com

AUDIO/VIDEO SYSTEMS AND COMPONENTS

Bose Corp.
The Mountain
Framingham, Massachusetts
01701-9168

508-766-1099

www.bose.com

Denon
Denon Electronics
19 Chapin Road
P.O. Box 867
Pine Brook, New Jersey
07058-9777

973-396-0810

www.denon.com

Harman Kardon
250 Crossways Park Drive
Woodbury, New York
11797

516-496-3400

www.harmankardon.com

Hitachi America, Ltd.
Home Electronics Division
1855 Dornoch Court
San Diego, California
92173

619-661-0227

www.hitachi.com/tv/

Infinity Systems, Inc.
250 Crossways Park Drive
Woodbury, New York
11797

800-553-3332

www.infinitysystems.com

JBL Consumer Products
80 Crossways Park West
Woodbury, New York
11797

800-336-4525

www.jbl.com

JVC Company of America
1700 Valley Road
Wayne, New Jersey
07470

800-526-5308

www.jvc.com

Kenwood USA Corporation
P.O. Box 22745
Long Beach, California
90801-5745

310-639-9000

www.kenwoodusa.com

Mitsubishi Digital Electronics America, Inc.
9351 Jeronimo Road
Irvine, California
92618

949-465-6000

www.mitsubishi-tv.com

Onkyo USA Corporation
18 Park Way
Upper Saddle River, New Jersey
07458

201-785-2600

www.onkyousa.com

Panasonic Consumer Electronics
1 Panasonic Way
Secaucus, New Jersey
07094

201-348-7000

www.panasonic.com

Pioneer Electronics, Inc.
2265 East 220th Street
Long Beach, California
90810

310-952-2000

www.pioneerelectronics.com

Polk Audio, Inc.
5601 Metro Dr.
Baltimore, Maryland
21215

410-358-3600

www.polkaudio.com

RCA
Thomson Multimedia, Inc.
10330 North Meridian Street
Indianapolis, Indiana
46290-1976

317-587-3000

www.rca.com

Sony Electronics
3300 Zanker Rd.
San Jose, California
95134

800-222-7669

www.sel.sony.com

Toshiba America Consumer Products, Inc.
82 Totowa Road
Wayne, New Jersey
07470

973-628-8000

www.toshiba.com

Yamaha Electronics Corporation, USA
6600 Orangethorpe Avenue
Buena Park, California
90620

714-522-9105

www.yamaha.com

BATTERIES

Duracell, Inc.
Berkshire Corporate Park
Bethel, Connecticut
06801

203-796-4000

www.duracell.com

NEC Electronics, Inc.
2880 Scott Blvd.
Santa Clara, California
95050-2554

408-588-6000

www.necel.com

Panasonic Industrial Co.
2 Panasonic Way
Secaucus, New Jersey
07094

201-348-7010

www.panasonic.com

Tadiran
2 Seaview Blvd.
Port Washington, New York
11050

516-621-4980

www.tadiranbat.com

CABLES AND NETWORKING

Belden Wire and Cable
P.O. Box 1980
2200 U.S. Highway 27 South
Richmond, Indiana
47374

765-983-5200

www.belden.com

D-Link Systems, Inc.
53 Discovery Dr.
Irvine, California
92618

949-788-0805

www.dlink.com

Linksys
17401 Armstrong Ave.
Irvine, California
92614

949-261-1288

www.linksys.com

Micro Computer Cable Company, Inc.
12200 Delta Dr.
Taylor, Michigan
48180

734-946-9700

www.microccc.com

Monster Cable Products, Inc.
455 Valley Drive
Brisbane, California
94005

415-840-2000

www.monstercable.com

Smart Cable Company
7403 Lakewood Drive #14
Lakewood, Washington
98499

253-474-9967

www.smart-cable.com

CELLULAR PHONES

Ericsson
North American Headquarters
6300 Legacy Drive
Plano, Texas
75024

972-583-0000

www.ericsson.com

Motorola, Inc.
1303 E. Algonquin Rd.
Schaumburg, Illinois
60196

800-331-6456

www.motorola.com

Nokia Americas
6000 Connection Drive
Irving, Texas
75039

888-665-4228

www.nokiausa.com

CELLULAR PHONE SERVICES

AT&T Wireless Services, Inc.
7277 164th Ave. NE, Bldg. 1
Redmond, Washington
98052

425-580-6000

www.attws.com

Cingular Wireless
Glenridge Highlands Two
5565 Glenridge Connector, Ste. 1401
Atlanta, Georgia
30342

404-236-6000

www.cingular.com

Nextel Communications, Inc.
2001 Edmund Halley Dr.
Reston, Virginia
20191

703-433-4000

www.nextel.com

Verizon Wireless
180 Washington Valley Rd.
Bedminster, New Jersey
07921

908-306-7000

www.verizonwireless.com

COMPUTER ACCESSORIES

CompuKit
97 Sunfield Ave.
P.O. Box 6351
Edison, New Jersey
08818

800-683-3567

www.compukit.com

Northwest Computer Accessories
2135 S.E. 6th Avenue
Portland, Oregon
97214

503-232-6324

www.nwca.com

Targus, Inc.
1211 N. Miller Street
Anaheim, California
92806

714-765-5555

www.targus.com

COMPUTER HARDWARE

Acer America Corp.
2641 Orchard Parkway
San Jose, California
95134-2073

408-432-6200

www.acer.com/us/

Apple Computer, Inc.
1 Infinite Loop
Cupertino, California
95014

408-996-1010

www.apple.com

Dell Computer Corporation
1 Dell Way
Round Rock, Texas
78682

512-338-4400

www.dell.com

Gateway, Inc.
610 Gateway Drive
North Sioux City, South Dakota
57049

858-846-2000

www.gateway.com

Hewlett-Packard Company
3000 Hanover St.
Palo Alto, California
94304

650-857-1501

www.hp.com

IBM Corporation
New Orchard Road
Armonk, New York
10504

914-499-1900

www.ibm.com

Sony Electronics
3300 Zanker Rd.
San Jose, California
95134

800-222-7669

www.sel.sony.com

Toshiba America, Inc.
Computer Systems Division
9740 Irvine Blvd.
Irvine, California
92618-1697

949-583-3000

www.csd.toshiba.com

COMPUTER MONITORS

CTX International, Inc.
16720 E. Gale Avenue
City of Industry, California
91745

626-709-1000

www.ctxintl.com

LG Electronics
1000 Sylvan Ave.
Englewood Cliffs, New Jersey
07632

201-816-2000

www.lgeus.com

NEC-Mitsubishi Electronics Display of America
1250 N. Arlington Heights Rd., Suite 500
Itasca, Illinois
60143-1248

800-632-4662

www.necmitsubishi.com

ViewSonic
381 Brea Canyon Road
Walnut, California
91789

909-444-8888

www.viewsonic.com

COMPUTER AND CONSUMER ELECTRONICS RETAILERS

Amazon.com, Inc.
1200 12th Ave. South, Suite 1200
Seattle, Washington
98144

206-266-1000

www.amazon.com

Best Buy Co., Inc.
7075 Flying Cloud Dr.
Eden Prairie, Minnesota
55344

952-947-2000

www.bestbuy.com

Circuit City Group
9950 Mayland Dr.
Richmond, Virginia
23233

804-527-4000

www.circuitcity.com

CompUSA, Inc.
14951 N. Dallas Parkway
Dallas, Texas
75240

972-982-4000

www.compusa.com

Computer Discount Warehouse (CDW)
200 N. Milwaukee Ave.
Vernon Hills, Illinois
60061

847-465-6000

www.cdw.com

Crutchfield
1 Crutchfield Park
Charlottesville, Virginia
22911-9097

800-955-3000

www.crutchfield.com

PC Connection
Route 101A
730 Milford Rd.
Merrimack, New Hampshire
03054-4631

603-355-6005

www.pcconnection.com

COMPUTER SOFTWARE

Adobe Systems, Inc.
345 Park Ave.
San Jose, California
95110-2704

408-536-6000

www.adobe.com

Autodesk, Inc.
111 McInnis Parkway
San Rafael, California
94903

415-507-5000

www.autodesk.com

Intuit
2535 Garcia Avenue
Mountain View, California
94043

650-944-6000

www.intuit.com

Lotus Software
IBM Software Group
One Rogers Street
Cambridge, Massachusetts
02142

617-577-8500

www.lotus.com

Microsoft Corporation
One Microsoft Way
Redmond, Washington
98052-6399

425-882-8080

www.microsoft.com

DIGITAL CAMERAS

Canon U.S.A., Inc.
One Canon Plaza
Lake Success, New York
11042

516-328-5000

www.usa.canon.com

Kodak
343 State St.
Rochester, New York
14650

585-724-4000

www.kodak.com

Nikon
1300 Walt Whitman Road
Melville, New York
11747

800-645-6687

www.nikonusa.com

Olympus America, Inc.
2 Corporate Center Drive
Melville, New York
11747

800-645-8160

www.olympusamerica.com

Sony Electronics
3300 Zanker Rd.
San Jose, California
95134

800-222-7669

www.sel.sony.com

DIGITAL SATELLITE SYSTEMS

DIRECTV
2230 E. Imperial Hwy.
El Segundo, California
90245

310-535-5000

www.directv.com

DISH Network/Echostar
5701 S. Santa Fe Dr.
Littleton, Colorado
80120

303-723-1000

www.dishnetwork.com

ISPS AND ONLINE SERVICES
America Online
22000 AOL Way
Dulles, Virginia
20166-9323

703-265-1000

www.aol.com

CompuServe Interactive Services
5000 Arlington Centre Blvd.
Columbus, Ohio
43220

614-457-8600

www.compuserve.com

EarthLink, Inc.
1375 Peachtree St. 7 North
Atlanta, Georgia
30309

404-815-0770

www.earthlink.com

MSN
Microsoft Corporation
One Microsoft Way
Redmond, Washington
98052-6399

425-882-8080

www.msn.com

KEYBOARDS AND MICE
KeyTronic Corporation
4424 North Sullivan Rd.
Spokane, Washington
99214

509-928-8000

www.keytronic.com

Logitech
6505 Kaiser Drive
Fremont, California
94555

510-795-8500

www.logitech.com

Microsoft Corporation
One Microsoft Way
Redmond, Washington
98052-6399

425-882-8080

www.microsoft.com

Mitsumi Electronics Corporation
5808 W. Campus Circle Dr.
Irving, Texas
75063

972-550-7300

www.mitsumi.com

MEDIA PLAYER SOFTWARE
MusicMatch
16935 West Bernardo Drive
San Diego, California
92127

858-835-8360

www.musicmatch.com

RealOne
RealNetworks, Inc.
2601 Elliott Ave., Ste. 1000
Seattle, Washington
98121

206-674-2700

www.real.com

Windows Media Player
Microsoft Corporation
One Microsoft Way
Redmond, Washington
98052-6399

425-882-8080

www.microsoft.com/windowsmedia/

WinAmp
Nullsoft/America Online
22000 AOL Way
Dulles, Virginia
20166-9323

703-265-1000

www.winamp.com

MEMORY

Centon Electronics, Inc.
20 Morgan
Irvine, California
92618

949-855-9111

www.centon.com

Kingston Technology Corporation
17600 Newhope St.
Fountain Valley, California
92708

714-435-2600

www.kingston.com

PDAS

Audiovox Communications Corporation
555 Wireless Boulevard
Hauppauge, New York
11788

631-233-3300

www.audiovox.com

Casio
570 Mount Pleasant Ave.
Dover, New Jersey
07801

888-204-7765

www.casio.com/personalpcs/

Handspring, Inc.
189 Bernardo Ave.
Mountain View, California
94043

650-230-5000

www.handspring.com

Hewlett-Packard Company
3000 Hanover St.
Palo Alto, California
94304

650-857-1501

www.hp.com

NEC USA, Inc.
2371 S. President's Dr., Suite A
West Valley City, Utah
84120

888-632-8701

www.neccomp.com/MobilePro/

Palm, Inc.
5470 Great America Pkwy.
Santa Clara, California
95054

408-878-9000

www.palm.com

Sony Electronics
3300 Zanker Rd.
San Jose, California
95134

800-222-7669

www.sel.sony.com

Toshiba America, Inc.
Computer Systems Division
9740 Irvine Blvd.
Irvine, California
92618-1697

949-583-3000

www.csd.toshiba.com

PDA CASES AND ACCESSORIES

Brenthaven (cases)
300 Harris Avenue
Bellingham, Washington
98225

360-752-5537

www.brenthaven.com

iBIZ Technology (accessories)
2238 W. Lone Cactus Dr., Suite 200
Phoenix, Arizona
85027

623-492-9200

www.ibizcorp.com

Pentopia (styli)
60 Commerce Drive
Trumbull, Connecticut
06611

203-381-4854

www.pentopia.com

Pharos (GPS navigators)
411 Amapola Avenue
Torrance, California
90501-1478

310-212-7088

www.pharosgps.com

Socket Communications (cards and connectors)
37400 Central Court
Newark, California
94560

510-744-2700

www.socketcom.com

Targus, Inc. (cases and accessories)
1211 N. Miller Street
Anaheim, California
92806

714-765-5555

www.targus.com

PERSONAL VIDEO RECORDERS

ReplayTV
SONICblue
2841 Mission College Blvd.
Santa Clara, California
95054-1838

408-588-8000

www.replaytv.com

TiVo, Inc.
2160 Gold Street
P.O. Box 2160
Alviso, California
95002-2160

877-367-8486

www.tivo.com

PORTABLE MP3 PLAYERS
Audiovox Communications Corporation
555 Wireless Boulevard
Hauppauge, New York
11788

631-233-3300

www.audiovox.com

Creative Labs, Inc.
1901 McCarthy Boulevard
Milpitas, California
95035

800-998-5227

www.creative.com

RCA Lyra
Thomson Multimedia, Inc.
10330 North Meridian Street
Indianapolis, Indiana
46290-1976

317-587-3000

www.lyrazone.com

SONICblue Incorporated
2841 Mission College Blvd.
Santa Clara, California
95054-1838

408-588-8000

www.sonicblue.com

PRINTERS
Brother International Corporation
100 Somerset Corporate Boulevard
Bridgewater, New Jersey
08807-0911

908-704-1700

www.brother.com/usa/

Canon U.S.A., Inc.
One Canon Plaza
Lake Success, New York
11042

516-328-5000

www.usa.canon.com

Epson America, Inc.
3840 Kilroy Airport Way
Long Beach, California
90806

562-981-3840

www.epson.com

Hewlett-Packard Company
3000 Hanover St.
Palo Alto, California
94304

650-857-1501

www.hp.com

Lexmark
740 West New Circle Rd.
Lexington, Kentucky
40550

859-232-2000

www.lexmark.com

REMOTE CONTROLS

Crestron Electronics, Inc.
15 Volvo Drive
Rockleigh, New Jersey
07647

201-767-3400

www.crestron.com

One for All Remotes
Universal Electronics
6101 Gateway Drive
Cypress, California
90630-4841

714-820-1000

www.ueic.com

Philips Pronto
Philips Electronics North America
1251 Avenue of the Americas
New York, New York
10020-1104

888-486-6272

www.pronto.philips.com

REMOVABLE STORAGE MEDIA AND MEMORY CARDS

IBM Microdrive
IBM Corporation
1133 Westchester Avenue
White Plains, New York
10604

800-426-4968

www.storage.ibm.com/hdd/micro/

Iomega Corporation
4435 Eastgate Mall
San Diego, California
92121

858-795-7000

www.iomega.com

Kingston Technology Corporation
17600 Newhope St.
Fountain Valley, California
92708

714-435-2600

www.kingston.com

Pretec Electronics Corporation
40979 Encyclopedia Circle
Fremont, California
94538

510-440-0535

www.pretec.com

SanDisk
140 Caspian Court
Sunnyvale, California
94089

408-542-0500

www.sandisk.com

ROBOTS

Sony Aibo
Sony Electronics
3300 Zanker Rd.
San Jose, California
95134

800-222-7669

www.aibo.com

SCANNERS

Hewlett-Packard Company
3000 Hanover St.
Palo Alto, California
94304

650-857-1501

www.hp.com

Scanners

Microtek
3715 Doolittle Dr.
Redondo Beach, California
90278-1226

310-687-5800

www.microtekusa.com

Visioneer, Inc.
5673 Gibraltar Drive, Suite 150
Pleasanton, California
94588

888-229-4172

www.visioneer.com

SOUND CARDS

Adaptec
691 S. Milpitas Blvd.
Milpitas, California
95035

408-945-8600

www.adaptec.com

Creative Labs, Inc.
1901 McCarthy Boulevard
Milpitas, California
95035

800-998-5227

www.creative.com

SONICblue Incorporated
2841 Mission College Blvd.
Santa Clara, California
95054-1838

408-588-8000

www.sonicblue.com

VIDEO GAMES

Microsoft Xbox
Microsoft Corporation
One Microsoft Way
Redmond, Washington
98052-6399

425-882-8080

www.xbox.com

Nintendo of America
P.O. Box 957
Redmond, Washington
98073

800-255-3700

www.nintendo.com

Sony PlayStation
P.O. Box 5888
San Mateo, California
94402-0888

800-697-7266

www.playstation.com

GLOSSARY

.AVI Audio Video Interleave; Microsoft's file format (and extension) for Windows-compatible audio/video files.

.DOC The file extension for Microsoft Word documents.

.EPS Encapsulated PostScript; a file format, developed by Adobe, that stores graphics and text as PostScript language commands that a printer can read and print.

.EXE The file extension for an executable (program) file.

.GIF Graphics Interchange Format; an 8-bit (256-color) graphics file format. GIFs are widely used on the Web because they compress well.

.HTM or .HTML The file extension for Web pages on the Internet.

.JPG or .JPEG Joint Photographic Experts Group (pronounced "jay-peg"); a standard for compressing still images. Compression is achieved by dividing the picture into tiny pixel blocks, which are halved over and over until the appropriate ratio is achieved. Because JPEG is extremely effective in compressing large graphics files, it is widely used on the Internet.

.MP3 MPEG-1, Layer 3; an audio compression technology that results in near-CD quality sound compressed into one-twelfth the original file size. MP3 music files, played using software or a handheld device, make it possible to download high-quality audio from the Web and play it back on PCs or portable digital audio players. Developed in Germany by the Fraunhofer Institute in 1991.

.QT QuickTime; a sound, video, and animation format developed by Apple Computer. A QuickTime file can contain up to 32 tracks of audio, video, MIDI, or other time-based control information.

.RA RealAudio; a standard for streaming audio data over the Web. Developed by RealNetworks, RealAudio supports FM-stereo–quality sound.

.RM RealMovie; the video version of the RealAudio format.

.SHS Windows 95/98/NT "scrap" files—usually dragged onto the desktop to be used as shortcuts.

.TIF or .TIFF Tagged Image File Format; a common file format for storing bitmapped images. The images can display any resolution, and they can be monochrome, grayscale, or in full color.

.WMA Windows Media Audio; Microsoft audio file format.

.WMV Windows Media Video; Microsoft video file format.

.XLS The file format for Microsoft Excel spreadsheets.

.ZIP A file format for compressed files. When you compress files to a .ZIP file, you're said to be "zipping" them.

1.85:1 The most common wide-screen aspect ratio used in theatrical films.

2G Second-generation wireless; unlike analog first-generation products, 2G phones and networks incorporate digital technology.

2.35:1 The widest possible aspect ratio used in theatrical films.

2.4GHz band An unlicensed RF band (between 2.4GHz and 2.48GHz) used to carry signals from various types of wireless devices. Also called the *ISM band*.

3G Third-generation wireless; the upcoming third generation of cellular phones and networks, designed for high-speed data transfer in addition to standard voice communication.

4:3 The NTSC standard aspect ratio for traditional TVs; a 4:3 picture is four units wide by three units high. Also measured as 1.33:1.

5.1 Dolby Digital produces five separate surround channels plus one subwoofer channel—thus the "5.1" designation.

6.1 Surround format with six separate surround channels plus one subwoofer channel; used in Dolby Digital EX and DTS ES.

7.1 Surround format with seven separate surround channels plus one subwoofer channel.

8mm   Recording format for camcorders that uses a videocassette with 8mm tape.

16:9   The aspect ratio used in HDTV broadcasts; a 16:9 picture is 16 units wide by 9 units high. The 16:9 aspect ratio presents a wider image area than the traditional 4:3 ratio. Also measured as 1.78:1.

780p   One of the two main HDTV formats; transmits 780 lines of resolution with progressive scanning.

802.11a   More accurately described as IEEE 802.11a, this is an RF-based technology designed for larger wireless networks.

802.11b   More accurately described as IEEE 802.11b, this is an RF-based technology designed for home and small business wireless networks. Also known as *Wi-Fi*, 802.11b uses the 2.4GHz band.

1080i   One of the two main HDTV formats; transmits 1,080 lines of resolution with interlaced scanning.

A

A/D converter   Analog/digital converter; a processor that converts analog electrical signals into digital data. The converter samples the electrical signal every few milliseconds, and then the signal is quantized into a digital "word." The larger the digital word, the more accurate the sample.

A/V   Audio/video.

AC-3   Audio Coding 3; Dolby's digital-audio data compression algorithm, the standard format for prerecorded DVDs and HDTV broadcasts.

access point   A base station that connects portable wireless devices to a larger public network. Similar to a LAN access point.

acoustic suspension   A type of speaker enclosure that uses a sealed box to provide accurate, tight bass response.

active desktop   Enhanced functionality within Windows that enables Web pages to be turned into desktop items or wallpaper that are updated automatically.

active server page   A specification for a dynamically created Web that uses ActiveX scripting, usually via VBScript or JScript code. When a browser requests an ASP page, the Web server generates a page with HTML code and sends it back to the browser.

ADAT   Alesis Digital Audio Tape; a form of digital audio tape developed by Alesis for its digital multitrack recorders. It uses eight tracks of 16-bit/44.1KHz digital audio on consumer S-VHS tape.

address   The pointer to a particular Web page (also known as a *URL*). Also the specific identifier for a person's email inbox.

ADN   Advanced Digital Network; usually refers to a 56Kbps leased line.

ADR   Additional Dialog Recording; the process of replacing film dialog by overdubbing new vocals that are recorded during postproduction.

ADSL   Asymmetric Digital Subscriber Line; a type of DSL line where the upload speed is different from the download speed. (Usually the download speed is several orders of magnitude greater than the upload speed.)

adware   Stealth software that tracks your online activity and sends that data to a marketing or advertising company; some adware also uses that data to serve up replacement ads on specific Web sites.

AGP   Accelerated Graphics Port; a graphics interface specification, based on the PCI bus, designed for three-dimensional graphics.

AI   Artificial intelligence; the use of computers to solve problems and process information in ways that approximate human thought.

AIM   AOL Instant Messenger; America Online's instant messaging service.

algorithm   A mathematical process or formula used to create a number or solve a particular problem.

aliasing   Distortion caused by a low sample rate.

alpha geek   The de facto expert even the most experienced users turn to when they have a technical problem.

amplifier   An electronic device that uses capacitors or (in olden days) vacuum tubes to increase the strength of an electronic signal. An audio amplifier amplifies audio signals that are then output to one or more speakers.

AMPS   Advanced Mobile Phone System; the original standard specification for analog mobile telephony systems. To optimize the use of transmission frequencies, AMPS divides geographic areas into cells—hence the phrase "cellular phone."

analog   A means of transmitting or storing data using a continuously variable signal. Prone to signal degradation; does not always accurately reproduce the original.

anamorphic   A process that condenses the image in the source material to be expanded by the display device. Also a type of widescreen display format available on selected DVD discs, which features increased resolution when played back on a 16:9 ratio TV.

anchor   *See* hyperlink.

android   A machine made in human form.

Annie   An orphaned Web page, as in "little orphan Annie."

anonymizer   A Web site or service that enables anonymous Web browsing or email communications.

antialiasing   A technique used to smooth the *jaggies*.

antivirus program   A software program that scans for and cleans viruses from computer systems.

AOL   America Online, the largest commercial online service and ISP.

aperture   The opening in a camera lens that controls how much light goes through to the film or image sensor.

API   Application Programming Interface; a series of functions that programs can use to make the operating system perform basic operations. Windows, for example, has several classes of APIs that deal with telephony, messaging, and other operations.

applet   A simple program or utility designed to be executed from within another application.

application   Another word for a computer software program. Common applications include word processors, spreadsheets, and Web browsers.

application cache   High-speed, temporary, chip-based storage that is specifically designed for a given application.

APS   Advanced Photo System; a new film-based imaging system designed for better and better-documented photographs.

Archie   A (now outdated) tool for finding files stored on FTP servers.

archive   Storing computer files onto some type of long-term storage medium.

ARPANet   Advanced Research Projects Agency Network; the forerunner to the current Internet, developed in the late 1960s by the U.S. Department of Defense.

artifact   Misinterpreted information in a .JPG image, typically seen as color or line faults.

ASCII   American Standard Code for Information Interchange (pronounced "ask-ee"); a binary code used to represent English text characters as numbers, with each letter assigned a number from 0 to 127. By replacing text with numbers, computers can transfer information more easily.

ASDR   Attack, sustain, decay, and release; the four different stages of a sound's envelope.

ASIC   Application-Specific Integrated Circuit (pronounced "ay-sik"); a chip designed for a particular application rather than for an all-purpose microprocessor.

ASIO   Audio Stream Input/Output; a multichannel audio transfer protocol developed by Steinberg North America in 1997 for audio/MIDI-sequencing applications that allows access to the multichannel capabilities of sound cards.

ASP   *See* active server page.

aspect ratio   The ratio between the width and height of a video display. The NTSC television standard is 4:3, whereas HDTV uses a 16:9 ratio. Some wide-screen movies use an even wider ratio, either 1.85:1 or 2.35:1.

asymmetrical   A type of connection that operates at two different speeds upstream and downstream.

asynchronous A type of connection that permits data to flow in only one direction at a time. Also known as *half-duplex*.

AT commands Audio/telephony commands used to control all the functions that a telephone or data modem is capable of.

ATM Asynchronous Transfer Mode. (In the noncomputer world, stands for automatic teller machine.)

attachment A file attached to an email message.

attack In the world of audio, the beginning stage of sound's envelope.

audio Sound.

audio/video receiver A combination of amplifier and preamplifier that controls both audio and video inputs and outputs. Most a/v receivers include some sort of surround-sound decoder, either Dolby Pro Logic or the newer (and slightly more expensive) Dolby Digital. Also called an *a/v receiver*.

authentication The process of determining whether someone or something is, in fact, who or what it is purporting to be.

auto exposure A feature of digital cameras that automatically selects the optimal exposure settings for best image quality.

auto focus A feature of digital cameras that automatically focuses the camera lens on the main subject in the picture.

B

B2B Business-to-business; the exchange of products, services, or information between two or more businesses. (Contrast with B2C, which describes interaction between businesses and consumers.)

B2C Business-to-consumer; the exchange of products, services, or information between businesses and consumers. Also known as *retailing*.

B2E Business-to-employee; an approach to business management in which the focus of business is the employee rather than the consumer.

B2G Business-to-government; the exchange of products, services, or information between businesses and government entities.

back door Undocumented (and typically unauthorized) entry point into a system.

back door Trojan A *Trojan horse* file that opens a back door on your system for potential unauthorized remote access.

backbone A high-speed connection that forms a major pathway within a network or over the Internet.

backtracing software Software used to trace an attacker's identity and host ISP.

backup The process of creating a compressed copy of the data on your hard disk, to be used in case of an emergency.

balanced cable An audio cable that has two conductive wires, has a ground, and is often shielded. These cables are used to reduce interference and noise.

bandwidth The amount of data that can be transmitted in a fixed amount of time. For digital devices, bandwidth usually is expressed in bits per second (bps) or bytes per second (Bps). For analog devices, bandwidth is expressed in cycles per second, or hertz (Hz). Specific to audio, bandwidth refers to the range of frequencies a component can reproduce; the larger the bandwidth, the better the sound or picture.

banner ad A graphic advertisement placed on a Web page. Banner ads are typically rectangles about 460 pixels wide by 60 pixels high.

BASIC Beginner's All-purpose Symbolic Instruction Code; an early programming language that is still among the simplest and most popular of programming languages today. BASIC (sometimes written as Basic) continues to be widely used because it can be learned quickly, its statements are easy to read by other programmers, and support is available on most operating systems. Microsoft's *Visual Basic* adds object-oriented features and a graphical user interface to the standard text-based BASIC language.

bass reflex   A type of speaker enclosure that includes a precisely designed or "tuned" opening in the enclosure. Typically louder—though less accurate—than acoustic suspension speakers.

batch file   An executable file containing separate lines of commands—actually, "batches" of commands.

baud   The measure of how many bits a modem can send or receive each second.

bay   Within a PC's system unit, the space for installing an internal drive or peripheral.

BBS   Bulletin board system; an electronic online meeting and messaging system, accessible by dial-in modem connections, popular in the 1980s and pre-Internet 1990s. Freestanding BBSs have been mostly obsoleted by Internet-based message boards and communities.

beam   The process of transferring files or data from one device, such as a PDA, to another device, typically through an IrDA link.

beta   A prerelease version of a software program, typically in the process of being tested for bugs. (This process is called *beta testing*.)

BHO   Browser Helper Object; a small software program that attaches itself to your Web browser.

biamplification   The practice of using separate amplifiers to power the low-frequency and high-frequency speakers.

binary   Information consisting entirely of 0s and 1s. In the computer world, also refers to files (such as image files) that are not simply ASCII text files.

binhex   BINary HEXadecimal; a method for converting nontext (binary) files into ASCII.

biometrics   The science of measuring and analyzing unique biological identifiers, such as fingerprints, retinas, voice patterns, facial patterns, and so on.

BIOS   The basic input/output system that interacts with computer hardware.

biotechnology   The science of employing living organisms (or parts of organisms) to make or modify products, improve plants or animals, or develop microorganisms for specific uses.

bipole   A speaker design that generates equal amounts of in-phase sound both forward and backward. Typically used for rear-channel speakers in a surround-sound setup.

bit   Binary DigIT; the smallest element of computer storage, a single digit (0 or 1) in a binary system; 8 bits equal 1 *byte*. Physically, a bit can be a transistor or capacitor in a memory cell, a magnetic domain on disk or tape, a reflective spot on optical media, or a high or low voltage pulsing through a circuit.

bit depth   The number of bits used to represent colors or tones. 2-bit color is black and white; 4-bit color produces 64 colors or shades of gray; 8-bit color produces 256 colors; 16-bit color produces 32,000 colors; 24-bit color produces 16.7 million colors; 30/32-bit color produces billions of individual colors.

bit rate   The transmission speed of binary-coded data. *See* data rate.

bitmap   A binary representation of an image or font consisting of rows and columns of dots. The broader the color spectrum, the more bits are required for each pixel. For simple monochrome images, 1 bit is sufficient to represent each dot, but for colors and shades of gray, each dot requires more than 1 bit of data, hence "64-bit" graphics.

blackhole list   A list of *open mail relay servers*, created for the purpose of blocking all (typically spam) messages from those servers.

block list   A list of specific addresses and domains known to send spam.

Bluetooth   The specification for a particular wireless connection technology operating in the unlicensed 2.4GHz RF band. Bluetooth (developed primarily by phone maker Ericsson) was originally intended to be a "wire replacement" technology but has since been expanded to compete somewhat with the more powerful Wi-Fi standard. The name comes from a tenth-century Viking king named Harald Blåtand, who is credited with unifying the country of Denmark. Depending on which legend you believe, King Harald (the Danish "Blåtand" translates into the English "Bluetooth") either had a dark complexion and dark hair unusual among the fair-skinned Nordic blondes, or had teeth stained from eating too many blueberries. (The former legend is probably more accurate; the name Blåtand is derived from two old Danish words, "blå," meaning dark skinned, and "tan," meaning great man.)

board   A device that plugs into your computer's system unit and provides auxiliary functions. Also called a *card*.

Boolean   A system of logic developed by George Boole (1815–1864), an English mathematician and computer pioneer. Boolean operators (used in everything from logic statements to Internet searches) include AND, OR, and NOT and work with words in much the same way that arithmetic operators (addition, subtraction, and so on) work with numbers.

boot   The process of turning on your computer system. *Rebooting* is turning your system off and then back on, which can be done by pressing Ctrl+Alt+Del or pressing your PC's on/off button.

boot sector   The area located on the first track of a floppy or hard disk.

boot sector virus   A virus that infects the boot sectors of floppy disks, or the master boot record of hard disks.

bootable disk   A disk or diskette that can be used to start your system because the disk contains certain system files. *See* system disk.

bouncing   The process of taking multiple audio tracks and mixing them down into either a mono track, stereo track, or surround-sound mix.

bps   Bits per second; the standard measure of data transmission speeds.

break-out box   A box that attaches to a sound card and is used to house additional input/output jacks.

broadband   A high-speed Internet connection, via ISDN, cable, DSL, satellite, or T1 and T3 lines.

browser   Short for Web browser, a client software program that lets a computer or other device access and display HTML pages on the World Wide Web.

bubblejet   A type of nonimpact printer, similar to an inkjet, that uses heated ink to form images in a matrix format.

buffer   Memory-based storage for pending computing tasks; multiple print jobs are sent to a buffer where they wait in a queue for the printer to execute them.

buffer overflow   A bug in some programs that enables the program's data buffer to be overloaded with data, forcing the original program code out so the buffer can be rewritten with malicious code.

burner   A device that writes CD-ROMs or DVD-ROMs.

bus (1)   In the audio world, the output circuit of an audio mixer. Most mixers have multiple buses, each to route an audio signal to a different place. Both software and digital mixers use this same concept to route signals.

bus (2)   In the computer world, a common pathway, or channel, between multiple devices. The computer's internal bus is known as the *local bus*, or *processor bus*. It provides a parallel data-transfer path between the CPU, main memory, and peripheral buses. A 16-bit bus transfers 2 bytes at a time over 16 wires; a 32-bit bus uses 32 wires; and so on. The bus is composed of two parts: the address bus and the data bus. Addresses are sent over the address bus to signal a memory location, and the data is transferred over the data bus to that location.

bus speed   The internal speed of a computer's motherboard.

button   A raised object in a dialog box that can be "pressed" (by clicking it with a mouse) to perform certain operations.

byte   Eight bits, which the computer treats as a single unit. A byte is the unit most computers use to represent a character such as a letter, number, or typographic symbol. One thousand bytes is called a *kilobyte (KB)*, one million bytes is called a *megabyte (MB)*, and one thousand megabytes is called a *gigabyte (GB)*.

C

C prompt   The prompt issued by the DOS command interpreter when it is waiting for you to input a command.

cable modem   A device that connects your computer to the Internet through cable lines.

cache   A form of temporary storage, either in computer memory or on a computer's hard disk.

cache memory   The area of computer memory that stores the most recently accessed data. When a computer needs data once, chances are it will need it again, soon, so computer designers realized they could speed up the computer by storing the most recently accessed data in a high-speed storage area. Most caches are FIFO (first in, first out), which means that as the cache fills, the older data is thrown out. There are several types of cache on your computer, including application cache, disk cache, hardware cache, and processor cache.

CAD   Computer-aided design; refers to a wide range of programs (including the popular AutoCAD) used for designing any type of product.

camcorder   Video camera and recorder combined into a single unit.

card   A device that plugs into your system unit and provides auxiliary functions. You can add video cards, modem cards, and sound cards to your system. Also called a *board*.

Carnivore   The packet sniffer software used by the FBI to spy on suspected criminals and terrorists.

CCD   Charge coupled device; a light-sensitive chip used for image gathering.

CD   Compact disc; a laser-based digital format for storing high-quality audio programming.

CD-DA   Compact Disc Digital Audio; the initial incarnation of the compact disc.

CD-R   Compact Disc Recordable; a type of CD drive that lets you record once onto CD discs, which can then be read by any CD-ROM drive and, with proper formatting, by most audio CD players.

CD-ROM   Compact Disc Read-Only Memory; a type of CD that stores digital data for computer applications.

CD-RW   Compact Disc Rewritable; a type of CD that can be recorded, erased, and rewritten to by the user, multiple times. A CD-RW disc cannot be played in a conventional CD player or in a normal CD-ROM drive.

CDMA   Code Division Multiple Access; a spread spectrum technology for cellular telephone use.

censorware   Another word for content-filtering software.

central processing unit   *See* CPU.

certificate authority   The company that issues a digital certificate.

certificate store   The repository of digital certificates stored on your hard disk and accessed by your Web browser.

CF   Compact Flash; a small form factor memory card for removable data storage.

CGI   Common Gateway Interface; a standard way for a Web server to pass a Web user's request to an application program, receive data back from that program, and forward it to the user.

chain letter   A letter or email directing the recipient to forward multiple copies of the message to other people.

channel   One section of an audio track, usually carrying the sound for a single speaker.

chat   Text-based real-time Internet communication, typically consisting of short, one-line messages back and forth between two or more users. Users gather to chat in chat rooms or channels.

chat channel   A public chat on an IRC network, typically organized by topic.

cheese   The content of a commercial Web site that consists primarily of product pictures or other useless information.

chip   A small piece of semiconducting material (usually silicon) on which an integrated circuit is embedded. A typical chip is less than a square inch in size and can contain millions of electronic components (transistors). Computers consist of many chips placed on electronic boards called *printed circuit boards*.

chrominance   The color component of a video signal that includes information about the image's color (hue) and saturation.

churn   The customer turnover rate of any ISP or commercial online service; the percent of new customers minus the percent of old customers canceling is the churn.

circuit board   A thin plate on which chips and other electronic components are placed. Computers consist of one or more boards, often called *cards* or *adapters*.

clear GIF   A small, transparent graphics file used to create a *Web bug*.

click   The process of selecting an item onscreen; what you do with a mouse button.

click-through   A measurement of Web page advertising effectiveness; a click-through occurs whenever a user clicks a banner ad or link.

client   In a client/server relationship between two devices, the client is the device that pushes or pulls data from the other device (server).

clustering   Connecting two or more computers to behave as a single computer. Thanks to clustering, two or more computers can jointly execute a function, activity can be distributed evenly across a computer network, and systems can respond gracefully to unexpected failures.

CMOS   Complementary metal-oxide semiconductor (pronounced "see-moss"); a small, 64-byte memory chip on the motherboard that stores information your computer needs to boot up.

CMYK   Cyan, Magenta, Yellow, Black; the individual colors used to create color prints.

co-location   The process of having a Web server located in a different physical location from its host company, typically for security purposes.

coaster   What all those excess AOL tryout CDs end up being used as.

code signature   A sequence of binary code unique to a computer virus; used to identify each virus.

CODEC   COder/DECoder; an algorithm that reduces the number of bytes consumed by large computer files and programs.

color depth   *See* bit depth.

comb filter   An electronic component in a television or other video display that removes residual chrominance (color) information from the luminance (brightness) signal, thus enhancing fine picture detail.

Comdex   A trade show in which IT professionals have convened twice yearly for the past 20 years to unveil new products, announce burgeoning technology trends, and schmooze with other geeks from around the world. Since the trade shows' humble beginnings in 1980, Comdex has grown into the computer industry's premiere U.S. event.

compact disc   *See* CD.

compact flash   *See* CF.

companion virus   A file infector virus that creates a clone of the host file, which is then run instead of the original file.

component   A part of Windows incidental to the main program. A component can be an applet such as HyperTerminal or Notepad or a utility such as the DVD driver.

component video   A video signal that has been split up into its component parts: red (Pr), green (Y), and blue (Pb). Component video connections—found on higher-end TVs and DVD players—reproduce the best possible picture quality, with improved color accuracy and reduced color bleeding.

composite video   A single video signal that contains both chrominance (color) and luminance (brightness) and information. Composite video is typically delivered through a single "video" RCA jack connection and delivers a better-quality picture than an RF signal, but not as good as an S-Video signal.

compression   The process of compacting digital data.

compressor   A signal processor that reduces the gain of a signal by a set ratio when it exceeds the set threshold.

computer   A programmable device that can store, retrieve, and process data. Computers can store prerecorded lists of instructions, which we call *programs*. The computer's brain is the microprocessor, which is capable of doing math, moving data around, and altering the data after storing it in binary code. Most computers have a fast, short-term storage medium and a slower, long-term storage medium. The faster storage medium, known as *RAM*, is used to store information temporarily while you work and run applications. The long-term, permanent storage is your hard drive. To feed the computer information and tell it how to process the data, you need input devices such as your mouse and keyboard. The monitor, or output device, displays the results.

computer virus A computer program or piece of malicious code that attaches itself to other files and then replicates itself.

content filter Software that analyzes Web page content and blocks access to inappropriate content.

controller Any MIDI device that can be used to control any other MIDI-capable device. Generally, controllers are in the form of a keyboard, but they can also be drum pads, mixer controllers, and so on.

cookie A small file created by a Web site and stored on your computer's hard disk, used to track specific user information. Typically, a cookie records your preferences when using a particular site; cookies are also used to rotate the banner ads that a site sends so that it doesn't keep sending you the same ad, and to customize pages for you based on your browser type or other information you might have provided the Web site.

CPU Central Processing Unit; a complex silicon chip that acts as a computer's brain, taking requests from applications and then processing, or executing, operations.

cracker An individual who maliciously breaks into another computer system. (Not to be confused with a *hacker*, who typically does not have malicious intent.)

crossover An electrical circuit designed to separate an audio signal into different frequency ranges that are then routed to the appropriate speaker (such as a subwoofer).

CRT Cathode-ray tube; commonly called a *picture tube*. Used in all direct-view, all rear-projection, and some front-projection televisions.

cryptography The science of information security; the process of hiding or coding information either in storage or in transit.

CTS Carpal Tunnel Syndrome; hand pain and weakness that results from compression of the median nerve at the wrist. Often caused by repetitive hand and arm movements, such as extended typing at a computer keyboard.

cursor The highlighted area or pointer that tracks with the movement of your mouse or arrow keys onscreen.

cybercafé A coffeehouse that offers Internet access. Also called an *Internet café*.

cybersex Any type of sexual activity (even the virtual kind) that takes place online.

cyberspace Typically used to define the "there" that is the Internet. The word was coined by author William Gibson in his novel *Neuromancer*.

cybored The state of boredom entered into while you're waiting for slow Web pages to load.

cybrarian A librarian specializing in electronic sources.

D

D/A converter Digital-to-Analog converter; the processor on a sound card that converts the analog electrical signal into digital data.

daemon A Unix program or agent (pronounced "demon") designed to wait in the background while another program is running and execute only when required. Using a daemon, a program can simply hand off data to the smaller program and go on to more important things.

DAMPS Digital Advanced Mobile Phone System; the American standard for digital mobile telephony. Also known as *TDMA*.

DAT Digital Audio Tape; a digital linear tape that uses PCM to convert analog signals into a digital form.

data Information that is convenient to move or process. In the computer world, data is typically digital.

Data That android dude on *Star Trek, the Next Generation*.

data diddling The process of surreptitiously altering (but not deleting) the data on another computer system.

data rate   The throughput rate at which data can be sent from one device to another.

data-driven attack   A virus or Trojan attack on a computer system; the attack is launched when a file is downloaded and opened.

daughter window   Another name for a pop-up window.

DAW   Digital Audio Workstation; a computer that has been specially configured for work with audio.

dB   Decibel; the standard unit of measure for expressing relative power differences—otherwise known as *loudness*. One dB is the smallest change in loudness most people can detect; a 10-dB difference produces twice the volume.

DBS   Digital Broadcast Satellite (or Direct Broadcast Satellite); the satellite broadcasting system that uses a small 18-inch satellite dish to receive signals from a high-powered satellite in geosynchronous orbit.

dead link   A hyperlink on a Web page that doesn't lead to an active page or site—probably because that page no longer exists.

dead tree edition   The print version of something also available on the Internet.

decompression   The process of returning a compressed file to its original format.

decryption   The process of decoding encrypted data.

DECT   Digital Enhanced Cordless Telephone; a standard that defines the radio-based connection between two devices, such as a cordless phone and its base unit.

defragment   To restructure a disk so that files are stored in contiguous blocks of space, rather than dispersed into multiple fragments at different locations on the disk.

demilitarized zone   A server that sits outside a company's firewall and enables public access to specified content.

denial-of-service attack   An attack that floods a computer or network with data or messages that overwhelm and ultimately shut down the system.

depth of field   The depth in a scene from foreground to background that will be in sharp focus in a photograph or movie frame. Depth of field is affected by a combination of *aperture, focal length,* and distance from subject.

desktop   The entire screen area on which you display all your computer work. A typical computer desktop can contain icons, a taskbar, menus, and individual application windows.

device   A Windows file that represents some object—physical or nonphysical—installed on your system.

dial-up access   An Internet connection via a dial-up modem—*not* via always-on broadband.

dialog box   An onscreen window that either displays a message or asks for user input.

dictionary spam   A means of generating email addresses by matching common names with known domain names.

digerati   Really hip people in the digital world; the digital version of literati.

digital   A means of transmitting or storing data using "on" and "off" bits (expressed as "1" or "0"). Known for its highly accurate reproduction, with little or no degradation from the original.

Digital 8   Digital recording format for camcorders that uses standard 8mm or Hi8 cassettes.

digital camera   A still camera that uses a light-sensitive image sensor chip (typically a *CCD*), instead of film, to capture the image.

digital certificate   An electronic credential that confirms the identity of a person, server, or software manufacturer.

digital compression   Any algorithm that reduces the storage space required to store or transmit information.

digital signature   A form of digital certificate used to authenticate the identity of the sender of a message or the signer of a document.

digital television   Television signals broadcast digitally, the U.S. TV standard that will become mandatory in 2006. DTV comes in several different formats, each with varying types of picture resolution and sound quality. The highest quality of these formats are called *HDTV*.

digital zoom   A pseudozoom mode in some digital cameras that operates by cropping the outside of the image and enlarging the center. Typically produces lower-quality images than a comparable *optical zoom*.

DIMM   Dual Inline Memory Module; a small circuit board that holds memory chips. Unlike SIMMS (Single Inline Memory Modules), you can install memory one DIMM at a time.

dipole   A speaker design that generates equal amounts of sound both forward and backward, with the two sounds being out of phase. Dipoles are often used as surround speakers.

directory (1)   An index to files you store on your disk, often represented as a simulated file folder. Also known as a *folder*.

directory (2)   A search site that collects and indexes Web pages manually, either by user submission or editorial selection. Yahoo! is the Web's most popular directory.

discovery   The process wherein a remote device becomes aware of the network to which it is connected.

disk   A device that stores data in magnetic format. The three main kinds of disks are diskettes, hard disks, and optical disks.

disk cache   High-speed, temporary, chip-based storage that reserves an area of RAM to store data that has been accessed from the hard drive. If the data is requested from the hard drive again, the computer gets it from RAM, which is much faster.

disk compression   Taking the information that is stored, or will be stored, on a disk and compacting it so that it takes less space to store.

diskette   A portable or removable disk.

distributed computing   A form of peer-to-peer computing where multiple computers are connected to harness their total processing power; typically used for large projects that would otherwise require use of a supercomputer.

DIVX   A type of DVD disc with regulated playback; now obsolete.

DLP   Digital Light Processor; the technology that controls DMD front-projection displays.

DMD   Digital Micromirror Device; a type of projection video display that uses thousands of small mirrors, controlled by a DLP.

DNS   Domain Name System; translates Internet domain and host names to IP addresses.

DNS spoofing   An attack resulting from the hijacking of a computer's DNS name by an attacker; the DNS name is redirected to the attacker's IP address.

document   A piece of information in a computer file. A Web page is one kind of document, as is a Microsoft Word file.

Dolby AC-3   The previous name for Dolby Digital.

Dolby Digital   Surround-sound format, sometimes referred to as *5.1*. Incorporates six discrete digital audio channels: front left, front center, front right, surround left, surround right, and a "low frequency effects" channel for subwoofers.

Dolby Digital EX   Extended version of the Dolby Digital surround-sound format, with 6.1 channels. The extra channel is a matrixed rear surround channel positioned at the rear of the room, behind and between the left and right surrounds.

Dolby HX Pro   This circuit adjusts cassette tape bias during recording to extend dynamic headroom (the difference between the loudest and the softest audible signals) and improve the tape deck's capability to record high frequencies without distortion. Dolby HX Pro requires no decoding.

Dolby noise reduction   Noise reduction systems used on audio-cassette decks. There are several different types of Dolby noise reduction, including Dolby B, Dolby C, Dolby S, and Dolby HX Pro.

Dolby Pro Logic   The predecessor to Dolby Digital surround, with only four channels: front left, front center, front right, and a single "surround" channel. The single surround channel is typically sent to two or more rear speakers. Dolby Pro Logic channels are matrixed into a left and right output, whereas Dolby Digital uses six discrete outputs.

Dolby Pro Logic II   The successor to Dolby Pro Logic, a matrix format used to simulate a surround experience for material recorded in two-channel format. Also used to simulate real channel effects in some video games.

domain   The name of a site on the Internet. Domains are hierarchical, and lower-level domains often refer to particular Web sites within a top-level domain. Examples of domains are .com, .edu, .gov, and .org.

dongle   A device developed to prevent piracy. It attaches to a port on your computer and works as a key to unlock a particular software application.

DOS   Disk Operating System (pronounced "dahss"); the pre-Windows operating system for IBM-compatible computers. The generic term DOS is often used as shorthand for the more specific MS-DOS, the original operating system developed by Microsoft for the PC.

dot bomb   A defunct dot com.

dot com   A company whose primary business is Internet related.

double-click   Clicking a mouse button twice in rapid succession.

download   The process of receiving information or data from a server on the Internet.

dpi   Dots per inch; a measurement of printer resolution. The more dots per inch, the higher the resolution. A 400dpi printer creates 160,000 dots (400×400).

DRAM   Dynamic RAM; the most common type of random-access memory. It accesses information as it needs it, and then closes and goes on to something else. Because DRAM is random, pieces of information can be stacked one upon another without discarding the entire stack. The information in DRAM is not only dynamic and randomly accessed, it's also fast.

driver   The program support file that tells a program how to interact with a specific hardware device, such as a hard disk controller or video display card.

DSL   Digital Subscriber Line; a new ultrafast Internet connection using standard phone lines. Download speeds can approach 32Mbps. Often preceded by another letter,

denoting the type of DSL connection; for example, ADSL stands for Asymmetric Digital Subscriber Line, and SDSL stands for Symmetric Digital Subscriber Line.

DSP   Digital Signal Processor; a chip designed to manipulate analog information that has been converted into digital format. DSP circuitry is used in some surround-sound systems to create different simulated sound fields.

DSS   Digital Satellite System; *see* DBS.

DSSS   Direct Sequence Spread Spectrum; a wireless RF technology that fixes signals within a specific channel but uses engineered noise to reduce interference and improve security.

DTS   Digital Theater Systems; a 5.1 surround-sound format similar to Dolby Digital.

DTS ES   A 6.1 version of DTS surround sound; the extra channel is a matrixed rear surround positioned behind and between the left and rear surrounds.

DTV   *See* digital television.

DV   Digital Video; the recording, editing, and storing of video in digital formats. A digital video (DV) camcorder is a video camera that captures and stores images on a digital medium such as a DAT or compact flash card.

DVD   A two-sided optical disc that holds a minimum of 4.7GB, enough for a full-length movie. DVDs can store significantly more data than ordinary CD-ROMs can, and can play high-quality videos. (The acronym DVD actually doesn't stand for anything anymore; at one time it stood for Digital Versatile Disk, and at another Digital Video Disk.)

DVD-Audio   New audio-only DVD format that delivers better-than-CD-quality sound; competes with SA-CD.

DVD-R   DVD Recordable; a write-once, read-many storage format similar to CD-R, but for DVDs.

DVD-RAM   DVD Random Access Memory; a rewritable DVD disc format for data recording and playback. DVD-RAM drives typically read DVD-Video, DVD-ROM, and CD media.

DVD-ROM DVD Read-Only Memory; a DVD disc capable of storing data, interactive sequences, and audio and video. DVD-ROMs run in DVD-ROM or DVD-RAM drives, but not DVD-Video players connected to TVs and home theaters. Most DVD-ROM drives will play DVD-Video movies, however.

DVD-RW DVD ReWritable; a rewritable DVD format that is similar to DVD+RW but with less capability to work as a random access device. It has a read-write capacity of 4.7GB.

DVD+RW DVD+ReWritable; one of several competing rewritable DVD formats. Fully compatible with existing DVD and DVD-ROM drives.

DVHS Digital VHS; a new videocassette format that can record and play back 16:9 HDTV programming.

DVR Digital Video Recorder; a device that records programming digitally on a large hard disk. Also known as *personal video recorder (PVR)* or *personal television receiver (PTR)*.

dynamic range The difference between the loudest sound and the quietest sound that is produced or can be reproduced by a piece of equipment.

dynamic system monitoring The real-time scanning mode of a virus-scanning program.

E

e-commerce Electronic commerce, or business conducted over the Internet.

e-tailer A retailer engaging in e-commerce; an online merchant.

Easter egg A surprise embedded in a program, typically activated by some unusual (and undocumented) combination of keystrokes or user actions.

email Electronic mail; a means of corresponding to other computer users over the Internet through digital messages.

email bomb The sending of a large number of email messages to a single address, with the intent of flooding that person's inbox.

email gateway A proxy server for email.

email spoofing The practice of changing your name in an outgoing email message so it looks like the message came from somewhere or someone else. Spammers generally use spoofing to prevent people from finding out who they are. It's also used by general malcontents to practice mischievous and malicious behavior. However, spoofing can be a legitimate and helpful tool for someone with more than one email account.

emoticon Punctuation characters that suggest how an email should be interpreted by indicating the writer's mood. For example, a :) emoticon indicates that the message is meant as a joke. (The name "emoticon" is short for "emotion icon.") An emoticon is also called a *smiley*.

encryption The process of coding data into a format that can't be read, for security purposes. To read an encrypted file, you must possess the secret key or password that unlocks the encryption.

envelope The dynamic shape of a sound over time, commonly characterized by its attack, decay, sustain, and release.

equalizer An amplifier that can boost or cut specific frequencies.

error message An onscreen message that your operating system or application issues to tell you that you did something wrong or that a command could not be executed correctly.

Ethernet Perhaps the most common networking protocol. Ethernet is used to network, or hook computers together so they can share information.

executable file A program that you run on your computer system.

exploit An attack that takes advantage of a bug or hole in a piece of hardware or operating system.

extranet An intranet that is accessible to select computers that are not physically part of the company's own network, but not accessible to the general public.

F

FAQ   Frequently Asked Questions; a document that answers the most commonly asked questions about a particular topic. FAQs are often found in newsgroups and on some Web sites as a preparatory answer to the common questions asked by new users.

fast Ethernet   The same thing as Ethernet, only 10 times faster.

FAT   File Allocation Table; a special section of your disk that stores tracking data to help Windows locate files.

FAT32   The 32-bit file allocation table used in Windows 98 and subsequent Microsoft operating systems.

FDISK   A DOS and Windows utility that creates one or more partitions on a hard disk drive.

FDMA   Frequency Division Multiple Access; the division of the frequency band allocated for wireless cellular telephone communication into 30 channels, each of which can carry a voice conversation or, with digital service, digital data.

FHSS   Frequency Hopping Spread Spectrum; a type of frequency hopping that uses a broad spectrum of frequencies.

field   When using interlaced scanning, half a frame of picture information.

file   A collection of data, with its own unique name and location; files can be documents or executable programs.

File Allocation Table   *See* FAT.

file extension   Extensions identify the type of file to which they're attached. All programs and almost all data files use extensions, which are separated from the filename with a dot. For example, LETTER.DOC is a Word document. NOTEPAD.EXE is a text-editor program that comes with Windows. Before Windows 95, an extension could have only up to three letters or digits; beginning with Windows 95 (and already standard on the Macintosh platform), extensions can be of any length.

file infector virus   A virus that infects the code of executable program files.

file type   A specific type of file, associated with a specific application.

filename   The formal name assigned to a file; beginning with Windows 95 (and already standard on the Macintosh platform), a filename can be up to 256 characters long and include letters, numbers, characters, and spaces.

Finger   A software tool for locating users on other Internet sites.

FIR   Fast Infrared; infrared transmission that supports speeds up to 4Mbps.

firewall   Software or hardware that insulates a computer or network from the Internet or other networks. A firewall blocks unwanted access to the protected network while giving the protected network access to networks outside the firewall.

FireWire   A high-speed bus. FireWire is a serial connector, like USB, and allows you to add peripheral devices to your computer very easily, without having to open the box. FireWire, however, can transmit data 30 to almost 40 times faster than USB. That makes it very good for tasks such as getting video off a camcorder. For most devices, you don't need that much speed, but if you wanted to add a very fast hard drive to your PC, FireWire would be an excellent solution. FireWire was originally developed by Apple and is now also sold under the names iLink and IE-1394.

firmware   Low-level software that runs in a freestanding device (such as a digital camera) and typically controls the functionality and user interface.

flame   To communicate emotionally and/or excessively via electronic mail. In other words, to insult someone online.

flame war   What happens when an online discussion degenerates into a series of flames or personal attacks.

Flash   Multimedia technology, developed by Macromedia, that enables audio/video interactivity on specially designed Web pages.

flat response   The reproduction of sound without altering the intensity of any part of the frequency range.

floppy disk   Another term for *diskette*.

flow control   A procedure used to control the transfer of data between two devices.

flutter   High-frequency variations in pitch of a recorded waveform due to fast speed variations in a recorder or playback machine.

flying erase head   A type of recording head on a VCR that reduces or eliminates static when stopping and starting recording between scenes.

focal length   A lens measurement that determines the perspective (wide angle through telephoto) viewed through a camera lens.

folder   A way to group files on a disk; each folder can contain multiple files or other folders (called *subfolders*). In the DOS and Windows operating systems, folders were originally called *directories*.

forced frame   A technique for forcing a new Web page into a framed page from another site.

format   The process that prepares a disk for use.

FPTV   Front-projection television; a video display device that projects a picture onto the front of a separate screen.

frame   One single still image that when played in rapid succession with other frames creates a moving picture.

frames   An HTML technique for combining two or more separate HTML documents within a single Web page.

freeware   Computer software distributed at no charge. Unlike open-source software, the author retains the copyright, which means that the application cannot be modified without the author's consent.

frequency hopping   An RF technology that enables a single signal to jump from one frequency to another, to reduce interference and increase security.

frequency response   The range of frequencies accurately reproduced by a particular component; the wider the range, the better.

FTP   File Transfer Protocol; a series of protocols or rules that define how to transfer files across the Internet. FTP is a very popular way to send files across the Internet, and is not dependent on Web servers and browsers.

full duplex   *See* synchronous.

full-motion video   The display of movie clips on your PC in as realistic a form as possible.

function key   One of the special keys labeled F1 to F12, located at the top of your computer keyboard.

G

gain   Amount of amplification, measured in decibels.

gateway   A device that connects one or more other devices to an external network.

gateway computer   A computer on a network that hosts the connection to the Internet.

Gb   Gigabit; approximately 1,000 megabits.

GB   Gigabyte; 1,000 megabytes, more or less (1,024 to be precise).

Gbps   Gigabits per second.

GBps   Gigabytes per second.

GHz   Gigahertz (millions of cycles per second).

gloss   The amount of light reflected by the surface of a sheet of paper, relative to the paper's smoothness.

Google   The most-used search engine on the Web.

Gopher   A pre-Web method of organizing material on Internet servers. Created at the University of Minnesota—home of the Fighting Gophers!

GPS   Global Positioning System; a system of 24 satellites for identifying Earth locations, launched by the U.S. Department of Defense. By triangulation of signals from three of the satellites, a receiving unit can pinpoint its current location anywhere on Earth to within a few meters.

graphics   Picture files. Pictures, photographs, and clip art are all commonly referred to as *graphics*.

grayscale   An image consisting of a range of gray levels, as opposed to a broader range of colors or pure black and white.

GSM   Global System for Mobile (communications); a second-generation (2G) standard for digital cellular transmissions; widely used in Europe and in U.S. PCS 1900 systems.

GUI   Graphical User Interface (pronounced "gooey"). The look and feel of an operating system that uses graphical elements instead of character-based elements. A GUI lets you interact by using a mouse rather than by having to type in keyboard commands.

H

hacker   An individual who enjoys exploring the details of computer systems and programming code, typically by "hacking" into those systems and programs—but without causing any intentional damage. (Not to be confused with a *cracker*, who engages in intentionally malicious behavior.)

half-duplex   *See* asynchronous.

hard disk   A piece of hardware that stores large amounts of data for future access.

hardware   A piece of electronic equipment that you can actually touch. Your personal computer and all its peripherals are hardware; the operations of your PC are controlled by *software* (which you *can't* touch).

hardware cache   High-speed, temporary, chip-based storage that offers faster access time than CD-ROM hardware. By placing data in the hardware cache, you minimize the CD-ROM system's waiting time. Hardware cache speeds up access to the CD and the CD's performance.

HDTV   High-Definition Television; a subset of the new digital TV standard that reproduces pictures in either 780p or 1080i resolution, with a 16:9 aspect ratio and Dolby Digital 5.1 surround sound.

header   That part of a data packet or email message, normally hidden, that contains the sender's IP address and other technical information.

heading   The initial portion of an HTML document, specified by a special code.

headroom   The amount of gain an audio amplifier can produce before distorting.

Heuristic scanning   A method of scanning for computer viruses by looking for general viruslike behavior.

Hi8   High-resolution version of the 8mm camcorder format.

HID   Human Interface Device; any device (physical or virtual) used to control a computer consumer electronics product. Keyboards and mice are HIDs, as are the knobs and buttons on the front of an audio/video receiver.

hit   A single request from a Web browser to view an item (typically a Web page) stored on a Web server. If a Web page contains graphics, the graphic elements are counted as separate hits.

home page   The initial page screen of a Web site.

home theater   The attempt to reproduce, as accurately as possible, the experience of watching a film in a movie theater. Typically involves a high-quality video source (such as DVD), audio/video receiver, surround-sound speakers, and a large video display device.

HomeRF   An RF-based technology designed for home and small business wireless networks. HomeRF uses the 2.4GHz band and competes with both Wi-Fi and Bluetooth.

horizontal resolution   The sharpness of a video display, measured in terms of horizontal lines that can be resolved from one side of the screen to the other. Broadcast television has a horizontal resolution of 330 lines; DVDs deliver 500 lines; and HDTV can deliver up to 1,080 lines of horizontal resolution.

host   An Internet server that houses a Web site; any computer on a network that is a repository for services available to other computers on the network.

hover   The act of selecting an item by placing your cursor over an icon *without clicking*.

GLOSSARY

HTML   HyperText Markup Language; the document format used to build pages on the World Wide Web. HTML tags, or codes, define the structure and layout of a Web document. Hundreds of tags are used to format and lay out a Web page.

HTML email   Email messages that incorporate HTML code, just like Web pages.

HTTP   HyperText Transfer Protocol; the underlying communications protocol used to connect servers and browsers on the World Wide Web. For example, when you enter a URL in your browser, the browser sends an HTTP command to the Web server directing it to retrieve and transmit the requested page.

hub   Hardware used to network computers together (usually over an Ethernet connection). It's a small box with five or more RJ-45 connectors that accept cables from individual computers.

hybrid virus   A virus that combines the capabilities of multiple types of viruses.

hyperlink   Special text or graphics on a Web page that, when clicked, automatically transfers the user to the another Web page.

hypertext   Any text that contains links to other documents. When users click on hyperlinked text, another document is retrieved and displayed.

Hz   Hertz; a unit of measurement for the frequency of sounds. One Hz is equal to one cycle per second, and the range of human hearing is typically 20–20,000 Hz.

I

I/O   Input/Output. The flow of information to and from computers and peripherals.

IBM-compatible   All personal computers that are compatible (that is, can share software and operating systems) with the original IBM PC.

IC   Integrated Circuit; *see* chip.

ICANN   Internet Corporation for Assigned Names and Numbers; a nonprofit, private corporation responsible for overseeing the following aspects of the World Wide Web: assigning space for IP addresses, managing the domain name system, and taking care of the root server system.

ICMP   Internet Control Message Protocol; used by Internet routers to notify a host computer when a specified destination is unreachable.

icon   A graphical representation of an object onscreen. Typically, you click an icon to initiate a function.

ICQ   One of the first instant-messaging services; now owned by America Online.

IDE   Intelligent (or integrated) Drive Electronics; IDE connects mass-storage devices, such as hard drives or CD-ROMs, to a computer.

identity theft   The theft of personal ID and financial information, enabling the thief to assume the identity of the victim.

IEEE   Institute of Electronic and Electrical Engineers.

IEEE 1394   *See* FireWire.

IMAP   Internet Message Access Protocol; a protocol (similar to POP) used by email clients when connecting to email servers.

in box   The virtual container where unread email is stored.

infection   The process of a computer virus inserting itself into a computer file.

infrared data transfer   A means of sending voice or data signals using light transmitted in the infrared range.

inkjet   A type of nonimpact printer that uses drops of ink to form images in a matrix format.

install   How you get software from its box to your hard disk.

instant messaging   Text-based real-time one-on-one communication over the Internet. Not to be confused with *chat*, which can accommodate multiple users, instant messaging (IM) typically is limited to just two users.

interlaced scanning   A method of displaying television pictures where the picture is displayed in two halves (one of odd-numbered lines, one of even-numbered lines) that are interlaced to create the full picture.

Internet   The global "network of networks" that connects millions of computers and other devices around the world. The World Wide Web and Usenet are both parts of the Internet.

Internet Explorer   Microsoft's PC-based Web browser software.

interpolation   A way to increase the apparent size, resolution, or colors in an image by calculating the pixels used to represent the new image from the old one.

interstitial   Another name for a pop-up advertisement.

intranet   A private network inside an organization that uses the same type of software and services found on the public Internet.

intrusion detection system   Software or hardware that monitors a computer network or system for signs of an attack.

IP   Internet Protocol; the protocol that defines how data is sent through routers to different networks, by assigning unique IP addresses to different devices.

IP address   The identifying address of a computer or device attached to a TCP/IP network. TCP/IP networks use IP addresses to route messages to their proper destinations. The IP address is written as four sets of numbers separated by periods.

IR   *See* infrared.

IRC   Internet Relay Chat; an Internet-based network of chat servers and channels that facilitates real-time public text messaging (called *chats*) and file exchanges.

IrDA   Describes both the Infrared Data Association and the standard developed by that organization for infrared-based data connections.

IRQ   Interrupt Request; a signal used by a device to gain the attention of your system's microprocessor when it needs processing resources. Most PCs have 16 different IRQs, labeled 0 through 15.

ISDN   Integrated Services Digital Network; a digital communication system that can transmit voice or packet data over a regular phone line at rates between 64Kbps and 256Kbps.

ISM   Industrial, Scientific, Medical; *see* 2.4GHz band.

ISO number   The standard rating for film or CCD sensitivity. The higher the ISO number, the greater the sensitivity.

ISP   Internet service provider; a company that connects individual users (calling in using traditional phone lines) to the Internet. Some Internet service providers—such as America Online—also provide unique content to their subscribers.

iTV   Interactive Television; television with interactive content and enhancements.

J

jaggies   The stairstepped appearance of a curved or angled line in a low-resolution image. Increasing the resolution (number of pixels) will decrease or eliminate jaggies.

jargon   Technical language from a special activity or group, often gobbledy-gook that sounds more important than it really is.

Java   A programming language used to develop sophisticated interactive Web pages and applications. Java was created and licensed by Sun Microsystems and is not always supported by Microsoft applications.

JavaScript   A scripting language used to create advanced Web page functionality—rollovers, pull-down menus, and other special effects. JavaScript has more in common with HTML than it does with Java, which is a full-fledged programming language.

junk email   Another name for *spam*.

K

Kb   Kilobit; approximately 1,000 bits (1,024, to be precise).

KB   Kilobyte; 1,000 bytes, more or less. (Actually, it's 1,024 bytes.)

Kbps   Kilobits per second.

KBps   Kilobytes per second.

kernel   The central part of an operating system that oversees all other operations. The kernel loads first and stays in the memory throughout the operation of the OS.

key (1) A folder that contains specific settings in the Windows Registry.

key (2) A code—actually, a really big number—that works with a cryptographic algorithm to produce a specific encrypted result.

keyboard The thing that looks like a typewriter that you use to type instructions to your computer.

keylogger Software or hardware that records the individual keystrokes entered by a user.

keystroke logger *See* keylogger.

keyword A word that forms all or part of a search engine query.

KHz Kilohertz (thousands of cycles per second).

L

LAN Local Area Network; a communications network that serves users within a relatively small area. Most LANs serve just one building or a group of buildings. The users' individual PCs are workstations (clients) that access the servers as needed.

LAN access point A base station used to connect wireless devices to a local area network.

landscape mode Viewing an image where the width is greater than the height.

laser disc An older laser-based format for delivering audio/video programming on 12-inch discs. Laser discs deliver 425 lines of nondigital horizontal resolution, whereas DVDs deliver 500 lines, digitally.

laser printer A type of nonimpact printer that creates an electrostatic image of an entire page on a photosensitive drum, using a laser beam. An ultrafine coated powder (called *toner*) is applied to the drum, and then transferred to a sheet of paper, creating the printed image.

launch To start a program.

LCD Liquid Crystal Display; a flat-screen display device in which images are created by light transmitted through a layer of liquid crystals.

LCD projector A type of video projector that generates a picture using a liquid crystal display, which is then projected through a magnifying lens.

LD *See* laser disc.

LDAP Lightweight Directory Access Protocol; a type of service that acts like a virtual "white pages" to directories of email addresses.

legacy Older hardware that is not compliant with the Plug-and-Play standard.

lens A device, made of ground glass, for focusing light rays onto a CCD or film.

letterbox A way to display wide-screen images on a standard 4:3 aspect ratio video display, by introducing black bars above and below the picture.

light-valve projector A type of video projector that combines LCD and CRT projection technology.

limiter A signal processor used to keep audio signals from exceeding a set level.

line doubler *See* line multiplier.

line level The standard volume level for routing audio signals. For pro audio gear, line level is set at +4dBv and for consumer gear it is -10dBv.

line multiplier A circuit that doubles, triples, or quadruples the number of lines that make up a picture, perceptively increasing picture detail while decreasing the incidence of flicker and visible scan lines.

link *See* hyperlink.

Linux A Unix-like operating system that runs on many different types of computers. Many different versions of Linux are available, even though it's not necessarily a user-friendly operating system; in fact, it's not recommended for general consumer use (although it does have a cult following among programmers and dedicated Microsoft haters). Linux was created by Linus Torvalds while he was a college student at the University of Helsinki in Finland. Instead of making it proprietary and trying to sell it, Torvalds gave it away, so anyone who wanted to develop for it could do so.

list merchant A company that buys and sells mailing lists.

Listserv A form of email mailing list.

LNB   Low Noise Blocker; a small amplifier located on the arm of a satellite dish that receives digital satellite transmissions.

log file   A computer file that contains a record of specific user or program activity.

log in   The requirement that one "registers" with one's computer or network before being granted access.

LPT   The typical designation for a computer's connection to a printer or other device through a parallel port. The name originally stood for "line printer terminal," but the LPT port can be used for other devices as well, such as a video camera.

luminance   The brightness or black-and-white component of a color video signal; determines the level of picture detail.

lurker   Someone who reads message board and discussion group postings, but seldom (if ever) participates himself.

M

macro   A series of instructions, using a simple coding language, used to automate procedures in a computer application; macros are typically attached to individual documents or templates.

macro virus   A macro that contains malicious code.

mailing list   A discussion group conducted using email.

malware   "Malicious software," shorthand for any virus, Trojan, or worm.

mattress tag   A Web site disclaimer or TOS that few, if any, users read or pay attention to—much like those "do not remove under penalty of law" tags found on new mattresses.

Mb   Megabit; one million bits, more or less.

MB   Megabyte; approximately one million bytes (1,048,576, to be precise).

Mbps   Megabits per second.

MBps   Megabytes per second.

MBR   Master Boot Record; a software routine placed at the very beginning of a hard disk that analyzes the disk partition table, loads the hard disk's boot sector into system memory, and then passes control to the boot sector.

megapixel   A way of measuring image resolution in digital photography. One megapixel equals a million pixels; the higher the megapixel rating, the better quality the picture.

memory   Temporary electronic storage for data and instructions, via electronic impulses on a chip.

menu   A selection of items or services.

meta search   A search of searches; a process where queries are submitted to multiple search engines or directories simultaneously.

META tag   A special HTML tag that identifies a Web page's contents. META tags do not have any influence on the appearance of the page, but instead hold information such as keywords for search engines, descriptions of the site, and update histories. The information in META tags is often used in the indexes of search engines.

MHz   Megahertz; one million hertz. (A hertz is a measurement of frequency; in the case of computers, the speed of a microprocessor is measured in megahertz.)

microprocessor   The chip inside your system unit that processes all the operations your computer can do; a microprocessor includes a CPU and is the brain of any computing device.

Microsoft   The company that developed and publishes the Windows operating system and hundreds of other best-selling programs, including Office, Excel, and Word.

MIDI   Musical Instrument Digital Interface (pronounced "middy"); a standard protocol for communication between musical devices such as synthesizers and PC sound cards. At minimum, MIDI defines the codes for a musical event, such as a note's pitch, length, volume, and other attributes, such as vibrato, attack, and delay time. The MIDI standard is supported by most synthesizers, allowing MIDI music to be played by an orchestra of separate MIDI instruments.

MIME   Multipurpose Internet Mail Extensions; a protocol that specifies how binary files are encoded, so that any email program can correctly interpret the file type.

Mini DV   Digital video recording format for camcorders that uses an ultrasmall cassette.

mirror   A copy of a Web site, located on a different server on the Internet. Many sites "mirror" their information on multiple servers to prevent overloading of their main site.

modem   Modulator-Demodulator; a hardware device that enables transmission of digital data from one computer to another over common telephone lines via modulating and demodulating. It's the most common way in which people connect to the Internet.

modifier   A symbol that causes a search engine to do something special with the word directly following the symbol. Three modifiers are used almost universally in the search engine community: **+**, **-**, and " ".

modulator   That part of a radio that oscillates a radio wave to a specific frequency.

molecular manufacturing   *See* nanotechnology.

monitor   The thing that looks like a TV screen that displays all your computer text and graphics.

monopole   The most common type of speaker that fires in only one direction (forward); compare with *bipole* and *dipole* speakers that fire in two opposing directions.

Mosaic   The very first Web browser, developed in 1993 by the National Center for Supercomputing Applications (NCSA) at the University of Illinois at Urbana-Champaign.

motherboard   The big board that makes up the bulk of the insides of your system unit. The motherboard holds your main microprocessor and memory chips and also contains slots to plug in additional boards (cards).

mouse   The handheld device with a rollerball and buttons you use to navigate through Windows and other graphical applications.

mouse potato   A person who spends too much time in front of his or her computer.

MPEG2   The method of compressing digital video signals used by DVDs, digital broadcast satellites, and digital and high-definition television.

ms   Millisecond.

MS-DOS   The Microsoft-specific version of DOS.

MSN   Microsoft Network; Microsoft's commercial online service and ISP.

MUD   Multi-User Dungeon (or Dimension); a multiple-user simulated environment, used either for gaming or for community.

multimedia   The combination, usually on a computer, of interactive text, graphics, audio, and video.

multipartite virus   A virus that combines file infection and boot sector infection.

multiplier   The function that determines the speed of the processor, which, in turn, is a multiple of the bus speed.

multitasking   The capability to run more than one application at a time.

multitrack recording   The process of recording multiple sound sources to individual isolated tracks that are synchronized to record and play back in time.

mW   Milliwatt; one-thousandth of a watt.

N

nanite   *See* nanomachine.

nanobot   A specialized *nanomachine* designed to repeatedly perform a specific task or set of tasks. Nanobots (also called *nanorobots*) have dimensions measured in *nanometers*.

nanomachine   A mechanical or electromechanical device whose dimensions are measured in *nanometers*. Also called a *nanite*.

nanometer   One-millionth of a millimeter.

nanorobot   *See* nanobot.

nanotechnology   A branch of engineering that deals with the design and manufacturer of electronic circuits and mechanical devices built at the molecular level of matter. Also called *molecular manufacturing*.

Napster A (now defunct) peer-to-peer file-sharing network developed to trade mass amounts of music files over the Internet. Napster was forced to shut down under a barrage of copyright lawsuits from the major music labels.

Net Shorthand for *Internet*.

Net police Self-appointed individuals who try to impose their standards on other Internet users; most often seen in newsgroups, mailing lists, and other similar online communities.

netiquette The etiquette of the Internet.

Netscape Navigator Netscape's Web browser software.

network Two or more computers connected together. The Internet is the largest network in the world.

newbie Newer, inexperienced user.

newsgroup A special-interest discussion group, hosted on Usenet.

newsreader A software program used to read Usenet newsgroup messages.

Ni-Cad Nickel Cadmium (pronounced "ny-cad"); a type of rechargeable battery used in portable computers and devices. To prevent damage to the battery, Ni-Cad batteries should be completely discharged before recharging.

NIC Network Interface Card; an add-on card that enables a computer to be connected to a network.

NiMH Nickel Metal Hydride; a type of rechargeable battery used in portable computers and other devices. Has a longer life than Ni-Cad batteries, and can be recharged at any time without damage.

NNTP Network News Transport Protocol; the protocol used by client and server software to carry Usenet postings across the Internet.

node Any single computer connected to a network.

nomepage A home page with little or no content.

NTSC National Television System Committee; the industry group that established the current North American analog broadcast TV standard. Sometimes refers to the standard itself.

O

OBEX Object Exchange; an industry protocol that describes how data objects are transferred from one device to another.

OCR Optical Character Recognition; the reading of text on paper and translation of those images into a form that computer users can manipulate. When a text document is scanned into the computer, it is turned into a bitmap, or picture, of the text. OCR software identifies letters and numbers by analyzing the light and dark areas of the bitmap. When it recognizes a character, it converts it into ASCII text.

OEM Original Equipment Manufacturer; a company that buys computers in bulk from a manufacturer, and then customizes the machines and sells them under its own name. The term is a misnomer because OEMs aren't the original manufacturers.

OLE Object Linking and Embedding. The Microsoft standard for creating automatically updated links between documents; also the standard for embedding a document created by one application into a document created by another.

OMR Open Mail Relay; an unprotected server that can be used to initiate mass emailings.

online communications Any and all communications between one computer and another over phone lines, via modem.

opacity A measurement of how easily light passes through paper.

open source Software for which the underlying programming code is available (free) for users to make changes to it and build new versions incorporating those changes.

operating system The core system software that lets you (and your software programs) communicate with your hardware.

optical zoom A traditional zoom lens that enables you to move the focus closer to the subject, thus enlarging the image.

OS Operating system.

oscillator   An electrical device that uses varying voltages to oscillate at different frequencies, thereby producing musical notes.

overclocking   Running your processor at a speed faster than it's rated. Most processors can run faster than their rated speed with some sacrifice of reliability.

oversampling   A technique in which each sample coming from the D/A converter is sampled multiple times. The samples are then interpolated creating an antialiasing effect.

P

P2P   Peer-to-peer; a communications network where two or more computers work together as equals, without benefit of a central server.

packet   Part of a larger piece of data. When sent from one device to another (or over the Internet or other networks), data objects are typically broken up into multiple packets for easier transmittal.

packet sniffer   A software program that examines the contents of data packets flowing over a network or the Internet.

packet switching   The method used to move data around the Internet, in small, easily manageable packets.

PAL   The European broadcast standard.

PAN   Personal Area Network; a small network comprised of all the personal electronics devices used by a single person.

pan-and-scan   A technique used to display the most important parts of a wide-screen image on a narrower 4:3 ratio screen. The name comes from the panning and scanning necessary to keep the focus on the most important part of the scene, which is not always in the direct center of the picture.

parallel   A type of external port used to connect printers and other similar devices.

password   A special encrypted "word" (composed of any combination of letters and numbers) that one enters to obtain access to a computer, network, or Web site.

password cracker   Software than can decrypt passwords or otherwise disable or bypass password protection.

paste   To place data cut or copied from another location into a new location.

patch   A sound created by a synthesizer. The term comes from the early days of modular synthesis when modules were "patched" together to produce different sounds.

patch bay   An electrical panel that, ideally, contains an input and output for the various devices used in an audio studio. It serves as a central point to connect the various devices together.

path   The collection of folders and subfolders (listed in order of hierarchy) that hold a particular file.

payload   The deliverable aspect of a computer virus; the noticeable effects of a virus attack.

PC   *See* personal computer.

PC Card   A credit-card–size memory or I/O device that fits into a desktop PC, portable PC, and some PDAs. Formerly known as a *PCMCIA card*.

PCM   Pulse Code Modulation; a way of encoding audio data as a series of pulses, with each pulse defining a binary 1 or 0.

PCMCIA   Personal Computer Memory Card International Association; an industry group formed to promote the adoption of credit-card–size memory and I/O devices.

PCMCIA card   *See* PC Card.

PDA   Personal Digital Assistant; a handheld device that organizes personal information, combining computing and networking features. A typical PDA includes an address book and a to-do list. Some function as cell phones and fax senders. Unlike portable computers, which use a keyboard for input, most PDAs incorporate a stylus and some sort of handwriting recognition capability. PDAs are sometimes called palm, pocket, or handheld PCs.

peer-to-peer   *See* P2P.

peer-to-peer file-swapping   The act of exchanging files among similar computers over a peer-to-peer network.

peripheral   Add-on hardware device for a computer system, such as a printer or a modem.

personal computer   A multifunction hardware unit that includes a hard disk, memory chips, microprocessor chip, and monitor. Personal computers perform tasks when enabled by *software* entered into memory.

personal firewall   Firewall software designed for a home or small-business PC.

pervasive computing   The use of numerous, easily accessible computing devices to conduct everyday activities.

PGP   Pretty Good Privacy; one of the most popular tools for a form of public-key encryption.

phreaker   An individual who cracks into telecommunications systems.

PIM   Personal Information Manager; a computer program that manages contact and scheduling data.

PIN   Personal Identification Number; a secret code number that must be entered by the user to gain access to a particular device or service.

PING   Packet INternet Groper; an Internet utility that determines whether a particular IP address is online. Administrators use it to test and debug a network by sending out a packet and waiting for a response.

pink noise   A random audio signal that has equal energy across its frequency range.

PIP   Picture-In-Picture; the display of a second picture in a small window within a larger picture.

pixel   The individual picture elements that make up a video image. The unit of measurement used in measuring the quality of screen displays.

pixelization   The stairstepped appearance of a curved or angled line in a digital image; *see* jaggies.

PKC   Public Key Cryptography; *see* public-key encryption.

plain-text email   Email messages that incorporate text only, without any HTML code.

plasma display   A flat-panel video display that uses plasma gas to "light up" individual pixels in a picture.

playlist   A list of songs that can be organized in the order to be played. Most media player programs and portable digital players let you create customized playlists of songs.

Plug and Play   Hardware that includes its manufacturer and model information in its ROM, enabling Windows to recognize it immediately upon startup and install the necessary drivers if not already set up.

plug-in   A type of program that integrates with a larger application to add a special capability to it.

point-to-point   A direct connection of one device to a second device.

polymorphic virus   A file-infector virus that is capable of changing itself as it travels from one system to another.

POP (1)   Point of Presence; a telephone number that gives you dial-up access. Internet service providers (ISPs) generally provide many POPs so that users can make a local call to gain Internet access.

POP (2)   Post Office Protocol; a protocol used to retrieve email from a mail server.

POP (3)   Picture-Outside-Picture; a second, smaller picture, typically on a widescreen TV, that displays outside the main picture window.

pop-under window   A pop-up window that hides itself behind other open windows on your desktop.

pop-up menu   The context-sensitive menu that appears when you right-click an object.

pop-up window   A small browser window, typically without menus or other navigational elements, that opens seemingly of its own accord when you visit or leave another Web site.

port (1)   An interface on a computer to which you can connect a device. Personal computers have various types of ports. Internally, there are several ports for connecting disk drives, display screens, and keyboards. Externally, there are ports for connecting modems, printers, mice, and other peripheral devices.

port (2)   A virtual access point into a computer. Internet services use specific ports on computers used as Web servers.

port scanner   Software that looks for open ports on other computers. Also called *port sniffer*.

portal   A Web site that provides a gateway to the Internet, as well as a collection of other content and services. Most of today's portals (Yahoo!, Excite, and so on) started life as search engines or directories.

portrait mode   Viewing an image where the height is greater than the width.

POTS   Plain Old Telephone Service; traditional wired telephone service.

ppi   Pixels per inch.

PPP   Point-to-Point Protocol; a technical protocol that defines how Internet Protocol (IP) data is transmitted over serial point-to-point links.

preamplifier   An amplifier that is used to boost a low-level signal up to line level (approximately up 60dBv). Audio preamps also typically control or switch the various inputs from audio and video sources.

printer   The piece of computer hardware that lets you create hard-copy printouts of your documents.

private key   A secret key that can be used, either by itself or (in public-key encryption) in conjunction with a public key, to decrypt encrypted messages.

processor   The brains of the entire computer. The processor, which is where a computer's instructions are decoded and executed, performs all of its logical operations.

processor cache   The usually small amount of high-speed Static RAM (SRAM) that can significantly improve CPU performance. This cache resides between the CPU and the main system memory.

program   A term used interchangeably with *software*, a program is an organized list of instructions that tells a computer what to do. In other words, software is an executable version of a program; without programs, computers are useless.

progressive scanning   A method of displaying television pictures where the picture is displayed in a single pass, instead of the two fields used with *interlaced scanning*. A progressively scanned picture more accurately reproduces fast action and minimizes the visibility of flicker and scan lines. Typically denoted by a "p" after the resolution number, as in 480p (480 lines of resolution, progressively scanned).

protocol   An agreed-upon format for transmitting data between two devices.

proxy server   A server that buffers all incoming and outgoing communications between a network and the Internet.

PSTN   Public Switched Telephony Network; the traditional, old-fashioned, wired telephone network.

PTR   Personal Television Receiver. *See* DVR.

public key   A key, provided by some authority, that, when combined with a private key, can be used to decrypt encrypted messages.

public-key encryption   A means of encrypting data and messages using a combination of public and private keys.

pull-down list   A button with a down arrow that, when clicked, displays a list of further options or items.

PVR   Personal Video Recorder. *See* DVR.

Q

QoS   Quality of Service; the guaranteed performance for an application or process.

quantize   Forcing the notes in a MIDI sequence to fall on the nearest beat.

query   A word, phrase, or group of words, possibly combined with other syntax or operators, used to initiate a search with a search engine or directory.

queue   The list of print jobs that are ready for printing, paused, or currently printing. (Not to be confused with Que, the company that published this book!)

GLOSSARY

R

rack   A special type of storage shelf used to house pro audio gear.

RAM   Random Access Memory; a common type of temporary computer memory that functions as a machine's primary workspace. The more RAM your computer has, the more efficiently it will operate.

RAS   Remote Access Services; a Windows NT feature that allows remote users to log in to a LAN using a modem, X.25 connection, or WAN link.

raster   A pattern of horizontal lines displayed on a computer or TV monitor. As the part of a monitor's screen that is actually being used to display images, it's a bit smaller than the physical dimensions of the display screen itself. It varies for different resolutions.

read   How data is absorbed from a disk to your system's memory.

receiver   A component that combines a preamplifier, amplifier, and radio in a single chassis. Receivers that include inputs and outputs for video sources and display are called *audio/video receivers*.

Recycle Bin   The "trash can" on the Windows desktop that temporarily holds deleted files.

region codes   The codes embedded in DVD discs that define the global regions in which the disc can be played.

Registry   The Windows registration file that stores all configuration information.

Registry Editor   A utility (REGEDIT.EXE) used to edit the Windows Registry.

remailer   A service used to send anonymous email; the remailer strips out the header from the original message, then remails the now-anonymous message to its intended recipient.

removable media   Information storage that allow users to remove the stored information if necessary. Examples of removable media include disks and magnetic tapes.

resolution   The degree of clarity an image displays. The term is most often used to describe the sharpness of bitmapped images on monitors, but also applies to images on printed pages, as expressed by the number of dots per inch (dpi). For monitors, screen resolution signifies the number of dots (pixels) on the screen. For example, a 640×480 pixel screen can display 640 dots on each of 480 lines, or about 300,000 pixels. For television monitors, resolution is typically measured in terms of horizontal lines that can be seen or resolved. (*See* horizontal resolution.)

restore   The process of returning a backed-up file to its previous location, often from a disk or tape to a hard drive.

reverb   The persistence of an acoustic signal after the original signal has ceased.

RF   Radio Frequency; a means of transmitting and receiving signals via modulated radio waves.

RFC   Request For Comments; the process for creating new standards on the Internet.

RGB   Red, Green, Blue; the additive color model used in video displays.

right-click   The act of hovering over an item and then clicking your right mouse button; this often displays a pop-up menu of commands related to the object selected.

ripping   Copying music from a CD to your computer's hard disk.

robot (1)   *See* spider.

robot (2)   A machine designed to execute one or more tasks repeatedly, with speed and precision.

ROM   Read-Only Memory; a storage chip that typically contains hard-wired instructions for use when a computer starts up.

root directory   The main directory or folder on a disk.

router   A piece of hardware or software that handles the connection between two or more networks.

RPTV Rear-Projection Television; a video display device that uses three CRTs (or some similar method of light generation) to project a picture backward within a cabinet onto a mirror, which then reflects the picture onto the back of a translucent screen.

RSA A public-key encryption technology created by Ron Rivest, Adi Shamir, and Leonard Adleman of RSA Data Security, Inc. The key has two parts, one private and one public; both parts are required for decryption. Used in Netscape Navigator, Microsoft Internet Explorer, and other applications that require industrial-strength encryption, the RSA algorithm has become a standard, especially for data sent over the Internet.

RSI Repetitive Strain Injury; ailments of the hands, neck, back, and eyes due to computer use.

RTFM Read The F***ing Manual; a typical response to newbies asking stupid technology-related questions.

S

S/N Signal to Noise; *see* signal-to-noise ratio.

S/PDIF Sony/Philips Digital Interface; a digital-to-digital audio file transfer format. Carries up to 24-bit data.

S-VHS Super VHS; a variation on the standard VHS format that delivers sharper pictures (400 lines of resolution versus 240 lines for standard VHS).

S-Video A four-pin connection that transmits the chrominance (color) and luminance (brightness) portions of a video signal separately, for improved color accuracy and reduced distortion.

SA-CD Super-Audio CD; a new CD-based format that delivers better-than-CD-quality sound. Competes with *DVD-Audio*.

sampling frequency The rate at which measurements of an audio signal are taken during A/D and D/A conversion. A higher sampling rate makes for a higher-fidelity audio signal.

sandboxing The process of running a program within an isolated (or virtual) environment, thus protecting the computer system from any ill effects of virus infection during the test.

scan lines The horizontal lines, scanned one after another, that comprise the picture on a video display. (Don't confuse with *horizontal resolution*, which measures the visible number of lines in a display.)

scanner (1) A device that converts paper documents or photos into a format that can be viewed on a computer and manipulated by the user.

scanner (2) *See* sniffer.

scavenger bot *See* spambot.

screen saver A utility that prolongs the life of your monitor by blanking the screen—or providing a continuously moving image—while your monitor is not in use.

script kiddie A would-be cracker who isn't a technically adept programmer.

script language An easy-to-use pseudo-programming language that enables the creation of executable scripts composed of individual commands.

script virus A computer virus written in ActiveX, Java, JavaScript, or another computer script language.

SCSI Small Computer System Interface (pronounced "scuzzy"); the standard port for Macintosh computers, also common in PCs and Unix boxes. SCSI is really a family of interfaces, ranging from the relatively primitive SCSI-1 to the spiffy new Wide Ultra2 SCSI. SCSI hard drives are commonly used for audio applications because they generally can read and write data faster than can an IDE drive.

scumware Another word for *spyware*.

SDSL Symmetric Digital Subscriber Line; a type of DSL in which the upload and download speeds are the same.

search engine A Web server that indexes Web pages, and then makes the index available for user searching. Search engines differ from directories in that the indexes are generated using *spiders*, where directories are assembled manually. Search engine indexes typically include many more Web pages than are found in directories.

search site Generic term for a Web site that offers either a search engine or directory (or both).

search term *See* query.

secure server   A Web *server* that uses encryption to provide protected credit-card transactions.

semiconductor   A substance, usually a solid chemical element or compound, that can conduct electricity under some conditions but not others, making it a good medium for the control of electrical current. Its conductance varies depending on the current or voltage applied to a control electrode, or on the intensity of irradiation by infrared, visible light, ultraviolet, or X rays.

sequencer   A device that stores MIDI data.

serial   A type of external port used to connect communication devices, such as modems and PalmPilots.

server   A central computer on a network that responds to requests for information from one or more client computers. On the Internet, all Web pages are stored on servers; in a client/server relationship between two devices, the server is the device that is controlled by commands from the other device (client).

session hijacking   An attack where the attacker commandeers use of a computer, typically using some sort of back-door Trojan, to use that computer to attack another computer or network.

session key   A temporary key used to encrypt or decrypt a specific message.

setup   How you configure your system (or individual software or hardware).

shareware   Computer software distributed free, but requiring purchase to use beyond an initial period of time (or to use the full feature set).

shortcut (1)   A combination of two keys on your keyboard that, when pressed simultaneously, execute a specific function.

shortcut (2)   An icon on the desktop used to represent an application; click a shortcut to launch an application, or right-click to view and modify its properties.

shouting   WRITING IN ALL CAPS!

shutter   That part of a camera that opens and closes to control how long the film or CCD is exposed to light.

shutter speed   The length of time the shutter remains open when shooting an image.

SIG   Special Interest Group; a topic-specific subgroup within a larger organization.

signal-to-noise ratio   A measurement of the content portion of an audio or video signal in relation to the noise contained in the signal, expressed in decibels (dB). A higher S/N ratio indicates a quieter or less noisy signal. As an example, VHS VCRs have S/N ratios in the 40dB range, whereas DVDs have S/N ratios approaching 65dB.

signature   The identifying information you put at the bottom of all your email correspondence.

signature scanning   A method of scanning for computer viruses by matching known sequences of binary code.

SIMM   Single Inline Memory Module; a narrow circuit board that holds memory chips. It plugs into a SIMM socket on a motherboard or memory board. Unlike memory chips, SIMMs are measured in bytes rather than bits.

site   A unified collection of Web pages on the Internet.

sleeper   A virus or worm that resides, hidden, on a system, awaiting the delivery of its payload at some later date.

SLR   Single Lens Reflex; a film-based camera that enables you to look through a viewfinder and see through the lens.

SM   SmartMedia; a small memory storage card, similar to *Compact Flash*.

SMART   Self-Monitoring, Analysis, and Reporting Technology; an open standard within hardware and software that automatically monitors a disk drive's health and reports of potential failure. All major hard-drive manufacturers use SMART to detect imminent disk problems and report the danger to the computer user.

smart phone   A next-generation (3G) digital cellular phone that offers enhanced data and communications capabilities.

SmartMedia   *See* SM.

SMB Server Message Block; a file-sharing protocol that Windows uses to share files and resources, such as printers, across a network.

SMPT Simple Mail Transfer Protocol; the primary protocol used to send email from server to server on the Internet.

SMS Short Message Service; similar to paging, a service for sending messages of up to 160 characters to mobile phones.

snail mail Traditional U.S. Postal Service (USPS) mail.

sniffer Software used to determine a computer's online availability.

SNMP Simple Network Management Protocol; a set of standards used to manage communication between devices connected to a TCP/IP network.

social engineering A nontechnological means of conning another person into revealing user names, passwords, and other private information.

software A digital program that instructs a piece of hardware to perform a specific task.

sound card The card that processes audio data on a PC. It's often a PCI card, but it can also be USB or FireWire based—or it can be built into the computer's motherboard.

spam Junk email. Some people define spam as any unsolicited email. A narrower definition is unsolicited advertising, most commonly for credit cards, weight-loss methods, and pyramid schemes.

spamblock Any characters you insert in the middle of your email address to confuse spambot software.

spambot An automated software program that trolls the Web, Usenet newsgroups, and public message boards, looking for email addresses that are later used in spam mailings. (The name is short for "spam robot.")

spamming The act of sending large numbers of unsolicited email messages.

spamouflage When a spammer spoofs the sender's email address in a spam message.

spider A software program that follows hypertext links across multiple Web pages, but is not directly under human control. Spiders scan the Web, looking for URLs, automatically following all the hyperlinks on pages accessed. The results from a spider's search are used to create the indexes used by search engines.

spool Lining up multiple print jobs in a queue. These print jobs are said to be "spooled" to the printer.

spread spectrum A coding technique where a digital signal is spread among a range of frequencies, to reduce interference and increase security.

spreadsheet Software that simulates a paper spreadsheet, or worksheet, in which columns of numbers are summed for budgets and plans. A spreadsheet appears onscreen as a matrix of rows and columns, the intersections of which are identified as cells. Spreadsheets can have thousands of cells and can be scrolled horizontally and vertically to be viewed.

spyware Software used to surreptitiously monitor computer use (that is, spy on other users).

SQL Structured Query Language; a language used to send queries to databases.

SRAM Static RAM; RAM that retains data bits in its memory as long as power is being supplied. Unlike DRAM (dynamic random access memory), which stores bits in cells consisting of a capacitor and a transistor, SRAM does not have to be periodically refreshed.

SSL Secure Sockets Layer; a form of encryption used in secure servers.

standby mode A special mode on newer computer systems that powers down disk drives and monitors without actually shutting off the computer itself; often called *sleep* mode.

Start menu The menu used to start most Windows programs and utilities; visible when the Start button is clicked.

startup diskette A special diskette used to start Windows if something is wrong with the information on your hard disk.

stateful packet inspection A method of firewall protection that matches incoming traffic with outgoing requests.

stealth virus   A virus that hides itself when running, to avoid detection.

STN   Spanking the Net; surfing the Web for adult-oriented material.

streaming   Refers to the continuous transmission of data, typically audio or video, so it can be processed as a steady stream. With streaming, the client browser or plug-in can start displaying the data as sound and pictures before the entire file has been transmitted.

stylus   A penlike device used to operate the touch screen on a PDA.

subwoofer   A speaker specially designed to reproduce a range of very low frequencies—typically 20Hz–200Hz. Subwoofers are common in home theater systems to enhance the reproduction of low bass in movie soundtracks.

suite   A set of applications designed to work together. A suite typically includes word processing, spreadsheet, presentation graphics, and database programs.

SuperDisk   A portable storage medium from Sony that can hold up to 120MB of data; SuperDisk drives can read and write information to and from older 3 1/2-inch disks.

surge suppressor   A device that protects your system from unwanted power-line surges.

surround sound   The experience of being surrounded by sound from a video or audio source. Typically achieved with a surround-sound decoder (either Dolby Digital or Dolby Pro Logic) and multiple speakers.

SVGA   Super Visual Graphics Array; a graphics display of 1280×1024 pixels, using 16 million different colors.

symmetrical   A type of connection that operates at the same speed both upstream and downstream.

symmetric-key encryption   A means of encrypting data where both parties (sender and recipient) have access to the same private key.

synching   The process of linking two devices together to exchange data or work from the same documents. For example, a DAT can be synched to a PC and be used to store audio data while still being controlled by the PC.

synchronous   A type of connection that permits data to flow in two directions, simultaneously. Also known as *full-duplex*.

sysop   System Operator; a person responsible for the physical operation of a computer system or network.

system disk   A disk containing the operating system and all files necessary to start your computer.

system file   A key file used by the computer's operating system.

system unit   That part of your computer system that looks like a big beige box. The system unit typically contains your microprocessor, system memory, hard disk drive, floppy disk drives, and various cards.

T

T-1   A leased-line connection capable of carrying data at 1.5Mbps; typically used for fast Internet connections to large corporations.

T-3   A leased-line connection capable of carrying data at 44.7Mbps.

tab   The top of a "page" in a dialog box; many dialog boxes display multiple sets of data on a series of tabs.

table   A collection of data organized into rows and columns.

Taskbar   The bar at the bottom of the screen (normally) in Windows; the Start button and temporary buttons for active applications appear on the Taskbar.

TCP/IP   Transmission Control Protocol/Internet Protocol; the protocol used for communications on the Internet. It coordinates the addressing and packaging of the data packets that make up any communication.

technospeak   *See* jargon.

telecommunications   How your computer talks to other computers, using a modem.

telephoto lens   A camera lens with a focal length greater than 50mm; makes far subjects appear closer than through a standard lens.

Telnet   An older command and program used to log in to and access data stored on an Internet server.

terabyte   One thousand gigabytes.

terminal   A device with a screen and keyboard that relies on a mainframe or another computer for intelligence.

THD   Total Harmonic Distortion; a measurement of the noise generated by an amplifier or receiver. The lower the number, the better.

thread   A group of related messages in a newsgroup, mailing list, or message board.

thumbnail   A miniature representation of a page or image. Thumbnails often take considerable time to generate, but provide a convenient way to browse through multiple images before retrieving the one you need. A number of programs let you click on the thumbnail to retrieve the item it represents or view the picture at a larger size.

THX   A set of high-fidelity standards, above and beyond the Dolby Digital standard, for both home theater equipment and prerecorded programming.

Time Division Duplexing   A scheme wherein two different transmissions can share the same frequency for full-duplex communication, by dividing each frequency into time slots; the two transmissions alternate transmitting and receiving at preset intervals.

timecode   Timecode is a signal that contains a chronological record of the absolute time in a recording. It is used for synchronizing different recorders and for electronic editing. Timecode was initially invented for motion pictures as a method of synchronizing the pictures recorded in the frames of a camera with the sound recorded on a tape recorder.

toner   Ultrafine coated powder, typically stored in some sort of cartridge, used by laser printers to create printed images on paper.

TOS   Terms Of Service; the legal restrictions you allegedly agree to before you enter a Web site.

Tray   The area of the Windows Taskbar that holds icons for "background" utilities, such as the Windows clock.

Trojan horse   A malicious program that pretends to be another, harmless program or file.

troll   A user who posts only to inflame other newsgroup or mailing list users.

TrueType   A scalable font technology that renders fonts for both the printer and the screen. Originally developed by Apple, it was enhanced jointly by Apple and Microsoft.

Twain   The standard used to acquire digital images from scanners and digital cameras.

tweeter   A speaker designed to reproduce very high frequencies, typically those over 5KHz or so.

U

UBE   Unsolicited Bulk Email; another name for *spam*.

UCE   Unsolicited Commercial Email; another name for *spam*.

unbalanced   A connector that has a positive conductor that's surrounded by the negative conductor.

Uncle Joe   A Web site that loads very slowly. (As in the character of Uncle Joe from the old *Petticoat Junction* TV show.)

undelete   Unerase. Bring a file back from the dead.

uninstall   Deleting a software application—and all its associated files, drivers, and associations—from a computer system.

Unix   A computer operating system. Unix is designed to be used by many people at the same time and has TCP/IP built in.

upgrade   To add a new or improved peripheral or part to your system hardware. Also to install a newer version of an existing piece of software.

upholstery   Useless graphics on a Web page.

upload   The act of copying a file from a personal computer to a Web site or Internet server.

UPnP   Universal Plug and Play; a standard that uses Internet and Web protocols to enable various devices (PCs, peripherals, and so on) to be plugged into a network and automatically know about one another.

URL Uniform Resource Locator; the address of a Web page.

USB Universal Serial Bus; an external bus standard that supports data transfer rates of 12Mbps (12 million bits per second). One USB port can connect up to 127 peripheral devices, such as keyboards, modems, and mice. USB also supports hot plugging and Plug-and-Play installation.

Usenet A subset of the Internet used to exchange messages between users, using topic-specific *newsgroups*.

Uuencode When it was new, uuencode stood for Unix-to-Unix encode, but gradually it became a universal protocol for transferring files between platforms such as Unix, Windows, and Macintosh. It's a set of algorithms that converts files into a series of 7-bit ASCII characters that can be transmitted over the Internet.

V

V-Chip Government-mandated chip included in newer television sets that can block the display of inappropriate programming.

value The program setting that defines a specific key in the Windows Registry.

vaporware New computer software that's been announced but never seems to be released.

VCR Video Cassette Recorder; a device that records audio and video signals on videotape cassettes.

Veronica Very Easy Rodent Oriented Netwide Index to Computerized Archives; an early method of indexing and searching Gopher servers.

VGA Video Graphics Array; a graphics display of 640×480 pixels with 256 colors.

VHS Today's standard videocassette format.

VHS HiFi A variation on the standard VHS format that includes high-fidelity stereo sound. VHS HiFi VCRs can also play back tapes encoded with Dolby Pro Logic surround sound—although they can't reproduce Dolby Digital soundtracks.

VHS-C A recording format for camcorders that uses standard VHS-format tape in a smaller-shelled cassette.

video Picture.

virtual memory Hard disk space used by Windows as transient memory.

virus A bad, nasty, evil computer program that can infect your computer system and cause untold damage to your data. *See* computer virus.

virus scanner A computer utility, typically part of an antivirus program, that searches for suspicious program code.

Visual Basic Based on the BASIC computer programming language, Microsoft's Visual Basic was one of the first products to provide a graphical programming environment and a paint metaphor for developing user interfaces. With Visual Basic, a programmer can add or delete code by dragging and dropping controls, such as buttons and dialog boxes, instead of worrying about syntax details.

Visual Basic Script Also called VBScript or VBS, this is an extension to Microsoft's Visual Basic language specifically designed for developing World Wide Web applications. VBScript is widely used as the scripting language in Active Server Pages.

VPN Virtual Private Network; a network in which some parts are connected via the public Internet, but encrypted, so that the network is "virtually" private.

VRAM Video RAM (pronounced "vee-ram"); a memory chip designed specifically for video applications.

W

WAIS Wide Area Information Servers; a software program that enables the indexing of huge quantities of information across the Internet and other networks.

WAN Wide Area Network; a connection between two or more local area networks (LANs). Wide area networks can be made up of interconnected smaller networks spread throughout a building, a state, or the globe.

WAP Wireless Application Protocol; a standard for providing cellular phones, pagers, and other handheld devices with secure access to email and text-based Web pages. WAP features the Wireless Markup Language (WML), a streamlined version of HTML for small-screen displays. It also uses WMLScript, a compact JavaScript-like language that runs in limited memory.

war driving   The act of driving around a business district with specific electronic equipment, looking for insecure wireless networks.

warez   Pronounced "wheres," this is illegally distributed software, from which normal copy protection has been cracked or removed.

watt   A unit of power of energy.

Web   *See* World Wide Web.

Web beacon   *See* Web bug.

Web browser   *See* browser.

Web bug   A small, typically transparent graphics file (typically 1×1 pixel) hidden in an HTML email message, that is loaded from an advertising site and drops cookies on your hard disk.

Web ring   A navigation system that links related Web sites together. Each ring links sites that pertain to a particular topic.

WEP   Wireless Equivalent Privacy; the encryption and security protocol for Wi-Fi networks.

white noise   A random noise that contains an equal amount of energy per frequency band. That is, 100–200, 800–900, and 3000–3100. Pink noise has an equal amount of energy per octave. The bands 0–200, 800–1600, and 3000–6000 all contain the same amount of energy.

WHOIS   An Internet lookup service used to trace the owner of a specific Web page or domain.

wide screen   A picture with an aspect ratio wider than 4:3 or 1.33:1.

wide-angle lens   A camera lens with a focal length less than 50mm; it gives a wider field of view than normal lenses.

WiFi   The 802.11b wireless networking standard; short for "wireless fidelity."

wildcard   A character that substitutes for one or more characters within a query. For example, the * wildcard typically substitutes for any combination of characters.

Windows   The generic name for all versions of Microsoft's graphical operating system.

WLAN   Wireless LAN; a local area network composed of wireless connections between devices.

woofer   A driver within a speaker enclosure that uses a large cone to reproduce bass frequencies.

word   One sample of audio data.

wordclock   A sync pulse that lets devices determine the start of each digital word. When multiple digital devices are connected together, it's vital that each device knows where a digital word starts and stops; otherwise, dropout or distortion can result.

World Wide Web   A subset of the Internet that contains HTML pages.

worm   A parasitic computer program that replicates but does not infect other files.

wow and flutter   Measures the accuracy of a cassette deck's playback speed; the lower, the better.

write   How data is placed on a disk.

WYSIWYG   What You See Is What You Get (pronounced "whizzy wig"); refers to display or printouts that accurately reflect the original documents or images.

WWW   *World Wide Web*.

X

XGA   eXtended Graphics Array; a graphics display of 1024×768 pixels, with 65,000 colors.

XLR   A connector that's used to carry balanced audio signals.

XML   eXtensible Markup Language; a scripting language designed especially for Web documents that lets programmers create customized tags which provide functionality not available in HTML. Not only does it make the language easier to understand, it also lets you search and extract information. This can be particularly helpful for use in databases.

XNS   eXtensible Name Service; combines the technology of XML with Web agents.

Y–Z

Yahoo!   The most popular portal and directory on the Web.

Zip drive   A portable storage medium from Iomega that can hold between 100MB (originally) and 250MB of data.

zombie (1)   A computer that has been hijacked by another computer, typically with malicious intent.

zombie (2)   A dead program or process that occupies memory but is no longer functional but will not go away.

A TOUR OF TECHTV

TechTV is the only 24-hour cable television network dedicated to showcasing the impact technology has on our everyday lives and the world at large. By creating and delivering entertaining and insightful programming regarding today's and tomorrow's technology news, events, products, and people, TechTV enables viewers to stay current and connected with all things related to technology.

Offering more than a cable television channel, TechTV delivers a fully integrated Web site. TechTV.com enhances the TV viewing experience with compelling companion content and interactivity.

TechTV is owned by Vulcan Inc.

AUDIENCE

TechTV appeals to people who are excited by and curious about the many aspects of technology. By using technology as the backdrop, TechTV entertains, amazes and provides its viewers with insight into how technology enriches our lifestyles and the world around us.

WEB SITE

TechTV.com allows viewers to participate in programming, provide feedback, interact with hosts, send video emails, and further explore the latest tech content featured on the television cable network. In addition, TechTV.com has one of the Web's most extensive technology-specific video-on-demand (VOD) features, offering users immediate access to more than 5,000 videos, as well as expanded tech content of more than 2,000 in-depth articles.

INTERNATIONAL

TechTV is the world's largest producer and distributor of television programming about technology. TechTV delivers a 24-hour international version via satellite that reaches all of Asia, the Pacific, and the Middle East. TechTV Canada is a "must-carry" digital channel that launched in September 2001.

NETWORK PROGRAM GUIDE

Big Thinkers

$$\beta \iota g \; \mathcal{T} h \div \iota n K e R \int$$

www.techtv.com/bigthinkers

Explore the future of technology through insightful and down-to-earth interviews with the industry's most influential thinkers and innovators of our time.

Call For Help

www.techtv.com/callforhelp

Host Chris Pirillo translates technical jargon into plain English, provides computing tips, answers live viewer questions, and interviews guests who help demystify technology. It's interactive, informative, and above all, fun.

CyberCrime

www.techtv.com/cybercrime

Hosts Alex Wellen and Jennifer London take an inside look at fraud, hacking, viruses, identity theft, and invasions of privacy, to keep users secure and aware of the potential dangers on the Internet.

Extended Play

www.techtv.com/extendedplay

Host Adam Sessler provides comprehensive reviews of the hottest new games on the market, and previews of games in development and tips on how to score the biggest thrills and avoid the worst spills in gaming.

Eye Drops

www.techtv.com/eyedrops

Breathtaking, beautiful, compelling, insightful, and sometimes even a little scary, but always entertaining, *Eye Drops* has something for everyone. *Eye Drops* showcases today's best computer-generated animated short subjects.

Fresh Gear

www.techtv.com/freshgear

Host Sumi Das takes an in-depth look at the coolest new products out there from color PDAs to ultra-light notebooks, digital cameras to PVRs, virtual operating rooms to wearable computers. Catch reviews of the latest products, get advice on what to buy and what to bypass, and explore the technologies of tomorrow.

Future Fighting Machines

www.techtv.com/futurefightingmachines

Future Fighting Machines takes a look at the latest in military hardware and gadgets, from electromagnetic energy weapons, to high-tech soldiers' uniforms with built-in mine detectors, to flying spying micro-robots.

Max Headroom

www.techtv.com/maxheadroom

In a cyberpunk future where television is the fabric that binds society, Max Headroom is a computer-generated TV host at Network 23.

The Screen Savers

www.techtv.com/screensaver

TechTV's daily live variety show hosted by Leo Laporte and Patrick Norton features guest interviews and celebrities, remote field pieces, product advice and demos, and software reviews.

The Tech Of...

www.techtv.com/thetechof

From the food we eat, to the sports we play, to buildings where we work, technology has a profound impact on the way we live. *The Tech Of…* is an engaging series that goes behind the scenes of modern life and shows you the technology that makes things tick.

Tech Live

www.techtv.com/news

Tech Live focuses on the technology world's most important people, companies, products, and issues and how they affect consumers, investors, and the industry through interviews, product reviews, advice, and technology analysis.

Technogames

www.techtv.com/technogames

Homemade machines, robots, and electronic devices face off in a high-tech international competition from London's Millennium Dome. Innovation and technical excellence are tested as robots compete at cycling, swimming, high jump, rope climb, solar-powered marathon, and shot put.

TechTV's Titans of Tech

www.techtv.com/titansoftech

Through insightful interviews and in-depth profiles, *Titans of Tech* offer viewers an informed look at where the new economy is headed. These specials profile technology's most important movers and shakers—the CEOs, entrepreneurs, and visionaries driving today's tech economy.

Tomorrow's World

www.techtv.com/tomorrowsworld

The BBC's *Tomorrow's World* takes a look at the latest innovation and discovery in medicine, space, entertainment, sports, transportation, and law enforcement. Featuring reports from every corner of the globe, *Tomorrow's World* is a fascinating, informed, and fact-based view of the future of technology.

INDEX

F

F-Secure Inc.Web site, 428
Facemail program, 234
FactMonster Web site, 87
faded images, fixing (Photoshop
Elements), 79
fair access policies, satellite broad-
band access, 64
Fair Labor Standards Act of 1938,
328
fake desktop prank, 107
Family Fun Game Finder online
games, 132
family tree sites, 295
FamilySearchWeb site, 295
fantasy football sites, 269
Fantom USB 2.0, 306
Farnsworth, Philo T., 257
Fast ForWord program (learning-dis-
abled), 273
FastCPU utility, overclocking (Palm),
74
FCC (Federal Communications
Commission), 64, 68, 423
Federal Emergency Management
Agency (FEMA) Web site, 347
Federal Highway Administration
Web site, 347
Federal Radio Commission, 67
Feed The Pig game, 112
Fellowes.com Web site, 66
Fermi, Enrico, 372
Feynman, Richard, 375
File & Web Sharing, disabling (Mac
OS X), 9
file extensions
dangerous types, 11
forced, 107
File Transfer Protocol. *See* FTP
files
backups, 17
deleting from hard drive (Tolvanen
Eraser), 252
encrypting, 16
sending
via AOL Instant Messenger, 54
via Yahoo! Messenger, 53
Filez application (Palm), 66
fill flash, applying (Photoshop
Elements), 321
fill light, 319
film scanners, 318
FilterGate tool, 250

filtering email (Outlook Express), 234
Findgift.com Web site, 149
FindLaw Web site, 86
FindSounds.com Web site, 224
fingerprint IDs, 232
Fink, Unix application installer utility,
29
firewalls
enabling (Windows XP), 14
function of, 14
hacker pranks, 255
hardware, 14
installing, 14
limitations, 196
Mac OS X
BrickHouse, 342
built-in, 342
configuring, 14
Shields Up, 342
ShieldsUp utility, 14
testing, 14
Tiny Personal Firewall, 14
vulnerabilities (Windows XP), 14
ZoneAlarm, 14
FireWire (IEEE 1394/iLink), 32,
227-228
First Thanksgiving Web site, 365
FirstGov Web site, 86
FishSearch.com Web site, 86
Fitlinxx.com Web site, 192
fitness
commercial sites, 193
noncommercial sites, 193
FitnessZone Web site, 12
fixes, operating system bugs, 10
Flag Etiquette Web site, 186
flagging messages (Outlook), 232
Flash Player, adding to PDAs, 244
flatbed scanners, 318
Fleming, Sir Alexander, 287
FlightGear game, open source pro-
ject, 130
FlightSearch.com Web site, 86
FlipDog.com Web site, 86
Flo Control Project Web site, 359
floppy disks, files, copying to, 111
Fly Feastin' game, 133
FOLDER.HTT file (Windows), 139
folders
backgrounds
changing (Mac OS X), 141
changing (Windows 98), 141
customization (Windows 98), 139

Font Magic tool, 206
fonts
1001 Fonts Web site, 135
Font Magic tool, 206
Windows True Type, converting to
Macintosh format, 341
FoodTV.com Web site, 293
Fool.com Web site, 111
Forbes Magazine Web site, richest
nerds listing, 142
forced file extensions, 107
Forchetti.org Web site, 32
foreign language programs, 184
Forgotten Password Wizard (Windows
XP), 98
Forrester Research Web site, 418
FORTRAN (Formula Translation), 126
Fortune Teller Web site, 220
forwarding email (EmailStripper), 232
FoundMoney.com Web site, 293
Fract-o-rama (Linux), 376
frames, Web design mistakes, 94
Franklin, Benjamin, 187
fraud (online)
auctions, 420
credit cards, 420
Nigerian Letter Scam, 420
Free Graphics Web site, 126
Free Networks.org Web site, 119
Free Software Foundation, 280
free Web hosts, 89-90
FreeAgent reader (Usenet news-
groups), 103
FreebieList.com Web site, 90
FreeBSD Web site, 342
FreeCharge battery charger, 230
FreeDB.org Web site, automatic song
list tracker, 25
Freedom Scientific Web site, 113
FreeDonation.com Web site, 194
FreeFind.com Web site, Webmaster
search services, 87
Freemazes.com Web site, 299
FreePhotoshop.com Web site, 210
Freeplay.net Web site, 230
FreeRip 1.13 for Windows, 25
freeware sources, 202
Fresh Devices Web site, 350
Fresh Diagnose tool, 350
Freshmeat Web site, 155
FreshRPMS.net Web site, 285
Friday Five Web site, 359
Frito Files Web site, 279

G

Web browsers